Research on Mathematical Thinking of Young Children

Research on Mathematical Thinking of Young Children

Six Empirical Studies

Edited by

LESLIE P. STEFFE

NATIONAL COUNCIL
OF TEACHERS OF MATHEMATICS

Library of Congress Cataloging in Publication Data:

Main entry under title:

Research on mathematical
thinking of young children

Includes bibliography.
1. Mathematics--Study and teaching (elementary)--Addresses, essays, lectures. 2. Learning, Psychology of--Addresses, essays, lectures. I. Steffe, Leslie P. II. National Council of Teachers of Mathematics.
QA135.5.R47   372.7   75-22461

Printed in the United States of America

Table of Contents

LESLIE P. STEFFE

Introduction

Acknowledgments

The studies reported in this monograph have been influenced by the work of many professors. In the current zeitgeist in mathematics education, it is easy to underestimate the impact of the foresightedness of a rather small number of professors in mathematics education who did much of their work during the decades circa 1950-1970. Two of the most influential contributors, directly and indirectly, to the works of this volume are Myron Rosskopf, past Professor of Mathematics and Chairman of the Department of Mathematical Education, Teachers College, Columbia University; and Henry Van Engen, Professor Emeritus of Mathematics Education, the University of Wisconsin. Their work stimulated others to examine the formation of operational characteristics of basic mathematical concepts in children of school age. This effort made clear the necessity of the interdisciplinary nature of research in mathematics education. The emphases and substance of research in cognitive-developmental psychology, especially Piagetian, proved most timely and, we hope, most fruitful.

Professor Charles D. Smock, Professor of Developmental Psychology at the University of Georgia, provided many insightful suggestions. His influence, however, transcends the contents and ideas in this monograph; one application of cognitive-developmental theory to mathematics education has been translated into action through his efforts. Others who have directly influenced the contents of this volume are Thomas Romberg, Professor of Mathematics Education, the University of Wisconsin and John LeBlanc, Associate Professor of Mathematics Education, Indiana University. Professor Romberg was dissertation director for Thomas Carpenter, author of Chapter VII, and Professor LeBlanc was thesis advisor for Richard Lesh, author of Chapter V.

Conferences

In 1967, the National Science Foundation, the National Council of Teachers of Mathematics, and the Department of Mathematics Education, University of Georgia, cosponsored a conference on needed research in mathematics education. The conference was general in nature in that it included major papers on needed research in the learning of mathematics, in the teaching of mathematics, and in mathematics curriculum. It was felt by most of the participants that the conference was well-conceived and well-directed for one of the first national conferences on needed research in mathematics education. But, from this conference, it was clear that follow-up efforts aimed at more specific areas of research in mathematics education would be needed--the scope of research in mathematics education is too broad to be dealt with adequately at any one conference.

Subsequently, a conference was held on Piagetian cognitive-development research and mathematical education. This second conference was sponsored jointly by the National Council of Teachers of Mathematics, the Department of Mathematical Education, Teachers College, Columbia University, and the National Science Foundation. The proceedings from this conference consisted of 14 major papers. These papers were successful in identifying the state of the knowledge in the area of cognitive development research in mathematics education and in highlighting promising areas for further research.

It was clear to some of those participating in the conference, however, that the papers were theoretical and experimental in nature and did not, to any great extent, deal with mathematics pedagogy and Piagetian cognitive-development theory. Consequently, a symposium was held on Piagetian cognitive-development research and mathematical laboratories at Northwestern University in 1973 as part of the dedication ceremonies for their new education building. These papers ranged from theoretical expositions of cognitive-development theory to practical expositions of teacher education programs.

These two conferences and one symposium, in addition to theoretical papers, empirical research, and related projects by mathematics educators and psychologists, attest to the exploding interest in the United States in the area of application of cognitive-development research in mathematics education research and development. The papers of these conferences and the symposium are significant contributions to literature in mathematics education. However, the concepts and principles contained in the papers are far from being universally applied (or acknowledged) in educational practice in mathematics education in the schools and colleges of the United States. Such a state of affairs is not necessarily undesirable in view of (1) the lack of formal training in cognitive-development of professional educators in mathematics education and (2) the state of the applied research of cognitive-development to mathematics education. As difficult as it may have been to institute changes in the school mathematics curriculum in the 1950's and 1960's, the mathematical preparation of professional mathematics educators in those two decades far excels psychological preparation of mathematics educators in the 1970's. Even so, there has been a dramatic Piagetian renaissance in mathematics education in the United States over the past ten years. Much work remains to be done, however, if the children in the schools are to realize the potential benefit of recent advances in knowledge derived from cognitive-development theory and research.

On an Outline of a Program of Research

A massive amount of theory and data exists which describes the development of mathematical and scientific concepts in children from the onset of the formation of the permanent object through adolescence--much of that theory and data was generated by the Genevan school within a specific epistemological framework. This theory and data, while it is extremely rich, certainly was not generated by researchers primarily interested in the establishment of scientific pedagogy. As such, it cannot be indiscriminately applied with the hope that, somehow, such application will improve the state of affairs in mathematics education.

Generally, mathematics educators are concerned with the child's learning aspects of various mathematical systems in school mathematics--the natural numbers, the integers, the rational numbers of arithmetic, the rational numbers, the real numbers, polynomials, Euclidean geometry, transformational geometry, linear spaces, matrix theory, and finite systems, to name some. Cognitive-development theory can contribute to an understanding of how it is a child acquires knowledge of these mathematical systems through its description of cognitive operations children acquire and the mechanism through which children acquire them. A mathematics educator cannot stop there, however, because the cognitive operations demanded by mathematical systems may be distinguishable from (but include) the cognitive operations described in cognitive-development psychology. Mathematics educators do not yet know how to utilize the cognitive operations studied in cognitive development psychology in the further acquisition of cognitive operations demanded by the mathematical systems mentioned. In fact, few attempts have been made toward the identification of relationships between the cognitive operations studied in developmental psychology and the cognitive operations demanded by the mathematical systems. For example, (1) if a child is or is not in possession of cognitive operations normally attributed to the grouping structures vis-à-vis Piaget, what does this say about his knowledge or acquisition of the integers, of the rational numbers of arithmetic, or even the rational number system? Or, (2) if a child does or does not possess the proportionality scheme or the INRC Group, what does this say about his knowledge or acquisition of measurement, of the rational numbers, of finite algebraic systems?

Not only, then, is it critical to test for possible relationships between the cognitive systems of the child and knowledge of the systems of mathematics, it is also critical to learn how the mental operations normally attributable to the grouping structures, figurative structures, and the formal operational structures are utilized by the child in the acquisition of mathematical content whose structural properties are not necessarily isomorphic to those genetic structures. All of this information is difficult to acquire, but until the story is told, critical assumptions will have to be made in the application of cognitive-development theory to mathematics education--assumptions which, of course, may not be untenable.

Assuming the validity of certain critical assumptions alluded to above, applications of cognitive-development can be made to mathematical education in which learning-instructional models can be formulated and tested empirically. Such a model may not attain the status of a theory but can be used to both describe and prescribe learning-instructional phenomena concerning mathematics until it proves unusable in terms of the desired objectives and/or learning process.

LESLIE P. STEFFE
CHARLES D. SMOCK

On a Model for Learning and Teaching Mathematics

Piaget (1971, p. 21; 1973a, p. ix) has expressed the convictions that (1) experimental pedagogy must remain distinct from psychology but, yet, utilize psychological principles, and (2) hypotheses derived from psychology must be subjected to empirical verification (or refutation) rather than be accepted only on the basis of deduction. While it would seem unnecessary to restate these two convictions, education has a history of embracing a particular theory or point of view based on overly simplistic deductions and then, when educational practice has shown the transparency of these deductions, abandoning that theory. Piagetian cognitive-development theory may be no exception to this general pattern in education because it is, in the main, the theoretical basis on which the "mathematical laboratory" is built.

The mathematical laboratory, according to Smock (1973) has "remained only loosely or ambiguously defined (p. 1)." If that assertion remains true after substantial attempts are made at an unambiguous definition, then the mathematical laboratory would have to rely on only sloganese or personal testimony for its justification as an instructional approach. Until and unless mathematics educators return to the beginning and ask "how do children learn?" rather than "how do we teach?" the fundamental dimensions of educational and instructional problems facing the mathematics educator will remain unidentified. If we confront this basic question, it is possible to proceed with the task of characterizing what is meant by a "mathematical laboratory." The emphasis, then, is to be placed not on methodology and learning activities but, rather, on the learning characteristics of the child as he acquires particular subject matter and content and methodology constructed for that special purpose.

The preparation of this chapter was supported, in part, by the Mathemagenic Activities Program, Follow Through, C. D. Smock, Director, under Grant No. EG-0-8-522478-4617 (287), Department of HEW, USOE.

The problems of characterizing the mathematical laboratory can best be understood in the context of the issues involved in developing a theory of mathematical *learning* and *instruction.* Bruner points out (1964b) that most theories of learning and development are descriptive rather than prescriptive. While this may be the case, a theory of mathematical instruction for children must be based in the developmental constraints of concept learning, a theory of learning relevant to mathematical concepts, and in mathematics itself if the theory is to have validity. Consequently, rather than focusing on instruction with little regard for learning or on learning with little regard for instruction, analysis of school mathematics requires that learning and instruction be considered simultaneously. Even then, little progress will be possible if mathematics and cognitive development are ignored.

One of the best examples of an analysis and synthesis of cognitive development theory, fundamental mathematical structures, and mathematics instruction for the early school years has been presented by two Russian educational psychologists, El'konin and Davydov (1974). Following Vygotskii, a child's mental development is viewed as being ultimately determined by the content of the knowledge studied. They feel that researchers who study the development of mental operations (notably Piaget) concentrate only on those processes which are maximally independent of specific subject matter. El'konin and Davydov are critical of this approach because it leads to a view that the sources of mental development lie in the individual independently of the specific historical conditions of existence and characterize the child's mind in absolutist terms. On the other hand, they do not ascribe to Bruner's hypothesis that "any subject can be taught effectively in some intellectually honest form to any child at any stage of development." Such an assumption makes reference to abstract forms of teaching fundamentals of any subject to a child of any age, but forms of instruction must be found that are suitable for each specific piece of content *and* given age level.

Piaget (1971, p. 21), however, clearly differentiates experimental pedagogy from psychology. Experimental pedagogy is concerned less with the general and spontaneous characteristics of the child than with their modification through pedagogic processes. Moreover, in commenting on the value of developmental stages in educational sciences, Piaget (1971, p. 171) rejects the notion of inflexible stages characterized by invariant chronological age limits and fixed thought content. As an interactionist, Piaget (1971, pp. 171-73) advocates that the cognitive structural changes that come about through maturation and those that derive from the child's individual experience be considered as separate factors in intellectual development. Also, Piaget (1964a) maintains that mathematical structures can be learned if the structure of interest can be supported by simpler, more elementary structures. Consequently, while the Genevans' work has not been in experimental pedagogy but has dealt with the development of the child independent of particular subject matter curricula, experimental pedagogy does not stand in opposition to cognitive-developmental psychology. Rather, experimental pedagogy is complementary to it, with the potential of contributing knowledge of the developmental processes.

Piaget rejects the notion of inflexible stages characterized by invariable chronological age limits and fixed thought content. Yet, El'konin and Davydov make a central issue out of whether to characterize a given age level in terms of processes for which a developmental period is concluded or in terms of the processes for which that developmental period is beginning. The former is rejected because it would lead to presentation of educational exercises that demand only previously formed intellectual processes for solution and to the further assumption that intellectual development is inviolable and independent of the content and methods of presentation of subject matter. El'konin and Davydov, thus, believe that development of psychological processes underlying the learning of mathematics not only *do not precede* instruction in mathematics but are formed in the process of learning.

El'konin and Davydov's point of view is consistent with the leading role ascribed to instruction by Soviet psychologists (Kilpatrick and Wirszup 1969, p. v). But El'konin and Davydov do not separate methods of instruction from the content of what is to be learned nor from the general cognitive development of children. El'konin and Davydov test experimental curricula based on measurement processes, but their experiments do not provide conclusive evidence that the cognitive development of the children was altered. The experiments shed some light on symbolization capabilities of concrete operational children in highly structured measurement exercises, but little evidence is presented which would lead one to believe these concrete operational children were, as a result of the instruction in measurement, in the formal reasoning stage vis-à-vis Piaget. Thus, the contribution of school learning to cognitive development (in a Piagetian sense) remains to be adequately tested.

The important contribution of El'konin and Davydov is the detailed analysis of fundamental mathematical structures and the explication of the yet unconfirmed hypothesis that cognitive development of children can by altered by school instruction in mathematics. Their analysis of the fundamental mathematical structures led them to the conclusion that the concept of quantity, with its roots in the ordering structures, should be the starting place for school mathematics. The task of analyzing the similarities and differences of the fundamental mathematical (including those mentioned by El'konin and Davydov) and genetic structures is an important first step (Beth and Piaget, 1966).

One important difference is that mathematical structures are the object of reflection by the mathematician but genetic structures are manifested only by the child's behavioral-action structures, which are determined by his assimilation of past experiences. A second major difference is that form is *independent* of the content in the mathematical structure but in genetic structures the form is *inseparable* from content. Finally, in the mathematical structures axioms are the starting point of formal deduction whereas in genetic structures the laws are the rules which the child's deductions obey.

Similarities in the structural types are twofold: (1) operations in the mathematical structures correspond to operations in the genetic structures; and (2) the axioms of the mathematical structures correspond to the "laws of combination" in genetic structures. It is these operational genetic structures which El'konin and Davydov identified as being maximally independent of specific subject matter. The basic content of the genetic structures, however, are classes and relations which, in synthesis, form the basis of cardinal and ordinal number in the logical domain and of quantity and of measurement in the infralogical domain. On the face of it, then, it seems as if El'konin and Davydov's declaration of genetic structures as maximally independent of school mathematics is unjustified. It is true, however, that profound structural differences exist in the genetic structures of concern and certain of the mathematical structures which are used as the basis for the content of school curricula. These structural differences are a central issue in the determination of the applicability of genetic structures to mathematical learning. Mental operations associated with such mathematical structures may or may not be accounted for by the mental operations ascribed to the genetic structures. If the latter case is so, El'konin and Davydov *may be* essentially correct in asserting that the psychological processes are developed concomitant with learning. Piaget (Beth and Piaget, 1966, p. 189), however, proposes that the construction of mathematical entities is an elaboration of the elements of natural thought and the construction of mathematical structures is an enlargement of particular mathematical entities.

The Piagetian hypothesis is, at least, intriguing--it suggests that the individual *constructs* his own mathematics. The testing of the hypothesis, however, is extraordinarily complex due to the structural differences alluded to above. So, two programs of research would seem to be necessary. On the one hand, the logical and mathematical veracity of Piaget's system, concentrating on similarities and differences between genetic and mathematical structures, requires both logical and empirical study. On the other hand, models (albeit preliminary) for learning and instruction of mathematical concepts need to be developed where that development explicitly includes theoretical as well as empirical components. It is this second program of research which is of basic concern in this monograph.

Piagetian theory offers several principles which can be utilized in the construction of such a model (Piaget, 1971, 1973b; Smock, 1970, 1973). First, equilibration theory provides a theoretical model of knowledge acquisition with specification of the factors that regulate acquisition. Second, two distinct levels of cognitive functioning--figurative processes and operative processes--are identified as necessary for understanding learning and development. Third, cognitive capacities determine the effectiveness of training and these cognitive capacities are influenced by four factors that contribute to cognitive development. Fourth, the learning environment must be considered from both the points of view of the genetic structures and the mathematical structures. The implication of some of these principles for the development of an instructional model and for research relevant to that model is presented below.

General Factors Contributing to Cognitive Development

Piaget (1964a) has identified the major factors contributing to the development of cognitive growth of children as including: (1) maturation, (2) experience, (3) language, and (4) equilibration.

Maturation

The proposition that *maturation* is a major determinant of cognitive growth is not, of course, a novel idea. What is new in Piaget's analysis is the explicit inclusion of a maturational *component* as a modulating factor to the experimental and/or experiential contribution to development progress. The constraining role of maturation is supported by, for example, the fact that transitive reasoning seldom has been observed in children below four years of age. The evidence indicates great difficulty in a child's learning transitivity of, for example, " as many as" during the stage of preoperational representation (even when apparently appropriate learning experiences have been encountered). Such evidence cannot be taken as *proof* that maturation is responsible, but it certainly suggests that instrinsic physio-biochemical processes play a prominent part in development of thinking. Subjecting a child to learning "experience" does not appear sufficient to insure he will understand the concept of transitivity.

Experience

Experience in and of itself may not be sufficient to explain conceptual learning of children but no one denies its importance for intellectual growth. But, if experience was sufficient, all one would have to do to "teach" transitivity would be to give the child sufficient exposure--and he would learn. But, unfortunately, it is not that simple.

Physical Experience and Mathematical Experience. Piaget (1964a) has analyzed "experience" into two components: physical and logico-mathematical experience. Imagine, for example, that a child matches objects of Set A one-to-one with objects of Set B through overt (practical) actions; i.e., he places one object from Set A in correspondence with one object from Set B, etc., until all the objects of one (or both) of the sets are exhausted. Then, he takes the objects of Set B and likewise matches them with the objects of another set, C. Does this matching constitute a physical experience or a logico-mathematical experience? It could be either, depending on the cognitive level of the child.

One cannot differentiate between the two types of experiences through observation of the child's overt acts of matching. The crucial determiner of the type of experience is whether the Sets A and C are "related" by the child by virtue of the comparisons of A and B and then, B and C. If the child is not able, through reasoning (mental operations), to determine the relation between A and C, then the experience gained through overt matching of the objects of A and B and B and C was, by definition, physical in nature. The relation between the Sets A and B in this case was a function of the physical arrangement of the objects and would not exist for that child in the absence of perceptual input. That is, the *relation* remains *external to the child* and thus is destroyed upon rearrangement of the objects of the sets. When the two sets of objects are in a state for physical comparison, the child definitely obtains knowledge about the objects--either they match or they don't--but, for that knowledge to be mathematical in nature, the *relation* must be conserved by the child when the objects are moved to new states and the child must be able to engage in reasoning involving the properties of the relations that go beyond the perceptually or graphically "givens."

The distinction between a physical experience and a mathematical experience is essential to the understanding of the growth of mathematical concepts. Knowledge based on physical experience alone is knowledge of static states of affairs and, if a child is wrong, it is easy to demonstrate that to him. However, knowledge derivable from mathematical experience is another matter; if a child is wrong, it is difficult, if not impossible, to convincingly demonstrate, or even to get the child to accept verbal explanation of the correct answer. For example, if a child fails to *align* the two endpoints when comparing length of sticks, it is quite easy to correct the mistake. If, however, he fails to display transitive reasoning in a task, one or two examples is not likely to teach him the concept.

Physical knowledge, then, is the construction of the invariants relevant to the properties of objects (i.e., states) and is based on "experience" through direct contact with objects through one or more of the five senses. For example, one may touch something and it is hard, cold, hot, soft, supple, etc. Or, one may see something--an object is red, a diamond cutting glass, the shape of a banana, etc. The source of mathematical experience, however, is assumed to be the abstractions from coordination of actions vis-à-vis object; i.e., transformation of the "states" associated with series of discreet physical experiences. The critical difference is that the mathematical knowledge gained demands that a pair (or set) of physical objects not be defined by the temporal-spatial (perceptual) similarities, but rather by the invariant relations among or between objects. Overt (perceptual) actions alone are not sufficient for mathematical experience. As already noted, a child may match the objects of two equivalent collections and the knowledge gained from the actions and perceptual consequences may be no more than physical knowledge. Often cited as an example of mathematical experience is the realization by a child that it makes no difference *how* you count a collection of objects--you get the same number. Such knowledge is gained only through counting the collection in at least two or more ways; i.e., coordination of mental, as well as practical, actions.

Linguistic Transmission

Language, the third factor in the growth of mathematical concepts, is considered a part of the experience of the child, but deserves special consideration because of its special quality and status within the total realm of experience. Information contained in a verbal communication will not, necessarily, increase a child's understanding of a mathematical concept. Bailey (1973), for example, presented a transitivity problem to 40 first graders, 40 second graders, and 40 third graders who were in the top two-thirds of their class according to teachers' judgments. Each child was presented a transitivity of length problem. Those children who did not solve the problem were told the correct relations between the two sticks. For example, if a child took a stick B and first compared it with C, and then with A, and found that A and B were the same length and B and C were the same length, but could not infer the relation between A and C, he was told A and C were the *same length*. After the verbal instructions, the child was asked to explain why A was as long as C. Of 24 children who could not infer the correct relation between A and C, only five would give a satisfactory explanation of why A and C were of the same length *after* the verbal instructions.

It would appear that for children in the stage of preoperational representation (or even in the transitional stage), any attempt to teach mathematics concepts only through verbal or symbolic means will be unsuccessful. But, because words and symbols are an important part of mathematics, their specific functions must be clarified. Until then, a carefully arranged interplay between the spoken words which symbolizes a mathematical concept and the sets of actions performed in the process of constructing a tangible representation of the concept should be maintained. In short, a mathematical vocabulary should be developed *during* the course of activities used to explicate and provide embodiments for a concept to be learned. The particular blend, of course, will be determined by the specific activity and characteristics of the child.

Equilibration and Learning

Of the four factors which contribute to the growth of mathematical concepts, Piaget considers equilibration to be most fundamental. Equilibration is a self-regulatory mechanism that balances the invariant biological adaptation processes of assimilation and accommodation. Assimilation refers to the process by which novel events are integrated into the existing mental structures. The complementary process of accommodation concerns the alteration of mental structure under the pressure of this new information.

Learning, in this context, refers to the process by which new information is assimilated into available cognitive structures *and* to the modification of those structures (accommodation). Mathematical learning, then, appears to be more than association of stimulus and response. The *association* of 6 with (2 x 3) is important and no one doubts it can be conditioned (or memorized) using appropriate instructional strategies. Teaching which assumes a stimulus-response view of learning runs the risk of promoting physical knowledge and not mathematical (or operational) knowledge. However, because learning is generally thought to be provoked by situations external to the learner, it is necessary to analyze the levels of learning relevant to particular mathematical concepts or structures.

If our assumption is correct, there should be a differential emphasis on assimilation and accommodative activity depending on the level of understanding of a particular concept. Assimilative task structures would emphasize "play" and/or self (child) regulated activities until the child's behavior indicates the essential elements of a concept have been assimilated. Then, more task situations (including modeling and verbal exploration), as well as situations designed to utilize and generalize the relevant concepts to new situations, should be introduced. The appropriate balancing and sequencing of the assimilative-accommodative activities (practical and mental) requires considerable theoretical and observational skills of the instructor. At the same time, the basic ideas and associated techniques can be identified and used as guidelines for a Piagetian type of learning environment.

Levels of Mathematical Concepts. Relations, classes and number take a relatively long period to develop as operational concepts in the child, appearing perhaps as late as nine to ten years of age. The stages of cognitive development in Piagetian theory are identified as sensorimotor, intuitive preoperational, concrete operational, and formal operational with the movement from one stage to the next being clearly marked by "transitional" phase characteristics. Our assumption is that mathematical concepts go through similar "stages" (called levels) as the child "learns" a concept; e.g., in the case of relations, either children have little or no knowledge of relations, or they are able to engage in reasoning involving the properties of the relations, or they are oscillators --at times, in restricted situations, they appear as if they are able to reason involving relations, but that reasoning is limited and can be extinguished quite easily. Finally, as the assimilation-accomodation activities are "balanced," the child now "feels" he "understands" and insists on the "logical necessity" of the concept.

Learning-Instructional Phases for Mathematical Concepts

Phase I: Exploration

Equilibration, the balancing of assimilatory and accommodatory activity, is a useful theoretical construct to help determine the criteria for learning activities in mathematical instruction. Exploratory activities have been identified by Piaget as representing a preponderance of assimilatory activity; i.e., modification of the environment to match the existing cognitive structures. As such, exploration is conceived as an essential first step in mathematical instruction and learning. This first phase corresponds to the first level of mathematical concepts identified; i.e., to essentially "no concept" and to the emergence of the second level (rudiments of a concept). At these two levels of mathematical concept development, emphasis is on the *constructive* thinking by the child. It is a period of concept formation and not analysis. Exploratory activities can vary along two dimensions: the *type and structure of the material* and the *degree* of *direction* given to the child. However, it is important to keep in mind that the child needs to structure (assimilate) the activities but in a direction relevant to the particular concept learning desired.

Multiple Embodiment Principle. In order to illustrate the above principles using particular concepts, imagine that one-to-one correspondence is the concept of interest. The "no concept" phase of one-to-one correspondence corresponds exactly to the preoperational stage of development. Children who display lack of one-to-one correspondence first must be allowed to engage in undirected exploratory activities, using physical objects that later will be used in more directed activities. For example, the child may be given assortments of beads, bird cutouts, blocks, discs, animal cutouts, toy animals, toy cowboys, toy soldiers, etc., and allowed free play time with these materials. Most children will attempt to place cowboys and Indians on horses, dress dolls, stack dishes, stack blocks, string beads, categorize animals or bird cutouts, align soldiers in rows and give each guns, etc. Further, this type of *practical play* is extended *by the child* into symbolic play; i.e., such as waging wars, keeping house, setting tables, etc. The length of time and number of free play activities which should be encouraged is determined by the frequency of "transitional indication" in the child's behavior and two additional principles: (1) *multiple-embodiment* and (2) *mathematical variability* (Dienes, 1971).

The first (multiple-embodiment) states simply that in play activities, the child should use as many different material sets as appropriate so long as each material set is conducive to construction (by the child) of the concept. Consider a particular free play activity where the preoperational child places cowboys and Indians on horses. Through this assimilatory activity, the child can gain the physical knowledge that indeed the cowboys and Indians fit on the horses. The situation is set for an adult to create a disequilibrium for the child by asking the child if there are enough cowboys and Indians so each horse would have a rider. To find out, the child has to change his practical activity to answer that question. Now if the child correctly achieves that task, the next step is to introduce new materials but maintain the original goal (one-to-one matching); e.g., are there enough dresses so one could be put on each doll?

If the child does not initiate specified goal-directed activities following suggestions, the adult may then demonstrate that there are enough cowboys and Indians so each horse has a rider. Such *imitation* learning (accommodatory activities) provides the conditions to employ the principle of multiple-embodiment for subsequent learning tasks and even, at times, imitative behavior across task situations. The adult must, always, be sensitive to the type of knowledge the child is acquiring in the imitative activities; i.e., knowledge acquisition under imitative conditions has a high probability of being at the level of "physical knowledge" if children are in the preoperational stage. By remaining sensitive to this, the adult will avoid expecting the child to build an understanding of higher-order concepts prior to acquiring the necessary prerequisite concepts.

Mathematical Variability Principle. It was pointed out above that free play activities can, through appropriate intervention, be changed into more directed learning activity for children. The second dimension of task activity that can be modified by the adult involves the application of the mathematical variability principle (Dienes, 1971). In contrast to the multiple embodiment principle where the mathematical content is held constant and the materials varied, the mathematical variability principle varies the mathematical content. For example, in case of one-to-one correspondence, the relation being considered can either be changed to a new relational category altogether (e.g., length relations or family relations) or to a relation within the category of matching relations (i.e., more than, fewer than, as many as). Both of these types of variations can, if appropriately used, create cognitive conflict to be resolved by the child.

In summary, it has been pointed out that "play" can vary from free play to directed play, where the directed play is a natural extension of free play. Further, the principles of multiple embodiment and mathematical variability provide guidelines for setting the stage for transition from the level of physical experience to mathematical experience. However, dramatic short-term success in teaching mathematical concepts to preoperational children is not to be expected. More success can be expected with children in the transitional stages (which corresponds here to the second level of mathematical concepts), but again, the short-term success will undoubtedly be modest. During the developmental phase of preoperational representation, it is advocated that the *learning-instructional* phase conditions be held relatively constant; i.e., use the explorations with variations based on the mathematical variability and multiple embodiment principles.

Phase II: Abstraction and Representation

The second learning-instructional phase, that of abstraction and representation, is based in part on the distinction between physical experience and logico-mathematical experience. Abstraction from properties of objects (physical experience) are called simple abstractions; e.g., hardness, sharpness, etc. Reflective abstraction (logico-mathematical experience) involves abstraction from the *actions performed on* (or with) objects *or* representations of those actions. Reflective abstraction is represented by the case of a child counting a string of beads from one end, then from the other, and realizing that the number of beads is independent of the manner of counting them; i.e., which is selected first, which second, which third, etc. The beads are there, but the knowledge gained had to do with the actions with the beads and the capability of representing and reviewing the actions. Or a child may pair elements from two sets until one is exhausted prior to the other; re-pairing the elements in a different way provides the conditions necessary to make the abstraction that no matter how the pairing is done, the one set will always contain more elements than the second set. It is clear that a child may be "playing" but still be engaged in reflective abstraction. Thus, the teacher need not be restricted to "play" activities as long as the child reveals capacity to make the higher level abstraction.

The child may engage in reflective abstraction but not achieve stable representation of newly gained knowledge. Representations may be figurative (e.g., images) derived from drawings or perception of a collection of symbols, etc., and not available to the child at a later time. For example, if a child compares a green stick with a red stick and finds the green stick to be shorter than the red stick, any one of

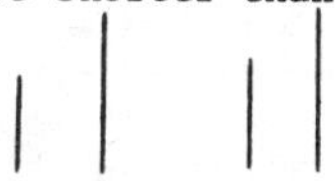

$G < R$, $G < R$, or G R

might be used as a static, immediate representation. There, reflective abstraction and representation together contribute to a higher level of concept formation than expected in the first learning-instructional phase in that rudiments of mathematical concepts are present and can be utilized in a limited way (2nd level of concept formation).

Phase III: Formalization and Interpretation

The learning-instructional phase of formalization and interpretation completes the proposed learning cycle for mathematical concepts. The mathematical concept base-ten numeration system will be used to illustrate the three learning-instructional phases, with emphases on formalization and interpretation (Phase III). The concept was selected because no data are presently available that show the numeration systems are part of the natural cognitive development of children.

We assume the child is at the concrete stage of operations and the operational structures related to classification and relations are available to him. It must be noted that because a child is at this developmental stage does not mean he knows base ten numeration nor that figurative representation of the concept has been achieved. What use the child is able to make with his knowledge of classes, relations, and number may be in the absence of formalization of numeration concepts. Therefore, the only prerequisites required are the completion of a learning cycle concerning the ordering of the digits 0, 1, 2, 3, 4, 5, 6, 7, 8, and 9; ability to write them from memory, and to do simple addition problems.

Any natural number can be written in expanded notation. Consequently, the coefficients, the base, and the exponents can all be allowed to vary in employing the mathematical variability principle. Usually, the base is held constant (base ten is used) and only the exponents and coefficients are allowed to vary.

Imagine that a small group of children are given a collection of various assortments of materials, such as geometrical shapes, checkers, dried beans, etc., and are allowed to engage in free play with the materials, building whatever they wish--castles, houses, roads, forts, etc. The first type of direction which could be given to the children is to find "how many piles, with a certain number in each pile, can be made from the objects." The mathematical variability principle should be employed by varying the number in each pile or the total number of objects in each collection. The multiple embodiment principle should be used by changing the type of objects (thus setting a new problem each time) or the type of collection to be formed. The essential aspect is that a collection of objects always can be partitioned into *subcollections* with the *same number* in each and *one other subcollection* with relatively *fewer objects* in it; e.g., a collection of twenty-six objects can be partitioned into four subcollections with six per subcollection *and* two objects in the nonequal set.

One of the first bits of logico-mathematical knowledge the children generally acquire is the sameness of the *number* of objects in the total collection before and after the partitioning process. That is, the child discovers, through his actions, that a pile of objects can always be put back the way it was before the partition (reversibility) and that no objects were added or subtracted; therefore, the number of objects before and after piling is the "same" even though the child *does not* know how many things there are.

Specifically, if a child starts with some objects, makes three piles with six per pile, and one pile of four, the child should know that the total number of objects in the original pile is the same as the number of objects in three piles of six and one pile of four, without knowing there

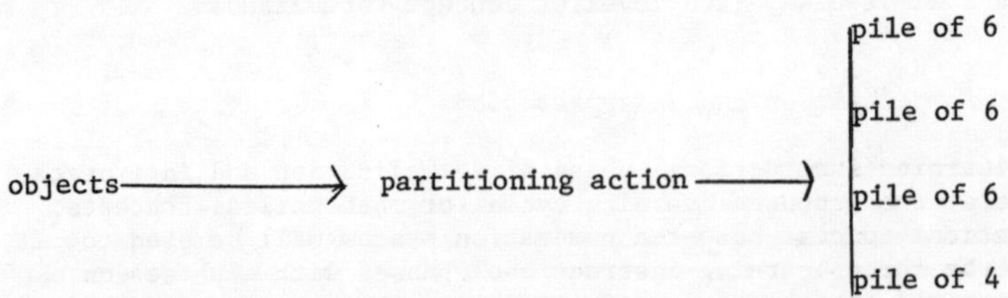

are 22 objects. The mathematical variability principle (varying the number of objects in each pile) should help the child to the realization that no matter how many are in each pile, the total number in *all* the piles is equal to the total number of objects. When a child discovers this, he has made a transition from the first learning-instructional phase (exploration) to the second learning-instructional phase (abstraction and representation).

At this point, the operational basis for constructing the concept of a numeration system has been laid. The goal of the second learning-instructional phase is to have the child construct a notational system and construct the place-value concept. Generally, the two-digit numerals are worked on at different age levels than are the three-digit numerals, which in turn are worked on at different age levels than are the four-digit and higher-digit numerals (the generalization of place value).

After the children first enter the second learning-instructional phase they are able to partition a collection into subcollections and know that the number of objects in the original collection is the same as that in all the subcollections. Capitalizing on this knowledge and the ability of the children to engage in rational counting, place-value concepts may be developed. However, until the children can represent any collection of a tens and b ones (where a and b are digits) as "ab," they are not ready to learn the number names for the two-digit numbers and order the numbers from 0 to 100. The number names and the order relation are included in the next learning-instructional phase because the knowledge gained to this point is to be systemized by the children. The basis for the learning which is to take place has been laid in counting out piles of ten. However, the main goal of the formalization-interpretation phase is to, again, systemize the whole numbers from 0 to 100 using the number names. Formalization takes place in the sense that a notational system is developed and organized by the child. The organization of the notational system is based on the abstraction and representation accomplished at the second phase and on the new element of an *order relation*. The order relation is an essential part of the third learning-instructional phase for the concept of numeration. Without it, the third phase would have little meaning. The order relation, however, is based on one-to-one correspondence, so that preliminary cycles will have to have been completed with regard to one-to-one correspondence and number.

Some Problems

The foregoing model for learning and teaching mathematical concepts needs critical examination in view of other theoretical constructs in an attempt to build the best first approximation of a model possible. That refinements are possible is easily recognized, as a host of theoretical constructs exist which have not yet been integrated into the model. Some of these constructs are figurations and operations, the concept of decentering, and egocentrism of the child. Moreover, a great deal of difference may exist between the model's applicability to mathematical concepts shown to be part of the general development acquisition and those not. Further, no attempt has yet been made to apply the model to geometrical and spatial concepts. It may well be that a model for learning concepts in those areas is greatly different from a model for learning numerical concepts. However, reason does exist that the above model is applicable to geometrical and spatial concepts as Piaget views the grouping structure as a basic structure of mental operations in the infralogical domain. In any case, it is clear that theoretical refinement of the posited model is necessary and that the model needs to be studied across different mathematical concept areas for applicability. Certainly, there are no a priori reasons that a single model is sufficient to account for the learning of disparate mathematical concepts.

The theoretical problems associated with the model should not preclude empirical study of the validity of certain crucial implications of the model. Especially important are such factors as:

1. Are the four factors contributing to the development of certain mathematical concepts critical to the learning of those concepts which have not been shown to be part of the natural course of intellectual development?

2. Can those mathematical concepts not (yet) shown to be developmental phenomena be ordered along the three levels comparable to the concepts known to be part of the developmental process?

3. What is the validity of the learning-instructional strategy involving the mathematical variability and the multiple embodiment principle, in the context of sequencing learning conditions according to the exploration, abstraction-representation, and formalization-interpretation phases?

4. What is validity of learning-instructional phases? Does a structural integration take place only after appropriate overt actions are internalized through reflective abstraction? That is, is the phase of formalization and interpretation identifiable distinct (psychologically) from the phase of abstraction and representation? Reflective abstraction, as a theoretical construct, is appealing, but does it have psychological credibility in mathematics learning?

The experimental studies reported in the following chapters offer a preliminary test of the notion of reflective abstraction in learning of classes and relations by children who had not yet consolidated concrete operational structures. The set of principles inherent in the model described above together with analysis of the relevant genetic structures and mathematical structures were used as guides for the design of the learning materials. No attempt was made to isolate one or more of the underlying factors which may have contributed to resultant learning. The preliminary model was applied in its totality in all of the training studies so that complex interactions of principles in the model were not explored in the learning of selected aspects of classes and relations.

The learning material utilized in the experimental studies did not progress beyond the abstraction and representation phase, except, of course, for cases in which children themselves went into the third phase. The initial learning-instructional tasks were intended to operationally define the concepts for the children. These learning-instructional tasks were written within the constraints of the learning-instructional phase, Exploration. The children were allowed time to engage in free play activities, but direction from the experimenters was included in a highly controlled context to insure that each of the children engaged in overt activities necessary to operationally define the concepts. It was not expected that the children would progress beyond physical knowledge in these initial tasks. The multiple embodiment principle and the mathematical variability principle were employed in such a way that each material set of interest and each concept of interest were included in these initial tasks. A carefully designed schedule for the introduction of terminology was followed throughout the learning materials.

Other learning-instructional tasks were constructed intending to maximize the possibility of children engaging in logical-mathematical experience. These tasks differed from the initial tasks in that they included operations on, or properties of, the concepts involved (e.g., transitivity, asymmetry, class intersection). Hindsight and foresight (anticipation) activities were utilized in the design of these higher-order tasks. No attempts were made to include figural representations or written representations of the higher-order tasks. The tasks always included manipulatable objects. Internal representations of tasks (images or verbal thought) or spoken language were encouraged, but no controls were included to maximize such representation except in the case of terminology developed to communicate the concept elements (e.g., "pair," "partner," "more than"). The time devoted to the two learning-instructional phases was held constant.

In the study by Steffe and Carey (Chapter II) the mathematical structures of equivalence and order relations were used as mathematical models in the construction of the learning materials. The content of the relational structures was length relations defined for open curves of finite length. In the experiment, each child was used as his own control so that information was available prior to the experiment on conservation and transitivity of length relations. The relationship of relational structures to genetic structures has been discussed elsewhere (Steffe, 1973)--similarities and differences pointed out earlier in this chapter were kept in mind, where the similarities were emphasized owing to the status of relations in cognitive development.

The study by Owens (Chapter III) was also concerned with the reflective abstraction and representation of relational structures. Owens, however, employed two relational categories, matching relations and length relations, where each category included equivalence and order relations. Owen's test of whether reflective abstraction took place in the children demanded that the children be able to apply learned properties of matching relations to length relations, where the length relations were only operationally defined. The learning materials, just as in the Steffe and Carey study, employed the foregoing posited model. Owens not only demanded the learned relational properties be transferred to a different relational category in a test for possible reflective abstraction, but he also administered a problem to the children which demanded that transitivity of matching relations be employed in its solution.

In the study conducted by Martin L. Johnson (Chapter IV), rather than attempting to induce properties of equivalence and order relations property by property, children were immersed in total seriation tasks. This decision was predicated on the theory that relational properties emerge as a result of a total scheme of classification or seriation rather than the other way around. It was felt that reflective abstraction would be given the maximal opportunity to operate in a relatively short period of time (16 instructional days out of 22 consecutive instructional days) with content shown to be developmental phenomena.

Lesh, in the study reported in Chapter V, did not begin with mathematical structures in his learning program but, rather, conducted a pilot investigation using the genetic structures as his starting point. On the basis of the genetic structures, Lesh generated three sequences of tasks, one dealing with seriation, one with number,and one with classification. The tasks were subjected to empirical validation as to their sequential nature and difficulty. A transfer of learning experiment was then carried out where training was given on seriation and classification and transfer to the number tasks tested. The preliminary model presented above was utilized in the construction of the learning materials for the transfer of learning experiment.

A fundamental issue raised by Lesh's experiment was mentioned in discussion of the El'Konin-Davydov experiment. The mental operations Lesh worked with were taken from the genetic structures. Because Lesh was dealing with such fundamental concepts, it was possible for him to proceed as he did. However, Piagetian theory has less to offer concerning possible genetic structures underlying more advanced concepts, and even if mathematical structures are considered, mental operations underpinning these structures may be different from those underpinning genetic structures. In that the results of Lesh's training study are positive, more experiments need to be conducted designed to shed light on mental operations underlying the child's concept of number.

The study by David C. Johnson (Chapter VI) was concerned basically with educational technology. No attempt was made to experimentally determine basic mental operations underlying the child's concept of number. Rather, it was assumed that Piagetian theory was essentially correct as it is concerned with relations and classification. The experimenter was explicitly aware of structural differences in mathematical structures and genetic structures dealing with classes and relations, but he emphasized the similarities rather than the differences.

Of the experiments reported in this monograph, David C. Johnson's experiment provides the best test of the construct "reflective abstraction" in the case of learning concepts shown to be developmental phenomena. In the learning material, children were given definite opportunities to engage in mathematical as well as physical experiences. The transfer tests all demanded mathematical knowledge for successful completion, whereas the achievement measures demanded only physical knowledge. So, a test was possible of the amount of mathematical knowledge the learning material produced in the children.

The study conducted by Carpenter (Chapter VII) was concerned with development of mental operations regarding measurement. The study was not experimental in nature but was related to the previous studies in the monograph by virtue of the content of the tasks, the variables controlled, and its developmental nature. In particular, Carpenter tested the degree to which young children possess the logical structures necessary to assimilate and apply information from measurement processes and attempted to identify some factors involved in the development of measurement concepts. The study provides, within a scope limited by the tasks and factors studied, baseline data for designing experiments relevant to specific questions implied by the model.

LESLIE P. STEFFE
RUSSELL L. CAREY

Learning of Equivalence and Order Relations by Four- and Five-Year-Old Children

Elkind (1967) has categorized Piaget's conservation problems into two categories, conservation of identity and conservation of equivalence.

> *Regardless of the content of these problems, they routinely involve presenting the subject with a variable (V) and a standard (S) stimulus that are initially equivalent in both the perceptual and quantitative sense. The subject is then asked to make a judgment regarding their quantitative equivalence. Once the judgment is made, the variable stimulus is subjected to a transformation, $V \rightarrow V'$, which alters the perceptual but not the quantitative equivalence between the variable and standard. After completion of the transformation, the subject is asked to judge the quantitative equivalence between the standard and the transformed variable (p. 16).*

In the above conceptualization, a judgment of conservation may be relative to conservation of a quantitative relation or to the identity of V and V'. Even though the possibility of two judgments exists, "It is probably true, nonetheless, that from the point of view of the subject, the conservation of identity is a necessary condition for the conservation of equivalence (Elkind, 1967, p. 17)."

Aspects of conservation exist which are not completely clarified by Elkind's characterization. For example, consider the relation "as many as." If the elements of a set A are in one-to-one correspondence with the elements of a set B, the A has as many elements as B, and vice versa (denoted by A ~B). In a conservation problem involving "~", if the child is asked to make a "quantitative judgment," one must be assured that the child associates at least a one-to-one correspondence with the phrase "as many as." That is, one must be assured that a conservation problem is not a test of terminology. The establishment of the initial comparison is also basic to conservation of length relations between two objects. One may take the point of view,

---

This paper is based on Research Paper Number 17 of the Research and Development Center for Educational Stimulation. University of Georgia, Athens, Georgia (Carey & Steffe, 1968).

moreover, that even though a child may point to the longer of two sticks, he may be basing his judgment on two endpoints only without regard to the relative position of the remaining two endpoints. In this case, one should not be willing to accept that he perceives the initial relation. Clearly, a comprehension of relational terms is a prerequisite to problems in conservation of the relation. The phrase "the same length as" has a quite different referent than does "as many as." While both are equivalence relations they still are different relations. Thus, there seems to be no reason to believe that the ability to conserve one of the two relations implies the ability to conserve the other. Smedslund (1964), in a study of concrete reasoning, observed that 31 children failed one of the two conservation problems involving "same as" and "longer than" while 32 failed both and 97 passed both, which supports the contention that the ability to conserve a particular relation does not imply an ability to conserve another. Moreover, in a conservation problem, the initial relation need not be an equivalence relation. It may be, in fact, an order relation (e.g., "fewer than").

Whether the initial judgment in a conservation problem always involves a judgment of quantitative equivalence is not completely clear. For, if A and B are curves of finite length, then A is the same length as B if and only if L(A)=L(B), where L(A) is a number denoting the length of A, and L(B) is a number denoting the length of B. If T(B) is a transformation of B which is length preserving, then L(B)=L(T(B)) implies that A is the same length as T(B). If children cannot associate a number with A and B, then there is no reason to believe that "the same length as" has any quantitative meaning for them. Therefore, under these conditions, there would be no reason to expect children to conserve a quantitative equivalence between A and B. It is entirely reasonable to expect children not to be able to associate a number with a segment but yet be capable of establishing a relation not necessarily involving number between two or more segments, for Piaget, Inhelder, and Szeminska (1960) make a sharp distinction between "qualitative" and "operational" measurement.

> *Qualitative measuring . . . which consists in transitive congruence differs from a true metrical system in that the latter involves changes of position among the subdivisions of a middle term in a metrical system . . . whereas in qualitative measuring, one object in its entirety is applied to another (p. 60).*
>
> *While conservation, and hence qualitative transitivity, are achieved at a mean age of 7 1/2, measurement in its operational form . . . is only achieved at about 8 or 8 1/2 (p. 126).*

Before presenting length relations to children below six years of age, it seems necessary, then, to define the relations on a basis that does not assume number. Such a definition follows. Let A, B, and C be segments. A is the same length as B if, and only if, when segments (or their transforms) lie on a line in such a way that two endpoints coincide (left or right), the two remaining endpoints coincide. A is longer than B if, and only if, the remaining endpoint of B coincides with a point between the endpoints of A. Also, in this case, B is shorter than A.

The above definitions are acceptable from a mathematical point of view as the length of a curve is the least upper bound of the lengths of all inscribed polygons. Intuitively, then, one could think of the length of a curve as the length of a line segment where, of course, the lengths are identical. It is essential to note that in the definitions given, children do not have to assign numbers to segments through measurement processes. The definitions are given entirely in terms of a line, the endpoints of curves, betweenness for points, and coincident points on a line and are consistent with Piaget's (1964a) view that "learning is possible in the case of . . . logical-mathematical structures, but on one condition--that is, the structure you want to teach . . . can be supported by simpler, more elementary, logical-mathematical structures"(p. 16). The relations "same length as," "longer than," and "shorter than," as defined, and their properties are more elementary and logically precede measurement. The definitions given above are the results of an attempt, on the part of the investigators, to define the relations in as simple a manner as possible but in such a way that they are still mathematically acceptable.

The relations need not be presented to children by the use of words alone as they may be defined operationally, i.e., defined by physical operations with concrete objects. The physical operations eventually need to be performed by the child himself, because central to Piaget's theory is the fact that the child is active; he gains knowledge through his own actions.

Operationally, then, for a child to find a relation between two "rods," say rod A and rod B, he must place the rods side by side and align two of the endpoints. The relative extension of the two remaining endpoints then determines the relation(s). If rod A is in fact shorter than rod B the child, upon placing A by B, can determine that fact. Through an equivalent action or the same action the child also can determine that B is longer than A. It is through the coordination of these actions that logical-mathematical structures evolve for the child as "coordination of actions before the stage of operations needs to be supported by concrete material. Later, this coordination of actions leads to the logical-mathematical structures"(Piaget, 1964a, p. 12).

If a child establishes a relation between two curves in accordance with the operational definition given, then to conserve the relation, the child must realize that the relation obtains regardless of any length-preserving transformation on one or both of the curves. In other terms the child must realize that, after such a transformation, if the curves are moved back side by side as in the original state, the ends will be still in the same relative positions. Viewed in this manner, the conservation of the relation is essential for the transitive property. Take the example of a child who is presented with two fixed line segments, say, of the same length but not obviously so, and a third segment the same length as the first two and then questioned about the relative lengths of the two fixed segments (which he must not overtly compare). The child must realize that once he has established a relation between the lengths of two segments, the relation obtains regardless of the proximity of the segments.

If conservation of identity is viewed in terms of quantity, then there is little logical reason to expect "conservation of identity" to be involved in conservation of length relations as discussed above. While the length of an object is a number assigned to the object, it is not necessary for a child (or an adult) to know the lengths of two segments in order to establish a length relation between them, on an operational basis. The only aspect of identity involved, then, would seem to be that the child would have to affirm that the segment is the same segment no matter how it is moved around.

The length relations as operationally defined and mathematically defined do have certain properties. The relation "the same length as" is reflexive, symmetric, and transitive and the relations "longer than" and "shorter than" are nonreflexive, asymmetric, and transitive. Because for any curve A, A is the same length as itself and not longer or shorter, it would seem that, at least in a relational sense, what sometimes passes for a test of conservation of identity is no more than a test of the reflexive and nonreflexive properties. Although it is not true for equivalence relations in general, if it is assumed that for each curve A there is a curve B such that A is the same length as B, the reflexive property of "the same length as" can be deduced from the symmetric and transitive properties. For if "~" denotes "the same length as," A~B and B~A implies A~A for each curve A. This logical interdependency gives little hope for conservation of identity to be necessary for transitivity.

In addition to the properties of the relations, the following statements are logical consequences of the definitions of the relations given. (1) A shorter (longer) than B is equivalent to B longer (shorter) than A; (2) if A is the same length as B then A is not shorter (longer) than B; (3) if A is shorter (longer) than B then A is not longer (shorter) than B.

Questions and Hypotheses of the Study

Few data exist concerning proficiency levels of four-and five-year-old children in establishing length relations in accordance with the operational definition given. For open curves, the operational definition is extended as follows. To establish a length relation between two open curves A and B, a child must (1) place each curve on a line in such a way that two endpoints (left or right) coincide, (2) compare the relative position of the two remaining endpoints, and then (3) on the basis of (1) and (2), determine what relation holds. Given that a child is able to establish a length relation between two curves, it is hypothesized that he will be able to conserve the relation established. This hypothesis is advanced due to the fact that for a child to establish a length relation, he must attend to relative positions of the endpoints of the curves as well as ensure that the curves are on a line. Even though the actions of establishing length relations between curves are physical actions, for a child to carry the physical actions out spontaneously, it would seem that the child must be operational in a Piagetian sense. If such is the case, a multitude of potential physical actions would be possible, which should include use of the properties and logical consequences of the relations. A second hypothesis is then advanced. If a child is able to conserve length relations established, it is then hypothesized that he would be able to use properties and logical consequences of the relations. It must be made explicit that it is not hypothesized that use of the reflexive and nonreflexive properties precedes conservation of length relations. Rather, it is hypothesized that conservation of length relations is necessary for use of the reflexive and nonreflexive properties as well as the asymmetric and transitive properties. It is further hypothesized that use of relational properties and consequences will be consistent with logical interdependencies of those properties.

All of the above hypotheses are advanced only for children who have not received formal instruction on relations. Because any hypothesis advanced for children who have received specific instruction must by necessity be at least provisionally instruction-specific, a list of specific questions is presented rather than hypotheses. The first list is a question asked for four- and five-year-old children who have not been engaged in formal instruction on establishing length relations; the second list is questions asked for four- and five-year-old children who have been engaged in formal instruction only on establishing length relations; and the third list is questions asked for four- and five-year-old children who have been engaged in formal instruction on establishing length relations, conserving length relations, and using properties and consequences of length relations.

Question asked for four- and five-year-old children with no formal instruction on length relations.

1. What is the proficiency level of children when spontaneously establishing length relations between two curves?

Questions asked for four- and five-year-old children with formal instruction only on establishing length relations.

2. What is the proficiency level of children when establishing length relations between two curves?
3. Does formal instruction only on establishing length relations improve the proficiency level of children when establishing length relations?
4. Are children able to conserve length relations when the asymmetric property and logical consequences are involved as well as when they are not involved?
5. Are children able to use the reflexive and nonreflexive properties?
6. Are children able to use the transitive property of length relations?
7. Is the ability to use the reflexive and nonreflexive properties necessary (or sufficient) for children to conserve relations?
8. Is the ability to use the reflexive and nonreflexive properties necessary (or sufficient) for children to use the transitive property of length relations?
9. Is the ability to conserve length relations necessary (or sufficient) for children to use the transitive property of length relations?

Questions asked for four- and five-year-olds with formal instruction on establishing length relations, conserving length relations, and using properties and consequences of length relations.

Questions (5)-(9) are repeated here as questions (10)-(14).

15. Does formal instruction on conserving length relations; on the reflexive, nonreflexive, and asymmetric properties; and on consequences of length relations improve the ability to (1) use the reflexive and nonreflexive property, (2) conserve length relations, and (3) use the transitive property of length relations?

Procedure

Subjects

The subjects were 20 four-year-old and 34 five-year-old children.

At the initiation of the study, the range of ages was 47-57 months for the group considered as four-year-olds and 59-69 months for the group considered as five-year-olds. The children were in three self-contained classrooms with some of both age groups in each room. The verbal maturity and intelligence of the children were measured by the Peabody Picture Vocabulary Test and Stanford Binet Intelligence Scale, Form L-M (Table 1). The mean for the intelligence of the four-year-olds was modestly higher than that for the five-year-olds.

Table 1
Verbal Maturity and Intelligence

	Verbal Maturity		*Intelligence*	
Age Group	Range	Mean	Range	Mean
4	83-119	102.6	98-145	119.6
5	55-120	97.7	81-130	109.1

According to the Hollingshead Two Factor Index of Social Position, the social classes of the children ranged from I (high) to V (Table 2). Category III for each age group contained the greatest number of children.

Table 2
Social Classes by Age Group

Age Group \ Social Class	I	II	III	IV	V
4	3	4	9	4	0
5	3	8	13	6	4

*Instructional Sequence and Measuring Instruments**

Instructional sequences. Three instructional sequences were constructed especially for the study. Instructional Sequence I was designed to develop the ability of children to establish a length relation between two curves; Instructional Sequence II was designed to develop the ability of children to use the reflexive and nonreflexive properties; and Instructional Sequence III was designed to develop the ability of children to conserve length relations and use the asymmetric property and logical consequences. The following principles were employed in the design of the sequences.

1. Mathematical concepts are not implicit in a set of physical materials. A child gains mathematical knowledge from a set of physical materials by the actions he performs on or with the materials.

*Sample items are given in the Appendix.

2. Mathematical concepts should not be presented to young children through the use only of the symbols of mathematics or verbalizations. Explanations which accompany the child's actions, however, may facilitate his acquisition of mathematical concepts.

3. There should be a continuous interplay between the spoken words which symbolize a mathematical concept and a set of actions a child performs while constructing something that makes the concept tangible.

4. In order to teach a concept, it is necessary to use different assortments of physical materials and different types of activities all of which are related to the development, by the child, of the same concept(s).

5. The principle of reversibility should be employed (i.e., returning a transformed set of conditions to an original set of conditions).

6. Situations must be contrived in which the children are led to multiple focusing (e.g., if A is the same length as B, then B is also the same length as A).

7. Situations must be contrived which involve more than one child so that the children may interact.

8. The principle of equilibration should be employed.

Measuring instruments. Five instruments were constructed to measure pupil capabilities. The first instrument, the Length Comparison Test, was designed to measure the ability of children to establish a length relation between two curves. Six different material sets were used. Three items, one a "longer than," one a "shorter than," and one a "same length as" item, were presented to the child in the case of each material set for a total of 18 items.

The second instrument, the Conservation of Length Relations Test, consisted of two parts. In the first part of each of the 18 items, the children were asked to compare the lengths of two curves. Since the material used in the items differed from those in either Instructional Sequence I or the Length Comparison Test, these 18 first parts were considered as an Application Test for Instructional Sequence I (hereafter called the Length Comparison Application Test). The second part of each item involved the ability of the child to conserve the length relation he had just established. Nine of the items also involved the ability of the child to use the asymmetric property of "longer than" and "shorter than" or logical consequences. These nine items comprised an instrument which will be designated as the Conservation of Length Relations: Level II Test. The remaining nine items comprise an instrument which will be designated as the Conservation of Length Relations: Level I Test.

"Yes" was the correct response in the case of the nine items of the Level I Test. "No" was the correct response for each of the nine items of the Level II Test. The children were required to respond in the presence of a perceptual conflict so that if a child based his response on visual perception he would give an incorrect response. Three distinct length-preserving transformations were used to produce the perceptual conflicts. Also, different material sets were utilized.

The third instrument, the Reflexive and Nonreflexive Test, consisted of six items of a diversified nature. Three of the items involved the reflexive property of "the same length as" and three items involved the nonreflexive property of "longer than" or "shorter than." Five different material sets were employed. "Yes" was the correct response to the items involving the reflexive property, and "No" was the correct response to the remaining three items.

The fourth instrument, the Transitivity Test, consisted of six items where "Yes" was the correct response for three items. For these items, each of the relations "longer than," "shorter than," and "the same length as" was included. "No" was the correct response for the remaining three items. Each of the latter three items involved transitivity of "the same length as." It was not possible for the child to use a non-transitive hypothesis to arrive at a correct response because all of the perceptual cues were biased against a correct response and the child was not allowed to directly compare the two curves under consideration.

Instructional and Evaluational Sequence

Small group instructional procedures were utilized in each room. An instructional group generally consisted of six children with teacher aides present to guide the remaining children. After the Length Comparison Test was administered, Instructional Sequence I was administered for a sequence of seven sessions of 20-30 minutes per session. Due to small-group instructional procedures, the total instructional time spanned more than seven days for any one class. However, any one child was involved in only seven instructional sessions. The Length Comparison Test, the Length Comparison Application Test, the Conservation of Length Relations Test, the Reflexive and Nonreflexive Test, and the Transitivity Test were administered during the days immediately following the last instructional session. The Length Comparison Test was not administered a second time to one class because that class earned a high mean score on the first administration of the test. The material in Instructional Sequence I was administered to that class, however, to support the interpretation of the remaining tests.

Instructional Sequence II and III began immediately after the testing period following Instructional Sequence I. Instructional Sequence II was administered in three sessions of 20-30 minutes per session and Instructional Sequence III was administered in five sessions of 20-30 minutes per session. The second administration of the Length Comparison Application Test, the Conservation of Length Relations Test, the Reflexive and Nonreflexive Test, and the Transitive Test began one day after the last instructional sequence.

Testing Procedures

The children were tested on a one-to-one basis. The items were assigned at random by test to each child so that each had a different sequence of the same items. All tests were administered by specially trained evaluators.

The Length Comparison Test was scored on a basis of the number of correct comparisons a child was able to perform. The Conservation of Length Relations Test was administered at one sitting so that a child would be forced to respond "Yes" or "No" in a random sequence. If a child established a relation, regardless of whether he established a "correct" or "incorrect" relation, he was tested on his ability to conserve that relation. In the case of the Transitivity Test, unless a child established two correct comparisons, no measure was obtained on his ability to use the transitive property of that relation.

Design

Length Comparison Test. An analysis of variance technique was used to study the profiles of four- and five-year-old children with regard to the Length Comparison Test on the first and second administration (Greenhouse and Geisser, 1959). In particular, the design allows for testing of the hypothesis that the profile of mean scores on the first and second administration does not differ for the four- and five-year-olds as well as providing a test for possible differences in the mean scores on the first and second administration across age. An item analysis was also conducted.

Conservation of Length Relations Test. The Conservation of Length Relations Test consisted of nine items for which a response of "Yes" was correct and nine items for which a response of "No" was correct. One may think of each student's response set as being an ordered 18-tuple where each element is either "Yes" or "No." If each response set is considered to be a random sample from 2^{18} such response sets, it has probability of 2^{-18} of occurring (Feller, 1957, p. 29). If a child guessed during the test, then one may consider his responses as being nothing more than an 18-tuple of "Yes's" or "No's" for elements, where "Yes" or "No" for any one entry each had probability of 1/2 of occurring. In this case, his response set may be considered as a random sample, and the probability he obtained at least six correct "Yes" responses and six correct "No" responses is not greater than .06.

For a child to be classified as being able to conserve length relations and conserve length relations involving the asymmetric property and logical consequences, he then must have at least six of the nine items which were written to exemplify Level I and six of the nine items which were written to exemplify Level II correct. In such case, the child is said to meet criterion for Level I and II.

If one considers the nine items written at either Level I or Level II regardless of the nine items written at the other level, a probability of only approximately .02 exists that a child responded correctly to eight or nine items at that Level if he guessed. Thus, if a child does not meet criterion for Level I and II one may consider his responses to one of the two items sets written at Level I or Level II. Clearly, a high probability exists that those children who scored at least eight or nine correct for a particular item set may have responded to those items on a basis other than guessing. Such children may be candidates for being classified at just Level I or Level II. One cannot, however, with any degree of confidence, assert that in fact such children did not possess a response bias unless the remaining nine items are considered. For example, if a child was able to score an eight or nine on Level I items and responded on a basis of guessing on Level II items, then a probability of only .02 occurs that the child had at most one correct "No" response. If this unlikely event occurred, whether a response bias existed or whether the child responded on the basis of the perceptual cues is an open question. For a child to meet criterion for just Level I or Level II then, he must respond correctly to eight or nine items of the Level in question and no less than two and no more than five items of the other level. It must be pointed out that the criterion is a conservation one since it is known that children do respond on the basis of perceptual cues (Steffe, 1966).

A principal component analysis was conducted using all 18 items to aid in the interpretation of the above criteria. Item difficulties were determined as well as internal consistency reliabilities, both of which also can be used in interpretation of the criteria established. In order to check the hypothesis that the distribution of total scores did not differ from a theoretical distribution based on random responses, a "goodness of fit" test was employed (Seigel, 1956, pp. 42-46).

In order to detect any significant changes in the number of children meeting criterion on the conservation of length relations test for Level I and II from the first to second administration, the McNemar test for significance of changes was used. (Seigel, 1956, pp. 63-67). Thus, those children meeting criterion were given a "1" and those not meeting criterion were given a "0," so only nominal scale of measurement was employed. According to Seigel, the "McNemar test for the significance of changes is particularly applicable to those 'before and after' designs in which each person is used as his own control in which measurement is in the strength of either a nominal or ordinal scale (p. 63)." Explicitly, the null hypothesis is: H_0: For those children who change, the probability P_1 that any child will change from C (criterion) to ~C (noncriterion) is equal to the probability P_2 that he will change from ~C to C. The alternative hypothesis is: H_1: $P_1 < P_2$.

Reflexive and Nonreflexive Test. The set {Yes, No} represents possible responses for the six items of the Reflexive and Nonreflexive Test. Other responses were possible, but they occurred with zero probability in the testing sessions. Because there are 2^6 different sextuples with "Yes" or "No" as elements, if a child guessed, the probability that any one of the 2^6-tuples occurred is 2^{-6}. Under these conditions, the probability of a child obtaining at least five or six correct responses is approximately .11. It must be pointed out, however, that children do respond on the basis of perceptual cues, so that the actual probability that a child who does not possess the ability to conserve length could obtain five or six may be much lower than .11.

If a child responded on the basis of a bias (always says "Yes" or "No"), then he would not obtain a five or six. Moreover, if a child possesses only the ability to use either the reflexive or nonreflexive property, he also would not achieve a five or six. Hence, the performance criterion of a total score of five or six was established. A "goodness of fit" test was employed to test the hypothesis that the distribution of total scores does not differ from a distribution based on random responses. In order to detect any significant changes in the number of children meeting criterion from the first to second administration, the McNemar test for significance of changes was used. Explicitly, the null hypothesis is H_0: For those children who change, the probability P_1 that any child will change from C to ~C is equal to the probability P_2 that he will change from ~C to C. The alternative hypothesis is: H_1: $P_1 < P_2$.

Transitivity Test. Based on the average item difficulty of the Length Relations Application Test, a parameter was established (average item difficulty) which may be regarded as an efficiency level of the child's ability to establish length relations between curves. Using this parameter, r, the probability that a child could establish a correct relation in each of the two necessary overt comparisons on any item (comparisons between A and B and between B and C, where ARB and BRC and R is the relation) in the Transitivity Test was r^2. The calculation assumes that the comparisons are performed independently.

If a child responded on a random basis to a relational question concerning A and C (such as, "Is A longer than C?"), the probability p of a correct response on any item is $r^2/2$. Using this value of p, a performance criterion was established and a "goodness of fit" test performed on the distribution of total scores to the theoretical distribution of total scores based on guessing.

To establish whether the ability to conserve length relations is necessary (sufficient) to enable children to use the transitive property, an inspection was made of those children who met criterion on each test instrument. If the ability to conserve length relations is necessary for the ability to use the transitive property, then each child who attains criterion on the Transitivity Test must also meet criterion on the Conservation of Length Relations Test. If the ability to conserve length relations is sufficient for the ability to use the transitive property, then each child who meets criterion on the Conservation of Length Relations Test must also meet criterion on the Transitivity Test. Other interdependencies were investigated in the same way.

Results of the Study

The results of the study are partitioned as follows: Length Comparison Test; Length Comparison Application Test; Conservation of Length Relations Test; Reflexive and Nonreflexive Test; Transitivity Test; and Conservation and Transitivity Relationships.

Length Comparison Test

The results of an internal-consistency reliability study (Table 3) revealed that the reliabilities associated with the total test scores were quite substantial and support analyses of the data. In the case of the first administration, the reliabilities for the subsets were also substantial. For the second administration, however, the reliability for the six items which were designed to measure the ability of children to establish the relation "shorter than" was low. Various reasons may be given, the most apparent of which is the high mean and relatively small standard deviation (Table 4). It is known that easy tests may be unreliable.

No differences were statistically discernible for the variable Age using the total scores as the dependent measure (Table 5) although the mean score for the second administration was significantly greater than the mean score for the first administration. No interaction of Age and

Table 3
Reliabilities of Length Comparison Test: First and Second Administration
(Kuder-Richardson #20)

Test	Reliability	
	First Administration	Second Administration
Total	.91	.83
Longer Than	.82	.71
Shorter Than	.87	.43
Same Length As	.77	.73

Table 4
Mean and Standard Deviations of Length
Comparison Test: First and Second Administration

Test	First Administration		Second Administration	
	$\overline{X}$	S.D.	$\overline{X}$	S.D.
Total	10.68	5.35	14.55	3.53
Longer Than	4.38	1.91	4.94	1.43
Shorter Than	3.29	2.32	5.12	1.07
Same Length As	3.00	2.02	4.49	1.70

Table 5
ANOVA Summary
Length Comparison Application Test

Source of Variation by Test	F
Total Scores	
A (Age)	2.65
B (Tests: First vs. Second Administration)	22.45**
AB	< 1
Longer Than	
A (Age)	< 1
B (Tests)	2.85
AB	< 1
Shorter Than	
A (Age)	3.42
B (Tests)	26.35**
AB	< 1
Same Length As	
A (Age)	2.04
B (Tests)	14.18**
AB	2.80

$^{**}p < .01$

Tests occurred that indicate that the difference between the means for each group on the second administration was not significantly different than the differences between the means for each group on the first administration.

On the subtest "longer than," the children started with relatively high mean scores (68 and 75 percent for the four- and five-year-olds, respectively) and ended with mean scores 78 and 86 percent, a nonsignificant gain, statistically. In the case of the subtest "shorter than," a large gain was noted for both the four- and five-year-olds (from 43 to 76 percent for age four and from 62 to 91 percent for age five). Again, Age was not significant. In the case of the subtest "same length as," a substantial increase was again present (48 to 57 percent for age four and 46 to 80 percent for age five). Age was again nonsignificant as was the interaction of Age and Tests. On the basis of the test scores alone, one may hypothesize that an interaction occurred. The nonsignificant interaction may be due to the power of the statistical test involved.

All the correlations computed between test scores on the first and second administration with the variables Verbal Maturity, I.Q., Age, and Social Class were low, although some differed significantly from a zero correlation. Age correlated significantly (Total test--.42, Shorter Than--.41, Same Length As--.42; $p < .02$) with scores on the second administration except for the subtest "longer than." The correlation coefficient between Social Class and the subtest "same length as" on the first administration was also statistially significant (-.41, $p < .02$) but negative.

Length Comparison Application Test

In order to ascertain whether the ability of children to compare lengths of curves was restricted to six specific material sets, the Length Comparison Application Test was administered and a correlation study conducted using scores of eight tests (the total tests and subtests thereof for the second administration of Length Comparison Test and for the first administration of Length Comparison Application Test). The correlation of .81 between total scores (Table 6) along with the significant pair-wise correlation of the respective subtests indicates a high degree of relationship.

Table 6
Correlation Matrix
Length Comparison Test (Second Administration) and
Length Comparison Application Test (First Administration)

Test	1	2	3	4	5	6	7	8
LCT								
1. Total	1.00	.82**	.79**	.88**	.81**	.71**	.78**	.65**
2. Longer		1.00	.52**	.53**	.77**	.71**	.77**	.58**
3. Shorter			1.00	.57**	.69**	.60**	.65**	.59**
4. Same As				1.00	.58**	.50**	.56**	.48**
LCAT								
5. Total					1.00	.83**	.93**	.89**
6. Longer						1.00	.79**	.60**
7. Shorter							1.00	.72**
8. Same As								1.00

**Significantly different from zero correlations; $p < .01$

The Length Comparison Application Test was administered twice, once before the completion of Instructional Sequences II and III and once after. The pupil performances on the second administration are of interest because Instructional Sequence III contained additional exercises on length comparisons. However, no apparent changes in the mean scores were observable across administrations (Table 7). All the reliabilities on the first administration were substantial (Table 8). On the second administration, the reliability of the subtest "shorter than" was very low. A high mean score and small standard deviation may contribute to this reliability.

Table 7
Means and Standard Deviations of Length Comparison Application Tests

Test	First Administration $\overline{X}$	First Administration S.D.	Second Administration $\overline{X}$	Second Administration S.D.
Total	14.10	3.89	14.44	3.14
Longer Than	5.02	1.39	5.16	1.22
Shorter Than	4.34	1.81	4.86	1.03
Same Length As	4.74	1.50	4.42	1.58

Table 8
Reliabilities of Length Comparison Application Tests (Kuder-Richardson #20)

Test	Reliability First Administration	Reliability Second Administration
Total	.85	.76
Longer Than	.71	.63
Shorter Than	.77	.18
Same Length As	.68	.65

The correlation of the variables Verbal Maturity, I.Q., Age, and Social Class with the total test scores and subtest thereof on the first and second administration were low (-.12 to .39). All but one of the significant correlations involved Age. This is consistent with the correlations reported earlier for the Length Comparison Test.

Conservation of Length Relations Test

An internal consistency reliability study was conducted for each test administration. The range of the reliabilities was .81 to .88. The item difficulties (Table 9) and means (Table 10) for the Conservation of Length Relations Tests indicated that performance of children on Level I and Level II items was similar for the first test administration. There was a major difference, however, for the second administration in that Level I items were considerably less difficult that Level II items, items which remained at about the same difficulty level for both test administrations.

A principal component analysis was conducted (Table 11). Factor 1 of the first test administration was a bipolar factor where the items at Level I loaded negatively and the items at Level II loaded positively. Four of the five positive loadings which exceeded .5 were items involving the asymmetrical property of "longer than" or "shorter than." The remaining

Table 9
Item Difficulty of Conservation of Length Relations Tests

	Item	Difficulty: First Administration	Difficulty: Second Administration
Level I	1	.59	.83
	2	.39	.69
	3	.55	.85
	4	.49	.87
	5	.51	.83
	6	.51	.77
	7	.37	.73
	8	.49	.85
	9	.39	.73
Level II	1	.47	.46
	2	.43	.58
	3	.49	.44
	4	.59	.58
	5	.43	.44
	6	.43	.52
	7	.57	.56
	8	.43	.46
	9	.49	.58

Table 10
Means and Standard Deviations of Conservation of Length Relations Test: Level I and Level II

Level	First Administration $\bar{X}$	First Administration S.D.	Second Administration $\bar{X}$	Second Administration S.D.
Level I	4.29	3.17	7.13	2.56
Level II	4.33	2.80	4.62	2.92

positive loading which exceeded .5 involved the statement, "If A is the same length as B, then A is not longer than B." The six items which had loadings greater than .5 for Factor 2 of the first test administration included four items which involved logical consequences of the relations, one of which involved the asymmetrical property of "shorter than" and one of which tested conservation of "the same length as."

Of the two identifiable factors of the second test administration, the items which had loadings greater than .5 were all Level II items for Factor I and Level I items for Factor 2. Moreover, each Level II item had a loading greater than .5 on Factor 1. These factors clearly may be a result of the item difficulties for the second test administration.

Table 11
Principal Component Analysis of Conservation of Length Relations Tests

Item Level		First Administration 1	First Administration 2	Second Administration 1	Second Administration 2
Level I					
Longer Than	1	-.5179	.4928	-.1938	.6206
	2	-.8139	.3029	.0778	.7065
	3	-.7534	.1310	.3150	.4925
Shorter Than	4	-.6982	.3444	-.2794	.5122
	5	-.6776	.4312	-.2651	.4185
	6	-.7831	-.0674	-.1996	.7985
Same Length As	7	-.6903	.5853	-.3807	.8069
	8	-.7261	.2393	-.3466	.3631
	9	-.8440	.4050	-.4118	.7599
Level II					
Longer Than	1	.5748	.4854	.5134	.3771
	2	.3730	.5885	.7704	.2654
	3	.6523	.0404	.8291	.2600
Shorter Than	4	.8592	.2577	.5999	.1304
	5	.7244	.5162	.7887	.2206
	6	.4528	.5671	.5580	.0838
Same Length As	7	.5512	.6195	.7462	.2527
	8	.3729	.2845	.6475	.2374
	9	.3865	.7055	.7429	.1681
Percent Communality		45.57	21.61	41.67	33.00

These principal component analyses justified identifying two levels of items in the Conservation of Length Relations Test.

Level I criterion was met by one four-year-old and three five-year-olds for the first test administration. Of these four children, only one five-year-old met criterion for Level I and II on the second test administration, and the four-year-old met criterion for Level I. The remaining two children did not meet any criterion on the second test administration. A total of four four-year-olds and six five-year-olds met criterion for Level I on the second test administration.

In case of the first test administration, seven children scored eight or nine on Level II items but at most five on Level I items. Of these seven, five had only a zero or one on Level I items. One of the remaining two children met criterion for Level I and II on the second test administration. The other child did not meet any criterion on the second test administration. No child met criterion for Level II only on the second administration.

After Instructional Sequence I, three four-year-olds and three five-year-olds met the criterion for Level I and II. Five four-year-olds and fourteen five-year-olds met the same criterion after Instructional Sequence II and III. According to the McNemar Test, the change for the five-year-olds was significant ($\chi^2 = 6.67$; $p < .01$), but the change for the four-year-olds was not.

If children do, in fact, respond "Yes" or "No" in a random fashion to items presented, then the distribution of total scores should not depart from a binomial frequency distribution based on random responses, except for chance fluctuations. The actual frequency distribution of scores for each group by Conservation Level did statistically depart from a theoretical distribution at the .01 level (Table 12).

Table 12
Comparison of Theoretical and Actual Frequency Distribution
Conservation of Length Relations

Test By Age	χ^2
Four-Year-Olds	
Level I, First Administration	744.5**
Level I, Second Administration	1712.8**
Level II, First Administration	140.8**
Level II, Second Administration	69.6**
Five-Year-Olds	
Level I, First Administration	351.3**
Level I, Second Administration	2071.5**
Level II, First Administration	267.0**
Level II, Second Administration	495.9**

**$p < .01$

The correlation between the Level I and Level II total scores with Verbal Maturity, Age, and Social Class was not significantly different from a zero correlation except for the correlation between I.Q. and the Level II total scores on the second test administration. This correlation of .34 was low.

Reflexive and Nonreflexive Test

The reliabilities for the Reflexive and Nonreflexive Test were .43 for the first test administration and .53 for the second test administration. A contribution to the low test reliabilities was the existence of more than one factor in the test (Table 13). In case of each test administration, the items loaded on two factors. Factor 1, in case of the first test administration, was a combination of the reflexive property and the type of transformation and Factor 2 was a combination of conservation involving the nonreflexive property and the type of transformation. It is noted that for both factors, two of the items involving the same property loaded with a higher value than the third. The third item always involved a different transformation from the two others, which involved the same transformation. These factors clearly justify the criterion established because for a child to know that a curve is the same length as itself, he must also know it is not longer or shorter than itself.

Table 13
Principal Component Analysis for the Reflexive and Nonreflexive Test

Item	*First Administration* 1	2	*Second Administration* 1	2
Nonreflexive				
1	.1971	.6889	.7808	.0553
2	-.1639	.6452	.8748	.0444
3	.1975	.3252	.5354	-.0007
Reflexive				
4	-.9071	-.0168	-.0819	.7808
5	-.9341	.1090	-.0586	.8334
6	-.4188	.0184	.0940	.3311
Percent Communality	52.63	26.88	42.45	35.84

The item difficulties for the first test administration ranged from .24 to .51 with four item difficulties below .40. The item difficulties for the second test administration ranged from .37 to .88 with only one difficulty below .40. All of the item difficulties increased from the first to second administration with the greatest increase for the items involving the reflexive property. A change from 2.12 to 3.75 in the means for the first and second administration reflected the modest increase in item difficulty.

One four- and one five-year-old earned a score of five or six on the first test administration. The number of four- and five-year-olds meeting the criterion on the second test administration increased to six and nine, respectively. The two children who met the criterion on the first test administration did not meet the required level of performance on the second administration. However, the number of students who changed from noncriterion to criterion was greater than the number of children who changed from criterion to noncriterion ($\chi^2 = 8.50$, $p < .01$). There was also an increase in the number of children that responded correctly to all the reflexive items but did not meet the criterion. The change was from seven to twenty-one from the first to the second test administration.

When the distribution of total scores by the four-year-olds was considered, it was found that the frequency distribution for both the first ($\chi^2 = 32.8$) and second ($\chi^2 = 50.7$) test administration departed statistically at the .01 level from a binomial distribution. The theoretical and actual frequency distributions of scores earned by the five-year-olds on the first ($\chi^2 = 37.7$) and second ($\chi^2 = 31.3$) test administration also departed statistically at the .01 level.

All correlations of the total scores with the variables Verbal Maturity, I.Q., Age, and Social Class were low. However, the correlations between total scores and Social Class were significantly different from zero.

Transitivity

The reliabilities for both test administrations for the Transitivity Test (.50 and .45) were low. This may be expected because the principal component analysis (Table 14) revealed the existence of more than one factor in the test. For the first test administration, two items (one involving transitivity of "shorter than" and one "longer than") loaded greater than .5 on Factor 1. Factor 2, first administration, is a combination of transitivity of "longer than" and "same length as." For the second test administration, Factor 1 involved transitivity of "same length as," and Factor 2 involved transitivity of "shorter than" and "longer than," a clear dichotomy.

Table 14
Principal Component Analysis for the Transitivity Test

Item	Relation	First Administration 1	First Administration 2	Second Administration 1	Second Administration 2
1	Same Length	.4362	.4998	.8001	-.0065
2	Same Length	.2940	.4637	.5762	.3157
3	Shorter than	.6970	-.1967	.1468	-.4648
4	Longer than	.5621	-.5222	.1204	-.5562
5	Same Length	.3424	.2903	.4260	-.0658
6	Same Length	.4241	-.0545	.7806	-.1921
Percent Communality		44.44	27.90	61.50	11.11

The mean scores for the first and second administration were 2.00 and 2.67, respectively, an increase which reflected the increase in item difficulty for each item. Only one item on any administration had a difficulty that exceeded .5. Four four-year-olds and five five-year-olds met the criterion (a total score of five or six) for transitivity on the first test administration. A total of fifteen students met the criterion on the second administration of which five were four-year-olds and ten were five-year-olds. Five students that met the criterion on the first test administration did not meet the criterion on the second administration. Three of these students were unable to make the necessary length comparisons upon which to base the transitive property. Therefore, only two students may have lost transitivity. The level of performance of one of these two students may involve a chance fluctuation since transitivity was exhibited three out of five times on the second test administration.

The actual frequency distributions of scores earned by the four-year-olds on the first ($\chi^2 = 6.5$) and on the second ($\chi^2 = 9.1$) test administrations did not depart statistically at the .05 level from a binomial distribution based on random responses. Since the actual frequency distributions for the four-year-olds did not depart from the theoretical distribution, no four-year-olds were considered to have the ability to use the transitive property of the length relations involved. In the calculation of the theoretical binomial distribution based on guesses, a probability p for correct responses was .30. This value is based on an efficiency level of .78 as calculated from the Length Comparison Application Test, first test administration.

The actual frequency distribution of scores earned by the five-year-olds on the first ($\chi^2 = 17.2$) and second test administration ($\chi^2 = 74.9$) did depart statistically from a binomial distribution at the .01 level. The main departure for the first administration scores was in the number of 0 and 1 scores. An increase in frequency of total scores in the range of 3 to 6 was noted in the results of the second test administration.

An investigation of characteristics of children not meeting the criterion and those meeting the criterion revealed little difference between the mean age for the two levels of performance of any one group. There was a small difference between the mean Verbal Maturity scores and for the mean I.Q. scores. Correlation between the variables Verbal Maturity, I.Q., Age, and Social Class and the levels of performance were not statistically significant.

Relationships Among the Variables

On the first test administration, two children met criterion on the Reflexive and Nonreflexive Test. Neither of these children met criterion on the Transitivity Test or criterion on Conservation of Length Relations: Level I and II Test. One child met criterion only in the case of the Conservation of Length Relations: Level I Test. On the second test administration, only one child out of the 14 who met criterion on the Reflexive and Nonreflexive Test met criterion on the Transitivity Test. This child did not meet the criterion on the Conservation of Length Relations: Level I Test or on the Conservation of Length Relations: Level I and II Test. However, seven of the 14 children who met criterion on the Reflexive and Nonreflexive Test met criterion on the Conservation of Length Relations: Level I and II Test, and three children met criterion in the case of Conservation of Length Relations: Level I Test.

Four children met criterion of Length Relations: Level I Test but not on the Level II Test for the first test administration. Two of these children met criterion on the Transitivity Test and one met criterion on the Reflexive and Nonreflexive Test. The two children meeting criterion on the Transitivity Test did not meet criterion on the Reflexive and Nonreflexive Test. Only four out of the ten children who met criterion on the Conservation of Length Relations: Level I Test but not the Level II Test on the second test administration met criterion on the Reflexive and Nonreflexive Test. None of the ten met criterion on the Transitivity Test.

On the first test administration, only one out of the six children who met criterion on the Conservation of Length Relations: Level I and II Test met criterion on the Transitivity Test. None of these six children met the criterion on the Reflexive and Nonreflexive Test. On the second test administration, seven of the 19 children who met criterion on the Conservation of Length Relations: Level I and II Test met criterion on the Reflexive and Nonreflexive Test. Seven different children met criterion on the Transitivity Test. Five children did not meet criterion on the Reflexive and Nonreflexive Test or on the Transitivity Test.

On the first test administration, only two of five children who met criterion on the Transitivity Test met criterion on the Conservation of Length Relations: Level I Test. One of these five children met criterion on the Reflexive and Nonreflexive Test. On the second test administration, seven of the ten students who met criterion on the Transitivity Test also met criterion on the Conservation of Length Relations: Level I and II Test, but only one child met criterion on the Reflexive and Nonreflexive Test.

Conclusions, Discussions, and Implications

Length Comparison Test

Before or after Instructional Sequence I on length comparison, the performance of four-year-old children in establishing a relation between two curves is not different from that of five-year-olds. It appears that four- and five-year-old children easily learn the relation "longer than" through informal experiences or testing facilitates learning of this relation. Beilen and Franklin (1962) did find that testing facilitates first-grade children's acquisition of measurement tasks which, in addition to the fact that testing was conducted for all three relations, leads to the conclusion that children acquire "longer than" through informal experience to a greater extent than "shorter than" or "the same length as."

Instruction on establishing length comparisons does significantly improve the ability of both four- and five-year-old children to establish length comparisons. The instructional experiences utilized in this study involved a continuous interplay between language and manipulation of objects as Bruner and Kenney (1964) recommend. This interplay was an endeavor to eliminate experiences dependent solely upon language and not real practical action, which Adler (1964) considers a failure of formal education and which should have aided the children in not responding on a perceptual basis when establishing length relations as suggested by Wohlwill (1960).

The ability of four- and five-year-old children to make length comparisons involving the relations "longer than," "shorter than," and "same length as" is not limited to situations in which they learned to establish these relations -- as the children had the ability to use the relations in novel length comparison situations. The formal experiences with concrete materials was sufficient for a majority of the children to reach an overt operational level with length comparisons, a level of performance which was retained over the several months this study was in progress.

There appears to be little, if any, relation between the variables of Verbal Maturity, I.Q., Age, and Social Class and the ability of four- and five-year-old children to make length comparisons involving "longer than," "shorter than," and "same length as." This is similar to Beilen and Franklin's (1962) findings that I.Q. was not a factor in first-grade children's learning to measure length.

Conservation of Length Relations

The definitions given for length relations and conservation of these relations (i.e., that the relation obtains regardless of the proximity of the curves) seem to have been supported by the results of the study. On the Length Comparison Application Test, first administration, the mean score was 78 percent (14.10 out of 18 items) with a standard deviation of only 3.89. At this point in time, the children in the study were able to associate a relational term with an overt comparison of curves in such a way that they were able to discriminate among the comparisons denoted by "longer than," "shorter than," and "the same length as." The particular relation a child established on the first administration of the application test through overt comparison was a function of the proximity of the curves involved. This is supported by the fact that at most two children could be classified at only Level I and at most four children could be classified as meeting criterion on the Conservation of Length Relations: Level I and II Test (those four who met criterion on both the first and second administration of the Conservation of Length Relations Test). With the exception of these last four children and possibly the former two, there is no evidence that at the time of the first administration of the Length Comparison Application Test an overt comparison constituted a logical-mathematical experience for the child making the comparison. The overt comparison was certainly not sufficient for the child (using Piaget's terms) to disengage the structure of the relation he established. It certainly may be the case that the relation for the child not only was a function of the proximity of the curves but was a function of the external physical situation so that the child did not think about the relation in the absence of the external situation. In Bruner and Kenny's (1964) terms, the child had not internalized the relation; or in Lovell's (1966a) terms, the child was not aware of the significance of his actions in the overt comparison of the curves.

The definitions of Level I and Level II were well supported by the principal components analysis on the first administration. This analysis shows that the items written at Level I and Level II involve differential abilities. In particular, for the pretest, the items written at Level II which involved the asymmetrical property of "longer than" or "shorter than" loaded on Factor 2 as well as an item involving a logical consequence of "the same length as." On the second test administration, the items written at Level I were much less difficult than those written at Level II, which certainly contributed to the factors present in the principal component analysis.

Level I items were constructed to measure the extent to which the children realize that the length relation they established between two curves is independent of the proximity of the curves. As noted, before the administration of Instructional Sequences II and III, only about 12 percent of the children could be categorized at Level I. After the administration of Instructional Sequences II and III, however, the evidence indicated that about 57 percent of the children could be categorized at that Level. At the same two points in time, the percents were 8 and 37 with regard to Level I and II, which was a statistically significant change. It must be emphasized that the children in this 37 percent not only were able to establish a relation between two curves and retain the relation regardless of the proximity of the curves but were able to use the asymmetric property and logical consequences of the relation under consideration. It is certainly true that the experiences contained in Instructional Sequences II and III did not readily increase the children's ability to use logical consequences of the relations they were able to establish.

The data suggest that the mean I.Q. for the five-year-old children who met criterion for Level I and II was greater than the mean I.Q. for those who did not meet criterion. The correlation of total scores for Level I and II with the variables of Verbal Maturity, I.Q., Age, and Social Class were not significant with the possible exception of a low correlation between I.Q. and Level II posttest scores.

Reflexive and Nonreflexive Properties

Very few four- and five-year-old children were able to use the reflexive and nonreflexive properties on the first administration of the Reflexive and Nonreflexive Test. Elkind (1967) apparently would identify the ability to use the reflexive property as conservation of identity even though he did not subdivide conservation of identity with regard to the reflexive and nonreflexive properties. An effort is made here not to confuse conservation of identity with the ability to use the reflexive and nonreflexive properties nor to confuse conservation of length with conservation of length relations.

Some four- and five-year-old children have the ability to use the reflexive property but not the nonreflexive property. Instructional experience on length comparisons appear to be sufficient for such children to exhibit the reflexive property, as 14 percent of the sample were able to use the reflexive property on the first test administration as compared to four percent who were able to use both properties.

Instructional Sequences II and III significantly increased the ability of four- and five-year-old children to use both properties. On the second test administration 41 percent of the sample were able to use only the reflexive property and 30 percent of the sample were able to use both. Only 29 percent of the sample did not display an ability to use the reflexive or nonreflexive properties. These conclusions substantiate Piaget's theory that experience is a necessary but not a sufficient condition for the development of logical thought processes because all the children received the same selected experiences. Certainly the data substantiate that the ability to use the reflexive property is different from and precedes the ability to use the nonreflexive property.

There appears to be little, if any, relation between the student variables Verbal Maturity, I.Q., Age, and Social Class and scores earned by four- and five-year-old children on the Reflexive and Nonreflexive Test. Only correlations involving Social Class were significantly different from zero, but these correlations were low.

Transitivity

Few five-year-old children were able to use the transitive property after only instructional experience in establishing length relations. At this point in time, only 16 percent of the five-year-olds used the transitive property. At the same point in time, the distribution of total scores for the four-year-olds did not statistically depart from a binomial distribution based on random responses, so no four-year-old was considered able to use the transitive property of length relations. Some children performed poorly because of their inability to establish the two initial comparisons, an inability Smedslund (1963b) considers as a reason for failure of some young children to use the transitive property.

Instructional Sequences II and III did increase the ability of five-year-olds to use the transitive property, since the percent of five-year-olds able to use the transitive property increased to 31. These same experiences did not increase the ability of four-year-old children to use the transitive property because again the distribution of total scores for the four-year-olds did not statistically depart from a binomial distribution based on guessing. The number of five-year-olds that used transitivity of length relations is below that found by Braine (1959) but above that found by Smedslund (1964). It appears that these experiences were not logical-mathematical experiences that readily increase children's ability to use the transitive property. All the children may not have had a mental structure sufficient to allow assimilation of the information.

The mean Verbal Maturity and I.Q. of five-year-old children who were able to use the transitive property appeared to be slightly higher than for those who do not use this property. However, the correlations between these two variables and transitivity scores earned by the total sample was not statistically different from zero. Also, there appears to be little, if any, relationship between the variables Age and Social Class and the ability of four- and five-year-old children to use the transitive property.

Relationships Among the Variables

The relationships of reflexive and nonreflexive properties, conservation of length relations, and transitivity of length relations will be discussed on each of the first and second test administrations.

On the first test administration only two children met criterion on the Reflexive and Nonreflexive Test so that a discussion of relationships is not appropriate. However, on the second administration, 30 percent of the children met criterion. Of this 30 percent, only one child met criterion on the Transitivity Test. Because there were 10 children who met criterion on the Transitivity Test, it is quite apparent that the ability to use the reflexive and nonreflexive properties as measured here is not a necessary or a sufficient condition for the ability to use transitivity of length relations. This observation is quite consistent with the fact that the reflexive property of "the same length as" does not imply the transitive property of "the same length as" nor does the nonreflexive property of "longer than" or "shorter than" imply the transitive property of these two relations, on a logical basis. Conversely, the transitive property of "longer than" or "shorter than" does not imply the nonreflexive property of these two relations. Because on a logical basis the reflexive property of "the same length as" is (under restricted conditions) a consequence of the symmetric and transitive properties of "the same length as," and because some children could use the reflexive property but not the transitive property, there may be factors which enable children to use the reflexive property before they are able to use transitivity (e.g., spatial imagery or the definition of "the same length as"). In fact, the results indicate that the reflexive property may be necessary for transitivity. This observation may be due to the possibility that use of the reflexive property in this study was more of a "learned response" than a logical-mathematical process.

It also appears that use of the reflexive and nonreflexive properties is not a necessary or sufficient condition for being able to conserve length relations. Of the 30 percent who met criterion on the Reflexive and Nonreflexive Test, only seven children met criterion for the Conservation of Length Relations: Level I and II Test. This observation is consistent with the logical relationships of the properties of the relations. However, the data do not contradict the fact that being able to use only the reflexive property may precede an ability to conserve length relations at Level I and, therefore, Level II. The data of this study support the contention that conservation of identity is not unitary in nature. Certainly, if a child judges that a stick is the same length as itself, he must also judge that it is not longer or shorter than itself, or a contradiction would be present. On a logical basis and on a psychological basis, when one considers "conservation" problems, it is necessary to consider the properties of the relations which may be involved.

For those nineteen children who met criterion on the Conservation of Length Relations: Level I and II Test, seven met criterion on the Transitivity Test. Since only ten children met criterion on the Transitivity Test, it seems that conservation of length relations: Level I and II is necessary for transitivity. The fact that two of three children who met criterion on the Transitivity Test but not for conservation length relations: Level I and II, did not meet criterion for conservation of length relations: Level I or for reflexivity and nonreflexivity, indicates an inaccurate assessment. The above data are consistent with Smedslund's (1963b) observation that what he calls conservation of length is a necessary condition for what he calls transitivity.

The study involves implications for further research and development. Among these implications, the following are relevant. (1) With the exception of the transitive property, it may be important to first introduce the properties, relationships, and consequences of the relations involved at the point in time in which the children are first able to associate a relational term with an overt comparison and before perceptual conflict is introduced. The children could then observe, with perceptual support, the properties, etc., involved. If the children were thus able to learn that the relation(s) they establish is (are) not a function of the proximity of the curves involved, they may be able to use the properties, etc., in the absence of perceptual support, and indeed, even in the presence of perceptual conflict. (2) The relations "as many as," "more than," and "fewer than," and their properties are basic in the development of the cardinal numbers. For this reason, an analogous study as suggested in (1) above is important. (3) If children are able to learn particular equivalence or order relations and their properties, relationships, and consequences, are they able to transfer this knowledge to other such relations given knowledge of that relation? (4) On a logical basis, the relations involved in this study are basic to measurement. Moreover, the relation of "more than," "fewer than," and "as many as " are basic to cardinal numbers. Are the relations basic also on a psychological basis?

Appendix

Sample Items of Measuring Instruments

Length Comparison Test

Material Set I

Materials:

One green stick; 3 pieces of white string, one being longer than, one shorter than, and one the same length as the green stick

Directions:

Item 1. Using these pieces of string, find a piece longer than this green stick.

Item 7. Using these pieces of string, find a piece shorter than this green stick.

Item 14. Using these pieces of string, find a piece the same length as this stick.

Conservation of Length Relations Test

Level I--Longer Than

Materials:

One green straw; 3 red straws, one being longer than, one shorter than, and one the same length as the green straw

Statement:

Using these red straws, find a straw longer than this green straw.

Transformation:

________________ green

____________________ red (move the red straw)

Question:

"Is this red straw still longer than this green straw?"

Level II--Longer Than

Materials:

One green straw; 3 white pipe cleaners, one being longer than, one shorter than, and one the same length as the green straw

Statement:

Using these pipe cleaners, find a pipe cleaner longer than this green straw.

Transformation:

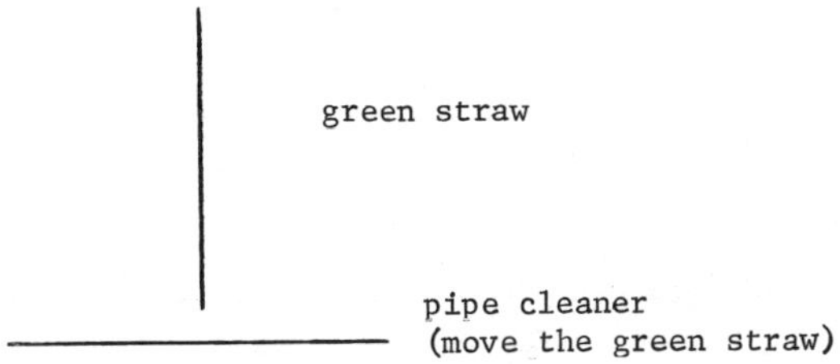

green straw

pipe cleaner
(move the green straw)

Question: "Now is the green straw longer than the pipe cleaner?"

Reflexive and Nonreflexive Test

Materials:

1 cardboard with M-L Diagram. 1 6-in. flannel strip

Statement:

Look at the length of this strip.

Transformation:

Look at the strip here.

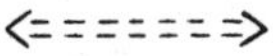

Look at the strip here.

Question:

"Now, is the strip longer?"

Transitivity Test

Materials:

A red stick and a green stick of the same length attached to a cardboard as follows:

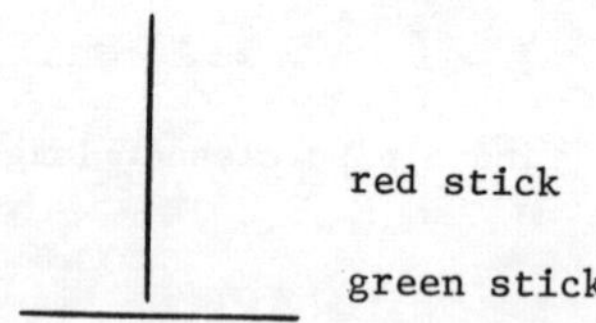

A white stick the same length as the red and green sticks for the child's use.

Question:

(a) "Is the red stick the same length as your stick?"
(b) "Is the green stick the same length as your stick?"
(c) "Is the green stick shorter than the red stick?"

DOUGLAS T. OWENS

Learning of Equivalence and Order Relations by Disadvantaged Five- and Six-Year-Old Children

Hilgard (1964, pp. 405-410) has suggested that there is a continuum of research studies along the dimension from pure research on learning to applied research on classroom practice. He specified six steps along this continuum: (1) learning research without regard for educational relevance, e.g., animal studies; (2) learning research using human subjects, but without concern for educational practice; (3) research on learning which is relevant to school learning, because school children and content are studied; (4) studies conducted in special laboratory classrooms on the feasibility of some educational practice; (5) tryout in a normal classroom; (6) developmental steps. In the first three of these steps the investigator is not primarily concerned with immediate application of his results to the classroom. In the second triad of steps, the researcher is expressly interested in classroom practice.

An analogous argument can be made for the existence of a continuum of types of research ranging from basic research on cognitive development to eventual classroom practices based upon cognitive development theory. From the Genevan studies it appears that Piaget and his colleagues are interested in the nature of cognitive development without particular concern for educational practice. Similarly, in many of the training studies which have been reported (Beilin, 1971), the experimenter is not primarily interested in developing curriculum for schools. The present study may be categorized at a level analogous to step (4) above. The investigator's goal is to make application of cognitive development theory to curriculum used in the classroom.

The experiment reported in this chapter is based on a doctoral dissertation in the Department of Mathematics Education at the University of Georgia (Owens, 1972).

The Problem

The purposes of this study were fourfold: (1) to determine the effectiveness of a set of activities designed to teach conservation and the transitive property of the matching relations "as many as," "more than," and "fewer than" to a group of economically disadvantaged five- and six-year-old children; (2) to determine the effect of the learning activities on the ability of the children to use properties of matching relations other than the specific properties upon which instruction was given; (3) to determine the effect of the learning activities on the ability of the children to conserve and use relational properties of length relations "as long as," "longer than," and "shorter than"; (4) to determine relationships among matching and length relations.

Operation and Structures

An operation, a concept central to Piaget's developmental theory (1970, pp. 21-23), has four properties. First, an operation is an action which can be carried out in thought as well as executed physically. The second characteristic of an operation is that it is reversible; the action can be carried out in one direction and in the opposite direction. Third, an operation always assumes some invariant (conservation). The fourth property is that every operation is related to a system of operation called a structure.

Piaget (Beth & Piaget, 1966, p. 172) believes that mental structures of the stage of concrete operations (from age 7 or 8 to age 12, approximately) may be reduced to a single model called "groupings." Piaget has postulated eight major groupings and a ninth preliminary grouping of equalities (Flavell, 1963, p. 195). If x and y represent grouping elements and "+" and "-" represent grouping operations, then each grouping has the following five properties (Piaget, 1964c, p. 42):

1. Combinativity, $x + x' = y$;
2. Reversibility, $y - x = x'$;
3. Associativity, $(x + x') + y' = x + (x' + y')$;
4. General operation of identity, $x - x = 0$;
5. Special identities, $x + x = x$.

In Grouping I, Primary Addition of Classes, the elements are classes which are ordered in a chain of inclusions $A \subset B \subset C$, etc. Addition, "+," is interpreted as the union of classes and "-" as set difference relative to a supraordinate class. Thus $A + A' = B$ where $A' = B - A$, since $A \subset B$, and "0" represents the null class (Flavell, 1963, pp. 173-74).

In Grouping V, Addition of Asymmetrical Relations, consider the seriation $0 < A < B < C < D$, etc. If $0 < A$, $0 < B$, $0 < C$, etc., are denoted by a, b, c, etc., and $A < B$, $B < C$, $C < D$, etc., are denoted by a', b', c', etc., respectively, then combinativity $(a + a' = b)$ is interpreted as transitivity of the relation when written as given (Beth & Piaget, 1966, p. 177).

In an additive system of relations, such as Grouping V, reversibility takes the form of what Piaget calls *reciprocity* (Beth & Piaget, 1966). Reciprocity consists of either permuting the terms of the relation (denoted by R), reversing the relation (R'), or both (R"). Thus, $R(A < B) = B < A$, $R'(A < B) = A > B$, and $R''(A < B) = (B > A)$. Concerning reciprocity Beth and Piaget (1966) stated:

> *If we combine additively the relation $(A < B)$ with its R, R', and R", we have:*
>
> *(1) $(A < B) + (B < A) = (A = B)$ which is true in the case where the relation is $\leq$.*
>
> *(2) $(A < B) + (A > B) = (A = B)$ id.*
>
> *(3) $(A < B) + (B > A) = (A < B)$.*
>
> *Thus in all three cases there is no anullment, but the product is either an equivalence or the relation with which we started unchanged.* [p. 177]

Piaget indicated that statements (1) and (2) hold for partial order relations, such as "less than or equal to." Apparently (1) should be interpreted as, if $A \leq B$ and $B \leq A$ then $A = B$. This is precisely the anti-symmetric property of a partial order relation. Moreover, if "$<$ " is an order relation such as "less than" for example, then $A < B$ and $B < A$ contradict the asymmetric property and cannot hold simultaneously. In (3) $A < B$ and $B > A$ are logical equivalents and can hold simultaneously for order relations as well as for partial orderings. Thus, $R''(A < B) = B > A$ is evidently the form of reciprocity characteristic of Grouping V since the R and R' cannot be combined with the original asymmetrical relation.

The general identity is not the absence of a relation, as in the case of the null class, but an equivalence relation. A special identity takes the form of $(A < B) + (A < B) = (A < B)$, and associativity is limited to the cases in which no special identity is involved (Beth & Piaget, 1966, p. 178).

Development of the Concept of Measurement

Number

From Piaget's (1970, pp. 37-38) analysis of children's mental processes, he has concluded that the development of the concept of number is a synthesis of operations of class inclusion and operations of order. So long as the elements of a class have their qualities, Grouping I and Grouping V cannot be applied to the same elements simultaneously, but the basis of the notion of number is that the elements are stripped of their qualities, such that each element becomes a unit. As soon as the qualities of the elements are abstracted, Grouping I and Grouping V can no longer function separately but must necessarily merge into a single new structure (Beth & Piaget, 1966, pp. 259-67). "Class inclusion is involved in the sense that two is included in three, three is included in four, etc." (Piaget, 1970, p. 38). Since the elements are considered to be equivalent the only way to tell the elements apart is to introduce some order. The elements are arranged one after another spatially, temporally or in the counting sequence (Piaget, 1970, p. 38).

Van Engen (1971) disagrees with Piaget's notion of number.

> *The difficulty with this conception of number is that it does not distinguish between the elements of a set and the relation that exists between two or more elements of the set. The study of the order of whole numbers is the study of a relation that exists between two numbers and has the usual properties of an order relation.*[p. 40]

Van Engen (1971, pp. 37-39) suggests that, from a mathematical point of view, the cardinal numbers are standard sets of a particular kind. For example, $5 = \{0, 1, 2, 3, 4\}$. To determine the cardinality of any set S, it is necessary to find one of the standard sets to which S is equivalent. This is accomplished by constructing a one-to-one correspondence or by counting. "From the point of view of mathematics, the relations 'as many as,' 'more than,' and 'fewer than' are basic to the development of number"(Van Engen, 1968, p. iii). On the basis of these relations, the cardinal numbers can be ordered, and the counting set can be formed.

These matching relations may be operationally defined between two sets A and B of physical objects as follows. Place an a beside a b until all the a's or b's are exhausted. If both sets are exhausted simultaneously, then there are as many a's as b's. If set B is exhausted and set A is not exhausted, there are more a's than b's and fewer b's than a's.

The relation "as many as" is thus another way of expressing set equivalence and is an equivalence relation. If "there are as many a's as b's" is indicated by "$A \approx B$" for equivalent sets A and B, then "$\approx$" is reflexive ($A \approx A$); symmetric (If $A \approx B$ then $B \approx A$); and transitive (If $A \approx B$ and $B \approx C$ then $A \approx C$). The relations "more than" and "fewer than" are order relations, for if $A > B$ indicates "there are more (or fewer) a's than b's," then ">" is nonreflexive ($A \not> A$); asymmetric (If $A > B$ then $B \not> A$); and transitive (If $A > B$ and $B > C$ then $A > C$). The relations "more than" and "fewer than" are examples of asymmetrical transitive relations of which Piaget wrote. They also exhibit the reversibility property. For if there are more a's than b's, then there are fewer b's than a's , and conversely. Thus, from the mathematical point of view of Van Engen and from the psychological perspective of Piaget, the matching relations are involved in the development of the number concept.

Measurement

Measurement has been described as "a process whereby a number is assigned to some object"(Steffe, 1971, p. 335). From this definition it follows logically that number is a prerequisite of length. Sinclair (1971) has stated that the

> *first measurement concept (length) is achieved rather later than that of number;. . . There is an even greater time lag...between acquisition of the corresponding conservation of length concept and the simple numerical conservations. Although the psychological construction is parallel, dealing*

> *with continuous elements is very much more difficult than dealing with discontinuous units.*[p. 153]

Sinclair (1971) has presented empirical evidence which is consistent with the logical conclusion that number precedes length in development. However, the explanation given is that length is achieved later than number because it is more difficult to deal with continuous elements than with discrete objects. Relations also provide a basis for the development of measurement in elementary school children. The relations "as long as," "longer than," and "shorter than" are comparisons of the relative lengths of segments, but for children they can be defined on objects such as sticks or straws. In the present study, a concept of number was not required in establishment of either the matching relations or length relations. However, the materials for the length relations were continuous objects, and the materials for the matching relations were discrete. Thus, Sinclair's (1971) hypothesis raises the question of whether the ability to use the matching relations precedes the ability to use length relations in the tasks of conservation and transitivity.

For an operational definition of the length relations, consider two segments A and B. A is as long as B if whenever A and B

> ...*(or their transforms) lie on a line in such a way that two end points coincide (right or left), the two remaining end points coincide. A is longer than B if and only if the remaining end point of B coincides with a point between the end points of A. Also, in this case, B is shorter than A.*[*Carey and Steffe, 1968, p. 31*]

The relation "as long as" thus defined is an equivalence relation and has the reflexive, symmetric, and transitive properties as does the matching relation, "as many as." The relations "longer than" and "shorter than" are order relations and possess the nonreflexive, asymmetric, and transitive properties analogous to the relation "more than."

Conservation and Transitivity

In Piaget's (1952) classical conservation of number tasks, a child is asked to establish that there are as many objects in a set A as in set B. Then one of the collections, say A, is taken through a physical transformation. Then the child is asked, "Are there as many *a*'s as *b*'s, or does one have more?" Van Engen (1971, p. 43) has argued that this task may be measuring whether or not the child conserves the one-to-one correspondence rather than conservation of number. In this study a task similar to the above example is considered to be a measure of conservation of the relation "as many as." It is not necessary that conservation be limited to cases of equivalence. For example, in a task given by Smedslund (1963b) a child was asked to establish that one stick was longer than a second stick and to maintain that the one stick was longer after a conflicting cue was introduced. While Smedslund called the task "conservation of length," a similar task in the present study is called "conservation of the relation 'longer than.'" Thus, order relation conservation is also included.

Conservation is studied from the relational point of view and transitivity is necessarily a relational property. Thus, the relationship between the development of conservation and attainment of transitivity is approached from the standpoint of relations. In his earlier writing, Piaget (1952, p. 205) reported that as soon as children can establish a lasting equivalence (that is, conserve the equivalence), they can at once use the transitive property. "The explanation is simple: the composition of two equivalences [transitivity]* is already implied in the construction of a single lasting equivalence between two sets, since the different successive forms of the two sets seem to the child to be different sets" (Piaget, 1952, p. 208).

Similarly, Northman and Gruen (1970) argue that transitivity is involved in equivalence conservation. Suppose the subject establishes A equivalent to B (A = B). When an equivalence-preserving transformation T is performed, the subject establishes (covertly) A = T(A). Then, transitivity is used in order to deduct T(A) = B or to conserve the equivalence of A and B.

Smedslund (1964) has argued that from a logical point of view, conservation precedes transitivity in the child's development. Consider three quantities which are related by a transitive relation @. Assume that a child established A@B. B (or A) must undergo some transformation, T, before B is compared with C; otherwise, A and C can be compared perceptually. Hence B = T(B) (or A = T(A)) must hold from one comparison to the other.

In a later discussion of training research Piaget (Beth & Piaget, 1966, p. 192) also alluded to an ordering in the attainment of conservation and transitivity. He reported that Smedslund easily induced conservation of weight by repeatedly changing the shape of a small clay ball and checking the weight on a scale. Smedslund was not successful in obtaining immediate learning of the transitive property.

Basic Questions of the Study

Among equivalence and order relations in the primary school curricula are set relations, based on matching finite sets of objects, and length relations, determined by comparing relative lengths of objects. It appears from Piaget's theory of grouping structures that if a child has, for example, Grouping V: Addition of Asymmetrical Relations in his cognitive structure, he can use logical properties of any such relations. In this study, an attempt was made to: (1) provide experiences for five- and six-year-old children in which the transitive property of the relations "as many as," "more than," and "fewer than" could be observed empirically by the children, and in which conservation of these relations could be observed through reversing a transformation; and (2) determine the effectiveness of the treatment in inducing the logical-mathematical properties of these relations and of the length relations "as long as," "longer than," and "shorter than."

Specifically, the following questions are basic to the study where most, but not all, arise from Piaget's theory.

---

*Added by the Author.

1. What is the effect of selected experiences on the ability of children to establish, conserve, and use properties of equivalence and order relations?

2. What is the effect of age on the ability of children to establish, conserve, and use properties of equivalence and order relations?

3. To what extent does an experimentally induced capability to conserve and use transitivity of matching relations transfer across relational categories to conservation and transitivity of length relations?

4. To what extent does an experimentally induced capability to conserve and use transitivity of matching relations transfer to remaining properties of matching relations?

5. What is the effect of a pretest on the ability of children to establish, conserve, and use properties of relations with or without selected experiences?

6. Is the ability to conserve matching relations related to the ability to use the transitive property of matching relations?

7. Is the ability to conserve length relations related to the ability to use the transitive property of the length relations?

8. Is the ability to conserve matching relations related to the ability to conserve length relations?

9. Is the ability to use transitivity of matching relations related to the ability to use transitivity of length relations?

10. Is the ability to solve a problem involving transitivity of a matching relation related to performance on a test of conservation or transitivity of matching relations which utilizes a standardized interview technique?

11. What are the intercorrelations among the variables of the study?

Method

The subjects of the study were 23 kindergarten and 24 first-grade children of the William Fountain Elementary School, Atlanta, Georgia. Kindergarten children were randomly selected from 35 children of two classes whose ages were in the range (5:1)[1] to (5:10) at the outset of the study. Grade one children were randomly chosen from 48 children of three classes with ages between (6:1) and (6:10) at the outset. The school was chiefly composed of Negro children from low income families. With one exception, the children in the sample were Negro.

---

[1]5 years, 1 month.

Tests

The thirteen tests described below were constructed to measure the abilities of the children to establish relations, conserve relations, and use relational properties.

The *Matching Relations (MR) Test* was designed to measure the ability of a child to establish matching relations and the *Conservation of Matching Relations (CMR) Test* was designed to measure the ability of a child to conserve a matching relation, provided that he could establish the relation. These two tests were administered simultaneously. In the example presented in Figure 1, a child was given five blue discs glued on a piece of cardboard and six red discs (i). He was instructed to pair the red discs and the blue discs. After the pairing (Figure 1--ii), the examiner asked two questions, "Are there as many red discs as blue discs?" and "Are there more red discs than blue discs?" After the second response the examiner rearranged the red discs (Figure 1-iii) and repeated the same two questions. In each case the correct answer to one question was "yes" and to the other "no." In each item, the rearrangement was perceptually biased in favor of the incorrect conclusion. The first two questions comprised an item of the MR Test. All four questions were considered in the CMR Test.

Figure 1

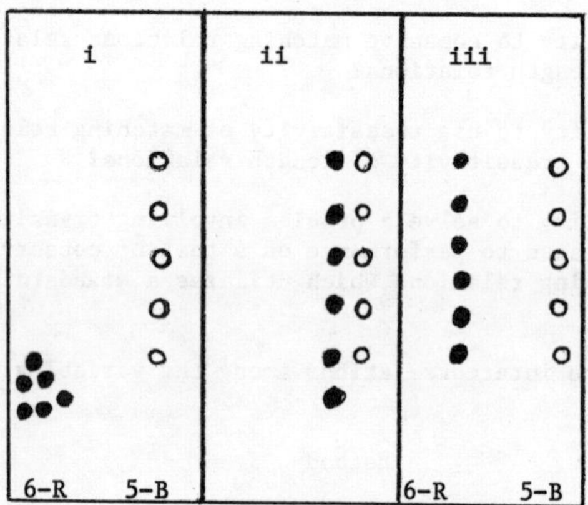

The *Length Relations (LR) Test* was designed to measure the child's ability to establish length relations. The *Conservation of Length Relations (CLR) Test* was designed to measure the ability of a child to conserve length relations. These two tests were given together in the same way as the MR and CMR Tests. In each item the child was asked to establish a length relation between two sticks (or straws) by answering two questions. Then the sticks were rearranged to produce a perceptual bias against the correct conclusion, and the questions were repeated.

The purpose of the *Transitivity of Matching Relations (TMR) Test* was to measure a child's ability to use the transitive property of matching relations. On a TMR item a child was presented three collections A, B, C, of physical materials, arranged in clusters. Suppose, for example, that there were fewer *a*'s than *b*'s and fewer *b*'s than *c*'s. The child was instructed to pair the *a*'s and *b*'s and was then asked, "Are there fewer *a*'s than *b*'s?" The examiner then put the *a*'s into a cup which sat nearby and said "Pair the *b*'s and *c*'s." After the pairing the examiner asked, "Are there fewer *b*'s than *c*'s?" The examiner then placed the *c*'s in another cup and asked, "Are there fewer *a*'s than *c*'s?" and "Are there more *a*'s than *c*'s?" (or "Are there as many *a*'s as *c*'s?") Note that the sets A and C were not "paired" and that the objects were screened at the time of the transitive inference.

The *Transitivity of Length Relations (TLR) Test* was designed to measure the ability of a child to use the transitive property of the length relations. On each item, as in the TMR test, a child was asked to establish the relation between two sticks, A and B. Stick A was placed in a box and stick B was compared with another stick C such that the same relation held between B and C as between A and B. Then stick C was placed in a box and two questions, relative to A and C, were asked.

The purpose of the *Symmetric Property of the Matching Relations (SMR) Test* was to determine the child's ability to use symmetry of the relation "as many as." For an item of SMR test the child was presented two collections A and B of objects and instructed to pair the objects. After the pairing the examiner asked two questions: "Are there as many *a*'s as *b*'s?" (Response), "Are there more (or fewer) *a*'s than *b*'s?" (Response). Then the examiner put the two collections into two cups and asked, "Are there as many *b*'s as *a*'s?" (Response), and "Are there more (or fewer) *a*'s than *b*'s?"

The *Symmetric Property of the Length Relations (SLR) Test* was designed to measure the ability of a child to use symmetry of the relation "as long as." In this case the child was asked to compare two sticks (straws) to determine that stick A was as long as stick B and that an order relation did not hold. Then the examiner placed the two sticks into two boxes and asked, "Is stick B as long as stick A?" and the previous question involving an order relation.

The *Test of the Asymmetric Property of the Matching Relations (AMR)* was designed to measure the ability of a child to use the asymmetric property of the relations "more than" and "fewer than." The child was presented two collections, for example, with more *a*'s than *b*'s and instructed to pair them. After the pairing the examiner asked, "Are there more *a*'s than *b*'s?" After the response the examiner placed the two collections into two cups and asked, "Are there more *b*'s than *a*'s?" and "Are there more *a*'s than *b*'s?"

The purpose of the *Test of the Asymmetric Property of the Length Relations (ALR)* was to measure the child's ability to use the asymmetric property of "longer than" and "shorter than." On an item of this test the child compared two sticks related by an order relation. Suppose a child established correctly that stick A was shorter than stick B. The examiner then placed each stick into a box and asked, for example, "Is stick B shorter than stick A?" and "Is stick A shorter than stick B?"

The *Reversibility of Matching Relations (RMR) Test* was designed to measure the child's ability to use the following property: if there are more (fewer) *a*'s than *b*'s, then there are fewer (more) *b*'s than *a*'s. On a given item, the child was presented with two collections A and B of objects such that an order relation held. After the child had paired the objects, the examiner asked, "Are there more (fewer) *a*'s than *b*'s?" The examiner then put the objects into two cups and asked, "Are there fewer (more) *b*'s than *a*'s?" and "Are there as many *b*'s as *a*'s?"

The *Reversibility of Length Relations (RLR) Test* was designed to measure the ability of a child to use the following reversibility property: if segment A is longer (shorter) than segment B, then segment B is shorter (longer) than segment A. After the child compared two sticks, the examiner asked, "Is stick A longer (shorter) than stick B?" Then, the examiner placed the sticks into two boxes and asked, "Is stick B shorter (longer) than stick A?" and "Is stick B as long as stick A?"

On each of the MR, LR, CMR, CLR, TMR, and TLR Tests there were two items which in fact exhibited each relation. Thus there were six items on each of these tests. The SMR and SLR Tests contained three items each. The AMR, ALR, RMR, and RLR Tests had two items for each of two order relations, or four items per test. The total number of items was 58. The relations (MR, LR) Tests involved situations under which the stimuli were arranged to aid the child in establishing the relation. The questions of the conservation (CMR, CLR) Tests were administered under conditions of perceptual conflict. All other items were administered under screened stimuli conditions. The child was not asked to give reasons for his answers on any of the structured items.

The *Transitivity Problem (TP)* was designed to measure the ability of a child to solve a problem which involved transitivity of a matching relation with minimum guidance from the examiner. The situation involved a cardboard box from which the front and top were removed. The box was divided into halves by a partition as shown in Figure 2. Ten checkers were attached to the bottom inside one half of the box and ten tiles were attached in the other side. Twelve buttons lay on the table in front of the box. After the objects were identified, the examiner said, "Find out if there are as many checkers as tiles. You may use the buttons to help you find out." In general the examiner gave as little guidance as was possible, but if the child failed to respond at some point, the examiner directed the next step toward solution. When a response was given, the examiner asked for an explanation.

Figure 2

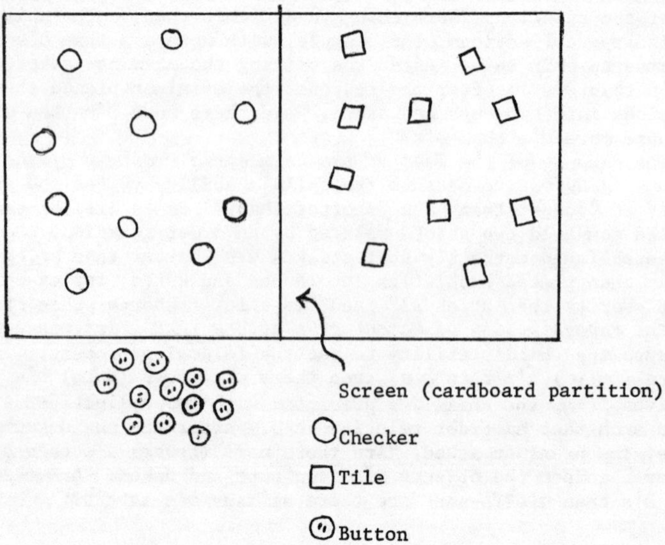

Screen (cardboard partition)

Checker

Tile

Button

Scoring Tests

An item was scored "pass" provided that a child answered correctly all the questions contained in the item and "fail" otherwise. The number of items scored "pass" by a child on each test was considered to be his score on the test. For the purpose of comparing these data with other studies it was desirable to distinguish children for which evidence existed that they could use a property from those for which no such evidence existed. This was accomplished by setting a criterion score based on a random model. It was assumed that a child could use a relational property if and only if he met the criterion on a particular test. Four of the six items was the criterion set on each of the CMR, CLR, TMR, and TLR Tests. The probability of reaching this criterion by guessing was at most .038.

For the Transitivity Problem, the following four levels of ability to apply the transitive property were identified: 1--the child neither consistently established relations nor used the transitive property; 2--the child established relations but did not use the transitive property; 3--the child both established relations and used the transitive property without adequate justification; 4--the child established relations, used transitivity, and gave adequate justification for his conclusion. The consensus of two of three judges' ratings, based on transcripts of audio tapes, was taken as the child's rating on the Transitivity Problem.

Instructional Activities

All of the instructional activities were designed for use in small instructional groups and involved manipulative materials. In some activities each child had his own set of materials. Other activities involved one set of materials for the entire group. In the latter cases, the instructor or one child performed the manipulations, but all of the children entered into discussion. Materials for instruction varied from materials such as small toys to neutral material such as checkers, tiles, or colored wooden discs. Colored sticks, straws, etc., represented segments for length comparison.

The purpose of Unit I, *Matching Relations*, was to develop the ability of the children to establish matching relations. The relations were introduced by having children pair the objects from two finite sets. It was noted that the sets may or may not be in one-to-one correspondence. When the sets A and B were equivalent, the phraseology "there are as many *a*'s as *b*'s" was used. "More than" was introduced second, and "fewer than" was introduced as the reverse of "more than." It was emphasized that if a relation holds between two sets (in a fixed order) then no other relation holds.

Unit II, *Length Relations*, was designed to develop the ability of children to establish length relations. The relations were introduced by placing the ends of two sticks together, observing the remaining ends, and associating the name of the appropriate relation. After "longer than" was discussed, "shorter than" was introduced as the reverse. The equivalence relation "as long as" was the third length relation considered.

The purpose of Unit III, *Conservation of Matching Relations*, was to develop the ability of children to maintain relations between sets when the physical matching of the objects is destroyed. The principle of reversibility of a transformation was emphasized by having the children return the objects, following a transformation, to the position in which the relation was established. Combinations of perceptual screening, perceptual conflict, child transformations of his own materials, and instructor transformations in a group situation were used in Unit III and Unit IV, *Transitivity of Matching Relations*. Unit IV was designed to develop the ability of children to use the transitive property of the matching relations. The chief method of the transitivity training was what has been termed fixed practice with empirical control (Smedslund, 1963a). The instructor gave explicit instructions for comparing sets A and B, then B and C. Sets A and C were compared after the child made a prediction of the relation between them.

Design

Age (five-and six-year-olds) was used as a categorization variable because of its importance in cognitive development. Treatment was a second major factor of which two levels existed, a Full Treatment and a Partial Treatment. The Full Treatment consisted of all four units described earlier and the Partial Treatment consisted of Units I and II. Transfer shall be inferred from a significant difference in favor of the full treatment group in performance on some property for which no instruction was given, provided that there is a significance in the same direction on a related property for which instruction was given.

In most of the learning research based on cognitive development theory, and in many other educational research studies, pretests are given to all subjects. However, due to the large time requirement of instructing and testing, a strictly pretest-posttest design was not considered feasible in the present study. However, it was desirable to obtain premeasures on some subjects, so a Solomon four group design was selected. Use of this design requires that part of the Full Treatment group and part of the Partial Treatment group be selected at random to have the pretest. Schematically, the Solomon four group design may be represented as follows:

Randomized assignment	G_1	Pretest:	Full Treatment	Posttest
to groups	G_2	Pretest:	Partial Treatment	Posttest
	G_3		Full Treatment	Posttest
	G_4		Partial Treatment	Posttest

Campbell and Stanley (1963) note that the results of an experiment using this design are more generalizable than those from a pretest-posttest design, because the effects of testing and the interaction of testing with the treatment are determinable, and randomization controls for initial biases between groups. They also suggest that experience with the Solomon four group design in a particular research area gives information about the general likelihood of the effects of pretesting in that area of research. It is desirable that this general information be obtained for learning research based on cognitive development theory.

Campbell and Stanley (1963) suggest that to analyze the data obtained from the Solomon four group design, the pretests may be disregarded except as another treatment, and only the posttest scores analyzed by analysis of variance. If there is no effect due to pretesting or no interaction of pretesting and treatment, then the pretest data may be used as a covariate in performing analysis of covariance on the data from the pretest groups. In the present study the first of these suggestions was followed, but the analysis of covariance was not performed due to the small pretest group size. Moreover, the pretest data were considered to be somewhat invalid because the examiners strictly adhered to the relational terminology preferred by the investigator. A more flexible testing procedure, adaptable to the child's language pattern, was used for the posttests.

Procedure

Children in the Full and Partial Treatment groups first had experience in establishing relations (Units I and II). Ten lessons on matching relations from Unit I and seven lessons from Unit II on length relations were given. Then the tests on relations (MR, LR), conservation (CMR, CLR), and transitivity (TMR, TLR) of each relational category were administered as pretests to the pretest group while the no-pretest group had only the relations tests. Following the pretests, the Full Treatment group had four lessons on conservation of matching relations (Unit III) and five lessons on the transitive property (Unit IV). Near the end of this instructional period the Partial Treatment group had two additional lessons on matching relations, but the remainder of the treatment period was spent in normal classroom activities.

Each lesson was of 20-30 minutes duration. There were four to six children in an instructional group. The investigator and two teachers' aides served as instructors and testers. Instructional groups were rotated among instructors each day. During testing the Full and Partial Treatment groups were balanced among testers in five untimed interviews per child, except that the Transitivity Problem session (sixth interview) was held entirely by the investigator. The test items given during a test session were randomly ordered for each child, independently of other children, and each pair of test questions of an item were randomly ordered for each item and each child.

Near the end of the study it was apparent that the full treatment had not extensively changed the language patterns of the children with regard to relational terminology. The investigator felt that strict adherence to predetermined terminology could make the tests invalid in terms of the concepts measured. Approximations to desired terminology, for example, "the same" for "as many as," was accepted in the posttests. Further, if a child were giving a "no--no" or a "yes--yes" response set to an item, the question was repeated using an alternate terminology. This was the only way in which the postests differed from those tests which were given as pretests, but this was considered to be sufficient to make the pretest data invalid per se. Thus, Pretest was retained as a factor but the data were disregarded.

Statistical Analyses

The data for the analysis of variance were vectors of 12 posttest scores for each individual. Multivariate analysis of variance was an appropriate statistical design. The design is represented diagramatically in Table 1. Three factors were considered at two levels each: Age--

five- and six-year-olds; Treatment--full treatment and partial treatment; and Pretest--pretest and no-pretest. The Age X Treatment interaction and the Treatment X Pretest interaction were of particular interest to the investigator, but the three-way Age X Treatment X Pretest interaction was not considered as one of the questions in the study. Thus, three separate multivariate analyses of variance were performed in which two factors and their two-way interaction were considered. Data for all cells of each factor were combined for the 2 X 2 factorial multivariate analyses. It was of particular interest to the investigator to determine the effects of the treatment, the pretest, and age upon each of the variables and to determine if two-way interactions existed. Thus, a univariate analysis for each of the 12 response variables was performed. In this regard Table 1 may be interpreted as 12 univariate designs in which the three main effects and pairwise interactions were of interest. Again the analyses were handled by consideration of three 2 X 2 factorial univariate analyses for each of the 12 variables and combining all cells within a factor under consideration.

Table 1

Diagram of the Design

Factors and Levels		Twelve Response Variables											
Treatment	Age	MR	CMR	TMR	SMR	AMR	RMR	LR	CLR	TLR	SLR	ALR	RLR
Full Treatment	Five												
	Six												
Partial Treatment	Five												
	Six												
Treatment	Pretest												
Full Treatment	Pretest												
	No Pretest												
Partial Treatment	Pretest												
	No Pretest												

Calculations for all of the MANOVA's and ANOVA's were performed by computer with the use of the computer program MUDAID (Applebaum and Bargmann, 1967). MUDAID provides multivariate and univariate analyses of variance for pairs of factors and pairwise interactions. Also, each multivariate pass provides matrices of intercorrelations among the response variables.

Each covariance matrix in a multivariate analysis contains estimates of the variances of the variables on the main diagonal and estimates of the covariances for pairs of variables in the off-diagonal positions. Each covariance matrix has an associated matrix of sums of squares and cross products. The sum of squares of error and sums of products of error are the residuals after the effects of the factors and interactions have been removed by subtraction of their sums of squares and sums of products from the respective totals. The correlations reported in this study were calculated from the covariance matrix derived from the matrix of sums of squares and products of error in the Treatment X Age analysis.

Chi-square tests for independence (Ferguson, 1966, pp. 192-208) were used to determine whether a relationship existed between levels of performance on the Transitivity Problem and Age. Chi-square tests were also made to determine relationships between conservation and transitivity within a relational category and to determine relationships across relational categories within corresponding measures. Chi-squares were calculated on the 2 X 2 or 2 X 3 tables where the frequencies were the number of children achieving a criterion or level of performance.

Results

Multivariate Analyses

None of the F ratios for any factor or two-way interaction were significant at the .05 level of significance in the multivariate tests. However, the F statistic for the main effect of Age was 1.95 in the Treatment versus Age multivariate analysis with 12 and 32 *df*. The critical value ($p < .05$) of F with 12 and 32 *df* is 2.07. Thus the factor Age approached significance, but no interpretation was made.

Univariate Analyses

Analyses of Variance for which F ratios were significant in the Treatment versus Age analyses are reported in Table 2. Table 3 contains analyses of variance for the cases of significance in the Treatment versus Pretest analyses. Any factor which was statistically significant in a Pretest X Age analysis was significant in the corresponding Treatment X Pretest or Age X Pretest analysis. Thus, analysis of variance tables are not presented for Pretest versus Age. Group means, as percents, for treatment and age groups are presented in Table 4. Age was the only significant ($p < .01$) effect for the variables matching relations (MR) and conservation of matching relations (CMR). In the first case, the mean for the six-year-olds was 87% and for the five-year-olds was 59%. On conservation the six-year-old group performed at a mean of 62% and the five-year-old group at a mean of 36%. It was not anticipated that Treatment would be significant for MR since all children had received instruction in matching relations.

Table 2
Treatment Versus Age Analyses of
Variance With Significant Effects

Source of Variation	Relations (MR) M.S.	Relations (MR) F	Conservation Of MR (CMR) M.S.	Conservation Of MR (CMR) F	Transitivity Of MR (TMR) M.S.	Transitivity Of MR (TMR) F	Symmetric Property Of MR (SMR) M.S.	Symmetric Property Of MR (SMR) F
Treatment (T)	.44	.16	2.19	.62	19.90	8.34**	2.32	2.69
Age (A)	31.53	11.79**	28.88	8.18**	2.36	.99	11.10	12.89**
T X A	.15	.06	1.49	.42	.16	.07	.15	.18
Error	2.67		3.53		2.38		.86	

	Asymmetric Property of MR (AMR) M.S.	Asymmetric Property of MR (AMR) F	Reversibility of MR (RMR) M.S.	Reversibility of MR (RMR) F	Length Relations (LR) M.S.	Length Relations (LR) F
Treatment	7.69	3.98√	2.60	1.97	1.00	1.01
Age	10.39	5.37	8.74	4.79*	5.87	5.89*
T X A	.14	.07	.47	.26	.53	.53
Error	1.93		1.83		1.00	

√($p < .10$), *($p < .05$), **($p < .01$)

Note: Each factor and interaction had 1 *df*; error 43 *df*.

Table 3
Treatment versus Pretest Analyses of
Variance with Significant Effects

	Transitivity of MR (TMR) M.S.	Transitivity of MR (TMR) F	Asymmetric Property of MR (AMR) M.S.	Asymmetric Property of MR (AMR) F	Symmetric Property of LR (SLR) M.S.	Symmetric Property of LR (SLR) F	Reversibility of LR (RLR) M.S.	Reversibility of LR (RLR) F
Treatment (T)	20.41	8.45**	8.37	4.10*	.21	.18	1.71	1.21
Pretest (P)	1.19	.49	5.39	2.64	4.71	4.09*	3.53	2.31
T X P	.00	.00	.39	.19	4.92	4.29	9.54	6.26*
Error	2.42		2.04		1.15		1.52	

*$p < .05$ **$p < .01$

Note: Each factor and interaction had 1 *df*; error 43 *df*.

Table 4
Group and Total Means, as Percents, for Each of 12 Variables

Variable	Treatment Groups		Age Groups		Totals
	Full	Partial	Six	Five	
MR	75	71	87	59*	73
CMR	53	45	62	36*	49
TMR	58	36*	51	43	47
SMR	81	48	81	48*	65
AMR	73	52*	74	50*	62
RMR	68	54	72	50*	61
LR	90	85	93	81*	87
CLR	62	52	63	51	57
TLR	47	51	50	48	49
SLR	62	58	67	54	60
ALR	64	57	68	53	61
RLR	72	62	65	70	67

*This pair of means was significantly different in a univariate analysis.

Treatment was a significant ($p < .01$) main effect for transitivity of matching relations (TMR). The full treatment group mean was 58% and the partial treatment group mean was 36%. Treatment was also a significant ($p < .05$) factor for the variable AMR in the Treatment versus Pretest analysis, and was close to significance at the .05 level in the Treatment versus Age analysis. In this case the means were 73% and 52% for the full treatment and partial treatment groups, respectively. Age was also a significant ($p < .05$) main effect for AMR as it was for SMR ($p < .01$) and RMR ($p < .05$). In each of these cases the six-year-olds performed at a higher level than the five-year-olds.

The F statistic for the factor Age and for the variable Length Relations (LR) was significant. However, in Bartlett's test (Ostle, 1963, pp. 136-137) the hypothesis of homogeneity of variances was rejected. Thus, no interpretation of the ANOVA was made.

There were no significant interactions in the Treatment versus Age analyses. There were, however, two Pretest X Treatment interactions ($p < .05$) for the variables in SLR and RLR. Pretest was not a significant main effect in the absence of interaction in any analysis. The cell means for the significant interactions are presented in Table 5. In each case the greatest mean was that of the full treatment group which had no pretest, and the least mean was that of full treatment group which had pretests. One possible interpretation of this interaction is that the pretests interfered with the effect of the treatment. However, this may be a misinterpretation since instruction was not given on the symmetric and reversibility properties of either category of relations, nor was there any indication of transfer to the properties of length relations from the instruction which was given. The interpretation which is accepted here is that the pretests had essentially no effect on the subjects' performance on the posttests.

Table 5
Cell Means as Percents: Treatment X Test Interactions

	SLR			RLR		
	Pretest	No Pretest	Total	Pretest	No Pretest	Total
Full Treatment	42	85	62	54	91	72
Partial Treatment	58	58	58	67	58	63
Total	50	71	60	60	74	67

Age was the most general effect in the study, but the surprising result was that Age was not significant for any length relational variable. In comparing means for length relational variables with means for matching relational variables, it may be noted that a grand mean of 87% for the variable Length Relations was equal to the mean for the six-year-old group on MR, which was significantly greater than the mean for the five-year-old group on MR. The grand mean of 57% for CLR was between the means of 62% for the six-year-old group and 36% for the five-year-old group on CMR. For TLR the mean of 49% was between the significantly different means for the full and partial treatment groups for TMR. The means of 60%, 61%, and 67% for SLR, ALR, and RLR, respectively, were between the respective matching relational means for the two ages, which were different because of an age effect in each case. Also, in each case the mean for the five-year-old group was greater for length than for the corresponding matching relations variable. Thus, while no factors were significant for the length relations variables, overall performance in each case was not decidedly different from performance on the corresponding matching relations variable. No formal statistical tests were made between variables across relational categories.

Transitivity Problem Results

In order to test the relationship between performance on the Transitivity Problem and the factors Treatment and Age, chi-square tests for independence were performed on contingency tables. The frequencies of Transitivity Problem ratings versus Treatment groups are presented in Table 6, and ratings by age frequencies are found in Table 7. Two children counted and no ratings were possible. While it is of interest to see the number of children at each of the four levels on the Transitivity Problem, categories 3 and 4 were combined into a single category, 3 or 4 (the child used transitivity), for the chi-square tests. This was necessary to increase the expected frequency for some cells. Frequencies are presented both ways but the chi-square tests were performed on the 2 X 3 tables.

Table 6
Contingency Table: Transitivity Problem
Ratings Versus Treatment Group

Treatment Group	Rating				
	1	2	3 or 4	3	4
Full Treatment	4	7	10	6	4
Partial Treatment	7	12	5	4	1

Table 7
Contingency Table: Transitivity Problem
Ratings Versus Age Level

Age Level	Rating				
	1	2	3 or 4	3	4
Six	3	7	12	8	4
Five	8	12	3	2	1

The chi-square calculated for Table 6 was 3.62 with 2 *df*, not significant at the .05 level. Thus while there appeared to be a tendency for more children in the full treatment group to get a rating of 3 or 4 and more children in the partial treatment group to get a rating of 1 or a rating of 2, the hypothesis of independence was not rejected. The chi-square calculated for Table 7 (2 X 3) was 8.97 with 2 *df* which is significant at the .02 level. Thus, the null hypothesis of independence was rejected, and the existence of a relationship between age and the level of performance on the Transitivity Problem was accepted. There was a tendency for six-year-old children to have the higher rating of 3 or 4, and for the five-year-old children to have the lower ratings of 1 and 2.

While the treatment was effective in improving the abilities of the children to perform the transitivity tasks of TMR, the treatment was not related to level of performance on the Transitivity Problem. On the other hand, there was no significant difference between ages in performance on TMR, but age level was related to level of performance on the Transitivity Problem. These results raise a question about the relationship between performance on the Transitivity Problem and the more structured tests.

Relationships Among the Variables

Chi-square tests were used to test for a relationship between level of performance on the Transitivity Problem and criterion performance on TMR and CMR. The frequencies of the ratings on the Transitivity Problem versus meeting the criterion on TMR and CMR are presented in Table 8 and Table 9 respectively. Chi-square tests were run on the 2x3 tables.

Table 8
Contingency Table: Ratings on Transitivity Problem Versus Criterion on Transitivity of Matching Relations

TMR Criterion	Rating				
Level	1	2	3 or 4	3	4
Criterion	1	7	8	5	3
Not Criterion	10	12	7	5	2

Table 9
Contingency Table: Ratings on Transitivity Problem Versus Criterion on Conservation of Matching Relations

CMR Criterion	Rating				
Level	1	2	3 or 4	3	4
Criterion	0	5	13	8	5
Not Criterion	11	14	2	2	0

The chi-square calculated for Table 8 was 5.45. The critical value of chi-square with 2 *df* is 5.99 ($p < .05$). Thus, the chi-square for level of performance on the Transitivity Problem versus Transitivity, as measured by TMR test, was near significance at the .05 level, but independence was accepted. The chi-square calculated for Table 9 was 22.43 ($p < .001$). There was a strong relationship between ratings on the Transitivity Problem and achieving the criterion on the CMR test.

The product moment correlations in the present study were calculated in the multivariate analysis by using the error covariance matrix from the Treatment versus Age Analysis. The reason for using this error matrix to calculate the correlations is that essentially all significant effects have been eliminated from the matrix and only nonsignificant effects remain. That is, the effects of Treatment and Age were statistically removed by subtraction, and only the (nonsignificant) effects of Pretest remain. The correlations are presented in Table 10. Since *df* for error in the analyses of variance was 43, there are 42 *df* associated with each correlation of Table 10. The critical values for correlations significantly different from zero are .30 ($p < .05$) and .39 ($p < .01$).

Inspection of Table 10 revealed that 47 of the 66 correlations were significantly different from zero and all were positive. Only two correlations were greater than .60 and 16 others were greater than .50. Of the 19 nonsignificant correlations, 13 were with or between LR and TLR. It was interesting that the only length variable with which LR was correlated was CLR. Indeed, each item of the CLR Tests was dependent upon an item of the LR Test. It appears that there is little relationship between each of LR and TLR and the remaining variables. In addition to TLR, three variables are not correlated with CLR. The nonsignificant correlations of SMR with RMR and RLR indicate a lack of relationship between the symmetric property of "as many as" and the reversibility property of either relational category. The additional nonsignificant correlation

Table 10
Intercorrelations Among the 12 Variables

	CMR	TMR	SMR	AMR	RMR	LR	CLR	TLR	SLR	ALR	RLR
MR	73**	57**	32*	59**	59**	22	35*	16	49**	55**	40**
CMR		51**	37*	59**	48**	30*	41**	40**	56**	48**	39**
TMR			44**	28	47**	07	24	28	51**	59**	32*
SMR				46**	27	43**	41**	36*	55**	51**	17
AMR					45**	43**	40**	26	54**	52**	41**
RMR						07	27	25	54**	46**	50**
LR							46**	15	27	24	20
CLR								11	53**	25	39**
TLR									47**	33*	23
SLR										64**	57**
ALR											40**

*p < .05, **p < .01

Note: Decimal points are omitted.

was between TMR and AMR. The remaining correlations with each matching relational variable were significant. It is interesting to note that CMR was correlated with each variable across both relational categories.

Whether or not a child in the present study attained the criterion on a particular test is a measure of the child's ability to use the relational property of the test. In order to examine the hypothesis that conservation ability precedes the ability to use the transitive property within a category of relations, 2 x 2 frequency tables, of those who did and did not use conservation and transitivity, were prepared. Chi-square tests for independence were then made on the contingency tables. The frequencies of children meeting criterion on CMR versus meeting criterion on TMR are presented in Table 11. Table 12 contains the frequencies of children in the sample who met the criterion on conservation versus those who met the criterion on transitivity of length relations. The calculated chi-squares with 1 *df* were 1.73 for Table 11 and .57 for Table 12. These nonsignificant chi-squares indicate independence between the ability to use conservation and the ability to use transitivity within the respective relational categories. These results are not completely consistent with the significant product moment correlation of .51 between CMR and TMR for the matching relations. However, in the case of length relations, the result is consistent with the nonsignificant correlation between conservation and transitivity.

Table 11
Contingency Table: Criterion on CMR Versus Criterion on TMR

Conservation of Matching Relations (CMR)	Transitivity of Matching Relations (TMR)	
	Criterion	Not Criterion
Criterion	9	10
Not Criterion	8	20

Table 12
Contingency Table: Criterion on CLR Versus Criterion on TLR

Conservation of Length Relations (CLR)	Transitivity of Length Relations (TLR)	
	Criterion	Not Criterion
Criterion	9	15
Not Criterion	9	14

Examination of Table 11 revealed that there were 8 children in the study who met criterion for transitivity but not conservation of matching relations. From Table 12 it may be observed that 9 children met criterion for transitivity but not for conservation of length relations. In each case, about one-half of the children who could use the transitive property within a relational category failed to conserve the relations of the same category. Thus, no evidence is provided by these data that, for the children in this study, the ability to conserve relations precedes the ability to use the transitive property. The case is different, however, in the case of the Transitivity Problem.

For consideration of whether the ability to conserve matching relations precedes the ability to conserve length relations, frequencies of children who achieved the criteria for CLR and CMR are presented in Table 13. Table 14 contains frequencies with which children in the study met the criteria for TLR and TMR as an indication of whether matching precedes length in development of the transitive property of relations. The calculated chi-squares were 6.33 for Table 13 and .87 for Table 14, each with 1 *df*. The value for conservation was significant ($p < .05$), and thus a relationship between meeting criterion on CMR and meeting criterion on CLR is indicated. These results are consistent with the significant correlation of .41 between CMR and CLR and the nonsignificant correlation between TMR and TLR.

Table 13
Contingency Table: Criterion on CLR Versus Criterion on CMR

Conservation of Length Relations (CLR)	Conservation of Matching Relations (CMR)	
	Criterion	Not Criterion
Criterion	13	10
Not Criterion	5	19

Table 14
Contingency Table: Criterion on TLR Versus Criterion on TMR

Transitivity of Length Relations (TLR)	Transitivity of Matching Relations (TMR)	
	Criterion	Not Criterion
Criterion	8	10
Not Criterion	9	20

The data of Table 13 gave no indication that conservation of matching relations precedes conservation of length relations for the children in this study. In fact, 10 children who met the criterion on CLR failed to achieve the criterion on CMR. On the other hand, there were 5 children who met criterion on CMR but failed to meet criterion on CLR. This evidence is in opposition to the suggestion that the ability to conserve matching relations precedes the ability to conserve length relations.

From Table 14 it may be observed that 9 children used (as defined by the criterion) the transitive property of matching relations but not length relations. On the other hand, 10 children used the transitive property of length relations but not of matching relations. These data gave no indication that, for the subjects of this study, the ability to use the transitive property in one relational category consistently preceded the ability to use the transitive property in the other relational category.

Presumably, a solution of the Transitivity Problem required use of the transitive property of the relation "as many as." However, other abilities were necessary for a solution. Thus, the fact that some children achieved the criterion on TMR but did not reach a solution in the Transitivity Problem is consistent with the logical conclusion.

What appears inconsistent with the logical conclusion is that seven children solved the Transitivity Problem but failed to reach the criterion on the transitivity (TMR) test (see Table 8). Of these seven, however, four made a score of three on the TMR test and thus gave evidence of some facility in transitivity. The failure of the other three children may be attributed to inaccuracy of measurement.

Another discrepancy between the data and the logical conclusion is the fact that 8 children used the transitive property (as defined by the criterion on TMR), but did not conserve matching relations. It is interesting to note that 5 of these 8 children were in the full treatment group. It is also of interest to observe that in the entire study, 13 children who had full treatment achieved the criterion on TMR while only 4 children in the partial treatment did so.

Discussion and Conclusions

The Effectiveness of the Treatment

The mean performance of the children in the full treatment group was significantly greater than the mean performance of the children in the partial treatment group on the Transitivity of Matching Relations Test. This was an indication that the treatment was effective in improving the ability of the children in using the transitive property of these relations. However, the results from the Transitivity Problem indicated no relationship between a student's membership in a treatment group and his level of performance on the Transitivity Problem. This apparent discrepancy may be interpreted by an examination of the tasks and the instructional activities. In the instructional setting the children were instructed to establish the relation between two sets, say A and B, and between B and a third set, C. The sets were constructed in such a way that the same relation existed between B and C as between A and B. The children were then asked to predict the relation between A and C and were given an opportunity to verify their prediction. Each item of the structured transitivity test followed this same procedure except that on the test the child did not have the opportunity to verify his conclusion. Also, in the testing situation the objects were screened at the time of the transitive inference, whereas this was not always the case in instruction. In the Transitivity Problem, the child was required to compare sets A and B, and sets A and C where A contained two more objects than B or C. He then was required to remove (either physically or mentally) two objects from the set A to form a new set which was equivalent to B and C before applying the transitive property of "as many as," and to conclude that B was equivalent to C. The reasonable conclusion then, is that the treatment improved the ability of the children to perform tasks very much like the treatment activities, but this improvement did not generalize to the Transitivity Problem, a higher order task.

These results are consistent with previous transitivity training studies. In a study with five- to seven-year-old children, Smedslund (1963c) found that none of the children acquired transitivity of weight due to practice. In another study he (Smedslund, 1963c) found that about 30% of a group of eight-year-old children acquired transitivity of weight by practice, while only 12.5% of a control group acquired transitivity. Thus, behavior indicative of transitivity has been obtained in some training studies, but it appears to be difficult to induce transitivity by practice.

It appears from Piaget's theory that if a child's cognitive structure contains the grouping of addition of asymmetrical, transitive relations, he can use the transitive property of any such relations, regardless of the concrete embodiment. Piaget (1952, p. 204) has indicated, on the contrary, that a formal structure of transitivity is not acquired all at once, but it must be reacquired every time a new embodiment is encountered. Sinclair (1971) has further suggested that properties of the concrete embodiments (such as discrete or continuous) will affect the attainment of psychologically parallel concepts.

In the present study, experiences in length relations were given to introduce an embodiment of the transitive relations in addition to the matching relations, but no instruction was given in transitivity of the length relations. The results indicate that while the treatment improved the ability to use transitivity of the matching relations, there was no corresponding improvement in the ability for the children to use transitivity of length relations. Thus, the conclusion was reached that the treatment was rather task specific and no generalized scheme of transitivity was induced.

This conclusion is consistent with Piaget's conjecture, and with the results of training studies in conservation. For example, Beilin's (1965) subjects improved in conservation of number and length when experiences were given. However, the training was not sufficient to foster generalization to conservation of area.

The results of the Asymmetric Property of the Matching Relations Test indicate that the treatment was effective in improving the ability of the children in the full treatment group in using the asymmetric property of the matching (order) relations. This may be interpreted not as a transfer of training, but as a direct consequence of the instructional activities. In each activity, the instructors stressed the relations which did not hold as well as the relation which did hold. Consider, for example, an activity in the differential treatment in which there were more a's than b's. After the transitive inference or conservation question, "Are there more *a*'s than *b*'s?" the instructor also asked "Are there as many *a*'s as *b*'s?" and "Are there fewer *a*'s than *b*'s?" If a child failed to answer "no" to each of these latter two questions, the instructor corrected the child by using the materials. The statement that there are not fewer *a*'s than *b*'s is equivalent to the statement that there are not more *b*'s than *a*'s. This logical equivalent (that there are not more *b*'s than *a*'s) is precisely the asymmetrical inference from the relation which does hold: there are more *a*'s than *b*'s. This situation may have been interpreted in this way by the children, so that the treatment effect was obtained for the asymmetric property.

The differential treatment contained four lessons on conservation of matching relations and five lessons on transitivity of matching relations. The conservation portion of the treatment was not successful in improving the conservation ability of the children in the treatment group. Many of the conservation training studies previously reported have indicated that conservation ability has been improved (Beilin, 1971). The conservation treatment in the present study was apparently either too short, or the activities were inappropriate for the subjects of the study. Another possible factor was that the transitivity instruction intervened between the conservation instruction and the testing period. This delayed the testing on conservation for one more week after instruction than the testing on transitivity. There remains the possibility that the conservation lessons were instrumental in fostering the improvement of performance of the treatment group in the transitive and asymmetric properties.

Matching and Length Relational Properties

The mean performance of the six-year-old group was higher than the mean performance of the five-year-old group on all matching relations tests except transitivity. It is not surprising that these cognitive abilities improved between the ages of five and six. The amazing result is that age had no significant effect on the abilities of the children in using any of the length relational properties. Consideration of the means indicated that performance on length relational properties was at about the same level as performance on matching relational properties. Consideration of criteria levels showed that more children attained conservation and transitivity of length relations than the corresponding properties of matching relations. Thus, from the point of view of relations rather than number and length, Sinclair's (1971) hypothesis is not confirmed for the children in this study.

Conservation and Transitivity Attainment

The result that about one-half of the children who used the transitive property in each relational category failed to use conservation of that respective category is at variance with results of previous studies. Smedslund (1964) found only 4 of 160 subjects who passed the test on transitivity and failed on conservation of discontinuous quantities, and only 1 subject was in the corresponding cell for length. Owens and Steffe (1972) observed only 4 of 126 instances (among 42 subjects) in which transitivity of a matching relation preceded conservation of that relation. Divers (1970) found that in 87% of the cases where transitivity of a length relation was attained, the relation was also conserved. In the studies cited, the results consistently indicated that attainment of conservation preceded attainment of the transitivity property. None of the studies involved instruction or practice, and the present results may be interpreted in terms of the treatment effect. The treatment was effective in improving performance on the test of the transitive property while the treatment had no effect on conservation performance for matching relations. Thus, some children in the treatment group met the criterion on the transitivity test who might otherwise not have attained transitivity. Only two children who used transitivity on the Transitivity Problem failed to exhibit conservation. This explanation applies, however, only to the matching relational category, because the treatment was not effective in improving the performance on transitivity of length relations.

Perhaps an interpretation can be made in terms of the characteristics of the children in the sample. Skypek (1966) conducted a study which involved both middle and lower socio-economic status children. It was found that among the low status children, the development pattern of cardinal number conservation was erratic. While the present study included no middle class group for comparison, it appears that the pattern of attainment of conservation and relational properties was irregular for these low economic status subjects.

MARTIN L. JOHNSON

Learning of Classification and Seriation by Young Children

The acts of classifying and ordering objects may be analyzed both psychologically and mathematically. Beth and Piaget (1966) have attempted to explain these acts psychologically by postulated models of cognition called "groupings." Two of the Groupings, Grouping I and Grouping V, deal with classes and asymmetric relations, respectively. These two groupings provide models for the cognitive acts of combining individuals in classes and assembling the asymmetrical relations which express differences in the individuals, or more specifically, models for classification and seriation.

The elements of Grouping I are classes which are hierarchically arranged. Somewhere between late preoperational and early or middle concrete operational stages the child can readily ascend such a hierarchy of classes by successively combining elementary classes into supraordinate classes ($A + A' = B$; $B + B' = C$, etc.) (Flavell, 1963). Furthermore, the child can just as easily descend the hierarchy, beginning with a supraordinate class and decomposing it into its subordinate classes, ($C - B' = B$, etc.). In addition, the child can destroy one classification system in order to impose a new and different one on the same data (Inhelder and Piaget, 1964).

Beth and Piaget (1966) point out that seriation behavior can be found in children from the sensory-motor stage onward, with operational seriation coming only after the child begins to anticipate the series and coordinate the relations involved in forming the series. An example is where a child is given elements A, B, C, D, E, F, G, etc., and is asked to arrange them according to some asymmetrical transitive relation. If the child finds a systematic method -- puts down the "smallest" of the elements (A) after carrying out pairwise comparisons, the "smallest" (B)

The experiment reported in this chapter is based on a doctoral dissertation in the Department of Mathematics Education at the University of Georgia (Johnson, M. L., 1971).

of the remainder (again after comparing in pairs), then again the "smallest" (C) of the remainder, etc. -- he understands in advance that any element E will be at the same time "larger" than any element already put down (A, B, C, D) and "smaller" than the remaining elements (F, G, etc.). Grouping V provides a model for the cognitive actions present in such an act of seriating objects.

Mathematically, classification and seriation can be interpreted as being logically dependent on equivalence and order relations. It is well known in mathematics that each equivalence relation serves as the basis for a classification of objects (Herstein, 1964) and conversely that every exhaustive classification of objects into distinct classes defines an equivalence relation, where objects are considered as being equivalent if they are classified together. For example, given a set of linear objects (A), with the instructions to "put all objects having the same length together," the set can be partitioned into disjoint subsets by using the mathematical properties of "same length as." On the other hand, nonreflexive, asymmetrical, transitive relations can serve as a basis for ordering a collection of objects, or for the act of seriation.

Classificatory behavior of young children has been the subject of a substantial amount of research in recent years. Inhelder and Piaget (1964) were among the first to systematically study the behavior of children as they attempted to form classes. These authors report behavior related to classificatory acts ranging from "graphic collections" (Stage I) in which the child forms spatial wholes, to true classification (Stage III). True classification appears when children are able to coordinate both the intension and extension of a class as shown by an ability to solve class inclusion problems -- somewhere around 8-9 years of age. Lovell, Mitchell, and Everett (1962) found behavior similar to that found by Inhelder and Piaget with only Stage III children being able to group objects according to more than one criterion; such as color, shape, or form. The fact that the basis of classification children use is age related was revealed by Olver and Hornsby (1966). Their research showed that collections made by very young children are based on perceptible properties of objects (color, shape, etc.) with an increase of functional based equivalence as children grow older. Other researchers (Maccoby and Modiano, 1966) reported that the choice of criteria for classification is a function of the child's culture. While this may be the case, Olmsted, Parks, and Rickel (1970) reported that the classification skills of culturally deprived children, including an increase in the variety of criteria used for classification, could be improved by involving the children in a systematic training procedure. Edwards (1969) also reported an increase in classification performance of children due to training. Other investigators (Clarke, Cooper and Loudon, 1969; Darnell and Bourne, 1970) reported that conditions of training, such as making the child aware of natural relationships or orderings among a set of objects, may facilitate the learning of equivalence relations.

Seriation behavior develops in stages similar to classification behavior (Inhelder and Piaget, 1964). Systematic or operational seriation appears in Stage III -- approximately eight years of age. Operational seriation is distinguished by (1) the discovering of a systematic way of forming a series and (2) the ability to insert new elements in an existing series without relying on trial-and-error procedures. Developmental stages consistent with the findings of Inhelder and Piaget have been reported by Elkind (1964) and Lovell, Mitchell, and Everett (1962).

Very little research has been reported in which training procedures were used in an attempt to facilitate seriation ability. Coxford (1964) reported that selected instructional activities had a facilitating effect on the seriation ability of those children who were already in a transitional stage. Holowinsky (1970), however, reported that any increase in seriation ability of four-, five- and six-year-old children in his sample was more likely due to age increases than to instructional activities. Clearly, the issue of training effects has not been resolved.

The current literature indicates that various factors influence the ability of a child to determine criteria for classification. Although the training research has not been completely unfavorable, classification has been approached only as a general categorizing process not including the major action in classifying -- the forming of equivalence classes. Hence, any relationship which may exist between the child's knowledge of the mathematical properties of an equivalence relation and his classification skills based on that relation has not been explicated.

Similarly, the current literature does not explicate any relationship which may exist between seriation ability and properties of order relations. Specifically, does a relationship exist between the child's knowledge of the transitive property of an asymmetric, transitive relation and the child's ability to seriate on the basis of that relation? Furthermore, it has not been determined whether seriation ability is relational specific or material specific. Conversely, because classification and seriation involves using mathematical relations, does classification and seriation training produce an understanding of the mathematical properties of the relations involved, specifically, the transitive property?

Purpose

The main purpose of this experiment was to determine the influence of training on the ability of first and second grade children to classify and seriate objects on the basis of length. A second purpose was to investigate the influence of such training on the child's ability to conserve and use the transitive properties of the above relations "same length as," "longer than," and "shorter than."

Other objectives were to determine if the subject's ability to use the transitive property of the equivalence relation "same length as" was related to his ability to classify on the basis of the relation; to investigate the relationship between the child's ability to use the transitive property of the relations "longer than" and "shorter than" and his ability to seriate on the basis of these relations; and to determine if the ability to seriate linear objects is material specific or relational specific.

Method

The Subjects

Eighty-one subjects, comprised of thirty-nine first grade children and forty-two second grade children were chosen for this study. Twenty-three first grade and twenty-four second grade children were from the

W. H. Crogman Elementary School, while sixteen first grade and eighteen second grade children were enrolled at the Cleveland Avenue Elementary School; both schools in Atlanta, Georgia. At the beginning of this study, March 16, 1971, the mean age for first grade was 80.8 months and for second grade 91.8 months.

The W. H. Crogman Elementary School is located near downtown Atlanta in a Model Cities area. All subjects from W. H. Crogman School who participated in this study were Negro. By virtue of having been in a Model Cities area, the educational programs of W. H. Crogman Elementary were enriched by the use of parents as "teacher helpers" and a well-planned extended day program for first and second grade children. Many of the children who participated in this study took part in home economics, art, music, organized physical education, and a variety of other activities.

Cleveland Avenue Elementary School is located in Southwest Atlanta and served a predominately Caucasian, middle-class student population. Of the thirty-four children in the sample from this school, thirty-two were Caucasian and two were Negro. Within each school, the sample was randomly selected from the existing first and second grade classes.

Description of Learning Material

Two instructional units were written for this study. Unit I consisted of six lessons designed to acquaint the students with the relations "same length as," "longer than" and "shorter than" and to make proper comparisons based on these relations. Unit II consisted of ten lessons designed to give experiences in classifying on the basis of the equivalence relation "same length as" and seriating on the basis of the order relations "longer than" and "shorter than." For example, lessons 1 and 3 of Unit II were primarily concerned with classifying sticks, straws, pipecleaners, and ropes on the basis of length. In lesson 2 the child was asked to determine the longest and/or shortest object from a collection of objects given to him. The procedure followed was to make pairwise comparisons until the longest (shortest) object was determined. In subsequent lessons, the child was asked to seriate collections of sticks and then mixed collections (strings, sticks, straws, pipecleaners) using a procedure consistent with Piaget's stage three behavior. At least two lessons required the child to insert additional objects into series already formed.

Instructional Schedule and Modes of Instruction

Instruction on Unit I began at W. H. Crogman School on the morning of March 18, 1971. Similar instruction began at Cleveland Avenue School on March 19, 1971. Because of having to alternate between the schools on consecutive days, twelve days were required for the completion of Unit I. Upon completion of Unit I, a Criterion Test (see *Criterion Test*) was administered. The children who met criterion were randomly placed into either an experimental or control group. The experimental group received instruction on Unit II while the control group received no further instruction. Instruction on Unit II began on April 14, 1971 with instruction being given at W. H. Crogman School in the morning and at Cleveland Avenue School in the afternoon. Ten instructional days were required for the administration of Unit II, ending on April 27, 1971. All instruction was carried out in groups of approximately six students in 20 minute sessions. Unit II was taught only by the investigator while teacher aides helped with the instruction of Unit I.

Tests

Instruments were constructed to measure the children's knowledge of the length relations, ability to conserve and use the transitive property of the relations, ability to seriate using the order relations, and ability to classify using the equivalence relation.

Criterion Test. A nine-item test was constructed to determine if, at the end of Unit I, the children understood the relations and terms used in the conservation and transitivity tests to be administered as pretests. To meet criterion on this test, the child had to meet criterion on each of the three relations, which was defined as correctly performing on two of the three questions asked about each relation. For example, the child would be asked (from a pile of sticks with a standard stick placed before the pile) to "find a stick the same length as the standard stick," "find a stick longer than the standard stick," and "find a stick shorter than the standard stick." Similar instructions were given for the other six items which included both sticks and strings. All questions were asked in random order to each child.

Conservation of Length Relations Test (CLRT). This test consisted of six items; two each concerning the relations "same length as," "longer than," and "shorter than." Two perceptual stimuli were given for each relation; neutral and conflictive. All of the materials were red and green sticks 3/8" in diameter differing in length by 1/8" within an item. In items with the neutral stimuli a red and green stick would be displayed and the child was asked "Is the red stick the same length as the green stick?" or "Is the red stick longer than the green stick?" or "Is the red stick shorter than the green stick?" The question asked would depend on whatever relation did hold between the two sticks. After the child had determined which relations did hold, one stick was moved right or left so that the left end of one stick coincided with the right end of the other. Three questions were now asked in random order. "Is the red stick the same length as the green stick?", "Is the red stick longer than the green stick?", "Is the red stick shorter than the green stick?"

The items with conflictive stimuli were administered in a slightly different way than the items with neutral stimuli. After the child had determined the relation that existed between the red and green sticks, they were moved to form a "T" and the three questions were then asked.

To receive a score of one on an item, the child had to answer the three questions correctly. The correct sequence of answers depended on the item being given. This test was given both as a pretest and a posttest.

Transitivity of Length Relations Test (TLRT). This test consisted of six items; two each for the relations "same length as," "longer than," and "shorter than." Two perceptual stimuli were present; screened and conflictive. All materials in this test consisted of red, blue, and green sticks all 3/8" in diameter and differing in length by 1/8". In each item, the child had first to determine the relation that existed between the red and blue sticks, then the blue and green sticks. To make an inference about the relation that existed between the red and green sticks the child was again asked three questions in random order as in the CLRT. On the items with screened stimuli the final inference about the length of the red and green sticks had to be made with the sticks in boxes and not visible by the subjects. This test was used both as a pretest and a posttest with scoring as in the CLRT.

Seriation Test. A 12-item test was constructed to assess the child's ability to seriate on the basis of "longer than" and "shorter than." Items 1-6 were based on the relation "longer than;" items 7-12 were based on "shorter than." Item 1 and item 7 required the child to seriate six sticks (free seriation), all 3/8" in diameter, differing in length by 1/8" with the shortest stick being 5 1/2" long. Item 2 and item 8 required the child to seriate six strings (free seriation) of the same length as the sticks in item 1 and item 7.

For the free seriation items, a point was given for each stick or string judged to be in the "correct place" with respect to the relation given. For example, when the child had indicated that his series was formed, he was then asked to show how the objects were in order from the longest to shortest (shortest to longest). Now, if, for instance, he was basing his ordering on "longer than," and he indicated that his series was formed from left to right, a point would be given for a stick *b* if *b* was shorter than the stick it immediately succeeded and at the same time longer than the stick it immediately preceded. A maximum of four points was awarded for each of the free seriation items.

Items 3, 4, 5, 9, 10 and 11 required the child to insert a stick into a series already formed. However, the sticks in the series were glued on an 8" X 16" piece of cardboard, spaced and staggered so that a baseline was not discernable, as in Figure 1.

Figure 1

Item #4 (seriated from longest to shortest - left to right).

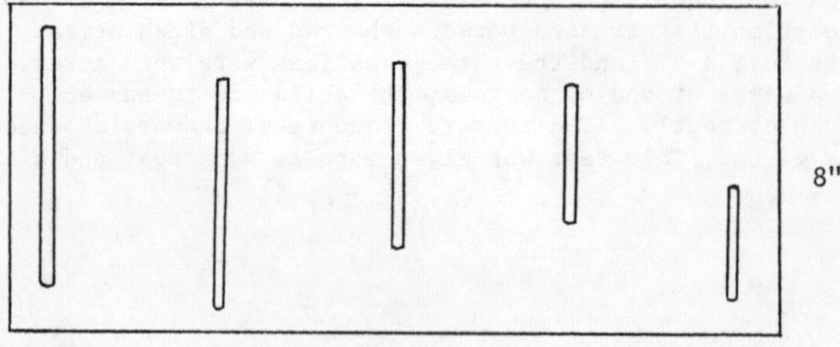

The series in items 3 and 9 consisted of four sticks, in items 4 and 10 five sticks, and in items 5 and 11 six sticks. In each case the sticks were equally spaced. Items 6 and 12 were also insertion items but the existing series had a visible baseline and the sticks could be moved about. One point was given for each correct answer.

Classification Test. This test consisted of 3 items; two requiring the child to group sticks on the basis of length and one in which the child had to determine the criteria used for sticks already grouped.

The materials for item 1 consisted of 12 green sticks, each 3/8" diameter with four of length 5", four of length 5 1/4" and four of length 5 1/2". One stick of each length was mounted on a piece of paper board. The three mounted sticks were pointed out to the child who was then instructed to "find all of the sticks that would go with this stick (5"), this stick (5 1/4") and this stick (5 1/2")." The nine sticks to be classified were in disorder before the child. A record of all sticks correctly and incorrectly placed was kept by the experimenter.

The materials for item 3 consisted of ten red sticks all 3/8" diameter, three of length 4", three of length 4 1/4", three of length 4 1/2", and one of length 4 3/4". The ten sticks were given to the child and he was instructed to "put all of the sticks together that belong together." A record of the child's actions was kept by the experimenter.

Item 2 required that the child determine the criteria used for grouping. The materials for this item consisted of fifteen sticks; five each at length 6", 6 1/4", and 6 1/2". The sticks were placed into three distinct piles about 15 inches apart on a table. Within a pile, sticks differed in color and diameter; with length being constant. The child was instructed to "Tell me why I have all of these sticks together in this pile (6"), in this pile (6 1/4") and in this pile (6 1/2")." If a correct answer was given, the child was asked to justify his answer. Upon justification, he was then asked, "Why do I have these sticks in different piles?" Again a justification for a correct answer was asked for. A record of all answers was kept by the experimenter.

The Experimental Design and Statistical Analysis. Two treatment conditions within two grade levels within two schools produced eight comparison groups. Table 1 is a layout of the design. S_1 and S_2 represent W. H. Crogman Elementary School and Cleveland Avenue Elementary School, respectively. The numerals "1" and "2" represent grades 1 and 2. The letters E and C represent experimental and control groups, and G_i (i = 1, ..., 8) represents the eight different groups.

Because the main purpose of the criterion test was to eliminate subjects who did not have a knowledge of the relations, no test of significance was performed on the criterion test data. It should be pointed out that all children met criterion on the Criterion Test.

A 2 X 2 X 2 factorial design utilizing analysis of variance (MUGALS)* was used to determine the effect of the two classification (School and Grade Level) and treatment variables on the seriation test. An analysis

*MUGALS (Modified University of Georgia Least Squares Analysis of Variance), Athens, Georgia, University of Georgia Computing Center, 1966.

Table 1
Outline of the Design

School	Grade Level	Treatment	Tests: Crit Test	CLRT Pre	TLRT Pre	Seri Test	Class Test	CLRT Post	TLRT Post
S_1	1	E	G_1	G_1	G_1	G_1	G_1	G_1	G_1
		C	G_2	G_2	G_2	G_2	G_2	G_2	G_2
	2	E	G_3	G_3	G_3	G_3	G_3	G_3	G_3
		C	G_4	G_4	G_4	G_4	G_4	G_4	G_4
S_2	1	E	G_5	G_5	G_5	G_5	G_5	G_5	G_5
		C	G_6	G_6	G_6	G_6	G_6	G_6	G_6
	2	E	G_7	G_7	G_7	G_7	G_7	G_7	G_7
		C	G_8	G_8	G_8	G_8	G_8	G_8	G_8

of covariance (MUGALS) was used to analyze the conservation and transitivity posttest scores using the respective pretests as covariates. An item by item analysis involving the treatment variable was performed on the classification test data using contingency tables and Chi-square test of independence. To determine relationships between transitivity, seriation, and classification, a series of contingency tables was constructed and tested with Chi-square tests of independence.

Results

Seriation Test

The overall mean for the seriation test was 12.51 with a standard deviation of 7.03. The total possible score by an individual on this test was 24. Table 2 contains the means for grades and treatment within groups.

Table 2
Means for Seriation Test

School	Grade	Experimentals	Controls
Crogman	1	12.83	6.55
	2	15.50	12.42
Cleveland	1	11.25	7.88
	2	20.00	13.56

Table 3 contains the difficulties of all dichotomous items on the seriation test. Because items 1, 2, 7, and 8 were nondichotomous the difficulties of these items are reported as p-values in Table 4.

Table 3
Item Difficulties of Dichotomous Items - Seriation Test

Item No.	Frequency of Correct Response	Difficulty
3	46	.57
4	33	.41
5	33	.41
6	46	.57
9	41	.51
10	36	.44
11	43	.53
12	44	.54

Table 4
P-Values for Nondichotomous Items*

	P-Values				
Item No.	Score 0	1	2	3	4
1	.26	.06	.17	.00	.51
2	.28	.16	.23	.03	.30
7	.27	.07	.12	.05	.48
8	.30	.12	.27	.05	.26

*p is the ratio of Ss who received score i (i = 0, 1, 2, 3, 4) for item x (x = 1, 2, 7, 8) to the total number of subjects answering.

Inspection of Table 3 shows that less than fifty percent of the children were able to correctly answer items 4, 5 and 10. Items 4 and 10 involved inserting a stick into a fixed five-stick series in which the sticks were ordered from longest to shortest (item 4) and from shortest to longest (item 10). It was expected that item 5 would be more difficult than item 4, because item 5 contained six sticks as opposed to five in item 4 and were arranged in a staggered series from longest to shortest. Because items 5 and 11 were identical except for order, the difference in difficulty was not expected. Furthermore, inserting a stick into a six-stick series with a baseline (items 6 and 12) appeared to be slightly easier than inserting into a six-stick series without a baseline (items 5 and 11).

Table 4 clearly shows that more children were able to correctly seriate sticks (items 1 and 7) than strings (items 2 and 8). Little difference in difficulty was found between performance on the "longer than" item using sticks (item 1) and the "shorter than" item using sticks (item 7). Similarly, little difference in difficulty was found between performance on the "longer than" item using strings (item 2) and the "shorter than" item using strings (item 8). It also appeared that children either could not put any objects in correct order (score of 0); could correctly order up to four or make two pairs of three, each correctly ordered (score of 2); or could correctly order all six objects (score of 4).

The analysis of variance for the seriation test is reported in Table 5. Both grade ($p < .01$) and treatment ($p < .01$) were highly significant main effects. No differences could be detected due to school. No significant first or second order interactions could be detected. It is clear that the experiences provided to the subjects in this study were sufficient to improve their seriation ability as measured by the seriation test.

Table 5
Analysis of Variance for Seriation Test Scores

Source of Variation	df	MS	F
S (School)	1	35.66	<1.00
G (Grade)	1	648.79	17.22**
T (Treatment)	1	452.92	12.02*
S x G	1	42.70	1.13
S x T	1	.25	<1.00
G x T	1	.02	<1.00
S x G x T	1	48.41	1.29
Error	73	37.68	

**(p < .0005), * (p < .001)

Conservation of Length Relations Test (Posttest)

Table 6 contains the means for all groups on the CLRT posttest. An interesting observation is that the means for first-grade controls were somewhat higher than means for first-grade experimentals across schools.

Table 6
Means for Conservation of Length Relations Test (Posttest)

School	Grade	Experimentals	Controls
Crogman	1	2.50	3.20
	2	4.50	4.08
Cleveland	1	2.25	4.25
	2	5.22	4.89

The CLRT was given both as a pretest and a posttest. A comparison of item difficulties on the pretest and posttest is given in Table 7. Overall, the items on the CLRT were easier on the posttest than on the pretest. Item 1, involving "same length as," was more difficult than item 2, also involving "same length as," on both administrations of the test. This is surprising since item 1 used a "neutral" situation while item 2 was a "conflictive" item. Divers (1970) found that different perceptual situations had little effect on conservation ability. Items 3 and 4, involving "longer than," were the easiest items on the posttest.

The results of the CLRT posttest were analyzed by analysis of covariance using the CLRT pretest as a covariate. The results of this analysis are reported in Table 8.

Table 7
Item Difficulties of Conservation of Length Relations Test: Pretest and Posttest

Item No.	Relation and Situation	Difficulty Pretest	Difficulty Posttest
1	Same Length As (N)	.35	.56
2	Same Length As (C)	.42	.63
3	Shorter Than (N)	.63	.67
4	Shorter Than (C)	.43	.70
5	Longer Than (N)	.35	.64
6	Longer Than (C)	.41	.64

Table 8
Analysis of Covariance for Conservation of Length Relations Test Scores (Posttest)

Source of Variation	df	MS	F
S (School)	1	14.45	6.39*
G (Grade)	1	10.68	4.72*
T (Treatment)	1	.67	<1.00
S x G	1	8.98	3.97
S x T	1	.42	<1.00
G x T	1	.34	<1.00
T x S x G	1	.98	<1.00
Error	72	2.26	

*($p < .05$)

The main effects of school and grade were both significant. In view of past research on conservation ability, it was expected that older children would be better conservers of length relations than the younger children; however, it was not expected that the school effect would be significant. No significance could be detected due to treatment. No statistically significant interactions were found; however, there was a possible suggested interaction between school and grade.

Transitivity of Length Relations Test (Posttest)

Table 9 contains the means for all children on the TLRT posttest. Item difficulties for the pretest and posttest are given in Table 10.

Inspection of Table 10 reveals that on the pretest, all items except item 3 were of near equal difficulty. It was not expected that item 3 would be easier than item 4 because item 3 required the child to make an inference about the relative length of sticks placed in boxes and not visible to the child. An interesting result was the change in difficulty of items 1 and 2 in a positive direction from pre-to posttest and a change in difficulty in a negative direction for items 3, 4, 5, 6 from pretest to posttest. The items involving the linear order relations were at least as difficult after the extensive training on strategies of seriation utilizing these relations.

Table 9
Means for Transitivity of Length Relations Test (Posttest)

School	Grade	Experimentals	Controls
Crogman	1	1.50	1.40
	2	2.50	1.33
Cleveland	1	2.13	2.50
	2	2.67	3.44

Table 10
Item Difficulties of Transitivity of Length Relations Test: Pretest and Posttest

Item No.	Relation and Situation	Difficulty	
		Pretest	Posttest
1	Same Length As (S)*	.33	.49
2	Same Length As (C)	.30	.43
3	Shorter Than (S)	.44	.38
4	Shorter Than (C)	.31	.28
5	Longer Than (S)	.33	.22
6	Longer Than (C)	.31	.30

*S: Screened, C: Conflictive

Table 11
Analysis of Covariance for Transitivity of Length Relations Test Scores (Posttest)

Source of Variation	df	MS	F
S (School)	1	14.96	6.31*
G (Grade)	1	2.12	<1.00
T (Treatment)	1	.59	<1.00
S x G	1	.001	<1.00
S x T	1	8.14	3.43
G x T	1	.12	<1.00
T x S x G	1	1.40	<1.00
Error	72	2.37	

*($p < .05$)

Table 11 contains the results of the analysis of covariance on the TLRT posttest with the TLRT pretest used as a covariate. Only the main effect of school was significant. No significant interactions were detected with only a possible interaction suggested between school and treatment.

The test statistics for the seriation test, the CLRT pre- and posttest, and TLRT pre- and posttest are contained in Table 12. Test correlations are given in Table 13. An unexpected result was that the seriation

Table 12
Test Statistics for Seriation, Conservation, and Transitivity Tests (N = 81)

Test	Number of Items	Possible Score	Mean	SD	Reliability
Seriation	12	24	12.5	7.03	.81**
CLRT (pretest)	6	6	2.58	1.98	.77*
CLRT (posttest)	6	6	3.84	1.98	.85*
TLRT (pretest)	6	6	2.03	1.47	.46*
TLRT (posttest)	6	6	2.11	1.66	.63*

**Alpha Coefficient, *KR-20

Table 13
Test Correlations

	Con. Pre.	Con. Post	Tran. Pre.	Tran. Post
Seriation	.21	.25*	.15	.26*
Con. Pre.		.65*	.45*	.38*
Con. Post			.43*	.33*
Tran. Pre.				.31*

*($p < .01$)

test did not correlate more than .26 with any other test. All correlations differed significantly from the zero correlation except the correlations between the seriation test and the conservation and transitivity pretest.

Classification Test

Item 1 on the classification test required the child to find and group into three distinct piles sticks similar to a given stick. From the children's responses, four performance categories were identified. They were: (a) the child did not attempt to classify sticks; (b) the child made some partial classes but did not exhaust the set of sticks to be classified; (c) the child exhausted the set but made some incorrect choices; and (d) the child correctly classified all sticks. Table 14 shows the number of subjects exhibiting each of the above four types of performance on item 1 by treatment, grade, and school. A Chi-square test of independence was performed for each main effect and performance. The control subjects performed comparably to experimental subjects on item 1. Thirty-six of forty-seven (76%) subjects at Crogman School were able to classify all sticks. The same percent of category d responses was found at Cleveland School; twenty-six of thirty-four (76%). A slight relationship ($\chi^2 = 6.78$, $p < .10$) was found between performance on item 1 and grade level.

Item 2 required the subjects to discover the criteria for classification. In this item sticks of different colors and diameters were presented in three distinct piles and the child was asked to give a reason for their being grouped together in separate piles. The child was also asked to tell why distinct piles were formed. Five distinct categories of

Table 14
Frequency Table: Performance on Item 1 Contrasted With Treatment, Grade, and School

		Performance			
		a	b	c	d
Treatment	E	1	7	4	29
	C	0	4	3	33
Grade	1	1	8	5	25
	2	0	3	2	37
School	Cr	1	7	3	36
	Cl	0	4	4	26

responses were identified. They were: (a) the child did not discover the criteria; (b) the child gave a correct reason for the piles being together but without justification; (c) a correct reason was given with justification; (d) in addition to justifying the reason for sticks belonging in distinct groups, the subject correctly gave a reason for sticks being in different groups but without justification for his reason; (e) all of (d) with justification. The overall performance of the subjects on item 2 is presented in Table 15 contrasted by treatment, grade, and school. A slight relationship was found ($\chi^2 = 9.26$, $p < .10$) between performance and treatment; however, a higher frequency of category (e) responses was given by the control subjects with a reversal for category (d) responses. Overall, it can be seen that about 75% of the subjects failed to discover the criteria for classification in item 2.

Table 15
Frequency Table: Performance on Item 2 Contrasted With Treatment, Grade, and School

		Performance				
		a	b	c	d	e
Treatment	E	29	1	2	6	3
	C	30	0	2	0	8
Grade	1	29	0	3	1	6
	2	30	1	1	5	5
School	Cr	35	1	3	2	6
	Cl	24	0	1	4	5

In item 3 the child was given ten sticks and asked to classify them as he desired where the sticks differed only in length. One stick was longer than all of the others, requiring the child to come to grips with forming a class with one element. Four categories of performance were identified: (a) no attempt was made to group the sticks; (b) the child made at least two piles with the sticks being placed incorrectly; (c) the child put all sticks in correct piles according to length except the longest sticks; (d) the child correctly classified all sticks, including the longest stick. The overall performance of the subjects contrasted by treatment, grade, and school is given in Table 16.

Table 16
Frequency Table: Performance on Item 3 Contrasted With Treatment, Grade, and School

		Performance			
		a	b	c	d
Treatment	E	5	17	3	16
	C	1	21	4	14
Grade	1	2	22	5	10
	2	4	16	2	20
School	Cr	4	22	6	15
	Cl	2	16	1	15

No significant relationship could be detected between performance on item 3 and treatment, grade, or school. However, the frequencies reported for grade 2 shows that second graders gave more correct category (d) responses than the first graders which indicates that more older children were able to deal with a class consisting of one member than their younger counterparts.

Classification and Transitivity

One purpose of the study was to investigate relationships between the ability to use the transitive property of "same length as" and classification ability on the basis of length. Tables 17, 18 and 19 contain the subjects' classification responses on items 1, 2 and 3, respectively, partitioned by transitivity score. The transitivity score was a result of the subject's performance on the transitivity items involving "same length as" on the TLRT posttest. Zero, one, and two were assigned as transitivity scores depending upon whether the subject correctly answered none, one, or both of the transitivity items. In order to increase cell frequencies, rows indicating intermediate levels of performance on the classification test were combined as explained by Guilford (1956). Tables 17 and 18 show that performance on item 1 and 2 was slightly related to

Table 17
Contingency Table: Classification Performance (Item 1) vs Transitivity Ability (same length as - Posttest)

Classification Performance	Transitivity Score		
	2	1	0
d	25	16	21
a-c	3	3	13

$\chi^2 = 5.73$, $p < .10$

transitivity ability of "same length as." No relationship could be detected between transitivity ability and classification performance on item 3. Perhaps transitivity was not needed to correctly perform the items on the classification test. However, the data in Table 17 indicate that at least 80% of the time, the child who scored 1 or 2 on the transitivity test performed at the highest level on the classification item.

In contrast, the data in Table 18 suggest that at least 85% of the time, the child who scored 1 or 0 on the transitivity test performed at the lowest level on classification item 2.

Table 18
Contingency Table: Classification Performance (Item 2) vs Transitivity Ability (same length as - Posttest)

Classification Performance	Transitivity Score		
	2	1	0
d-e	10	2	5
a-c	18	17	29

$\chi^2 = 5.72$, $p < .10$

Table 19
Contingency Table: Classification Performance (Item 3) vs Transitivity Ability (same length as - Posttest)

Classification Performance	Transitivity Score		
	2	1	0
d	13	7	10
a-c	15	12	24

$\chi^2 = 1.91$, $p < .50$

Seriation and Transitivity

The relationship between seriation ability using the relations "longer than" and "shorter than" and the ability to use the transitive properties of these relations was also investigated. These results are presented in Tables 20 and 21. The transitivity score refers to whether

Table 20
Contingency Table: Seriation (longer than) vs Transitivity (longer than - Posttest)

Seriation Score	Transitivity Score		
	2	1	0
9-12	4	12	12
5-8	1	6	13
0-4	2	10	21

$\chi^2 = 3.91$, $p < .50$

Table 21
Contingency Table: Seriation (shorter than) vs Transitivity (shorter than - Posttest)

Seriation Score	Transitivity Score		
	2	1	0
9-12	2	10	12
5-8	5	11	14
0-4	7	5	15

$\chi^2 = 4.96$, $p < .30$

the child correctly answered none, one or both of the items on the transitivity test involving the relation "shorter than" or "longer than." The seriation score for each order relation ranged from zero to twelve.

The results of Chi-square tests of independence indicate that the hypothesis of independence between seriation ability and transitivity ability cannot be rejected beyond the .10 level of significance.

Other Relationships

It was expected that the ability to seriate sticks was related to the ability to seriate strings across relations. The results reported in Tables 22 and 23 show that a high relationship does exist between these two abilities. Inspection of Table 22 shows that of the 24 subjects who received a score of four, representing the correct seriating of six strings from shortest to longest, twenty-three also received a score of four for

Table 22
Contingency Table: Seriation of Sticks vs Seriation of Strings (Shorter Than)

Strings	Sticks		
	4	3-2-1	0
4	23	0	1
3-2-1	17	10	7
0	1	9	13

$\chi^2 = 41.03$, $p < .001$

seriating sticks from shortest to longest. However, of the forty-one receiving a score of four for seriating sticks from shortest to longest, only twenty-three received four for seriating strings. Similarly, Table 23 reveals that of 21 students receiving a score of four with strings, 18 received a score of four for sticks while of 39 who received a score of four for sticks, only 18 received a score of four for strings, all seriation based on the relation "longer than." Not only were the abilities related, but clearly seriating strings was somewhat more difficult than seriating sticks.

Table 23
Contingency Table: Seriation of Sticks vs Seriation of Strings (Longer Than)

Strings	Sticks 4	Sticks 3-2-1	Sticks 0
4	18	3	0
3-2-1	18	15	3
0	3	2	19

$\chi^2 = 54.54$, $p < .001$

Table 24
Contingency Table: Insertion Ability (Baseline vs Non-Baseline)

Baseline	Non-Baseline 2	Non-Baseline 1	Non-Baseline 0
2	17	10	8
1	4	9	7
0	2	11	13

$\chi^2 = 13.83$, $p < .01$

A strong relationship was also found between the abilities to insert a stick into an existing series of sticks with a baseline and without a baseline, shown in Table 24. Seventy-four percent of the subjects who correctly inserted the stick into the two non-baseline items also correctly inserted the stick into the two baseline items while only fifty-four percent of the subjects who inserted correctly into the two baseline items could also insert correctly into the two non-baseline items.

Discussion

The results of this study clearly confirm the hypothesis that seriaability of "linear" objects can be improved by training. It is also clear that seriation ability improves with age and, if trends hold, little ability to seriate "linear" objects can be expected below six years of age. The experiences provided in this study to the first grade children were sufficient to cause their mean performance (12.04) on the seriation test to be comparable to the mean performance of the second grade children who did not have the experiences (13.49). Being black or white appeared to have little or no effect on the subject's seriation ability.

The extent of the subjects' seriation ability, in terms of being operational in a Piagetian sense, must be questioned when one considers the overall performance on the transitivity test. In particular, the treatment appears to have had no effect on the children's ability to use the transitive property of the order relations involved in the study. In fact, no significant relationship could be detected between transitivity of "longer than" and "shorter than" and the ability to seriate using these relations. This finding is not consistent with the hypothesis presented by Beth and Piaget (1966) and confirmed by Elkind (1964) that transitivity is necessarily present when a child exhibits behavior characterized as stage three seriation behavior. The question is raised concerning what is "operational" seriation behavior. In this study, children were able to seriate strings and sticks, as well as insert additional sticks into a series already formed without any trouble but could not use the transitive property of "longer than." Such responses would indicate that the seriation training was successful in training the children to use an algorithm which was not part of an operational scheme. If this was the case, it would be expected that the relationship between seriation and transitivity would be negligible. If, however, the children were now "operational" then these findings suggest that contrary to Piaget's hypothesis, seriation behavior does not necessarily imply transitivity. In any case, it is clear that we need additional guidelines as to what constitutes operational behavior and more effective ways of measuring such behavior.

Throughout the training sessions outlined, it was frequently pointed out that if object a was the same length as object b, then the spatial position of a and b did not alter this relationship. Furthermore, if a was longer (or shorter) than b, then a would remain longer (or shorter) than b regardless of their spatial position. Even though such procedures were part of the classification and seriation training little or no difference was detected between the experimental and control groups in the performance on the CLRT. However, a significant school and grade effect was found. While the school and grade differences were expected in view of past studies, the non-significant treatment effect was unexpected. Although the procedures in this study differ somewhat from the procedures used in a study by Sigel, Roeper and Hooper (1966), they report that classification training improved ability to conserve quantity. Carey and Steffe (1968) report that selected experiences significantly improved the ability of four- and five-year-old children to conserve length. The experiences provided by Carey and Steffe were similar to the experiences provided to the sample in this study.

The results of the classification test indicate that it was somewhat easier for children to classify sticks on the basis of self-selected criteria than to discover the criteria used for sticks already classified. While little difference was found in performance (as noted by frequencies of response) on items one and three due to school and treatment, it was clear that second grade children did better on both of the items. On item three, the difference in response frequencies indicated that second grade children were able to form a class with only one element more consistently than the first graders. This finding was consistent with Piaget's observation that the concept of a singular class appears in a child around eight or nine years of age.

The hypothesis of a relationship between the child's classification ability and his ability to use the transitive property of the equivalence relation of "same length as" was not confirmed. The lack of a relationship may be explained, at least partially, in two ways: (1) A two-item test may not give a true assessment of transitivity ability. Past research reveals that much controversy exists over methodological issues and at the age at which children acquire the transitive property. Braine (1959), using a non-verbal technique, reported that children can use the transitive property of length relations as early as four and one-half years of age. On the other hand, Smedslund (1963b) reports that operational transitivity occurs around seven years of age and that Braine failed to assess transitivity. (2) Transitivity was not needed to do the classification tasks. In the case of item one, this could possibly have been the case since over half of the subjects receiving a score of zero on the transitivity test (indicating failure to correctly answer both transitivity items) performed at the highest level on this item. On item 2, over 50% of the subjects performed at the lowest level of performance across transitivity scores. Over half of the subjects receiving zero on transitivity also performed at the lowest levels of performance on item 3. Such results suggest that transitivity was not necessary for the classification items in this test.

In view of the findings of this study, questions may be raised concerning the feasibility of placing certain topics and activities in the early elementary mathematics curriculum. Consider the topic of formal linear measurement which is now being introduced by some curriculum developers as early as first grade. According to Piaget, Inhelder, and Szeminska (1960), prerequisite to understanding linear measurement is the ability to conserve length and to use the transitive property of length relations. The findings of this study indicate that about half of the first and second grade children used did not show evidence of these prerequisites. In view of this, perhaps, as pointed out by Huntington (1970), the teaching of formal linear measurement should be delayed until approximately third grade.

The idea of ordering numbers (such as 3 comes after 2 and 3 comes before 6) is one commonly taught at first and second grade. It seems reasonable that children at these grade levels would also have many experiences in ordering sets of physical objects. Certainly, such an activity is less abstract than ordering cardinal numbers per se. An example of such an ordering would be to order sticks on the basis of "longer than." This study has shown that many children at first and second grade cannot perform such ordering, causing one to question whether the child has a concept of "five," "six," "seven," etc. when he arranges them in order or if he is just recalling the order from his rote counting process. It has been shown that seriation ability, as related to linear objects, can be improved with certain experiences. It still needs to be shown whether similar results can be found with other relations.

The early elementary mathematics curriculum includes activities in forming and describing "sets" and operations with "sets." However, basic to forming sets of objects is the notion of classifying objects on the basis of certain properties of qualitative characteristics of the objects. As noted, Inhelder and Piaget (1964) have shown that children go through various stages in determining criteria for grouping. This study has shown that while children of six or seven years of age can sort sticks on the basis of length, they experience great difficulty when given a collection of sticks already partitioned on the basis of length and asked to tell why they were grouped together. This finding implies that children will experience difficulty in determining the reason or reasons X number of objects has been placed in a set. For example, suppose A = {January, February, March, April, May, ___________}. Will the child "discover" the criteria for grouping and add June to the set? Teachers should be aware that this type of problem may be quite difficult for six- and seven-year-old children.

Finally, the present study has raised questions concerning relationships between classification, seriation and transitivity ability. While some answers are given, it is not at all clear what kind of experiences children should have between the ages of four and eight in order to facilitate development of structures needed in logical activities.

RICHARD A. LESH

The Generalization of Piagetian Operations as It Relates to the Hypothesized Functional Interdependence between Classification, Seriation, and Number Concepts

Piaget's analysis of the cognitive evolution of number and other logical-mathematical concepts relies heavily on the psychological viability of analyzing, ordering, and equating concepts (or tasks) on the basis of their underlying operational structures. Two studies, a pilot study and a training study, were conducted in order to investigate the legitimacy of Piaget's emphasis on the operational nature of mathematical concepts. In the pilot study, a Piagetian task analysis was used in order to obtain three parallel sequences of tasks which were graded in difficulty and which pertain to seriation, number, and classification concepts, respectively. These three sequences of tasks were used to investigate the interdependent development of classification, seriation, and number concepts. The results of the pilot study were then used to organize and interpret a training study. In the training study, the possibility of inducing learning which would transfer between logical-mathematical tasks that are characterized by isomorphic operational structures was investigated. Specifically, in the training study, an attempt was made to obtain transfer from classification and seriation tasks to number tasks and to delimit the nature of the transfer that occurred.

Before reporting the results of these studies, an interpretation of Piaget's description of the development of classification, seriation and number concepts is given. In this interpretation, the operational nature of logical-mathematical concepts is discussed and tasks that were used in the two empirical studies are presented.

The experiment reported in this chapter is based on a doctoral dissertation in the College of Education at Indiana University (Lesh, 1971).

Operational Concepts

One useful definition of the word "concept" can be stated as follows. A concept has been attained when one can, within a given universe of experience, distinguish instances from noninstances of the concept. On the basis of this definition, at least two subcategories can be distinguished within the class of concepts. An example of the first of these types is the concept of "red." This type of concept may be referred to as a *concrete concept* since all of the information that is necessary in order to distinguish instances from noninstances is directly given in the perceptual field. Another type of concept may be referred to as an *operational concept* in that it involves abstractions, not just from directly perceived properties of objects, but also from relations between objects, or from operations (or transformations) that are performed on objects (Piaget, 1971, p. 26).

Mathematical concepts can involve operations in at least two ways. Some concepts (e.g., set union "+") inherently involve the mastery of a system of operations. Other concepts are operational because they arise only after a system of operations has been mastered. As an example, consider the concept of a class.

The Concept of a Class

A class of objects does not exist in isolation. In order to form a class of objects C, one must be able to determine not only what elements are in C but also what elements are not in C (call this class C') relative to some subsuming class S.

A kindergarten child can be presented with three clear plastic boxes containing 8 yellow balls, 3 yellow cubes, and 8 green cubes respectively. If he is asked, "Are there more yellow things or more balls?" the response is often "more balls." An analysis of children's responses (Inhelder & Piaget, 1964) reveals that the difficulty is not that young children misunderstand the intent of the question. The difficulty seems to be that when the child's attention is drawn to the class C = (balls), the subsuming class S = (yellow things) is cognitively destroyed. Hence, the child may end up by comparing the size of the class C with the size of the class C' = (yellow cubes).

Similarly, other tasks indicate that when attention is directed toward a subsuming class, its subclasses are often confused with overlappings (Vygotsky, 1962, pp. 56-65). Based on the careful analysis of children's responses to such tasks, Inhelder and Piaget (1964, Ch. 1-4) have concluded that a concept of a class C relative to a subsuming class S requires the coordination of the operation "+" (i.e., class union, S = C + C'), with its inverse "-" (i.e., separation of classes, C = S - C').

Three Basic Types of Logical-Mathematical Operations

A group of mathematicians, the Bourbaki group (Bourbaki, 1948), wanted to isolate a small number of "matrix structures" which would be fundamental to all of the various branches of mathematics in that no one of them could be reduced to the others and that all other mathematical structures could be derived from these by combination, differentiation, or specialization. Through regressive analysis, three basic types of structures were isolated which can be roughly characterized as follows (Grize, 1960, pp. 72-81):

1. *Algebraic structures*, the prototype of which is the group. These structures were distinguished in that their form of inverse operation was *negation*.

2. *Ordering structures*, the prototype of which is the lattice. These structures were distinguished in that their form of inverse operation was reciprocity.

3. *Topological structures*, involving the concepts of neighborhood, limit and continuity.

Just as the axiomatician can analyze mathematical structures in forms of component structures and can look for the fewest and weakest axioms that will be sufficient to account for a given structure, the developmental psychologist can look at tasks that children perform and characterize them in terms of the system of operations or relations that they involve. Piagetians (Beth & Piaget, 1966, p. 186) have isolated three basic types of cognitive operations that are roughly equivalent to three types of structures determined by the Bourbaki group. Distinguished by their form of inverse, these types of cognitive operations are:

1. Operations whose form of inverse is negation, as in the set union *operation* + that gives rise to classification concepts.

2. Operations whose form of inverse is reciprocity, as in the ordering *relation* < (less than) that gives rise to seriation concepts.

3. Geometric *transformations*.

Of course, a child may not be consciously aware of the operations and relations that are implicit in his activities. For example, when a pencil A is shorter than a pencil B, and B is shorter than a pencil C, kindergarten children may be able to conclude that A will be shorter than C. Further, they can use this fact long before they are explicitly aware of the transitive property of order relations or of the system of relations that the transitive property implies. As another example of the intuitive mastery of a concept, children commonly use perfectly correct rules of grammar long before they are explicitly aware of these rules.

Intuitive Mastery of Operational Concepts

In mathematics as in language acquisition, it may be typical for children to use rules (or systems of operations) before concious awareness is attained. The intuitive mastery of a system of operations may be somewhat analogous to the acquisition of an unconscious habit. What is at first a habitual pattern (i.e., structure) for using a system of operations to achieve some end later becomes a program in the sense that various substitutes can be inserted without disturbing the overall act. The unconscious application of a system of operations becomes more and more probable in the performance of concrete tasks, and it is in this sense that one can speak of the intuitive mastery of a given operational structure.

It is clear that children typically come to master a wide range of tasks that are characterized by isomorphic operational structures over a relatively short period of time. For example, in the case of the ordering relation $<$, a child usually becomes able to put cubes in order according to size at about the same time he becomes able to put pencils in order according to length, at about the time he can put circles in order according to diameter, etc.

A question which arises is, "How might one go about teaching children an intuitive understanding of the order relation $<$?" In order to teach a concept such as "red," the child can simply be shown examples and counterexamples of red objects. However, in order to give a child an intuitive understanding of the relation $<$, the situation is not as simple.

The Concept of a Series

Consider the relation $<$ as it pertains to the task of putting ten 3/8" dowel sticks (varying in length by 1 cm, the shortest of which is 9 cm) in order according to length (Inhelder & Piaget, 1964, Ch. 9).

The earliest responses that children are able to give when confronted with such a task consists of unconnected, uncoordinated pairs of shorter and longer sticks (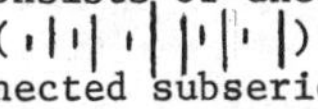). Later, children are able to produce two or three unconnected subseries (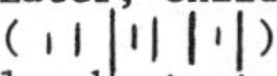). This is accomplished by choosing the stick that is apparently shortest (i.e., usually without making any active comparison), then some stick that is longer than the first stick selected, followed by a stick that is longer than the second one selected, etc., until the child is forced to choose a stick shorter than the last one selected. At this level of mastery of the seriation task, the child is often unable to select the shortest stick first, then the shortest of those remaining sticks, etc., until all of the sticks have been put in order. Such a response would require that the child be able to coordinate the relation "longer than" (i.e., longer than the sticks already selected) with the relation "shorter than" (i.e., shorter than those sticks remaining). Indeed, even if a child is able to correctly seriate a collection of sticks, he may still be quite unable to insert a "forgotten" stick (i.e., an eleventh intermediate stick in the series) without breaking up the ordering and reconstructing the entire series. Insertion of a "forgotten" stick requires simultaneous consideration of the relation "longer than" and its inverse "shorter than." Thus, the concept of a series involves the gradual coordination of the relation "longer than" and its inverse "shorter than."

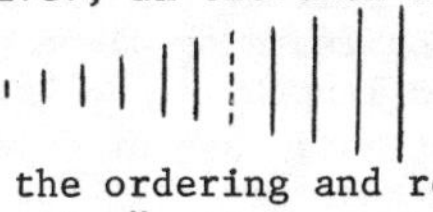

Mathematically, the relation that characterizes the above seriation task is a strict partial ordering, the formal definition of which follows.

Definition: < is a strict partial ordering on a set S if < is a set of ordered pairs of elements in S such that:

1. For every element a in S, (a,a) is not in < (nonreflexive property).

2. For every pair of elements a, b in the set S, if (a,b) is in < then (b,a) is not in < (asymmetric property).

3. For any three elements a, b and c in the set S, if (a, b) is in < and if (b,c) is in < then (a, c) is in < (transitive property).

From this definition it can be seen that, apart from the fact that the relation < involves giving a response to pairs of objects (in some arbitrary set), it is primarily properties 1, 2, and 3 that define < . Further, it is clear that these three properties stipulate that an understanding of the relation < implies a corresponding mastery of the relation "not < " plus an ability to simultaneously consider pairs of relations.

Mathematically, the three basic types of logical-mathematical structures were defined by the Bourbaki (1948) in terms of their form of inverse and their manner of combination. Therefore, Piaget has held that psychologically operations (or relations) are not understood in isolation, but only as they relate to whole operational structures (Beth & Piaget, 1966). That is, an operation (i.e., operation, relation, or transformation) is not first learned and later assigned its properties (i.e., commutative property, associative property, etc., or reflexive property, transitive property, symmetric property, etc.). Rather, the meaning of an operation is derived from the structure of which it forms a part. For the seriation task described above, it was not until the comparison "longer than" came to be coordinated with the comparison "shorter than" that the comparison attained the status of a strict partial ordering relation. This point will be reconsidered in the next section; however, for now, the following observation should be made.

It is quite possible, that, for a specific finite set of objects, a pseudorelation between objects can be learned as simple S-R associations to pairs of objects without any accompanying understanding of the relation per se. As a trivial example of this phenomenon, one could take a set of ten ordered Cuisenaire rods (||||||||||) and teach a young child to say, "They are not equal in length" for any pair of rods which could be presented from the ordered set of ten rods. Such learning alone would not indicate an understanding of the relation ≠ (in length).[1] Rather, the child may have learned only a property of a particular set of objects. No understanding would be required of the relation per se. For the purposes of this paper, less concern will be given to a child's apprehension of S-R associations to pairs of objects in a specific set than to a child's apprehension of certain relational <u>structures</u> in a wide range of situations.

---

[1]If two identical Cuisenaire rods (A and B) are glued to a piece of paper with arrows drawn on the paper as follows (⇄) and if a third identical rod, C, is used by a child to compare with rods A and B, he may say that A = C (in length) and B = C (in length), but still maintain that A ≠ B (in length).

The Formalization of Operational Structures

The preceding section posed an apparent instructional dilemma because of a phenomenon which can be called *structural integration*. Structural integration occurs when lower order concepts are brought together into a whole (i.e., structure) and when the properties of the lower concepts depend partly or entirely on the characteristics of the whole.

Structural integration occurs fairly often in mathematics. Two examples have already been given. The mastery of the set union operation +, and the ordering relation $<$, both involved structural integration. In order to come to an understanding of either of these individual operations, a child must consider the operation to be part of a system of operations. But this fact causes a "chicken-egg" sort of instructional dilemma. It appears that in order to master an operation, a child must master a system of operations. But in order to master a system of operations, the individual operations must be mastered.

Mathematicians can formalize a mathematical structure (e.g., define a strict partial ordering relation) by starting with certain axioms, undefined terms, or accepted rules of logic, and construct theorems and definitions on the basis of these. That is, axiomatics terminates endless regressions by beginning with undefined terms and it avoids circularity by arbitrarily choosing a starting point which has not been demonstrated.[2] Psychologically, however, one is not afforded the luxury of beginning with indefinables, axioms, or accepted rules of logic.

For example, in the case of the ordering relation $<$, the nonreflexive, asymmetric, and transitive properties cannot be used as self-evident concepts. Before the relation $<$ has been coordinated with its inverse, each of these properties is repeatedly and often emphatically denied by children (Inhelder & Piaget, 1964). Even such mathematically primitive concepts as Hilbert's order axiom (If B is between A and C, then it is also between C and A) are not a priori intuitions for children until the betweenness relation has been subsumed within a system of relations (Piaget & Inhelder, 1971, p. 144).

The Genetic Construction of Operational Structures

In order to teach children a concept of redness, one can present examples and counterexamples of red objects. In a certain respect, the abstraction of operations can be achieved through a similar process. That is, operations are abstracted from many different situations in which the

---

[2]Gödel (1934) demonstrated the impossibility of establishing the noncontradiction of any deductive theory solely by methods borrowed from this theory or from weaker systems. The verification of the completeness and noncontradiction of a system and the independence of its axioms must be tested by the use of mathematical models. However, as soon as lower systems are subordinated to higher, only systematic wholes are guaranteed an autonomous existence (Beth & Piaget, 1966, p. 272). Referring to exactly this point, Bertrand Russell is known to have quipped, "Mathematics is the subject where we never know what we are talking about, nor if what we are saying is true."

operation occurs. Piaget has held that these situations in which operations occur are the child's actions. Logical-mathematical knowledge is seen as beginning, not with an awareness of self (a priori intuitions) or of things, but with the coordination and recognition of their interactions. That is, an operation is an internalized *scheme* of interactions, where the scheme of a set of actions is their common operational essence.

> *The scheme of an action is, by definition, the structured group of the generalizable characteristics of this action, that is, those which allow the repetition of the same action or its application to a new content. . . . This is why such schemes have a completely general significance and are not characteristic merely of one or another of the actions of a single individual. (Beth & Piaget, 1966, p. 235)*

For example, in order to teach a child the relation < , he can be given a variety of experiences ordering many kinds of objects according to various criteria. To expect a child to abstract the relation < by working with only one set of objects (e.g., Cuisenaire rods) would be as unlikely as expecting the child to abstract redness by showing him only one red object.

Thus, internalizing schemes of actions means abstracting the common operational essence from a number of isomorphic interactions. In the case of the seriation operation, one might give the child the following types of experiences:

1. put Cuisenaire rods in a row according to length,
2. put dowel rods in order according to length,
3. put cylinders in a row according to height,
4. put cylinders in a row according to diameter,
5. put circles in a pile according to diameter,
6. put cubes in a row according to size,
7. make a tower of cubes according to size,
8. put spheres in order according to size,
9. put spheres in order according to color,
10. put sandpaper in a pile according to roughness.

None of the materials above inherently embody the relation < . Rather, each set of materials can be used to coordinate the relevant scheme of interactions. These various sets of materials can then be used to help the child abstract the relevant system of operations. However, the abstraction which takes place is not from the objects per se, but from the systems of interactions that were coordinated using the objects.

Reflexive Abstraction

In the previous section certain similarities which exist between teaching children a concept such as redness through experiences with objects and teaching children an operation through experiences performing actions on objects were pointed out. However, there are also certain dissimilarities between these two types of abstractions. In order to abstract a concept of redness from a set of objects, the child simply needs to isolate the relevant property. However, as long as the single interaction is isolated, it can have little significance to the child as the archetype of an operation. To abstract operations from one's own actions consists not simply of taking note of individual isolated interactions, it requires the reconstruction of these actions on a higher plane. Individual interactions gradually take on new significance (reflexive abstraction) as they are modified by being treated as part of a whole operational structure.

Reversibility

The key to the emergence of a whole system of schemes of interactions is the appearance of the inverse to the given scheme. This reversibility phenomenon is attained when the child exhibits a recognition of the fact that the combined application of a scheme followed by its inverse is equivalent to the identity scheme. According to this definition reversibility implies not only the emergence of the inverse scheme but also the identity scheme and combination of pairs of these.[3] Thus, the attainment of reversibility implies the existence of an operational system which in turn elevates the scheme to the status of an operation as part of the structured whole.

For Piaget, an operation is an internalized scheme of interactions that is reversible and that is dependent on other schemes with which it forms an operational system characterized by laws that apply to the whole structure (Beth & Piaget, 1966, p. 234). Further, he has held that the simplest such structures include not just the original scheme of actions, but also at least its inverse, identity schemes, and combination of pairs of these.

Genetic Circularity

It should be clear from the above description that the evolution of operational structures would not be conceived as beginning with individual isolated operations which are successively linked together. Rather, the evolution of structures of operations would be visualized as occurring simultaneously with the evolution of the operations that the structure subsumes. Thus, both the structure and its operations simultaneously crystalize out of a system of schemes of actions as it becomes progressively coordinated (genetic circularity).

While the coordination of a system of schemes of actions is achieved progressively, its completion is marked by a momentary acceleration in this construction as the child shifts to a qualitatively higher level of thought. As a result of this reorganization, new self-evidence typically appears

---

[3]One could easily argue that the emergence of the identity scheme is equally as important as the emergence of the inverse and choose to call this event the child's recognition of Identity (Berlyne, 1965). Or one could argue that the child's ability to combine pairs of schemes is the significant event (Lunzer, 1960a, p. 32) and call the event Combination. The choice of terms seems somewhat arbitrary, however, in the sense that Reversibility, Identity, and Combination should each be implied no matter which of the three terms one wishes to emphasize.

with regard to concepts whose definitions depend upon the application of the given structure. Thus, certain operational concepts (such as the concept of a series, or class) and certain properties (such as transitivity) arise out of structured wholes of operations, the completion of which explains the necessity of its elements insofar as their meanings are dependent on that whole.

Piaget's Groupings

Because of the fact that a formalization of the most elementary operational structures which are mastered by children are globally similar to a mathematical group, Piaget has coined the word "grouping" to refer to such structures. The concept of a grouping is believed to be useful (1) due to the ability of children to internalize any particular action that is included within a given scheme of action at "about" the same time and, (2) since the internalization of a scheme of action automatically implies the internalization of a structure of internalized actions, the simplest of which includes the scheme, its inverse, identity schemes, and combinations of pairs of these.

It should be emphasized that a grouping is not some sort of "a priori" cognitive structure (à la Gestalt psychology) which imposes itself on the thought of a child. There is no more reason to attribute a priori existence to Piaget's groupings in the minds of children than there is to attribute a priori existence to the Pythagorean Theorem in the mind of Pythagoras. The theorem was not a form into which Pythagoras' experiences fell. It was a necessary consequence of the progressive organization of Pythagoras' experiences. There is an important psychological distinction between a form that is assumed to exist a priori in a child's mind and a form that is a product of equilibration (i.e., progressive organization) and which could not have developed otherwise.

Cognitive Characteristics of Preoperational Children

Children who have not yet mastered a given system of operations are characterized by at least the following cognitive characteristics: syncretic thinking, centering, and fixed state thinking.

Syncretic Thinking

Children who are able to copy a 3 x 3 array of circles (ooo ooo ooo   ooo ooo ooo), and who have stated that each of the two arrays contains nine circles, are often convinced that the two arrays no longer contain the same number of circles after one of the two arrays has been partitioned into three clusters (ooo ooo ooo ooo ooo ooo). Children have difficulties coordinating part-whole relationships within numerical aggregates. When attention is drawn to a numerical whole, the parts (or units) are cognitively neglected. When attention is directed toward component parts, the whole is often cognitively destroyed.

That is, children tend to view sets of objects *syncretically*, or as a global unanalyzed whole, rather than analytically.

Gast (1957) has shown that the ability to determine the cardinality of a set depends on the homogeneity of its items. He found an initial stage in which virtually complete homogeneity of the elements is required; a second in which perceptual diversity is possible within certain limits of qualitative resemblance; and a final state in which the objects may belong to several disjunctive classes (also see Piaget, 1952; Dodwell, 1962; and Elkind, 1964). The concept of a unit is by no means an a priori intuition for young children.

Fixed State Thinking

Preoperational children tend to focus on successive states of an object or set of objects rather than on the operations that connect these states. For example, if a kindergarten child is asked to represent (by drawings, by gestures, by multiple choice selections from pictures) the successive positions occupied by a stick in falling from vertical to horizontal ( ), the task proves to be surprisingly difficult.

While kindergarteners are usually able to represent the beginning vertical position and the final horizontal position, intermediate positions often present great difficulties. Young children may not only fail to represent intermediate positions correctly, they may even fail to recognize a correct representation when it is shown to them (Piaget & Inhelder, 1971). Thus, preoperational children seem unable to integrate a series of states of an object into a continuous whole--or a transformation.

As another example consider two identical transparent bowls one of which contains six beads and the other five and two identical opaque boxes in front of each bowl (Figure 1). If the beads are taken from the bowls and placed one for one into the boxes until each box contains five beads, young children may believe that there are not the same number of beads in

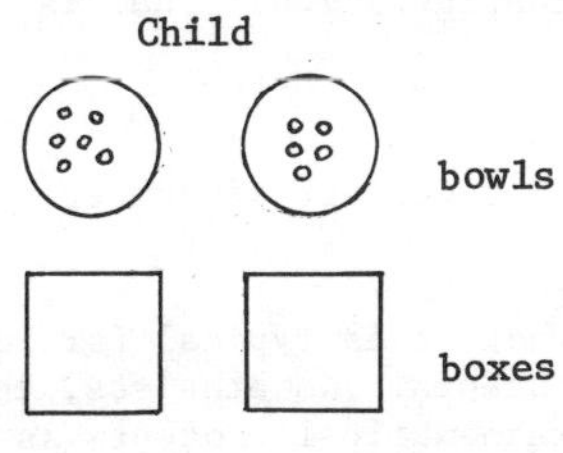

Figure 1

the two boxes, indicating that a yellow bead is left in one bowl while all of the blue beads have been used. Further, if the child is told that there are five beads in one of the boxes and is asked to guess how many beads are in the other, he will typically answer in accordance with his judgment of equality or inequality. If he had previously stated that the two sets were unequal, he will likely guess almost any number other than five. Thus, young children seem to believe that the cardinality of a set may somehow be affected by the source of its elements.

Preoperational children tend to base their judgment solely on isolated configurations that are before them at any given moment. This cognitive preference was reflected in the above task in that children typically make their incorrect numerical judgment based on the only number-relevant information that was available in the final state of the task situation--the source of the objects.

Centering

Another task can be posed which illustrates one of the cognitive characteristics that accompanies thinking in terms of unconnected fixed states. Place two cylindrical glasses in front of identical boxes, each of which contains thirty half-inch beads (Figure 2). The child is directed to take a blue bead in one hand, a yellow bead in the other and to put the beads into the two cylindrical glasses at exactly the same time. After ten beads have been put into each of the two glasses, the child may believe

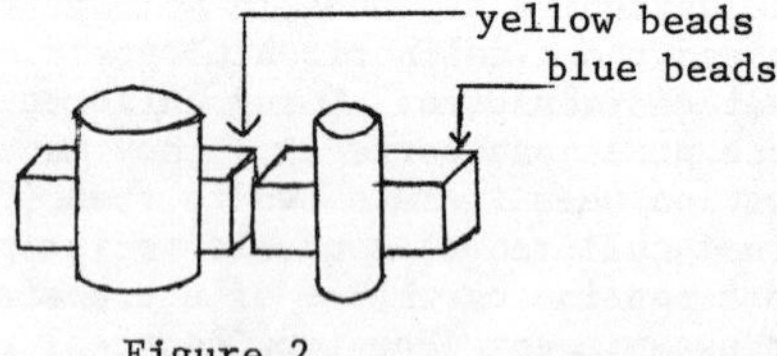

Figure 2

that there are more beads in the glass where the beads reach a higher level.

Children not only focus their attention on momentary conditions of an object or set of objects, they also *center* on only the most salient perceptual features of a given configuration. That is, they may notice height but neglect thickness.

The Concept of Number

It has been argued that it is typical for logical-mathematical concepts to be operational concepts. Nonetheless, the involvement of operations in the formation of many mathematical concepts is much less obvious than in the two examples cited thus far. In particular, the operational nature of early number concepts has been contested throughout the history of mathematics education. One of the most eloquent arguments against nonoperational points of view concerning the origin of number concepts has been given by Dewey (McLellan and Dewey, 1914), whose views are summarized in the following statements:

> Number *is not (psychologically) got* from *things, it is put* into *them (p. 61).*
>
> . . . *This abstraction is* complex, *involving two factors: the difference that makes the individuality of each object must be noted, and yet the different individuals must be grasped as one --a sum (p. 25).*

Thus, in considering a group of seven red circles, Dewey would contend that the concept "redness" is a qualitatively different sort of concept than the concept of "sevenness." Whereas redness can be directly perceived in the circles, sevenness only becomes a property of the circles due to operations that are performed on the circles.

Modern mathematics educators have often cited children's responses to Piagetian number conservation tasks in order to help verify the point of view expressed by Dewey. Nonetheless, universal acceptance has not been given to any one of the various possible interpretations which exists concerning the relationship between a child's understanding of number concepts and his ability to respond correctly to conservations of number tasks. In the following two sections, conservation-like tasks will be given which will help to establish an interpretation of the significance of conservation tasks. In addition, the examples may help to clarify the way children come to master elementary number concepts.

Qualitative Cognitive Growth

Implicitly taking the position that correct conservation responses are largely unrelated to the child's level of understanding of the concept of number, certain psychologists and educators have attempted to explain the mastery of conservation tasks by children in terms of their gradual mastery of the fact that a spatially displaced set of objects can be returned to their original positions (or slight modifications of this argument). It seems likely that an understanding of empirical return is a necessary (but not sufficient) condition for mastery of conservation tasks. However, the insufficiency of this explanation is illustrated by the following example.

Suppose a circular string of circumference four inches is put in the shape of a square (□). The child is told that the string is a fence and that a cow can eat the grass inside the fence. Then the string is changed into the shape of a 1-1/2 inch by 1/2 inch rectangle. The child is asked if the cow still has the same amount to eat (□→▭).

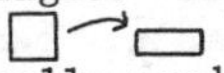

Understanding of empirical return is an almost equally good explanation of conservation of area in the above task, in spite of the fact that area is not conserved for this task as can be seen if the string continues to be transformed into two line segments of length two inches (□→▭→▬).

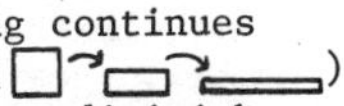

Kindergarten children often respond correctly that the area diminishes as the square becomes more rectangular. However, to assume that these children understand the concept of area would be incorrect. Further questioning may indicate that those children who responded correctly were basing their judgments on the height of the rectangles. (Incorrect answers usually focus on the width. Only seldom will a child judge the areas to be the same.) Thus, children often respond correctly by basing their judgments on the wrong information.

Children older than five years of age (and in fact many adults) often assert that the area remains the same. Further, they may maintain this conviction almost until the area disappears in the limiting case. Such adults certainly do not understand less than the average kindergarten child. They have shifted to a *qualitatively* higher level of thought which brings with it new factors as sources for incorrect judgment. A fundamental fact which Piaget's research makes abundantly clear is that cognitive growth from birth to maturity does not simply get qualitatively better and better; qualitative reorganizations also occur. His theory addresses itself to these qualitative changes. Learning is not simply a matter of associating right answers to questions.

If one's emphasis is on a child's understanding of the concept of number, it is crucial to be able to account for the differences between Piaget's conservation of number tasks and the area task described above. That is, it is important to be able to explain how children come to understand that *number* is invariant under simple displacements. Too often invariance (or conservation) has been treated as a unitary sort of concept, as though invariance of what (i.e., number, mass, volume, area, etc.) were relatively unimportant.

Rejectable Explanations of the Initial Attainment of an Operational Concept of Number

With respect to logical-mathematical knowledge, Piaget has considered the most relevant aspects of intelligence to be, not what a child perceives, but the rules of organization which the child gradually develops in order to control and use the information he receives. Although an adult may feel that he perceives "nineness" in a 3 x 3 array of circles (⁣ooo ooo ooo), he may be more skeptical regarding the purely perceptual origin of "nineness" in the following configuration (ooo ooo ooo). The sensation of perceiving "nineness" appears to be similar to what happens when one looks at a hidden picture puzzle. Once the picture is distinguished, it is difficult to realize how it had ever been disguised (Bruner, 1968, Ch. 5).[4]

Many examples could be given which would bear witness to the fact that any concept of number which does not involve at least the operations of giving an order to objects which previously had no order (seriation), identifying in some sense objects which are not in fact identical (classification), and coordinating part-whole relationships in order to grasp the concept of units can involve only the most rudimentary and superficial concept of number. Until children have mastered these elementary operations, they not only fail to realize that number is invariant under simple displacements, they also deny each of the properties that define the concept of number. For instance, tasks can be posed in which nonconservers will deny the validity of Peano's Axioms of (1) that a numerical whole is equal to the sum of its parts, (2) that addition is commutative (or associative), (3) the existence of an identify element (or inverses), and (4) the relationship between cardinal and ordinal numbers (Piaget, 1952). Such tasks can be used to determine progressively reduced developmental levels at which a nonoperational concept of number could exist.

Having reduced the level of development at which a nonoperational concept of number could exist, the question remains whether an early operational number concept must ultimately, or at some still lower level, evolve out of some sort of nonoperational concept. One might still hold that some nonoperational concept (although exceedingly rudimentary) is actually

---

[4]Wohlwill (1968) has summarized some of the distinctions between perception and conception as seen by the Gestalt school (Kohler, Wertheimer, Bruner, Brunswick, and Piaget).

a first approximation to a later, more refined concept. On the other hand, it may equally well be that any nonoperational concept of "number," far from being a first approximation to a more mathematically viable concept of number, is actually a detriment to later learning. To clarify this possibility, consider the following analogy.

A child who could select a red crayon from his box of crayons would likely be considered to have attained a primitive concept of redness. To be sure, the concept would be quite elementary to a spectrometrist, who must analyze incoming light from far away stars. Nonetheless, under limited conditions, the concept would likely suffice as a first approximation if it did not deny any of the properties that characterize a later, more sophisticated notion of redness.

Conversely, a concept which could not in some sense be construed as being a first approximation to a later, more sophisticated concept would not be considered to be a concept of redness. Thus, if the child's red crayons were broken in half and he were taught to recognize it only by its shorter length, the learning which would accrue would not be a concept of redness. Even though the child might always be able to select the red crayon from his box upon command, he might be responding to length cues rather than to color cues. Such a training procedure would be foolish, of course, since redness is at least as easy to teach a child as shortness. It does little good to trick a child into giving a correct response to erroneous cues and it does little good to trick him into correct responses which he does not understand. However, while these maxims seem to be so much a matter of common sense concerning the concept of redness, they are commonly violated concerning children's instruction pertaining to number concepts. Children are often tricked into giving correct arithmetic responses which they do not understand and/or into giving correct responses to erroneous cues.

For example, while a child can often be tricked into giving the correct numerical responses to the following arrays of objects (· : ∴ :: ⁙, etc.), the concept that the child may be learning may not be a concept of number. The essence of making numerical judgments involves learning to avoid making judgments on the basis of shape or pattern. A training procedure based on standard dot patterns may encourage preoperational children toward tendency to judge numerical wholes on the basis of gross configuration (or area covered) rather than on appropriate cues.

Dot patterns, Cuisenaire rods, counting discs, and arithmetic blocks can each be useful models in order to help children come to an understanding of number concepts. However, even if a dot pattern (⁙ ⁙) can eventually be used as a model to represent the number 10, it is important to remember that it is a constructed representation. That is, the model only comes to embody the number 10 after certain systems of operations have been coordinated relative to the model. Until a child has coordinated these operations into elementary systems, his thinking will tend to be fixed and syncretic with respect to tasks that are characterized by the structure, and he will tend to center on only one aspect of models that are presented.

Initially Purely Verbal or Symbolic Concepts of Number

The preoperational thinking of young children seems to be so different from that of an adult that for the child many adult-like words and responses must mean something very different from the meaning an adult assigns to them. It is difficult to say exactly what the statement 5 + 3 = 8 may mean to a little child whose thinking is characterized by fixed thinking, syncretic thinking, and centering; but it is well known that even without proper understanding, children are quite capable of memorizing large quantities of verbal or symbolic material. Thus, misunderstandings are often not detected until an entire facade of ill-conceived notions collapses. In early elementary school arithmetic, this collapse typically occurs when children reach regrouping concepts involving "borrowing" and "carrying."[5]

The improvement of langauge may aid in the acquisition of an operational concept, if the activation of language can facilitate the coordination of operations and enable the child to be less dominated by perceptual forces (Bruner, 1964). Nonetheless, appeals to an initially purely verbal-symbolic concept to explain the development of an operational number concept is insufficient. Piaget (Ripple & Rockcastle, 1964) has stated:

> *Words are probably no short-cut to a better understanding . . . . The level of understanding seems to modify the language that is used, rather than vice versa. . . . Mainly language serves to translate what is already understood; or else language may even present a danger if it is used to introduce an idea which is not yet accessible (p. 5).*

The fundamental problem appears to be to determine to what underlying concepts the language and symbols that children use are being attached (Bruner, Olver & Greenfield, 1966, p. 47).

The Genetic Development of the Concept of Number

On the basis of parsimony, Piaget's description of the development of number concepts is quite pleasing since an operational number concept need not be assumed to evolve out of some sort of nonoperational concept. Piagetians (e.g., Piaget, 1952; Inhelder & Piaget, 1964) have furnished an impressive quantity of data to substantiate the hypothesis that elementary number concepts (the assignment of numerals to sets whose elements are regarded as classed and ordered) develop in parallel to, and as a synthesis of, the development of elementary classification and seriation concepts. This appears to be so since the intellectual coordinations involved in forming series and classes are also involved in forming seriated classes (i.e., numbers). However, Piaget's analysis of the cognitive evolution of number and other logical-mathematical concepts relies heavily on the psychological viability of analyzing, ordering, and equating concepts (or tasks) on the basis of their underlying operational structures.

---

[5]Roughhead & Scandura (1968) and Brownell & Chazal (1935) have reported findings which indicate that rote verbal or symbolic learning may actually cue out the kind of reorganizing activity which seems necessary for a child to come to an operational understanding of number.

Ordering and Equating Operational Structures

For Piaget, cognitive growth is viewed as a process of gradually coordinating systems of operations through the dual process of assimilation (i.e., inner organization) and accommodation(i.e., outer adaptation).

As the child's perceptual activities become coordinated, he becomes cognizant of more features of what is perceptually before him at any given moment (i.e., less centering, syncretic thinking, and fixed state thinking). This increased awareness demands greater coordination, which in turn produces still more analysis of perceptual givens. In short, what we have is an activity that organizes reality while coordinating its own functioning. The tendency in adaptation is constantly in the direction of greater equilibrium of the functioning structure in the face of external disturbances and demands for internal consistency (i.e., coordination) (Piaget, 1960). Further, each relative equilibrium state carries with it the ability to detect new sources of disequilibrium and hence the seeds of its own destruction. What we have here is a sort of concrete analogue to the fact established by Gödel (1934) concerning the impossibility of establishing the noncontradiction of a deductive system solely by methods borrowed from this system or weaker systems.

This progress toward greater equilibrium, together with the proposition that operations exist psychologically only within structured operational wholes, yields a basis for ordering and equating operational concepts (or tasks). As a trivial illustration, one would expect that the task of putting cylinders (which vary according to height and diameter) into 4 x 4

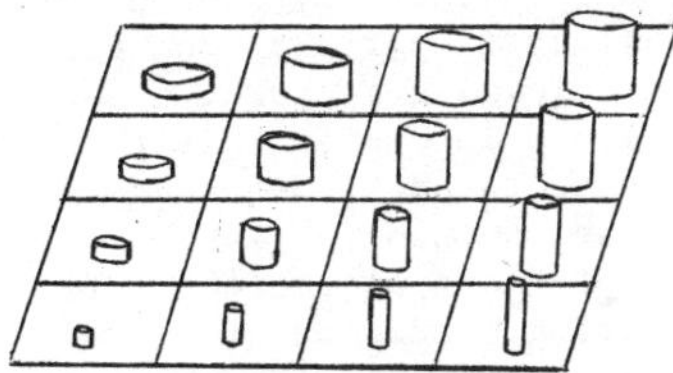

Figure 3

matrix would be mastered no sooner than the task of putting ten dowel rods in order according to length. This is because the operational structure that characterizes the dowel rods task is included within the structure that describes the task involving a matrix of cylinders (Figure 3).

Intra-individual Variability

While Piagetians have amassed a large amount of data to support the contention that tasks with isomorphic operational structures are mastered at "about" the same time, it is also well known that intra-individual variability commonly occurs concerning a child's ability to perform tasks which are characterized by a single operational structure (Piaget, 1971, p. 173).

As an example of the phenomenon of intra-individual variability, consider the following tasks. Six pennies are placed in front of a kindergarten child, and ten pennies are placed in front of an adult. The child is then asked to "Make it so we both have the same number of pennies." Another similar task can be posed using small one-inch cubes instead of pennies. The problem is markedly more difficult using pennies than using one-inch cubes. Using cubes, the problem is commonly solved by kindergarteners following the sequence of steps illustrated in Figure 4. The child is aided in making the two groups equal in number by being able to make them the same shape. Using pennies, the child is forced to be more analytic in his consideration of the two groups. Therefore, if one were to consider a set of tasks all of which are characterized by the same

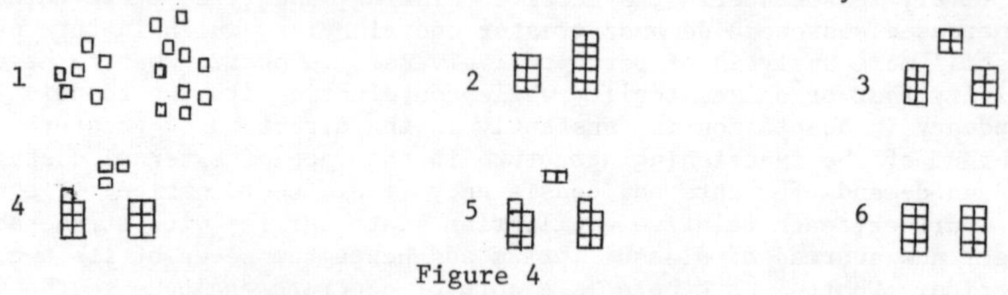

Figure 4

system of operations, the tasks would vary somewhat in difficulty due to the relative involvement of factors such as: syncretic thinking, fixed state thinking, and centering.

Ordering and Equating Tasks

The intra-individual variability, which is part of Piaget's theory concerning a child's ability to perform concrete tasks which are characterized by a single operational structure, has caused understandable confusion among those who would interpret this theory. This confusion seems to have developed, at least in part, because of a common failure to distinguish between the invariant sequential mastery of various tasks which involve the application of these operations. To illustrate this distinction, consider the following situation.

Suppose that tasks T_1 and T_1' both involve the application of an operational structure S_1. The theory predicts that tasks T_1 and T_1' (and all other tasks characterized by operational structures S_1) should be mastered at "about" the same time, subject to a certain amount of intra-individual variability, and subject to certain side conditions of equivalence between the two tasks.[6] Hence, one might visualize a given child's mastery of all tasks that are characterized by a particular operational structure, as in Figure 5.

In particular, then, it would only in general be true that tasks T_1 and T_1' are mastered at the same time. For instance, it could happen that task T_1' was mastered before T_1.

Now suppose that another task T_2 was found to be characterized by an operational structure S_2, and further suppose that structure S_2 includes (or subsumes) S_1. On the basis of the subsumption of structure S_1 by S_2,

---

[6]That is, the two tasks would have to be equally facilitating. They would have to be relatively equivalent concerning the degree to which they require the child to decenter, be more flexible, be more analytic (i.e., less syncretic), etc.

one could conclude that structure S_2 would be mastered by a child no sooner than structure S_1. Nonetheless, this fact would not necessarily imply that

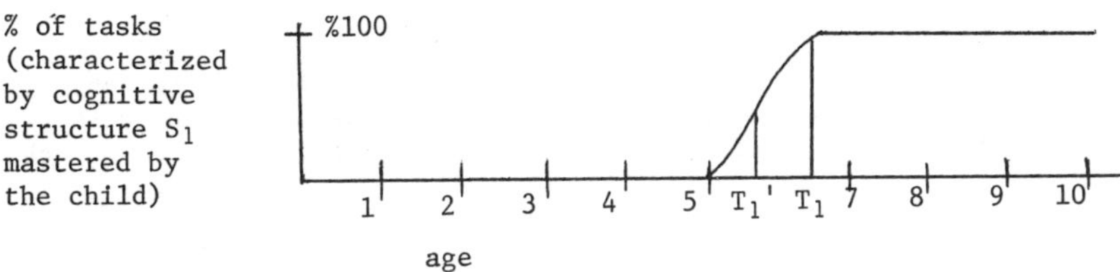

Figure 5

task T_2 would be mastered no sooner than task T_1. In fact, the situation could occur as illustrated in Figure 6. That is, although it is in general true that tasks characterized by structure S_2 are mastered no sooner than tasks characterized by structure S_1, this might not be the case with respect to particular tasks T_2 and T_1. It could happen that task T_2 would be mastered

% of tasks (characterized by cognitive structure S_1 or S_2) mastered by the child

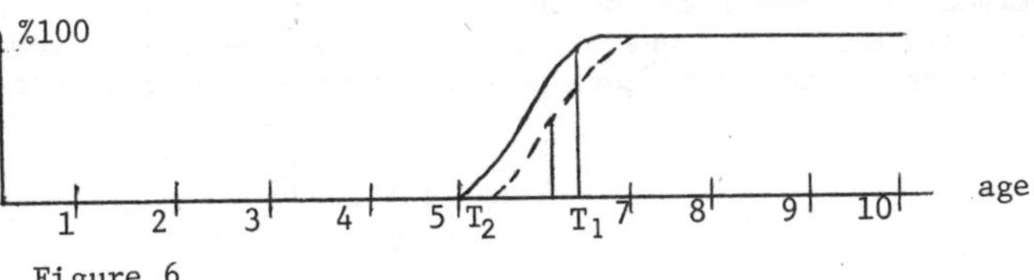

Figure 6

before task T_1.

Lunzer's Hypothesis

Lunzer (1960a, pp. 30-32; 1960b) has attempted to reconcile the fact of intra-individual variability with the quantity of evidence that Piagetians have produced showing that children attain the general ability to internalize *all* logical-mathematical action schemes into reversible structures over a relatively short period of time. That is, children usually master all three types of logical-mathematical groupings at about six or seven years of age--subject to variations due to factors such as experience, social transmission, and equilibration (Piaget, 1964a).

Lunzer has suggested that the crucial step that is taken by children at about six or seven years of age is when they become capable of making two judgments simultaneously, and this ushers in the beginning of Piaget's period of Concrete Operations.

It is, no doubt, quite true that a generalized ability to make two simultaneous judgments is a prime factor accounting for the great cognitive reorganization which takes place in children at about six or seven years of age. In fact, this seems to be only another way of defining Piaget's concept of reversibility. What is for Piaget the coordination of an operation with its inverse is for Lunzer the ability to make two simultaneous judgments. However, Piaget has believed that it is fruitful to distinguish at least three types of logical-mathematical operations (Beth & Piaget, 1966, p. 186). In terms of simultaneous judgments, these operations would perhaps be distinguished as follows.

1. Operations involve coordinating two properties of a set of objects.
2. Relations involve coordinating two comparisons between objects.
3. Transformations involve coordinating two perceptions of an object.

The main factor that enables all three types of groupings to be mastered during the same general age range may well be the fact that each involves the coordination of an operation with its inverse. Nonetheless, the three basic types of logical-mathematical operations may retain certain unique characteristics that enable them to be distinguished from one another as distinct psychological entities (Elkind, 1964).

It is only in such special instances as the synthesis of the classification and seriation groupings to form the number group that Piaget has hypothesized functional interdependence between concrete operational structures. The relationship between the number group and the classification or seriation groupings is predicted to be closer than the relationship between the classification and seriation groupings. The relationships between specific actions within a given scheme are closer than the relationships between groupings that are formed from distinct schemes.

The Pilot Study

A theory which hypothesizes the invariant sequential mastery of certain operational structures while allowing for intra-individual variability concerning a child's ability to perform tasks which are characterized by these structures has remained a source of controversy. For example, certain psychologists (e.g., Kohnstamm, 1967) have asserted that the fact of intra-individual variability renders meaningless the practice of ordering and equating tasks on the basis of underlying operational structure. Such criticisms suggested a pilot study, the primary experimental objective of which was to investigate the interdependent development of classification, seriation, and number concepts.

While helping to confirm the psychological viability of analyzing, ordering, and equating tasks on the basis of their operational structures, the pilot study was to serve the dual function of furnishing the theoretical scaffolding which would be necessary for structuring and interpreting a transfer of training study. Toward these ends, three parallel sequences of Piagetian tasks were obtained (denoted by S1, S2, . . ., S7; N1, N2 . . ., N6; and C0, C1, C2,. . ., C6) which were graded in difficulty and which pertained to seriation, number, and classification respectively. Each of these three sequences was determined by ordering tasks according to the theory outlined in preceding sections and selecting those tasks which would, in fact, exhibit a relatively invariant sequential mastery. For example, the seriation tasks were related in such a way that the probability would be small (<15%) that a child would be able to correctly respond to task

S(n + 1) before he is able to respond to task S(n); and similarly for the other sequences of tasks. Once formulated, these three sequences were to be used to investigate the interdependent development between concept areas.

The easiest task in the seriation series involved copying a circular string of beads (S1) or copying a string of beads in the inverse direction (S2). Progressively more difficult seriation tasks involved reconstructing a set of ten ordered Cuisenaire rods (S3), putting ten dowel rods in order according to length by trial and error (S4), or without trial and error (S5), inserting dowel rods into a completed series (S6), and reconstructing a 4 x 4 matrix of cylinders (S7). The simplest classification task involved producing "nongraphic collections" (see Inhelder and Piaget, 1964, p. 19-20, for an explanation of classification by graphic collections) when attempting to classify objects within a set of yellow cylinders, yellow cones, green cubes, and green pyramids (C1). More difficult classification tasks involved anticipating criteria for exhaustively subdividing sets of objects (C2), repartitioning sets of objects according to differing criteria (C3), reconstructing a 5 x 5 classification matrix (C4), and hierarchically classifying a set of objects (C5). The most difficult classification task (C6) was a quantitative inclusion task (Inhelder & Piaget, 1969, Chapter IV). The simplest number tasks involved copying a row of seven circles (N1) and partitioning a set of sixteen pennies into four equal sets (N2). More difficult number tasks involved equalizing a set of ten pennies and six pennies by taking pennies from the larger set (N3) and copying a 3 x 4 array of circles (N4). The most difficult number tasks were four distinct types of number conservation tasks.

After a child had copied a row of seven red circles (), conservation task N5a required the child to realize that his row still had the same number of circles as the model row after the circles in the model row had been pushed closer together (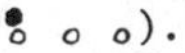). Conservation task N5b tested the child's understanding of the fact that the number of circles in a 3 x 4 array () does not change when the circles are regrouped into three 2 x 2 arrays. Task N6 involved two subtasks, one in which beads were placed into two separate and different shaped glasses by the child (N6a), and the other in which six beads were placed into two separate identical red cardboard boxes in a one-to-one fashion where the beads came from piles of beads of different cardinality (N6b).

Procedure

Each of the three sequences of tasks was administered individually to each of 160 kindergarten children during the last month of the 1969-1970 school year. The children participating in these studies represented rather typical small town Indiana communities. Although I.Q. test scores were not available for kindergarten children in the schools involved, typical achievement test and I.Q. test performance of older children in the participating schools were about average for the state of Indiana. Severely mentally handicapped children had been identified (and placed in special classes which were not used in the study) through the combined use of a Bender Perceptual Development Test, a Boehm Test of Basic Concepts, and a Draw-a-Man General Intelligence Classification Test. Scores for the children used in the pilot study sample on each of these tests were distributed from below average to superior for their age group. The ages of the children (83 boys, 77 girls) ranged from 5 years 4 months to 6 years 7 months. Each of the 160 children took the task batteries on three successive days. Each of the three batteries of tasks required from 10 to 20 minutes to complete. The order in which the test batteries were administered was varied. One-sixth of the children were chosen at random to take the seriation battery of tasks on the first day, the number battery on the second day, and the classification battery on the third day. Similarly, one-sixth of the children took the task batteries in one of the other six permutations of the order: seriation, number, and classification.

Results

Tasks on the pilot study batteries were each scored on a pass-fail basis. A summary of the results of the pilot study are recorded in Figure 8, which should be read as illustrated in Figure 7. Figure 7 indi-

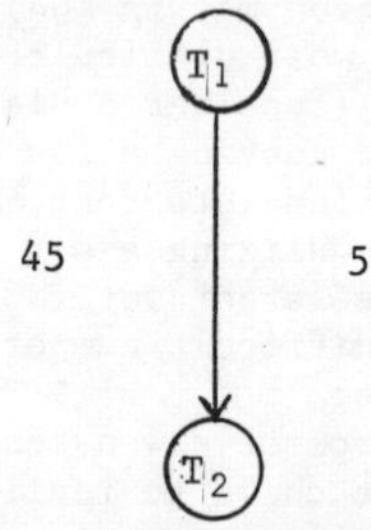

Figure 7

cates that of the 160 children who participated in the pilot study, 45 responded correctly to task T_1 but not to task T_2, and 5 responded correctly to task T_2 but not to task T_1. Other children either missed both tasks or responded correctly to both tasks. Thus, Figure 7 reveals that, on the basis of a sample of 50 children who responded incorrectly to exactly one task, the chances are approximately 90 percent, i.e., $90\% = 45/(45 + 5) = 45/50$ that a given child will correctly respond to task T_1 before task T_2.

The tasks are related in difficulty approximately as illustrated in Figure 8. The easiest tasks are at the top of the figure and children appear to proceed in a parallel fashion through each of these three series of tasks. That is, tasks which are at approximately the same level in Figure 8 are comparable in difficulty, whereas tasks which are at different levels differ significantly as to degree of difficulty.

The existence of a high correlation between cognitive development in these three concept areas is also evidenced by the following information. By assigning each child an ordered three-tuple (x,y,z), where x, y, and z correspond to the child's scores on the seriation, number and classification batteries respectively, scatter diagrams and Pearson's product-moment coefficients were obtained.

Figure 8

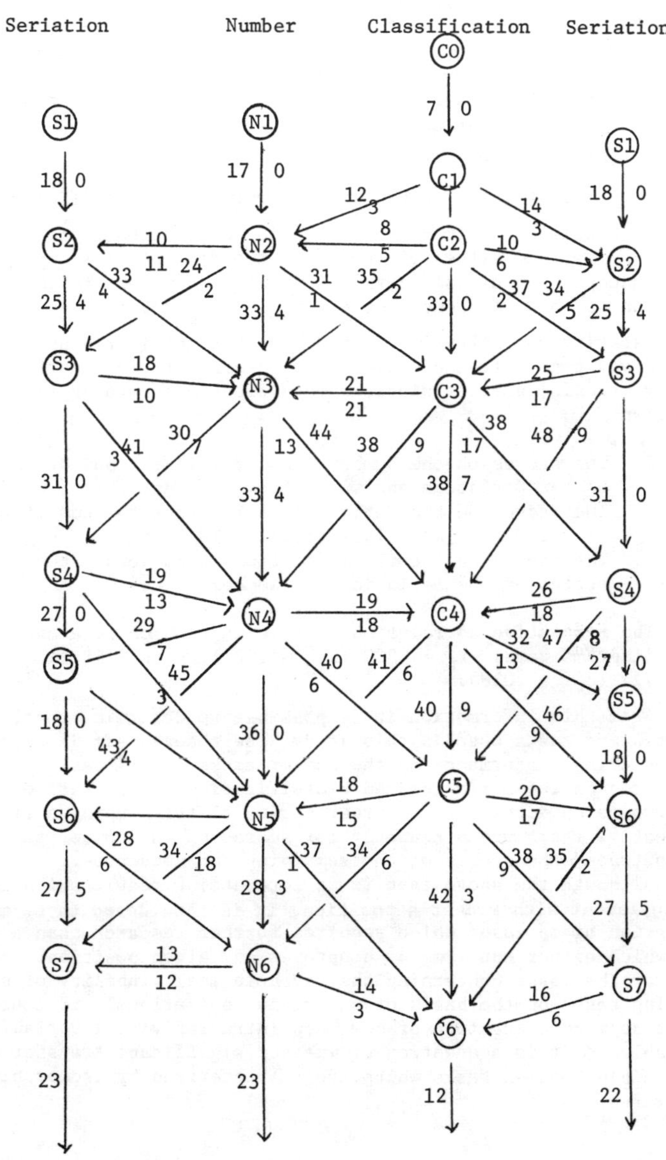
Seriation
Number
Classification
Seriation
C0
S1
N1
C1
S1
S2
N2
C2
S2
S3
N3
C3
S3
S4
N4
C4
S4
S5
S5
S6
N5
C5
S6
S7
N6
C6
S7

Although the correlation coefficients between these three series of tasks were high (r_{ns} = .695, $\sigma_{r_{ns}}$ = .041; r_{nc} = .650, $\sigma_{r_{nc}}$ = .046; and r_{sc} = .609, $\sigma_{r_{sc}}$ = .050), the nature of the relationship between the three areas is by no means established. In particular, a causal connection between these series based on transfer of learning with respect to underlying operational structures (as opposed to simply a high probabilistic correlation) has not been established. However, several facts are of interest in this regard from the information that was obtained.

It was noted that correlation coefficients r_{ns} = .695 ($\sigma_{r_{ns}}$ = .041) and r_{nc} = .650 ($\sigma_{r_{nc}}$ = .046) were both greater than the correlation coefficient r_{sc} = .609 ($\sigma_{r_{sc}}$ = .050). Such a result, if significant statistically, would be consistent with Piaget's hypothesis of closer operational ties between number and either of the other two concept areas than between seriation concepts and classification concepts. However, (with the possible exception of the difference between r_{ns} and r_{sc}) the above results did not attain statistical sifnificance and were not considered as evidence confirming any theoretical position. To obtain more information concerning this hypothesis, scatter diagrams were plotted recording the following information:

1. The scores on the Number Tasks versus the sum of the scores on the Seriation and Classification Tasks.
2. The scores on the Seriation Task versus the sum of the scores on the Number and Classification Tasks.
3. The scores on the Classification Tasks versus the sum of the scores on the Seriation and Number Tasks.

The respective correlation coefficients which were obtained from these diagrams were: r_n = .809 (σ_{r_n} = .027), r_s = .751 (σ_{r_s} = .035), r_c = .724 (σ_{r_c} = .038).

From this information it is possible to determine that, for the children and tasks used in this study, the chances are 95 percent better of predicting performance on the number tasks on the basis of the sum of the scores on the seriation and classification tasks than of predicting performance on either of the other series of tasks using a similar method. Apparently, there was a tendency for scores on the number task sequence to lie "between" the scores on the remaining two sequences.

Although the above fact is an interesting result which appears to be consistent with Piaget's position, it is considered to be more of an indication of an issue which requires further research than a piece of data which either confirms or disproves any given position. Further, the heart of the issue concerning the psychological viability of ordering and equating tasks on the basis of underlying operational structures seems to be not so much a question of how much intra-individual variability is allowable as it is a question of whether significant transfer of learning is possible between tasks which are characterized by isomorphic operational structures.

The Training Study

The key issue toward which the training study was to be directed was to determine whether transfer of learning could be induced between tasks involving similar underlying operational structures. Since Piaget has predicted number to be a synthesis of seriation and classification operations, the decision was made to try to induce number concept learning through teaching seriation and classification concepts.[7] It was hoped that the seriation and classification concepts would bear a similarity to the number concepts only due to underlying operational structure. However, Lunzer's hypothesis suggested that precautions should be taken to demonstrate that if transfer was obtained it was not due only to the ability to make two judgments simultaneously. Toward this end, a short study was conducted to determine two tasks which involve only transformations and which would be roughly equivalent in difficulty to tasks N5 and N6 from the pilot study. If such tasks could be found, it was hypothesized that transfer from learning classification and seriation operations would produce gains in the understanding of number concepts, while very little gain would be made concerning spatial concepts involving only transformations.

The two tasks which were selected involving only spatial transformations were Task T6: Piaget's three mountain problem concerning the child's ability to accurately conceive of points of view other than his own (Piaget & Inhelder, 1967, Chapter VIII), and Task T7: Piaget's task dealing with horizontal axes relative to the water level in an inclined bottle (Piaget & Inhelder, 1967, Chapter VIII). Tasks N5, N6, T6 and T7 were administered individually to 100 kindergarten children (50 boys, 50 girls). The results of the study are shown in Figure 9.

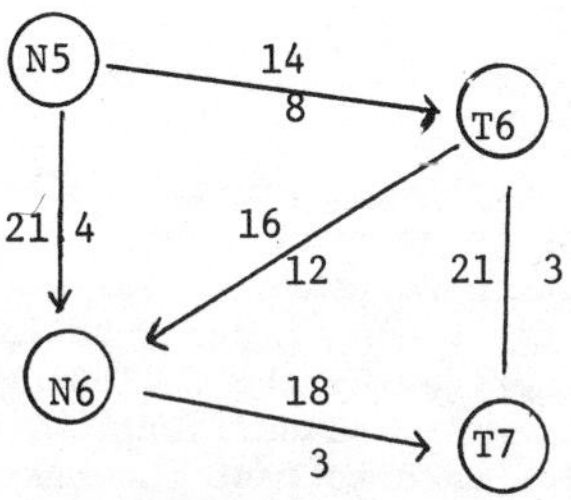

Figure 9

---

[7]Training studies such as those conducted by Sigel, Roeper, and Hooper (1966), Churchill (1958a), and Lasry (1969) offered hope that such training might be possible.

Subjects for the Training Study

The results of the pilot study were used to select twenty kindergarten children who were matched according to cognitive development relative to seriation, classification, and number concepts. That is, children were selected who could correctly respond to tasks S1, N2, and C1, but who responded incorrectly to task S3, N3, and C3, and who could thus be assumed to be incapable of responding correctly to more difficult tasks in any of the three sequences of tasks.[8] The children participating in the training study were all kindergarten children from one of the schools that had been used the previous year in the pilot study.

The above twenty children were divided into two groups which were equivalent in age (range: 5 years 3 months to 6 years 2 months), boy-girl distribution, performance on tasks S2 and C2, and performance on the following three tests: Bender Perceptual Development Test, Boehm Test of Basic Concepts, and the Draw-a-Man General Intelligence Classification Test.

Procedure

The training study involved two and a half weeks between Thanksgiving and Christmas vacations. Training sessions involved groups of five children each and lasted about a half hour each school day. The training group participated in laboratory type sessions to be described in the following section. These training sessions aimed at teaching children all and only the operations which were involved in the tasks of the classification sequence or the seriation sequence of the pilot study. Short stories were read to the control group followed by discussions of social studies problems, community helpers, or social roles. In this way, the control group was given special treatment, presumably different from that of the training group only in content.[9]

Instructional Philosophy

The immediate instructional aim of the training study was to teach children to master those structures of operations which characterized the tasks in the classification sequence or the seriation sequence in the pilot study. That is, the training group children were taught to perform tasks which were characterized by the following four groupings of operations: classification, multiplicative classification, seriation, and multiplicative seriation. The criterion used to test the mastery of the above groupings

---

[8]Seventeen children in the pilot study had responded correctly to tasks S1, N2, and C1, but not to tasks S3, N3, or C3. None of these children responded correctly to any of the more difficult tasks in the three sequences.

[9]For a complete account of this training study, including a complete day-to-day account of the training sessions, see Lesh (1971).

of operations was that the child be able to correctly respond to all of the tasks in the classification sequence and the seriation sequence from the pilot study.

To teach the children to master the above four groupings, the following instructional philosophy was employed. For each task which had appeared in either the seriation sequence or the classification sequence of the pilot study, other tasks were devised which were characterized by the same structure of operations but which utilized perceptually different materials. For example, in the case of Task S5 (putting ten dowel rods in order according to length), a set of isomorphic tasks was given in the section of this paper titled "The Genetic Construction of Operational Structures."

Isomorphic sets of tasks relative to each of the tasks which were involved in the classification and seriation sequences of the pilot study were presented following the sequential order of difficulty which had been revealed in the pilot study. Thus, isomorphic sets of tasks were presented first for Task S1, then for C1, then for S2, then for C2, etc.

In the process of encouraging children to actively apply seriation and classification schemes in tasks which required progressively higher degrees of coordination and flexibility, the following training variables were introduced as by-products. Children were taken from tasks which required only a semi-anticipation of the result of the application of an operation to a set of objects, through a trial and error period in which semi-anticipation was successively corrected by hindsight, to a period characterized by the attainment of reversibility of the relevant operations in which the results of operations could be genuinely anticipated (i.e., foresight). Further, children were gradually required to overcome their cognitive tendencies toward centering and syncretic thinking. Nonetheless, it should be stressed that decentration and analytic thinking were considered to be primarily by-products of the gradual coordination of the schemes of actions rather than conversely. The primary focus of the training procedure was to coordinate schemes of actions which lead to the groupings of seriation, multiple seriation, classification and multiple classification.

In addition, children in the training group became acquainted with the meaning of the following words relative to the correct completion of their seriation and classification tasks: *alike, different, order, some, all,* and *more than.* Although the use of language was considered to be useful in helping children to organize their seriation and classification activities, the emphasis of the training procedure was on coordination rather than on the use of language. For the most part, the use of language was left to the spontaneous application by the children. Little effort was made to refine the children's use of language except in the instances noted above.

Posttest: Results

The posttest was given individually to each of the twenty children who participated in the study. The results were striking. None of the ten children who had been in the control group were able to respond correctly to any of the six tasks on the posttest. In contrast, four of the ten children in the training group responded correctly to all of the number tasks (i.e., N5, N6a, and N6b). One other training group child responded correctly to only Task N5b, and one responded correctly to only Task N6b. Thus, the training group significantly out-performed the control group. Of equal importance, however, is the fact that none of the ten children in the training group were able to respond correctly to either of the transformation tasks T6 or T7.

Conclusions

The training group's sessions aimed at teaching children those operations and operational structures which were involved in the seriation and classification tasks of the pilot study. The posttest revealed that transfer of learning from the experience which the training group had received induced improved understanding concerning number concepts. Further, the nature of this transfer was determined by the fact that whereas transfer was obtained to tasks involving number concepts, no transfer was obtained to tasks involving only spatial transformations.

Children who had simply learned to make two simultaneous judgments would have been expected to perform better on not only the number tasks, but also on the transformation task of the posttest. However, this was not the case, even though the number tasks and the transformation tasks had been shown to be comparable in difficulty. Other conjectures such as maintaining that the training group had simply had more practice in dealing with concrete materials must similarly be rejected since one would expect to find comparable improvement on both the number tasks and the transformation tasks of the training study.

The results of this study seem to bear witness to the fact that children may indeed be capable of abstracting the operational essence from the series of tasks which are characterized by isomorphic operational structures. That is, children appear to be capable of internalizing *schemes* of actions. Further, once these schemes are internalized as reversible structures (i.e., groupings), they appear to generalize to new situations which involve the same scheme. Therefore, the results of the study appear to significantly strengthen the psychological viability of ordering and equating operational concepts (or tasks) on the basis of their underlying operational structure. Further, the fact that no transfer was obtained from the seriation and classification instruction to tasks which involve only spatial transformations indicates that Piaget's distinction between three basic types of cognitive logical-mathematical operations may be quite a fruitful sort to make. There may be certain qualitative psychological differences between the types of operations which have been referred to in the present article as operations, relations, and transformations.

Since Piaget's analysis of operational concepts (and number concepts in particular) relies heavily on the psychological viability of analyzing, ordering, and equating tasks on the basis of their underlying operational structures, his description of the development of such concepts was strengthened by the results of this study. For Piaget, operational concepts such as the concept of number need not be assumed to evolve out of some sort of initially nonoperational (e.g., purely perceptual-linguistic) concept. Rather, an operation is an internalized *scheme* of actions which is reversible and which depends on other operations, with which it forms a structured whole characterized by laws of totality (Beth & Piaget, 1966, p. 234).

Two facts should perhaps be mentioned concerning the fact that children who spontaneously mastered all of the tasks in the seriation and classification sequences of the pilot study out-performed the ten children in the training group of the present study.

1. While a concept of number might involve only seriation and classification operations, conservation of number tasks involve transformations as well. For this reason, if the goal is to teach children that number remains invariant under simple spatial transformations, it seems likely that the child will have to be taught all three types of logical-mathematical operations (i.e., operations, relations, and transformations). However, the purpose of this study was not to isolate sufficient conditions which will insure the child's mastery of conservation tasks. Rather, it was to produce transfer of learning due to similarities in underlying operational structures.

2. Cognitive operations are perhaps never mastered in any absolute sense during the period of concrete operations. This is because children are not actually aware of the systems of operations which they bring to bear in various logical-mathematical settings. Mastery of a given operational structure means that a child is able to apply the system of operations in a wide range of concrete situations. Further, it seems likely that the more situations in which a child has learned to apply a given operational structure, the greater will be the chance that the structure can be applied to a new setting. What we have here is near tautology; the wider the applicability of a given cognitive operational structure, the greater will be the chances that the structure will be applied in any given situation. Maximum transfer can be expected from learning of greater generality.

Children in the training group were given a relatively small number of tasks representing each operational structure which characterized the tasks in the seriation and classification sequences of the pilot study. Therefore, it is not unreasonable to suppose that their level of mastery of the relevant structures of operations would have been somewhat less than that of a child who could spontaneously respond correctly to all of the seriation and classification tasks. Thus, the degree of transferability which one would expect from such learning would be somewhat less than for spontaneous problem solvers.

Since training studies are frequently interpreted as encouraging the acceleration of a child's cognitive development, a disclaimer concerning the unqualified desirability of acceleration should be emphasized. From the point of view of this paper, Piaget's theory can perhaps be most useful in providing guidance to broaden the conceptual basis underlying those mathematical topics that are of greatest importance to mathematics educators.

If Piaget's analysis of the development of logical-mathematical concepts is taken seriously, then for many concepts that are most fundamental, learning may have to be much more broadly based than many educators have been willing to admit. So, while acceleration of a single isolated concept is no doubt possible, even this acceleration should only be possible within limits that are imposed by the breadth of the child's conceptual bases.

In order to come to an understanding of the concept of number, children may have to have certain experiences seriating and classifying objects, as well as certain experiences concerning spatial transformations. The exact nature of these experiences may be able to be determined by analyzing, ordering, and equating tasks on the basis of their underlying operational structures.

Figural models can be very useful in order to help children come to an understanding of logical-mathematical concepts. But, according to Piaget before a model can be used as an image to represent a mathematical concept certain systems of operations will usually have to be coordinated relative to the model. For mathematical concepts, figural models are typically constructed representations. That is, mathematical properties will usually have to be put into the object using systems of operations before the properties can be abstracted.

DAVID C. JOHNSON

Learning of Selected Parts of a Boolean Algebra by Young Children

Literature pertaining to theoretical as well as empirical study of the thinking of young children is quite abundant. Although used extensively by psychologists, this literature remains largely untapped by mathematics educators. However, for mathematics educators interested in cognition, the research literature surrounding the work of the Geneva School provides a framework for (1) explaining how mental operations basic to mathematical thought develop, (2) identifying structural characteristics of thought as they undergo change with age, and (3) forming a theoretical basis for certain curricular decisions and experiments in the learning of mathematics.

The present study was designed with the following purposes: (1) To determine if specific instructional conditions improve the ability of young children of various ages and intellectual levels to (a) form classes, (b) establish selected equivalence or order relations; and (2) to investigate that if specific instructional conditions improve abilities outlined in (a) and (b) of (1) above, whether transfer occurs to (a) other class-related activities and (b) the transitive property of the selected equivalence and order relations.

Grouping Structures

Piaget (Beth and Piaget, 1966, pp. 158-162) has identified four main stages in which structural characteristics of thought are qualitatively different. They are: (1) sensory-motor, preverbal stage; (2) the stage of preoperational representation; (3) the stage of concrete operations;

The experiment reported in this chapter is based on a doctoral dissertation in the Department of Mathematics Education at the University of Georgia (Johnson, D.C., 1971).

and (4) the stage of formal operations. Concrete operations are a part of the cognitive structure of children from about 7-8 years of age to 11-12 years of age. Piaget (1964c, p. 42) postulates that this cognitive structure has the form of what he calls groupings, of which five properties exist. Eight major groupings are identified, each of which satisfies the five properties. The idea of an operation is central to these groupings. Piaget (1964c) views an operation as being an interiorized action, always linked to other operations and part of a total structure. Piaget's claim is that operations are fundamental to the understanding of the development of knowledge. The groupings are the structures of which the operations are a part. The difference in the groupings resides in the various operations which are structured. The elements of two groupings are classes and asymmetrical relations which correspond to the cognitive operations of combining individuals in classes and assembling the asymmetrical relations which express differences in the individuals.

It must be made clear that the Geneva School is concerned with describing transformations that intervene between the input of a problem and the output of a solution of the problem by a subject. As Bruner (1959) put it, "Piaget proposes to describe them [the transformations] in terms of their correspondence to formal logical structures [p. 364]." At a certain stage, a child becomes capable of solving a variety of problems not possible at an earlier stage, but is still not able to solve other problems which contain elements of a more advanced stage. In short, Piaget has provided a structure of intelligence which can be used to account for success or failure of children when solving certain problems.

Because the grouping structure is used as a tool to characterize the thinking of the young child, it is interesting to give an interpretation. In *The Psychology of Intelligence*, Piaget apparently selects special classes for part of his elements in the first grouping. These classes must satisfy the following pattern: $\phi \subset A_1 \subset A_2 \; . \; . \; . \subset \cup A_\sigma$, where $\sigma \varepsilon A$ and A is the index set. If "$\subset$" is interpreted to mean "$\subseteq$," then the above sets constitute a lattice, which is a partially ordered system in which any two elements have a greatest lower bound and a least upper bound. Clearly, "$\subset$" is a partial ordering of the sets in question since it is (a) reflexive, (b) antisymmetric, and (c) transitive. Moreover, for any two elements A_α and A_β, $A_\alpha \cap A_\beta$ is the greatest lower bound and $A_\alpha \cup A_\beta$ is the least upper bound.

This lattice structure is not all that is included in the first grouping. Classes of the form $A'_\sigma = A_\gamma - A_\sigma$ where $A_\sigma \subset A_\gamma$ are also included. The classes A'_σ included along with the elements of the lattice are the elements of this first grouping. If one interprets Piaget's (1964c) "+" to be "$\cup$," then he gives (embedded in a zoological classification) statements analogous to the following [p. 42]:

1. Combinativity, $A_\sigma \cup A'_\sigma = A_\gamma$;
2. Reversibility, If $A_\sigma \cup A'_\sigma = A_\gamma$ then $A_\sigma = A_\gamma - A'_\sigma$;
3. Associativity, $(A_\sigma \cup A'_\sigma) \cup A'_\gamma = A_\sigma \cup (A'_\sigma \cup A'_\sigma)$;
4. General Operation of Identity, $A_\sigma \cup \phi = A_\sigma$;
5. Special Identities, (a) $A_\sigma \cup A_\sigma = A_\sigma$, (b) $A_\sigma \cup A_\gamma = A_\gamma$ where $A_\sigma \subset A_\gamma$.

When considering definitions of a Boolean Algebra such as recorded in

Modern Algebra by Birkhoff and Maclane [1958, pp. 336, 337], it can be noted that aspects of a Boolean Algebra are inherent in Grouping I. For example, there are two binary operations "$\cap$" and "$\cup$" with all of the usual properties (such as commutativity and associativity) and a binary relation "$\subseteq$" which orders the subclasses. Also, $\phi \cup X = X$ if X is a class in the system.

Grouping I also describes essential operations and relations involved in cognition of simple hierarchies of classes. Proficiency with the use of the class inclusion relation is viewed by Piaget as essential in the establishment of operatory classification. Two abilities, described by structural properties, are of particular importance in this proficiency. The first is the ability to compose classes (combinativity) and decompose classes (reversibility), and the second is the ability to hold in mind a total class and its subclasses at the same time, made possible through combinativity and reversibility; or as will be seen later, through an ability to think of two attributes at the same time.

Due to the centrality of the class inclusion problem as a test of operatory classification, Piaget (1952) reported an early study with children of ages four to eight. A major part of the investigation involved presenting the children individually with materials similar to the following: wooden beads, the majority of which were brown; blue beads, the majority of which were square; and flowers, the majority of which were poppies. Typical kinds of questions asked were the following: (a) Are there more wooden beads or more brown beads? (b) Would a necklace made of the wooden or of the brown beads be longer? or (c) Would the bunch of flowers or the bunch of poppies be bigger? The questions were quite difficult for children under seven, but children over seven performed quite well. The main reason attributed to the failure of the younger children was that they supposedly could not think simultaneously of the whole and its parts, as mentioned above.

Continuing the "additive" operations, Piaget delineates two groupings entitled "Addition of Asymmetrical Relations" and "Addition of Symmetrical Relations." The asymmetrical relations referred to are interpreted here as strict partial orderings, i.e., orderings that are (1) transitive, (2) asymmetric, and (3) nonreflexive. Moreover, if such relations are linear, then the set A on which the relation is defined is a chain and hence is a lattice. The general properties of a grouping may be applied. Combinativity can be interpreted under the more general notion of relation composition. That is, $A \alpha B$ and $B \alpha C$ implies $A \alpha C$ which is an expression of transitivity. Reversibility by reciprocity includes permuting the terms of the relation as well as reversing the relation, i.e., the reciprocal of $A \alpha B$ is $B \propto A$. The composition is associative by virtue of the transitive property and has special identities. Addition of symmetrical relations involves several distinct categories of relations; some transitive, some intransitive, some reflexive, and some nonreflexive.

Piaget (1964c) also describes groupings based on multiplicative operations, i.e., those which deal with more than one system of classes or relations at a time. Two of these groupings are called Bi-Univocal Multiplication of Classes and Bi-Univocal Multiplication of Relations. In the former, an example is given by the following: If C_1 and C_2 denote the same set of, say, squares, but $C_1 = A_1 \cup A_2$ and $C_2 = B_1 \cup B_2$ where A_1 denotes red squares, A_2 blue squares, B_1 large squares, and B_2 small squares, then $C = C_1 \cap C_2 = (A_1 \cap B_1) \cup (A_1 \cap B_2) \cup (A_2 \cap B_1) \cup (A_2 \cap B_2)$. In other words, a matrix or double entry table of four cells has been generated with the component classes of C_1 on one dimension and those of C_2 on the other. In the case of Bi-Univocal Multiplication of Relations, an example could be seriating a collection of sticks according to lengths and diameter (thickness). A double entry table would thus be defined. If L denotes length and T thickness, then the matrix could look as follows. All the objects in the first row are the same thickness but different lengths while the objects of the first column are the same length but different

$$
\begin{array}{ccccc}
L_1T_1 & L_2T_1 & L_3T_1 & L_4T_1 & \ldots \\
L_1T_2 & L_2L_2 & L_3T_2 & L_4T_2 & \ldots \\
L_1T_3 & L_2T_3 & L_3T_3 & L_4T_3 & \ldots \\
L_1T_4 & L_2T_4 & L_3T_4 & L_4L_4 & \ldots \\
\ldots & & & &
\end{array}
$$

thickness. It must be pointed out, however, that L_1T_1 denotes *at least* zero objects, so that equivalence as well as order relations are potentially involved in this process. The structural properties of these latter two groupings are not discussed--except to say that multiplication of classes allows a child to classify according to two or more classification systems at once--or to consider an object as possessing two or more attributes simultaneously, and that multiplication of relations allows a child to seriate a collection of objects according to two or more order relations at the same time.

In general, classification (which involves equivalence relations) and seriation (which involves asymmetric relations) are at the heart of the theory of Piaget. When asked to classify, children below the age of five usually form "figural collections." By age seven, children can sort objects, add classes (form unions), and multiply classes (cross classify). However, genuine operatory classification does not exist until age eight when children can solve the class inclusion problem. Although $(A + A' = B)$ is logically equivalent to $(A = B - A')$, many children have difficulty with the latter having mastered the former as shown by a failure to state $B > A$ (B contains more than A). The conservation of the whole (being able to hold the class B in mind when focussing on A) and the quantitative comparison of whole and part $(B > A)$ are the two essential characteristics of genuine class inclusion (Piaget, 1964c, p. 117).

Recognizing that empirical research exists which provides evidence for existence of the above groupings (i.e., replications studies) and that experiments exist which have been designed to test the theory (i.e., training studies), the present study was of a slightly different nature, but was embedded in existing psychological, mathematical, and logical theories and structures. Just how it was embedded is made clear as the study is laid out. It must be emphasized that the study was not done to test Piaget's theory or to replicate already known results, such as those produced by Smedslund (1963c), Bruner and Kenney (1966), and Shantz (1967), but an employment of the theory in an applied research problem. To be sure, controversies exist concerning the validity of the theory (e.g., see Kohnstamm (1967), Braine (1959)).

Method

The theory of Piaget is a theory of development which subordinates learning to development in contrast with behavorial theories which attempt to explain development in terms of learning (e.g., Gagné's work). As a corollary, one could view mathematical experiences (e.g., school instruction) as not being assimilated in any genuine way in the absence of requisite cognitive structure. More specifically, it would appear that work on classifications and relations would bear little fruit for children in the stage of preoperational representation. However, as Sullivan (1967) comments: "If learning should be geared to the child's present developmental level as Piaget insists, then the problem of matching the subject matter to the growing conceptual ability of the child (i.e., present cognitive structure) is a relevant consideration [p. 19]."

Learning Material

Classifications and relations were the broad topics about which learning material was constructed. The basic connectives considered in the learning material were conjunction, disjunction, and negation, as well as selected mathematical relations. The learning material, described in detail elsewhere (Johnson, D., 1971), was conducted to provide children with experiences in forming (1) classes, (2) intersection and union of classes, (3) the complement of a class, and (4) relations between classes and between class elements. Physical objects were employed so that each child could be actively involved. Some free play was permitted and interaction with peers was encouraged. The learning material was administered in 17 instructional sessions each lasting about 20 minutes. The first three sessions were designed to provide experiences in forming classes. Hula hoops and other representations of closed curves were used in all sessions to motivate formation of classes. In sessions IV, V, and VI work was done on the intersection and the complement of the intersection of classes. The children were put in a conflict situation when it was pointed out that an object could not be placed inside two nonoverlapping hula hoops simultaneously. For example, if the children were instructed to place red objects in one hula hoop and triangular shapes into another hula hoop, the problem would arise as to where the red triangles should go. Sessions VII and VIII included activities concerning formation of the union of classes. Sessions XII, XIII, XIV, and XV contained activities designed to operationally define the relations "more than," "fewer than," and "as many as." The remaining sessions involved review on formation of classes involving complementation, intersection, and union. Five basic posttests were then constructed to measure achievement and transfer.

Posttests

Connective Achievement Test (CA). The connective test was designed to measure an ability to use the logical connectives "and," "or," and "not." Two sets of physical objects were used in the testing. One set consisted of Dienes' Logic Blocks used in the learning sessions (CA_1) and the other set consisted of physical objects which had not been used in the learning sessions (CA_2). Ten items were written using each set where the items were isomorphic across sets except for the differences in the objects used. Six warm-up questions were included for each set of objects to insure that the children understood basic attributes of the objects. The phraseology "Put in the ring *all* the things that are ..." preceded the directions in each of the 12 warm-up and 20 test items. The directions for the ten items involving physical objects which had not been used in the learning sessions were:

1. Either sticks or they are clothespins.
2. Either sticks or they are not blue.
3. Not blue discs.
4. Red discs.
5. Clothespins and they are blue.
6. Either sticks or they are green.
7. Not blue and they are not clothespins.
8. Not red.
9. Discs and they are sticks.
10. Red and they are not sticks.

Relation Achievement Test (RA). This 25 question test was designed to measure understanding of the relations "more than," "fewer than," "as many as," "same shape as," and "same color as." For each of the first three relations, objects used in the items were mounted on pieces of posterboard in a vertical, horizontal, and circular arrangement, for a total of nine items. The set of number pairs used for the "as many as" relation was $\{(6, 6), (7, 7), (8, 8)\}$. The set used for the "more than," and "fewer than" relation was $\{(5, 6), (6, 7), (7, 8)\}$. A "more than," "fewer than," and "as many as" question was asked for each item to insure that when a child said, for example, "There are more A's than B's," he also knew that there were neither fewer A's than B's nor as many A's as B's. An example question would be, "Are there fewer A's than B's?" For the 16 shape and color items, eight cards (containing two objects each) were constructed, two for each pair in the set { (same shape, same color), (same shape, different color), (different shape, same color), (different shape, different color)}. Each card was used for two items, a shape item and a color item. The tester pointed to the appropriate object and asked: "Is this the same shape as that?" and "Is this the same color as that?" The next three tests to be described are transfer tests with the exception of the intersecting ring items in the Multiplication of Classes and Relations Test.

Multiplication of Classes and Relations Test (MU). This test was constructed to measure the ability of children to use two or more criteria at once. Parts of this test were similar to the nine matrix tasks designed by Inhelder and Piaget (1964, pp. 60-61), which were either four-cell or six-cell matrices with from five to eight choices located below the matrix. For the purpose of testing the ability of children to multiply classes and relations, six material sets spanning across each of the following three types of arrays were utilized: (1) 3 x 3 matrices, (2) 2 x 2 matrices, and (3) ring intersection. The six sets were defined by the pairs in the following set: { (shape used in learning material, color used in learning material), (shape, color used in learning material), (color, number), (shape, shading), (shape, size), (color, size)}. Exactly one material set was used in the construction of each of the six 3 x 3 matrices, of each of the six 2 x 2 matrices, and of each of the six intersecting ring patterns. Although the intersection ring activity was not performed during the unit, it was very similar to some activities and was thus considered as an achievement measure. The matrix items were never solved in the instructional unit and hence were viewed as transfer measures. For each of the eighteen items described, a strip of four response choices was constructed. For the matrix items each response strip included (1) the correct missing object, (2) an object from the same column but a different row than the missing objects, (3) an object from the same row but a different column than the missing object, and (4) an object having one attribute not represented in the matrix. For each pair of intersecting rings, corresponding response strips included (1) an object from the left ring, (2) an object from the right ring, (3) the object logically belonging in both rings (possessing both attributes), and (4) an object having one attribute not represented in either ring.

Class Inclusion Test (CI). This 16 item test was included as a transfer measure for two reasons. First, whenever a class and its complement are specified, the idea of inclusion is implicit. Second, as already noted, Piaget views successful solution of the class inclusion problem as indicative of operatory classification.

Factors affecting the ability to solve inclusion problems are: (1) presence of an extraneous object, (2) three or more proper subsets present, (3) equal numbers in a set and its complement, (4) mingled items, (5) items not visually present, (6) addition or subtraction of an item after initial comparison. These factors were utilized in designing the items of this test. Two other factors included were: (7) items of an infinite nature, and (8) items where subset comparison is made through the use of an outside set of objects. Eight items involved factor 1; two, factor 2; three, factor 3; nine, factor 4; one, factor 5; two, factor 6; two, factor 7; and two, factor 8. With the exception of two items, the number of objects in subclasses for each item was assigned to the items randomly where the numbers were members of the set { 2, 3, 4, 5}.

The first 14 items (items numbered 1-14) included two questions. An example item is where there were five blue tops, three blue guns, and two turkeys. The experimenter had the child point to the toys and to the tops. The two standard questions, "Are there more toys than tops?", and "Are there more tops than toys?" were then asked. The last two items were analogous to one another in that each included Factor 8. In addition to two standard questions, two other questions were asked concerning comparison of the outside set of objects with the set of objects of direct concern. For example, one item contained pictures of seven animals (four horses and three rabbits) and four dots arranged proximal to the horses. Two questions were asked requiring the child to compare the horses and dots, and the animals and dots as well as the two standard questions.

Transitivity Test (TR). This 10 item test was designed to measure the ability of children to use the transitive property of the relations tested for in the Relation Achievement Test. Two items were designed to test for the transitivity property of each of the five relations. A "left to right" and a "right to left" matching were used in the testing for the transitive property of the relations "as many as," "more than," and "fewer than." The triplets of numbers of objects used for testing for the above three relations were (7, 7, 7) and (8, 8, 8) ; (8, 7, 6) and (9, 8, 7) ; and (6, 7, 8) and (7, 8, 9) respectively. The test was used as a transfer measure to determine if an ability to use transitivity is improved by instruction on the relations of concern.

An example of a transitivity item for matching relations is where there were seven red discs and seven green discs mounted in rows on posterboard. The child was directed to match a pile of seven blue discs with the red discs and judge the relation between the two sets. The red discs were then covered. The child was then directed to match the blue discs with the green discs and judge the relation between the two sets. The green discs were then covered. Three questions were then asked; "Are there as many red discs as green discs?" "Are there more red discs than green discs?" and "Are there fewer red discs than green discs?". An analogous procedure was used for transitivity of the equivalence relations involving color and shape, except only two questions were asked, one for the appropriate equivalence relation and one for its accompanying difference relation.

Sample

The subjects for the study were chosen from four kindergarten and four first grade classes located in or closely adjacent to Athens, Georgia. All of these children were administered an Otis-Lennon Ability Test during March 24-April 1, 1970. A total of 99 first graders and 97 kindergarteners were tested. Two levels, Primary 1 and Elementary 1, of the Otis-Lennon Mental Abilities were utilized. The Primary 1 level is designed for pupils in the last half of the kindergarten and Elementary 1 level is designed for pupils in the last half of the first grade. The test items sample the mental processes of classification, following directions, qualitative reasoning, comprehension of verbal concepts, and reasoning by analogy. K-R 20's for the Primary and Elementary Levels are .88 and .90 respectively. The two categorization variables, then, were chronological age and IQ. Only those children who had an IQ in the interval (80, 125) and a CA either in the interval (64, 76) or (77, 89) for kindergarten and first grade, respectively, were included in the study. The children were further categorized by the two IQ intervals (80, 100), (105, 125). Children within the four categories thus defined were then randomly assigned to an experimental or control group after an ordered random sample of 80 subjects had been selected, 20 in each category. Thirty-five alternates were also selected for a total of 115 children in the sample.

Administration of the Tests

Administration of CA. The CA was administrated to six subjects at a time. Three subjects were seated adjacent to each other on one side of a table and the other three were seated facing them on the opposite side of the table. Subjects were separated by cardboard partitions so they could not see each other. Each subject was given a rope ring and some objects to classify. No objects were initially inside the rope rings. The order of test questions was initially randomized. The investigator read all the directions clearly and repeated if necessary. All subjects were given sufficient time to make their responses. The experimenter stood behind the subjects and recorded each response as correct (correct set of objects was placed in ring) or incorrect (either items omitted or at least one incorrect item placed in ring).

For subtest CA_1 if all the proper objects were placed in the ring and nothing extra was placed there the answer was considered as correct. One point was given for correct answers and no points were given for incorrect answers. Subtest CA_2 was scored in a similar way. Since the tests were parallel, Subtest CA_3 was formed through the consideration of the responses to the items in Subtests I and II. The subjects were given credit for having a question right on Subtest III only if they had scored each corresponding question right on both CA_1 and CA_2. In considering Subtest CA_3, one point was given for each question judged as right by the above procedure. The normal testing time was approximately 23 minutes.

Administration of RA. For this test, the material sets were placed in a row on a low table in order from 1 to 17. Administration of items 1-9 (matching relations) was done first with the sequence of presentation randomized individually for each subject. Also the question sequence was randomized for each question for each subject. Cards 10-17 (shape and color relations) followed with the sequence of presentation also randomized for each subject. Here again, the question sequence was randomized for each subject. The eight "same shape" questions asked of cards 10-17 composed items 10-17 for this test and the eight "same color" questions composed items 18-25 respectively. For each card, the response was scored correct if the color and shape questions were both correct. The tester recorded the "yes" and "no" responses for each question asked. Average testing time was approximately twelve minutes.

Administration of MU. The eighteen material sets for this test were placed in order (1-18) on a low table similar to that used with the RA. Each strip of four response choices was centered and placed directly below the respective matrix or ring item. The sequence of presentation of the eighteen items was randomized for each subject. The tester recorded the response choice pointed to on each response strip. Average testing time was approximately twelve minutes.

Administration of CI. The 16 items were partially randomized for each subject. The exceptions were that items numbered 3 and 4, and 13 and 14 were presented in pairs in the natural order and items numbered 15 and 16 were presented last in the natural order. An item was scored

Table 1
Formation of Subtests

Test Type	No. of Items	Subtests	Content of Subtest
	10	CA_1	First ten items of CA
Achievement	10	CA_2	Last ten items of CA (novel material)
Tests	10	CA_3	Intersection of Tests CA_1 and CA_2
	25	RA	Same as RA
	6	MU_r	Last six items of MU (intersection rings)
	6	MU_3	First six items of MU (3x3 matrices)
Transfer	6	MU_2	Second six items of MU (2x2 matrices)
Tests	16	CI	Same as CI
	10	TR	Same as TR

as correct only if the two standard questions were correctly answered.

Administration of TR. Items were arranged in a row on a low table. Administration of the six items for matching relations was conducted followed by the four items for the color and shape relations. Within this constraint, the items were randomized independently for each subject. A transitivity item was scored as correct only if all questions were correctly answered.

Design of Study and Method of Analysis

The basic design of the study was The Posttest-Only Control Group Design presented by Campbell and Stanley (1963). This design calls for initial randomization followed by an experimental treatment given to the experimental group. Twelve major multivariate analyses of variance null hypotheses were tested.

H_1: The mean vectors of the experimental and control groups are not different on the achievement measures.
H_2: The mean vectors of the experimental and control groups are not different on the transfer measures.
H_3: The mean vectors of the kindergarten and first-grade subjects are not different on the achievement measures.
H_4: The mean vectors of the kindergarten and first-grade subjects are not different on the transfer measures.
H_5: The mean vectors of the low and high IQ subjects are not different on the achievement measures.
H_6: The mean vectors of the low and high IQ subjects are not different on the transfer measures.
H_7: There is no significant interaction of IQ with Treatment on the achievement measures.

H_8: There is no significant interaction of Grade with Treatment on the achievement measures.
H_9: There is no significant interaction of Grade with IQ on the achievement measures.
H_{10}: There is no significant interaction of IQ with Treatment on the transfer measures.
H_{11}: There is no significant interaction of Grade with Treatment on the transfer measures.
H_{12}: There is no significant interaction of Grade with IQ on the transfer measures.

Test statistics and an item analysis were computed for each of the subtests composing the transfer and achievement measures. Two point biserial correlation coefficients, a phi coefficient, and a difficulty index were computed for each item. A point biserial correlation coefficient represents the degree of correlation existing between a dichotomous and a continuous variable. In the study, IQ measures and the total test score formed by the composite of posttest scores were considered continuous variables. The dichotomous variables are the individual items scored as either correct or incorrect. Correlations involving IQ and total scores provide indices of validity and reliability respectively. Essentially, a phi coefficient is, with minor modification, a chi-square calculated on a two-way contingency table to test for independence of two random variables. The table was defined by experimental and control groups, and the ratio of subjects passing or failing each item to the total responses on that item.

The null hypotheses were tested with the use of Multivariate Analysis of Variance (MANOVA) procedures. Program MUDAID (Multivariate, Univariate, and Discriminant Analysis of Irregular Data) was used for the MANOVAs where the five achievement and four transfer measures were the response variables for all combination of independent variables taken two at a time. Therefore six MANOVAs and 27 ANOVAs were calculated; one for each IQ (I) by Age (A), IQ by Treatment (T), and Age by Treatment. Levels of IQ were 80-100 (L) and 105-125 (H); levels of Treatment were experimental (E) and control (C); and levels of Age were five-year-olds (K) and six-year-olds (F).

Results

The results of the analyses are presented in this section. All data analyzed in the item analysis section were obtained from all 111 subjects and alternates administered all the posttest measures. The multivariate analyses are limited to 80 subjects selected for the study.

Item Analysis

A phi coefficient was calculated for each of the 99 items. Utilizing a significant ϕ ($p < .05$), items which were discriminators between the experimental and control groups were found for each test. From the array of data in Table 2, it can be easily seen that there was only one item which discriminated in favor of the control group out of the total 99 items.

Table 2
Frequency of Items: Discriminators and Nondiscriminators

		Discriminators		Nondiscriminators
No. of Items	Subtest	Experimental	Control	
10	CA_1	8		2
10	CA_2	7		3
10	CA_3	8		2
25	RA	7	1	17
6	MU_r	5		1
6	MU_3	4		2
6	MU_2	2		4
16	CI	0		16
10	TR	7		3

Two of the subtests deserve special discussion in that all or a majority of the items of those tests were nondiscriminators. First, in the case of the RA test, the 16 items which involved usage of the relations "same shape as" and "same color as" were extremely easy for all subjects, and thereby were excluded from all other analyses. Second, four of the six items composing the MU_2 test were nondiscriminators. It appeared that much guessing was done on this test, as the average score was approximately the same as chance would allocate. One of the four nondiscriminators on MU_2 was excluded from all further analyses. Ten other items were also excluded from the analysis with undesirable item characteristics (very hard or very easy items with low or negative biserial correlations with the total test or IQ). Nine of these ten items were nondiscriminators; six for the achievement measures and three for the transfer measures. Seventy-two items were retained for the analysis of variance.

Multivariate and Univariate Analysis

The necessary subtest information is tabulated in Table 3. The internal-consistency reliabilities are quite substantial indicating good homogeneity of the test items. The multivariate and univariate analyses of variance are given for the direct achievement measures (CA_1, CA_2, CA_3, RA, MU_r) and transfer measures (MU_3, MU_2, CI, TR) for the two classification variables (Age and IQ) each considered in conjunction with the treatment variable, and also considered in conjunction with each other.

Table 3
Subtest Statistics

No. of Items	Subtest	Reliability (KR-20)	Grand Mean
9	CA_1	.72	5.09
7	CA_2	.65	3.70
9	CA_3	.74	3.88
9	RA	.82	5.89
5	MU_r	.67	1.39
6	MU_3	.70	3.23
5	MU_2	.58	2.35
13	CI	.75	3.78
9	TR	.79	6.13

Analyses of achievement measures. For the purpose of testing the hypotheses related to achievement, the five achievement subtests were considered concomitantly as response variables in the MANOVA and were considered singly in ANOVAs. In the MANOVA analysis of T vs I, the likelihood ratio test statistic $\chi^2 = 113.30$ was significant ($p < .01$), indicating significant differences in the mean vectors for all effects. As indicated in Table 5, the main effects due to T and I and the interaction of T and I were significant. The test of all F values in Table 5 is done

Table 4
Subclass Means: T vs. I (Achievement Subtests)

Subtest	Low	High	Means
Experimentals			
CA_1	5.35	7.40	6.38
CA_2	4.15	5.95	5.05
CA_3	4.25	6.35	5.30
RA	5.50	8.60	7.05
MU_r	1.55	2.85	2.20
Controls			
CA_1	3.20	4.40	3.80
CA_2	2.05	2.65	2.35
CA_3	1.80	3.10	2.45
RA	3.25	6.20	4.72
MU_r	0.55	0.60	0.58
Means			
CA_1	4.28	5.90	5.09
CA_2	3.10	4.30	3.70
CA_3	3.02	4.72	3.88
RA	4.38	7.40	5.89
MU_r	1.05	1.72	1.39

Table 5
F Values for MANOVA of Achievement Subtests[a]

Analysis	Factor	F
	T	29.66**
T vs. I	I	10.06**
	T x I	2.52*
	T	20.32**
T vs. A	A	< 1
	T x A	1.13
	I	5.43**
I vs. A	A	< 1
	I x A	1.13

a* = .05 level of significance
** = .01 level of significance

using p and (N-3-p) degrees of freedom where p is the number of response variables and N is the number of subjects. In this analysis p is 5 and N is 80. Also, $F_{.05}$ (5, 72) = 2.35 and $F_{.01}$ (5, 72) = 3.28.

In order to further interpret the main effects of T, I, and T x I, five univariate analyses were performed. The results in terms of F values for these analyses and also for T vs A and I vs A are included within Table 6. It is noted that for each of the five response variables there existed a significant F ($p < .01$) for both T and I. This indicated that performance of children of E and C and also of L and H were significantly different

Table 6
ANOVA F Values for Achievement Measures[a]

Type Variation	CA_1	CA_2	CA_3	RA	MU_r
T	60.22**	114.20**	80.54**	17.31**	44.97**
I	23.98**	22.56**	28.65**	29.30**	7.76**
T x I	1.64	5.64**	1.59	< 1	6.65**
T	13.37**	8.92**	13.96**	23.90**	4.69*
A	< 1	1.25	< 1	< 1	< 1
T x A	< 1	< 1	< 1	< 1	1.09

a* = .05 level of significance
** = .01 level of significance

on all achievement subtests.

Significant interaction ($p < .05$) of T with I occurred only on CA_2 (involving "and," "or," and "not") and MU_r. The significant interaction indicates that on these subtests the performance of control subjects was not like the performance of experimental subjects across the two levels of IQ. Table 4 indicates that on these subtests, the higher IQ experimental subjects performed better than any other group.

In the MANOVA analysis of T vs A, the likelihood ratio test statistic $\chi^2 = 71.43$ was significant ($p < .01$), indicating significant differences in the mean vectors for all effects. The only main effect that

Table 7
Subclass Means: T vs. G (Achievement Subtests)

Subtest	Kindergarten	First Grade	Means
Experimentals			
CA_1	6.35	6.40	6.38
CA_2	5.00	5.10	5.05
CA_3	5.30	5.30	5.30
RA	6.75	7.35	7.05
MU_r	2.40	2.00	2.20
Controls			
CA_1	3.45	4.15	3.80
CA_2	1.95	2.75	2.35
CA_3	2.00	2.90	2.45
RA	4.90	4.55	4.72
MU_r	0.40	0.75	0.58
Means			
CA_1	4.90	5.28	5.09
CA_2	3.48	3.92	3.70
CA_3	3.65	4.10	3.88
RA	5.83	5.95	5.89
MU_r	1.40	1.38	1.39

was significant in this analysis, as indicated in Table 5, was T. Again, univariate analyses were performed to further interpret the main effect. As shown in Table 6, significance ($p < .01$) was achieved on each of the five subtests if and only if the effect was T.

The final two-way analysis dealt with the factors of I and A. The likelihood ratio test statistic $\chi^2 = 27.41$ was significant ($p < .01$) indicating significant difference in the mean vectors presented for all effects. As indicated in Table 5, the only main effect that was significant was I. Hence, for the effects of I and A, considered concomitantly, significant

Table 8
Subclass Means: I vs. A (Achievement Subtests)

Subtest	Kindergarten	First Grade	Means
Low			
CA_1	4.00	4.55	4.28
CA_2	2.80	3.40	3.10
CA_3	2.75	3.30	3.02
RA	4.40	4.35	4.38
MU_r	0.90	1.20	1.05
High			
CA_1	5.80	6.00	5.90
CA_2	4.15	4.45	4.30
CA_3	4.55	4.90	4.72
RA	7.25	7.55	7.40
MU_r	1.90	1.55	1.72
Means			
CA_1	4.90	5.28	5.09
CA_2	3.48	3.92	3.70
CA_3	3.65	4.10	3.88
RA	5.82	5.95	5.89
MU_r	1.40	1.38	1.39

differences on achievement existed between the two levels of intelligence used in the study. Table 6 shows that again all F values for the I effect were significant ($p < .01$). As can be seen from Table 8, for all five subtests the mean scores of the high intelligence group were greater than for the low intelligence group and first graders performed better (but not significantly) than or approximately equivalent to kindergarteners. On the basis of the results listed in Tables 5 and 6, hypotheses H_1, H_5, and H_7 were rejected and H_3, H_8, and H_9 were accepted. Hence, for the achievement scores, the factors IQ and Treatment significantly affected performance. First graders performed better, but not significantly better, than kindergarteners on all achievement measures.

Analyses of Transfer Measures

The four transfer subtests were the response variables considered concomitantly in MANOVAs and separately in ANOVAs for the purpose of testing the hypotheses related to transfer effects. For the MANOVA analysis of T vs I, the likelihood ratio test statistic $\chi^2 = 60.19$ was significant ($p < .01$) for all effects. As illustrated in Table 10, the main effects due to T and I were significant but the interaction of T with I was not significant. The test of all F values in Table 10 is done using p and (N-3-p) degrees of freedom as was the case with the achievement

Table 9
Subclass Means: T vs. I (Transfer Subtests)

Subtest	Low	High	Means
Experimentals			
MU_3	3.15	4.45	3.80
MU_2	2.10	3.40	2.75
CI	2.20	5.00	3.60
TR	5.80	8.35	7.08
Controls			
MU_3	2.60	2.70	2.65
MU_2	1.85	2.05	1.95
CI	3.10	4.80	3.95
TR	4.15	6.20	5.18
Means			
MU_3	2.88	3.58	3.22
MU_2	1.98	2.72	2.35
CI	2.65	4.90	3.78
TR	4.98	7.28	6.12

Table 10
F Values for MANOVA of Transfer Subtests[a]

Analysis	Factor	F
T vs. I	T	7.18**
	I	11.75**
	T x I	1.00
T vs. A	T	5.69**
	A	< 1
	T x A	< 1
I vs. A	I	9.68**
	A	< 1
	I x A	< 1

[a]** = significance of factors beyond the .01 level

measures. However, for the transfer measures p is 4 and N is 80. For the new value of p, $F_{.05}$ (4, 73) = 2.49 and $F_{.01}$ (4, 73) = 3.59.

To assist the investigator in interpreting the main effects of T, I, and T x I more precisely, four univariate analyses were performed. F values for these analyses and also T vs A and I vs A are reported in Table 11. For MU_3 and TR significance was maintained ($p < .01$) for the main effect T.

Table 11
ANOVA F Values for Transfer Measures[a]

Type Variation	MU_3	MU_2	CI	TR
T	8.80**	5.59*	< 1	18.95**
I	3.26	4.91*	13.33**	27.77**
T x I	2.40	2.64	< 1	< 1
T	8.25**	5.11*	< 1	14.03**
A	< 1	< 1	< 1	< 1
T x A	< 1	< 1	1.86	< 1
I	2.88	4.45*	13.30**	22.47**
A	< 1	< 1	< 1	1.06
I x A	< 1	< 1	< 1	< 1

a* = .05 level of significance
** = .01 level of significance

A significant F ($p < .05$) was computed for MU_2 but a nonsignificant F was computed for CI. The results were slightly different for the main effect of I. Here, significance ($p < .01$) was established for CI and TR, and for MU_2 there was significance at the .05 level. No significance was found for the main effect of I on MU_3. It is not known why the main effect of I was significant for MU_2 and not for MU_3. One possible explanation is that the subjects of greater intelligence were able to use the fewer cues available in MU_2 more proficiently than subjects of lesser intelligence. Table 9 indicates that significant differential performance always favors the experimental and high IQ groups.

For the MANOVA performed on the pair of factors T and A, the likelihood ratio test statistic $\chi^2 = 26.04$ was significant ($p < .01$), indicating significant differences for all effects. Only the main effect of T was significant ($p < .01$) as indicated in Table 10. Treatment was significant ($p < .01$) for MU_3 and TR, and was significant ($p < .05$) for MU_2, as given in Table 11. Hence, for those three variables, performance of subjects in the two levels of T differed significantly. Table 12 reveals that for all variables for which the main effect of T was significant, Experimentals outperformed Controls.

The last two-way analysis was done with the pair of factors I and A. The likelihood ratio test statistic $\chi^2 = 35.48$ was significant ($p < .01$) indicating significant differences in the mean vectors for all effects. As illustrated in Table 10, only the main effect of I was significant ($p < .01$). Table 11 reveals that the main effect of I was significant ($p < .01$) for

Table 12
Subclass Means: T vs. G (Transfer Subtests)

Subtest	Kindergarten	First Grade	Means
Experimentals			
MU_3	3.60	4.00	3.80
MU_2	2.75	2.75	2.75
CI	3.45	3.75	3.60
TR	6.90	7.25	7.08
Controls			
MU_3	2.60	2.70	2.65
MU_2	1.80	2.10	1.95
CI	4.70	3.20	3.95
TR	4.85	5.50	5.18
Means			
MU_3	3.10	3.35	3.22
MU_2	2.28	2.42	2.35
CI	4.08	3.48	3.78
TR	5.88	6.38	6.12

Table 13
Subclass Means: I vs. G (Transfer Subtests)

Subtest	Kindergarten	First Grade	Means
Low			
MU_3	2.60	3.15	2.88
MU_2	1.95	2.00	1.98
CI	3.05	2.25	2.65
TR	4.70	5.25	4.98
High			
MU_3	3.60	3.55	3.58
MU_2	2.60	2.85	2.72
CI	5.10	4.70	4.90
TR	7.05	7.50	7.28
Means			
MU_3	3.10	3.35	3.22
MU_2	2.28	2.42	2.35
CI	4.08	3.48	3.78
TR	5.88	6.38	6.12

CI and TR and was significant ($p < .05$) for MU_2. Hence, IQ plays an important role in performance measured by those variables. No other significant main effects were found. Table 13 indicates that responses favored the high intelligence and first-grade levels.

From the results indicated in Tables 10 and 11, hypotheses H_2 and H_6 were rejected and H_4, H_{10}, H_{11}, and H_{12} were accepted. Therefore transfer to related areas was found to differ significantly depending on levels of I and T. As with the achievement measures, the more intelligent subjects performed better than the less intelligent subjects and the experimental subjects performed better than the control subjects.

Discussion

There is substantial evidence in this study that kindergarten and first-grade children can be taught (1) to form classes using intersection, union, and negation, and (2) to make correct "prenumber" comparisons of sets of objects. Mastery was not required, although significant differences were noted between Experimentals and Controls. Furthermore, this increase in achievement was accompanied by some transfer to related activities. The main effects of Treatment and IQ were very significant on both achievement and transfer measures but the main effect of Age was not significant on any measure.

It is quite important for understanding the results of this study to distinguish between two types of experience--physical experience and logical-mathematical experience. According to Piaget (1964a) physical experience "consists of acting upon objects and drawing some knowledge about the objects by abstraction from the objects [p. 11]." Piaget (1964a) states further that in logical-mathematical experiences "knowledge is not drawn from the objects, but it is drawn from the actions effected on the objects [p. 12]." If a child is asked to place all the objects possessing a given attribute inside a ring, he can be shown his mistakes and they can be corrected. This type of activity is basically in the realm of physical knowledge. However, suppose that a child claims that there are more dogs than animals after he has pointed to the dogs and animals independently. It is impossible to correct his mistakes in a way similar to that of the previous example. With the exception of the MU_r subtest, all the achievement measures fell in the realm of physical knowledge. Hence, the treatment was very effective for imparting physical knowledge. However, the MU_r subtest and the transfer measures must be considered when investigating the production of logical-mathematical knowledge.

Activities with intersecting rings were provided in the unit but in a format that differed from the intersecting ring test items. Although Experimentals performed significantly better than Controls on the MU_r subtest, it can be noted that neither group performed extremely well. Furthermore, Controls appeared to consider the three regions formed by the intersecting rings as nonoverlapping regions. Hence, improvement can be explained by hypotheses other than a genuine improvement in the formation of intersections. In the case of the CI subtest, the treatment did not produce significant differences. On this measure, intelligence produced the only significant effect. However, operatory classification was not achieved by either IQ group because the higher IQ group scored about 37 percent and the lower group only scored about 25 percent ,where the expected mean based on guessing is 20 percent . Improvement on the transitivity items can be attributed to clarity of language rather than to usage of the transitivity property. Items based on the relation of shape and color contributed greatly to the rather high mean scores of the Transitivity subtest. Mean scores for Controls and Experiments on matching relations were 30 and 55 percent, respectively, whereas the analogous mean for the shape and color relations were 86 and 97 percent, respectively. The matrix items provided the strongest evidence for an improvement in logical thinking, although the Genevans claim that it is difficult to distinguish between graphic and operational solutions. There was some evidence that the most substantial improvement existed for the high ability first graders.

In conclusion, the unit produced substantial improvement in physical knowledge but very little improvement in operatory classification. When considering the results of the study and observing the way in which addition and subtraction are presented in school mathematics curricula, a serious problem is revealed in that children are being presented with concepts they are conceptually unable to handle. In a subtraction problem such as 9 - 5 = 4, if a child thinks that the difference is larger than the minuend he might just as well write something like 5 - 9 = 4.

Although there was nearly a significant difference in achievement between kindergarten and first-grade children on CA_2, it is recommended that instruction similar to that used in the unit begin at the kindergarten level because there were no significant differences in achievement between these grades on any subtest. However, more research with a more generalized population is highly recommended before final grade-level placement is decided upon. For example, a much deeper investigation is needed concerning the actual relations that exist between the words "and," "or," and "not" and the growth of conjunction, disjunction, and negation concepts respectively. These should be investigated at various grade levels in conjunction with other concepts such as conservation of various relations as discussed by Piaget. The positive transfer made to the transitive property of the equivalence and order relations used in the unit was an interesting outcome. Various properties of the multitude of equivalence and order relations existing in the mathematics curriculum warrant similar investigations. It was noted that relations such as "same shape as" and "same color as" and the transitive property of these relations were very easy even for kindergarteners. Very little, if any, instruction is required in kindergarten for such relations.

IQ should be considered when arranging instruction based on the concepts in this study. Three of the reasons for this are as follows: (1) there was significant interaction ($p < .05$) of treatment with IQ on MU_r with the best performance by the high IQ subjects, (2) among the best discriminators between levels of intelligence was RA, and (3) the intelligence factor was significant on the transfer subtests CI and TR. This is worthy of note because these two subtests occupy key positions in the theory of Piaget. IQ was the only factor where significance was attained for CI. In such areas as those just mentioned, a thorough analysis needs to be made concerning the relation that exists between Piaget's classification of mental operations and the degree to which these operations are measured on various IQ tests. Such investigation could have far-reaching implications for arranging mathematics instruction at various age levels.

At this point in time it is uncertain exactly what abilities the 3 x 3 and 2 x 2 matrix questions and the intersecting ring questions are measuring. There exists good, but inconclusive, evidence that the intersecting ring questions are measuring the same type of ability as the matrix questions. Future investigations need to incorporate other methods when investigating the intersection concept. It is assumed that the improvement in cross classification was done through the "intersection of attribute" activities of the unit. However, it is strongly recommended that the relation existing between two attributes and a total cross classification be investigated further. As indicated previously, Piaget has hypothesized that cross classification, as measured by matrix activities, develops at about age seven and the intersection of simple attributes at about age nine. The present study shows that instruction in one area will perhaps hasten the development of the other operation. Any such transfer is important to education.

THOMAS P. CARPENTER

The Performance of First- and Second-Grade Children on Liquid Conservation and Measurement Problems Employing Equivalence and Order Relations

Conservation or invariance of a given property under certain transformation is basic to the process of measurement of that property. One of the essential features of measurement or comparison of quantities is that the transformations used in the measurement or comparison process do not change the relation between the quantities.

Studies by Piaget, Inhelder, and Szeminska (1960) indicate that this logical interdependence of conservation and measurement is reflected in the development of these concepts in children. However, although Piaget et al. (1960) extensively document relationships between conservation and measurement failures in a variety of situations, their tasks share certain common features which may have influenced their conclusions. First, most of the measurement tasks required relatively sophisticated measurement manipulations. Second, in all comparisons distracting cues were perceptual; and if correctly applied, measurement processes yielded the correct response. There is evidence that certain conclusions of Piaget et al. (1960) resulted from this lack of experimental variability.

They concluded that young children are dominated by the immediate perceptual qualities of a situation. However, the results of another investigation (Carpenter, 1971a) indicate that young children respond to numerical cues with about the same degree of frequency as perceptual cues. As a consequence the children in this study demonstrated an ability to interpret and apply aspects of the measurement process earlier than indicated by Piaget et al. (1960).

In the current study the relation between young children's responses to perceptual and numerical cues on liquid conservation and measurement problems was systematically investigated. A second dimension of the study was to investigate the effect of equivalence and order relations on young children's performance on conservation and measurement of liquid quantities.

The experiment reported in this chapter is based on a doctoral dissertation in the College of Education at the University of Wisconsin (Carpenter, T. P., 1971).

A third dimension of the study was to provide insight into young children's conception of a unit of measure and their understanding of the relation between unit size and number of units.

Mathematical Definition of Measurement

Mathematically, measurement can be discussed in terms of a function mapping the elements of a given domain into some mathematical structure (usually a subset of the real numbers) in such a way as to preserve the essential characteristics of the domain. First a structure must be established on the domain by applying some empirical procedures to define equivalence and order relations ($\sim$ and $<$ respectively) to compare elements of the domain. Generally order relations are established by demonstrating equivalence between one quantity and a proper subset of the other quantity. Thus, logically the definition of equivalence relations precedes the definition of order relations. Similarly empirical procedures are used to define an operation "*" that is both commutative and associative to combine elements of the domain.

Specifically, in the case of liquid measure we could say that two quantities of liquid are equivalent if they both exactly fill identical containers. Quantity A is greater than quantity B if it fills one of the containers with some left over. The operation is defined by simply pouring one quantity of liquid into the other.

Once the domain has been given a recognizable structure, a function μ that maps the domain into a subset of the real numbers and preserves the essential characteristics of the structure of the domain must be defined. For liquid measurement this means that given liquid quantities ℓ_1, ℓ_2, and ℓ_3

1. $\mu(\ell_1) = \mu(\ell_2)$ if and only if $\ell_1 \sim \ell_2$

2. $\mu(\ell_1) < \mu(\ell_2)$ if and only if $\ell_1 < \ell_2$

3. $\ell_3 \sim \ell_1 * \ell_2$ implies that $\mu(\ell_3) = \mu(\ell_1) + \mu(\ell_2)$ assuming that ℓ_1 and ℓ_2 do not intersect.

The measurement function for liquid quantities is defined by arbitrarily selecting a quantity of liquid ℓ_0 as a unit. Then any other quantity of liquid is compared with successive multiples of ℓ_0 until a multiple $n\ell_0$ is found such that $n\ell_0$ is less than or equivalent to the given quantity which in turn is less than $(n + 1)\ell_0$. (A multiple $n\ell_0$ is defined to be a quantity of liquid equivalent to $\ell_0 * \ell_0 * \ldots * \ell_0$ in which there are n terms.) Next a quantity ℓ_1 is chosen such that $10\ell_1$ is equivalent to ℓ_0, and a multiple of ℓ_1 is joined to $n\ell_0$ such that $n\ell_0 * n_1\ell_1$ is less than or equivalent to the given quantity which in turn is less than $n\ell_0 * (n_1 + 1)\ell_1$. Similarly ℓ_2 and n_2 are chosen such that $n\ell_0 * n_1\ell_1 * n_2\ell_2$ is less than or equivalent to the given quantity which is less than $n\ell_0 * n_1\ell_1 * (n_2 + 1)\ell_2$. Continuing in this manner a decimal number $r = n.n_1n_2n_3\ldots$ can be constructed and used to define the function μ mapping the domain of liquid quantities onto the set of positive real numbers by $\mu(\ell) = r$, where ℓ is the given quantity above.

When the function μ_0 is defined by arbitrarily selecting a quantity ℓ_0 as a unit, a different function μ_1 can be defined by choosing a different quantity ℓ_1 and using it to generate μ_1. For liquid measurement functions the relation between the functions μ_0 and μ_1 is the form

$\mu_0 = k\mu_1$, where k is a positive real number and $k > 1$ when $\ell_0 < \ell_1$ and $0 < k < 1$ when $\ell_0 > \ell_1$. In other words, for these functions there is an inverse relationship between the unit size and the number of units.

It should be noted that a basic assumption in attributing a structure to the domain and defining the function from the domain to the set of positive real numbers is that the property that is being measured does not change under certain transformations and is not affected by the empirical procedures used to define the relations and operation on the domain. This assumption pervades the entire measurement process. One of the essential characteristics of a measurement function is that it preserves the relation between elements of the domain that it measures. Thus, it is critical that neither the empirical procedures employed to compare elements of the domain directly or the procedures used to define and apply the measurement function affect the relation between elements.

Related Research

For Piaget et al. (1960) this assumption that certain properties remain constant under certain transformations is the central idea underlying all of measurement. It is upon this assumption that these authors have based their investigations of the development of measurement concepts. Based on their studies of length, area, and volume they proposed a stagewise development of measurement which is interrelated with the development of conservation.

The measurement problems in these studies can be divided into two broad classes which correspond to the two major divisions within the mathematical definition of measurement described above, those strictly employing empirical procedures directly to elements of the domain and those employing the measurement function. In the first class of problems, objects of the domain were directly compared on the basis of a given attribute without assigning a number to the attribute. These problems include the classical conservation problems in which one of two objects equivalent in some way is transformed to appear larger or smaller than the other. To conserve, a child must not respond on the basis of the immediate appearance of the objects but rather must recognize that the objects were equivalent in the earlier state and the relation between them did not change. All comparisons were visual and measurement functions were not introduced. For example, in studying the development of area concepts, Piaget asked children to compare two identical rectangles made up of six squares each and arranged in a two by three configuration. After a child agreed that the two rectangles were the same size, the squares in one of the rectangles were moved to create a different shaped region. The child was then asked to compare the size of this new region with that of the undistorted rectangle.

In the second class of problems, measurement functions were applied in which different units of measurement were used. In some problems children were given several different sizes of units and in others the units were such that fractional parts were required to cover the object being measured. In this class of problems the objects being compared were never visually comparable. Thereby, in order to accurately judge the correct relation measurement was necessary. Furthermore, children were required to perform the measurement operations so that they not only had to correctly apply the information from the measurement process, but also had to carry out the measurement manipulations. For example, in studying the development of area measurement functions, children were asked to compare different shaped figures by measuring with different units. In one set of problems children were given enough units to cover the figures, but the units were of different sizes and shapes. Some were squares, some were rectangles (two squares), and some were triangles (squares cut diagonally in half). In another set of problems children were given a limited number of square cards which they had to move by successive iteration from one part of the region being measured to the next. Some regions were shaped in such a way that it was impossible to cover them with the given units without intersecting the exterior of the region. Thus, it was necessary for the children to consider fractions of units.

Based on children's responses to these problems Piaget et al. (1960) concluded that the development of measurement and conservation is integrally related and that the same general pattern of development persists across all types of measurement operations. The earliest stages (Stages I and IIA) are characterized by a dependence on one dimensional *perceptual* judgments. Conservation is not present and transformations from prior stages are completely ignored. Children are unable to apply measurement processes in any meaningful manner; and quantities are compared on the basis of a single, immediate, dominant dimension. In Stage IIB children begin to make a number of correct judgments as long as distortions in quantities being compared are not too great. Correct judgments in Stage IIB are largely a result of trial and error. Children have a dim concept of conservation and some notion that greater quantities measure more units. In Stage IIIA children begin to conserve and measure using a common unit of measure. However, they fail to recognize the importance of a constant unit of measure and often count a fraction of a unit as a whole or equate two quantities that measure the same number of units with different size units of measure. In Stage IIIB children successfully conserve and measure. They recognize the importance of different units of measure and understand the inverse relationship between unit size and number of units. It is not until Stage IV, however, that children finally discover the mathematical relation between area and volume and their respective linear dimensions.

Studies by Lovell, Healey, and Rowland (1962); Lovell and Ogilvie (1961); and Lunzer (1960b)--which employed items similar to those used by Piaget et al. (1960)--generally supported their conclusions regarding the development of measurement concepts. On the other hand, whereas these studies implied that conservation is a prerequisite for measurement, Bearison (1969) used measurement operations to teach children to conserve. Nonconservers were provided with experiences in which they compared two quantities of liquid in terms of the number of identical beakers containing the two quantities. Bearison (1969) concluded that:

> *The effects of training facilitated the conservation of continuous quantity and transferred to the conservation of area, mass, quantity, number, and length. The explanations offered for conservation by the trained conservers were identical to those elicited from a group of "natural" conservers, and the effects of conservation were maintained over a 7-month period (p. 653).*

In another set of studies integrating counting and conservation concepts Carpenter (1971b) and Wohlwill and Lowe (1962) found that simply counting the elements in the conservation of discrete object problems does not substantially improve performance. However, Almy, Chittenden, & Miller (1966) and Greco, Grize, Papert, & Piaget (1960) found that "conservation of number" (invariance of the number assigned to a set of discontinuous elements under a reversible transformation) precedes the standard equivalence conservation, which involves invariance of the relation between equal quantities.

Whereas Piaget et al. (1960) considered both the empirical procedures applied directly to the domain and the application of the measurement function, two Soviet researchers, P. Ya. Gal'perin and L. S. Georgiev (1969), have concentrated their efforts on the application of the measurement function, especially the role of the unit in defining the function. They administered a series of measurement problems to a group of Soviet kindergartners in which the children were asked to measure and compare quantities of rice in various situations. Based on these studies, Gal'perin and Georgiev (1969) concluded that young children taught by traditional methods have a number of serious misconceptions regarding the measurement process because of a lack of a basic understanding of a unit of measure. They found young children to be indifferent to the size and fullness of a unit of measure and to have more faith in direct visual comparison of quantities than in measurement by a given unit.

In a replication of the Gal'perin and Georgiev investigation with American first graders, Carpenter (1971a) found responses similar to those in the Soviet study. However, based upon the results on four additional items and a different interpretation of the results of the Soviet items, the conclusion was made that young children are not indifferent to the size and fullness of units of measure; but just as in Piaget's conservation problems, they are only capable of making one-dimensional comparisons and therefore do not focus on both unit size and number of units at the same time. Furthermore, Carpenter (1971a) hypothesized that young children do not rely primarily on visual comparisons, as both Piaget and Gal'perin and Georgiev have concluded, but rather they respond on the basis of the last stimulus available, be it visual or numerical.

Carpenter's (1971a) investigation also raised questions regarding the role of equivalence and order relations in conservation and measurement problems. Measurement problems in which equal quantities were made to appear unequal by measuring them with different sized units of measure were significantly more difficult than similar items in which unequal quantities were made to appear equal. Similar results were found favoring inequality when the same unit was used to measure and compare two different quantities. These results, which suggest that with regard to certain aspects of the measurement process a stable concept of nonequivalence may precede a stable concept of equivalence, run counter to the above logical construction of these concepts in the definition of the measurement function.

In his basic works on number and measurement (Piaget 1952, Piaget et al. 1960), Piaget does not differentiate between items employing different relations between sets. He has attempted to assess the child's conception of number, length, weight, etc. of a single quantity and has used equivalent sets as an experimental convenience. Elkind (1967), Van Engen (1971), and Wohwill and Lowe (1962) have questioned Piaget's procedure of using what Elkind (1967) calls "conservation of equivalence" tasks to assess conservation of number, length, weight, etc. For example, Elkind (1967) hypothesized that "identity conservation" (invariance of a quantitative attribute --e.g., numerousness, weight, volume--under a reversible transformation) precedes equivalence conservation. This hypothesis has been supported in studies by Hooper (1969) and McMannis (1969), while a study by Northman and Gruen (1970) found no differences between the two types of conservation.

In a study directly testing the effect of equivalence and order relations on performance on conservation items, Zimiles (1966) found no significant difference in difficulty between conservation tasks using equivalent sets of discrete objects and conservation tasks using non-equivalent sets of discrete objects in which the direction of the non-equivalence appeared to be reversed after the transformation. However, there was evidence that a substantial amount of individual inconsistency of performance between items could be attributed to differences in equivalence and nonequivalence conditions.

Steffe and Johnson (1971) also found that items which contained equal numbers of items in the sets to be compared demanded different abilities than items that employed the same number of items in both sets. In several other studies both equivalence and nonequivalence items have been administered. Although these studies were not designed to test for differences between the two types of tasks, their results were examined to determine whether differences did in fact exist. Analysis of individual items in studies by Carey and Steffe (1968) and Harper and Steffe (1968) indicated no clear-cut differences in difficulty between equivalence and nonequivalence items. On the other hand, in a study of conservation of discontinuous quantity with children between 2 and 4 years old, Piaget (1968) found a significantly greater number of correct answers in non-equivalence situations. Beilin (1968) and Rothenberg (1969) also reported significantly more correct answers to problems in which the relations between sets were nonequivalence; however, their tasks were not traditional conservation problems, and experimental variables appeared to favor the nonequivalence situations.

From a slightly different perspective, the results of three studies in which the type of inference required of the children rather than the relation between the sets being compared was investigated (Beilin 1964, Carey and Steffe 1968, and Griffiths, Shantz, and Sigel 1967), indicate that problems that require judgements of equality are more difficult than problems that require judgments of inequality. In one favoring equivalence Uprichard (1970) found that treatments in which children learned to classify sets on the basis of equivalence were mastered more quickly than treatments in which children classified sets on the basis of "greater than" or "less than," and learning sequences that began with equivalence were more effective than sequences that began with either "greater than" or "less than."

Several factors may explain this rather mixed collection of results regarding the role of equivalence and order relations in conservation and measurement problems. First, certain of the nonequivalence problems may not have required true conservation judgments. For example, if unequal quantities are made to appear equal by measuring them with different size units so that they measure the same number of units, it is still possible to accurately compare the quantities on the basis of unit size with no reference to the previous state. Second, although there does not appear to be any difference in difficulty between equivalence and nonequivalence problems with discrete objects, there is some evidence that suggests that equivalence-nonequivalence differences may exist for problems comparing continuous quantities where precise judgments of equality are more difficult than judgments of inequality. Fleishmann, Gilmore, and Ginsburg (1966) and Smedslund (1966) found that a number of young children (as many as 20%) fail to maintain choices of equality even when no apparent conflict is introduced.

Purpose and Procedures

The major purposes of this study were (1) to assess the degree to which young children possess the logical structures to assimilate and apply information from measurement processes and (2) to identify some of the factors involved in the development of measurement and conservation. Specifically, the question as to whether conservation and measurement failures are primarily the result of a dependence on perceptual cues, the order of the cues or an interaction of the two was investigated. That is, an attempt was made to determine whether young children respond differently to visual and numerical cues in conservation and measurement problems or whether they simply respond to the last cue available to them.

Another purpose of the study was to determine the role of equivalence and order relations in children's performance on conservation and measurement problems. Three different combinations of order and equivalence relations were studied.

1. Equivalence: Equal quantities were transformed to appear unequal.

2. Nonequivalence I: Unequal quantities were transformed so that the dominant dimension in each quantity (height of the liquid in conservation problems--number in measurement problems) was equal.

3. Nonequivalence II: Unequal quantities were transformed so that the direction of the inequality appeared to be reversed.

For most Nonequivalence I problems the correct relation between quantities could be determined from the distracting cues by simply focusing on the appropriate dimension (for example by focusing on the size of the unit rather than the number of units). To determine whether any possible differences favoring Nonequivalence I were simply the result of this sort of pseudo conservation, differences between measurement problems in which it was not possible to visually distinguish the larger unit were assessed.

Whether recognizing that an increase in one dimension of a quantity may be compensated for by a decrease in another dimension (when holding the quantity constant) is important in young children's conservation judgments was also investigated. Piaget (1952) asserted that this recognition of compensating relationships is a significant factor in the development of conservation. By contrasting performance on measurement problems in which it was possible to visually distinguish this compensating relationship to problems in which it was not, information concerning the importance of this factor for young children's conservation judgments was obtained.

Finally, young children's understanding of the following basic measurement concepts was investigated.

1. Quantity A is equivalent to quantity B if and only if $\mu(A) = \mu(B)$, and quantity A is less than quantity B if and only if $\mu(A) < \mu(B)$.

2. In order to compare quantities on the basis of measurement, the same measurement function (the same unit) must be used to measure both quantities.

3. When equivalent quantities are measured with different units, an inverse relation exists between unit size and the number of units.

In order to conduct the investigation, the following items were administered to a group of 129 first and second graders.

1. Conservation of continuous quantity.

   Equivalence. The child was shown two identical glasses containing equal amounts of water and was asked to compare the amount of water in the two glasses. If he said that there was more water in one of the glasses, some water was poured from this glass into the other glass; and this process was repeated until the child agreed that there was the same amount of water in the two glasses. Then one of the glasses of water was poured into a taller, narrower glass, and the child was again asked to compare the amounts of water.

   Nonequivalence I. The child was shown two identical glasses containing unequal amounts of water and was asked to compare the amounts of water in the two glasses. Then the glass containing the smaller amount of water was poured into a taller, narrower glass such that the height of the water was the same as the height of water in the glass containing more water, and the child was again asked to compare the two amounts of water.

   Nonequivalence II. The child was shown two identical glasses containing unequal amounts of water and was asked to compare the amount of water in the two glasses. Then the glass containing the smaller amount of water was poured into a taller, narrower glass such that the height of the water was higher than the height in the glass containing more water, and the child was again asked to compare the two amounts of water.

2. Measurement with visibly different units.

   Equivalence. The child was shown two glasses containing equal amounts of water and was aked to compare the amounts of water in the two glasses. If he said that there was more water in one of the glasses, some water was poured from this glass into the other glass; and this process was repeated until the child agreed that there was the same amount of water in the two glasses. Then the water in each glass was measured into two opaque containers using visibly different units of measure so that one glass of water measured three units and the other measured five. Then the child was again asked to compare the two amounts of water.

Nonequivalence I. The child was shown two glasses containing unequal amounts of water and was asked to compare the amount of water in the two glasses. Then the water in each glass was measured into two opaque containers using visibly different units of measure such that both glasses measured three units. Then the child was again asked to compare the two amounts of water.

Nonequivalence II. The child was shown two glasses containing unequal amounts of water and was asked to compare the amount of water in the two glasses. Then the water in each glass was measured into two opaque containers using visibly different units of measure so that the greater quantity of water measured three units and the other measured four. Then the child was again asked to compare the two amounts of water.

3. Measurement with indistinguishable different units.

Equivalence. This task was the same task as the equivalence task in measurement with visibly different units, except the smaller unit appeared larger. One glass measured five units and the other measured four.

Nonequivalence I. This task was the same task as the nonequivalence I task in measurement with visibly different units, except the smaller unit appeared larger. Both glasses measured four units.

Nonequivalence II. This task was the same task as the nonequivalence II task in measurement with visibly different units, except the smaller unit appeared larger. The greater quantity of water measured six units and the other measured seven.

4. Measurement of unequal-appearing quantities with the same unit.

Equivalence. The child was asked to compare two equal quantities of water in two different-shaped containers, one tall and narrow and the other short and wide (i.e., the final state in the equivalence task of conservation of continuous quantity). Then the water in each glass was measured into two opaque containers using the same unit (each glass measured four units) and the child was asked to compare the two amounts of water.

Nonequivalence II. The child was asked to compare two unequal amounts of water in the two different-shaped containers (the final state in the nonequivalence II task of continuous quantity). Then the water in each container was measured into two opaque containers using the same unit (the glass that appeared to have more water measured four units and the other measured five), and the child was again asked to compare the two amounts of water.

5. Measurement with the same unit into apparent inequality.*

Equivalence. Using the same unit of measure, four units of water were measured into two different-shaped containers and the child was asked to compare the two quantities of water.

Nonequivalence II. Using the same unit of measure, five units of water were measured into a short, wide container and four units were measured into a tall, narrow container and the child was asked to compare the two quantities of water.

In order to keep the number of tasks administered to each child reasonable, items were split into two groups and each group was administered to a different set of children. Sixty-one children in Part A received all three conservation problems and both sets of problems in which quantities were measured with two different units. All three sets of problems were administered with each of the three relations. Sixty-eight children in Part B received all the measurement problems with Equivalence and Nonequivalence II relations.

Thus, the problems in Part A fit a 3 x 3 repeated measures design where the factors were Problem Type (continuous quantity conservation and the two measurement problems with different units) and Relations (Equivalence, Nonequivalence I, and Nonequivalence II). The problems in Part B fit a 2 x 4 repeated measures design where the factors were Problem Type (all four measurement problems) and Relations (Equivalence and Nonequivqlence II).

The hypotheses of interest tested in Part A are as follows.

H_1: There is no significant difference between performance on Equivalence and Nonequivalence II items for any of the problem types.

H_2: There is no significant difference between performance on Equivalence and Nonequivalence I measurement problems in which the larger unit of measure is not visually distinguishable.

H_3: There is no significant difference between performance on Equivalence and Nonequivalence I items for conservation problems or for measurement problems in which the larger unit is visually distinguishable.

H_4: There is no significant difference between performance on conservation problems and corresponding measurement problems.

H_5: There is no significant difference between performance on measurement problems in which it is possible to visually distinguish the larger unit and those in which it is not.

H_6: Neither mean performance nor any of the above contrasts are significantly affected by grade, sex, or the order in which the items were administered.

---

*These tasks are simply the tasks in (4) with the stimuli appearing in a different order.

Hypotheses H1, H5, and H6 were also tested in Part B. In addition, the following hypotheses were added:

H_7: There is no significant difference in performance between measurement problems in which correct visual cues are followed by distracting numerical cues and corresponding problems in which correct number cues are followed by distracting visual cues.

H_8: There is no significant difference in performance between measurement problems in which the correct measurement cues appear before distracting visual cues and those in which they appear after the distracting visual cues.

Subjects. This study was run over a nine-day period in the spring of 1971 in a predominantly rural community near Madison, Wisconsin, with a population of about 4,000. The subjects (*S*s) for the study were selected from three of the five first grade classes and two of the five second grade classes in one of the two elementary schools serving the community. The sample, which included all students in the five classes except three who were absent on the testing days, consisted of 75 first graders and 54 second graders. The age range of the first graders was 6 years, 5 months to 9 years, 8 months with mean age 7 years, 5 months; and the range of the second graders was 7 years, 7 months to 9 years, 5 months with mean age 8 years, 4 months.

Procedures. *S*s were randomly assigned to two groups, 61 *S*s to Part A and 68 to Part B. Each *S* within each group received the same basic set of problems; however, the order of the problems was randomized for each *S*.

All items were administered in a small room apart from the classroom by one experimenter (E), a stranger to the *S*s. The *S* sat at a table opposite the E. Procedures and protocols were kept as consistent as possible between items; however, certain procedures were randomly varied between *S*s in order to control for responses based on experimental variables.

Piaget (1968) and Siegel and Goldstein (1969) found that young children tend to respond to the last choice available to them in a conservation problem. Thus, if the E said, "Is there the same amount of water in the two cups or does one have more?" the *S* may respond that one has more because "more" was the last choice given to him. Therefore, some of the *S*s were asked, "Is there the same amount of water in the two cups or does one have more?" and the others asked, "Does one cup have more water in it or is there the same amount in each cup?". For each *S* the "same-more" order was the same for all problems.

For some *S*s the smaller quantity was always measured first in nonequivalence problems, and for others the larger quantity was always measured first. Both of these variations were randomly assigned to *S*s.

Problems were administered in two sittings. *S*s in Part A received five problems the first day and four several days later, and *S*s in Part B had four problems the first day and four the second. Although reasons for responses were solicited and recorded, answers were judged correct or incorrect without regard to the explanations given.

Analysis. Item totals, reasons for responses, and types of errors were recorded for each item. The following categories were used to classify reasons for correct responses:

1. Reversibility: If the quantities were transformed back to their former state, they would again appear in the correct relation (equal or unequal).

2. Statement of operation performed: The water was just poured into a different container and this did not change the relation between the quantities.

3. Addition--subtraction: Nothing was added or taken away.

4. Compensation, proportionality: The liquid was higher but the container was narrower. One measured more units but the units were smaller.

5. Sameness of quantity: It's the same water.

6. Reference to the previous state: They were the same before when the water was in identical glasses.

7. No reason, unclassifiable: No reason was given or an incomprehensible reason was given.

Incorrect responses were sorted into two broad categories.

1. Dominant dimension: *S*s incorrectly chose (a) the taller container of water or (b) the quantity that measured the greater number of units.

2. Secondary dimension: *S*s incorrectly chose (a) the wider container or (b) the quantity measured with the larger unit.

Hypotheses were tested using a multivariate analysis of variance program of J.D. Finn (1967). In this program, analysis is conducted using single degrees of freedom-planned contrasts, and freedom is allowed to specify the contrasts of interest. This flexibility especially suited the purpose of this study in which specific contrasts, rather than overall differences between factors, were of interest.

The Finn program yields standard errors for each of the variables and also estimates the magnitude of the effects for the specific contrasts and their standard errors. Thus, 95% confidence intervals have been plotted for each of the problems and for each of the significant contrasts.

Based on the results of previous research it was predicted that there would be no significant difference between performance on Equivalence and corresponding Nonequivalence II problems. However, Nonequivalence I problems were expected to be easier than problems employing the other two relations except in the set of measurement problems in which the larger unit was not visually distinguishable. Since the Nonequivalence I relation was expected to operate differently than the other two relations, contrasts between problems involving the Nonequivalence I relation were conducted independently of contrasts between problems involving the other two relations.

In both Part A and Part B, four MANOVAs were employed. The first contained all contrasts that were predicted to have no significant effect, Equivalence--Nonequivalence II contrasts, and all contrasts between measurement problems in which the larger unit was not visually distinguishable. The second MANOVA contained all contrasts that were expected to be significant and all contrasts for which there was insufficient prior evidence to make a prediction. Thus, the second MANOVA contained contrasts between problem types and contrasts between Nonequivalence I and the other two relations. The third and fourth MANOVAs tested for effects due to grade, sex, and order in which the items were administered. What this partitioning effectively did was to hypothesize a model, to test the goodness of fit of this model (the first MANOVA), to test whether the parameters of the model are nonzero (the second MANOVA), and to test whether the model or the parameters of the model are significantly influenced by grade, sex, or the order of administration of the items (the third and fourth MANOVAs).

Testing for the effect of order presented certain problems. Since the order of items was randomized, every *S* received a different order of items, eliminating the feasibility of partitioning into each distinct order. Therefore, the effect of the order of the items was determined by a procedure proposed by Zimiles (1966). He found that the first item administered often significantly influenced performance on all subsequent items. *S*s administered easier first items performed better on all subsequent items than *S*s administered a more difficult first item. No differences were found, however, due to variations in the second item administered. Thus, *S*s were partitioned into order groups based on the first item they received.

Results

Part A. The results of individual items in Part A, the reasons given for responses, and the types of errors are summarized in Table 1. The means for individual items surrounded by 95% confidence intervals have been plotted in Figure 1. Since the individual items are scored on a 0-1 basis, the mean can be interpreted as representing the fraction of *S*s correctly responding to the item. Similarly the confidence intervals can be interpreted in terms of percents. For example, there is a 95% probability that between 27% and 56% of the population would respond correctly to the Equivalence conservation item.

There was very little diversity in the reasons given for correct responses. Practically all the *S*s either referred to the previous state of the quantities or noted the compensating relationship between unit size and the number of units or between height and width. Comparisons between reasons given by *S*s who were successful on the items in which it was possible to distinguish the compensating relationship between unit size and number of units but were unsuccessful on problems in which it was not are enlightening. Seven of the eight *S*s who either (1) correctly answered at least two of the measurement problems in which the larger unit was distinguishable but none of the problems in which it was not or (2) correctly answered all three of the problems in which the larger unit was distinguishable and at most one of the problems in which it was not, gave compensation as the reason for at least one of their correct responses.

Figure 1. 95% Confidence Intervals for Items in Part A

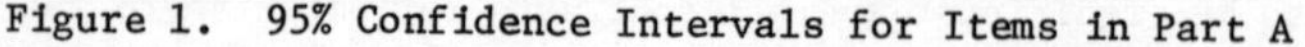

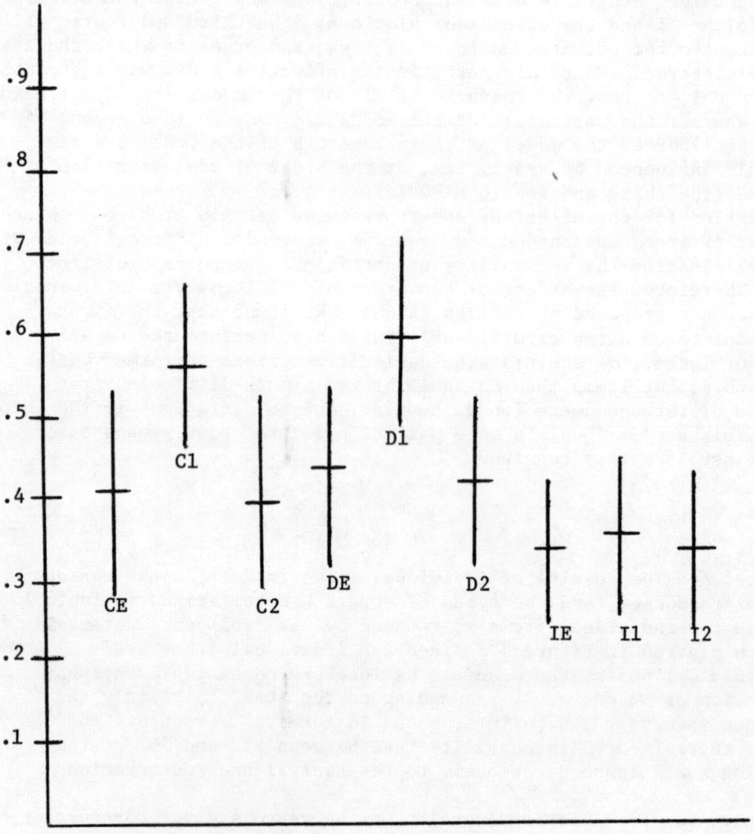

C = Conservation of continuous quantity
D = Measurement with visibly different units
I = Measurement with indistinguishably different units
E = Equivalence
1 = Nonequivalence I
2 = Nonequivalence II

The tests of the hypotheses are summarized in Table 2 and Table 3.

Table 2
MANOVA--Relation Contrasts foı Part A

Source	df	MS	F	P
Multivariate	4,24		.0769	.9887
H1a: CE = C2	1	.0164	.0830	.7755
H1b: DE = D2	1	.0164	.1021	.7518
H1c: IE = I2	1	.0164	.0450	.8336
H2: IE = I1	1	.0164	.0984	.7563

Degrees of freedom for error = 27
C = Conservation
D = Measurement with visibly different units
I = Measurement with indistinguishably different units
E = Equivalence
1 = Nonequivalence I
2 = Nonequivalence II

Table 3
MANOVA--Problem-Type and Equivalence--Nonequivalence I Contrasts

Source	df	MS	F	P
Multivariate	5,23		30.5264	.0001
I = 0	1	6.7776	67.1332	.0001
H5: D = I	1	.4376	3.6255	.0677
H4a: DE + D2 = CE + C2	1	.0164	.1180	.7339
H4b: D1 = C1	1	.0164	.0608	.8072
H3: DE + CE = D1 + D2	1	1.8074	11.6189	.0021

Degrees of freedom for error = 27
C = Conservation
D = Measurement with visibly different units
I = Measurement with indistinguishably different units
E = Equivalence
1 = Nonequivalence I
2 = Nonequivalence II

These results indicate that there are no significant differences between Equivalence and Nonequivalence II relations for any of the problems tested. There is a significant difference between Nonequivalence I and the other two relations except in the case of the measurement problems in which the larger unit is not visually identifiable. No significant differences were found between the conservation and measurement problems or between the two types of measurement problems.

These results are summarized in the model in Table 4. The parameters of the model are all positive and significant except for θ. θ was included in the model because (1) it approaches significance and (2) this effect was significant in Part B (see below). Ninety-five percent confidence intervals for each of the parameters have been plotted in Figure 2.

Figure 2. Confidence Intervals for Parameters of the Model in Part A

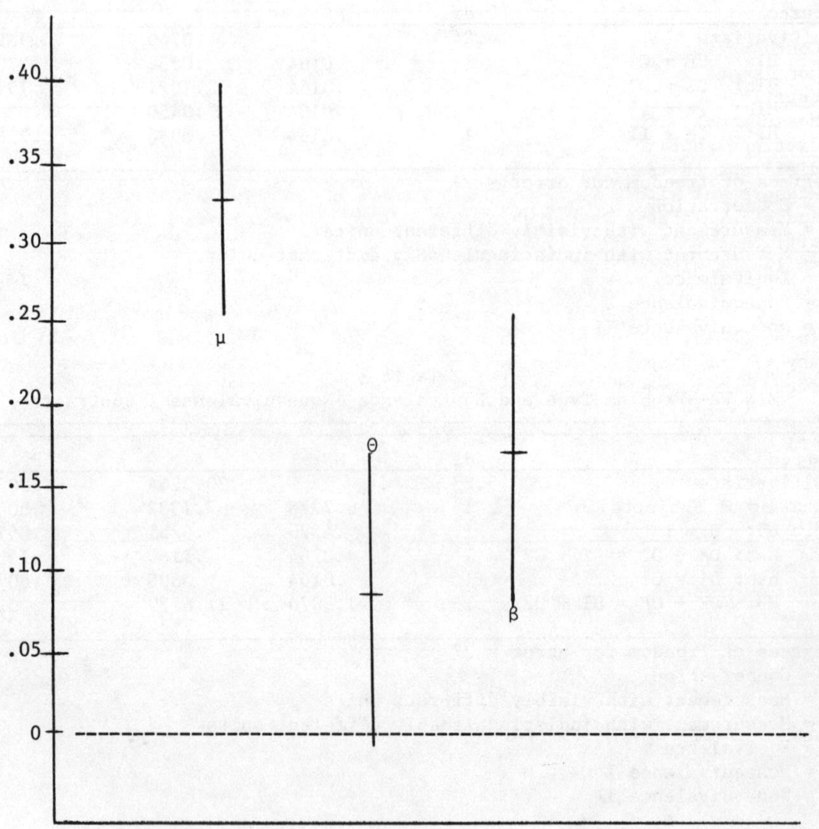

Table 4
Item Means for Problems In Part A

Problem type	Relation		
	Equivalence	Nonequiv. I	Nonequiv. II
Conservation continuous quantity	$\mu + \theta$*	$\mu + \theta$*$+ \beta$	$\mu + \theta$*
Measurement with distinguishably different units	$\mu + \theta$	$\mu + \theta$*$+ \beta$	$\mu + \theta$*
Measurement with indistinguishably different units	μ	μ	μ

*θ is not significant in Part A.

Significant differences between grades were found for overall means ($p = .0001$), but no significant effect due to grade level was found for any of the hypotheses tested ($p > .42$). No significant differences were found due to sex or order in which the items were administered ($p > .16$).

Part B. The results of individual items in Part B, the reasons given for responses, and the types of errors are summarized in Table 5.

Table 5
Number of Subjects in the Major Response Categories in Part B

Item	DE	D2	IE	I2	ME	M2	VE	V2
Total Correct	22	26	11	13	47	48	64	58
Reason for correct response								
Reversibility	0	0	0	0	0	0	0	0
Statement of operation performed	0	0	0	0	0	0	0	0
Addition-Subtraction	0	0	0	0	0	0	0	0
Compensation, proportionality	5	10	0	0	0	0	0	0
Sameness of quantity	0	0	1	0	0	0	0	0
Reference to previous state	14	11	6	8	45	46	59	55
No reason given or unclassifiable reason given	3	5	4	5	2	2	5	3
Total incorrect	46	42	57	55	21	20	4	10
Type of error								
Taller container or greater number of units	46	40	57	53	21	17	4	7
Wider container or larger unit	0	2	0	2	0	3	0	3

D = Measurement with visibly different units
I = Measurement with indistinguishably different units
M = Measurement with the same unit into apparent inequality
V = Measurement of unequal-appearing quantities into the same unit
E = Equivalence
2 = Nonequivalence II

and the means for individual items surrounded by 95% confidence intervals have been plotted in Figure 3.

Figure 3. Confidence Intervals for Items in Part B

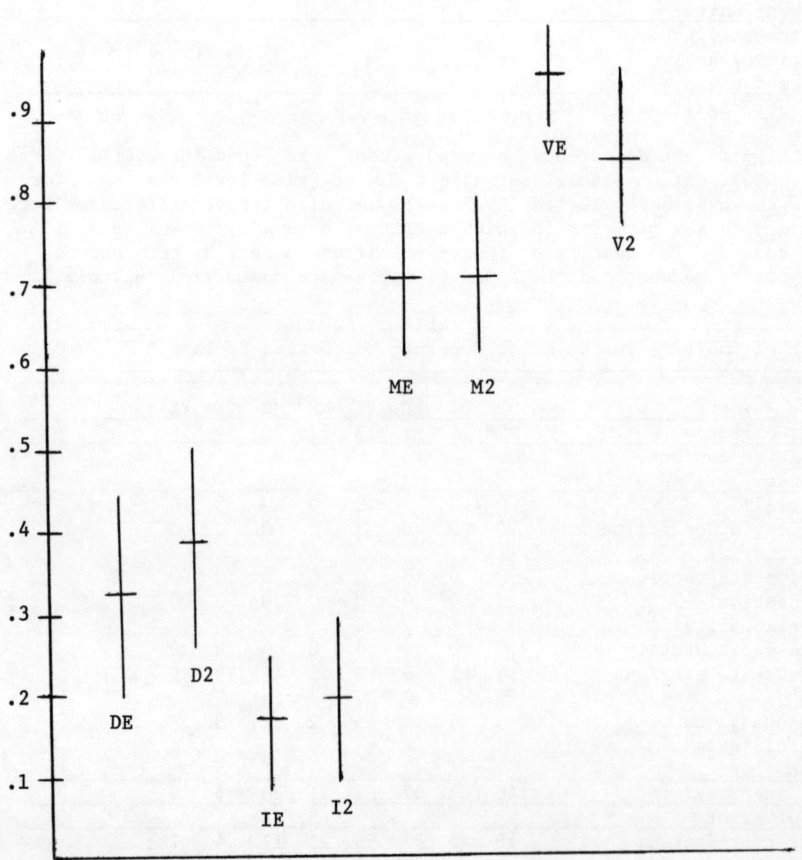

D = Measurement with visibly different units
I = Measurement with indistinguishably different units
M = Measurement with the same unit into apparent inequality
V = Measurement of unequal-appearing quantities with the same unit
E = Equivalence
2 = Nonequivalence II

As in Part A, virtually all of the reasons for correct responses fall into two categories; and except for the problems in which quantities were measured with distinguishably different units, virtually all the correct responses were based on reference to the previous state. Two of the five *S*s who correctly answered both of the problems in which the larger unit was distinguishable but neither of the problems in which it was not gave compensation as the reason for their response.

Only one *S* missed every item. Another *S* completely ignored the number cues, even though he successfully counted the number of units; consequently, he missed all the problems in which quantities were measured with the same unit but answered correctly the items in which quantities were measured with different units. A third *S* who was in the "more-same" protocol group responded "same" to every item. On the measurement problem with indistinguishably different units, only two of the *S*s were able to use the information from the measurement operation to correctly identify the larger unit. The rest were unable to apply the inverse relationship between unit size and number of units to this problem and simply responded incorrectly on the basis of the unit that looked larger. Between 85% and 89% of the *S*s gave the same response to corresponding Equivalence and Nonequivalence II problems.

The analysis summarized in Table 6 indicates that there is no significant difference between Equivalence and Nonequivalence II relations.

Table 6
MANOVA--Relation Contrasts for Part B

Source	df	MS	F	P
Multivariate	3,37		1.6369	.1970
IE = I2	1	.0000	.0000	1.0000
DE = D2	1	.2353	1.9335	.1721
ME = M2	1	.0000	.0000	1.0000
VE = V2	1	.5294	4.6109	.0379

Degrees of freedom for error = 40
D = Measurement with visibly different units
I = Measurement with indistinguishably different units
M = Measurement with the same unit into apparent inequality
V = Measurement of unequal-appearing quantities with the same unit
E = Equivalence
2 = Nonequivalence II

Consideration of the univariate analysis indicates that the contrast between problems in which unequal-appearing quantities are measured with the same unit approaches significance at the .01 level adopted in this study and would be significant if a .05 level had been adopted. None of the other contrasts even approach significance. The analysis in Table 7 indicates that there is a significant difference between each of the four types of measurement problems in Part B.

These results are summarized in the model in Table 8. The parameters of the model are all positive and significant. Ninety-five per cent confidence intervals for each of the parameters have been plotted in Figure 4.

Figure 4. Confidence Intervals for Parameters in Part B

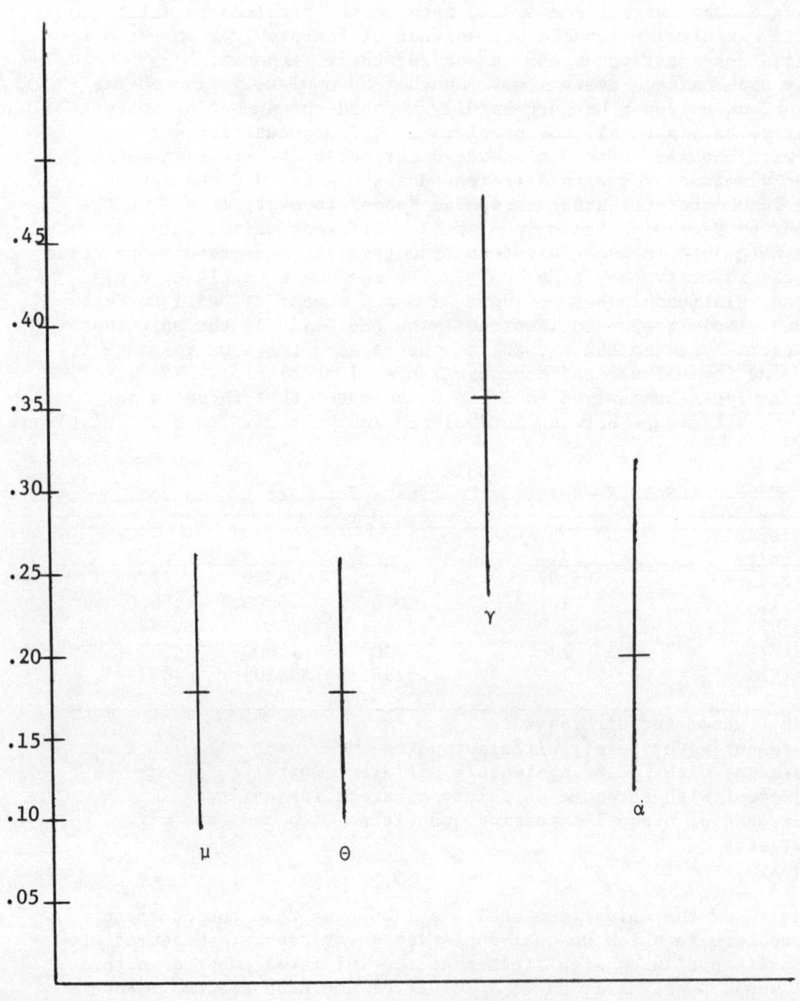

Table 7
MANOVA--Problem-Type Contrasts for Part B

Source	df	MS	F	P
Multivariate	3,38		70.8403	.0001
H5: D = E	1	2.1176	20.3702	.0001
H6: D = M	1	8.4706	33.6859	.0001
H7: M = V	1	2.4853	19.5404	.0001

Degrees of freedom for error = 40
D = Measurement with visibly different units
I = Measurement with indistinguishably different units
M = Measurement with the same unit into apparent inequality
V = Measurement of unequal-appearing quantities with the same unit

Table 8
Means for Items in Part B

	Relation	
Problem Type	Equivalence	Nonequiv. II
Measurement with distinguishably different units	$\mu + \theta$	$\mu + \theta$
Measurement with indistinguishably different units	μ	μ
Measurement into different-shaped containers	$\mu + \theta + \gamma$	$\mu + \theta + \gamma$
Measurement from different-shaped containers	$\mu + \theta + \gamma + \alpha$	$\mu + \theta + \gamma + \alpha$

No significant differences were found due to grade, sex, or the order in which the items were administered. Sex and order effects approached significance ($p = .02$) for the contrast between the two measurement problems in which a single unit was used, but did not even approach significance for any of the other contrasts ($p > .13$).

A and B comparisons. Four items were given in both parts of the study. The 95% confidence intervals for corresponding items do intersect (Figure 5); however, comparison of corresponding item means indicates that the fact that differences between measurement problems using visibly different units and those using indistinguishably different units are significant in Part B but fail to reach significance in Part A can be attributed entirely to between-study differences in performance on the problems employing indistinguishably different units.

Figure 5. Confidence Intervals for Items Appearing in Both Parts A and B

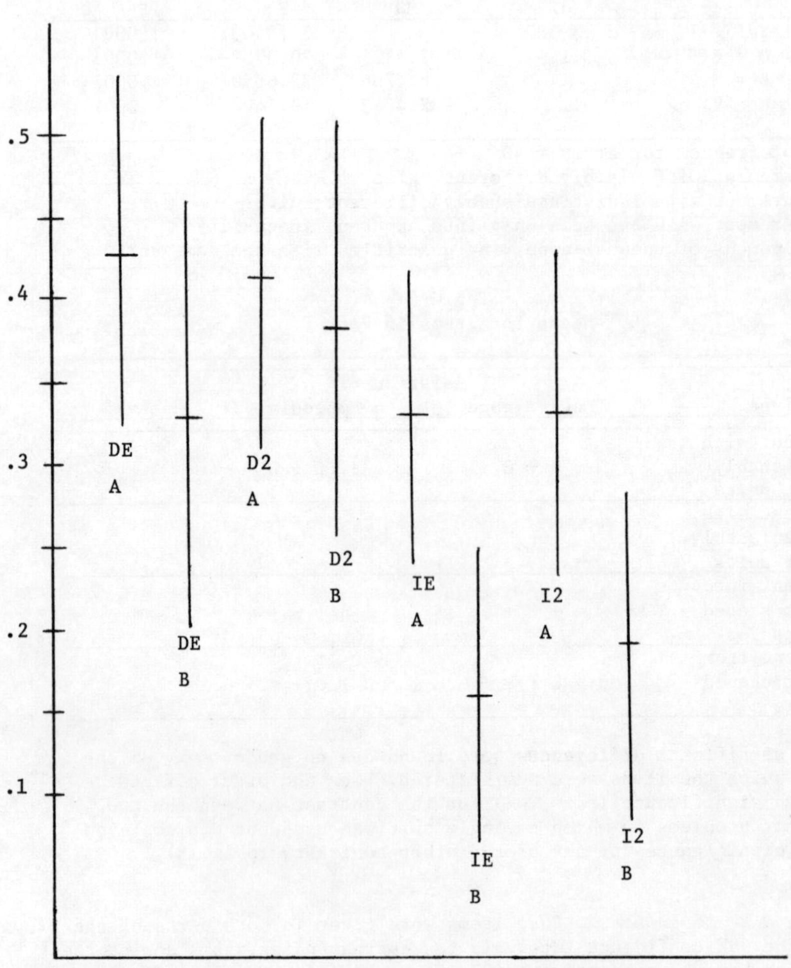

D = Measurement with visibly different units
I = Measurement with indistinguishably different units
E = Equivalence
2 = Nonequivalence II

Analysis of variance for contrasts between conservation of continuous quantity and measurement problems in which quantities were measured with the same unit into apparent inequality (i.e., the final state of the conservation problems) is summarized in Table 9, indicating significant differences favoring the measurement problems. These results should be interpreted somewhat cautiously in that the two types of problems were administered in different sets of problems in the series.

Table 9
ANOVA--Conservation of Continuous-Quantity Measurement into Apparent Inequality Contrast

Source	df	MS	F
Between	1	11	14.6**
Within Cells	127	.76	

$^{**}p < .01$

The results in Figure 5, however, indicate that for the four problems that were administered in both parts, performance was generally higher in the part containing the conservation problems; so the danger of interaction with other problems favoring the measurement problems is probably not too great.

Furthermore, in Part A no significant difference was found between conservation problems and corresponding problems in which quantities are measured with different units. In Part B problems in which quantities are measured with the same unit were found to be significantly easier than corresponding problems in which two units are employed. The combination of these results confirms that problems in which quantities are measured with the same unit are easier than corresponding conservation problems.

Summary and Conclusions

It appears that it is not simply the perceptual properties of the stimuli that produce errors in conservation problems. There is no significant difference in difficulty between conservation problems and corresponding measurement problems in which the distracting cues are numerical. The position of Piaget (1952, 1960), Bruner, Olver, and Greenfield (1966) and others that young children are highly dependent on perceptual properties of events and that conservation problems occur because the immediate perceptual properties of the conservation problems override the logical properties that imply conservation, has been based on tasks in which distracting visual cues always appeared last. The results of the current investigation, however, demonstrate that misleading numerical cues produce the same errors as misleading visual cues.

The failure of young children to respond primarily on the basis of visual cues is even more striking in the contrast between conservation problems and the problems in which quantities are measured into apparent inequality and the contrast between the problems in which quantities are measured with distinguishably different units and the problems in which quantities are measured into apparent inequality. The problems measuring quantities into apparent inequality, in which correct measurement cues are followed by misleading perceptual cues, are significantly easier than either corresponding conservation problems, in which both sets of cues are visual, or corresponding problems in which quantities are measured with different units, where correct visual cues are followed by incorrect numerical cues.

These results, which could be interpreted to imply that numerical modes dominate visual modes, should be regarded with some caution. Zimiles (1963) has suggested that conservation failures may result from *S*s basing their judgments on the E's manipulations of the quantities being compared. For example, if two rows of blocks which the *S* has judged equivalent when they are arranged in one-to-one correspondence are spread out, the *S* says that the longer row has more because the act of spreading the blocks out implies to him that the length of the rows is the dimension he is being asked to compare.

In the current investigation, the experimental procedures emphasize the measurement cues, which means that the correct choice is emphasized in the problems employing a single unit of measure but the incorrect choice is emphasized in the problems employing different units of measure and the conservation problems.

Thus, it appears that the most significant factor in determining which cues young children attend to is the order in which the cues appear. Problems in which correct cues appear last are significantly easier than corresponding problems in which correct cues are followed by misleading cues. As noted above, however, the order of the cues was not the only factor that was found to affect responses.

In general, there does not appear to be any significant difference between conservation and measurement problems employing Equivalence relations and corresponding problems employing Nonequivalence II relations. Nonequivalence I problems are significantly easier than corresponding problems employing Equivalence or Nonequivalence II relations except in problems in which it is not possible to identify the larger unit. These results imply that the relation between quantities being compared does not affect performance, and the Nonequivalence I problems are easier simply because they do not require genuine conservation, since accurate comparisons can be made from the final states of the quantities.

Measurement operations have some meaning for the majority of students in the first and second grades. By the end of the first grade, virtually all students recognize that quantities are equal if they measure the same number of units and quantity A is greater than quantity B if A measures more units than B. Only 3 of the 129 *S*s tested did not respond to any questions on the basis of measurement cues; and only 2 of the 3 definitely ignored the measurement cues. The other *S* simply responded "same" to all problems.

This does not mean, however, that first- and second-grade students have totally correct measurement concepts or are able to accurately apply measurement processes. As few as 25% of the *S*s tested completely understood the importance of using a single measurement function, and only 6% were able to discover the relation between measurement functions from the results of the measurement operations. Only 70% of the *S*s were able to use measurement results if they were followed by conflicting visual cues. Only 59% of the *S*s demonstrated any knowledge that variations in unit size affected measurement results, and as few as 40% of the *S*s were able to apply this knowledge to problems in which quantities were measured with different units. This figure dropped to 25% when the larger unit was not visually distinguishable, and only 6% of the *S*s were able to use the results of measurement operations to determine the larger unit when it was not visually apparent.

The conclusion that by the end of first grade virtually all children, even those in Stages I and IIA, have some concept of measurement appears to contradict Piaget's (1960) conclusions that measurement concepts do not begin to appear until Stage IIB. This apparent conflict is due to the fact that Piaget employed less structured measurement tasks. In order to have any measurement cues to respond to, *S*s had to measure themselves. In the current investigation the measurement cues were forced upon the *S*s; therefore, even *S*s in the earliest stages had number cues to guide or distract their reponses.

The results of the two sections of this study with respect to the importance of recognizing the compensating relation between dimensions are ambiguous. Significant differences between the problems in which it is possible to distinguish the larger unit and those in which it is not were found in Part B but not in Part A. In Part A, however, about 7% of the *S*s tested did find the problems in which the larger unit was distinguishable easier than the problems in which it was not, and the pooled results indicate there exist significant differences. Consideration of this fact and examination of the confidence intervals for the parameter Θ indicate that probably at least 10% of the population sampled require that the distracting cues contain compensating relations in order to conserve. These conclusions should be regarded with some caution, however, since the discrepancy between the results in Parts A and B indicates that there may be some interaction between tasks administered to the same *S* that affects the parameter Θ.

In general there were no significant differences due to sex, order of items, or protocol variations. The fact that only one *S* in the entire investigation consistently responded either "more" or "less" to all problems indicates that by the end of the first grade few children still respond to conservation problems on the basis of the last alternative offered to them.

Thus, of the factors under consideration in this study it appears that centering on a single dominant dimension is the major reason for most conservation and measurement failures and the development of conservation and measurement concepts can be described in terms of increasing ability to decenter.

In the earliest stage children respond on the basis of a single immediate, dominant dimension. The dimension may be either visual or numerical, depending on the problem. In the next stage children are capable of changing dimensions, but in each problem they still focus on a single dimension. In this stage some children are capable of pseudo conservation and correctly solve Nonequivalence I tasks but not Equivalence or Nonequivalence II tasks. Children in this stage occasionally conserve by focusing on the earlier state but are incapable of simultaneously considering the immediate state of the quantity and the state prior to the transformation and deciding which set of cues provide a legitimate basis for comparison. They generally explain their responses by referring to the prior state and seem to purposely ignore the current state of the quantity. Children around this stage probably show the most gains in conservation training research, but the gains may be in a very narrow sense. It seems likely that most training simply serves to redirect the object of the child's centering without providing him with the flexibility of thought that is necessary for progression to later stages. Thus the child may learn to conserve by simply centering on a different aspect of the problem but still lack the flexibility of thought that conservation implies.

Finally, children gain the flexibility to consider several conditions of a quantity simultaneously and can choose the condition that provides a rational basis for comparison; however, it is not until a later stage that they are able to consider the consequences of the comparisons between different states and use the information from both conditions to discover the correct relation between the sizes of different units based on the number of units two comparable quantities measure.

KENNETH LOVELL

Summary and Implications

The research papers that have been presented represent a concerted effort to investigate the thinking of children in the age range 4 to 8 years. Five of the six papers have dealt with aspects of the training and acquisition of logical structures and the sixth with the acquisition of structures involved in conservation and measurement. Accordingly, we must begin by briefly commenting on what is known of the effects of training. Beilin (1971) has given an extensive review of the broad position on the effects of training as it was at the end of 1970, and the position at the time of writing this chapter has not materially changed. If the training of conservation or of logical operations (classification and relational skills) is considered, training does often appear to effect an improvement in performance. At least, the training appeared to work in the hands of its proponents. The Geneva workers would probably concur, although they would stress that training has no effect if some vestige of operativity is not already present (Inhelder and Sinclair, 1969). For both those who tend to give credence to the Piagetian conceptual framework and for those who do not, the problem is (as Beilin points out) to define what is meant by true operativity. If strong criteria are insisted on it is difficult to refute the Piagetian position. But if weaker criteria are used it is easier to disconfirm it. However, it would not be profitable to pursue this particular point here, vital as it may be. Rather the results of the experiments in terms of the effect of training on performance on the posttests are considered.

Even if the issue of operativity is not pursued, other issues that could influence interpretations of the experiments remain. First, it is not possible for the reader to know much about the quality of the training in a particular study. While it is true the standard procedures can be laid down, one cannot be sure (unless present) of the general atmosphere and quality of the interaction between experimenter and pupils. Second, there is the question of the size of the groups involved in the training programmes. The writer is well aware of the difficulties in selecting pupils and of the work involved. But it must be pointed out that it is possible for fluctuation to be present in data obtained from small groups. My experience leads me to suggest that when small groups are themselves randomly selected from small numbers of children, it is possible for the small groups to be different with respect to some relevant variables. In such cases, even when results are obtained at some acceptable level of statistical significance, they cannot necessarily be trusted too far. In the five papers involving training, summary information is contained in Table 1. The results of these studies, then, can be generalized only to

Table 1
Number of Children in the Samples of the Training Studies

Paper	Numbers of Children	Children Were:
Steffe and Carey	20 four-year-olds 34 five-year-olds	
Owens	23 Kindergarteners 24 First Graders	Randomly assigned to full and partial treatments
Johnson, M. L.	39 First Graders 42 Second Graders	Selected from two schools
Lesh	20, selected from a larger group used in pilot study	Randomly assigned to experimental and control groups
Johnson, D. C.	115 children of which 35 were alternates	Randomly selected from two age levels and two intelligence levels and then randomly assigned to experimental and control groups with ten per cell.

similar samples. While it is possible that the groups were different with respect to some relevant variables, there is no way that this can be ascertained. A third issue is one that was raised by Smedslund (1964). He argues that in every concrete reasoning task there should be clear distinction made between *percept, goal object and inference pattern.* The first resides in the stimulus situation as apprehended by the subject; the goal object is what the child is told to attain, such as quantity or length; while inference pattern is formed by the set of premises and conclusion, e.g., transitivity or conservation. He argues that each factor can only be studied with the other two held constant -- this being a necessary condition for the discovery of exact relations. For his study, 160 children were involved ranging in age from 4-3 to 11-4 and evenly distributed over age and sex. The tasks[1] were administered individually. The results strongly point to the fact that when the generality of concrete reasoning is studied over variations in percepts, goal objects, and inference patterns, concrete reasoning has a very limited generality over the period of

[1]These included class inclusion, multiplication of classes, reversal of spatial order, conservation of discontinuous quantity, multiplications of relations, transitivity of length, conservation of length, addition and subtractions of one unit, transitivity of discontinuous quantity.

its acquisition. Indeed, in such circumstances, it appeared to be acquired in one restricted situation at a time, and only the grosser regularities -- such as differences in average item difficulty -- were observed. However, when the interactions between different inference patterns were studied, with goal objects and percepts held constant, the position was different. Such a study is, of course, of great importance, since concrete reasoning is assumed to be reflected in certain types of inference patterns. In Smedslund's investigation, the comparison between conservation and transitivity of length approached methodological perfection in the sense that only inference patterns varied, and goal objects and percepts were virtually constant. In this situation, only one child passed the test of transitivity and failed the test of conservation. Smedslund assumed that this was a case of diagnostic error and that conservation of length preceded transitivity of length.

Another issue (although not unrelated to the third) involves the developmental links between partial structures. Inhelder (1972) quotes earlier work of the Genevans into the question of whether elementary measurement of length can be helped by the application of numerical operations. Their conclusion was that interactions between numerical and ordinal ways of dealing with the problem of either judging or constructing lengths tend to produce conflict, and it was this which led to the final resolution of the measurement task, since conflict was overcome only by the child's own efforts to find "compensatory and coordinating actions." They argued that psychologically speaking, conflicts give rise to the recombination of existing partial structures in order to reestablish the equilibrium which has been destroyed, and hence, conflicts give rise to new constructions. Inhelder argues from biology, where new combinations can only take place inside what are called *reaction norms,* that new combinations in cognitive development can only occur within narrow zones of assimilating capacities. The structural levels of thought, while being at the very origin of the generation of new combinations, at the same time impose limits on the new constructions that can be produced.

Closely linked with the contents of the last paragraph is the fact that in scholastically backward, and particularly in school-educable retarded children, the attainments of concrete operational thought are extremely erratic from situation to situation (Lovell, 1966b). Both in everyday life and school situations, it would appear that their experiences bring far fewer conflicts, and/or they have very narrow zones of assimilating capacities. It is thus somewhat trite to say that given training experiences may not be assimilable to children of limited ability. There may well be, of course, something of a "chicken-egg" problem here. However, Owens quotes the study of Skypek who found the developmental pattern of cardinal number conservation was likewise erratic among pupils from lower socio economic- status homes.

These, then, are some of the issues which must be borne in mind when considering the results of the experimental studies and their educational implications.

The Research Results and the Educational Implications

The paper by Steffe and Carey is discussed first. It should be remembered that the measured intelligence of the children was normally distributed in both age groups (although both means were well above the average of 100), and the distribution of social classes to which the children belonged was also a normal one. Even on the first application of the Length Comparison Test, many children in both age groups could establish relations between two curves, especially in the case of "longer than." The remaining results are summarized in Table 2.

Table 2
Summary of Results of the Study by Steffe and Carey

Training	Results on Posttests
(Involving the interplay of language and action.)	
Instructional Sequence I.	A significant improvement in the number of correct responses, in comparing the lengths of two curves, especially in the case of the relations "shorter than" and "same length as."
Instructional Sequences II and III.	1. Little improvement in the number of correct responses in the comparison of lengths of two curves, since children came to the first application of the test fairly well able to discriminate among the relations. 2. A significant improvement in performance in respect of the Length Conservation Test: Level I. The percent of children categorized at Level I increased from 12 to 57. 3. The percent of children categorized at both Levels I and II of the Length Conservation Test increased from 8 to 37 -- a statistically significant increase. 4. A significant improvement in the ability of the age groups to use both reflexive and nonreflexive properties. In the posttest some 41 percent were able to use the reflexive property and 30 percent both properties. 5. No four-year-olds were able to use the transitive property either before or after the instructional sequences, but the percent of five-year-olds able to use the transitive property increased from 16 to 31.

The variables IQ, Verbal Maturity, Age, and Social Class had no significant effect on the posttest scores in the case of the Length Comparison Test, the Length Comparison Application Test, Length Conservation Test Levels I and II, and the test of Reflexive and Non-Reflexive properties. This argues a case that the appropriate instructional activities may profitably be undertaken with similar populations of four- and five-year-olds. In our present state of knowledge we cannot specify, in advance, which children will benefit from such instruction and which will not, but the results clearly suggest that some will. In the case of the Transitivity Test, those five-year-olds who could use the transitive property had slightly higher scores in IQ and on the Verbal Maturity Test, but there is no case at all for attempting any instruction using similar populations with a view to improving the use of the transitive property before five years of age, and even at that age results are likely to be limited. The Conservation of Length Test Level II involves a different ability, and is more difficult than Level I. This is clearly in line with Smedslund's argument. Here, goal object and inference pattern are invariant, but percept changes. Again on the second administration of the test of reflexive and nonreflexive properties only 30 percent met the criterion, and of these only one child met the criterion on the Transitivity Test, although there were nine others who did meet the latter criterion. From this it may be deduced that the use of reflexive and nonreflexive properties, as measured, is neither a necessary nor a sufficient condition for the ability to use the transitive property of length relations. However, there are unavoidable changes between these tasks in percepts, and inference patterns. Consequently, the necessary change in percepts may have influenced the relations between the tasks, although this is not certain.

The paper by Douglas T. Owens is concerned with five- and six-year-old Negro children who were disadvantaged in the sense that they came from low-income families. No measures of IQ were given. A rather small number of children were subdivided into a Partial Treatment and Full Treatment group, with the former group receiving Instructional Units I and II, and the latter Instructional Units I, II, III, and IV. Unit III was designed to develop the ability of children to maintain relations between sets when the physical matching of objects was destroyed, while Unit IV was to help the children use the transitive property of matching relations. Transfer was inferred from a significant difference in favor of the full treatment group in performance on some property for which no instruction was given, provided that there was a significant change in the same direction on a related property for which instruction was given. On the posttest, the scores on the Transitivity of Matching Relations test improved significantly and scores on the test of the asymmetric property of matching relations improved significantly ($p < .01$). It very much looks as if the Instructional Units III and IV improved the performance of children on tasks which were similar to the activities involved in the treatment, but that there was no transfer to the Transitivity Problem, nor to the Transitivity of Length Relations Test. Again Unit III did not result in any improvement in the conservation ability of the Full Treatment Group. On the other hand, age was a factor influencing performance on all matching relations tests other than transitivity. But it had no effect on the abilities of children to use length relational properties.

We should not be too surprised that more children attained conservation of length relations than conservation of matching relations, and more children attained transitivity of length relations than transitivity of matching relations. In each case we have inference patterns constant but different goal objects and percepts. The source of the difference in difficulty between items on length and items on matching lies either in the nature of the goal object, or differences in percepts. While in Smedlund's study there was a tendency for conservation and transitivity of quantity to precede, respectively, conservation and transitivity of length, there were exceptions. With this rather small sample of somewhat limited background experience, these particular results can be accepted without too much surprise. Again, studies have generally shown that most children use conservation of a particular relational category before they use the transitive property for that category. In this study, however, about one-half of those using the transitive property in a particular category failed to conserve that category. As Owens suggests, these results may be to some extent interpreted in terms of the treatment effect. But we must not forget the erratic performance of dull and/or disadvantaged children. It seems that for them concrete reasoning has very narrow applicability for a much longer period compared with normal pupils, and that every situation, or nearly so, has to be tackled afresh. Put the other way around, there is little transfer of training. This erratic performance is also frequently seen in individual examinations using the various versions of the Binet Test of measured intelligence.

The educational implications of this study may be read as follows. For samples of similar children it is likely that instruction in the activities indicated is likely to improve performance only on closely related tasks. Such children must, of course, be given a full range of relevant experiences -- the opportunity to assimilate -- but teachers must not be disappointed in their slower progress and in their greater specificity with respect to performance, compared with pupils from more advantaged homes. There seems little evidence at present that the growth of logical thinking as such, in this type of pupil, will be aided by training.

We now turn to the study of David C. Johnson. In this study the children were drawn from kindergarten and from first grade. Only those children with an IQ between 80 and 120 were included in the study. Precise details of social class are not given. The aims of the investigation were (1) to determine if specific instruction improved the ability of the children both to form classes and establish selected equivalence and order relations, and (2) to see if transfer of training took place to certain other selected tasks. The five posttests measured respectively:

1. The ability to use the logical connectives "and," "or," and "not." (Test CA)

2. Understanding of the relations "more than," "fewer than," "as many as," "same shape as," and "same color as." (RA)

3. The ability to use two or more criteria at once. (MU)

4. The ability to solve class inclusion problems (CI). Success on this demands operatory classification in Piaget's view.

5. The ability to use the transitive property of the relations tested in the RA Test (TR).

From these tests five achievement and four transfer tasks were selected. For the sake of clarity these are listed in Table 3 for the benefit of readers, as it is otherwise difficult to hold in mind the differences between the achievement and transfer measures.

In considering the results it should be remembered, as was pointed out earlier, that for each age and IQ level there were only 10 children in the experimental and 10 in the control group. However, for all five achievement tests, the F values for Treatment and Intelligence were significant at the one percent level, although the mean score on MU_r remained low even in the experimental group. The F value for Age was not significant. In the case of the four transfer tests, the F value for Treatment was significant in the case of MU_3, MU_2, and TR, although the mean score

Table 3
Tests of the David C. Johnson Study

Achievement Tests	Content
CA_1	First ten items of CA
CA_2	Last ten items of CA (novel material)
CA_3	Intersection of Tests CA_1 and CA_2
RA	As RA
MU_r	Last six items of MU (intersection rings)
Transfer Tests	
MU_3	First six items of MU (3 x 3 matrices)
MU_2	Second six items of MU (2 x 2 matrices)
CI	Same as CI
TR	Same as TR

in the experimental group for MU_2 remained rather low. Against this, the F value in respect of intelligence was significant in the case of MU_2, CI, and TR. But age was not a significant variable.

Looking at the evidence as a whole it seems that, for similar populations, using the kinds of instructional activities undertaken in the study, help can be given in forming classes using intersection, union, and negation, and in making "prenumber" sets of objects. Moreover, there was some transfer to related activities. But Johnson rightly asks whether there was any real improvement in operativity. That cannot be answered for certain, since it depends on the criteria we decide on to define operativity, as was indicated earlier. As was pointed out above, the performance of the experimental and the control groups on MU_r remained low in spite of the fact that the former group did significantly better than the latter group. Moreover, as Johnson points out, the type of performance of children in the control group mitigates against interpreting it as an inability to form interesting rings. The treatment did not produce a significant improvement in the case of the CI Test, and although intelligence was a factor in performance on this test, neither the experimental nor the control group reached operatory classification. Inhelder and Piaget (1964, p. 164) bring evidence that graphic solutions to matrix items reach a maximum at age of six years, after which graphic solutions decline and operational solutions increase. It is, therefore, difficult to be sure, considering the ages of the pupils engaged in this study, that the improvement in the performance of the experimental group on the matrix items implied an improvement in logical thought. Again in the case of the transitivity test, the author suggests that improvement can be attributed to clarity of language rather than to the use of the transitivity property as such. Thus, looking at the data as a whole, it is possible that these children acquired physical knowledge and an increase in figurative knowledge, but not in logical-mathematical knowledge, except perhaps for those five-year-olds with high-measured IQ. Once again, it seems that the kinds of instruction given can be of considerable use to similar samples of children, but teachers must not think that it will necessarily bring about a growth in logical thought.

Johnson makes an important point when he advocates the need for a study of the actual relations that exist between the words "and," "or," and "not," and the growth of conjunction, disjunction, and negative concepts, respectively. It would also have been useful in this, and other studies, if a principal components analysis had been carried out in order to establish how the test scores cluster together and hence make possible some estimate of the abilities underlying the various tasks. This might have thrown light on what abilities the 3 x 3 and 2 x 2 matrix questions, and the intersecting rings questions, measure in these age groups.

A study concerned with the learning of classification and seriation is reported by Martin L. Johnson. Two groups of first- and second-grade children were involved. One was drawn from a Model Cities area and consisted of Negroes, and the other group came from a middle-class Caucasian neighborhood. No measured IQs are given. After the teaching of Unit I, pupils meeting the criterion test involving the relations "same length as," "shorter than," and "longer than," were randomly assigned to an experimental and control group. The members of the former group were given Instructional Unit II, which was designed for experiences in classifying objects on the basis of the equivalence relation "same length as," and in seriating on the basis of order relations "longer than," and "shorter than." The Conservation of Length Relations Test and Transitivity of Length Relations Test were used both as pretests and posttests, with the respective pretests used as covariates, whereas the Seriation and Classification Tests were used as posttests only.

Both grade and treatment significantly affected performance on the Seriation Test. In Item 1 of the Classification Test, both experimental and control groups did equally well, but in Item 2, where children had to discover the criteria for objects already classified, there was a slight relationship between treatment and improved performance ($.05 < p < .10$) where school and grade had no effect. Indeed, 75 percent of the subjects failed to achieve the criteria for classification. In the case of Item 3 (requiring the formation of a class with one element) neither school, grade, nor treatment was significantly related to performance, although more Grade 2 than Grade 1 pupils gave complete solutions. However, the fact that school and grade, but not treatment, affected posttest performance on the Conservation of Length Relations Test was, perhaps, somewhat surprising, and we shall come back to this point in a moment. Again, only school, and not treatment, affected the posttest performance of the Transitivity of Length Relations Test.

A number of issues are immediately raised by the results. First, the abilities involved in seriating sticks and strings are clearly related, but the seriation of the former is easier than the seriation of the latter. This is an example of percept and materials changing, with goal object and inference pattern remaining constant. There is also a marked relation between the ability to insert a stick into an existing series of sticks with and without a baseline. And while the ability to seriate a set of "linear" objects can clearly be improved with training (the ability also improves with grade) in the case of both ethnic groups, we remain uncertain whether the level of logical thinking or the operativity of the pupils increased, or whether some rule was learned which enabled them to seriate more easily. The fact that no significant relation was found between transitivity of "longer than" and "shorter than" and the ability to seriate using the relations, might suggest that the training helped pupils to use an algorithm. On the other hand, it could be that more pupils had become operational in the Piagetian sense, but that the ability to seriate does not imply transitivity. Only a more precise study of the relationship between seriation and transitivity, keeping goal objects and percepts as constant as possible, will throw light on the latter problem.

If, however, the training did not improve operativity, then some of the other results are more understandable. For example, treatment did not affect performance on Items 2 and 3 of the Classification Test, on the Conservation of Length Relations Test, and on the Transitivity of Length Relations Test. Such results would be in keeping with the view that operativity was not increased by the treatment, as would the fact that performance on Items 1 and 2 of the Classification Test was only slightly related to the transitivity performance of "same length as," and performance on Item 3 not at all. On balance, it seems likely that the level of logical thinking was not increased, but grade did affect performance on some tests.

The study of R. A. Lesh concerns the interdependence of classification, seriation, and number concepts. Three parallel sequences of tasks (indicated by C1, C2 ---- C6: S1 ---- S6: N1 ------ N6) were devised to exhibit a relatively invariant sequential mastery, so that there would be only a small chance that a child could respond to the $(n + 1)^{th}$ task before he could respond to the nth task. The tasks were tried out by having them administered individually to each of 160 children aged 5 years 4 months to 6 years 7 months, living in a typical small town. This was in the nature of a pilot experiment leading up to a training study in which an answer was sought to the question of whether significant transfer of learning is possible between tasks which are characterized by isomorphic operational structures. In this case, the attempt was made to bring about the elaboration of number concepts through teaching seriation and classification concepts. But, in the training study, an answer to another question was sought: namely, would such training transfer to two tasks involving only spatial transformations which were roughly equivalent in difficulty to tasks N5 and N6 ?

The two spatial tasks chosen were Piaget's "three mountains" tasks (T6) and Piaget's tasks dealing with horizontal axes relative to the water level in an inclined bottle. We are not told how these particular tasks were made equivalent in difficulty to tasks N5 and N6, nor the exact details of materials and procedures used in these experiments. Experience shows that there are subtle changes in pupils' performance on these two tasks, depending on the precise task, on the materials used, and on the wording used in questioning (Lovell, 1972). Children are often at different stages on the two tasks, and, indeed, the level of performance may differ within a task because of changes in experimental procedure.

For the training study, another 20 children were chosen, aged 5 years 3 months to 6 years 2 months. These had correctly responded to tasks S1, N2, and C1, but had failed on tasks S3, N3, C3, and, from the experience gained in the pilot study, were most unlikely to respond correctly to tasks N5 and N6. The pupils were divided into an experimental and control group , with each individual in one group matched for sex and scores on certain other tests with an individual in the other group. Moreover, the primary purpose of the training was to get the pupils to coordinate schemes of actions which would lead to the groupings of seriation, multiple seriation, classification, and multiple classification; these, in turn, hopefully leading to increased decentration and analytic thinking.

The training successfully carried over to the number tasks but not to the spatial tasks, in the sense that the experimental group outperformed the control group on the former tasks, whereas none of the experimental group responded correctly to tasks T6 and T7. It would appear, as the author says, that training can enable some pupils to internalize schemes of actions which can be generalized to new situations involving the same schemes; in other pupils the transfer will be limited or nonexistent. The difficulty is that we do not know whether or not those in the experimental group who were able to pass tests N5 and N6 after the training were at some level of "transition" stage at the beginning. Basically we need to know more about the schemes available to children at the beginning of the training period than we are told in this and in all the other studies reported. But the author seems aware of the need to know more about the schemes at the outset. Indeed, he makes the point that the evidence is in favor of Piaget's distinction between three basic types of logical-mathematical operations being a useful one, and points out that children who spontaneously mastered all facts in the classification and seriation tasks of the pilot study outperformed the 10 children in the experimental group on number tasks. The schemes of the former were obviously different in some way from those of the latter. Lesh further points out that while the number concept involves only classification and seriation operations, the conservation of number also involves transformations. Clearly the schemes of some children in the experimental group permitted the handling of the relevant spatial transformation in the number field, while the schemes of other children did not. Such transformation had not been part of the training program. Yet, none of the pupils in the experimental group had schemes appropriate for the successful completion of tasks T6 and T7. Now, it is true that the scheme is a generalizable aspect of coordinating actions that can be applied to analogous situations, while schemes are coordinated among themselves in higher order structures. Moreover, tasks T6 and T7 depend for their successful completion on schemes and structures that enable them to handle aspects of projective and Euclidean space, respectively. Piaget is clear that the elaboration of logical-mathematical structures depends on maturation, social interchange, education and culture (cross cultural studies confirm this), and above all, on self-regulation. It would seem, then, that the structures involved for the successful completion on tasks T6 and T7 require different experiences from those required for N5 and N6: not that experience is a sufficient condition for the elaboration of structures, but that it is a necessary one. The discrepancy between performance on N5 and N6 on the one hand and T6 and T7 on the other, is not unexpected with this age group. The intra-individual variability in performing tasks characterized by a single operational structure is also likely to depend in part on experience and familiarity with materials, but to be sure we need to know much more about information processing in children than we know at present.

The author points to the rather narrow base of the training program and suggests that those pupils who spontaneously solved the classification and seriation tasks have better developed schemes than members of the experimental group, since the former did better than the latter on the number tests. This, he argues, is a case for more widely based teaching programs than many mathematics educators have admitted to hitherto. With this point the writer would heartily agree. We require widely based but directed programs, involving both action and language in small-group work. There seems little doubt that one can accelerate the performance of children on a particular task or on ones closely related to it, but the extent of transfer depends on the nature of the scheme available at the beginning of the teaching and on the width of zone of the pupil's assimilating capacity.

So far we have considered five studies. The effects of the training programs are briefly summarized in Table 4.

Table 4
Summary of the Training Programs

Group	Nature of Training	Effects of Training
1. Four- and five-year-olds. Normal spread of IQ and social background.	To establish length relations between two curves, to use reflexive and nonreflexive properties and to conserve length relations.	Improved ability to compare the lengths of two curves, in conservation of length relations, in use of reflexive and nonreflexive properties. Limited improvement in use of transitive property by 5-year-olds.
2. Five- and six-year-olds. Disadvantaged Negro children.	To establish length relations, to conserve matching relations, and to use the transitive property of matching relations.	Improved performance on transitivity of matching relations -- a task similar to activities involved in treatment. No transfer to other tasks.
3. Kindergarten and first-grade children with measured IQ 80-120. No precise details of social background.	To form classes, intersection and union of classes, complement of classes, relations between classes and between class elements.	Improved performance on all five direct achievement tests and on three of the transfer tests, although not on the test of Class Inclusion. Some doubt remains as to whether there is any improvement in regard to operativity.
4. First and second grade children: Negroes and middle-class Caucasian pupils. No IQ's given.	To classify on basis of equivalence relation "same length as," and seriate on basis of order relations "longer than," "shorter than."	Improved performance on Seriation Test. No improvement on Classification Test, Conservation of Length Relations Test or Transitivity Test.
5. Aged 5:3 to 6:2. Drawn from small Indiana community. A spread of ability.	To classify and seriate.	Improved performance on number tests but not on tasks involving spatial transformations.

In summary form, the overall picture can be quickly grasped. Suitable teaching programs aimed at improving children's understanding of certain mathematical ideas can profitably be undertaken with kindergarten, grade 1, and grade 2 children, providing such children are not slow learners and do not come from disadvantaged homes. With such populations, some children's performance will improve more than would have been the case without directed experiences, and in some instances, there may be some transfer of training. But it remains uncertain whether there will be any real improvement in operativity as the result of narrowly based experiences -- further, there remains the problem of the criteria used to define operativity. In the writer's view, the kinds of training included in these experiments could be incorporated into teaching programs in which small groups of children work through the various directed activities. It is, of course, important that children are not unduly pressed when the schemes available to them are far from those required for the tasks. If this is indeed the case, they are likely to assimilate the ideas with distortion, turn away in distaste, or have a tenuous grasp of the ideas in question. Readers will also have noticed that here and there in the papers, age, grade, and intelligence significantly affect the posttest results. This surely suggests that a longer period of varied experiences and better developed schemes, or earlier developed schemes in the case of higher intelligence, play a marked role in understanding mathematical ideas.

As against this, the one study reported among disadvantaged children suggests that teachers must not be disappointed when there is improvement in performance only on tasks very close to those that have been taught. Teachers must be prepared for limited improvement and limited transfer effect. In the case of school-educable retarded children, a number of studies have shown (Lovell, 1971a) that the intercorrelation coefficients calculated for performance on tasks administered individually on Piagetian lines are much lower than in the case of normal children. The schemes available to a child of chronological age and mental age seven years on a Binet type scale, must be different in ways we do not understand from one of chronological age ten and mental age seven. The fact that there is so much less transfer in dull and disadvantaged children does not imply that the kinds of teaching activities that these papers have discussed should be denied them. But teachers have to move carefully to maintain motivation and interest, be more sensitive to the capacity of such children to assimilate their experiences, and be ready to defer such activities for a few months. At the same time, our experience suggests that such children need more direction, sensibly applied in the teaching, than do abler and more advantaged children.

We must, of course, bear in mind that the posttests were given immediately after the training period ended. None of the studies reported giving a posttest, say, six months later. It is not possible to conjecture what the findings would have been on the latter occasion. This is a reason for long term follow-up studies of children, for which the writer argues a case later.

Three other points must be made.

1. In Almy's (1970) study, which involved a large number of second-grade children, it was found that performance was irregular across Piaget-type tasks. The results obtained in the present studies are consonant with the view that, even at 7-8 years of age, intellectual structures are still in a formative stage.

2. These studies have thrown no light on the question of the analytic set--or on the awareness on the part of the child that certain logical relations inhere within the situation. This demands a certain suspiciousness on the part of the child when faced with a task. We cannot tell from these studies whether the child is unable to elaborate the logical structures as necessary, or whether he can but fails to in the sense that he is not "switched on" to the implications of the situation.

3. It might appear from these studies that training in these types of activities was good in itself, for so often performance in closely related tasks improved although there was little transfer to other tasks. This may well be the case, but we cannot be sure. Young children appear to elaborate logical structures out of their interaction with their general environment, as they play and as they experiment with the world about them. It could be that direct activities, however skillfully and humanely applied to hold the interest of children, could nevertheless have a deleterious effect in the long run in the sense that we do not know how well such directed activities can be incorporated into the ongoing structures without, so to speak, any damage.

The sixth study, that of T. P. Carpenter, did not involve training. Rather, he was looking at the performance of 75 Grade 1 and 54 Grade 2 children on tasks involving the conservation and measurement of liquids. More specifically, Carpenter attempted to determine if young children responded differently to visual and numerical cues or simply to the last cue available. At the same time, the study was designed to find the role of equivalence and order relations in conservation and measurement problems. In order to reduce the number of tasks given to any one child, the three conservation problems, and both sets of problems (Nos. 2 and 3) in which quantities were measured with two different units, were administered to 61 of the children; the three relations being tested for all three sets of problems (Part A). The remaining 68 children were given all the measurement problems (Nos. 2, 3, 4, 5) with Equivalence and Nonequivalence II relations (Part B). We have no precise details of the social background of the children other than that they were drawn from a predominantly rural community in Wisconsin.

Some interesting data emerge. In Part A, 25 of the 61 children were correct on the Equivalence conservation item with a 95 percent probability that between 27 percent and 56 percent of the population would respond correctly to this item. These figures give readers some idea of the frequency of correct response to what has been the most usual type of conservation problem. But in the case of correct answers to all the tasks in Part A the reasons adduced fell almost completely under two main headings: (1) reference to the previous state, or (2) a compensating relationship between height and width, or between the number of units and unit size. Moreover, the evidence indicates that there are no significant differences either between the conservation and measurement problems or between the two types of measurement problems given. Furthermore, there are no significant differences in performance between Equivalence and Nonequivalence II relations for any of the problems given.

In Part B it is important to note the following three points: (1) the great difficulty in measurement with indistinguishably different units, (2) how much easier the tasks were which involved measurement of unequal-appearing intervals with the same unit, and (3) the ease of the items involving measurement with the same unit with apparent inequality. Indeed, there is a significant difference between each of the four types of measurement problems in Part B with respect to performance. Furthermore, there is no significant difference in respect of difficulty between Equivalence and Nonequivalence II relations, although in the case where unequal-appearing quantities are measured with the same unit, the difference in difficulty is significant at the p = .05 but not at the p = .01 level. Nearly all the reasons for the correct responses were based on reference to the previous state. The author argues with some reason that from a consideration of the performance on the four items given in both Part A and Part B, when quantities are measured with the same unit they are easier than corresponding conservation problems.

This study indicated that there is no difference in difficulty between conservation problems and corresponding measurement problems in which the distracting cues are numerical; and that misleading numerical cues can produce the same errors as misleading visual ones. The fact that these children found the tasks in which quantities were measured with the same unit into inequality so easy is good evidence that they do not respond only, or even primarily, on the basis of visual cues. Carpenter argues that the most significant factor in determining which cues young children attend to is the order in which the cues appear. The present writer would like to see more evidence for this, although to be fair to the author, he does clearly point out, as he must, that the order of cues is not the only factor found to affect responses.

The evidence also suggests that relations between quantities being compared does not affect performance, since there is no significant difference in performance between conservation and measurement problems employing Equivalence relations and corresponding problems employing Nonequivalence II relations -- here we have different percepts but the same goal object (quantity) and inference pattern (comparison of quantities). And apart from the situation in which it is impossible to identify the larger unit, Nonequivalence I problems are less difficult than the corresponding problems employing Equivalence and Nonequivalence II relations, since the correct relation between quantities could be found from the distracting cues by focusing on the appropriate dimension; e.g., focusing on the size rather than the number of units.

Carpenter points out that by the end of the first grade almost all children recognize the quantities are equal if they measure the same number of units, and quantity A is greater than quantity B if A measures more units than B. The writer's experience generally confirms these ages or grades, except for very dull children. It is, of course, true as the author asserts, that children in grades 1 and 2 do not have well-developed concepts of measurement nor are they able to measure accurately in all instances. In a more structured situation, such as Carpenter employed, the measurement cues were forced on the pupils, whereas Piaget employed less structured tasks in which children had to measure themselves in order to have any measurement cues to respond to. Thus, the beginning of understanding with respect to measurement came earlier in this study than in Piaget's experiments. The present writer has pointed out elsewhere (Lovell, 1971a) that the structure of a problem affects its difficulty for children. This is as true at the level of formal operational thought as at the age of onset of concrete operational thought. Moreover, this point does indicate that some kinds of well-structured problems can be introduced to Grade 1 children, and indeed in kindergarten, in the form of play with water and sand.

The author concludes that the major reason for most conservation and measurement failures lies in centering on a single dominant dimension, and the development of concepts of conservation and measurement can be thought of in terms of the increasing ability to decentre. He proposes that children pass through four stages, and these can usefully be compared with four steps proposed by Inhelder (1972), which were determined through learning experiments involving conservation and class inclusion. Unfortunately we do not know how consistent, in respect of a stage, a child was across all the tasks Carpenter undertook, any more than we know how consistent a child was in passing or failing a task he undertook. However, his proposals were:

1. The child responds on the basis of a single dominant dimension, which can be either visual or numerical depending on the task set.

2. The child is capable of changing from one dimension to another, but within any one task he tends to remain focused on one dimension. Sometimes, conservation results from the child keeping the earlier state in mind, but he is unable to consider both the earlier state prior to the transformation and the present state at one and the same time, and deciding which set of cues provides the right basis for comparison. Children at this stage seem to ignore the present state and refer only to the former state ("they were the same before"). The author suggests that it is children at this transition stage who gain most from training in conservation, but such gains are on a narrow front and without a basis for movement to a later stage and hence to an improvement in operativity. Certainly the Geneva school would claim that training is ineffective except for those at a transition stage.

3. The schemes now permit the child to consider a number of conditions of a quantity, simultaneously, and choose the one that provides a rational basis for a comparison.

4. The child can now use the information from the prior and present state and find the correct relation between the sizes of different units based on the number of units which the two comparable quantities measure.

Inhelder's paper gives details of proposed stages found in learning experiments involving conservation and class inclusion:

1. Two different systems of evaluation (e.g., number of sticks and lengths of sticks) could be elicited, but neither was sufficiently developed to permit their integration. The two separate systems were activated successively, and the child did not feel there was any contradiction.

2. In place of the two evaluative schemes being evoked successively, both seemed to be present almost simultaneously. But the pupil could not conceive of a new solution which could take both schemes into account. However, he is conscious of contradictions.

3. An attempt is now made at integrating the two evaluative schemes, but it is inadequate. There are compromise solutions in the form of partial compensations.

4. The different schemes can now be integrated. Thus in respect of two lines of equal length composed of matches of different lengths the reply might be "You have more matches but they are shorter." A scheme no longer operates a post hoc correction on another but rather there is a reciprocal adjustment.

Inhelder states that in all the processes that have come to light in the training experiments carried out at Geneva, development takes place in a similar way except in one group of problems. In those involving logical operations in the strict sense of the word (e.g., class inclusion), the regulatory mechanisms found at stage (2) which yield the awareness of contradictions are not followed by the compromise solutions of stage (3) but by complete logical compensations which later result in correct solutions (4).

The suggestions of Carpenter, also of the Geneva school, have been mentioned since the importance of studying the growth of partial structures is raised in the next section.

Some Suggestions for Further Research

The studies that have been presented have been carefully designed and skillfully executed, and the suggestions which follow are in no sense to be taken as a reflection on them, but rather they should be regarded as lines for research in the future. The research reported has been concerned with the period of four to seven or eight years of age -- a period in which Piaget characterized the child's thinking as a semi-logic, or a one-way mapping, and the suggestions made here necessarily relate to the same period and the years that immediately follow. Unfortunately, psychology has not yet provided a valid theory of cognitive development which is presented in detailed process terms. Piaget has given us great insights and his developmental theory of intellectual growth provides a useful conceptual framework in which the teacher can consider the ideas he wishes his pupils to develop, although it still leaves large gaps in our knowledge. However, his theory is constantly developing as new problems are raised, new methods developed to deal with these, and existing models adjusted or refined to account for these findings. The following broad research areas are suggested.

1. Many studies have enumerated the items which a child passes or fails. This certainly has its place either in training, or in the frequent monitoring of children in a longitudinal study. But perhaps at this moment of time more emphasis should be placed on carefully recording the precise nature of the response both in respect of action and verbalization. We need far more knowledge about the exact stage of development of the relevant schemes of a child at the beginning of the training. It would appear from the Geneva evidence that children at the lowest operative levels get little from the training. But when items are scored on a pass or fail basis we do not see the detailed base line, or detailed development of the schemes which lead to a correct solution to the problem. Such information is greatly needed.

Again when training programs employ two or more procedures (e.g., numerical [number of matches] and ordinal [length of matches] ways of dealing with problems of constructing or judging lengths) we need to see the interaction between schemes at various points or steps. At some point conflict ensues, and in the view of the Geneva school it is conflict that triggers the reciprocal assimilation between schemes which provides the final resolution of the problem. Note carefully, however, that the different schemes which are assimilated and integrated may not all be at the same developmental level. Much research is required here as,we know little about the effect on each other of the various activities in which the child engages.

Such studies are likely to throw light on the nature of the schemes (in respect of mathematical ideas) available to normal as compared with dull and disadvantaged pupils. It would also be likely to shed light on the important problem of transfer. In short, such studies are likely to throw light on processes that impel the pupil forward. The classical Piagetian structural model must be supplemented. We need more information on the growth of schemes underpinning mathematical ideas and the way in which they become integrated with other schemes.

In keeping with what has just been said, readers are reminded again of the views of Smedslund regarding the importance of studying the growth of inference patterns holding constant percept (as far as possible) and goal object and also of the point made by Pinard and Laurendeau (1969) that until we know more than we do now, the *structure d'ensemble* criterion should be investigated to see to what extent the different Piagetian groupings are achieved in synchrony on tasks related to the same conceptual content and same material. Hamel and van der Veer (1972) attempted to carry out the suggestion of Pinard and Laurendeau involving Multiple Classification and Multiple Seriation tasks. Using their method of scoring, the correlation between performance on these tasks was around +0.6 even when measured intelligence has been partialled out. The authors are well aware that some children may solve this kind of problem by means other than using operational schemes -- as we saw earlier. However, they also make two points. First, the amount of information affects problem-solving behavior at the stage of concrete operational thought. Second, there is a need for a longitudinal study of individual children as they move from the preoperational to the concrete operational stage of thought, to see to what extent different operatory schemes develop in synchrony, and how performance is affected by irrelevant variables. The views of Hamel and van der Veer strongly support the general views just proposed by the writer.

2. In connection with what has been just said it seems to the writer that an information processing model of some of the tasks that have been attempted in these papers could be of importance. It is true that at the Université de Montréal work in this field has been in progress for some time, although the results are not widely known yet. In order to encourage readers who have easy access to a computer, a brief sketch of a little of the Montreal work is given.(See Baylor et al. 1973.) In, say, weight seriation and length seriation tasks, a video-tape record is made of the child solving, or attempting to solve, the problem given. The actions and words of the child are then transcribed onto a protocol. The protocol is carefully analyzed, in respect of both the task environment and of the subject's intellectual structures as revealed by his behaviors. The pupil's behavior on the task is then simulated by writing a set of rules or program which can be interpreted by a digital computer. When the program is executed a close reproduction of the child's behavior is obtained. It can also generate further protocols on new but similar problems.

Baylor gives an example which related to the weight seriation task. The child is presented with seven white two-inch cubes and a sensitive balance. The former all looked alike but were identified by different letter names. Their weights varied from 100.2 gms to 106.5 gms so that the pupil was forced to use the balance to judge the relative weights of the cubes. He was not allowed to put more than two cubes on the scale at any one time. Examples are given of the recognizable strategies found in the task and programs are given for the various "stages" of strategies employed, namely:

1. A juxtaposition of pairs without any coordination between pairs;

2. The child tries to coordinate his successive weighings of pairs;

3. Successive weighings are coordinated.

The derivation of predictions from the model forms the basis for further experimental studies. Data from the latter may, of course, demand modifications in the model; in the way one could come to a number of recyclings through the series. For example, if a pupil at stage (3) was presented with two extra cubes and asked to intercalate these into the series, would he behave as the model predicts? If he does not, then why not? The model would have to be appropriately amended in this case.

At the time of writing, Baylor et al. had a program which would simulate behavior over both a task which involved the seriation of sticks (taking only two at a time) and the weight seriation task, for a program must ever be made more general. At the same time these writers point out that there are certain aspects of Piagetian theory that have not yet found adequate nontrivial representations in the information processing models (e.g., such competences as the onset of reversible, asymmetric operations, and the ability to envisage, say, a cube as weighing more than its neighbor to the right and at the same time weighing less than its neighbor to the left). Thus, at present, an information-processing model and a Piagetian model must remain complementary, although the former may, as the result of future research, give operational definitions to the Piagetian insights that cannot be represented at present.

At the moment a small amount of work has been carried out in England involving information processing in respect of the class inclusion problem and the conservation of quantity, but details of the work are not yet available. In the writer's view this is a potentially useful research area as it may well throw great light on the nature of the partial structures; that is, schemes in the process of development, and of the interaction between schemes when a complete solution is developing. It may also throw light on the partial structures of able and less able children, and on the question of transfer.

3. More research is required into the growth of schemes leading to success in the class inclusion problem. Piaget believes that successful performance in this problem demands operatory classification, while Inhelder (1972) points out that the experience at Geneva suggests that training in the class inclusion problem has positive effects on performance on the conservation problems. In D. C. Johnson's study, children were given experience in forming classes, in forming intersections and unions, and in forming the complement of a class. The Class Inclusion test administered as a posttest involved the following factors: presence of an extraneous object, three or more subsets present, equal numbers in a set and its elements, mingled items, items not visually present, addition or subtraction of an item after an initial comparison. Now it is true that whenever a class and its complement are specified, the idea of inclusion is implicit. But apparently the training was of little avail when it came to the CI items. Further detailed studies involving the growth of schemes relating to the CI problem, taking into account variables such as Johnson used, are likely to be of value. They would also throw further light on the growth of schemes in relation to the amount of relevant and irrelevant information provided in the problems. And it might develop that greater transfer to other tasks such as conservation might be found, as Inhelder suggests.

Beilin reviews the relevant evidence concerning training studies in class inclusion. After reviewing the evidence provided by Kohnstamm and the counter-evidence of the Geneva school, together with other studies, he concludes that training can lead to the successful conclusion of this logical ability. Whether operative achievement from instruction and training results is still unresolved, since conceptual and operational definition of operativity have yet to be made. This need not detract the mathematics educator. He wishes to know whether the "pay off" in respect of transfer to other skills is greater if the emphasis is put more on class inclusion.

4. While the present papers involve fundamental logical structures vital to mathematics, which are elaborated with greater or lesser understanding in the move from semi-logic to concrete logical thought, we should not be content with these alone. We need to establish, in a whole range of abilities from very able to school-educable retarded, more knowledge as to the stages through which pupils pass in elaborating the concepts involved in, say, the numeration system or in the properties of the natural number system. And we need far more information in respect of the growth of spatial and geometrical concepts and how these develop in comparison with numerical ones. Again, we need more information on whether topological concepts develop prior to Euclidean and projective concepts in the child's representation of space. Lovell (1959), Lunzer (1960a), and Martin (1973) have doubted this. But the evidence of Laurendau and Pinard (1970) must also be considered. The outcome of this argument is important for it would give guidance in respect of the order in which spatial ideas should be introduced to young children.

5. Research is needed along the lines argued by Steffe (1973). In his paper he has attempted to outline some possible relations between the cognitive systems of the child and the mathematical systems of finite cardinal and ordinal number. Moreover, he argues that it seems likely that some mathematical structures may be more parsimonious models of cognitive operations than the genetic structures proposed by Piaget. For example, he reasons a case for suggesting that, on the basis of information which we have at present, the structures of connected, asymmetrical, transitive relations is more parsimonious as a logical model of seriation than is Piaget's Grouping V (Addition of Asymmetrical Relations). But more research is needed to establish if this is the case.

Again, since logical identity (essentially an equivalence relation) is an integral part of the Piagetian grouping structures, a great deal more knowledge needs to be established concerning its development, and of the relation between its development and the growth of seriation and classification behaviors. Moreover, although logical identity, set equivalence, and set similarity are all equivalence relations, they may have different roles in the child's elaboration of the concepts of cardinal and ordinal number. Here, too, research is needed, and Steffe lists a number of problems to be investigated holding in mind Piaget's Grouping I (Primary Addition of Classes).

6. Some of the basic research which we have suggested will require time both to execute and implement. Meanwhile children have to be educated. Thus, I also believe that a longitudinal study of children is important in which the style of teaching is kept constant over a period of years even though the same teachers do not remain with the pupils throughout the period. This involves great problems. For example, even if the style

of teaching remains constant over a number of years, the vigour and enthusiasm of individual teachers may not. In my view we need to compare the performance and understanding of pupils towards the end of the elementary school, whose teaching can be characterized since kindergarten and Grade 1 as carefully directed activities of the kinds indicated in these papers, with pupils who have been taught on more traditional lines. This is a formidable task. For one thing, the directed activities to induce an understanding of mathematical ideas would have to be done in a manner to hold the interest of pupils since children in the elementary school look upon mathematics as a tool with which to solve real-life problems, and not as a purely intellectual exercise. Again, the ability to compute quickly and accurately is a skill that all pupils need. Bluntly, our research to date has been too short-termed. In respect of the present studies, for example, it is unlikely that we shall ever know what happened to the mathematical understanding of these people in later school life. Do any improvements brought about by such directed activities enable the pupil to elaborate the concept of time any more easily, or have a surer grasp of the properties of the natural number system in the sixth grade? The design and execution of such a study would present formidable problems, but until it is tackled we shall not have accurate data on the long-term effects of a consistent style of teaching mathematics over a number of years.

The writer is, of course, well aware of the results of the Almy (1970) study, in which a large number of children who had had prescribed mathematics and science programs since kindergarten (AAAS, GCMP and SCIS) were compared with pupils whose mathematics and science activities were planned by the teacher. In the second grade both groups of children did about as well on Piaget-derived tasks; so there was no indication of superior logical thought in either group. However, two points need to be made in respect of the Almy study. First, we cannot be sure how well the presribed programs were implemented; that is, of the quality of the teaching. Attention was drawn to this danger in the opening paragraphs of this chapter. In any study the writer had in mind the quality and style of teaching would be controlled as far as possible. If this were not possible from kindergarten to grade 6, it might be possible from kindergarten to grades 3 or 4. Second, the follow-up study of Almy was in the second grade; the writer has in mind a much longer study. It is, of course, unlikely that we should ever be able to maintain a style of teaching across all areas of school life, and we have no idea what effect on the growth of logical thinking the mathematics programs alone would have.

While mathematics educators must necessarily believe in the particular programs they advocate, we shall not know the long term effects of such programs until a well-designed experiment is undertaken. Beilin, in his extensive review of the literature in the training and acquisition of logical structures, argues that since the child can construct a conceptual system out of many materials and techniques, even those not intended by the researcher, the basic pattern of organizations is internal. That is to say, the growth of the logical operational system is under the control of a genetic mechanism and permits the growth of intellectual structures through interactions of environmental inputs. Put simply, we want to know what the long-term effects are of particular environmental inputs on the growth of logical thought and the grasp of mathematical ideas. And can young pupils assimilate particular inputs, as in the case of directed activities in mathematics, without any ill effects?

REFERENCES

Adler, M. J. Some educational implications of the theories of Jean Piaget and J. S. Bruner. *Canadian Educational and Research Digest,* 1964, 4, 291-305.

Almy, M., Chittenden, E., & Miller, P. *Young children's thinking: Studies of some aspects of Piaget's theory.* New York: Teachers College Press, 1966.

Almy, M. *Logical thinking in second grade.* New York: Teachers College Press, 1970.

Applebaum, M., & Bargmann, R. E. A fortran II program for MUDAID: Multivariate, univariate, and discriminant analysis of irregular data. *NONR 1834,* 39, Urbana: University of Illinois Press, 1967.

Baylor, W., Gascon, J., Lemoyne, G., & Pothier, N. An information processing model of some seriation tasks. *Canadian Psychologist,* 1973, 14, 167-196.

Bailey, T. On the measurement of polygonal paths by young children. Unpublished doctoral dissertation, University of Georgia, 1973.

Bearison, D. J. Role of measurement operations in the acquisition of conservation. *Developmental Psychology,* 1969, 1, 653-660.

Beilin, H. Perceptual-cognitive conflict in the development of an invariant area concept. *Journal of Experimental Child Psychology,* 1964, 1, 208-226.

Beilin, H. Learning and operational convergence in logical thought development. *Journal of Experimental Child Psychology,* 1965, 2, 317-339.

Beilin, H. Cognitive capacities of young children: A replication. *Science,* 1968, 162, 920-921.

Beilin, H. The training and acquisition of logical operations. In M. F. Rosskopf, L. P. Steffe, & S. Taback (Eds.), *Piagetian cognitive-development research and mathematical education.* Washington, D.C.: National Council of Teachers of Mathematics, 1971.

Beilin, H., & Franklin, I. C. Logical operations in area and length measurement: Age and training effects. *Child Development,* 1962, 33, 607-618.

Berlyne, D. E. *Structure and direction in thinking.* New York: John Wiley & Sons, 1965.

Beth, E. W., & Piaget, J. *Mathematical epistemology and psychology.* Dordrecht-Holland: D. Reidel, 1966.

Birkhoff, G., & Maclane, S. *A survey of modern algebra.* New York: Macmillan, 1958.

Bourbaki, N. L'architecture des mathématiques. *Le Lionnais,* Paris, 1948, 35-37.

Braine, M. D. S. The ontogeny of certain logical operations: Piaget's formulation examined by nonverbal methods. *Psychological Monographs: General and Applied,* 1959, 73 (5, Whole No. 475).

Brownell, W. A., & Chazal, C. B. The effects of premature drill in third-grade arithmetic. *Journal of Educational Research,* 1935, 29, 17-28.

Bruner, J. S. Inhelder and Piaget's *The growth of logical thinking:* I. A psychologist's viewpoint. *British Journal of Psychology.* 1959, 50 363-370.

Bruner, J. S. The course of cognitive growth. *American Psychologist,* 1964, 19, 1-15. (a)

Bruner, J. S. Some theorems of instruction illustrated with reference to mathematics. In E. R. Hilgard (Ed.), *Theories of learning and instruction.* Sixty-third Yearbook of the National Society for the Study of Education, 1964, 306-336. (b)

Bruner, J. S. *Toward a theory of instruction.* New York: Norton, 1968.

Bruner, J. S., Goodnow, J. J., & Austin, G. A. *A study of thinking.* New York: John Wiley & Sons, 1956.

Bruner, J. S., & Kenney, H. J. Representation and mathematics learning. In L. N. Morrisett & J. Vinsonhaler (Eds.), *Mathematical Learning, Monographs of the Society for Research in Child Development,* 1964, 30 (1, Serial No. 99).

Bruner, J. S., & Kenney, H. J. On multiple ordering. In J. S. Bruner, R. R. Olver, & P. M. Greenfield, et al., *Studies in cognitive growth.* New York: John Wiley & Sons, 1966.

Bruner, J. S., Olver, R. R., & Greenfield, P. M., et al. *Studies in cognitive growth.* New York: John Wiley & Sons, 1966.

Campbell, D. T., & Stanley, J. C. Experimental and quasi-experimental designs for research on teaching. In N. L. Gage (Ed.), *Handbook of research on teaching.* Chicago: Rand McNally, 1963.

Carey, R., & Steffe, L. P. An investigation in the learning of equivalence and order relations by four-and-five-year-old children. *Research Paper No. 17, Georgia Research and Development Center in Educational Stimulation.* Athens: University of Georgia, 1968.

Carpenter, T. P. The role of equivalence and order relations in the development and coordination of the concepts of unit size and number of units in selected conservation type measurement problems. *Technical Report No. 178, Wisconsin Research and Development Center for Cognitive Learning.* Madison: The University of Wisconsin, 1971. (a)

Carpenter, T. P. The performance of first grade students on a nonstandard set of measurement tasks. *Technical Report No. 211, Wisconsin Research and Development Center for Cognitive Learning.* Madison: The University of Wisconsin, 1971. (b)

Churchill, E. M. The number concepts of the young child: Part I. *Researches and Studies,* 1958, 17, 34-49. (a)

Churchill, E. M. The number concepts of the young child: Part II. *Researches and Studies,* 1958, 18, 28-46. (b)

Clarke, A. M., Cooper, G. M., & Loudon, E. H. A set to establish equivalence relations in pre-school children. *Journal of Experimental Child Psychology,* 1969, 8, 180-189.

Coxford, A., Jr. The effects of instruction on the stage placement of children in Piaget's seriation experiments. *Arithmetic Teacher,* 1964, 11, 4-9.

Cochran, W. G. The comparison of percentages in matched samples. *Biometrika,* 1950, 37, 256-266.

Darnell, C. D., & Bourne, L., Jr. Effects of age, verbal ability, and pre-training with component concepts on the performance of children in a bidimensional classification task. *Journal of Educational Psychology,* 1970, 61, 66-71.

Dienes, Z. P. *Building of mathematics.* (Rev. ed.). London: Hutchinson, 1971.

Divers, B. P., Jr. The ability of kindergarten and first grade children to use the transitive property of three length relations in three perceptual situations. Unpublished doctoral dissertation, University of Georgia, 1970.

Dodwell, P. C. Children's understanding of number and related concepts. *Canadian Journal of Psychology.* 1960, 14, 191-205.

Dodwell, P. C. Children's understanding of number concepts: Characteristics of an individual and of a group test. *Canadian Journal of Psychology,* 1961, 15, 29-36.

Dodwell, P. C. Relations between understanding of the logic of classes and of cardinal number in children. *Canadian Journal of Psychology,* 1962, 16, 152-160.

Edwards, J. Effects of instruction and concomitant variables on multiple categorization ability. *Journal of Educational Psychology,* 1969, 60, 138-143.

Elkind, D. Piaget's conservation problems. *Child Development,* 1967, 38, 841-848.

Elkind, D. Discrimination, seriation, and numeration of size and dimensional differences in young children: Piaget replication study VI. *Journal of Genetic Psychology,* 1964, 104, 275-296.

El'konin, D. B., & Davydov, V. V. Children's capacity for learning mathematics. L. P. Steffe (Ed.), *Soviet studies in the psychology of learning and teaching mathematics*, Vol. 7, 261, School Mathematics Study Group, 1974.

Feller, W. *An introduction to probability theory and its applications.* New York: John Wiley & Sons, 1957.

Ferguson, G. A. *Statistical analysis in psychology and education.* New York: McGraw-Hill, 1966.

Finn, J. D. *Multivariance: Fortran program for univariate and multivariate analysis of variance and covariance.* Buffalo, State University of New York, 1967.

Flavell, J. H. *The developmental psychology of Jean Piaget.* Princeton: D. Van Nostrand Company, 1963.

Fleischmann, B., Gilmore, S., & Ginsburg, H. The strength of nonconservation. *Journal of Experimental Child Psychology*, 1966, 4, 353-368.

Gal'perin, P. Ya., & Georgiev, L. S. The formation of elementary mathematical notions. In J. Kilpatrick & I. Wirszup (Eds.), *Soviet studies in the psychology of learning and teaching mathematics*, Vol. 1. School Mathematics Study Group, 1969.

Gast, H. Der Umgang mit Zahlen und Zahlbegilden in der frühen Kindheit. Z. Psycholo., 1957, 161, 1-90. Cited in I. E. Sigel & F. H. Hooper (Eds.), *Logical thinking in children.* New York: Holt, Rinehart, & Winston, 1968, p. 97.

Gödel, K. Über formal unetscheidbare Sätze der Principia Mathematica und verwandter Systeme I. *Mathematiker Zeitschrift*, 1934, 39, 176-210, 405-431.

Greco, P., Grize, J., Papert, S., & Piaget, J. Problems de la construction du nombre. *Études d'épistémologie génétique.* Vol. 2. Paris: Presses Université de France, 1960.

Greenhouse, S. W., & Geisser, S. On methods in the analysis of profile data. *Psychometrika*, 1959, 24, 95-112.

Griffiths, J. A., Shantz, C. A., & Sigel, I. E. A methodological problem in conservation studies: The use of relational terms. *Child Development*, 1967, 38, 841-848.

Grize, J. B. Du groupment au nombre. In P. Greco, J. B. Grize, S. Papert, & J. Piaget, Problems de la construction du nombre. *Études d'épistémologie génétique.* Paris: Presses Université de France, 1960, 11, 69-96.

Guilford, J. P. *Fundamental statistics in psychology and education.* New York: McGraw-Hill, 1956.

Hamel, B. R., & van der Veer, M. A. A. Structure d'ensemble, multiple classification, multiple seriation and amount of irrelevant information. *British Journal of Educational Psychology*, 1972, 42, 319-325.

Harper, E. H., & Steffe, L. P. The effects of selected experiences on the ability of kindergarten and first grade children to conserve numerousness. *Technical Report No. 38, Wisconsin Research and Development Center for Cognitive Learning.* Madison: The University of Wisconsin, 1968.

Herstein, I. N. *Topics in algebra.* Waltham: Blaisdell Publishing Company, 1964.

Hilgard, E. R. A perspective on the relationship between learning theory and educational practices. In E. R. Hilgard (Ed.), *Theories of learning and instruction.* Sixty-third Yearbook of the National Society for the Study of Education, 1964, 402-415.

Holowinsky, Ivan. Seriation actions in preschool children. *Journal of Learning Disabilities*, 1970, 9, 34-35.

Hooper, F. Piaget's conservation tasks: The logical and developmental priority of identity conservation. *Journal of Experimental Child Psychology*, 1969, 8, 234-249.

Huntington, J. R. Linear measurement in the primary grades: A comparison of Piaget's description of the child's spontaneous conceptual development and the SMSG sequence of instruction. *Journal for Research in Mathematics Education*, 1970, 1, 219-232.

Hyde, D. M. An investigation of Piaget's theories of the development of the concept of number. Unpublished doctoral dissertation, University of London, 1959.

Inhelder, B. Information processing tendencies -- empirical studies. In Farnham - Diggory, S. (Ed.), *Information processing in children.* New York: Academic Press, 1972.

Inhelder, B., & Piaget, J. *The growth of logical thinking from childhood to adolescence.* Translated by A. Parsons & S. Milgram, New York: Basic Books, 1958.

Inhelder, B., & Piaget, J. *The early growth of logic in the child: Classification and seriation.* Translated by E. A. Lunzer, London: Routledge and Paul, 1964.

Inhelder, B., & Sinclair, H. Learning cognitive structures. In P. Mussen, J. Langer, & M. Covington (Eds.), *Trends and Issues in Developmental Psychology.* New York: Holt, Rinehart, & Winston, 1969.

Johnson, D. C. An investigation in the learning of selected parts of a boolean algebra by five- and six-year-old children. Unpublished doctoral dissertation, University of Georgia, 1971.

Johnson, M. L. Effects of selected experiences on the classification and seriation abilities of young children. Unpublished doctoral dissertation, University of Georgia, 1971.

Kilpatrick, J., & Wirszup, I. (Eds.). Preface. *Soviet studies in the psychology of learning and teaching mathematics,* Vol. II. School Mathematics Study Group, 1969.

Kohnstamm, G. A. *Piaget's analysis of class inclusion: Right or wrong?* Translated by M. Peck-O'Toole & G. Uildriks-Bone, The Hague: Mouton & Co., 1967.

Lasry, J. C., & Laurendeau, M. Apprentissage empirique de la notion d'inclusion. *Human Development,* 1969, 12, 141-153.

Laurendeau, M., & Pinard, A. *The development of the concept of space in the child.* New York: International Universities Press, 1970.

Lesh, R. A. The generalization of Piagetian operations as it relates to the hypothesized functional interdependence between class, series, and number concepts. Unpublished doctoral dissertation, Indiana University, 1971.

Lovell, K. A follow-up study of some aspects of the work of Piaget and Inhelder on the child's conception of space. *British Journal of Educational Psychology,* 1959, 29, 104-117.

Lovell, K. Concepts in mathematics. In H. J. Klausmeier & C. W. Harris (Eds.), *Analyses of concept learning.* New York: Academic Press, 1966. (a)

Lovell, K. In The developmental approach of Jean Piaget: Open discussion. In M. Garrison, Jr. (Ed.), *Cognitive models and development in mental retardation. Monograph supplement to the American Journal of Mental Deficiency,* 1966, 70 (4) ,84-89. (b)

Lovell, K. The development of some mathematical ideas in elementary school pupils. In M. F. Rosskopf, L. P. Steffe, & S. Taback (Eds.), *Piagetian cognitive-development research and mathematics education.* Washington: National Council of Teachers of Mathematics, 1971. (a)

Lovell, K. *The growth of understanding in mathematics: Kindergarten through grade three.* New York: Holt, Rinehart & Winston, 1971. (b)

Lovell, K. Intellectual growth and understanding in mathematics. Paper presented at the meeting of the American Educational Research Association, New York, 1971. (c)

Lovell, K. Intellectual growth and understanding mathematics. *Journal for Research in Mathematics Education,* 1972, 3, 164-182.

Lovell, K., Mitchell, B., & Everett, I. R. An experimental study of the growth of some structures. *British Journal of Psychology,* 1962, 53, 175-188.

Lovell, K., & Ogilvie ,E. The growth of the concept of volume in junior high school children. *Journal of Child Psychology and Psychiatry*, 1961, 2, 118-126.

Lovell, K., Healey, D., & Rowland, A. D. Growth of some geometrical concepts. *Child Development*, 1962, 33, 751-767.

Lunzer, E. A. *Recent studies in Britain based on the work of Jean Piaget.* London: National Foundation for Educational Research in England and Wales, Occasional publication, 4, 1960. (a)

Lunzer, E. A. Some points of Piagetian theory in the light of experimental criticism. *Journal of Child Psychology and Psychiatry*, 1960, 1, 191-202. (b)

Martin, J. L. An investigation of the development of selected topological properties in the representational space of young children. Paper presented at the meeting of The American Educational Research Association, New Orleans, 1973.

McLellan, J. A., & Dewey, J. *The psychology of number.* New York: D. Appleton, 1914.

McManis, D. L. Conservation of identity and equivalence of quantity by retardates. *Journal of Genetic Psychology*, 1969, 115, 63-69.

Maccoby, M., & Modiano, N. On culture and equivalence: I. In J. S. Bruner, R. R. Olver, & P. M. Greenfield, et al., *Studies in cognitive growth.* New York: John Wiley & Sons, 1966.

Northman, J. E., & Gruen, G. E. Relationship between identity and equivalence conservation. *Developmental Psychology*, 1970, 2, 311.

Olmsted, P., Parks, C. V., & Rickel, A. The development of classification skills in the preschool child. *International Review of Education*, 1970, 16, 67-80.

Olver, R. R., & Hornsby, J. R. On equivalence. In J. S. Bruner, R. R. Olver, & P. M. Greenfield, et al., *Studies in cognitive growth.* New York: John Wiley & Sons, 1966.

Ostle, B. *Statistics in research.* Ames: Iowa State University Press, 1963.

Otis, A. S., & Lennon, R. T. *Manual for administration: Otis-Lennon mental ability test.* New York: Harcourt, Brace & World, 1967.

Owens, D. T. The effects of selected experiences on the ability of disadvantaged kindergarten and first grade children to use properties of equivalence and order relations. Unpublished doctoral dissertation, University of Georgia, 1972.

Owens, D. T., & Steffe, L. P. Performance of kindergarten children on transitivity of three matching relations. *Journal for Research in Mathematics Education*, 1972, 3, 141-154.

Piaget, J. Classes, relations et nombres: *Essai sur les "groupements" de la logistique et la réversibilité de la pensée.* Paris: Vrin, 1942.

Piaget, J. *The child's conception of number.* London: Routledge and Kegan Paul, 1952.

Piaget, J. Equilibration and the development of logical structures. In J. M. Tanner & B. Inhelder (Eds.), *Discussions on child development.* Vol. 4. London: Tavistock, 1960.

Piaget, J. Development and Learning. In R. E. Ripple & V. N. Rockcastle (Eds.), *Piaget rediscovered.* A report of the conference on cognitive studies and curriculum development. Ithaca, New York: Cornell University Press, 1964. (a)

Piaget, J. Mother structures and the notion of number. In R. E. Ripple & V. N. Rockcastle (Eds.), *Piaget rediscovered.* A report of the conference on cognitive studies and curriculum development. Ithaca, New York: Cornell University Press, 1964. (b)

Piaget, J. *The psychology of intelligence.* London: Routledge and Kegan Paul, 1964. (c)

Piaget, J. Quantification, conservation, and nativism. *Science,* 1968, 162, 976-979.

Piaget, J. *Genetic epistemology.* New York: Teachers College Press, 1970.

Piaget, J. *Science of education and the psychology of the child.* Translated by D. Coltman, New York: Viking, 1971.

Piaget, J. Forward. In M. Schwebel & J. Raph (Eds.), *Piaget in the classroom.* New York: Basic Books, Inc., 1973. (a)

Piaget, J. *To understand is to invent: The future of education,* New York: Grossman, 1973. (b)

Piaget, J., & Inhelder, B. *The child's conception of space.* Translated by F. J. Langdon and J. L. Lunzer. New York: Norton, 1967.

Piaget, J., & Inhelder, B. *The mental imagery of the child.* Translated by P. A. Chilton. New York: Basic Books, Inc., 1971.

Piaget, J., Inhelder, B., & Szeminska, A. *The child's conception of geometry.* New York: Harper and Row, 1960.

Pinard, A., & Laurendeau, M. "Stage" in Piaget's cognitive development theory: Exegesis of a concept. In D. Elkind & J. H. Flavell (Eds.), *Studies in cognitive development.* New York: Oxford University Press, 1969.

Ripple, R. E., & Rockcastle, V. N. (Eds.). *Piaget rediscovered.* A report of the conference on cognitive studies and curriculum development. Ithaca, New York: Cornell University Press, 1964.

Rothenberg, B. B. Conservation of number among four-and-five-year-old children: Some methodological considerations. *Child Development*, 1969, 40, 383-406.

Roughhead, W. G., & Scandura, J. M. What is learned in mathematical discovery. *Journal of Educational Psychology*, 1968, 59, 282-289.

Saltz, E., & Sigel, I. E. Concept overdiscrimination in children. *Journal of Experimental Psychology*, 1967, 73, 1-8.

Seigel, S. *Nonparametric statistics for the behavioral sciences.* New York: McGraw-Hill Book Company, 1956.

Shantz, C. U. A developmental study of Piaget's theory of logical multiplication. *The Merrill-Palmer Quarterly*, 1967, 13, 121-137.

Siegel, L. S., & Goldstein, A. G. Conservation of number in young children: Recency versus relational response strategies. *Developmental Psychology*, 1969, 1, 128-130.

Sigel, I. E., & Hooper, F. H. (Eds.). *Logical thinking in children.* New York: Holt, Rinehart and Winston, 1968.

Sigel, I. E., Roeper, A., & Hooper, F. H. A training procedure for acquisition of Piaget's conservation of quantity: A pilot study and its replication. *British Journal of Educational Psychology*, 1966, 36, 301-311.

Sinclair, H. Number and measurement. In M. F. Rosskopf, L. P. Steffe, & S. Taback (Eds.), *Piagetian cognitive-development research and mathematical education.* Washington, D. C.: National Council of Teachers of Mathematics, 1971.

Skypeck, D. H. The relationship of socio-economic status to the development of conservation of number. Unpublished doctoral dissertation, University of Wisconsin, 1966.

Smedslund, J. The acquisition of transitivity of weight in five- to seven-year-old children. *Journal of Genetic Psychology*, 1963, 102, 245-255. (a)

Smedslund, J. Development of concrete transitivity of length in children. *Child Development*, 1963, 34, 389-405. (b)

Smedslund, J. Patterns of experience and the acquisition of concrete transitivity of weight in eight-year-old children. *Scandinavian Journal of Psychology*, 1963, 4, 251-256. (c)

Smedslund, J. Concrete reasoning: A study of intellectual development. *Monographs of the Society for Research in Child Development*, 1964, 29 (Serial No. 93).

Smedslund, J. Microanalysis of concrete reasoning, I: The difficulty of some combinations of addition and subtraction of the unit. *Scandinavian Journal of Psychology*, 1966, 7, 145-156.

Smock, C. A model for early childhood education. Unpublished manuscript, University of Georgia, 1970.

Smock, C. Discovering psychological principles for mathematics instruction. Paper presented at the Northwestern symposium on cognitive development research and mathematical laboratories, 1973.

Steffe, L. P. The performance of first grade children in four levels of conservation of numerousness on three IQ groups when solving arithmetic addition problems, *Technical Report No. 14, Wisconsin Research and Development Center for Cognitive Learning.* Madison: The University of Wisconsin, 1966.

Steffe, L. P. Thinking about measurement. *The Arithmetic Teacher,* 1971, 18, 332.

Steffe, L. P. Relationships between mathematical and genetic structures: Cardinal and ordinal number. Paper presented at the meeting of the National Council of Teachers of Mathematics, Houston, 1973.

Steffe, L. P., & Johnson, D. C. Problem solving performance of first-grade children. *Journal for Research in Mathematics Education,* 1971, 2, 50-64.

Sullivan, E. V. Piaget and the school curriculum: A critical appraisal. *The Ontario Institute for Studies in Education,* 1967, No. 2.

Uprichard, A. E. The effects of sequence in the acquisition of three set relations: An experiment with preschoolers. *The Arithmetic Teacher,* 1970, 17, 597-604.

Van Engen, H. Foreward. In R. L. Carey & L. P. Steffe, An investigation in learning of equivalence and order relations by four- and five-year-old children. *Research Paper No. 17, Georgia Research and Development Center in Educational Stimulation.* Athens: University of Georgia, 1968.

Van Engen, H. Epistemology, research and instruction. In M. F. Rosskopf, L. P. Steffe, & S. Taback (Eds.), *Piagetian cognitive-development research and mathematical education.* Washington, D. C.: National Council of Teachers of Mathematics, 1971.

Vygotsky, L. S. *Thought and language.* Cambridge: MIT Press, 1962.

Wohlwill, J. F. The abstraction and conceptualization of form, color, and number. *Journal of Experimental Psychology,* 1957, 53, 304-309.

Wohlwill, J. F. A study of the development of the number concept by scalogram analysis. *Journal of Genetic Psychology,* 1960, 67, 345-377.

Wohlwill, J. F. From perception to inference: A dimension of cognitive development. In I. E. Sigel & F. H. Hooper (Eds.), *Logical thinking in children.* New York: Holt, Rinehart & Winston, 1968.

Wohlwill, F. J., & Lowe, R. C. An experimental analysis of the development of the conservation of number. *Child Development,* 1962, 33, 153-167.

Wolf, R., & Kolpfer, L. Program TSSA' test scorer and statistical analysis 2. *Computer Program Library: Social Sciences Division,* Chicago: University of Chicago, 1963.

Zimiles, H. A note on Piaget's concept of conservation. *Child Development,* 1963, 34, 691-695.

Zimiles, H. The development of conservation and differentiation of number. *Monograph of the society for Research in Child Development,* 1966, 31.

Y0-CLE-924

Max Heindel

The
Message of the Stars

BY

MAX HEINDEL

AND

AUGUSTA FOSS HEINDEL

AN ESOTERIC EXPOSITION OF

NATAL AND MEDICAL ASTROLOGY

EXPLAINING THE ARTS OF

READING THE HOROSCOPE AND DIAGNOSING DISEASE

SEVENTEENTH EDITION

The Rosicrucian Fellowship

INTERNATIONAL HEADQUARTERS

MOUNT ECCLESIA, OCEANSIDE, CALIFORNIA, U.S.A.

ENGLAND

L. N. Fowler & Co., Ltd. 29, Ludgate Hill

London, E. C. 4

THIRD PRINTING
PAPER COVER EDITION
MARCH, 1976

THE ROSICRUCIAN FELLOWSHIP
OCEANSIDE, CALIF., U.S.A.
92054

PRINTED IN THE UNITED STATES OF AMERICA
BY WOOD & JONES
PASADENA, CALIFORNIA

CHAPTER I.

Evolution as Shown in the Zodiac

IT IS a matter of common knowledge among mystics that the evolutionary career of mankind is indissolubly bound up with the divine hierarchies who rule the planets and the signs of the Zodiac, and that the passage of the Sun and the planets through the twelve signs of the Zodiac, marks man's progress in time and in space. Therefore it is not to be wondered at, that in the course of their investigations into the spiritual development of mankind, the writers have also encountered much that deals with the Zodiac which is the boundary of our evolutionary sphere at the present time. So much has been perceived in *the memory of nature* that sheds light upon obscure passages of the Bible, that notes have been made from time to time of different points, but how to collect and collate these dissociated writings into a united whole, has been a great problem for a long time. Even now, the writers know and feel that what they are bringing forth is only a very, very weak attempt to set before the students that great body of facts which have come to them through the memory of nature. They feel, however, that this will give a new and more profound meaning to the old symbols, and that by passing on what has been found they put themselves in line to receive more light.

Concerning the future evolution of planets; the Rosicrucian Cosmo-Conception teaches, on page 256, that "when the beings upon a planet have evolved to a sufficient degree, the planet becomes a Sun, the fixed center of a Solar System. When the beings there have evolved to a still greater degree, and consequently it has reached its maximum of brilliancy, it breaks up into a Zodiac and becomes, so to speak, the womb of a new Solar System. Thus the Great hosts of Divine beings who, until then, were confined upon that Sun gain freedom of action upon a great number of stars whence they can affect, in different ways, the system which grows up within their sphere of influence. The planets or man-bearing worlds within the Zodiac are constantly being worked upon by these forces but in various ways according to the stage they have reached in evolution. Our Sun could not have become a sun until it set out from itself all the beings who were not sufficiently evolved to endure the high rate of vibration and the great luminosity of the beings who were qualified for that evolution. All the beings upon the different planets would have been consumed had they remained in the Sun. This visible Sun, however, though it is a place of evolution for beings vastly above man, is not by any means, the Father of the other planets, as material science supposes. On the contrary, it is itself an emanation from *the central*

Sun, which is the invisible source of all that IS in our solar system."

"Our visible Sun is but the mirror in which are reflected the Rays of energy from the Spiritual Sun, the real Sun is as invisible as the *real* man."

From this teaching it is apparent that the great spiritual hierarchies which are now guiding our evolution, have had their training for this path in previous schemes of manifestation, also that what *they* are now doing, *we* shall some day do *for others.* Already the foremost among our race are treading the path of initiation, and have thereby advanced into stages, far beyond the general status of our present humanity. It has been learned that those who have gone through the Mercurial School of the lesser Mysteries, and have graduated from the School of the Greater Mysteries are now preparing human evolution for the Jupiter Period. They have entered the planet Jupiter, by way of one of the Moons, which serves as a stepping stone. Others there are, unfortunately, who have gone the other way. We read in the Rosicrucian Cosmo-Conception, that even as the whole population of the earth was at one time expelled from the present Sun because of their inability to keep up with the vibrations of the beings thereon, thus hindering them and being hindered themselves, so also it became necessary in the Lemurian Epoch, to expel a number of the stragglers from earth. Thus the Moon was cast out into space to revolve as a Satellite around our present planet.

Those unfortunates are gradually degenerating and the time will come when they will all go to the planet Saturn, which is the door to Chaos. Thence they will be expelled to inter-planetary space to await the time when, in a new system, there will be a favorable condition for their further evolution.

The Gate of Life and Death

Thus the Zodiac and the planets are as a book in which we may read the history of Humanity during past ages, and they also give a key to the future which is in store for us. In the famous Zodiac in the Temple of Denderah, Cancer is not pictured as we have it in modern days. There it is a beetle, a scarab. This was the emblem of the soul, and Cancer has always been known in ancient times, as well as among modern mystics, to be the sphere of the soul, *the gate of Life* in the Zodiac whence the spirits coming into rebirth, enter our sub-lunary conditions. It is therefore aptly ruled by the Moon which is the planet of fecundation, and it is noteworthy that we find Capricorn, which is its opposite, ruled by Saturn the *Planet of Death and Chaos,* who is mystically depicted as "the reaper with his scythe and hour glass in hand." These two opposite signs are therefore turning points in the soul's career. Cancer and Capricorn respectively mark the highest ascent of the Sun into the Northern Hemisphere, and its lowest descent into the South. We observe that during the summer when the Sun is in the sphere of Cancer and allied signs, fecundation and growth are the order of the day. But when the Sun is in the South, in Capricorn, we have winter, when nature is dead. The fruits of the summer are then consumed and assimilated by us. As a circle dance of the Sun among the twelve signs determines the seasons of the year *when direct,* causing the germination of myriads of seeds cast in the earth, also the mating of the fauna, which then makes the world alive with the sights and sounds of manifested life, and at another time leaves the world dumb, dull and drear in winter's gloom, under the sway of Saturn, so by the slower backward movement, known as the *Precession of the Equinox,* does it produce the great changes which we know as Evolution. In fact, this precessional measure of the sun marks the birth and death of races, nations and their religions, for the pictorial Zodiac is a symbolical presentation of our past, present and future development.

Capricorn

Capricorn, the goat, is not a goat at all as we know that animal, but part fish and part goat. Its Saturnine rulership, and the fact that it receives the Sun at the dawn of each New Year, naturally by analogy associates it with the beginning of precessional epochs. It represents the stage in evolution covering transition from fish, through amphibia to the mammalian form. The belligerency of the goat is well known, and an apt symbol of the struggle for existence, in which the weak perish unless able to outdistance their foes. This phase of the matter is sometimes expressed in the symbol, when drawn as part fish and part antelope. Jacob, in the forty-ninth chapter of Genesis, pronounces blessings upon his children, which symbolize the twelve signs. There he speaks of Naphtali as a *"hind"* let loose; thus a very apt symbol of Capricorn, for when the Sun is there at each winter solstice, it is starting a race through the circle of twelve signs, which it must complete in a given time—a year.

Sagittarius

When the Sun leaves Capricorn, by precession, it enters the sign Sagittarius, and this is pictured in the symbolical Zodiac as a Centaur, part horse and part man. Thus it shows aptly, the fact that we have evolved through the animal stage into the human. The centaur is in the act of drawing his bow, showing that there is something for which the human spirit, on its pilgrimage through matter, is seeking, that it aspires to something that lies beyond it, as a lofty ideal, for the bow points upward to the stars.

Scorpio

The next step in human unfoldment is not so much along the physical lines as along the mental. Its nature is shown by the Sun's passage through the sign Scorpio, which is pictorially represented as a *serpent* or *scorpion,* emblems of cunning and subtility. It is plain from this symbol that the first faculty of the mind evolved by infant humanity was *cunning,* and we still see that that is a characteristic trait among the lower races, the lower classes and the lower natures even among our present-day humanity.

Libra

But when the Sun enters the sign Libra, '*The Scales,*' by precession, the balance of reason gives him a new start upon the evolutionary path. Under the care of divine instructors man had at that time advanced to the point where because of this new faculty, reason, he could be made fully responsible to nature's laws, and thus reap what he had sown, that he might learn the lesson of life by actual experience, be able to reason out the connection between cause and effect and in time learn to govern himself so as to progress further upon the path.

Virgo

Thus, under the guidance of the spiritual hierarchies, focused through the signs of *Capricorn, Sagittarius, Scorpio,* and *Libra,* were his physical, moral and mental attributes acquired, and he was equipped to commence the spiritual side of his evolution. The germ of this progress is hidden in the celestial virgin, the sign *Virgo,* which is the vehicle of the immaculate conception, the heavenly mother of Christ; not of one Christ only, but of many. This is one of the most sublime signs of the Zodiac and one of the most mystical, so fraught with hidden meaning that its full import cannot be fully understood save when viewed by the internal light of spiritual illumination. Yearly, at the winter solstice, the immaculate Madonna is ascendant at midnight, when the new born Sun commences to rise to the task of growing the grain and grape, to save humanity from the cold and famine, which would inevitably result were he to remain in the southern declination. The Sun is therefore an apt symbol of the Savior, born to feed his flock on the spiritual bread of life. But, as we must have eyes attuned to light to see the sun, so must the Christ be born within before we can perceive spiritual light. As Angelus Silesius says:

"Though Christ a thousand times in Bethlehem be born
And not within thyself, thy soul will be forlorn.
The Cross on Golgotha thou lookest to in vain
Unless within thyself it be set up again."

Therefore, by the precessional passage of the Sun through the sign Virgo, the germinal impulse was given towards the birth of Christ within man. The *mystic marriage* of the lower self to the higher, the *immaculate conception,* and the *divine motherhood* which nourishes deep in its bosom, unseen by a scoffing world"*the new born Christ,*" are actual experiences of a growing number of people. And without the celestial prototype, fructified by the solar precession, this would be an impossibility; neither has this ideal been realized in such fullness during the past ages as today. The reason of this will appear when we take up the joint consideration of opposite signs of the Zodiac.

Leo

A great future is in store for this offspring of the celestial virgin. Listen to the wonderful prophecy of Isaiah: "For unto us a child is born, unto us a Son is given, and the government shall be upon his shoulders and his name shall be called *Wonderful, Counsellor,* the *Mighty God,* the *Everlasting Father,* the *Prince of Peace.* Of the increase of His government and peace there shall be no end."

Humanity is to rise to a wonderful spiritual height and this is symbolized by the Sun's precessional passage through the royal sign Leo, pictorially represented by the king of beasts, the lion. This is an apt allusion to the King of Creation, who will then embody the three great virtues of the Master Man, Strength, Wisdom and Beauty.

It is wonderful to trace the various phases of the religions given to the Great Aryo-Semitic Race from the time they were "called out" in the latter third of the Atlantean Epoch, to the end of the Aquarian Age, when a new race will have been definitely born. This aspect of the Zodiac will form the subject of the following pages. It will shed light on many of the most obscure passages of the Bible, as only study of this Cosmic Science can.

When we consider the Zodiac in its religious as well as its evolutionary aspects, by means of the six pairs of opposite signs into which the twelve may be divided, we also commence with Cancer and Capricorn, for the reason given in the previous article, namely: that these are the solstitial points where the Sun reaches its highest and lowest declination.

Considered in this manner, we find that there are two sets of three pairs of signs, the first being Cancer and Capricorn, Gemini and Sagittarius, Taurus and Scorpio. In these pairs of signs we may read the history of human evolution and religion, in the early, the middle and the latter third of the Atlantean Epoch. In the other three pairs of signs, Aries and Libra, Pisces and Virgo, Aquarius and Leo, we find the key to man's development during the Aryan Epoch. This is also divisible into three distinct periods, namely: the *Aryan Age,* from Moses to Christ, which comes under Aries-Libra; the *Piscean Age,* which takes in the last two thousand years under Pisces-Virgo Catholicism; and the two thousand years which are ahead of us, called the *Aquarian Age,* where the signs Aquarius and Leo will be illuminated and vivified by the solar precession, for the upliftment of the Son of Man (Aquarius), by the Christ within, the Lion of Judah (Leo), to the estate of Superman.

It must not be thought, however, that the Atlantean Epoch only lasted while the Sun by precession went through Cancer, Gemini, and Taurus, a period of only six thousand and a few hundred years; far from it; but there are spirals within spirals and recapitulation takes place in the epochs and races, so that we may know what is the general destiny by looking at the Sun's passage through these signs and therewith taking this import and symbolism into consideration. It may also be said that the further we advance the smaller do the spirals become, the shorter the time in which a given improvement is made, because of the proficiency we attained in former ages, and therefore it is extremely probable that this present is the last lap, that the coming Aquarian Age is the final preparatory school day which will fit us for the new age, the Sixth Epoch, and that this will begin when the Sun by precession enters Capricorn.

This, of course, would mean that the Second Advent must take place just before that time, and though it seems to us that so many signs point that way, still it is a mere surmise and may not have any truth in it at all. Thousands of people have been misled during all the ages that we know of, to think that Christ would soon be here; it is, however, better that we are looking forward to it than if we should say with some, that it will never take place. In that case the Great Day would find us unprepared and we should find ourselves among the stragglers who are unfit to attend the wedding feast of the Higher Self to the lower because lacking the "soul-body," the "wedding garment," necessary to enfold them.

Cancer-Capricorn (♋—♑)

The Sun's passage by precession through the sphere of Cancer with its opposite sign Capricorn, designates the early third of the Atlantean period, which was intensely watery, as the whole earth was covered by a dense, drenching fog. The Niebelung, or "Children of the Mist," lived then in the basins of the Earth. Cancer was not then represented by the same symbol as today; in ancient times, it was pictorially figured as a beetle or scarab. This was the signature of the soul, for then mankind was much less body than soul.

The sign Cancer is watery in its nature, and the fish part of Capricorn, the opposite sign, also helps to symbolize this state of life under water when the Sun went through the watery sign Cancer by precession. The Moon, the planet of fecundation, points mystically to this period of germination, when mankind first commenced to exercise the Creative function at the dictates of desire inculcated by the Lucifer Spirits. Thus mankind opened the Gate of physical Life through Cancer, and strayed into the terrestrial sphere, but opposite stood Saturn, the ruler of Capricorn, ready to slay them with his scythe, and usher them through the Gate of Death back into the spiritual realms where they are at home.

Capricorn was the opposite of Cancer and embodied the ideal that as the goat climbs the mountains, so man must leave the basins of Atlantis and come up from the mist.

Gemini-Sagittarius (♊—♐)

Our condition during the middle third of the Atlantean Epoch is illustrated in the Sun's passage through the sign Gemini, the twins, which aptly represent infant humanity. During this age the division of soul from soul by the veil of flesh, which we call the body, became more noticeable, for the atmosphere had already cleared to a considerable extent, and the faculties of the spirit had become more focused in its physical instrument. With this delusion of the personal self, there came at once the idea of "me" and "thee," "mine" and "thine," our individual interests commenced to clash with those of others, so that a tragedy such as that recorded between Cain and Abel became possible. Nor was the shedding of blood confined to human beings, for we learn from the Bible that "Nimrod was a mighty hunter". This savage ideal was expressed in the Celestial Centaur, Sagittarius, with his bow and arrow.

But both of these pairs of opposites, Cancer-Capricorn and Gemini-Sagittarius, may be considered pre-historic hieroglyphics of a development accomplished in Sidereal years, long past, though none the less important on that account. Our own times, with the development prescribed for them, are symbolically represented in the two pairs of signs within the fixed cross, the Bull, the Lion, the Serpent and the Man.

For that reason the two pairs of opposites comprising the fixed signs, Taurus-Scorpio, and Leo-

Aquarius, are mentioned in the Bible, and we shall find that our modern systems of religion are full of allusions to the three pairs of opposites, Aquarius-Leo and the two adjacent pairs of signs, Aries-Libra and Pisces-Virgo. These three pairs of opposites are, as already stated, emblematic of the development in the entire Aryan Epoch. In the *early* third of this Epoch, the Sun by precession went through the sign Aries, the *middle* third of it finds the Sun in Pisces, by precession, and during the last third the Sun will go through the sign Aquarius. Then the solstitial point Capricorn will see the inauguration of a new cycle or age.

The spiritual preparation for this development commenced about thirteen thousand B. C. when the Sun by precession, was in the sign Libra, the Balance, the last time. Different phases of this germinal impregnation of the people then living were carried on during the precessional travel of the Sun through Virgo, Leo, and culminated in Cancer about eight thousand B. C. when the last of Atlantis was destroyed by water, substantially as related by the Egyptian priests to Plato. We shall see presently how the germinal ideals, given to humanity in those far, by-gone days have grown and flowered into factors of human development and spiritual standards of the greatest importance.

Taurus-Scorpio (♉—♏)

In the latter third of Atlantis, egoism had developed to a far greater degree than before, the spiritual sight had been lost by the large majority of the people who then lived entirely on the material plane and gloried particularly in their material possessions.

The Bull was very properly worshiped by them, being an emblem of strength necessary to conquer the material world. It was, on account of its prodigious strength, an invaluable aid in all their work. The proverb about "the flesh pots of Egypt" has remained illustrative to the present day, to show how abundantly that animal supplied their physical need of food, the milk of the female being also an important article of diet. The possession of many cattle was therefore ardently desired by the ancient infant nations, and the worship of the Bull was inaugurated under the solar precession through Taurus during earlier Great Sidereal Years, and was continued to the comparatively modern times, when the Sun by precession went through the sign of the Celestial Bull for the last time.

At that point when the Sun entered the sign of the Lamb, Aries, the Aryan religions were inaugurated. The Religion of the Lamb is to hold sway for the next Great Sidereal Year, while the Sun by precession passes around the twelve signs of the Zodiac, as the religion of the Bull has held sway during the previous celestial year from the time the Sun entered Taurus, until it left the same sign on its next passage.

New religions, however, are not revealed in their

fullness at the beginning; they are started and go through a period of gestation long before the religion which they are to succeed ends its material existence, and similarly, an ancient religion about to be abrogated survives long after the religion which succeeds it has become the official source for upliftment of humanity. The original Semites, chosen to inaugurate the worship of the Lamb, Aries, during the Aryan Epoch, were taken from "Egypt," the home of the Bull "Taurus." Not our modern Egypt however. The story of Pharaoh, who endeavored to prevent their emigration and was drowned, has reference to Atlantis which was submerged thousands of years before Moses is supposed to have made his escape with the Israelites through the "Red Sea." The facts underlying the story are that a multitude of people left the land where the bull "Taurus" was worshiped, (Atlantis or Egypt) whose inhabitants were then drowned, to seek a "promised land" beyond the water which had engulfed an *"ungodly nation."* There they were dedicated to the worship of the "Lamb" Aries which had been slain in "Egypt" (Atlantis); through its blood these pioneers had been preserved from death, and it was thus "the Lamb, slain from the foundation of the (present) World" which we call *the Aryan Epoch.* Noah's escape presents another phase of the same occurrence relating that the mists which had enveloped Atlantis condensed to rain, and flooded the basins of the earth, leaving a clear atmosphere in which the Rainbow was seen for the first time at the opening of the New Age, the Aryan Epoch, where a new Covenant was made with the pioneers of the polity then ushered in.

Atlantis was the home of the Bull, Taurus, and when the Sun, by precession, was leaving that sign the last time, the Religion of the Lamb Aries was definitely ushered in. Thenceforth, the worship of the Bull was abrogated and when any of the pioneer race, brought out from the ancient Atlantean dispensation by the blood of the Lamb, Aries, backslid and worshiped the Taurean "Calf," they acted contrary to the law of progress and were therefore "Idolaters," and an abomination to the divine hier archs whose task it was to guide them during the ages preceding the advent of Christ. On account of repeated transgressions many were "lost," and they are the Jews of today who still retain their Atlantean traits (see Cosmo-Conception).

Apart from the Astrological key, the Bible is truly a closed book, but with this key, the matter is different. In the Old Testament reference is made to two classes of animals: Bulls, which were Taurean, and Sheep and Goats, which were Arian. These alone were used as Sacrifices. (Turtle doves were permitted as a concession to poverty). All the principal characters of the Old Dispensation were shep herds (*Arian*) and Christ also announces Himself as the Great Shepherd.

In the New Testament we find another animal,

the Fish, attaining great prominence, and the apostles were called to be "Fishers of Men," for then the sun by precession was nearing the cusp of Pisces, the Fishes, and Christ spoke of the time when the Son of Man (Aquarius) shall come. Thus our evolutionary journey is mapped out in the hidden astrological allusions of the Bible.

The student now has a line on the march of events, which it is well to keep in mind.

Jesus taught the multitudes in parables but explained the mysteries of the Kingdom to His disciples. Paul gave spiritual meat to the strong, but the milk of doctrine to the multitude, for there has always been an exoteric and an esoteric side to every religion. Taking Taurus, the sign of the Bull, to symbolize the worship of that animal as practiced in Egypt, Persia and other countries at that time, then we shall find that the opposite sign, Scorpio, symbolizes the esoteric doctrine of the priesthood, who were the guardians of the ancient Atlantean Mysteries.

In this connection we will note first that the sign Scorpio is represented in the pictorial Zodiac by a Scorpion or Serpent, and we wish to impress particularly on the student's mind that the Scorpion has its *sting in the tail,* while the Serpent has the *venom in its teeth.* This is very significant, as we shall see presently.

On looking up the word "serpent" in the Bible, we shall find that there are about seven words that have thus been translated; but one of them, which was borrowed from Egypt, is *Naja.* This word is found on the old tablets in the ancient temples of Egypt where Osiris, the Sun God, is hailed when arising from the primordial deep. He was then crowned with glory and has the Uræus Naja, *an emblem of cosmic wisdom.* The Uræus was a part of a serpent's body, with its head depicted as protruding from a point in the forehead just above the nose, where the human spirit has its seat; and Christ therefore referred to the ancient Serpent-Initiates, when He said: "Be ye wise as serpents."

In ancient Egypt the King wore a crown adorned by *a double serpent, Uraeus* or *Naja,* which seemed to protrude from his forehead when the crown was placed upon his head. This was to symbolize the fact that he held the double office of King and Priest by virtue of his sublime wisdom. In India, also, the guardians of the Mystery Teachings were called Nagas or Serpents. In the Icelandic "Eddas," the Northern Vedas, Siegfried, the truth seeker, slays the serpent, tastes of its blood and then becomes wise. Nor, to elaborate on the statement made above, is it necessary to go outside our own religion for proof that the serpent is the symbol of wisdom, for the Christ Himself said: "Be ye wise as serpents." The serpent is certainly not sufficiently sagacious to warrant a literal meaning of this saying; but when we understand that when the creative fire is drawn upwards through the serpentine spinal cord it vibrates the pituitary body and the pineal gland, connecting the Ego with the invisible worlds by opening up a hidden sense, the allusion is perfectly clear.

There is, however, a lower phase of spiritual development, symbolized in ancient times by placing the Uræus or serpent at the navel, to show that the mediumistic faculties in the solar plexus had been developed. Mediumship is a negative phase of spiritual sight or hearing possessed by a person who, under the control of an outside intelligence, prophesies. This undesirable phase of seership was represented in the Zodiac by the symbol of the Scorpion, which has the sting in its tail. In the Serpent Initiate the Creative Cosmic Fire was drawn upward through the head to serve a spiritual end; in the Medium the creative energy is expressed for selfish, sensual ends through the procreative organ ruled by Scorpio.

The point between the eyebrows, whence the serpent of wisdom protrudes, is *the seat of life*, whereas all that opens the womb is subject to *the sting of death*, contained in the Scorpion's tail.

If we now turn with this information to our Bible, we shall find that a great many things, previously obscure, will become clear. As said, the Egyptian word for this Uræus or serpent is Naja and it was borrowed by the Israelites who expressed the negative faculty of mediumship by affixing the feminine ending "oth," giving *Naioth;* while those able to function consciously in the spiritual worlds were given the positive, male plural ending "im," and were called *Naim*. If we read the nineteenth chapter of first Samuel with this understanding we shall readily see that the incident there narrated was of a mediumistic nature. David had become afraid of Saul and he went with Samuel to "Naioth." This is supposed by Bible translators to be a place, and maybe a village was so named. But if that was the case, it was because the people who lived in that place were Naioth, or mediums. They were called prophets in the chapter before us, and it is significant that as soon as anyone came within their camp, he commenced to prophesy or speak under control. Even Saul, who came there, anxious to get David away that he might slay him, was seized by the spirits and prophesied, to the amazement of all present.

In the New Testament we are told that the Christ went to the city of Nain and there raised *the Son of a Widow*. In the Latin Testament, this city was not called Nain, but *Naim*. And it is very significant that all three, Naim, Naioth and Endor, where the sorceress that assisted Saul is supposed to have lived, are in the same locality by Mount Tabor.

Every Freemason knows that the brethren of that Order are called "Sons of the Widow." And it is stated in the Bible that Hiram Abiff, the Master Builder of Solomon's Temple, was the Son of a Widow, a cunning craftsman. We cannot in the present article repeat the Masonic Legend which tells the reason why. This we have given in the book on "Freemasonry and Catholicism" and also in our books on the Rosicrucian Philosophy. But suffice it to say that in the Bible story to which reference has been made, we have one of the Naim, a Widow's Son or initiate of the old Serpent School, for the priests of Egypt were *"phree messen,"* children of light. Each had within, the ancient Serpent Wisdom. But a new religion was being inaugurated, and it was necessary to raise the ancient Initiates to the Mysteries of the Coming Age. *Therefore the Christ, the Lion of Judah, Lord of the new Kingdom, went to the Widow's Son of Naim* and raised him up by the strong grip of the Lion's paw. And we may here emphasize that the first Initiate under the new system was Hiram Abiff, the highest Initiate of the old system, who, by this new initiation given him by the Christ, became a *Christian,* pledged to bear the *Rose* and the *Cross,* which were the symbols of the New Mystery Teachings of the Western World and he was then given the symbolical name, Christian Rosenkreuz.

Thus from the time when the Sun entered the sign Aries by precession, it became a crime for the chosen people to worship the bull exoterically, or to partake of the esoteric Serpent wisdom. And for a similar reason *it is Idolatry when people of the West take up the Eastern religions, Hinduism, Buddhism and kindred teachings.* For in the Aryan

Epoch, only the Aryan Religions, the religions of the Lamb, have the proper effect on the human evolution. All previous systems are detrimental to the Western people; and in time those also who are now in the East, the Orientals, will be forced to embrace this religion, or be left far behind in evolution.

The Aryan Epoch

Aries—Libra (♈—♎)

The Aryan Epoch may be divided into three eras; but they are all served by the religion of the Lamb. The first division covers the time when the Sun, by precession, went through the sign Aries, the Lamb. Jesus was born when the Vernal equinox was in about seven degrees of Aries; so the twenty-three degrees which lie on the other side belong to the Old Testament period, when the chosen people were in captivity and lost in the wilderness of the world; the new religion had not then found its place. Then the Christ came and inaugurated this new teaching definitely. He came not to destroy the old prophecies and the law, but to give us something higher when they shall have been fulfilled. The sign opposite Aries is Libra, the scales or balance of Justice; and therefore we are told in the new religion that there will come a day of judgment (♎), when Christ shall appear to give to every man according to the deeds done in the body.

Pisces—Virgo (♓—♍)

Christ was the Great Shepherd (♈), but He

called His disciples to be "fishers of men," for the Sun by precession was then leaving the sign of the Lamb and entering Pisces, the sign of the fishes. Therefore a new phase of the Aryan religion was opening up. The Bishop's mitre is also in the form of a fish's head.

The New Testament, therefore, does not mention the Bull or the Lamb, but references to the fishes are numerous. We also find the celestial virgin (♍) prominent and the wheat ear of Virgo is the Bread of Life, to be gained only through immaculate purity. Thus Christ fed the multitude on fish (Pisces) and loaves (Virgo).

Before the time of Christ, the new religion of the Lamb (Aries), could get no foothold. Moses, the erstwhile leader, could not bring the chosen people to the "promised land." That was reserved for Joshua, the son of Nun. Joshua is the Hebraic for "Jesus" and the Hebrew word "Nun" means "fish" (Pisces). It was thus foretold that the religion of the Lamb (♈) would attain prominence during the precessional passage of the Sun through the sign Pisces, the fishes.

This prophecy has been fulfilled, for during the two thousand years which have elapsed since the birth of Jesus, the Western religion has been taught by a celibate priesthood, worshiping an immaculate virgin, symbolized by the celestial sign Virgo, which is the opposite of Pisces. This same priesthood has also enjoined the eating of fish and forbidden the use of flesh (♈ ♉) on certain days. When the children of Israel left the flesh pots of Egypt, where the Bull (♉) was slain, they left it by the blood of the Lamb (♈). But in the Piscean dispensation no shedding of blood is enjoined and flesh eating is condemned as a sin at certain times, for man is now taught to forsake the lusts of the flesh and also lusting after the flesh.

This ideal was tried under the Aryan dispensation, when the chosen people were yet in the Wilderness, so called, but without success; they would not have the heavenly manna. Now, however, man is being weaned from the cannibalistic practice, and in the seven hundred years which remain before the Aquarian age is definitely ushered in, we will, in all probability, have made great strides, both in overcoming the lust of the flesh and the lust after the flesh. For Virgo, the immaculate celestial virgin, and the ears of wheat contained in the sign, show both these ideals as profitable to soul growth at the present time. Jupiter, the planet of benevolence and philanthropy, which rules Pisces, has been a prominent factor in promoting altruism during the past two milleniums.

Aquarius—Leo (♒—♌)

It is often said, and rightly so, that the boy is father of the man. And on the same principle we may say that the Son of Man is the Super-Man; therefore, when the Sun by precession enters the celestial sign Aquarius, the water-bearer, we shall have a new phase of the religion of the Lamb, exoterically; and the ideal to be striven for is shown in the opposite sign, Leo.

The Moon, which is the habitat of the autocratic Race Ruler and Lawgiver, Jehovah, is exalted in Taurus, the sign of the Bull, and all Race religions, even the Mosaic phase of the Aryan religion of the Lamb, demanded a sacrificial victim for every transgression of that law. But the Sun is exalted in Aries, and when the great Sun spirit, Christ, came as High Priest of the Aryan religion, He abrogated sacrifice of *others* by offering up *Himself as a perpetual sacrifice* for sin.

By looking to the mother ideal of Virgo during the Piscean Age, and following the Christ's example of sacrificial service, the immaculate conception becomes an actual experience to each of us, and Christ, the Son of Man, Aquarius, is born within us. Thus, gradually, the third phase of the Aryan religion will be ushered in and a new ideal will be found in the Lion of Judah, Leo. Courage of conviction, strength of character and kindred virtues will then make man truly the King of Creation, worthy of the trust and the confidence of the lower orders of life as well as of the love of the Divine Hierarchs above.

This, the mystic message of Man's evolution, is marked in flaming characters upon the field of heaven, where he who runs may read. And when we study the revealed purpose of God, we shall in turn learn to conform intelligently to that design, thereby hastening the day of emancipation from our present cramped environment to the perfect liberty of free Spirits, risen superior to the law of Sin and Death, through Christ, the Lord of Love and Life.

It is for us to decipher this message, and solve the Riddle of the Universe.

CHAPTER II.

The Measure of Amenability to Planetary Vibrations

WHEN judging a horoscope it is of prime importance that we take into consideration the social and racial standing of the individual, for configurations which are of great significance in the horoscope of an educated Caucasian, may mean little or nothing in the figure of a Chinese coolie and vice versa. Neglect of this factor would inevitably lead to false conclusions, as we shall now explain.

It is a mystic maxim that the lower in the scale of evolution a being is placed the more certainly it responds to the planetary rays, and conversely the higher we ascend in the scale of attainment the more the man conquers and rules his stars, freeing himself from the leading strings of the Divine Hierarchies. This yoke was not, however, placed upon man in order to restrain him needlessly, but just as we in our ordinary life restrain a child from doing things in ignorance, which would hurt it, and maybe cripple it for life, so also are we restrained by the Divine Hierarchies through the planetary aspects in such a manner that we do not hurt ourselves beyond recovery in the experiences of life.

But coupled with this guidance there is of course the measure of Free Will, which grows as we evolve. The child in our midst has really very little free will, being subject not only to its parents but to the servants, if such there be in the household, and to everybody with whom it is associated, all exercising control over it for its own good. As the child grows, this measure of restraint is by degrees relaxed, and in the course of years the child will learn to exercise its free will. This method has been followed by the Divine Hierarchies in the case of man. Infant humanity was absolutely guided by Divine rules without having any Will at all; "Thus shalt thou do, or not do," were injunctions laid upon them which must be implicitly obeyed, otherwise the Divine displeasure was at once shown by such strenuous manifestations as appealed to infant humanity's mind, namely, lightning, thunder, earth-quakes and great visitations of plagues. This was for their collective guidance; for individual restraint there were strict laws, commandments and ordinances. Tribute must be paid continually to the Divine Leader and offered up on the altar as sacrifices, and for every offense against the law a certain sacrifice of material goods must be made. Fear was the dominant keynote of that dispensation: for "The fear of the Lord is the beginning of righteousness." This regime was carried on under the planetary conditions of Mars and the Moon. Mars, being the home of the dominant Lucifer Spirits, gave to mankind the energy necessary that evolution may be accomplished; this martial energy was of the very greatest importance, particularly of course in the earlier stages. The Moon, which is the home of the Angels, under their Divine Leader Jehovah, gave to infant humanity that child-like brain-mind which is amenable to rulership, and bends itself readily before authority.

These with Saturn were the only planetary rays which affected mankind as a whole during the Lemurian epoch, and if a horoscope were erected for any of the people who lived then, it would be unnecessary to enter the places of the other planets, because they could not respond to their rays. Even today a great part of mankind has not evolved very far beyond that point, a large class, particularly among those we speak of as the lower races, and even the lower classes of our western world being dominated principally by these planetary rays. Under their impulses they act with automatic certainty in a specific manner, and it is possible to predict exactly what they will do under a certain aspect of these planets, because they live entirely in their emotions and are scarcely, if at all, responsive to the intellectual vibrations of Mercury. Neither can they appreciate such emotions as signified by Venus or its octave, Uranus; they respond solely to the lower nature, the animal passions. They move under the impulses of Mars and the Moon respecting sex and sustenance. Their pleasures are of the lowest and most sensual nature, they live like animals altogether in the physical, and their creed is "eat, drink and be merry." Their desires run chiefly to "wine and women," for they have not as yet awakened to the charm of song; neither has beauty had a chance to enchant the savage heart at this stage of development for that comes from the Venus rays which are beyond such people. Woman is to the man of that stage only a beast of burden and a convenience.

Meanwhile "Father Time" represented by the planet Saturn, keeps the score, and wields over them the whiplash of necessity to drive them forward on the evolutionary path, meting out to each the fruits of his labor at the harvest time between lives. When the man has cultivated the savage virtues of bravery, physical endurance, etc., he dreams in the post-mortem existence of new fields to conquer, and sees where he was lacking and why his desires were frustrated because of lack of implements. Gradually the constructive martial ray and the Saturn cunning fertilize the lunar brain which he is building, so that in time he learns to make the crude implements necessary for the attainment of his primitive ambitions. Even today we see the same cunning traits of character, the same crude crafts displayed in and by the lower races for the purpose of irrigating land, mining ores or milling grain. All those earliest implements were the result of the planetary rays of Saturn, Moon and Mars, impinging on the primitive brain of infant humanity.

A little further along the path of evolution, in

the Atlantean epoch, the Lords of Venus and the Lords of Mercury came to the earth for the purpose of giving a further impulse to the mental and emotional development. It was the task of Venus to combat the lower emotions and raise the brutish animal passion of Mars to the softer and more beautiful Venus-love. She was to add beauty to strength, and to attain that ideal the Lords of Venus fostered the plastic arts, painting and sculpture. These were not taught men of the general public at that time; the ideals which are to be developed in a race are always first taught to the most advanced ones in a mystery temple, and at that time initiation included no spiritual instruction, but consisted of an education in the liberal arts. Sculpture taught how the beautiful may be incorporated in physical form. It called attention to the body and idealized the softly curved lines. The result is now incorporated in our own race body, for it should be thoroughly understood that in a mystery school an ideal is not taught today simply to be forgotten tomorrow or in the next generation, but ideals are inculcated so that in time they may become a part of the very life, soul and body of the race. Compare the race body of the modern civilized man with that of the Indian, the Bushman, the Hottentot, etc., and you will find that there is indeed beauty added to strength.

It may be objected that we are degenerating compared with what is shown in the Hellenic Arts, but that is positively not so; it is rather that we have not yet attained to that highest ideal. In ancient Greece the mystery temples occupied a much more prominent position than today; the beautiful form was idolized to the detriment of the mind notwithstanding the fact that Greece had a Plato and a Socrates. The Lords of Mercury who had charge of the development of mind, at the time when the Lords of Venus exercised their great influence on the emotions, had not then been able to make a universally strong impression on the early humanity. We are well aware even today that it hurts to think, but it is easy to follow the emotions. At the present time the middle class of the West is much further advanced than the ancient Greeks because of the influence of these two planetary rays in our lives. Woman naturally excels in the highly imaginative Venus faculty, because of her part in the creative function which aids in moulding the body of the race. On that account her figure has the graceful curves which naturally express beauty, while man has the worldly-wise intellect fostered by the Lords of Mercury, and is the exponent of reason, the creative agency of physical progress in the world's work.

We always long for, admire, and aspire to what we lack. In days of savagery when kicks and cuffs were her daily fare woman longed for a caress from her lord. The Venus ray gave her beauty and made her an adept in the feminine arts which have conquered the masculine heart, so that now man plays the role of protector on the plea that woman is not mentally competent; meanwhile he is becoming that which he admires in her; he is more gentle and kind, Venus is conquering Mars, but the Mercury delusion of intellectual superiority needs another influence to conquer it. And this, woman is now supplying by her aspiration. As she mastered martial brutality by Venus beauty, so also, will she free herself from Mercurial bondage by Uranian intuition.

To primitive man, driven by the whip-lash of Saturnine necessity, when not by the animal lust and passions of Mars and the Moon, the world looks gloomy. Fear is the key-note of his existence; fear of animals; fear of other men; fear of the nature forces; fear of everything around him. He must ever be watchful and on the alert, vigilance is eternally the price of safety. But when evolution makes him amenable to the influences of Venus and Mercury, they soften his emotions and brighten the mentality; he begins to regard love and reason as factors in life. The Sun also begins to brighten his outlook upon life, and sunshine in the nature of man during this phase of his evolution partly dispels the gloom of Saturn. Thus, by degrees, as man evolves and becomes responsive to the music of the spheres, one string after another in the celestial harp strikes the kindred chord in the human soul and makes him amenable to its vibrations, so that as a tuning fork which is struck, awakens the music in other tuning forks of even pitch within reasonable distance, so the planets in our solar system have in evolutionary succession struck various chords that have found an echo in the human heart.

But the strings on the celestial Lyre of Apollo are not all in harmony, some are in actual discord, and while man responds to some he must necessarily remain, at least partially, unresponsive to others. In fact, before it is possible to respond perfectly to the rays of Venus it is necessary for man to conquer Mars to a considerable degree, and bring him under control so that certain undesirable martial traits in his nature will be kept in the background, while others, which may be valuable, are retained. The Venus love which is willing to give all for the loved ones cannot dwell side by side in the heart with the Mars ray which demands all for self. Therefore the savage must learn to conquer himself in a certain measure ere he may become the more civilized family man of modern times. Under the unrestrained passionate rays of Mars and the Moon, parents bring children into the world and leave them to take care of themselves almost as animals do, for they are products of animal passion. The females are bought and sold as a horse or cow or else taken by force and carried away. Even so late as the mediaeval dark ages, the knight often carried away his bride by force of arms, practically in the same manner that the male animals battle for the possession of the female at mating time.

Thus we see that the first step toward civilization requires that a man conquer one or more of the planets to a certain degree at least. Unbridled passion such as generated by the primitive Mars rays is no more permissible under the regime of modern civilization, neither is the tenet that "might is right" any longer admissible, save in wars when we return to barbarism. The Mars quality of physical prowess, that at one time made it a virtue to attack others and take away property, is no longer admired in the individual. It is punished by various means, according to law, though it is still effective as far as nations are concerned, who go to war under this primitive impulse for purposes of territorial aggrandizement. However, as said, Mars has been conquered to a great degree in civil and social life in order that the Venus love might take the place of the Mars passion.

As previously noted, the children of primitive man were left to their own resources, as soon as they had been taught to defend themselves in physical warfare. With the advent of Mercury another method is observable. The battle of life nowadays, is no longer fought with physical weapons alone. Brain, rather than brawn determines success. Therefore the period of education has been lengthened as mankind advanced, and it aims principally at mental accomplishments because of the Mercurial rays which accompany the Venus development of modern civilization. Thus man sees nature from a more sunny side when he has learned to respond to the

Sun, Venus, Mercury, Mars, Moon and Saturn, even if only in a very slight measure.

But although these various stages of evolution have gradually brought man under the dominance of a number of planetary rays, the development has been one-sided, for it has aimed to foster interest solely in things over which he has a proprietary right: *his* business, *his* house, *his* family, *his* cattle, farm, etc., are all vitally important, and must be taken care of. *His* possessions must be increased, if possible, no matter what happens to the possessions, family, etc., belonging to anyone else, that not being his concern. But before he can reach to a higher stage of evolution it is necessary that this desire to appropriate the earth, and retain it for himself if possible, must give way to a desire to benefit his fellowmen. In other words, Egoism must give way to Altruism, and just as Saturn by wielding the whip lash of necessity over him in his primitive days brought him up to his present point of civilization, so also Jupiter, the planet of altruism, is destined to raise him from the state of man to superman where he will come under the Uranian ray in respect to his emotional nature, where passion generated by Mars will be replaced by Compassion, and where the childlike consciousness of Lunar origin will be replaced by a Cosmic consciousness of the Neptunian ray. Therefore the advent into our lives of the Jupiterian ray marks a very distinct advance in the human development. As taught in the Rosicrucian

Cosmo-Conception, we are to advance from our present Earth period into the Jupiter period, and therefore the Jupiterian ray marks that high stage of altruism which will then be a prominent factor in our relations, one with the other, and it will be readily understood that before we can really respond to the rays of Jupiter we must in a measure cultivate altruism, and conquer the egoism that comes through the Mercurial reasoning power. We have learned to conquer some of the phases of Mars and the Moon, we may have also learned to conquer some of the lower phases of Mercury and Venus; the more we have overcome these the better we shall be able to respond to the highest vibratory forces emanating from these planets; yes, if we strive earnestly we shall some day be able to overcome even the highest stage of the Venus love, that always attaches itself to an object which is owned by us. We love our children because they are ours; we love our husbands and wives because they belong to us; we take pride, Venusian pride, in their moral characteristics or Mercurial pride in their accomplishments; but Christ set a higher standard: "Unless a man leave his father and mother he can not be my disciple." The idea that we should neglect our fathers and mothers or that we must hate them in order to follow Him was far from His mind, of course, but father and mother are only bodies; the soul that inhabits this body of the father and mother is to be loved, not the mere physical garment. Our love should be the same whether the person is old or young, ugly or beautiful. We should look for the beauty of the soul, for the universal relationship of all souls and not mind so much the relationship of the bodies. "Who are my mother and my brothers," said the Christ, and pointed to his disciples, those who were at one with Him in His great work. They were closer to Him than any brother could be on account of mere physical relationship. This attitude constitutes an upward step from the Venus love which places the emphasis on the physical garments of the loved ones and leaves out of consideration the soul that is within. The Jupiterian love on the other hand takes cognizance only of the soul, regardless of the body it wears. The Mercurial or reasoning phase of mentality is also changed by response to the altruistic Jupiter. Cold calculation is out of the question. One who feels the expansive ray of Jupiter is big hearted, first, last and all the time, and in every respect; big hearted where his emotions are concerned, his love; big hearted where all the things of the world are concerned. "A jovial fellow," is an apt expression. He is welcomed and loved by everyone he meets because he radiates not the common selfishness, but a desire to benefit others that breeds in us a feeling of trust, diametrically opposed to the sense of distrust we instinctively feel when we come in contact with a Saturn-Mercury man.

It is a matter of actual experience to astrologers endowed with spiritual sight that every man's planetary rays produce certain colors in his aura, in addition to the basic color which is the stamp of the race to which the man belongs. The man with the thin, sickly blues of a commingled Saturn and Mercury, is to be pitied rather than censured for the avarice and gloom which are his constant attitude of mind; he sees everything in the world through the auric mirror which he has created around himself; he feels that the world is cold, hard and selfish, that therefore it is necessary for him to be more selfish and more cold in order that he may protect himself. On the other hand, when we see the divine blue ray of Jupiter tinted with perhaps the fine gold of the Uranian nature we realize how differently such an exalted individual must view the world from the other's sordid way of seeing things. Even those who have the faintest Jupiterian tinge are in a world filled with sunshine, flowers blooming, everything in nature gay and glad. And by looking at the world through such an atmosphere they call forth from other sources a similar response, as the tuning fork previously mentioned generates a vibration in another of an even pitch.

After what has been said it will not be difficult to understand that the Uranian characteristics, where love becomes compassion, give wisdom that is not dependent upon reasoning, a love that is not fixed upon one object alone, but includes all that lives and moves and has its being; being similar to the characteristics that are to be evolved by humanity during the Venus period when perfect love shall have cast out all fear, when man shall have conquered all the lower phases of his nature and love shall be as pure as it is universally inclusive.

When these Uranian vibrations are felt by advance in the higher life through aspiration, there is great danger that we may throw away the fetters of law and convention before we are really ready to govern ourselves by the law of Love divine, that we may disregard the laws that are in the world, that we may not render unto Caesar that which is Ceasar's, whether in obedience or coin, that we may not be careful of avoiding the appearance of evil, that we may think that we have so far transcended the ordinary stage of humanity that we can live as super-humans, that the passion of Mars has in our case been changed to Uranian compassion, which is sexless. Under such misapprehensions, many people who endeavor to tread the path disregard the laws of marriage and enter into relationships as soulmates and affinities. They feel the Uranian ray, but cannot quite respond to its sublime purity, therefore they experience a counterfeit Venusian sensation which usually ends in adultery and sex-perversion, so that instead of the natural animal passion of Mars having been transmuted to the compassion of Uranus it has as a matter of fact, degenerated into something that is far worse than the fullest sex expression of the martial rays committed in a frank and proper manner. This is a danger that cannot be too strictly guarded against and it behooves every one who endeavors to live the higher life not to try to aspire to the Uranian rays until he at first becomes thoroughly imbued with the altruistic vibrations of Jupiter, for more misery is brought into the world by those who have aspired too high and fallen low, than by those who are not sufficiently aspiring. "Pride goeth before a fall," is an ancient and very true proverb, which it behooves every one of us to take to heart. The Christ took part in the marriage at Cana. Marriage is a regular Christian institution, and must exist until abolished in the kingdom to come; there the bodies we have will not wear out and therefore there will be no need of marriage to generate new ones.

Let it also be understood that the minister who marries cannot truly mate people, therefore the presence of the basic harmony for true marriage should be determined before the marriage ceremony.

As we have seen in the foregoing, Mars, Venus and Uranus mark three stages in the emotional development of man. During the stage where he is only amenable to Mars, animal passion reigns supreme and he seeks unrestricted gratification of all his lower desires in the intercourse with his fellowman but particularly with the opposite sex; during the stage where he becomes amenable to the rays of Venus, love softens the brutality of his desires and the animal passions are somewhat held in leash; he is even, under the higher phases of this planet, ready to sacrifice himself and his desires for the benefit and comfort of the loved ones. When he has evolved to the point where he can feel the rays of Uranus, the passion of Mars gradually turns to compassion; there the love of Venus which is only for one particular person, becomes all inclusive so that it embraces all humankind regardless of sex or any other distinction, for it is the divine love of soul for soul which is above all material considerations of whatever nature.

The mentality also evolves through three stages according to the amenability of the person to the vibrations of the Moon, Mercury and Neptune. While man is only amenable to the lunar influence, he is childlike and easily guided by the higher powers, which have led him through the various stages mentioned in our previous chapters. Under the stellar ray of Mercury he gradually develops his intellectual powers and becomes a reasoning being. As such, he is placed under the law of cause and effect, made responsible for his own actions, so that he may reap what he has sown and learn thereby the lessons that human life has to teach him under the present regime. Being inexperienced, he makes mistakes in whatever direction indicated by the afflictions to Mercury in his horoscope and consequently he suffers a corresponding penalty of sorrow and trouble. If he has not the mentality to reason on the connection between his mistakes and the sad experiences growing from them, during his life time, the panorama of life, which unfolds in the post-mortem state, makes this clear, and leaves with him an essence of "right feeling" which we know as "conscience."

This conscience keeps him from repeating past mistakes, when the feeling generated has become sufficiently strong to overbalance the tendency to yield to the particular temptation which caused him suffering. Thus he gradually develops a spiritual consciousness which is above and beyond human reason, but which nevertheless is also connected with reason in such a manner that when the result has been reached, the man who has this Cosmic Consciousness knows the reason why such and such a thing is and must be, or why he ought to take a certain action. This Cosmic Consciousness is developed under the ray of Neptune and differs from that intuitional right feeling developed under the ray of Uranus in the very important fact that while the person who has developed the Uranian quality of intuition arrives at the truth instantaneously without the necessity of thinking over the matter or reasoning, he is unable to give anything but the result; he cannot connect the various steps of logical sequence whereby the final result was reached. The man or woman, however, who develops the Neptunian faculty, also has the answer of any question immediately and is able to tell the reason why that answer is the proper and right one.

The faculty of intuition built up from the Martial base of passion, through the Venusian stage of love, and the Uranian ray of compassion, depends upon the ability of the person involved *to feel very intensely.* By love and devotion, the heart is attuned to every other heart in the universe and in this way it knows and feels all that may be known and felt by any other heart in the universe, thus sharing the divine omniscience that binds Our Father in Heaven to His children and through the direct heart to heart touch with that omniscience the person obtains the answers to whatever problem is placed before him.

The noblest men of all ages, Christian saints of the most transcendent spirituality, have attained their wonderful development through the spiritual rays of this planet because of the intense feeling of Oneness with the divine and with all that lives and breathes in the universe.

But there are others who are not thus constituted and they are not able to walk that path. These, through the Moon, Mercury and Neptune have developed their intellect and attained the same results plus the Neptunian power of idealization.

This is a very important point and it is only brought out in the Western Wisdom Teachings, for while it was formerly taught that the spirit involves itself in matter and thereby crystallizes itself into form which then evolves, the Western Wisdom Teachings tell us that there is in addition a third factor in universal advancement, namely, *Epigenesis;* the faculty whereby the spirit may choose a course that is altogether new and independent of what has gone before. We see the expression of this in all kingdoms relative to form, but in the human kingdom, epigenesis expresses itself as genius, a creative instinct, which makes man more akin to the divine than any other of his accomplishments. This is developed under the Neptune ray when that planet is well placed in the horoscope. There is of course also such a thing as an evil genius, a destructive faculty developed under an afflicted Neptune.

Only the most sensitive people in the world feel the rays of Uranus and Neptune at the present time. To feel these vibrations the connection between the dense physical body and the vital body, which is made of ether, must be rather loose for where these two vehicles are firmly interlocked the person is always of a materialistic turn, and cannot respond to the higher and more subtle vibrations from the spiritual world. But when the stellar rays from these two planets impinge upon a person whose vital body is loosely connected with the physical, we have what is called a sensitive. The direction and quality of this faculty depends upon the placement and the aspects of the two planets mentioned, however. Those who are particularly under the domination of an adverse aspect of the Uranian ray, usually develop the more undesirable phases of clairvoyance and mediumship. They easily become the prey of entities from the invisible world who have no regard for their victims' desire, even if in a weak manner these should protest. Such mediums are generally used in simple trance communications and in a few cases known to the writer have lived very beautiful and happy lives because of their implicit belief in the spirits that dominated them. In these cases the spirit-controls were of a better class than usually met with. But as this Uranian faculty is built up through Mars and Venus, passion is prominent in such natures and under the influence of obsessing spirits many of these people are driven into gross immorality. Vampirism and kindred disreputable practices are also engendered by the perverse use of the Uranian ray in mediums.

Neptune may be said to represent the invisible worlds in more positive aspects and those who come under the evil rays of this planet are therefore brought in touch with the most undesirable occupants of the invisible worlds. Actual obsession whereby the owner of a body is deprived of his vehicle takes place under the ray of Neptune and no materializing seance could ever be held if it were not for this stellar vibration. Magic, white or black can never be put to practical use save under and because of this Neptunian vibration. Apart from this ray it will remain theory, speculation and book learning. Therefore the Initiates of every Mystery School, Spiritual Seers who have full control of their faculty, and Astrologers are amenable in varying degrees to the ray of Neptune. The Black Magician and the

Hypnotist, who is a twin brother to him, are also dependent upon the power of this stellar ray for use in their nefarious practices.

The highest human development at the present time, namely, the soul unfoldment which is undertaken in the mystery temples through initiation, is directly the result of the Neptune ray, for just as evil configurations lay men liable to assault by invisible entities, so the good configurations of Neptune are particularly required to enable a man to unfold by initiation his whole soul powers and become a conscious agent in the invisible worlds. Let us remember, however, that good or evil configurations are not the result of chance or luck, but are the product of our own past acts; the horoscope shows what we have earned by our past living and therefore what we are entitled to in the present life.

Moreover it should always be kept in mind that *the stars impel but do not compel;* because a man or woman has an evil configuration of Neptune or Uranus it is not unavoidable that they should go into active evil Mediumship and Black Magic and thereby make life harder for themselves in the future. Their opportunity to do so and the temptation will come at certain times when the heavenly time markers point to the right hour on the clock of destiny. Then it is time to stand firm for the good and for the right; being forewarned through a knowledge of Astrology one is also forearmed and may the easier overcome when such an aspect culminates.

Thus we have seen that man is amenable to the planetary rays in an increasing measure as he advances through evolution, but the more highly he becomes developed spiritually the less he will allow the planets to dominate him, while the younger soul is driven unresistingly along the tide of life in whatever direction the planetary vibrations impel him. It is the mark of the advanced soul that he keeps the true course regardless of the planetary vibrations. Between these two extremes there are naturally all gradations, some amenable to the rays of one planet, some to another. The bark of life of men and women is often driven upon the rocks of sorrow and suffering, that they may learn to evolve within themselves the will power that finally frees them from all domination by the ruling stars. As Gœthe, the great mystic, said,

"From every power that holds the world in chains,
Man frees himself when self-control he gains."

And it may be asked, have we run the gamut of vibrations when we have learned to respond to all the seven planets which are mythically represented as the seven strings on Apollo's Lyre? In other words is Neptune the highest vibration to which we shall yet respond? The Western Wisdom Teachings tell us that there are two more planets in the universe which will be known in future ages and that these will have an influence in developing qualities of so transcendent a nature that we cannot now understand them. The number of Adam, man or humanity, is nine, and there are nine rungs upon the stellar ladder by which he is ascending to God; up to the present time he has climbed only five of these rungs; Mercury, Venus, Mars, Jupiter and Saturn, and not even the vibration of these has he by any means learned; Uranus and Neptune are slowly coming into our lives; they will not become active in the same manner and to the same degree that for instance, the Moon and Mars are at the present time until many ages have passed. But even when we have learned to respond to them there are two more of which we shall know something later on; it is the opinion of the writers that these are probably not felt by any except those who have graduated from the Greater Mystery School and by the Hierophants of that sublime institution.

In conclusion to this article on the Amenability of Man to Planetary Vibrations we quote from the Rosicrucian Mysteries the article on Light, Color and Consciousness:

"Truly, *God is One and Undivided.* He enfolds within His Being all that is, as the white light embraces all colors. But He appears three-fold in manifestation, as the white light is refracted in three primary colors, Blue, Yellow and Red. Wherever we see these colors they are emblematical of the Father, Son and Holy Spirit. These three primary rays of Divine Life are diffused or radiated through the Sun and produce *Life, Consciousness and Form* upon each of the seven light bearers, the planets, which are called the 'Seven Spirits before the Throne.' Their names are, Mercury, Venus, Earth, Mars, Jupiter, Saturn and Uranus. Bode's law proves that Neptune does not yet belong to our solar system and the reader is referred to 'Simplified, Scientific Astrology' by the present writer, for mathematical demonstration of this condition.

"Each of the seven planets receives the light of the Sun in a different measure, according to its proximity to the central orb and the constitution of its atmosphere, and the beings on each, according to their stage of development have affinity for some of the solar rays. The planets absorb the color or colors congruous to them, and reflect the rest upon the other planets. This reflected ray bears with it an impulse of the nature of the beings with which it has been in contact.

"Thus the divine Light and Life comes to each planet, either directly from the Sun, or reflected from its six sister planets, and as the summer breeze which has been wafted over blooming fields carries upon its silent, invisible wings the blended fragrance of a multitude of flowers, so also the subtle influences from *The Garden of God* bring to us the commingled impulses of all the Planetary Spirits and in that vari-colored light we live and move and have our being.

"The rays which come directly from the Sun are productive of spiritual illumination; the reflected rays from other planets make for added consciousness and moral development and the rays reflected by way of the Moon give physical growth.

"But as each planet can only absorb a certain quantity of one or more colors according to the general stage of evolution there, so each being upon earth, mineral, plant, animal and man can only absorb and thrive upon a certain quantity of the various rays projected upon the earth. The remainder do not affect it or produce sensation any more than the blind are conscious of light and color which exist everywhere around them. Therefore each being is differently affected by the stellar rays, and the science of Astrology, a fundamental truth in nature, is of enormous benefit in the attainment of spiritual growth."

CHAPTER III.

WERE YOU BORN UNDER A LUCKY STAR?

HAVE you ever looked through a kaleidoscope at the patterns formed there by the many little pieces of varicolored glass, and noticed how the slightest disturbance of the position changes the pattern? Also, do you realize that it would be impossible, or almost so, to duplicate any pattern, no matter how much you were to turn; there is such a variety of effect. Similarly when you look into the heavens night after night you will notice changes among the planets, in fact such is the variety of changes that occur among them that it would be impossible to duplicate the position which they hold relatively to one another while you are reading this, for almost twenty-six thousand years. Thus in the planetary kaleidoscope there is, we might say, an infinity of patterns. When we realize that human beings are entering the world constantly and that each being is stamped at the first complete breath with the planetary pattern then in the sky, everyone must necessarily be different from everybody else. Nor should this statement about stellar influence create doubt when we consider that wireless waves of different lengths and different pitch sent out from a tiny man-made contrivance can make themselves felt and can register by mechanical operations involving expenditure of energy thousands of miles from their source. The planetary vibrations from those great orbs in the heavens make themselves felt millions of miles away as surely, as easily, and with equal certainty. We know that the angle of the solar ray determines whether it is winter or summer. We also know the effect of the Moon upon the waters, and it is within the experience of all that we feel more buoyant when the atmosphere is clear and dry than when it is moist and murky. And what determines these atmospheric conditions but the planets, the circling stars?

When we look up at this planetary kaleidoscope from time to time we see in the heavens various configurations which are pronounced lucky or unlucky according to whether they are formed between so-called benefics alone, such as Venus, Jupiter and the Sun, or planets said to be malefic such as Saturn, Mars or Uranus. When Jupiter and Venus are in close conjunction near the midheaven, it is a foregone conclusion that those who come into the world under this configuration will enjoy a measure of good fortune far above the average, and such persons would therefore be considered "lucky" in the extreme. On the other hand there are times when Saturn and Mars occupy the zenith position for souls that are born to suffer.

But why should one suffer and another be born under a lucky star? Why do the stars give good fortune to one and misfortune to others, and if we are born to "luck," whether good or bad, what is the use or where is the incentive to individual effort? If there is a law of nature which is established beyond doubt it is surely the law of Cause and Effect. Every cause must produce an adequate effect and nothing which we see as an effect can be without a pre-existent cause. Moreover, if this is a universal law it must apply to the conditions of birth as well as to subsequent life. Following up this idea the next question is: If our birth under a lucky or unlucky star is the effect of some prior cause, what may that be, or where and how was that cause generated? To that there can be only one answer; that we must have made the causes in some previous existence which now result in our birth under a lucky or an unlucky star. Thus by induction a belief in Astrology requires also a belief in a previous existence as well as in future lives, for while we are now reaping in our horoscopes the effects of our past lives we are also by our acts laying the foundations for a new horoscope which can only be worked out in a future life.

> "How closely luck is linked to merit
> Does never to the fool occur;
> Had he the wise man's stone, I swear it,
> The stone had no philosopher,"

said *Mephisto* sarcastically in "*Faust*" and it is true. If we are born under a lucky star it shows that we have earned the good fortune thereby indicated, by forethought, kindness, and our other virtues expressed in previous lives, for we cannot have friends unless we are friendly ourselves. If we happen to have Saturn and Mars instead of Venus and Jupier near the zenith, it shows that in the past we ourselves have not been kindly and friendly or we could not now express the opposite traits. But this is just the point where the study of Astrology should help us. It shows our limitations for the present and it points out the obvious remedies and *how to build for the future.* Can the leopard change its skin? No. Can the lion cease to prey? Absolutely impossible. Can the flower cease to bloom or the mineral to crystallize? Certainly not; because they are under laws which are as unchangeable as the laws of the Medes and Persians. *They have neither choice nor prerogative* but must obey the dictates of the group spirit which guides them along their path of evolution. But in this respect we differ radically from those lower kingdoms, we have both choice and prerogative. *We may do whatsoever we will* and that is a factor which is never shown in the horoscope, a factor that may be made to play an all important role in every life. It is not enough to be born under a lucky star to have a lucky life, for the horoscope shows only the tendencies and the person who is so well endowed will without question have an abundance of opportunities to make his life fortunate in the very highest degree. *But only in so far as he ex-*

erts himself to grasp opportunity on the wing, will that which is foreshadowed in his horoscope come to pass. And similarily with the person who is afflicted by the conjunction of two malefics in the midheaven or anywhere else in the horoscope. By his will, and the exercise of choice, which are his divine birthrights, *he may rule his stars* and make of the unlucky horoscope a fruitful life from a far higher standpoint than the other. The bark that has been tossed by the tempest harbors a joy when the haven of safety is reached that is not equaled on the ship that has always sailed on smiling seas.

"Who never ate his bread in sorrow,
Who never passed the midnight hours
Weeping, waiting for the morrow,
He knows not yet ye heavenly powers."

From the higher standpoint those who are living in the lap of luxury are to be pitied when their lucky stars give them all the good things of this world and cause them to forget that they are stewards and that the day is coming when their souls shall be required of them with an account of their stewardship. They shall then be forced to confess that they have failed to use the substance entrusted to them in the proper manner; while others under the strain and stress of life, expressed by the horoscopical squares and oppositions, have wrung from their unlucky stars a measure of victory. What wonder then if the king's messengers, the circling stars, take from the unfaithful steward that which he had and give to the other, changing the latter's adversity to prosperity in later lives. Thus the pendulum of luck and loss, success and failure swings through many lives till we learn to make our own "luck" by ruling our stars.

> "A god can love without cessation,
> But under laws of alteration
> We mortals need, in changing measure,
> Our share of pain as well as pleasure."

And it is this necessity for change that is ministered unto us by the circling stars which form configurations that we call good or evil, though they are neither from a higher standpoint; for no matter how good the horoscope, by progression of the stars evil configurations are sure to come and no matter how evil, there are always new opportunities for good given by aspects of the Sun, Venus and Jupiter to our planets at birth. *All that we have to do is to grasp the opportunity, and help our stars, that our stars may help us.*

Amulets, Birth-stones and Planetary Colors

In the windows of jewelers' shops and in cheap, ready made horoscopes one may often read that it is "*lucky*" for people born in a certain month to wear a particular stone or color. It means business to the jeweler and the astrological prestidigitator who produces "your horoscope" by a turn of the wrist from a box when you tell him in what month you were born. Both buy their instructive (?) literature at a nominal price per thousand, the principal cost being paper and printers' ink; there are no furrows in their foreheads from deep and earnest study of the problem.

But as the counterfeit coin argues the existence of the genuine, so also the fallacious information flippantly dispensed by people who cater to the sense of mystery and wonder which is deeply imbedded in human nature argues the existence of a genuine science of mineralogical correspondences with the stellar rays impinging upon all who inhabit our sub-lunar sphere; and when this is rightly understood and used, that which is loosely termed *luck* results; but then it is not really luck in the sense understood by the majority of people, for then it is *the result of accurate knowledge scientifically used,* and therefore the outcome is as inevitable as that water runs down hill.

The philosophy of planetary colors and mineralogy is that each of the Creative Hierarchies which is active in evolution works with the various classes of beings from mineral to man, and is responsible for the progress made by them. In the course of this work each Hierarchy naturally imparts to the beings with whom it labors some of its own nature and vibration. Thus each group of minerals, each species of plant and animal, vibrates to a certain keynote which blends with the vibration of the Group

Spirit, and the particular sign and planet with which he is most nearly attuned.

It has been taught by the Elder Brothers in the Rosicrucian Cosmo-Conception, that:

The Archangels, who were human in the Sun Period when the present animals started their evolution with a mineral-like existence, are now the Group Spirits of the animals.

The Angels, who were human in the Moon Period when the present plants commenced their evolution with a similar mineral constitution are now the Group Spirits of the plants. Man, who reached the human stage in the Earth Period, is now working with the new life-wave which started its evolution on the Earth as minerals. He is not far enough advanced to assume the role of Group Spirit, that being reserved for the future. In the Jupiter Period he will give them life as plants have, in the Venus Period he will bring out their desires and emotions as animals, and in the Vulcan Period he will give them a mind and make them human. That, however, is all in the future. At present he is working with them to the best of his ability, smelting them into iron bridges, ships and skeleton skyscrapers; he is pulling them into wires which wind around the world; he is grinding from them gems that glitter and grace the great in our social structure, and thus he is gradually establishing an intimate relationship with them and preparing to take charge of their evolution as a Group Spirit at some future time.

It is well known to students of Astrology that an astrological reading based upon the month in which an individual is born is worth little, for all the people born in the same month do not have the same experiences by any means, but if we consider the *day*, the *year* and the *place* we get a horoscope that is absolutely individual and totally different in detail from the horoscope of anyone else—and this is the point which concerns us for the present argument—the ruler is not the lord of the sign the Sun is in, except for children born at Sunrise, when the Sun is on the Ascendant. *It is the ruler of the rising sign, THAT is the determinator with regard to our mineralogical affinity,* because at the moment of conception when the seed-atom of our present physical mineral body was deposited the Moon was in that particular sign and degree, (or its opposite), and acted then as a focus of forces which have since crystallized into the vehicle we now wear.

The following table shows the affinity of each of the twelve signs with certain gems, metals and colors, and in that chart there are the elements for making an effective talisman by any individual who has the knowledge of how to cast a horoscope and blend the ingredients according to the requirements of the case. We have no scruples about telling how this is done, for it may help some to help themselves and others. The only harm it can do is that it might induce some unscrupulous person to make talismans for money and even then, if he is conscientious about the work, whoever obtains them will not be cheated, the re-action being upon the one who prostitutes the spiritual science for material gain.

BIRTH-STONES AND COLORS.				
Gems ruled by the signs.		Sign Rulers	Metals	Colors.
♈	Amethyst, Diamond	♂	Iron	Red
♉	Moss Agate, Emerald	♀	Copper	Yellow
♊	Crystal, Aqua Marine	☿	Mercury	Violet
♋	Emerald, Black Onyx	☽	Silver	Green
♌	Ruby, Diamond	☉	Gold	Orange
♍	Pink Jasper, Hyacinth	☿	Mercury	Violet
♎	Diamond, Opal.	♀	Copper	Yellow
♏	Topaz, Malachite.	♂	Iron	Red
♐	Carbuncle, Turquoise	♃	Tin	Blue
♑	White Onyx, Moonstone	♄	Lead	Indigo
♒	Sapphire, Opal	♄	Lead	Indigo
♓	Chrysolite, Moonstone	♃	Tin	Blue

To forestall a question we may say that ancient astrologers who have studied this aspect of the science have tabulated several hundred minerals of which the planetary affinities had been noted, but these works have been mutilated in the course of time, and are now not available. Paracelsus and also Agrippa, made considerable study of this subject, and with very important results; but its extensive consideration is outside the scope of this work, so the authors will confine their remarks to the essentials, indicating the way which others may pursue if they feel so inclined.

To illustrate how the mineral elements may be used to advantage let us take the following example: Suppose that in a certain horoscope ve find Sagittarius rising with its lord Jupiter on the Ascendant. Jupiter is then the ruling planet and so, according to our chart turquoise is the person's birthstone, tin, the metal with which he has affinity, and blue, his color. That means that it will help him express himself if he wears a turquoise, an amulet of tin, and dresses in blue whenever consistent with custom. That is true to a certain extent, but it is only a small part of the truth, and it is by no means the best use that may be made of this knowledge.

To indicate the better way, let us suppose that this person's figure shows severe afflictions by Mars and Saturn.

Mars afflicts three planets; his metal is iron. Venus is the opposite of Mars; her metal is copper, and consequently copper is an antidote for the martial vibrations.

Saturn afflicts one planet; his metal is lead.

Jupiter is his opposite and therefore the Jupiter metal, tin, is an antidote for the Saturnian vibrations.

With this in mind an amulet may be compounded of tin and copper; not exactly in the ratio of three to one, but with a mind on the bulk of the various planets, their density and the strength of the aspects it is desired to overcome, a matter which involves further study. The work itself should be done under auspicious planetary conditions. A Mars amulet, designed to give energy to one with a weak figure would be most successful if made in a Mars-hour on a Tuesday when both the Sun and Moon are in martial signs as happens in April and November. The same with amulets made for other planets. (See the Tables of Planetary Hours, in our *Simplified Scientific Astrology.*)

A gem or an amulet made on these principles is a focus for the stellar rays of the planets it represents and infuses vibrations of their nature into our auras all the while we are wearing it, just as surely as the wireless receiver attuned to a certain pitch catches the waves within its range; and we may blend the colors in the same manner to obtain help from them. As a matter of fact, it is the complementary color which is seen in the desire world that produces the effect of the physical colors. If it is desired to restrain one whose Mars is too prominent, the gems, colors and metals of Saturn will help, and such a person should have as little to do with iron (tools, machinery, etc.,) as possible, but if we want to help someone who is moody and taciturn, we may use the gems, colors and metals of Mars to advantage. In the final analysis the matter resolves itself into a question of judgment and common sense. With these, the knowledge concerning the essentials here given may be used by anyone to advantage.

When is the Best time to Be Born?

In the light of occult investigation of the subject it appears that birth is an advent we are powerless to control; therefore when we seem to control it in a slight degree we are really the agents of Destiny to precipitate or delay it till the proper moment has arrived. This view is also justified by the author's experience in Horary Astrology. The philosophy of Horary Astrology is that at the time one is impelled to ask a question concerning an important matter the heavens contain also the answer and a figure set for that time will contain the solution to the problem. But it should be particularly noted that the time to set the figure is when the inquirer asks the question of the astrologer, if this is done in person; when it is done by mail the astrologer sets the figure for the time he reads the question in the letter.

On a number of occasions we have received letters containing questions which bore marks of having been delayed by flood or fire, but the figure cast for the moment of reading gave the answer, showing that the delay had a part in the plan, nor should it surprise us that the great Intelligences which are the ministers of Destiny foresee and make allowance for contingencies beyond the grasp of the human mind. When the Infinite Mind bestows equal care upon the design of the anatomy of a fly, a mouse and a lion, may we not conclude that a similar attention to the minutiæ prevails in all departments of life and that when we seem to delay or precipitate birth we are really aiding nature to take its predetermined course as said in the opening sentence of this article.

Nevertheless people often ask the astrologer when is the best time to be born; young astrologers also frequently want to know this, not that they have any idea of controlling birth but so that on seeing a horoscope or being told a person's time of birth they may make a quick mental calculation as to whether the horoscope is good or bad. Such a judgment would, of course, be founded only on the position of the sun by sign and approximate house, hence general in the extreme. It may be said however that other planetary positions being equal, it is better to be born when the Moon is increasing in light from the new to the full than when she is decreasing from the full to the new for the growing Moon always increases vitality and furthers our affairs.

It is best to be born in April or August when the life-giving Sun is in its exaltation sign Aries or Leo, its home, for then we enter the sea of life on the crest-wave and are backed in the battle of existence by an abundant fund of vim and energy.

It is also good to be born in May or July when the life-light of the Sun is focused through the exaltation sign or home of the Moon, Taurus or Cancer, especially, as said, when the lesser light is increasing for those conditions, also furnish an abundance of vitality which is such a great asset in physical life.

With respect to the time of day most favorable for birth it may be said that children born about sunrise, or during the forenoon from 8 to 12 while the Sun is traversing the houses of friends and social prestige are the "luckiest" for they are helped on every hand. Children born between noon and midnight are less "lucky" the nearer the Sun comes to the Nadir, and then the "luck" turns again in favor of those born in the early morning while the Daystar is ascending towards the eastern horizon. They will have to carve their own way in the world, but opportunities will be given them in abundance.

We may therefore sum up our conclusions by saying that it is best to be born at Sunrise or in the forenoon, preferably in April or August when the Moon is increasing in light.

Finally it should always be borne in mind that there is no "luck," in the commonly accepted sense, for that which we have or lack in any respect is due to our own actions in the past, and in the future we may by proper application have what we now lack.

CHAPTER IV.

Reading the Horoscope

Introductory

WHEN the student of Astrology has learned to cast the horoscope correctly by the study of our "Simplified Scientific Astrology," or another reliable textbook, the next and most important part is to read its message. Astrology means "Star Logic" and we must seriously advise the student not to depend too much on authorities but to try to understand the basic nature of each planet, the influence of signs, houses and aspects; then by a process of reasoning to combine these and thus develop his own intuition which will serve him far better than the ability to quote like a poll parrot what some one else has said.

We would also advise the younger astrologer not to bother too much with the descriptions of physical appearance indicated in the horoscope. It is foolish to spend hours in studying over a phase of the subject which is of limited value. We give descriptions of the different physical types, but do so for the purpose of aiding the student to determine at sight the probable sign and planet rising when a person comes who does not know his birth hour. There are people for instance, who have a face perfectly resembling that of a sheep. If such a one were in doubt about the birth hour, we would at once look to Aries and experimentally try how Aries rising would fit with the other characteristics of that person; if we did so we should probably find our guess to be correct. Thus also the other signs and planets in signs exhibit distinguishing characteristics of valuable aid to the student in the direction mentioned.

The student should also endeavor to cultivate perfect confidence in the science of Astrology. There is *nothing empirical about character reading and diagnosis.* In those respects it is plain as A B C. *Predictions may fail* because the Astrologer is unable to determine the strength of will of the person for whom he predicts, but the latent tendencies are always accurately foreshown. The writers have found that where they do not personally know the people whose characters they read, their delineations are much deeper and more accurate than otherwise because then personal impressions and bias are absent and the mystic scroll of the heavens is more easily read.

There are three factors which bring to us the mystic message of the stars; the houses, the signs and the planets.

Each house represents a department of life; the signs are divisions of the heavens which by their placement relative to the houses indicate our basic temperament and attitude towards life; and the planets are the messengers of God which by their motion through the houses and signs bring to us the opportunities for soulgrowth which we need for our individual development. It is therefore necessary for one who wishes to learn to read a horoscope to become thoroughly acquainted with these three factors both separately and in their various combinations. The following discriptions may help to convey this knowledge:

The Houses

The houses are called "Mundane Houses," to differentiate between them and the "Celestial Houses" namely the twelve signs of the Zodiac; but generally they are designated as "houses" only.

It is the angle of the stellar ray which determines its effect in our lives; planets which are in the East affect our physical constitution, planets in the South near the zenith are factors for good or ill where our social position is concerned. If a planet is setting in the West at the time of our birth its ray strikes us in such a manner as to draw us to a certain type of marriage partner, and the planets under the earth, in the North, have an effect upon our condition in the latter part of life. Let us suppose for illustration of the point that someone is born at sunrise on a day when the Sun and Jupiter are in conjunction. Then they strike him from the eastern angle and give him splendid vitality. Another born on the same day at noon when Jupiter and the Sun are in the zenith position may have a very poor, weak body if other planets in the East are adverse, but the ray of the Sun and Jupiter falling on his birth figure from the South will certainly attract to him attention in his social sphere and make him the recipient of public favor and honor. Another born on the same day, when the Sun and Jupiter are setting in the West may be an outcast if planets in the East and South so decree, but the benefic ray of the Sun and Jupiter from the Western angle will make him beloved of his mate and successful in partnerships. These facts have been ascertained by observation and tabulation. Therefore the twelve sections of the circle of observation as seen from the birthplace are truly said to rule or govern various departments of life and thus people born on the same day may have the most diverse experiences.

The houses may be variously grouped according to the influence they exercise in our lives; there are "angular," "succedent" and "cadent" houses, also personal, spiritual, material, social and mystical houses.

Of the *angles,* the first house governs our personal self, and its opposite the seventh house, rules the one who is nearest and dearest to us, namely, the marriage partner. The fourth house determines conditions in our home and its opposite angle, the tenth house, shows our social standing in the community where we live. Thus the angles show collectively the sphere of our activities in life.

Of the *succeedent houses* the second shows our financial status with regard to that which we acquire by our own efforts and the opposite succeedent house, the eighth, shows whatever we may receive from others as legacies, etc. The other succeedent houses, the fifth and eleventh, show how our income may be spent, for the fifth house indicates the children of our body who have a legitimate claim to a share of our income, and the eleventh house shows the children of our brain, our hopes, wishes and aspirations which also draw upon our resources.

Of the two pairs of *cadent houses* the sixth is the house of voluntary service which we perform as our share of the world's work for an equivalent share in the world's wealth, and the twelfth house shows how we may be compelled to labor without remuneration under prison restraint if we do not work willingly. The sixth house shows also the state of our health and the twelfth tells if hospital treatment is necessary.

The other pair of cadent houses, the third and ninth, show whether our life and work will confine us to one place or require travel and changes of residence. In this respect the third house shows short journeys and the ninth house long travels.

The *personal houses* comprise the first, fifth and

ninth. The first house rules the constitution and peculiarities of the physical body. Planets and signs in that house put their stamp on it to make or mar according to the nature of its self-generated destiny. Our fifth house shows the quality of the love-nature of the soul and the line of its expression if it follows the line of least resistance; and the ninth house shows as much of the spirit as we can apprehend in our present limited state

The *material trinity of houses* consists of the second, sixth and tenth and shows the worldly possessions of man, his means of obtaining them and the enjoyment they bring him. Wealth, or its reverse, is shown by the second house, health, without which there can be no joy in any worldly possession, is shown by the sixth house; and the public prestige which is the chief source of gratification to the average human being, is shown by the tenth house.

The *social houses* are the third, seventh and eleventh houses and in them is shown the nature of our relations with various classes of souls we meet in life. Brothers and sisters to whom we are bound by the tie of blood are shown by the third house, the companion of our heart with whom our blood blends in another way, is shown by the seventh house, and the friends, more precious than pearls to whoever has earned friendship, are designated by the eleventh house.

The fourth and last trinity of houses is composed of the fourth, eighth and twelfth. In them are hidden the mysteries of the ante-natal life of the spirit, and the post mortem experiences immediately to follow the *terminus vitae*. On the material plane the fourth house signifies our condition in the latter part of life, the twelfth shows the sorrow which impresses us with the worthlessness of material things and the eighth indicates the nature of our exit from the world's stage.

An illustration may further help the student to understand how the heavens influence our life through the twelve houses. Suppose we are out driving and our road follows the seacoast, but a mile or so inland. A breeze is blowing from the ocean and as it passes over the country separating us from the sea, it brings upon invisible wings messages from that land, which evoke pleasure or aversion according to their nature. In one place, an aroma of new mown hay fills us with delight; perhaps we are nauseated by the noxious smell of jasmine on the next stretch of our journey; and later become really ill from the stench of stagnant marsh-water. But then we enter a forest, and soon its grateful pine balm restores the normal health and spirits.

In our journey from the cradle to the grave we carry the twelve houses with us in the auric atmosphere surrounding us, as the air envelops the flying earth. Each house mirrors part of the life; each holds some of our life lessons; each represents how we have worked or shirked before in a given department of life's tasks. At the appropriate time of life we reap from each house what we have sown in past lives, that is, unless we forestall the harvest in time. Is our eleventh house afflicted, do friends betray and forsake us, do they leave us heartsick, or nauseate us like the scent of jasmine and stagnant marsh-water? Then let us examine the horoscope, for it reveals what is hidden in our auric atmosphere. The friends sensed us, and we them, through the eleventh angle, and something ill-smelling must be there. It may be, we long to be befriended, more than to befriend others. Let us cease to be like the sickly, debilitating jasmine, and seek to manifest the sturdy strength of the invigorating pine tree; then we shall find friends flocking around, admiring our strength. Not all have such sturdy natures, but we can attract equally by kindliness, as soothing to sorrowing hearts as perfume of new mown hay to the sense, and thus we may rid the house of friends of affliction.

After the foregoing explanations, the houses may now be said to influence the affairs of life as follows:

First House rules the physical body and its constitution and appearance; it determines conditions in the childhood home while the person is under control of the parents.

Second House rules money, the financial fortunes; it shows what the person acquires by individual effort and to a certain extent what use he will make of it.

Third House rules brothers and sisters, neighbors, the instinctual mind, writings, short journeys and conveyances of travel.

Fourth House—That one of the parents who exercises the lesser influence in the person's life, conditions in the latter part of life, houses, lands, mines; everything pertaining to the earth.

Fifth House—Love, courtship and licentiousness, the legitimate and illegitimate attraction and social intercourse between the sexes prior to wedlock; children, educational institutions, books and newspapers, sports and amusements, stocks and speculations.

Sixth House—Health, service to be rendered by the person and also the condition and faithfulness of those who serve him.

Seventh House—The marriage partner, the public in general, competitors, partners, opponents in litigation, rivals.

Eighth House—Death, legacies, the marriage partner's finances, occult abilities or faculties latent but nearly ready for manifestation.

Ninth House—Religion, spiritual experiences and aspirations, dreams and visions, long travels, and law.

Tenth House—The parent who exercises most influence in the person's life, the honor and social standing of the person, his employer or judge, and the government.

Eleventh House—Friends, companions and well-wishers, hopes, wishes and aspirations, generally of a material nature, also stepchildren.

Twelfth House—Confinement in hospitals or prison, secret enemies and plots; sorrow and self undoing.

The Signs of the Zodiac

On either side of the Sun's path there are a number of fixed stars which are so grouped that they may be conceived as forming twelve constellations, and as they have certain characteristic influences ancient sages named them for the animals which express similar traits. These constellations are called the *natural* Zodiac and for all practical purposes it may be said that they occupy permanent positions relative to the other fixed stars of the firmament. This circle is divided into twelve sections starting at the first degree of Aries, which is occupied by the Sun at the vernal equinox.

On account of the precession of the equinox the Sun does not cross the equator at the same point each year, but it has been found that the first 30 degrees from the point where the Sun does cross the equator at the equinox have an effect similar to that ascribed to the constellation Aries; the next thirty degrees radiate a Taurian influence and so on with the other ten sections of thirty degrees each. Therefore the twelve sections measured from the vernal equinox are used exclusively in Astrology and called *signs* of the Zodiac, to differentiate them from the *constellations*. (For a thorough elucidation of the subject see "Simplified Scientific Astrology," under the caption "Intellectual Zodiac.")

These twelve signs of the Zodiac are variously divided according to their effect on humanity into Cardinal, Fixed and Common signs, also into Fiery, Earthy, Airy and Watery signs. What their influences are we shall endeavor to elucidate in the following sections.

The Cardinal Signs

Keyword "Activity."

The Cardinal Signs are *Aries, Cancer, Libra* and *Capricorn.* These signs are called Cardinal because when the Sun is in them he is in one of the four corners of the heavens; at a turning-point, where he is forced to take another direction. In Aries he is as far *East* as he can go; Cancer is the tropical point of the *North* where he gives the *perpendicular ray* at the Summer Solstice, and consequently the greatest *heat*. Libra is the extreme *Western* point of his path, where he turns away from the Northern Hemisphere, and in midwinter, at Christmas, he is in Capricorn at the farthest point *South,* where his *horizontal ray* leaves the people of the North in winter's icy grip. The effect of the angles, the first, fourth, seventh and tenth houses, is similar to the effect of the cardinal signs because these houses are at the East, North, West and South points of the horoscope. The nature and effect of cardinal signs and angles may be summed up in the words "Action" and "Initiative" (though each acts differently from the others,) therefore planets placed in cardinal signs and angles give zest to life according to the nature of the particular planet, sign and angle.

"Zodiac" means a circle of animals. The symbols of three of the cardinal signs are animalistic: *Aries,* the Ram; *Cancer,* the Crab; and *Capricorn,* the Goat. The fourth, Libra, the Scales, represents the ideal towards which this class must strive. None need poise so much as those under the impulsive influence of the cardinal ray; therefore the Balance was set in the heavens to direct their aspirations.

The Fixed Signs

Keyword "Stability"

The Fixed Signs are *Taurus, Leo, Scorpio* and *Aquarius.* Three symbols of the fixed signs are also bestial, violent and virulent; *Taurus,* the Bull; *Leo,* the Lion; and *Scorpio,* the Scorpion. The human figure of *Aquarius,* the Waterbearer, shows us the ideal towards which this class must strive. Instead of fighting, preying upon, or poisoning others in the struggle for existence they must learn to become humane, to be friends to all instead of foes.

The influence of the fixed signs rouses the *desire* nature, giving stamina and persistence in action.

When fixed signs are on the angles (the first, fourth, seventh and tenth houses), they exert a well nigh irresistible force, impelling the individual along a certain line. He may be slow and plodding, but is sure to be *persistent* in whatever he undertakes, and whatever talent he may possess in a certain direction will be exploited to its fullest extent. Setbacks which would take the courage from a person with cardinal signs do not daunt the man with fixed signs on the angles, he knows no defeat, and therefore he usually gains his goal in the end and achieves success by Concentration upon one point, and Persistence in following his chosen path. On the other hand such people are conservative to the last degree. They may see and desire improvements in various lines, but are exceedingly slow to adopt measures to accomplish the desired end; they never do this until thoroughly satisfied that a certain method will meet the requirements. In other words, people with fixed signs on the angles "look before they leap;" they look a long time and very, very carefully, but on the other hand, when they have once been won over to a certain cause they are faithful unto death, and no more ardent advocates can be found; their zeal is almost fanatical. On the whole, people with fixed signs may be said to be *the most reliable people* in the world, either for good or bad.

The Common Signs

Keyword "Flexibility"

Gemini, Sagittarius, Virgo and Pisces are called common signs, their intrinsic nature being best expressed by the keyword, Flexibility.

The forces working through the *cardinal* signs impinge upon the *dense body* and stir it to action.

The power of the *common* signs is *mental and spiritual,* giving purpose to action and incentive to nobility of life.

Therefore people influenced by stellar forces focused principally through *cardinal* signs are the workers of the world, not the toilers, but *executives,* who accomplish things industrially, and who bring into concrete existence schemes, great or small, of value in the world's work. *The common signs are all double;* two of them are human: *Gemini,* the Twins, and *Virgo,* the Virgin; the third, *Sagittarius,* the Centaur, is partly human; and only the fourth symbol, *Pisces,* the Fishes, is taken from the lower kingdom. None are violent, however, but intensely moral, intellectual and spiritual symbols.

Unstable as reeds they are swayed hither and thither; nothing appeals to them permanently, they desire nothing as much as change. No matter how well placed, they can seldom resist the lure of an opening in another city, the farther away, the better. Therefore the old maxim: "a rolling stone gathers no moss," applies particularly to this class, for their roving habits usually keep them poor. They spend as fast as they earn, or faster. Thus these people drift upon the sea of life propelled by the currents of circumstances. Outside conditions dominate them as they lack stamina to assert their own individuality.

The foregoing is true of the great majority who are under the rule and influence of common signs; they respond to the *lower phase* simply because the higher side is too high for all but a very few at our present stage of development. Those who make a success in the world because prodded by the cardinal and fixed influences, call them indolent and good-for-nothing, but were the former bereft of the cardinal or fixed energy which goads them to action, and placed under the common ray, they would soon realize its lack of power and learn compassion for those who must so live all their lives. What then is the lesson these people have to learn?

Comparative Effect of Cardinal, Fixed, and Common Signs on the Angles

While the nature of the cardinal signs is such that their rays stir our latent forces into action, and promote change, the most prominent quality of the fixed signs is Stability; but the student must beware of confounding stability with inertia. The action induced by the rays of cardinal signs may be changed into other channels with considerable facility, all they want being expression; the direction in which they express themselves is a secondary consideration. Not so with the fixed signs, when their ray impels to action in a certain direction it is next to impossible to stay the force or change it. On the other hand, if they deny expression in certain lines, the obstruction is almost insurmountable.

People of the fixed class lack ability to make their inventions commercially usable, a task for which the cardinal class is eminently fitted. Thus these two classes work hand in hand and between them they have transformed the wilderness of the world to a condition of comparative comfort, their efforts toward improvement are continually carried on, and in time the desert will be made to bloom like a rose.

As material success depends on ability to cope with material conditions, the cardinal class is particularly fortunate, for it is the chief executive factor in the world's work, and reaps a ready reward therefrom. The fixed class is not so prominently before the public, labors in laboratories and works experimentally to complete the processes and perfect the models which are later used in manufacture. Therefore this class also is a potent factor in life, and shares the material and financial success of the cardinal class.

The common class is a sharp contrast. Forces focused through *common* signs are *mental*, therefore people ruled by them are averse to strenuous physical action which is the forte of the cardinal class;

they labor only when lashed by the whip of necessity. They are also incapable of the slow but sustained effort put forth by the fixed class and are easily discouraged by obstacles. Thus they are leaners and not lifters. *Toilers* who do the bidding of the inventive and executive classes are recruited from people ruled by *common* signs. There is one sphere, however, where they shine, according to their ability to think. Being averse to work they have created a vantage-ground whence they may reap the benefits of the toil of others, of their inventive faculties and executive skill. To do this they become *promoters* who bring inventor and manufacturer together, *agents* who mediate between buyer and seller, *peddlers,* venders and all other *middlemen* who go between producer and consumer and *live on a commission;* also *literary* men who devote their talent to purposeless *fiction* belong to the class actuated by the lower phases of the force in the common signs.

The cardinal class is active, the common is restless, the fixed class is rigid, the common is flexible.

The Four Triplicities

The effect of the "Triplicities" is most marked in the rising sign and when the majority of the planets are grouped in one of them.

A fiery sign (Aries, Leo or Sagittarius), on the ascendant, gives much vitality, but it also makes the person prone to fevers and inflammatory disorders; and when the majority of the planets are in fiery signs they make it very difficult for the person to "keep cool" physically or mentally.

A watery sign (Cancer, Scorpio or Pisces) rising, gives much less stamina and predisposes to digestive, urinary and catarrhal troubles. If a person has many planets in watery signs his problem is to generate enough energy to keep warm, for this grouping gives a listless, indifferent disposition, except when Scorpio is rising or when many planets are in that sign.

Airy signs rising (Gemini, Libra and Aquarius,) give a nervous temperament and make the person liable to disorders of the lungs, heart and kidneys. Many planets in these signs give people literary and artistic inclinations.

Earthy signs rising (Taurus, Virgo and Capricorn), give fair vitality but a secret fear of disease arrests the vital processes in the body and poisons these people so that they become victims of chronic ailments oftener than those of the other groupings. The throat, stomach and intestines are specially threatened; rheumatism and gout are also frequently experienced. When a person has many planets in earthy signs it favors the acquisition of material wealth.

The Sun, The Moon and The Ascendant

We stated in our opening paragraph that there are Three Great Factors which convey to us the Mystic Message of the stars in general, namely, the "houses," the "signs" and the "planets." There are also three factors which play a specially important part in the individual horoscope, namely the Sun, the Moon and the Ascendant, which may be said to represent the spirit, the soul and the body.

Properly viewed the Sun, Moon and Ascendant are not really three separate horoscopical principles but represent two composite parts which when united constitute the human being. The "rising sign" and the "first house" together form an avenue for the fecundating influences of the Moon which there crystallize and form the etheric matrix that moulds the physical particles from the maternal body into a new vehicle; hence the astrological maxim that the ascendant at birth (or its opposite) is the Moon's place at conception. This composite body is the part of the human being which is born and dies after a relatively evanescent period of existence.

The other and immortal part of composite man which consists of the Ego and its finer vehicles is represented in the horoscope by the Sun and the Moon. The specific influence of these planets will be described when we have considered the rising sign.

The Rising Sign

As taught in "Simplified Scientific Astrology" it is the angle of the stellar ray which determines in what department of life it will be most prominently active; and it has been found by observation that the sign rising or ascending on the eastern horizon when a child is born is the principal factor in determining the basic constitution and form of the physical body. Further investigations have shown that the reason for this fact is that at the time of conception when the seed-atom was planted in the ovum the Moon, which is the Cosmic agent of fecundation, projected its fertilizing ray through the sign and degree which later rises at the moment of birth, (or its opposite). For that reason the rising sign and degree continue to be the avenue of ingress of the life-forces which build the body of the babe until the severance of the umbilical cord, and the nature of the rising sign is thus indelibly stamped upon the new vehicle and retained all through life.

In this connection it should be noted that conception is not necessarily coincident with the physical union of the parents, sometimes two weeks or even more elapsing ere the auspicious moment awaited by the Recording Angels or their agents strikes. At that time cosmic conditions are such that they will form a body which will facilitate the expression of the Ego seeking re-embodiment and aid it to work out its self-generated destiny. It should also be remembered by students that the moment of delivery is not the time of birth from the astrological point of view. The inhalation of the first complete breath usually accompanied by a cry, is the moment when the incoming Ego receives its stellar baptism. This renders it ever susceptible to the influence of the particular configuration of the stars existing at that moment, and therefore the stars affect each individual differently from all others, not even the horoscopes of twins being alike. It is also strongly emphasized that according to this explanation we do not have a certain "fate" because we were born at a certain time, but we are born at a particular time because we have a certain self-generated destiny to work out. That is a very important distinction for it substitutes divine law for divine caprice, it eliminates the element of "luck" and inspires man to mastery of "fate" by working with the Law. If we have made our present horoscope by our past actions in a past life, logically we are now preparing for future embodiment and may make it what we choose. If we strive to strengthen our body now, to overcome our faults, to cultivate new virtues, the Sun of our next life will rise under much more auspicious conditions than those under which we now live and thus we may truly rule our stars and master our fate.

When the last three degrees of a sign are rising, or when the first three degrees ascend at the time of birth the person is said to be born "on the cusp" between two signs and then the basic nature of the signs involved are blended in his or her body. Thus a person born when the three last degrees of Aries or the first degrees of Taurus were ascending would be neither purely Aries nor Taurus but a mixture of the qualities of the two signs.

The nature of the rising sign is also modified by

the presence of planets. The Sun and Mars increase vitality if well aspected but if afflicted they incline to fever and inflammatory disorders but they also favor rapid recuperation, and make the nature alert and energetic. A well-aspected Jupiter rising also increases vitality but inclines to corpulence; if the planet is afflicted that makes the circulation sluggish and thus gives a tendency to disorders of the blood. The foregoing remarks about Jupiter apply to Venus in a lesser degree. Saturn rising lowers the vitality and favors chronic ill-health in later life, but at the same time he gives such a tenacious hold on life that though the person may pray to be released he cannot die. Mercury, Moon, Uranus and Neptune make the body more high-strung and nervous than the average, usable specially for pioneers in music, literature, higher thought, science and the electrical arts.

Planets placed in the twelfth house are considered as being on the ascendant if within six degrees thereof, also all planets in the first house no matter how far from the rising degree; but if a sign be intercepted in the first house, planets placed therein will not have as strong an influence in the life as though the sign occupy the cusp.

CHAPTER V.

The Influence of the Twelve Signs When Rising

Aries, the Ram

ARIES is mythologically represented as a ram and the symbol describes most accurately those born under its influence; a pointed and protruding sheep-like nose, wide forehead, pointed chin and the resultant triangular face noted in many people, are unmistakable indications of their rising sign. Light brown or reddish tint of the hair is a pronounced characteristic of the Arian; the body is slender and well formed; if the first part of the sign is rising the body is shorter, and the complexion darker than given by the latter degrees.

Planets in the rising sign will modify the description, however, and the student must use his knowledge of the character of the planets in conjunction with the description of the Sign. The Sun and Mars make the complexion more florid, the Moon and Saturn make it paler and darker, Jupiter and Venus make the body more portly. Saturn shortens, Uranus and Mercury lengthen. This applies to all the signs, but is especially marked when a planet rises in the sign it rules. Mars in Aries rising would give fiery red hair and a face full of freckles. The Sun rising in Leo would give a florid complexion with flaxen hair, but if Saturn were there, instead it would shorten the body and darken the hair.

Aries people are bold, self-confident and impulsive; they aim to lead, dislike to follow, are always ready to take the initiative in any movement that appeals to them, but often lack persistence to carry their projects to a conclusion over serious obstacles.

The Sun, and Mars the Ruler, rising in Aries would intensify the above, but as a thorough explanation will be given under the heading "The Intrinsic Nature of the Planets," the student is referred thereto. We may mention it here, however, as a peculiarity that Aries people live through fevers to which others succumb. We have known their hair to fall out, and the temperature to remain four degrees above the usual maximum for many hours, without fatal result.

Taurus, the Bull

Taurus is represented by a Bull in the Zodiac, and the bodies generated under this sign are usually short and stocky. They have a strong neck with the bump of amativeness well developed, large lobe of the ear, heavy jaws, full face; nose short and stubby. Dark eyes and wavy hair frequently give them considerable beauty. The eye of the Taurian may never dart bolts of fire such as those wherewith the Arian would annihilate his enemies;

it is softer, but under provocation it becomes sullenly expressive of the passive resistance wherewith these people win their battles. It then marks the difference between the impulsive Aries and the stubborn Taurus. The inner phalange of the thumb is large and heavy, the calves well developed and the foot chubby. In walking the Taurian usually plants his heel first, and heaviest.

Taurus people are pre-eminently "thorough and steadfast" in everything they do: In love, in hate, in work or play, they persist in a given direction, and neither reason nor argument will turn them. They are verbose and argumentative in defense of their actions or opinions; they grasp new ideas slowly, with difficulty and conservatively, but once comprehended and espoused, they always remember what they have learned and defend their opinions to the last ditch.

The Sun rising in Taurus gives an unusually firm physique, and accentuates the Taurus pride in strength. *The Moon,* being the planet of fecundity, is exalted in this exceedingly fruitful sign; hence people with the Moon in Taurus have large families, particularly if the configuration is in the fifth house, for that designates children.

Venus, the ruler of Taurus, rising in that sign, makes the form beautiful as well as strong, also giving artistic ability and musical inspiration.

Gemini, the Twins

When Gemini is rising the body generated is tall and slender; the arms and limbs are particularly long, fingers slender, hair dark, eyes hazel. Gemini people are quick, active and alert in all their movements, habitual restlessness being noticeable in the expression of the eyes, which differs in that respect from more fixed tendencies of the eyes of those born under the two preceding signs, although of course we do not mean that the Arian always looks angry and the Taurian stubborn, nevertheless, there is a settled tendency in those directions noticeable when these people are not occupied in a certain direction; but the Gemini people have an expression which is much more vivid, changeable and past finding out. They have acutely inquiring minds, and always want to know the reason why, but often lack persistence to follow clews to the end, and thus they meet disappointment. Being tactful they avoid giving offense even under provocation, and are therefore generally liked by all; though their own affections are not deep. Two distinct classes are born under this sign; one, too fond of reading, should cultivate independent thought, instead of repeating other people's ideas, or aping their manners; the other is scientific, well balanced and reserved; a model for any person.

The Sun rising in Gemini brings out all the noblest traits of the sign; it makes the nature more settled and contented, gives more persistence and a particularly healthy and active body.

Mercury, the ruler, rising in Gemini, sharpens perception, gives ability as a writer, or speaker, but makes the person born with that position extremely irritable, vacillating and fond of change of scene and employment. Such people are best fitted for traveling salesmen.

Cancer, the Crab

The chief peculiarities of the crab are a clumsy body, slender limbs and powerful claws; people born with Cancer rising express them all. They have a large upper body, augmented in later years by a prominence of the abdomen acquired by overeating. The mandible or lower jaw is powerfully hinged to the cranium, the face is therefore widest between the ears, the mouth is also large, and the whole construction similar to the crab's claw. The face is full, the hair brown, the eyes blue, complexion pale and sickly, for the Cancer person has the least vitality of any. The limbs are extremely slender in proportion to the large upper body, so the structure appears "top heavy," and he walks with a "rolling" gait.

Cancer people are very fond of the home and its comforts, they are quiet, reserved and adapt themselves to conditions, hence they are easy to get along with; their anger is shortlived, and they hold no spite. Though lacking in physical prowess, they are no hypocrites, but always have the courage of their convictions; they voice and defend them too.

The Sun rising in Cancer brings out and accentuates all the good qualities mentioned above, giving more ambition and pride; it also increases the vitality, and is a particular boon in that respect to people with Cancer rising on account of their very low life force. Cancer, with its ruler, the Moon, governs the stomach and hence alimentation; Leo and its ruler, the Sun, have charge of the heart and circulation. If these signs and planets are well placed in the horoscope, they counteract most other afflictions and a long lease of life is assured, but if they are afflicted, much sickness results unless intelligent care is applied to modify the omen.

The Moon, the ruler, rising in Cancer, will give much instability to the nature, and Jupiter, being exalted there, will bring fortune and fame.

Leo, the Lion

The lion is the king of beasts and even in captivity is an embodiment of stateliness and pride. The typical Leos of the Zodiac also express pride in every movement and a stateliness which will not escape attention of the keen observer; the expansive chest, the massive shoulders, the strong arm and the large head contrast noticeably with the more slender but still muscular under body; and as Aries has the sheep face, so the typical Leo has certain feline features. The complexion is florid, eyes large and full, blue or grayish in color, expressing laughter, cheerfulness and content. The whole frame is well knit and strong, having great endurance and recuperative power.

It is really wonderful how the symbology of the signs is brought out in the different kinds of people born under them. People who are born under Leo always want to be noted; they are aggressive and want to attract attention everywhere they go. They aim to be leaders, never followers.

Leo rules the heart, and it is a marked characteristic that people with Leo rising unafflicted, have hearts bigger than their pocketbooks; they give generously of their time, money, or knowledge without thought of self. If the Sun rises in Leo, this trait becomes almost prodigality, but if Saturn is there to afflict instead, he will counteract it so that they will either circumscribe their gifts with conditions to such an extent that they retain practical control, or they will spend their means on themselves.

Leos are honest and faithful; being children of the day star, they love light and truth, are above subterfuge and aim straight at their object. Their will is firm to attain by honorable means. They make good orators and hold their audiences by personal magnetism. They are very attractive to the opposite sex, and the lower nature should be held firmly in check, otherwise serious trouble and heartache may ensue. The French, as a race, are ruled by Leo, and afford ample illustration of this point.

The Sun rising in Leo, unafflicted, gives a body of wonderful strength, vitality and recuperative power; superior in its wiriness to the body generated by the Sun in Taurus; but if Mars is afflicted in Leo, palpitation of the heart will ensue. Saturn here will cause regurgitation unless care is taken in early years to avoid strain.

Virgo, the Virgin

People born when Virgo is rising are above middle stature. The upper part of the head is much more developed than the lower, the weak chin, showing lack of will and the large brain indicating greatness of intellect, being therefore earmarks of the Virgo. The face is thin, the complexion sallow, the hair brown and the eyes hazel or grey. The feet are small, the toes turn inwards and give these people a peculiar labored walk.

Virgo people are very quick and active in youth; they learn with facility, and do not work hard for knowledge; they seem to breathe it in without an effort. They acquire linguistic and elocutionary powers most readily, are fluent writers but are often cynical, cold and unforgiving when they have been injured. They are extremists in their food, and make hygiene a fad; they often fancy that they have every imaginable disease, because Virgo is the sixth sign and has a certain affinity with the sixth house, denoting health and disease.

Mercury, the ruler, is also exalted here and gives pronouncement of all the good which otherwise might be expected from the Sun.

Virgo people are slender in youth, but when the

Sun of Life passes the Meridian and begins to throw its shadows toward the East, we find in them a tendency toward corpulence of body, particularly of that part ruled by Virgo, namely, the abdomen. They neglect to take exercise, and naturally on this account a sluggish condition of the intestines may set in which retains the poisons in the body and robs life of its joys, making one indifferent. In this fact lies the greatest danger of the Virgo people. Once they get into the rut of sickness, they actually "enjoy" poor health. They love to talk over their symptoms with other people, and they resent any thought or suggestion given to them that they are not sick, or that they can get well. The presence of Saturn in Virgo, or the sixth house, accentuates this tendency in the very highest degree, and therefore it is an almost infallible sign that the native will have or be subject to chronic illness, the nature of the disease being denoted by the aspect, and the afflicting planets.

In order to deal successfully with Virgo people when they have once become subject to disease, and get them out of it at all, it is necessary to be firm almost to the verge of cruelty. But though one may seem cruel in enforcing upon them the regime that is necessary to bring them away from themselves, this is really the greatest kindness that can be shown, for once these people are in the grip of sickness they stubbornly refuse to let go; they will resort to the most cunning, even childlike schemes to excite sympathy, particularly from strangers, and they will resent any effort to show them that they are not helpless invalids. At the very slightest suggestion of a hopeful nature, they sometimes lose their temper in the most unwarranted manner. But when at last they are given the deaf ear by everybody, when people who are in their immediate environment can be persuaded to show them no sympathy, then they may come to themselves. They need a shock to bring them out and away from their condition. And until they get that they never can be cured.

The Virgos make splendid nurses, if they can keep from taking on the conditions of the patient. The Virgo people never can bear to see blood shed or touch dead things. They feel bodily injury to others more than harm done to themselves, and are in fact splendidly described by the word "chicken hearted."

Libra, the Scales

Elegance may be said to express in one word the physical peculiarities of the Libran. The body is slender and graceful in youth; it becomes more plump as life advances, but even the portliness of the Libra body is pleasing. The complexion is smooth and clear, eyes are soft and blue with a kind expression; the mouth is unusually well formed and the teeth particularly fine and even.

Libra people have extremely strong conjugal affection, so strong, in fact, that it overshadows all other considerations. The Leos love their families, but their hearts take in all the world besides; not so the Librans; they are ready for any sacrifice to give comforts to those in their own immediate home circle, but they are also prepared to sacrifice any other family for their own, if necessary.

In most other traits the Librans express aptly the symbolism of their sign, a pair of scales, and their characteristics might be expressed in the word: "Changeability." They are people of "moods," because Saturn is exalted here and weighs upon the mind; the changes are sudden and extreme; they may follow a fad with as much zest as if their life depended upon it, and then, without a moment's warning, drop it and take up something entirely opposite; there are no half-way measures in the swing of the scales. Being naturally given to change, they are most adaptable to circumstances, and do not fret over reverses, but set about with vim and vigor to restore their fortunes.

Aries and Libra may be said to be the battlefields of the Sun and Saturn: Life and Death, Joy and Sorrow. The Sun is exalted in Aries, and vanquishes Saturn; hence the intrepidity of Aries people. In Libra the scales tip the other way; there Saturn is exalted, and conquers the Sun; this gives a softer tone to the Libran, whose kindly politeness contrasts markedly with the Arian's brusque address. Venus, the ruler of Libra, is not alone responsible for this trait, for Taurus people are blunt, though Venus rules. Venus rising in Libra gives artistic ability, Saturn turns the mind in scientific directions.

Librans usually have well shaped hands and feet, and are very proud of them.

Scorpio, the Eagle

The nose is the most prominent feature of the Scorpio; it is large, heavy, and hooked, resembling the bill of the eagle; the brows are bushy, the eyes sharp and piercing; the jaw is very heavy; the glint of the eye, and the set of the jaw indicate the great determination which is the most prominent characteristic of the Scorpio. The face is angular, complexion murky, and hair dark, with a peculiar ruddy tinge noticeable when the sun shines on it. The teeth are large and subject to early decay. The body is short and thickset, with a short, thick neck resembling that of the opposite sign, Taurus.

Scorpio people always stand up for their rights, and never submit to imposition, though prone to ride roughshod over others. They are full of worries over things that may happen, but never do, and thus make life a burden to those around them. Sarcasm that stings like a scorpion is ever upon the tip of their tongue, yet their love is strong, and their aspirations lofty. Thus there are two natures struggling in the Scorpios and they need much sympathy and forbearance from their friends. In the hour of danger they never flinch, but perform deeds of heroism with a disregard of self that amounts to foolhardiness. The mind is sharp, cool and collected, therefore Scorpio men make good army officers and excel in surgery. The Scorpio woman has a large family.

The Sun in Scorpio accentuates the good traits, and gives a love of mysticism; but Mars, the ruler, brings out the worldly side of the sign and makes scoffers and skeptics.

Sagittarius, the Centaur

People born with Sagittarius rising are even taller than those born under the opposite sign, Gemini, the men in particular having large hands and feet. The size and weight of the bony frame is often too much for the ligaments of the spine to support, so these people often develop a decided stoop in later years. The face is long and well formed, the nose well proportioned, dark kindly eyes and dark chestnut hair. The body is very active, but requires much rest, as the recuperative powers are below the average.

The symbol of this sign shows that there are two widely different classes born therein. One, designated by the animal body of the Centaur, is frankly in for "a good time;" they are sporty, soldiers of fortune, of roving proclivities, fond of games of chance, and ready to risk their all on the turn of a card, the speed of a horse, or a game of ball, while Aries or Scorpio people may become pugilists, and Taurus people take up wrestling as a profession. The sports of Sagittarius have no element of cruelty in them. Sagittarians when afflicted may become criminals;

their crimes are never violent, however, but rather results of their indulgence of the animal nature.

The other class is the extreme opposite, symbolized by the human part of the sign. Here is the man rising above the animal nature, bending the bow of aspiration and aiming at limitless space, signifying the loftiest longings of that immortal spark of incipient divinity we call the soul. This class is law abiding and of the highest morals; from it come the pillars of the church and beloved rulers of state famed for integrity, benevolence and justice.

The Sun rising in this sign is sure to bring preferment even to those born in lowly and obscure circumstances, and accentuate all good shown in the sign; so will Jupiter, the ruler.

Sagittarius rules the thighs and therefore, naturally, configurations from this sign, if afflicted are likely to cause accidents to those parts. And it is a notable fact that Sagittarians are very liable to broken bones under circumstances where people under other signs seldom meet injury.

In the eighth degree of Sagittarius we have the fixed star Antares, which has a very evil effect upon the sight. Two other nebulous spots in the Zodiac have a similar influence. One is Ascelli in Leo 6, the other Pleiades in Taurus 29. The Sun, or Moon, in one of those places and adversely configurated with one of the malefics, Saturn, Mars, Uranus or Neptune gives trouble with the eyes, according to the nature of the evil aspect; or, vice versa, if Saturn,

Mars, Uranus or Neptune are in one of the nebulous spots adversely configurated to the Sun or Moon a similar trouble will be experienced. Should a planet like one of the above named be in retrograde motion the aspect is much worse, for when the planet has ceased to retrograde and goes direct in the Zodiac again, it will pass over which ever one of these nebulous spots it is close to a second time and thereby cause an added damage. There may be, however, a compensating side to this aspect, for it sometimes happens that while an evil configuration to one of these nebulous spots, (and Antares is the worst,) deprives a person of his sight, a benevolent configuration awakens in him a second-sight which will mitigate the loss in a degree that only those who have that sight can appreciate.

The Sagittarian must learn to realize his ideals within instead of seeking them without. We are in this school of experience for the purpose of overcoming, and it is not by running away from one place to another that we gain experience. By staying in one place, by doing our very best to attain our ideals where we are, we make our ideals come true.

Capricorn, the Goat

Capricorn rising gives a short, slender, narrow-chested body with a thin neck, thin silky dark hair, a pale peaked face with small, weak eyes. It makes the chin pointed and turned upwards, the nose pointed and turned downwards, an impediment in the speech, ill formed lower limbs and an awkward walk. The vitality is very low, and these children are reared with great difficulty, but once infancy is past, they exhibit a tenacity that is truly amazing, and often become very, very old; they seem to dry up into a mass of wrinkled skin and bone that is all but imperishable, this, on account of the Saturn ray which rules Capricorn. It is noticeable also, that all who have that planet prominent in the nativity show the before mentioned wrinkling of the skin, even though they may retain corpulence conferred by other configurations.

Ambition and suspicion are ruling characteristics, an inordinate desire for recognition of their claims to superiority and advancement; also suspicion that others are trying to subvert or withhold the coveted prize, is ever with these people. It causes them much unnecessary worry, and may result in habitual melancholy, particularly if Saturn is afflicted. They ought to seek amusement outdoors, read funny stories and otherwise try to cultivate a sense of the humorous from childhood, for this is one of the saddest signs, and needs all possible encouragement.

Capricorn people are successful in detective work, where secret practices are used to trap others, and persistence is required to ferret out a mystery, for they never give up. The afflicted Capricorn is very revengeful, and if by Mars, may shed blood to satisfy a grudge. The Sun rising brings out the Justice, Purity and Honor of the sign, makes Captains of Industry such as forward the great enterprises of the world.

Aquarius, the Water Bearer

The stateliness and pride of those born under the sign of Leo are not missing in the typical Aquarian, but while in the Leo these qualities are of a lower, more bestial nature agreeable to the sign, they are manly pride and stateliness in the true Aquarian. Libra generates a beautiful body but more effeminate as it were, whereas the Aquarian beauty is truly manly or womanly; the fearless eye is kindly and drooping eyelashes are peculiar to this sign. The forehead is square, and the well developed poise tells of intellect, the large domed head shows the spiritual side of the nature and the chin is sufficiently developed to give purpose to all actions. Thus the typical Aquarian is the highest grade of humanity; but therefore, also exceedingly rare, for the variants produced in each sign from the typical, by the interposition of one or more planets are so different that the type is often unrecognizable in the majority of its features. Aquarians are most loyal to friends, therefore they attract many, keep them through life, and are much benefited by them. Like Capricorn, this sign is ruled by Saturn, and he gives to the Aquarian the same retiring nature and tendency to melancholy which marks the Capricornian, but also the persistence in following a given course;

and whatever financial success comes to these people is the result of continued and patient effort; Aquarians are very deliberate and longsuffering; they never act in a hurry, and therefore seldom have cause to regret their actions, save when reason has been stilled through play upon their sympathies, for under such circumstances they are readily imposed upon. The love nature is very strong, but they are not as demonstrative as the Leo. It is noteworthy that the qualities of opposite signs are always reflected; Leo in Aquarius, reflects love; Taurus mirrors the passion of Scorpio; the Gemini body is a reflex of the bony Sagittarius frame, etc.

The Sun and Saturn bring out more prominently the good traits of Aquarius; this sign, where Saturn rules, and Libra, where he is exalted, are therefore under his most benign influence. The Sun in Aquarius adds much hope and life to the nature, and thus counteracts the melancholy trait previously mentioned.

Pisces, the Fishes

The typical Piscean is short, flabby and fleshy with a waddling gait not unlike those born under the sign Cancer, but differs from them by having a stouter body. The feet are often turned in, but larger than those born under Virgo. The body is weak and deficient in recuperative force. The complexion is medium, the eyes blue, watery and expressionless, the nose large and flat.

There is a strong tendency to mediumship among the Pisces people, and therein is a danger greater than any other on earth. No one should "sit for development" and degenerate into the tool of low spirits, but Pisces people in particular are "lost" if taken control of. They cannot free themselves, either in this life or the next, because generally inert and devoid of will power. They are timid, and even the men are tearful on the slightest provocation; they love leisure more than comfort, and do no work which is not absolutely necessary to keep body and soul together. They love change of scene, rove about considerably, generally in an aimless manner. Being fond of good things to eat and drink, particularly the latter, and lacking will to curb their appetite when afflicted, they frequently indulge their craving to such an extent that they become habitual drunkards.

The Sun rising in Pisces gives more energy and ambition, Jupiter, the ruler, strengthens the morals, and Venus exalted in this sign, gives great musical talent, but accentuates the tendency to alcoholic indulgence, which mars the lives of so many splendid musicians.

When many planets are in Pisces, the person will have a hard life, because he or she will not want to take up life's burden, but will love to dream; such people become recluses; they seek to master the hidden arts, occultism and mysticism; are not guided by reason, but rather by their likes and dislikes, and unless they can find an occupation that is otherwise isolated from the ordinary business and trend of life they will feel out of place. They are prone to incur the enmity of people with whom they come in contact intimately; nobody seems to get along with them, and nearly everybody, whether he shows it or not, will take a dislike to them.

There is, however, a higher side to Pisces; the person who finds himself with Pisces on the ascendant is at the end of one cycle of progress and at the beginning of a new. He stands, as it were, upon the threshhold of something higher. Therefore, he is usually not able to live up to the possibilities of the sign which requires self-sacrifice and non-resistance in absolutely Christlike fashion. The tendency is therefore to drift upon the sea of life and dream dreams of future greatness. This tendency must be counteracted by every effort of the will, for otherwise life will be a failure, and later the stern whip of necessity will be applied to goad him or her into action.

CHAPTER VI.

THE INTRINSIC NATURE OF THE PLANETS

THE nature of gun powder which causes it to explode under certain circumstances is neither good nor bad, the quality of its action being determined by the way its power is used. When it furthers the welfare of the community it is called good, and evil when used in a manner derogatory to our well being; so also with the planets, they are neither good nor evil, each having its intrinsic nature and acting in a manner consonant therewith save as modified by the circumstances under which its powers are exerted. When we know the nature of a sign and the nature of a planet, we may combine the two, and thus obtain the correct reading of the stellar script by our own reasoning instead of depending upon authorities. For instance, the Sun is hot, full of vital force, and exercises an influence that buoys us up in body and spirit. When its rays fall upon us with moderate strength it makes us stronger and more cheerful, for there is an atmosphere of generosity, out-going love and kindliness in the Sun. Thus if the Sun at birth is in the weak sign, Cancer, naturally the effect would be to modify the weak constitution described in the foregoing signature of the signs; the heat of the Sun would give a more florid complexion to the Cancer person, the general health and recuperative powers would be materially augmented, not to speak of the changes that would be manifested in the disposition, giving more ambition, hopefulness and buoyancy to the temperament. Suppose, on the other hand, that the Sun is in Aries when that sign is rising at the birth of a person, then the fire of the Sun, added to the fire of the sign Aries, will increase the boldness and the intrepidity of the person to such a degree that they may become foolhardiness, particularly, if Mars, the ruler of Aries, is also there increasing the warlike tendencies. Those are traits of character, but the physical body will also suffer from this excessive heat, the blood will race through the veins of such a person like a Niagara of liquid fire, and fevers will be a frequent experience, as the superabundance of vitality burns out the physical casement. Were the cold, slow and sluggish Saturn there instead of the Sun and Mars, he might squelch almost all of the Aries characteristics both mental and physical. If we consider Aries symbolized by a stove in which a fire is burning, it would make the same difference whether the hot Mars, or the cold Saturn, were placed there, as it makes a difference whether we pour oil or water into the stove. Similarly, all the other planets produce various results, according to their intrinsic natures and their various combinations. For the sake of lucidity and ready reference, let us first set down the word which describes best the most salient characteristics of each planet.

The Sun	Life
Venus	Coalition
Mercury	Reason
The Moon	Fecundation
Saturn	Obstruction
Jupiter	Idealism
Mars	Dynamic Energy
Uranus	Altruism
Neptune	Divinity

In the foregoing, the essential natures of the planets have been given; where they are well aspected by another planet these natural characteristics are enhanced so far as the benefic planets are concerned, but when evilly aspected, the nature of Venus, which is love and rhythm, becomes folly, licentiousness and sloth; the philosophy, law-abiding tendencies, mercy and lofty aspirations of Jupiter turn into lawlessness, disregard of others, and low pursuits; the lofty spirituality of the Sun will express itself as just animal spirits and physical health. In regard to the planets of the lower nature, good aspects of Mars turn the desires toward constructive objects and well regulated activities, while evil aspects are responsible for the destructive expression of the desire nature. Saturn, when well aspected, gives mechanical and executive ability capable of directing the desire nature. It shows the brainy, persevering man able to cope with, and conquer, material obstacles; the organizer and the promotor; the scientific investigator, who follows material lines. As Jupiter, well aspected, denotes the high-minded philosopher, the worthy law-giver, the sincere and ardent priest, in fact, all who have high and lofty aspirations, so Saturn, when evilly aspected, denotes the evil-minded, creed-bound sectarian, the materialist, and enemy of society, whether church or state, As Jupiter gives the lofty, expansive and benevolent mind, so Saturn, evilly aspected, gives a sarcastic, concrete and narrow tendency.

It is wonderful to contemplate how the planetary forces balance each other so perfectly that universal equilibrium is maintained despite the disturbances of the 1700 millions who inhabit the earth alone, not to speak of other spheres. Every moment of time our actions, individually and collectively, interfere with terrestrial equipoise, and were not this instantly restored, the earth must leave its orbit, fly off at a tangent and be destroyed. Nor are physical disturbances most potent in disturbing or restoring balance, it being a fallacy to confound solidity and rigidity with strength, as most thoroughly explained in our lecture No. 19, "The Coming Force." A train has no strength itself, but must be solid because it is operated upon by an invisible gas called steam. There is no force in a rigid hammer; but when driven by a column of flexible liquid, like water, backed by an elastic cushion of compressed air, the force stored in the air drives the powerful hydraulic ram irresistibly through whatever comes before it. Likewise subtle, invisible, stellar rays are the factors which maintain our ponderous planet in its path, and spiritual disturbances generated by mankind are naturally the most subtle force which interferes with the earth's equipoise.

Each planet has its opposite, and therefore every time we radiate the quality of one planet, we call forth a counter current of corresponding force, and by the action and reaction of those forces in and upon us and our environment we learn the lessons of life. Do we vibrate to the love ray of Venus, instantly Mars comes to tempt, and tries to turn love to lust, but it depends upon *us* whether we remain steadfast in virtue or yield to vice. Do we court the ideal of Jupiter; do we aim to elevate the standards of church or state, instantly the Saturnine forces invite to self-aggrandizement and appeal to the passion for power. With *us* it lies to remain true to the ideal and reap laurels that last through eternity, or yield to the promise of present gain of worthless gold which we repay in sorrow when Saturn turns and becomes the chastiser. Each horoscope shows the tendencies in even the humblest life, and opportunity continually knocks. May we all be prepared to meet it as spiritual astrologers.

How to Test the Horoscope

It sometimes happens that a momentary mental aberration causes even the best of mathematicians to make a mistake in his figures and if an error occurs when casting a horoscope an immense amount of labor may be wasted before it is discovered. There is an easy method of verifying the figure in the main points by a glance at the position of the Sun. The cautious astrologer never neglects to make use of this method, and we would specially recommend it to beginners who are naturally more prone to miscalculate than those who have long experience.

When you have calculated the place of the Sun and entered it in its proper house and sign, note at once if its position coincides with its actual place in the sky at the time of day when the child was born. If the birth occurred about sunrise, the Sun must be near the ascendant; if in the middle of the forenoon the Sun should be somewhere in the eleventh house, if near noon the Sun will be found near the Midheaven in a correctly cast horoscope, and in the middle of the afternoon it is in the eighth house. A child born near sunset has its sun close to the cusp between the sixth and seventh houses, and if the birth occurs about 9 p. m., the Sun will be in or near the fifth house. When birth is at midnight the Sun is near the nadir, and a child born about 3 o'clock in the morning has the Sun in or near the second house.

If you find that the Sun is in its proper position

relative to the houses, you may confidently proceed with your calculations and place the other planets. If not, you have made a mistake which must be corrected before you go further.

When someone hands you a horoscope calculated by another astrologer and asks you to read it, look first at the time of birth and then see if the Sun is in its proper position relative to the houses, and the right sign as determined by the month, for if you start to read from an improperly cast horoscope you lay yourself liable to ridicule. Suppose Saturn were on the ascendant and you accuse that person of being melancholy; when he denies the indications and you discover that Mars and Mercury should be there in Scorpio, it is not probable that he will accept your explanations; he will more likely sneer at astrology and astrologers; nor can we deny that from his point of view such condemnation is justified. Therefore be careful to look at the Sun. Other mistakes may occur, but that is the most serious and the most easily detected.

CHAPTER VII.

The Children of the Twelve Signs

The Children of Aries

Born March 20th to April 21st.

ARIES is the home of Mars, the planet of dynamic energy, and is also the exaltation sign of the life-giving Sun, hence it is a very fountain of life and vitality as manifest in the sprouting of the millions of seeds which break through the earth's crust at spring time and change the white winter garment to a flower-embroidered carpet of green, making the forests a bridal bower for the mating beasts and birds.

This great vital force also finds its expression in the children of Aries; they bubble over with life and energy to such an extent that it is often very difficult to curb them sufficiently to hold them within the bounds of safety and common sense. They are self-assertive and aggressive to a degree, always in the lead for they scorn to follow, turbulent and radical in all their thoughts, ideas and actions. They are venturesome to the verge of foolhardiness.

We also find that they are greedy for the fruits of their labor, they never can get enough, and no matter how much they earn they are generally poor for they spend as freely and as thoughtlessly as they earn. They make splendid foremen and overseers, for, being so full of vital energy and ambition themselves, they have a faculty of infusing their energy into their subordinates or forcing them to work when necessary. But being too impulsive and reckless they lack the ability to originate for themselves. They are serious and ardent in all they undertake; they cannot go into anything half-heartedly, and therefore, if they once espouse a cause, social, political or religious, they will work for that cause with all the vim and vigor of their energetic nature. But if on the other hand an Aries child becomes addicted to a vice the whole intensity of its being is turned towards the gratification of that particular part of its lower nature. Therefore parents with Aries children have a great responsibility to set before them by precept and example the noblest and best form of conduct of which they are capable, for this is probably the most impressive sign in the zodiac, and the habits formed, the lessons learned in childhood and youth will generally cling to the person through life and make him either very good or very bad. Be particularly careful to inculcate abstinence from alcoholic liquors, for if an Aries child becomes addicted to that vice he is beyond saving and often becomes subject to delirium.

Children of Taurus

Born April 21st to May 22nd.

On the 21st of April the Sun enters the zodiacal sign of the Bull, Taurus, and remains in that sign until the 20th of May and therefore children born between those dates partake in a great measure of the characteristics of this sign. Taurus is ruled by Venus the planet of love, and therefore the children of Taurus have a basically amicable and kind disposition, but when they once have conceived an idea they cling to it with stubbornness, they are very resentful of contradiction and very difficult to convince that they have made a mistake; but when one has once succeeded in showing them that they are wrong their inherent love of justice and truth will prompt them to acknowledge their mistakes and try to rectify them. They have a very strong and determined will so that when they set up a goal for themselves or have made up their minds to do anything they usually keep on working with patience and persistence until they make a success of whatever they have undertaken. They also have good executive ability and are able to take leading positions where they have others under their command. Although they are amicable and agreeable when in the company of others they have a strong tendency to seek solitude and to become very self-centered. They seem to set up unconsciously a barrier between themselves and other people so that it is difficult to become intimately acquainted with them. Taurus children are very keen in their desires for material possessions and they are usually very fortunate also in acquiring them for besides having good earning power themselves they are often the recipients of inheritance. But they do not want wealth for the sake of having it as much as for the pleasure and comfort which they can get out of it; they are very fond of comforts and luxuries, art, music, drama and other refining influences of life.

The children of Taurus have an abundance of vitality to start with, but they are very apt to go to excess in work or play, waste their energy and become ill as a consequence. They are particularly attracted to the pleasures of the table. They revel in rich foods which later give them a tendency to digestive troubles, enlargement of the liver, heart disease and congestion of the kidneys. These diseases are very apt to make them uncomfortable in later life, therefore parents should inculcate in them above all things the virtue of frugality, not only by precept, but by example, for these Taurus children are very quick and they will readily see that "mother and father tell me to eat little but they eat all they want themselves." They should also be taught to take plenty of exercise as a means to promote health, for the children of Taurus are rather indolent in their manner. However, as said before, they have a most wonderful vitality *particularly if they are born at sunrise* and although they may become subject to the diseases mentioned they will usually have a long life and a fair measure of general good health, wealth and happiness.

Children of Gemini

Born May 22nd to June 22nd.

The children of Gemini are wonderfully quick-witted and bright; they also have the ability to express themselves clearly and to the point, therefore they are always good company. Conversation never lags when they are present, in fact they are sometimes given to monopolizing it entirely, but then they are often so interesting that other people are glad to listen. They acquire learning very rapidly and are very well informed on most subjects. They have a good memory so that what they have won is not lost, that is of course, provided the horoscope is otherwise well-aspected and configurated. Where it is seriously afflicted we find the faults of the Gemini pointing in the opposite direction; then they may be inveterate chatterboxes, shunned by everybody who can possibly get out of their way. The great point to remember with these children is that they have the ability of expression and a great deal may be done during the days of childhood to mould the character in such a way that it expresses itself in a manner congenial to others and to the general benefit of the child and its surroundings, and that will be of help to it later in life.

The children of Gemini are, generally speaking,

of a very kind and affable disposition, easy to get along with. They are able to adapt themselves to other people and to circumstances so that they become all things to all men and in that way they usually make many friends and few enemies. They are of a roving disposition and love to travel about from one place to another. They excel in scientific or clerical activities, as agents or representatives of others where their Mercurial talents find an avenue for expression.

From the moral point of view it is not good to have a flexible nature. The children of Gemini are only too easily made victims of flattery and therefore apt to be led unconsciously into paths of wrongdoing. It should be the aim of the parents of these children to hold before them the ideal of the straight and narrow path and emphasize the idea in their minds that that is never to be swerved from under any consideration.

The children of Gemini are very high-strung and nervous and therefore they are easily worried and irritated, which is reflected in their actions and their bodily health. On that account parents with children born in this month ought to be lenient with them in their flashes of temper for they are very quick-spoken under wrath; they need a soothing answer rather than reproof, in order that they may be helped to overcome while they are young and to strengthen their moral constitution in that respect. When the horoscope of a Gemini child is afflicted there is very apt to be some disorder of the lungs and Gemini children will be much helped if they are taught proper breathing exercises and calisthenics. It will at least minimize the tendencies and may entirely overcome them. Gemini children usually grow very tall and straight. They are fine-looking people with a quick walk and brisk movements, and they may be either light or dark complexioned according to the placement and configuration of the planets.

The Children of Cancer

Born June 22nd to July 23rd.

The watery sign Cancer is one of the weakest in the zodiac so far as vitality goes and when it is upon the eastern angle of a person's horoscope it always gives a rather weak body; but usually this does not apply to the children born during the time when the Sun is in Cancer, for the Sun is the giver of life, and these children are therefore more fortunate with respect to vitality than those children who have Cancer rising.

The children of Cancer are usually very timid and retiring, yet they want and need friendship and sympathy, though they are very sensitive about seeking it; but when they get well acquainted they can at times be very exacting with their friends, even autocratic in their ways of ordering them about. At the same time, it must be said they are very conscientious in all things entrusted to them, and use considerable discretion in whatever they do, so that one may safely trust them to keep a secret or execute a commission. The sign Cancer is ruled by the restless Moon, and therefore changes of residence, position, vocation, and of all matters, are quite frequent in the lives of these children. At the same time they cannot be called fickle and flippant for they are very tenacious whenever they have undertaken to do a certain work or undertaken a certain obligation; then they stay by it until it is finished. Neither do they run haphazard into anything; in fact, there are times when they are inclined to be too cautious. Especially where there is danger of injury they are almost cowards, and they are often given to anxiety and worry.

The Children of Leo
Born July 23rd to August 24th.

The sign Leo is ruled by the life-giving Sun, and it is called the royal sign of the Zodiac; therefore it confers upon the children which are born under its influence a noble, ambitious and aspiring nature. They are of the Master breed and make good leaders but poor followers. Being of a noble and lofty character themselves they scorn mean and sordid things, nor will they stoop to do a low act even under great provocation or the strong urge of self-interest. The love nature is very strong and ardent. No inconvenience or sacrifice is too great to serve those they love. They are loyal and true friends through thick and thin. Leo is a fixed sign and gives its children considerable will power, so that they are usually able to win their way to the top despite all handicaps and obstacles. They are very fixed in their opinions and if they espouse any cause they will usually stay by it and work for it in a most enthusiastic manner. They never do anything half-heartedly, for Leo being a fiery sign endows them with power, vitality and enthusiasm. Leo also gives its children a good memory. The foregoing tendencies are indicated when the Sun is fairly well aspected in the horoscope; but if it is afflicted by Mars, or any of the malefics, the nature is changed, so that the person becomes bombastic, blustering and domineering, one not to be trusted in any department of life, and an unfaithful, amorous husband or wife, or a disloyal friend, one who will not hesitate to stoop to any meanness. He is then just as bad as the Leo with the well aspected Sun is good, this on the principle that the brightest light always casts the deepest shadow. The principal fault of the Leos is a quick temper, but they do not hold spite, and when shown to have been in the wrong they are always ready to apologize and make amends. They are magnanimous, even to their bitterest enemies.

The Children of Virgo

Born August 24th to September 23rd.

Virgo, the Sixth sign of the zodiac, is ruled by Mercury, the planet of reason, expression and dexterity. It is said, and with considerable truth, that love is blind, for were one to see faults in the beloved one the master passion never would find expression. Therefore the children of Virgo who are governed so much by intellect are not sympathetic, but inclined to be cynical, critical and skeptical of anything that is not scientifically demonstrable to the reason and senses. They are very quick mentally, though only too often inclined to "strain at a gnat," and though they seldom "swallow the camel," they get into a rut where they become narrow-minded and bigoted. They are rather lazy themselves and fond of taking things easy, but they like to drive others, and can be very masterful with subordinates. On that account they often cause enmities of a lasting nature, but whenever they become friendly with any one they also make very good friends and treat their friends well. The Mercurial disposition infused by this sign brings many changes of environment and therefore new associations and friendships are constantly being formed. They are very acquisitive and always looking out for ways and means of bettering themselves financially, socially and economically. It may also be said that they deserve promotion for they are industrious to a degree where they see that a reward may be gained thereby. They are also very ingenious and versatile, fond of the study of science, particularly chemistry, diet and hygiene, and many among them become extreme food faddists. As Virgo is the Sixth sign these people take on Sixth house characteristics and are therefore very sensitive to suggestions of ill health, so that if they ever become enmeshed in the tentacles of disease they frequently lack the necessary will power to extricate themselves, with the result that they then usually become chronic invalids or perhaps rather they think themselves so, for it may be said that these people seem to resent any effort to cheer them up and get them out of the clutches of their particular illness, real or fancied. They seem in fact to *enjoy* bad health, and they are always looking for sympathy, though as we noted in the beginning of this reading, they are very slow to grant the same to others. If they can keep out of the clutches of disease, they often become excellent nurses and have a splendid influence upon the sick.

The Children of Libra

Born September 23rd to October 24th.

Libra is the seventh sign of the zodiac. The children which are born under this sign are ruled by the planet of love, Venus. The symbol of Libra in the pictorial zodiac is a pair of scales and this instrument describes graphically their principal characteristic. The children of Libra are very ardent in anything they do; they take up a vocation or an avocation with a zeal and enthusiasm which for the time being excludes all other things from their consideration, but after a while they may drop it just as suddenly, take up something else as a trade, a fad or a hobby, and pursue that with an equal energy and absorbing interest. This is in fact one of their principal faults, as they find it very difficult to settle down to anything definite, and continue it with patience and persistence until they have achieved success.

Libra is the sign where the Sun changes from the northern to the southern hemisphere; it crosses the equator there, and consequently the Sun is very weak at that point. It is the great life-giver going down into the dark winter months, and therefore Saturn, the planet of darkness, is exalted in Libra. Thus we find two natures very markedly expressed in children that are born under this sign; one is of the Sun, which is cheerful and optimistic, the other is that of Saturn, which is morose and melancholy. And this expresses itself in the changeable nature of the Libra children; sometimes they are up in the seventh heaven, optimistic and enthusiastic, cheerful and happy, then as suddenly and without any seeming cause the scale swings and they seem to be down in the dumps of worry and melancholy just as if they had not a friend in the world. As a matter of fact they make many friends, for they have a basically kind disposition engendered by the Lady of Libra, Venus, but they also have a quick temper, though fortunately they do not hold spite. They are exceedingly fond of pleasures in general and particularly lean toward art and music.

The Children of Scorpio

Born October 24th to November 23rd.

Scorpio is ruled by Mars, the planet of dynamic energy, and therefore the children born during that month when the Sun is passing through this sign are filled with a force that must have an outlet somewhere or somehow. They partake of all the Martial qualities, either good or bad, according to the way the Sun is placed and aspected, and they are always ready to take up an argument or a fight, either on their own behalf or for someone else; they are never content with half measures, either they go to one extreme or the other, good or bad. Those who show the good side of Scorpio have splendid constructive and executive abilities. They are brusque but honest and just, indefatigable workers, and always ready to sacrifice themeslves for the good of others by rebelling against oppression or in other ways unselfishly working for the cause they have espoused. But those who show the bad side of Scorpio not only refuse to work themselves but become demagogues who incite others to anarchy and lawlessness and destruction. These people are social fire-brands and very dangerous to the community. But there is one redeeming feature about them and that is that they are not underhanded; whatever they do is open and aboveboard. The children of Scorpio usually have a very uncertain temper and a sarcastic tongue that bites like the sting of the scorpion, when they turn that side of their nature. Therefore the parents of these children should take them in hand as early as possible and teach them self-control by every means within their power; also strive to soften the Mars ray and instil into them a more kindly spirit. This may be very difficult because the sign Scorpio gives a very determined nature, still, in childhood's years it is plastic to a certain extent and can be best worked upon then. They have a very strong and vivid imagination, with a clear, sharp and penetrating mind, also a personal magnetism that makes them very attractive to those with whom they come in contact. They seem to be most contented in military life where there is sharp and strict discipline. Particular care should be taken to teach these children sex hygiene, for the sign Scorpio rules the generative and eliminative organs, whose functions are stimulated by the presence of the Sun in Scorpio, so that if the person is not morally and physically clean, much trouble may be expected. These children also make excellent surgeons and if they are taught to use surgery only for constructive purposes they can do a great deal of good in the world. All this depends in a considerable measure upon the early training, for there is a destructive side to the Scorpio nature which would make it very dangerous from the spiritual viewpoint for such a person to take up a vocation that offers scope for malpractice; he would then contract a very heavy debt under the law of consequence, which must be paid in sorrow and suffering either in this or later lives.

The Children of Sagittarius

Born November 23rd to December 22nd.

Sagittarius is ruled by Jupiter, the great benefic planet, and it may be said generally that those who are born while the Sun is in this sign from November 23rd to December 22nd are well liked in the society where they move. They are of a hearty and jovial disposition, princes among men, hail-fellows-well-met, and their acquaintances are generally glad to see them. There are two very distinct classes born under this sign. In the pictorial zodiac, Sagittarius is represented as a centaur, half horse and half man, and one class of those who come to birth under its influence are well described by the animal part thereof, for they are of a sporty nature, ready to gamble on the speed of a horse at long odds or to stake their last dollar on a game of cards. They are fond of a "good time right straight through" and their moral nature is of low grade, aptly described by the animal part of the symbol, so that they have no scruples with respect to the indulgence of their appetites, passions and desires. They are lacking in respect for both the law and ordinary morals, hence they are often found among the criminal class. But those children of Sagittarius symbolized by the human part of the centaur, aiming the bow of aspiration at the stars, are as different from the above as day is from night, for they are extremely idealistic, moral, law-abiding, noble characters who win the respect of society in general and particularly of all with whom they come into intimate contact. Therefore they become in time the pillars of society and often receive positions of honor and preferment in State or Church as judges or divines. They are very orthodox and conservative in their opinions and punctilious to a fault in their observance of all customs and traditions of the times wherein they live, but they are not progressive, for they value the opinions of their contemporaries very highly and are seldom induced to espouse any progressive ideas which might jeopardize the respect of the community enjoyed by them. They are firm believers in the necessity of red tape. Withal, however, they are charitable and benevolent, tender and sympathetic; they can always be relied upon to aid any altruistic movement, and though they are of a kindly nature and endeavor to avoid quarrels in their own behalf, they sometimes fight with great zeal and courage for others who have been injured and in whose behalf their sympathies have been enlisted, hence they make admirable lawyers.

The Sagittarians are usually excellent conversationalists; they have a quick and ready wit and are fond of indulging in oratory. Their exhibitions of memory and interesting way of relating experiences always hold the audience. They are very proud and have great confidence in themselves.

The Children of Capricorn

Born December 22nd to January 20th.

Capricorn is ruled by Saturn, the planet of obstruction, therefore the vitality of these children is very low and they are difficult to raise, but once infancy is passed the Saturnine persistence makes itself felt and they cling to life with an amazing tenacity so that they often become very old. They are very much subject to colds and their principal source of danger is falls and bruises. The children of Capricorn are usually bashful and timid in the presence of strangers but when they have become used to people they show their domineering nature and endeavor to make everybody around them conform to their will. The Saturnine quality of the sign makes them jealous and suspicious of the motives of others. Therefore they are very fond of detective work. They will follow a trail with unerring instinct and unwavering perseverance that never gives up as long as there is the remotest chance of success. It is good to be friends with Capricornians and bad to make enemies of them, for they find it very hard to forgive a real or fancied offense or injury and always brood over any wrong done to them. On the other hand, if they once give their confidence or friendship they are also consistent in that direction. They are very ambitious and anxious to have their services recognized by other people and they have splendid executive ability because of the unusual qualities of forethought and concentration conferred by Saturn. They are born leaders and organizers but chafe under restrictions and dislike particularly to take orders from others. When they are placed in such a subordinate position and cannot have their own way they become gloomy, taciturn, moody, pessimistic, irritable, and given to worry. The children of Capricorn usually have a disinclination for marriage and are seldom at ease if they enter into that state. The union is usually childless or children are few.

The Children of Aquarius

Born January 20th to February 19th.

The children of Aquarius are of a rather shy, retiring nature. They like to keep their own company and counsel more than is good for them, for if this bent in the nature is allowed full scope, it has a tendency to breed melancholy and make them recluses. They have a quiet, unassuming manner which gains many friends for them and their home life is usually ideal. They are generally affectionate and of a very sweet and kind disposition; they are always ready to defer to the opinion of a loved one and ready to yield a point for the sake of harmony. Besides, Aquarius being a fixed sign they are very constant in their affection as well as in other things.

Aquarius is an intellectual sign and its children usually have a good mentality, because the Saturnine rulership gives depth to the mind, and the Uranian ray gives them intuition and an inclination towards science, literature and philosophy. They are remarkably persistent in whatever they undertake, and therefore usually succeed in the long run. As Aquarius is the 11th sign it partakes also of the qualities ruled by the 11th House; therefore the children of Aquarius are usually well liked among their associates and have many friends. The children of Aquarius are very proud and jealous of the esteem of others. Their principal fault is that on account of Saturnine traits they are somewhat given to worry. As with the Leos, they are strong in their likes and dislikes; they will do anything for those who have won their affection, but resent any attempt to drive them, and under such conditions are extremely stubborn; in fact they are very set in their mental attitude, and once an opinion has been formed it is not easily changed. They are so very sensitive to the mental condition around them that it affects their physical well being perhaps more than they are aware of for this is one of the most sensitive signs.

The Children of Pisces

Born February 20th to March 20th.

The children of Pisces are of a marked negative disposition, subject to varying moods, and are, like the children of Aquarius, very sensitive to the mental atmosphere in their environment. For that reason it is of the greatest importance that parents of these children should guard them during childhood against the influences of bad companions, for the old proverb about "bad company corrupting good manners" applies with ten-fold strength to these children, and they will absorb good or evil with equal facility. So until they have learned to choose for themselves the good things, it is especially necessary for their natural guardians to shield them. They also have a strong tendency to mediumship and if they are taken into seances there is a great danger that they may become controlled. Moreover, having such an extremely flexible nature they can never exert sufficient will power to free themselves from the influence when once they have been subjected to it, and it may ruin their whole life.

These children are very peaceable in disposition and suffer injury rather than fight for their rights, not because they do not care, for they are very jealous especially when born in the latter part of the sign, but because the Piscean nature is averse to exertion, and generally they do not want to take the trouble to fight for their rights. In plain English they are lazy. Therefore the parents should see that a certain amount of work is allotted to them during the earliest years, for it is then that the habits are formed and the nature is the most plastic. They can learn to be diligent with much less effort at that time than during the later stages of life. But once the children of Pisces have commenced doing a piece of work it will probably be a surprise to others to watch them and see the methodical way they go at it, making every move count until the task has been completed with seemingly very little effort on their part. Honesty is another of the virtues of the Pisces children; they are usually dependable and close-mouthed, so that they may be trusted with secrets in full confidence that they will not betray the trust.

The children of Pisces are generally kind and sympathetic, cordial and suave in manner, qualities which will of course bring them many friends. They are notoriously fond of good things to eat, they revel in rich foods, and are also prone to be fond of drink. If these tendencies are allowed to work themselves out they will of course ruin the life, and besides bring on a train of disease. Therefore the parents of these children should endeavor by precept and example to teach them the simple life, frugality and control of the appetite during the years when habits are formed, besides guarding them against too strenuous exercise which even the children of Pisces will not shun in childhood when the abundance of life force impels them. Then later in life these lessons will not be without their fruit. The chances are that the child which by the help of the parent has learned in childhood to rule its stars will be both healthy and hearty, respected and loved because of good habits, and will fully enjoy life. In short, these children need a very careful bringing up to save them from their evil tendencies and bring out the good, but that is just what such souls come to parents for. Their necessity is the parents' opportunity to make great and wonderful soul growth.

CHAPTER VIII.

The Sun, Giver of Life

THE Sun, being the center of the solar system, is recognized by all as the physical life-giver even when they do not believe in anything superphysical; it is patent to everyone from personal observation that the horizontal ray of the morning sun affects us differently from the perpendicular noon ray, and that in summer the rays carry a life-force which not only brings forth the verdure upon the fields, but also affects the human temperament, and endows us with vital energy, courage and a hopeful spirit foreign to the dark and gloomy winter months. This gloom is permanently noticeable in the temperament of people living in the far north, where the absence of sunlight makes life a struggle that saps the spirit of frolic, while in countries where abundance of sunlight lessens the cares of existence, the temperament is correspondingly vivacious and hopeful and sunny.

In the horoscope, the angle of each planetary ray at birth determines the department of life it will affect. If the child is born at the noon hour when the sun is at the Zenith, the daystar will appear in the 10th house of the horoscope and bring preferment professionally. If the child were born at midnight when the sun is directly under the place of birth its influence would be through the Fourth House, and it would brighten the old age of the child then born.

There are three unfortunate angles for the sun: Children born shortly after sunset have it in the Sixth House, which indicates sickness, and as the Sun is life-giver this position lessens the vitality and recuperative power. Birth in the middle part of the afternoon places the Sun in the Eighth House. This is the house through which the death-dealing forces act, and logically, the Lord of Life is out of place in the House of Death. The Second House shows what income we obtain by our own efforts, and as the Eighth House is opposite the Second it reveals the sources of revenue for which we do not personally exert ourselves, that is to say, legacies, pensions or grants of a public nature. We have known people with the Sun in the Eighth House to acquire vast sums, millions in one case, by speculation in municipal necessities. Such persons are often threatened by death and sometimes have many hairbreadth escapes, but even with the best of aspects to the Sun, a ripe age is seldom attained.

When a child is born shortly after sunrise the Sun is in the Twelfth House, which is the avenue whence we reap our sorrows, and it has been our experience that the early life of such a person is encompassed by trouble of one kind or another.

When the ascendant of a person is in doubt and

the place in the Zodiac which seems to fit nearest brings the Sun into the Twelfth House, the writer has often found that the exact ascendant may be ascertained by asking the person if his childhood's life was clouded by poverty of the parents and consequent limitation for a number of years just after birth. This in all cases where it has been found that all other events fitted in the horoscope proved a successful method of determining the true ascendant, so that the number of degrees from the ascendant to the Sun, the latter located in the Twelfth House, would indicate the years of poverty, for the Twelfth House makes for limitation in that respect, especially when the Sun is there at birth. When the Sun by progression has passed through the Twelfth House and comes into the ascendant, things begin to brighten for the person involved, and when in time it passes through the Second House he will have a period of financial success; but as stated the Sun in the Twelfth House, just above the ascendant, usually makes a very poor home for the child during the early years of life. If Pisces is there the cause will generally be found in slothfulness and a desire for drink on the part of the parents, which make them thus neglect their offspring.

The qualities imparted by a well placed Sun are dignity, strength of will and courage, both physical and moral, a lofty pride and a keen sense of honor and responsibility which make a person eminently reliable, a sterling honesty and a hatred of anything small, underhanded or tricky. It makes him steadfast in love, staunch in friendship and generous even to enemies. A dignified, exalted or well placed Sun brings friendship from people in a position to bestow substantial favors and aids the person materially in his endeavors to advance in life.

When the Sun is afflicted and weak by sign and position the opposite qualities are manifested; bombastic self-assurance and bluster, love of adulation and a desire to rule or ruin, but no courage to face opposition; indulgence of the lower nature and a waste of the vital force with a consequent loss of health and strength. When the Sun is weak the person is not to be depended on; he regards his promises as pie-crusts, made to be broken, and because of these traits such people always remain in obscurity.

In the world at large the Sun signifies employers and those in immediate authority over the person, such as judges and other government officers, and when the exigencies of life bring a person in contact with them he will receive at their hands whatever treatment is merited by his Sun.

The Sun being masculine is significator of the marriage partner in a woman's horoscope (and the feminine Moon serves a similar purpose in a man's figure), hence a well placed Sun is one of the indications that a man will make a good husband, and an unaspected, weak or afflicted Sun gives him a tendency to neglect his hearth and home.

As general significator of health the Sun rules principally in masculine figures, (and the Moon in feminine horoscopes), but both lights are important. It may be said however, that the health of a man is not so much endangered by afflictions of the Moon as by a weak Sun, and vice versa, a woman suffers more if her Moon is afflicted than if her Sun is evilly aspected.

The Sun in the Twelve Houses.

⊙1 *The Sun in the First House*

The Sun is the source of vitality. The First House signifies our constitutional condition and the home of our childhood, hence the Sun well aspected in the First House adds to the vitality of the rising sign and augments the recuperative powers. It brightens life during the days of childhood and stabilizes the nature, making the person more cheerful and companionable, ambitious to succeed in life, courageous in overcoming obstacles. The outlook on life is joyful and optimistic, hence the chances of success are increased. People with the Sun in this position love to lead and exercise authority over others; they are very jealous of the esteem of the community, upright and honest in their dealings.

When the Sun is afflicted in the First House it lowers the vitality, makes the person timid and vacillating, lacking in courage and ambition; hence the chances of a successful life are slim unless many aspects are good, thus modifying this condition.

⊙2 *The Sun in the Second House*

This shows the person will find favor with people in a position to further his material prosperity and will by their help gain a comfortable living, but it also gives a tendency to squander money on the principle that "what comes easy goes easy." Unless this trait be curbed it may bring about financial stringency, for it is not so much what we earn that counts as what we spend. We shall be poor with an income of a million if we spend two.

⊙3 *The Sun in the Third House*

This favors travel and makes the person bright and observing, eager to investigate conditions and things, for it imparts a scientific turn to the mind. It is a good position for writers as it helps to bring them to public notice and favor.

⊙4 *The Sun in the Fourth House*

In one sense this is a very unfortunate position because it deprives the person of the help of the solar influence during the major portion of life, which is on that account a constant uphill struggle, but as the Fourth House rules the latter part of life it is always a consolation to know that the declining years will be brightened by the Sun of success. That should make the burdens lighter to bear.

☉5 *The Sun in the Fifth House*

The Fifth House rules courtship, children, pleasure, education and publications; when the Sun is there it favors all these except children. It makes the person a favorite with the opposite sex, gives him much enjoyment of life, also success as a teacher, publisher or editor, but strangely enough, though the Sun rules the heart whence spring our children, his position in the Fifth House is distinctly unfavorable for their begetting. This is especially so if the fiery Fifth sign Leo is on the cusp. Then the fervent heat of passion seems to scorch the human plant ere it has time to grow. This tendency is modified to some extent when a watery sign is on the cusp, but when one of the partners has the Sun in the Fifth House the offspring are never numerous.

☉6 *The Sun in the Sixth House*

Seeing that the Sun is the Giver of Life it is evident that when it is confined in the Sixth House it is debilitated and the vital flow is obstructed; therefore people who have the Sun in that position are particularly liable to disease and slow to recuperate. On that account their diseases are frequent and long-drawn-out to an extent which often amounts to chronic invalidism.

If the person is an employee of someone else he will be efficient in his work; he will have no difficulty in obtaining well-paid positions but he will be very touchy towards his employers and make frequent changes under the pretext that his abilities are not sufficiently appreciated. If he is an employer, this position of the Sun is good for success in business, but indicates trouble with servants, who will be domineering.

If the configurations in the horoscope enable the person to shake off the grip of sickness the Sun in the Sixth House gives great ability in chemistry, preparation of health-food, and makes the person a capable nurse or healer.

⊙7 *The Sun in the Seventh House*

Partnerships are often unsuccessful because of the selfishness of the participants but he who has the Sun in the Seventh House will have no reason to complain in that respect for he will always attract someone with a high sense of honor when in need of a partner, and as marriage is the most intimate of all partnerships, the Sun in the Seventh House is a particularly fortunate position in that respect, because it will bring the person a mate who is absolutely steadfast and true, one who may indeed be depended upon as a helpmeet in all the exigencies and vicissitudes of life till death do part. As there is no earthly treasure equal to such an enduring love this is perhaps the best of all solar positions.

Should the person be unfortunate enough to become involved in litigation the Sun in the Seventh House promotes the favor of the judge and a successful outcome.

⊙8 *The Sun in the Eighth House*

The Eighth House is the angle of incidence through which the death dealing forces act, and as the Sun is the giver of life it is evident that this position is extremely detrimental as far as vitality is concerned, and it often brings a promising life to an early termination. It also often happens that when genius has gone begging all through life and passed the portal of death in obscurity it gains belated recognition, fame and immortality through this position of the Sun.

As the Second House signifies the financial condition of the person and shows what he does with the money he earns, so the Eighth shows what comes to him apart from his own efforts, that is to say, inheritances, the wealth of the marriage partner, etc. Therefore the Sun in the Eighth House shows an increase of wealth after marriage but also a tendency of the mate to be over-generous and squander the means.

☉9 *The Sun in the Ninth House*

This position brightens the mind and imbues the person with high ideals and lofty ambitions. It makes him generously tolerant of other people's opinions—noble and kind-hearted. There is an inner urge to solve the problems of life and learn the "whys" and "wherefores," hence the mind turns naturally toward philosophy, religion and law. And as we always excel in the things we love, people with the Sun in the Ninth House make excellent statesmen, lawyers and ministers of God. They shine in all intellectual and scientific pursuits. Their mission often takes them into foreign lands.

☉10 *The Sun in the Tenth House*

This is one of the surest signs of general success in life. The person rises by the favor of those above him in the social scale and obtains positions of responsibility and trust. He is much respected in the community and often honored by election to public office, and he may always be depended upon to justify the trust reposed in him.

☉11 *The Sun in the Eleventh House*

This is a good sign that the hopes, wishes and

aspirations of the person will be realized; it attracts people in a position to befriend him and with an inclination to do so.

☉12 *The Sun in the Twelfth House*

This is the signature of the lonely soul who as a recluse shuts himself off from his fellows. It brings with it a danger of conflict with the authorities or an inability to fit in with the family conditions and on account of the ensuing trouble the person goes into voluntary or enforced exile, living his life henceforth a stranger among strangers. Even when such extreme conditions do not prevail, the first third of the life is usually wasted in vain efforts to find a balance and settle down to some life work.

Like the Sixth House position of the Sun, this also favors work with the sick in hospitals, chemistry and laboratory work, or work with prisoners; it gives a love of the occult and leads to curious lines of research.

THE SUN IN THE TWELVE SIGNS.

☉♈ *The Sun in Aries*

Aries is the exaltation-sign of the Sun and hence this is the most powerful position of the central orb. There it radiates a vital force of unexampled strength which gives to the person a wonderful fund of energy wherewith to withstand the onslaughts of disease and should he be taken ill his powers of recuperation will quickly free him from the clutches of sickness. People having this position are principally liable to fevers on account of the fervent heat of the Sun in Aries. As Aries rules the head the excessive heat often dries up the scalp so that the hair cannot grow and the person becomes bald.

☉ ♉ *The Sun in Taurus*

A favorable position for the financial fortunes but it also gives a tendency to extravagance, especially in dress, and makes the person extremely fond of the opposite sex, sometimes with detrimental results. It gives great physical strength and the person loves to show off that people may admire his prowess. Taurus rules the larynx and therefore the Sun in Taurus adds strength to the vocal organs and gives the person a strong, pleasant voice.

☉ ♊ *The Sun in Gemini*

Gemini is a Mercurial sign and third in the gamut, hence this position gives a blended influence of the Sun, Mercury and the Third House. This favors expression of Mercury for it is the planet which stirs the vocal chords and produces sound in the Taurian larynx; it also favors writings and travel; the mind is brightened by the Sun in Gemini and when it is necessary or expedient to travel the person gains thereby physically and mentally. It gives a pleasant, affable disposition which makes him generally liked among his associates.

☉♋ *The Sun in Cancer*

Cancer is the fourth sign and is ruled by the Moon, hence, the Sun in Cancer is a mixture of the Sun, Moon and fourth House influences. In the natural horoscope (where Aries is on the Ascendant) Cancer is at the nadir, and with the Sun here, vitality is at its lowest ebb; therefore with this position one is apt to be indolent even when not sickly at all. He is harmless and avoids quarrels, hence is harmonious and agreeable in the home so long as he is not asked to work too hard. This position of the Sun makes the first part of the life barren of fruits but brings success in the later years. Cancer is a psychic sign and therefore the Sun in Cancer gives a tendency toward the occult, often with psychic experiences.

☉♌ *The Sun in Leo*

The Sun in Leo gives a masterful nature with a large measure of self-control, a keen sense of honor and a never-failing integrity. The person aspires to rule others but would scorn to take a mean advantage or to do anything to others that would not be in strict accord with the golden rule; the affections are deep and lasting. People with the Sun in Leo are staunch defenders of those they love, but equally strong in their aversions. Leo is the sign which rules the heart. Whatever people with the Sun in Leo do is done with a concentration of purpose which compels success. They make true friends and if one must have an enemy, a Leo will prove more honorable and magnanimous than any other.

☉♍ *The Sun in Virgo*

This is a combination of the solar, mercurial and Sixth House influences. It shows the successful middleman between the producer and consumer, subtle, extremely quick to see what will work to his advantage in the promotion of business, pleasant and sociable, agreeable to all from whom he expects to gain, but domineering to employees and fellow workers; a smooth talker but not necesarily insincere; he merely looks out for number one.

The Sun in Virgo makes good chemists, nurses and doctors, *not surgeons but drug-doctors;* they are firm believers in medicine and lots of it.

☉♎ *The Sun in Libra*

Libra is ruled by Venus and is the seventh sign, hence the Sun in Libra combines the influence of Venus with that of the Sun and the Seventh house, with the result that the person loves the marriage partner so devotedly that he excludes everyone else; for of a person with that position it may truly be said that "the Sun rises and sets" in the marriage partner.

Libra is also the exaltation sign of Saturn, and his influence is there at its best, giving an element of construction to the art of Venus. This is brought about as ability for architecture and the finer branches of decorative construction when the Sun is in Libra. This position also gives a fine, sonorous voice and vocal talent.

☉♏ *The Sun in Scorpio*

The Sun in Scorpio, when well aspected, gives great energy, courage and independence. It makes the mind active, and favors success in such occupations as those of the surgeon or soldier. It also tends to improve the finances after marriage, but tends to extravagance.

The Sun here afflicted gives the person a very blunt, brusque manner, a feeling that his judgment is better than that of others, and a tendency to ride rough-shod over anybody or anything that stands in his way. It often makes him indifferent to suffering, and may transform the surgeon into a vivisectionist.

☉♐ *The Sun in Sagittarius*

This gives lofty ideals and a noble aspiring disposition aiming to rise by raising others. It makes the person benevolent, philanthropic and therefore beloved among his associates. He is often the recipient of honors and appointments to positions of trust, and missions of a delicate nature, nor could a better selection be made, for such people are the souls of honor. This position will also bring success in religion, law and statesmanship for it gives an expansive mind fitted to grapple with the greater problems of life.

☉♑ *The Sun in Capricorn*

This is a good sign that the person will rise in life by the aid of the good-will of people in a higher position than himself; it shows that he will merit their trust and acquit himself well in a position of responsibility and trust; it makes him careful, prudent, faithful and honest. Judges with that position cannot be bought but will administer justice as they see it, to all comers. It gives an all round love of fair play and wins for those who have it the respect and esteem of all in their circle.

☉♒ *The Sun in Aquarius*

This is a combination of the Sun, Uranus and the Eleventh House influences. It gives the person an intuitive perception of the inner nature of things and a touch with the forces and ideas of the spiritual realms which leads him to take up when possible, new and advanced cults, or methods of healing such as Naturopathy, Electro-therapy, Astro-therapy, Magnetic Healing, etc. He is also drawn to scientific research and ultra-intellectual or strange religions. This position gives much popularity and firm friends among people who are in a position to bestow favors and further the person's attainment of his ambitions.

☉ ♓ *The Sun in Pisces*

Gives a retiring disposition and favors success in occupations removed from the public gaze such as prisons, hospitals, institutions for the poor, etc. If the person incur enmity of others, he will be vindicated whatever they may do to hurt his reputation. People with the Sun in Pisces have a strong tendency towards psychism, mediumship and the occult in general.

THE SUN IN ASPECT WITH OTHER PLANETS

♀ P ☌ ☉ *Venus parallel or in conjunction with the Sun* calls out the artistic side of the nature, making the person fond of music, art an poetry; it strengthens the love nature and if the configuration occurs in the Seventh House it is a positive testimony of unalloyed marital bliss. In the Second or Eighth House it leads to extravagance of the person or his mate; in Scorpio it is not good for the morals and in Pisces it leads to intemperance. These aspects strengthen the constitution, increase the popularity and make social intercourse smooth so that the person has many friends and keeps them.

As the orbit of Venus is so small she never forms the sextile, trine, square or opposition to the Sun.

☿ P ☌ ☉ *Mercury parallel or in conjunction with the Sun.* These are the only aspects formed between the two. They are good for the memory and mentality if Mercury is not closer to the Sun than three degrees, for then he is '*combust*' and his good qualities are burned up in the Sun's rays. It is most fortunate to have Mercury rise *before* the Sun at birth for he is the Lightbearer who holds the torch of reason before the Spirit which in the horoscope is symbolized by the Sun. When he rises after the Sun the mentality is not nearly so keen (unless other good aspects favor).

☽ P ☌ ☉ *The Moon parallel or in conjunction with Sun.* No matter in what sign or house the conjunction of the Lights occurs the person will be so strongly marked with the characteristics of that sign that lacking knowledge of his true Ascendant even the most competent astrologer is likely to be misled and judge him to be born with the sign rising in which the conjunction took place, and whatever matters are ruled by the House in which the conjunction occurs will play a very important part in the life. In the First House he is an out and out egotist with very little love for others save in so far as they serve his ends; in the Seventh, his world pivots on the mate; in the Tenth House or sign he will sacrifice all other considerations to rise in public life; in the Twelfth House or sign the conjunction will give a strong tendency to drink, bringing trouble; in the Third and Ninth Houses it will brighten the mind and induce travel from which he will benefit; in the Second House it will bring wealth, especially if in good aspect with Jupiter.

But if the conjunction of the Sun and Moon is closer than three degrees it has a tendency to deplete the vitality and if the conjunction is also a solar eclipse, *and the child survives*, this will be particularly noticeable, all through life. People who have such close conjunctions or eclipses become listless, dis-spirited and out of sorts every time there is a new Moon. The conjunction or eclipse does not seem to interfere with the good effects in other departments of life.

☽ ✱ △ ☉ *The Moon sextile or trine to the Sun.* The good aspects of the Sun and Moon make for general success in life, health, fair financial conditions, good home surroundings with faithful friends, and esteem in the community; they favor a rise in life because of the person's innate ability, which either gains for him the recognition of people in a position to help him rise, or impels him to carve his own way.

☽ □ ☍ ☉ *The Moon square or opposition to Sun* makes the person vacillating and unsettled in disposition, changeable and unable to pursue a settled course in life, rash to plunge into enterprises, but lacking the persistence or continuity of purpose to carry anything to a successful conclusion. For that reason such people become failures in life, especially in their dealings with women and people higher in the social scale such as employers, the authorities, judges, etc. They always have difficulty in obtaining employment and keeping their positions when they obtain them for they are hyper-sensitive and ready to take offense, with or without provocation. These configurations also affect the health, rendering the body liable to colds and making recuperation slow when sickness has overtaken the person.

♄ ✱ △ ☉ *Saturn sextile or trine to Sun* endows the person who is fortunate enough to so have it with some of the finest faculties in the gamut, for it brings out the best qualities in the two planets. It gives method, foresight and organizing, executive and diplomatic ability with the moral stamina to carry any project determined on to a successful conclusion despite delays and obstacles. Yet the person makes no enemies in so doing, for this configuration also makes him the soul of honor, kind and considerate; he would never stoop to do anything mean for he is very sincere and just in his dealings with all men, but on the other hand, when he believes a certain course of action to be right, he will never swerve therefrom though heaven and earth be moved against him. These aspects bring success in political or judicial positions also in connection with mining or agriculture. The person often benefits by legacy, but recognition and success are generally delayed till middle life.

♄ P ☌ □ ☍ ☉ *Saturn parallel, conjunction, square or opposition to the Sun* has a very detrimental effect where the resistance is fundamentally low; in Gemini and Sagittarius it gives a tendency to tuberculosis. It does least damage in the fixed signs where resistance is greatest, but even there when sickness gets a grip on the person it hangs on like grim death, for it lessens the power of the body to throw off disease quickly, hence recuperation is very slow,

These aspects are extremely adverse to that which is generally termed success, but they give an abundance of experience, so they are excellent from the standpoint of the soul. It may be truly said of the person who has them, that "the best-laid plans of mice and men gang aft agley," for no matter how carefully he may plan his affairs he will be subject to delays and obstacles which thwart his desires. His marriage is unhappy and is likely to end in divorce or early death of the partner. He has difficulty in finding and keeping employment, trouble with employers and authorities, a feeling as if he were held in leash all his life and denied expression in any direction. These are the outward experiences but they are generated by the inner nature, and until that changes he must suffer the whiplash of necessity. In the first place he has a tendency to crawl into a shell and shut himself in and others out. He is a pessimist and a kill-joy, has little or no regard for the feelings of others and is very obstinate. In the horoscope of a woman such an aspect signifies marriage to one much older who will hold her with a very tight rein; it augurs death of the husband and often several marriages which are ended by death or divorce.

These configurations often bring legacies, but either there is trouble and litigation over the bequests, or the person squanders the estate after he receives it. If Saturn is in his exaltation sign, Libra, the latter part of the life may be better because the person may have taken the lessons of life to heart and mended his ways.

♃ ☌ P ⚹ △ ☉ *Jupiter conjunction, parallel, sextile or trine to Sun.* The conjunction gives a tendency to apoplexy, especially if it occurs in Aries, but with that exception we may say that these configurations are sure indications of health, wealth and happiness. They give the person an abundance of vitality which is proof against very severe onslaughts of disease, and even when particularly unfavorable planetary influences succeed in breaking down his resistance, recovery will be so rapid as to seem miraculous. This nearly impregnable condition of health is all the more unassailable because it is backed by a disposition at once *sunny* and *jovial* and that latter characteristic also makes the fortunate possessors of these aspects beloved by all with whom they come in contact. Everybody is glad to see the person with the perpetual smile, but they do more than "smile"—they earn the friendship universally bestowed upon them by deeds of kindness, by words of sympathy, cheer or hope as the occasion may demand. They are trusted by everybody because they never betray a trust. They have clear heads, good judgment and executive ability so that they are well fitted to help others. These characteristics also favor their own financial fortunes, so they accumulate wealth, but theirs is never "tainted money;" they never benefit by the loss of others. They are religiously conservative and may be aptly described as "pillars of society." They shine particularly in government work.

♃ □ ☍ ☉ *Jupiter square or opposition to the Sun* is bad for the health because it gives a tendency to form bad habits. The person is far too fond of the so-called "good things of life," and very selfish in supplying his own comforts; he never exercises nor denies himself so the circulation becomes sluggish and as these people have a superabundance of blood this sluggishness is productive of various noxious growths and functional disorders; sometimes a fit of anger raises the blood pressure to such a point that a vessel bursts and ends the life or leaves the person henceforth a useless wreck.

These aspects give a bombastic haughty disposition with an inordinate love of display and thus induce extravagance both in social and business affairs with the result that the person sometimes finds himself involved in debt which he cannot pay and then it is but a step to the bankruptcy court. A false pride often prevents these people from working honestly for others; they would rather prey upon the public as gamblers, followers of races and other so-called sports where there is an opportunity to swindle people and get what they call an "easy" living until they land in the meshes of the law. Children with these aspects should be given special training in self-restraint, thrift and honesty; they will have a tendency to scorn and scoff at religion, but perhaps the memory of a devout mother may help to keep them straight.

♂ P ☌ ✱ △ ☉ *Mars parallel, conjunction, sextile or trine to Sun.* The conjunction gives a tendency to fever, especially if it occurs in Aries, the sign which governs the head, but it is curious that people with that configuration seem also to be able to endure a much higher temperature than others, and come unscathed through such a siege of sickness as would ordinarily prove fatal. With that exception these aspects all produce a super-abundance of vital energy which assures their possessor of the most radiant health all through life, they strengthen the constitution and make the person able to endure the harder tasks, and give him a dauntless determination and courage to face the greatest odds. Given a plan to follow he may be trusted to overcome all physical obstacles for he has both executive and constructive ability together with an indomitable will which refuses to recognize defeat. The disposition is frank and open but blunt and often brusque; they are too intensely bent on whatever they want to do to waste time in politeness and suavity; they brush the conventionalities aside without compunction and are therefore not liked by people of too fine sensibilities; they are, however, men and women of action and the foremost factors in the world's work; but for their enterprise and energy the world would move much more slowly.

Aspects to the Sun and Mars are absolutely necessary to give zest to life; even adverse aspects are better than none, for where these planets are unaspected the person is listless, vapid and he will never amount to anything no matter how good the figure may be in other respects.

♂ □ ☍ ☉ *Mars square or opposition to the Sun* also endows the person with an abundance of energy and the faculty of leadership, but these are turned to purposes of deviltry and destruction. The courage implanted by the good aspects becomes foolhardiness, the person has a loud, overbearing, swaggering manner and is ready to fight at the drop of a hat, he is always in opposition to constituted authority and ready to rebel wherever he sees a chance. He has an extremely fiery temper but holds no resentment. On account of these qualities he is universally disliked both by employers and his fellow-workers, is always in hot water and never stays long in any place for he is an agitator and trouble-maker. These aspects also dispose to accidents in which the person may be maimed, also to gunshot and knife-wounds, to scalding-burns and to fevers, inflammatory complaints, boils and eruptions.

♅ ✱ △ ☉ *Uranus sextile or trine to the Sun* makes the person intuitive, original, inventive and independent in his manner of conduct and personal appearance, also with respect to food and certain mannerisms; he is what people call eccentric, often conspicuous, yet not offensively so; given to pursuits and studies which people consider "queer" such as occultism and astrology, but also delving into the unknown after nature's secrets concerning electricity or the like. He often becomes a successful inventor if other aspects give the mechanical ability to work out his schemes. Uranus rules the ether and now that we are nearing the Aquarian age his vibrations will in increasing measure bring to our ken methods of using nature's finer forces and the people with the Sun sextile or trine Uranus will be the media to attract and interpret them for us as the aerials and receivers in a wireless station collect and transcribe the messages carried by the ether waves to which they are attuned. The person often rises in life through the friendship of people above him in the social scale. He is of a very high-strung temperament but has himself well under control, and rarely shows temper or anger. He is an out and out idealist.

♅ P ☌ □ ☍ ☉ *Uranus parallel, conjunction, square or opposition to Sun* makes the person very high-strung, nervous and of uncontrolled emotions, ready to fly into hysteria on any or no provocation. It predisposes to all nervous disorders such as St. Vitus dance, epilepsy and lack of coordination. It makes him impulsive and unreliable, without regard for the conventionalities, highly impatient of any human restraint upon his liberty and committed to the theory of affinities, soulmates and free-love, hence an undesirable marriage partner and likely to figure in divorce proceedings or scandals of an even worse nature.

There is also danger of trouble on account of connection with anarchistic plots where the inventive faculty may find scope in the construction of explosives and infernal machines. Unless these aspects are modified by other configurations these people are among the most dangerous to society. They are liable to accidents from lightning and electricity, and all through life they meet disappointment in every direction.

♆ ✱ △ ☉ *Neptune sextile or trine to the Sun* favors the possibility of developing the spiritual faculties, for he intensifies the spiritual vibrations in the aura. Many people with these configurations hear the harmony of the spheres and if Mercury, the lower octave of Neptune gives the requisite dexterity they become musicians of high inspirational nature. In others it breeds a love of the occult which leads them into the higher life but they usually approach it from the intellectual standpoint of psychic investigators; a few live the life and obtain first-hand knowledge.

♆ ☌ P□ ☍ ☉ *Neptune conjunction, parallel, square or opposition to the Sun* also brings the person in touch with the denizens of the invisible world by raising the vibrations in his aura, but these configurations attract the undesirable element such as met at the ordinary spiritualistic seance. In a watery sign Neptune induces the person to drink to excess and then the resulting acceleration of the vibratory rate frequently causes him to perceive the ugly, gruesome forms abounding in the lower realms of the invisible world, which are real elemental entities and not figments as believed by people who hear him tell what he sees during delirium tremens.

These aspects also make the person liable to be swindled by sharpers and confidence men, and easily hoodwinked.

It cannot be too strongly impressed upon readers and students that judgment is never to be formed on any planetary aspect or position apart from the balance of the horoscope. The unblended, basic nature of aspects is given so that students may recognize innate tendencies and be alert to overcome the evil and to cultivate the good. The free will of the individual can always modify the horoscope, as pointed out on pages 58 and 59, and in Chapter XXII of this book. ("A word to the wise."—EDITOR.)

CHAPTER IX.

VENUS THE PLANET OF LOVE

IN THE 13th Chapter of Paul's First Epistle to the Corinthians we find a eulogy of "love." The word used in the authorized version is "charity," but it ought to be read as "love." "Love suffereth long and is kind, love vaunteth not herself, is not puffed up, believeth all things, endureth all things . . . Whether there be prophecies they shall fail, whether there be knowledge it shall vanish away." He concludes that in time *faith* and *hope* will pass away because we shall know the things in which we now have faith and our hopes will have been realized, but love, he contends, remains forever. The keynote of Venus is "love," "harmony," and "rhythm," and if we want to know her nature we may profitably read that chapter and substitute "Venus" for "Love." Venus vaunteth not herself, is not puffed up, seeketh not her own, rejoices not in iniquity but in truth, beareth all things, believeth all things, endureth all things. These sayings are all true when applied to Venus for she furnishes the unifying bond between all members of the human family in whatever relationship they may be placed. It is the love-ray of Venus piercing deeply the heart of the mother which breeds in her the tender care wherewith she nourishes her offspring through helpless infancy. Venus sounds the love call of the youth and the maiden, gives and takes, smoothing out all the difficulties in the conjugal career. She is ever burning incense upon the altar of affection and from her garden of love come the flowers which scent even the most sordid souls with celestial perfume and raise them for the time being to the stature of gods.

But when Venus is afflicted, all these sublime qualities become tainted and take a hideous aspect according to the nature of their affliction. Squares and oppositions turn love to lust which makes the person revel in sensual gratification; the perception of beauty which expresses itself as art becomes slovenliness, the tendency to self-sacrifice, the giving of oneself for others is turned to selfishness and the person will then seem to use others to escape any task or effort not to his or her liking, laziness being one of the most prominent characteristics of an afflicted Venus.

Being feminine, Venus never reaches out toward others, but exerts a magnetic energy which draws them to her. Therefore she represents in a man's horoscope those of the opposite sex to whom the person is drawn, but in a woman's horoscope Venus describes the person's own attraction for the opposite sex and Mars the masculine planet shows who will be attracted by her charms.

Venus is essentially dignified in Taurus and Libra, and exalted in Pisces, and therefore her influence is most powerfully felt when she is placed in those signs. She is weak and afflicted when placed in either of the martial signs, Aries or Scorpio, where she is in her fall, or when she is in the mercurial sign, Virgo. The best House position for her is the Seventh where her influence will make the marriage serene and blissful.

Venus in the Twelve Houses

♀1 *Venus in the First House* has a tendency to spread sunshine over the child's home and make the early life happy. It gives an amiable character so that the person is well liked because of his social nature and friendly disposition. It brings out the love of music, art and a desire for pleasure. This is what may be called "a lucky position" for it makes the person very attractive to all with whom he or she comes in contact and in that way it tends to give general success in life. It is also very good for the general health.

♀2 *Venus in the Second House* is an indication of financial success in life. People with Venus in this position are usually very popular and are thus helped by their friends to lucrative positions. At the same time this position makes the person very wasteful and prodigal so that it tends to make him spend more than he earns.

The money is usually squandered on pleasure, dress and ornaments for self by a woman and for an amour by a man, and not infrequently leads to abuses which undermine the health. This position also shows gain by dealing in things ruled by Venus, such as dress goods, jewelry, music, etc.

♀3 *Venus in the Third House* has a particularly beneficial effect upon the mind, making the person cheerful, optimistic and inclined to look at everything from the bright side of life. It gives a love of music, art, literature and everything that has a refining influence, and unusual facility for expressing one's self in a happy, appropriate manner, either in speech or writing. It gives love of travel; the person will enjoy himself on his journeys and benefit by them. It also makes relations with brothers and sisters and neighbors and the people in one's immediate environment congenial.

♀4 *Venus in the Fourth House* shows happy conditions in the home, particularly in the latter part of life. It also indicates that an inheritance may be left to the person and that if he owns houses or lands he will gain much by them.

♀5 *Venus in the Fifth House* makes the person unusually affectionate and as a result he or she usually experiences a number of love affairs all of which run their courses smoothly. It indicates that the marriage will be fruitful and productive of lovely and loving children. It is a fortunate position for teachers and people connected with educational institutions, also for those engaged in publication of literature and for gain by speculation in stocks or similar securities.

♀ 6 *Venus in the Sixth House* gives the person faithful servants who will work for his interest if he is an employer. If he is an employee, it will make him well liked by his employers and fellow-workers. It is a fairly good position for health provided the person does not abuse it. That is to say, the constitution is harmonious, but not very strong. If the health is guarded with care it will remain in good condition for life, but a very little abuse may turn the scales the other way and make the person an invalid.

♀ 7 *Venus in the Seventh House* is one of the surest signs of domestic felicity. It signifies an early marriage and an increase of prosperity after that event. If the person finds it expedient to enter into partnership on a business basis the presence of Venus tends to make this relationship harmonious and beneficial. It is also a good sign that if litigation seems necessary some way will be found to settle the matter without actual rupture. This position is good for actors, singers, and others whose calling brings them before the public in a vocal capacity for it ensures a kind and sympathetic reception on the part of their audience.

♀8 *Venus in the Eighth House* will bring gain by marriage, partnership or legacy if it is well aspected, but if it is afflicted it brings loss and disappointment in love, or an extravagant marriage partner, and legal trouble over a will.

♀9 *Venus in the Ninth House* is a very fortunate position if Venus is well aspected, for being so highly elevated here it exercises considerable influence in the life and makes the disposition exceedingly kind, sympathetic and helpful so that by these qualities the person becomes much esteemed and sought after, particularly in charitable or religious work, for this position also brings out the devotional side of the nature. It gives a love of music, art and drama as well as everything that has an influence for soul upliftment. Whenever the person journeys from one place to another for gain or for pleasure, Venus in the Ninth House will smooth the path before him and make his trip thoroughly enjoyable. If Venus is afflicted in the Ninth House the person will long to do or to be all the foregoing things, but will find it exceedingly difficult, if not impossible to accomplish his desire.

♀10 *Venus in the Tenth House* is one of the best signs of general success in the life when well-aspected. The person who has this position becomes very popular, particularly with the opposite sex, and will rise in the social scale through marriage. It gives an ability to avoid trouble in life and extract from it all the pleasure there is in every situation. Comfortable financial circumstances attend upon the person all through life and foster a general attitude of optimism. When Venus is afflicted in the Tenth House the person is looked down on by those in his social environment and though he tries to ingratiate himself with those who are in the charmed circles, he will find himself left with snubs and insults. A hasty or ill-considered marriage is apt to make matters worse and bring him farther into disrepute, as a scapegrace.

♀11 *Venus in the Eleventh House* if well-aspected brings to the person hosts of friends who are willing and anxious to aid him in the realization of his hopes, wishes and desires, but it depends upon the nature and character of the sign wherein Venus is placed as well as on the strength of the aspects whether they will be able to do so or not. For instance, if Venus is in the Eleventh House in Aries or Scorpio, one of the martial signs where she is weak, and aspected only by sextiles from Mercury and the Moon, very little help can be expected of her compared to what she will give if she is in her own signs, Taurus or Libra, and aspected by trines from the Sun and Jupiter. In the case first cited, the friends drawn to the person may be ever so sincere in their wish to help but will not have the ability. In the latter case they will exert a powerful influence and will accomplish wonders. If Venus is afflicted in the Eleventh House it is very often found that the person attracts friends who impose upon him and use him for their own objects and when they have so used him to the fullest extent and he cannot serve their purpose any longer they throw him aside.

♀ 12 *Venus in the Twelfth House* if well-aspected indicates that the person will benefit from the things signified by this House, viz., occupations connected with prisons, hospitals or charitable institutions, or by work in a chemical laboratory or by some such secluded occupation where he does not come in touch with the public. It also favors study and practice of the occult and gives a tendency to secret, clandestine love affairs which will probably run smoothly if Venus is well-aspected, but if she is weak by sign, or afflicted in the Twelfth House she will cause trouble through jealousy, divorce and scandal, or sickness in confinement on account of over-indulgence of the passions, particularly if Venus is in Scorpio which governs the generative organs, or in Taurus which gives the same effect by reflex action, where it signifies self-abuse.

Venus in the Twelve Signs

♀ ♈ *Venus in Aries* lends ardor to the affections of Venus by blending them with the fire of Mars who is ruler of Aries and for that reason it makes the person very ardent in the expression of affection. This usually leads to popularity especially among the opposite sex and often results in a hasty marriage, but that kind of love is not and cannot be lasting. Eventually the fire of passion burns out the love and marriages brought about by this position are then fruit ful sources of domestic unhappiness. This position also inclines the person to be rash and impulsive whenever his sympathies are appealed to, so that he often helps an unworthy cause. Venus in Aries also inclines the person to general extravagance in his expenditures.

♀ ♉ *Venus in Taurus* is a splendid position for there she is essentially dignified and much stronger than in the other signs with the exception of Libra and Pisces where she is respectively dignified and exalted. It is a very favorable position for financial affairs, especially gains derived through the person's own efforts in whatever vocation in life he may have chosen. It gives a friendly and sociable disposition with the ability to inspire reciprocal feelings in others. People with Venus in Taurus are very set in their opinions concerning correct form and decorum, correct in speech and once they have formed an opinion they hold to it very tenaciously. They are generous but not extravagant.

♀ ♊ *Venus in Gemini* blends the beauty of Venus with the mercurial ability to express so that people who have this configuration are able to choose their words with singular facility and infuse in them a rhythm which is like music to the ears of a listener. Therefore this is one of the positions which make poets, provided of course that other indications in the horoscope support, for it should always be remembered by the student that no single aspect or position is in itself sufficient to mark a prominent characteristic. To do this the whole horoscope must be blended. This position has a very refining influence on the mind, inclining to a literary or artistic career. It makes the person beloved of his brothers and sisters, neighbors and other people in his immediate environment. This position also inclines to marriage and frequently to more than one union. It favors traveling both for gain and pleasure, especially short journeys.

♀ ♋ *Venus in Cancer* blends the characteristics of Venus with those of the Moon and the psychic watery nature of Cancer. Therefore this position gives the person a very fruitful imagination and he or she is very apt to come in touch with the inhabitants of the unseen world or at least take up some very devotional phase of religion; but this is dangerous because Venus is negative, attracting without selecting or discriminating, hence makes liable to domination by spirit controls and the dangers of mediumship.

♀ ♌ *Venus in Leo* is compounding love, for Leo rules the heart and whoever has this position will be tender-hearted to a degree. Contrary to the commonly accepted ideas there is a cruel streak in Leo, but when Venus is there, there is no more loving and tender sign in the zodiac, besides being that Leo is a fixed sign Venus in this position makes for an unparalleled assertion of the affections when once they have been placed and an unswerving loyalty to the object thereof. Being that Leo is the fifth sign Venus in Leo also gives success in entertainment or educational enterprises and the blending of the Venus ray with the solar brings favor from those above the person in the social scale.

♀ ♍ *Venus in Virgo,* the Sixth House sign gives the person a deep and tender sympathy for the sick and people with this position make good nurses. This position also favors occupation as a chemist, or a dietitian who is concerned with the preparation of foods for the maintenance or attainment of health. If the person has employees or subordinates under his management his relations with those people will always be very pleasant, and they will serve him well.

♀ ♎ *Venus in Libra,* the Seventh House sign is essentially dignified and strong. This is one of the positions which testify to a fruitful and congenial marriage or successful partnership. It gives musical and artistic ability and makes the person popular in public life. If engaged as a speaker or singer it ensures an appreciative audience whenever he appears in public.

♀ ♏ *Venus in Scorpio* is the worst position of all in which she may be placed, for here again the love ray of Venus blends with the martial fire of passion in the sign governing the genitals so that if there are no other redeeming and restraining influences in the horoscope love turns to lust and the unbridled gratification of an exaggerated sexual desire, especially if the Moon or Mars are there. This is apt to undermine the constitution and though that may not be apparent for a long time the effect of such a sapping of the vitality will some time be felt and cause a general breakdown, but that, of course, is nothing compared with the moral effect of the practices indicated by this passion. It should be said furthermore for the benefit of those who have this position that it does not matter whether such abuses take place in wedlock or not; Nature does not care whether they have been legalized by man-made law or not. From her standpoint they are a violation of the law of life and will be punished whether sanctioned by society or not. This position also gives a love of luxury and anything that stirs the emotions or wherein the senses may revel. Curiously enough it also sometimes gives a sense of deep religious devotion which then serves as an outlet for the overcharged feelings of the native. This position also creates jealousy and trouble in marriage and the reputation of the person is apt to be smirched. A well-aspected Venus in Scorpio is liable to bring a legacy.

♀ ♐ *Venus in Sagittarius.* This is another of her strongest positions for there her qualities blend with those of Jupiter, the planet of benevolence, to foster love and good-will among men.

Therefore also this position indicates a genial and optimistic disposition, a sympathetic, kind and generous heart, a love of God expressed in religious devotion, or love of man shown by philanthropy and charity. It indicates a refined mind, cultured, and fond of drama, art and music. It fosters the imagination and intuition and like the other double-bodied signs Gemini and Pisces, it inclines to plurality of marriages.

♀ ♑ *Venus in Capricorn,* the Tenth House sign, gives social success and popularity, but Venus does not blend well with Saturn, the ruler of Capricorn. There is therefore a slight tendency to melancholy in people who have Venus in that position. Nor are they ever secure in the favors which they receive from other people or in their popularity, for Saturn has a tendency to throw them down when they have reached the highest pinnacle. Therefore, though this influence may help them to climb the ladder of advancement in social circles or in business they are never safe in their position. This influence makes a person very jealous of honor and he takes it to heart when sometimes Saturn throws him down. Venus in Saturn's sign often causes the person to disregard the fact that disparity in ages is so fatal to happiness in marriage and hence if he marries young he takes someone who is much older than himself for a partner or if married in later years he selects someone who is still in the bloom of youth with the almost inevitable result that disagreement and dissolution of the marriage tie take place in the course of a few years. Frequently also people with this position of Venus marry for business or as a matter of convenience. In short Venus never reaches her legitimate expression of love in Saturn's House and therefore such unions are always a source of sorrow and disappointment to the contracting parties.

♀ ♒ *Venus in Aquarius* indicates a blending of the Uranian qualities, independence, impatience of restraint, disregard of convention, desire for originality, uncompromising sincerity and intuition, with those of Venus and as a result we find that people with this position refuse to be bound by the usual restrictive rules of society in their love affairs and follow their heart's inclination regardless of what others may say or think. They are firm believers in the theory of soul-mates, affinities, et cetera, and liable to act in the most unexpected manner with such startling suddenness that neither they nor anyone else are able to foresee what they may say or do next. But at the same time they are so loving and sincere in their convictions that friends never fail them and whatever success they attain in life is usually due to the efforts of friends to help them to realize their hopes, wishes and aspirations.

♀ ♓ *Venus in Pisces* is in her own exaltation sign where she again blends with the benefic ray of Jupiter and as Pisces is a watery sign this position signifies a powerful emotional nature, subdued and toned down by the element of sorrow inherent in the twelfth house sign. This position therefore indicates someone capable of feeling a sentiment such as that felt by our Savior when He said: "Come unto Me all ye that are weak and heavy laden and I will give you rest." Thus Venus in Pisces indicates a nature yearning and aching to assist those who are afflicted by bodily ills or suffering from sorrow. Moved by compassion such people often take up work in a prison or charitable institution where they find an outlet for their compassion. This position also gives an intense love of music and when other testimonies concur, considerable ability to express either vocally or instrumentally, for music is the most wonderful outlet for the deepest emotions of which the human soul is capable. People with Venus in Pisces are especially liable to financial imposition on the part of others and trouble through an illegal marriage.

Venus in Aspect with Other Planets

☉P☌♀ *The Sun parallel or conjunction Venus* calls out the artistic side of the nature, making the person fond of music, art and poetry. It also strengthens the love-nature and if the configuration occurs in the seventh house it is a positive testimony of unalloyed marital bliss. In the second or eighth house it leads to extravagance of the person or his mate, in Scorpio it is not good for the morals and in Pisces it leads to intemperance, but generally speaking, these aspects strengthen the constitution, increase the popularity and make social intercourse smooth so that the person finds many friends and keeps them.

As the orbit of Venus is so small she never forms the sextile, trine, square or opposition to the Sun.

☿☌P✱♀ *Mercury conjunction, parallel or sextile to Venus.* (Note.—Venus and Mercury are never more than 76 degrees apart, therefore they can only form the conjunctions, parallels and sextiles, but not the trine, square nor opposition.)

These aspects make the person cheerful and companionable with a good-natured disposition and a desire for society. They also give ability for music and poetry, especially if in the Ascendant and are a general indication of success in salesmanship, for such people are suave, affable and persuasive.

☽ ☌ P ✱ △ ♀ *The Moon conjunction, parallel, sextile or trine to Venus.* The Moon is a significator of marriage for a man and therefore the good aspects between Venus, the planet of love, and the Moon are good indications of a happy marriage when they occur in a man's horoscope. But in a woman's horoscope these aspects operate upon the health, for the Moon is the planet of fecundity and has rule over the female functions in particular which are so large a factor in the health of a woman; this latter is much strengthened by the good aspects of the Moon and Venus. These aspects make the person an orator with a fruitful imagination; give love of pleasure, music and art, and an engaging personality, very attractive to the opposite sex, because kindly, affectionate and sympathetic. They tend to general success in life and the person usually has sufficient for the day and the way.

☽ □ ☍ ♀ *The Moon square or opposition to Venus* is an indication of trouble in marriage for a man, because the wife described by an afflicted Venus will be slovenly and of dissolute habits which will destroy domestic happiness. In a woman's horoscope it indicates disturbance of the female functions and it also gives a tendency to digestive troubles and poor circulation when in the horoscope of either sex. These aspects also give a liability to trouble through slander and public scandal.

♄ ✱ △ ♀ *Saturn sextile or trine to Venus.* The good qualities of Venus are love and affection and the good qualities of Saturn are tact, diplomacy,method, system, justice, thrift and economy. We may therefore judge that when these two planets are configurated in good aspect they make the person faithful and true, just and methodical, qualities which make for success in all departments of life. Therefore a person with these aspects will be much sought as a friend and adviser, or as a person to be trusted with any commission requiring sterling honesty and ability. They make the person simple in his tastes and of unimpeachable morality, and give honor, esteem, health and easy circumstances.

♄ P ☌ □ ☍ ♀ *Saturn parallel, conjunction, square or opposition to Venus* brings out the evil qualities of the two planets and troubles which are thus generated usually come through the person's relations with the opposite sex. It makes him underhanded and scheming to gratify his passions often in an unusual manner and his perverted desires are usually directed against some one who is much younger than himself. If regular marriage relations are entered into, such a person is usually a demon of jealousy who makes life a burden for the marriage partner on account of his suspicious nature. People with these afflictions are also stingy in all money matters and exceedingly avaricious. They have poor business judgment and are therefore liable to losses, failure and bankruptcy.

♃ P ☌ ✶ △ ♀ *Jupiter parallel, conjunction, sextile or trine to Venus* is one of the best signs of success and general good fortune. It favors the accumulation of wealth and the enjoyment of all the luxuries of life. It is a good indication of a successful and happy marriage, social prestige and the respect of all with whom the person comes in contact. It gives the person a jovial, optimistic, generous and large-hearted disposition, and makes hospitable to a degree; interested and active in philanthropic measures, a liberal mind tolerant of the views of others even where he differs radically, fond of pleasure, traveling, parties, and capable of enjoying life to the fullest extent. These aspects also give a talent for music, especially if either planet is in Pisces.

♃ □ ☍ ♀ *Jupiter square or opposition to Venus* gives the same luxurious likings as the good aspects, but limits the ability to satisfy them; although such people make the most frantic efforts to present a fine front to the world, they are generally found out to be shams. Their lack of business ability is often responsible for failure and bankruptcy and they are very liable to suffer losses through the treachery of others. Love and marriage also are sources of sorrow for those whom Venus and Jupiter are afflicting. They are apt to be jilted before marriage or the marriage partner may prove faithless and may abscond. These aspects also produce an amorous nature likely to take liberties regardless of the laws of decency and to be faithless to marriage vows. They make people extremely self-indulgent and in Pisces they predispose to drink.

♂ * △ ♀ *Mars sextile or trine to Venus* will give an ambitious, aspiring and adventurous nature, amorous and extremely demonstrative in its affection, very fond of sports and pleasures. It gives the person an abundance of energy and business acumen, consequently he has a splendid earning capacity but he wastes money for he loves above all things to make a great outward show and display. Being a free spender he is also very popular among his associates, and being, as already said, of an amorous nature he marries either very early or the marriage is a very hasty one.

♂ ☌ P ♀ *Mars conjunction or parallel to Venus* does not always operate in the same manner, but is to be classed as a good or bad aspect according to circumstances and the matter to be judged. For instance, Mars conjunction Venus makes the person less blunt and domineering, more kind and polite; it is therefore good in that respect; but the conjunction also strengthens the passional nature, especially if it occurs in Scorpio; and in the Twelfth House it leads to self-abuse so that in those cases it is decidedly bad.

♂ □ ☍ ♀ *Mars square or opposition Venus.* See page 330.

♅ ✱ △ ♀ *Uranus sextile or trine to Venus* makes the person mentally alert, of quick intuitive perception and exceedingly magnetic, especially to the opposite sex; and he also attracts hosts of friends who will be a benefit and assistance to him. These aspects give love of art, music and poetry and are favorable indications of a happy marriage often at a very early age, or one suddenly consummated. They also sometimes bring the person love of a platonic nature.

♅ ☌ P ♀ *Uranus conjunction or parallel to Venus.* There is a doubt as to whether these aspects should be classed as good or evil, which must be settled in the individual horoscope where they occur for they may work either way, depending upon the other configurations. If Venus is otherwise afflicted in the horoscope, for instance the conjunction or parallel will further accentuate her evil qualities, but if she is well placed or aspected Uranus will bring out the nobler side.

♅ □ ☍ ♀ *Uranus square or opposition to Venus.* The square or opposition always brings trouble through the sex relation: a hasty, ill-considered union, quarrels, divorces, public scandals through clandestine intercourse and kindred irregularities, with loss of friends, prestige and popularity, exile from home and family and sudden financial losses through unexpected or unforeseen happenings. There is a general lack of balance, an erratic personality.

♆ ✱ △ ♀ *Neptune sextile or trine to Venus* makes an inspirational musician. It gives a fertile imagination and deep emotions, a nature that is pure and chaste, hence occasionally it leads to platonic unions and companionship of the most esthetic nature.

♆ ☌ P ♀ *Neptune conjunction or parallel to Venus* is to be judged on the same line as indicated in the case of Mars and Uranus.

♆ □ ☍ ♀ *Neptune square or opposition to Venus* makes the person liable to sorrow, loss and trouble, especially through the marriage partner or anyone else in whom he trusts. People with these aspects should be particularly careful to avoid anything which has in it an element of chance or speculation, for they are sure to lose, especially in dealing with large companies or corporations.

CHAPTER X.

Mercury, the Planet of Reason

MYTHOLOGICALLY Mercury is represented as a "Messenger of the Gods" and this is in line with the occult facts, for when infant humanity had been led astray by the martial Lucifer spirits and had fallen into *generation* it became necessary for the other divine hierarchies to take steps looking to a future *regeneration* and to further that object the Lords of Venus were brought to the earth to educate humanity in such a manner that love might be substituted for lust and men might thus be induced to aspire to something higher. While the Lords of Venus dealt with mankind in general the most precocious among them were taken in hand by the Lords of Mercury, whose wisdom-teaching is symbolically represented by the caduceus or *"staff of Mercury,"* consisting of two serpents twining around a rod and indicating the solution of the riddle of life, of "Whence have we come, why are we here, and whither are we bound?" showing the pupil the spiral path of *involution* by which the divine spark has buried itself in matter, also the spiral path of *evolution* by which humanity will eventually again reach the Father's bosom, and the short road of *Initiation* represented by the central rod around which the serpents twine. But to understand these Mysteries requires mind and reason. Mercury then is the mental educator of men and its place and position in the horoscope shows the status of the person's mind for whom it is cast.

Being the Messenger of the Gods to the other planets Mercury has no voice of its own and is even more dependent for expression upon the aspects of other planets than the Moon which rules the instinctual mind. So Mercury is really a focus through which the faculty of reason finds expression in the human being to act as a brake upon the lower nature and assist in lifting us from the human to the divine. Many may and do feel deeply, they may also have valuable knowledge, but they will be unable to express their feelings or share their knowledge with others if Mercury is lacking in aspects. Even a so-called evil aspect of Mercury helps to bring out what is within and is therefore better than none.

When Mercury is so placed in relation to the Sun that it goes *before* the luminary it has the effect of materially brightening the mind, for the Sun represents the Ego and it may therefore be said that then its path is illuminated by the lamp of reason. On the other hand if Mercury is so placed that it rises later than the Sun and thus follows *after* the luminary the Ego learns more by afterthought than by forethought for it walks comparatively speaking in the dark and must learn a great many of its lessons by experience.

As we have found that it is difficult for a number of young students to determine when Mercury goes before or after the Sun we may say in farther elucidation of that subject:

When Mercury is in a lower degree of the same sign as the Sun or in any degree of the previous sign then as a matter of course he rises *before* the Sun. To illustrate: If the Sun is in twenty degrees of Cancer and Mercury is in five, ten or fifteen degrees of that sign or if he is in any degree of Gemini, then he rises *before* the Sun.

But if he is in twenty-five degrees of Cancer which is a higher degree of the same sign, or if he is in any degree in Leo which is the sign succeeding Cancer, then he rises *after* the Sun and loses part of his good influence.

A retrograde Mercury is also a detriment to the faculty of reason. But in the year of life when Mercury by progression again turns direct, the reasoning faculties will improve correspondingly. Mercury is strong in the airy signs, Gemini, Libra and Aquarius, but he is exalted and therefore most powerful in Virgo. Mercury has special rule over agents and messengers, salesmen, postmen and other common carriers, people engaged in advertising or printing, literary men, writers, reporters, secretaries, clerks, stenographers and typewriters, commission men and other middle men, demagogues, confidence-men and thieves.

MERCURY IN THE TWELVE HOUSES.

☿ 1 *Mercury in the Ascendant, or First House* makes the person quick-witted and sharp according to the nature of the sign rising and the aspects of the planets which he receives. The fiery signs and the airy signs have the strongest influence in that respect. In Aries or Leo he is more impulsive than when rising in Sagittarius, but Gemini, Libra and Aquarius are best. When Mercury is rising in the watery signs Cancer or Pisces the intellect is dull, but rising in Scorpio where it is fired by the martial energy and armed with the venomous sting of the scorpion it has a somewhat similar influence to that of Mars in Scorpio though not quite so pronounced.

☿ 2 *Mercury in the Second House* is good for gain through mercurial occupations especially where the person is employed by someone else so that he appears in a true mercurial capacity as agent, messenger, clerk, writer or whatever else.

☿ 3 *Mercury in the Third House* and well-aspected has wonderful influence on the mental qualities of the native. It makes the mind serene and optimistic, inclined to study and research work. It gives fluency as a speaker and success by short journeys or travel and makes the relations of the person harmonious with his brothers. When Mercury is afflicted in the Third House it inclines to worry and pessimism, trouble and annoyance with sisters and brothers and when on short journeys.

☿ 4 *Mercury in the Fourth House* gives instability to home conditions. It signifies the homeless wanderer who is always moving from place to place unless a good aspect to Saturn comes in to steady him down. This is, however, a good aspect for people engaged in mercurial occupations which require a stationary residence, such as librarian, or literary men engaged in newspaper work, employees in printing establishments, commission houses, agencies and kindred organizations. If Mercury is afflicted by Saturn the home conditions of the person will cause him a great deal of worry.

☿ 5 *Mercury in the Fifth House* centers the mind upon education, amusements, courtships and children. If Mercury is well-aspected by Saturn or Jupiter it gives depth to the mind and makes the person successful in enterprises connected with education, publishing or public amusements. Good aspects from Mars or Venus give success in courtship but the adverse aspects of the planets make the person cruel; he is inconstant in affection toward those he professes to love, inclined to worry over affairs of his children, and superficial as a teacher. A good aspect from the Sun is an excellent indication of success in a government position, in an educational capacity.

☿ 6 *Mercury in the Sixth House* makes the mentality too active for the person's own good, for he is extremely ambitious and therefore liable to overtax himself to the detriment of his health, and the disability of the nervous system is most likely to express itself by a digestive disorder in the region governed by Virgo, the sixth sign, viz., the intestines. Such people are supersensitive to the conditions of others which affects their health bringing much trouble and worry in dealing with servants or subordinates. They are fond of the study of hygiene and diet and meet with considerable success in the practice of the chemistry of foods, particularly if Mercury is well-aspected. Adverse aspects of Saturn to a Sixth House Mercury make a chronic invalid of a most melancholy mind. The adverse aspects of Mars and Uranus are fruitful sources of suicide through brooding over disease.

☿ 7 *Mercury in the Seventh House* and well-aspected makes the person popular in literary and scientific circles. It is a good position for public speakers and all who are engaged in mercurial activities of a public nature. But if Mercury is afflicted the Seventh House position brings a great deal of hostile criticism of a public nature and is liable to involve the person in litigation either to defend himself against libel from others or on account of libel committed by himself. A well-aspected Mercury in the Seventh House indicates a successful marriage to a relative or an employee, but when Mercury is afflicted either the person or the marriage partner is of a nagging nature so that the married life is spoiled by constant quarrels and disputes on account of fickleness and faithlessness.

☿ 8 *Mercury in the Eighth House* when well-aspected gives gain through literary or scientific agencies, occupations or other mercurial pursuits provided they are carried on in partnership with someone else. This position also indicates that the person may receive a legacy and it is a good indication of the financial success of the marriage, but if Mercury is afflicted its position in the Eighth House indicates financial troubles for the marriage partner and litigation probably in connection with a legacy left to the native.

☿ 9 *Mercury in the Ninth House* and well-aspected gives love of religion, science, letters and law, a studious mind capable of delving deeply into profound problems of life and being, philosophic and philanthropic tendencies, and desire to travel far if need be in the pursuit of knowledge. This position gives facility in speech and writing and success in religion, philosophy, law or science. The mind is broad, flexible and adaptable, therefore the person is liable to change his views several times in his life on the various subjects which he has studied, but there will always be a good reason for adopting another viewpoint.

If Mercury is afflicted in the Ninth House he makes the person exceedingly unstable of mind, changeable as a weather vane in all his pursuits and activities. Such a person will never stay by anything long enough to try it out and therefore he will meet with a series of disasters all through life. Probably he may journey from one place to another in search of success but he will never find it until he learns to concentrate his energies upon one thing. This position is also a fruitful source of trouble with the law or legal affairs.

☿10 *Mercury in the Tenth House,* well-aspected, shows adaptability and resourcefulness such as enable the person to cope with all the contingencies of life. It makes a successful lecturer, publisher or writer and is also favorable to success in one of the occult occupations. If Mercury is placed in one of the airy signs the power of expression is much enhanced. Frequently people with Mercury in this position have several occupations, but usually they succeed best in a subordinate capacity.

☿11 *Mercury in the Eleventh House* brings a great many acquaintances among literary, scientific or other mercurial people, but none of them are sufficiently steadfast to be relied upon unless Mercury is very well aspected. This position has a tendency to make a person critical and cynical. It sharpens his intellect, however, and gives him a good flow of language.

☿12 *Mercury in the Twelfth House,* if well aspected gives a mind peculiarly fitted to delve into the mysterious, occult or secret things. This is especially the case if Mercury is between the Sun and Midheaven, that is to say if Mercury goes *before* the Sun or rises earlier than that luminary, for then all the light that is in the spirit seems to shine forth and make the person intellectually keen and bright. Therefore this is a good position for detective work as well as scientific or occult research work. Chemists of great ability have been produced under this aspect for such people have the faculty of going into the most minute details in things which seem microscopic and unimportant to others. When Mercury is in the Twelfth House and afflicted, especially by Saturn or Mars, also when *combust* or *behind the Sun* there is danger that the mind may become clouded and insanity may result. It may also be noted that the affliction will vary according to the way Mercury is aspected; if by Mars or Uranus the subject may be exceedingly violent, if by Saturn he will become melancholy, but whatever the cause, if Mercury is afflicted in the Twelfth House some form of limitation will restrain the spirit, for the Twelfth House is the house of limitation and confinement.

Deafness is also the result of this position of Mercury when severely afflicted by Saturn.

Mercury in the Twelve Signs

☿ ♈ *Mercury in Aries* makes the person very argumentative, fond of disputes, quick at repartee, with a tendency to exaggerate though not necessarily by design. If well-aspected he is broad-minded and tolerant of the opinions of others, of a studious nature, quick to grasp situations and ideas, neat and orderly. When afflicted Mercury in Aries makes people leap before they look, the mind is vacillating and there is a general recklessness about the person who is thus very unreliable and devoid of all sense of responsibility.

☿ ♉ *Mercury in Taurus* gives a mind that is not very soon made up but when it has once arrived at a conclusion it is almost as difficult to change as the laws of the Medes and Persians. However, being based upon thought and reason the judgment of these people is also extremely reliable. They believe thoroughly in the ancient adage that "Silence is golden" and are therefore close-mouthed. They are good counsellors and can be depended upon to keep a secret. At the same time they are not recluses, but have a pleasant, sociable disposition. They are fond of fun and recreation, they love music, art and literature, so they are thoroughly likable people if Mercury is well-aspected. But if Mercury is afflicted they become what the Scotch call "*dour,*" also obstinate, stubborn, secretive and avaricious.

☿ ♊ *Mercury in Gemini* makes a person fond of change and travel. He is always ready to investigate some new thing, or go to some other place for a change; in short, almost anything that is new appeals to him. At the same time if Mercury is well-fortified such people gain greatly by this fluidic state of the mind for they are shrewd and penetrating in their judgment so that they know good value when they see it and are not prejudiced by preconceived, set opinions. Therefore they are good business men and their ability to see a point makes them particularly good lawyers. They also succeed well as traveling salesmen.

☿ ♋ *Mercury in Cancer* gives a clear intellect, a good memory and superlative adaptability. People with this position fit into any place or occupation they may find and adapt themselves to the opinions and ideas of others. They love praise and flattery, therefore they are careful not to do anything whereby they may forfeit the good opinion of others.

☿ ♌ *Mercury in Leo* gives high ideals and aspirations, a positive, strong and persevering intellect which scorns to stoop to low and mean acts, and despises equivocation; is blunt and outspoken, quick-tempered, but kind-hearted and sympathetic. People with Mercury in Leo well-fortified have good organizing ability and make capable leaders. They love children and are also fond of pleasure. When Mercury is afflicted in Leo it makes the person fickle and inconstant in his affections, an unsuccessful gambler and speculator, a low and sensual nature.

☿ ♍ *Mercury in Virgo* is at the zenith of his power for there he is exalted, consequently when well-aspected it gives a clear, logical, scientific mind, eloquence and the ability to express oneself fluently in a number of languages. It gives the person a comprehensive, discriminating outlook upon life, his conclusions are usually practical and to the point because he also, like the Taurian Mercury, looks before he leaps. In short this characteristic is in a degree true of all the earthy signs. When Mercury is afflicted in Virgo it makes the man irritable, petulant and selfish, always looking for flaws in everything he comes across. People with Mercury in Virgo make excellent dietitians and chemists. They also have an unusual dexterity.

☿ ♎ *Mercury in Libra,* when well-aspected gives a broad, well-balanced mind with a love of art and music and an uncommon ability of expression. It brings success as a public speaker and sometimes as a singer. When Mercury is afflicted in Libra it indicates trouble by lawsuits through partnerships and an unfaithful marriage partner.

☿ ♏ *Mercury in Scorpio* gives a shrewd mind, a keen aspiration, a quick wit and a sharp tongue with biting sarcasm that can sting like the scorpion. The disposition is bold and stubborn, headstrong and difficult to get along with. But these people are extremely resourceful, dauntless and able to overcome difficulties which would crush others. They are attracted to the occult, as a needle is drawn to a magnet. When Mercury is afflicted they are subject to disappointment in everything they undertake, quarrelsome, skeptical and cynical, always holding opposite views to others.

☿ ♐ *Mercury in Sagittarius.* Though in detriment it is still a strong position of Mercury and if he is well-aspected it gives an exceedingly noble mind of a religious and philosophical turn, a mind which scorns the shackles of conventions where they interfere with freedom of thought and speech yet does not fly into paths that are contrary to the commonly accepted standards of moral usage and conduct. It always confines itself within the boundaries of law and order and people with Mercury in this position are therefore greatly respected in the community. Mercury in Sagittarius makes the person fond of travel to see the sights and scenery of nature and to investigate the customs of strange people. He is also fond of animals and pets. When afflicted it inclines to lawlessness, dishonesty, sophism and a twisted character.

☿ ♑ *Mercury in Capricorn* gives a critical and penetrating but somewhat suspicious mind with a thoughtful and diplomatic disposition. These people make splendid spies and detectives, having the ability to ferret out secrets in the most uncanny manner. They also have the persistence of Saturnians derived from the sign Capricorn so that they never give up until their object has been attained. This position gives a love of science, particularly chemistry. These people are much attracted to the occult, yet are practical and very thrifty. They hold on to what they get and always have something for a rainy day. When afflicted Mercury in Capricorn makes the person miserly, cruel, hard, malicious, vindictive and spiteful.

☿ ♒ *Mercury in Aquarius* gives the Uranian qualities of originality and independence and an unconquerable love of liberty to the mind so that people with Mercury in this position are apt to repudiate all the social conventions and live according to their highly idealistic conceptions. They often take no heed of fashion, and dress in a style entirely their own. They advocate ideas on social subjects which are a thousand years ahead of the world's development, among them the theory of soul-mates and affinities which is causing so much trouble in the world today because its advocates have not yet grown to the spiritual stature where they can separate it from sex and live the true Uranian love-life which is altogether spiritual. The foregoing delineations apply particularly where Mercury is aspected by Uranus and the people described by them are the extreme product of Mercury in Aquarius. All who have this position, however, are very intellectual, they have high ideals and aspirations, a love of popular science and mathematics and are usually attracted to the occult sciences also, especially to astrology, for they have a fine faculty for reading the horoscope. They are kind, sociable and fond of friends with the result that they usually attract large numbers of intellectual people to their circle of acquaintances. When afflicted this position makes the person disloyal and ready to prey upon his friends, or criticise and slander them.

☿ ♓ *Mercury in Pisces* the occult watery sign, seems to endow the mind with a certain psychic faculty which is not so much intuition as imagination. They think or imagine that something must be so and so and it is a startling fact that they are usually correct, but this ability brings them dangerously near to mediumship if Mercury is afflicted or when Neptune, the higher octave of Mercury, is in the Twelfth House. Therefore this is rather a dangerous position. If Mercury is afflicted by Saturn this position in Pisces makes the person liable to gloom and the mind will be subject to constant worry with a turn toward melancholy. Usually, people with Mercury in Pisces are of a kindly and benevolent disposition. This also is a good indication that success may be attained in chemistry and as a dietitian in the preparation of health foods.

Mercury in Aspect with the Other Planets

⊙ P ☌ ☿ *The Sun in parallel or conjunction with Mercury.* These are the only aspects ever formed and are good for the memory and mentality provided Mercury is not closer to the Sun than three degrees, for then he is "*combust*" and his good qualities are burned up in the Sun's rays. It is most fortunate to have Mercury rise *before* the Sun at Birth for he is then the Lightbearer who holds the torch of reason *before* the Spirit which in the horoscope is symbolized by the Sun. When he rises after the Sun the mentality is not nearly so keen (unless other good aspects favor).

♀ P ☌ ✱ ☿ *Venus parallel, conjunction or sextile to Mercury.* Venus and Mercury are never more than 76 degrees apart, therefore they can only form the conjunctions, parallels and sextiles, but not the trine, square nor opposition.

These aspects make the person cheerful and companionable with a good-natured disposition and a desire for society. They also give ability for music and poetry, especially if in the Ascendant, and are a general indication of *success* in salesmanship for such people are very suave, affable and persuasive.

☽ P ☌ ✱ △ ☿ *The Moon in parallel, conjunction, sextile or trine to Mercury* gives a receptive mind and a retentive memory, two very rare qualities and therefore these aspects, particularly the sextile and trine, are good indications of success in life, especially in one of the mercurial occupations, literary, clerical or traveling. People with these configurations are usually very verbose, particularly if the conjunction or trine occurs in airy signs or a sign of voice, for then the power of expression reaches a superlative degree and such people become able linguists and elocutionists; but unless there is some steadying influence people with configurations of Mercury and the Moon are not reliable because of their tendency to change their minds repeatedly in the most unexpected manner. They are inclined to look upon the bright side of life and are fond of pleasure, particularly travel.

☽ □ ☍ ☿ *The Moon square or opposition to Mercury* gives a poor memory and lack of mental stability with a tendency to indecision and worry, liability to brain storms and hysterics. These characteristics make the person unpopular and as the saying is, "unlucky."

♄ ⚹ △ ☿ *Saturn sextile or trine to Mercury* acts as a brake upon the flighty mind and gives it a seriousness, depth and concentration which is of inestimable value in life. The forethought and profound reasoning ability indicated by these aspects insure success in whatever vocation the person may pursue. The patient persistence which permits no temporary failure to stand in the way of ultimate success; their caution and diplomacy make such people invincible in the long run. Therefore they generally become prominent in connection with some serious enterprise such as secret societies, the church or even politics or governmental affairs. They are in demand for high positions in great undertakings where a steady hand is required on the helm. But they do not usually shine in public for they are very quiet, subdued and serious in their manner and demeanor; besides they are absolutely honest and fairminded, hence they make the very finest judges obtainable.

♄ ☌ P ☿ *Saturn conjunction or parallel to Mercury* gives depth to the mind, and forethought, together with all the other good qualities enumerated as resulting from the sextile and the trine if Mercury is otherwise well aspected, but not in so full a measure, or at any rate the person does not seem to be able to externalize them as readily, hence does not meet the same assured success as given by the good aspects. He also suffers from the tendency to melancholy denoted by the square or opposition, especially if the aspect occurs in one of the common signs or in Capricorn, and if in Gemini it interferes sadly with the dexterity. Such people tend to drop everything they take into their hands. These aspects also give an embarrassing timidity and if Mercury is afflicted the undesirable qualities enumerated as resulting from the square or opposition may be looked for.

♄ □ ☍ ☿ *Saturn square or opposition to Mercury* makes the person subject to trouble and delays all through life. He is thwarted on every hand by slander and secret enemies and this condition in time makes him bitter and sarcastic with the additional result that he is shunned by all who can possibly get away from him. This in time leads him to become a recluse who shuts himself away to brood over his troubles. Such a person sometimes becomes subject to melancholia of a most piteous character. These aspects also make the person cunning and untruthful. They give the same desire to study the occult conferred by the good aspects, but there is the great difference that while the good aspects of Saturn and Mercury incline one to the study of occultism from unselfish motives, the bad aspects impel him to ferret out nature's secrets for personal power or gain.

♃ ☌ P ✱ △ ☿ *Jupiter conjunction, parallel, sextile or trine to Mercury* is one of the finest assets in life, for it gives a cheerful, optimistic disposition with the ability to always look upon the bright side of things and keep up the spirits in hours of adversity. The mind is broad, versatile and able to reason correctly and to form a reliable judgment by careful deliberation. These people never give a hasty decision; they require time to think over whatever is presented to them, but once they have reached a conclusion it will be found incontrovertible. They are successful in law or literature and much respected for their honesty and sincerity. These aspects are particularly fortunate for people who travel for business or pleasure, for they will reap both benefit and enjoyment from a migratory mode of life; these aspects make them "healthy, wealthy and wise" beyond the average, and loved by everybody for the vital vibrations they radiate upon whomever they meet.

♃□☍☿ *Jupiter square or opposition to Mercury* gives a vacillating and wavering disposition so that the person cannot make up his mind when more than one course of action is open, hence people with these aspects often lose their opportunities through procrastination and lack of judgment, and must therefore often be classed as failures in life. They are liable to scandal and slander because of treacherous associates. They should not travel, for it will bring them loss and trouble. They should also be extremely careful in making contracts or agreements to do or deliver certain things at a specified time, for they will probably be unable to fulfill the requirements and thus trouble and loss will result.

♂✱△☿ *Mars sextile or trine to Mercury* gives a keen, sharp, ingenious and resourceful mentality. It makes the person enthusiastic over any proposition which appeals to him and he has also the ability to enthuse others and impress them with his views; an indefatigable worker in any cause which arouses his sympathies, but he is no visionary, and is interested only in concrete matters. These people love argument or debate, and they have an inexhaustible fund of wit and good humor, sometimes blended with a vein of sarcasm which always strikes its mark, yet never viciously nor maliciously. They also have remarkable dexterity and are able to turn their hands to whatever task is allotted and do it with a speed, facility and expedition that is astonishing, to say the least. They cannot do anything slowly or by halves; whatever they undertake must be done with a rush, and they put their whole energy into it so that they may accomplish the task and do it well, hence these aspects give success in life, in almost any line of endeavor these people may select, but most often in literature or the mechanical arts.

♂ ☌ P ☿ *Mars conjunction or parallel to Mercury* gives the same mental energy, enthusiasm and dexterity as the definitely good aspects, but whether these qualities are used for constructive and good purposes or for destructive and evil ends depends upon the sign, house position and other aspects. If the configuration occurs in a sign where either or both planets are strong and well-placed, as Mars in Aries or Capricorn, or Mercury in Gemini or Virgo, or if they are fortified by good aspects from the Sun, Venus or Jupiter, Mars conjunction or parallel Mercury will operate similarly to the sextile or trine, as stated in the foregoing paragraph, which see. But if Mars and Mercury are in one of the watery signs (Cancer, Scorpio or Pisces), or if either or both are afflicted by Saturn, Uranus or Neptune, the conjunction or parallel of Mars and Mercury will give the same evil tendencies as the square or opposition which are defined in the next paragraph.

♂ □ ☍ ☿ *Mars square or opposition to Mercury* makes people quickwitted, sharp and alert, quick tempered, impulsive and excitable, liable to jump at conclusions and act before they think with the inevitable result that they are always getting themselves or other people into trouble, hence they are dangerous associates. They are born prevaricators and utterly incapable of making a straight statement. It is just as natural for them to color or exaggerate their statements as it is to breathe. They are vitriolic in their wrath and their tongues are more poisonous than the bite of a rattlesnake, hence they are either feared or hated by those who are unfortunate enough to be bound to them by environment; all who can, shun them. They are bullies who are bound either to rule or ruin wherever they are, and they allow no obstacle to stand in their way which can be removed either by force or slander. They are the acme of selfishness, swagger and consummate egotism. The foregoing tendencies may of course be modified by other aspects, but if they are not, such people are a menace to society. If either Mars or Mercury is placed in the Sixth or Twelfth House or in any other position so that the bad aspect acts upon the health, there is a liability to nervous prostration, brain fever or insanity.

♅ ✱ △ ☿ *Uranus sextile or trine to Mercury* gives an original, independent and eccentric mind impatient of the fetters of fashion, tradition and convention. Such a person is strenuous in his efforts to hew a path for himself in complete liberty. Therefore this is the hall-mark of the pioneers in thought and invention, the sign of genius. Their ideas and ideals are exceedingly lofty, progressive and inspiring, in fact too much so in the opinion of the average man or woman who looks upon their actions as vagaries, the outcome of a diseased mind. Nevertheless they have plenty of friends on account of their kindly and sympathetic nature. These aspects are good for a literary or scientific pursuit, also for invention, particularly along lines which have to do with air or electricity.

♅ ☌ P ☿ *Uranus conjunction or parallel Mercury.* If Mercury is otherwise afflicted the conjunction and parallel are to be judged as bad aspects and read accordingly, but if Mercury is otherwise well placed and aspected the delineation given for the sextile and trine will apply.

♅ □ ☍ ☿ *Uranus square or opposition to Mercury* is the hall-mark of the true crank or anarchist who has extreme ideas in regard to tearing down the social structure and making reforms. People with these configurations are given to ranting and raving in public and their language is usually as cruel as the measures they advocate. Whatever ability they possess is usually turned to erratic purposes and they are often forced to make sudden changes on that account.

♆ ☌ P ✱ △ ☿ *Neptune conjunction, parallel, sextile or trine to Mercury* gives a mind peculiarly adapted to the occult art, particularly if the conjunction occurs in the Third or Ninth House or the trines are from the watery signs Cancer and Pisces. Such people usually succeed in occult science and often develop a supernormal faculty. They are particularly good as magnetic healers.

♆ □ ☍ ☿ *Neptune square or opposition to Mercury* gives a chaotic mind, liability to lack of memory, indolence and a disposition to dream the time away. There is a restless desire for fame and an inability to fit in anywhere. Such people are liable to fraud, deception and slander, also to commit suicide.

CHAPTER XI.

THE MOON, THE PLANET OF FECUNDATION.

FROM the Bible we learn that Jehovah made man in His image. We are also told that *angels* visited Sarah and proclaimed the birth of Isaac. They also foretold the birth of Samson and Samuel and the *angel* (not archangel) Gabriel came to Mary of Bethlehem to announce the coming birth of Jesus. According to occult science Jehovah and His angels are the guardians of the seed atoms, the basic factors in fertilization. The activities of the angels are directed to the maintenance of plant, animal and human life upon our earth. To this end their forces are focused by the wandering Moon through the twelve signs of the zodiac; they impinge upon the foetus in a creative manner during the period of gestation from the time of conception to birth.

Thus as the Moon measures the tides of the earth so also does she measure the soul's passage from the shores of eternity through the waters of the womb to the world of time. According to astrology Cancer is the home of the Moon. The ancient Egyptians pictured this sign as a scarab or beetle which was their emblem of the soul and they called Cancer *the sphere of the soul,* for it is said that through this moist watery sign fertilized by the lunar ray the seed atoms are projected into the womb of the prospective parent who is thus prepared for the period of gestation; and occult science adds to this that the seed atoms of the animal kingdom, which is still mindless and therefore not amenable to lunar influences in that direction, are projected through the watery martial sign *Scorpio* while the seed atoms of the inert plants are poured in through the Jupiterian sign Pisces just before the Sun enters Aries at the vernal equinox to awaken the plant seeds sleeping in Mother Earth, which have been fertilized by Pisces. Thus the human family has the longest period of gestation, the animal a somewhat shorter one and the plant the shortest of all.

The Moon also measures the period of postnatal growth so that the period of *childhood*, measured by the change of teeth is complete at about seven years of age when the Moon is *square* to her place at birth. The period of *puberty* is ushered in at about fourteen years of age when the Moon is in *opposition* to her place at birth and is marked by the change of voice in the boy and the commencement of the menses in the girl. At twenty-one years of age the Moon by progression has traveled three quarters of the circle of the horoscope from its place at birth. This finishes the period of incubation and the human being is considered to be full-grown, capable of exercising a franchise and taking care of his own affairs. Thus the distance traveled by the New Moon during the prenatal period of gestation in the mother's womb and the distance traveled by the progressed Moon during the twenty-one years of post-natal development in the womb of Mother Nature correspond exactly.

The Moon, like Mercury, has no basic nature of its own but serves to focus the qualities of the signs and other planets upon the human mind. She governs the tidal air in the lungs and the colorless lymph in the body, also the digestive activity and the sympathetic nervous system which automatically takes care of the process of digestion. She also governs the cerebellum, the mammae, the feminine functions and parturition as already explained.

People who are strongly under the influence of the lunar rays are of an easy-going, dreamy, indolent nature, adepts as architects of air castles which never materialize or assume concrete shape. They are very sociable and generally easy to get along with. They succeed best as cooks, housekeepers or in some domestic occupation or in one which has to do with liquids or a seafaring life.

The Moon being female indicates the marriage partner for a man so that in a man's horoscope affliction of the Moon would not be so apt to cause trouble in health as in married life and the horoscopes of the two sexes should therefore be read differently with respect to the Sun and Moon. If Saturn afflicts the Moon in a woman's horoscope it will affect her health, but the same aspect occurring in a man's horoscope will cause him trouble in married life. If the Sun is afflicted in a man's horoscope it will affect his health but in a woman's horoscope it would indicate trouble with her husband. At the same time however it should not be forgotten that both the Sun and Moon are vital factors in the health of both sexes but one sex is more affected by the Sun, the other by the Moon.

The Moon is the great time-marker of the universe. Without her our lives would be barren of events for although the Sun and the planets by their travel through the signs and houses indicate the years when certain tendencies shown in the horoscope may culminate in action, it invariably requires an aspect of the Moon to fertilize the aspect and make it bloom into physical manifestation. The Sun and the planets may therefore be likened to the hour-hand on the clock of destiny which shows the *year* when each phase of our destiny is ripe for the harvest and the Moon may be likened to the minute-hand which shows the *month* when the influences are due to culminate into action. In order to become fully conversant with the influences of the Moon we would advise students to read carefully the article on eclipses and new moon in our Simplified Scientific Astrology.

THE MOON IN THE TWELVE HOUSES.

☽ 1 *The Moon in the First House.* When the Moon is rising in the First House at birth and particularly in a common or cardinal sign she gives the person then born a very restless nature; he is constantly endeavoring to change his position.

environment and occupation, is ensouled by an insatiable wanderlust and always ready to roam. When the Moon is rising in a fixed sign there is a little more stability to the nature but even then the person will probably spend at least part of his time in a roving existence. People with the Moon in the First House are usually sensitives, especially if the Moon is in the psychic signs Cancer or Pisces. They have a very vivid imagination and are quite intuitive. This position of the Moon has a powerful influence upon health especially in a woman's horoscope and the aspects which the Moon receives determine the strength of the constitution. It is also a sign of success in such occupations as bring the person in close touch with the public.

☽ 2 *The Moon in the Second House* signifies fluctuating finances unless fortified by good aspects from Jupiter, the planet of opulence, or Venus the planet of attraction. Good aspects from the Sun make matters more settled in that respect.

☽ 3 *The Moon in the Third House* makes the mind extremely fertile in imagination with a strong liking for mental occupations, especially such as do not require continuity but are subject to constant change, like editing and reporting on newspapers where one must be on the alert for news and roam hither and thither for the purpose of gathering it. These people love the lime-light of publicity and if the Moon is strengthened by good aspects to Mercury they may reach a position of prominence.

☽ 4 *The Moon in the Fourth House* well-aspected indicates fortunate home conditions, especially toward the close of life but if the Moon is afflicted we may judge the reverse. This position also gives a tendency toward psychic experiences especially if the Moon is in its own sign Cancer or in Pisces, another watery sign. It also shows many changes of residence which will be fortunate or otherwise according to the other aspects of the Moon.

☽ 5 *The Moon in the Fifth House* in cardinal or common signs indicates a person of very changeable affections, fond of pleasure and gambling. It is a sign of a fruitful marriage particularly when in Scorpio. Even in a barren sign like Leo the Moon will give children when she is placed in the Fifth House. This question however, should always be judged from both horoscopes of the prospective parents, for should one be entirely barren, the Moon in the Fifth House in Leo or Virgo in the other horoscope, would not be sufficient help to mend the matter.

☽ 6 *The Moon in the Sixth House* is a poor position particularly in a woman's horoscope and any person with the Moon in that position will be better in a subordinate position employed by someone else than in a business venture of his own. Should he be placed in the position of employer he will find it difficult to keep servants or employees. They will change constantly.

☽ 7 *The Moon in the Seventh House* if well-aspected is fortunate for success in marriage, partnership and all dealings with the public for it makes the person popular. But if seriously afflicted it indicates a fickle, changeable marriage partner, loss through litigation, partnership and the general public which will then hold the person in disfavor.

☽ 8 *The Moon in the Eighth House* gives gain by marriage and legacy if it is well-aspected and it also increases the number of children though there is a chance that some of them may die. But if the Moon is afflicted the financial fortunes will change for the worse after marriage and if legacies do come they will bring lawsuits with them whereby the person will lose.

☽ 9 *The Moon in the Ninth House* when well-aspected gives a clean clear mind of a serious, religious, legal or philosophic turn according to the nature of the aspect. The person will travel far with both pleasure and profit for himself and sometime he will come into the lime-light of publicity. This position also gives a tendency to dreams and visions especially if the Moon is aspected by Neptune. If the Moon is afflicted the person will be too impulsive and jump to conclusions which are to his detriment. If he undertakes to travel he is liable to meet much trouble in consequence. He is also apt to make an ill-considered change in religion and be subjected to much censure on that account.

☽ 10 *The Moon in the Tenth House* is a sign of good fortune, popularity and prosperity if well-aspected. It brings the person prominently before the public and ensures favor especially from women, also the accumulation of property. It makes the mind deep and diplomatic, curious and inquisitive. When the Moon is afflicted the person is liable to incur hostility on the part of the public and reversals of fortune. Sometimes he becomes involved in public scandal and subject to censure.

☽ 11 *The Moon in the Eleventh House* if well-aspected gives many friends especially among women, but if she is afflicted those who come to the person under the guise of friendship do so in the hope that he may be of benefit to them.

☽ 12 *The Moon in the Twelfth House* if well-aspected gives success in such work as is performed in seclusion away from the public gaze, in prisons, hospitals or charitable institutions. There is also a liability to become involved in clandestine love-affairs but if the Moon is well-aspected the person will be able to keep this a secret. If the Moon is afflicted there is danger of secret enemies, trouble and persecution.

THE MOON IN THE TWELVE SIGNS

☽ ♈ *The Moon in Aries* gives a very independent type of mind which aims to hew out its own path in life whether right or wrong and is extremely quick to resent any interference from others. The person is ambitious and aggressive but lacks forethought, so that he is liable to meet with numerous setbacks. However, this position gives a dauntless courage and such people are not easily defeated. When they have failed in one direction they immediately try another venture and in the end their very persistence usually brings them into prominence in their line and gives them ultimate success, unless the Moon is afflicted; then they are prone to take up one occupation after another without giving themselves time to try honestly to make a success of any one.

☽ ♉ *The Moon in Taurus.* This is the Moon's exaltation sign and her effect is therefore very powerful for good if she is free from affliction and well-aspected. Then the fixed nature of Taurus tones down the changeability of the Moon which also blends with the Venus ray. Hence it makes the disposition gentle, self-reliant and determined. It gives perseverance, forethought and kindness, therefore the person attracts all the good things of life, health and wealth, friends and family, houses and lands with the ability to enjoy all these things for it makes him fond of pleasure, sociable and hospitable, a lover of art and music and all other things which make for the enjoyment of life.

☽ ♊ *The Moon in Gemini* gives a wide-awake intellect, fond of literature and science, resourceful and able to cope with emergencies, broad, liberal and alert for progressive ideas which are taken up with avidity. Hence such people are much attracted to literary occupations, particularly in the newspaper field where they may flit from one subject to another as required by their extremely restless mind. This position also gives an inordinate love of traveling, and desire for positions where one meets many people. Hence it favors such occupations as those of traveling salesmen, canvassers and the like.

☽ ♋ *The Moon in Cancer* gives a disposition which is kind, sociable and sympathetic, but indolent and averse to effort whether physical, moral or mental. These people love to drift with the tide and only bestir themselves when under the whiplash of necessity. They are often sensitive to psychic conditions, especially if the Moon is aspected by Neptune or Uranus and the nature of the aspect determines whether the influence is favorable or unfavorable. This position also gives a love of home and the comforts to be obtained there. It promotes the digestion and consequently the health if the Moon is well-aspected. If afflicted it has a tendency to give digestive troubles.

☽ ♌ *The Moon in Leo* has an illuminating influence on the mind. It gives a strong, self-reliant and aggressive disposition with ability for organization; therefore people with the Moon in this position usually attain to leadership in their immediate circle. They are honorable in financial and social matters, fair and magnanimous in their dealings with others, and very popular with other people.

☽ ♍ *The Moon in Virgo* increases the mental qualities if she is well-aspected; she gives a retentive memory, a love of study along scientific or occult lines and an ambition to excel. Chemistry is the favorite of these people among the sciences and they excel as dietitians. They are rather reserved and of quiet demeanor, disliking flattery or ostentation. Unless they devote themselves to dietetics they are more successful as the servants or employees of others than in business for themselves.

☽ ♎ *The Moon in Libra* is a fortunate position for the acquisition of friends and public popularity for it makes the person kind, sympathetic and agreeable, optimistic and fond of social pleasures. This position also gives good reasoning powers and the ability to form a correct judgment, love of art and music, sometimes considerable ability as a performer if assisted by other aspects.

☽ ♏ *The Moon in Scorpio* gives a courageous independent and energetic disposition. The person who has this configuration will not tolerate interference with his plans or submit to imposition. He is often very abrupt in his manners and blunt in speech, quick-tempered and not to be coerced by threats, but singularly amenable to kindness. He has a strong and stubborn will and determination to carry out whatever he undertakes. This position also gives a considerable attraction toward the occult sciences but if afflicted may lead to excess in gratification of the senses, trouble with women or difficulties in parturition.

☽ ♐ *The Moon in Sagittarius* gives an alert and active personality, a love of walking, riding or any other form of physical exercise, a roving disposition and love of travel in foreign countries, a fondness of animals, especially horses and dogs and an inclination for the study of religion, law, philosophy or the science of occultism. These people are very optimistic, good humored, jovial, and ideal companions unless the Moon is afflicted, then her position in Sagittarius is conducive to indolence and self-indulgence.

☽ ♑ *The Moon in Capricorn,* if well-aspected, gives abundance of help from people who are higher in the social scale so that whatever success there may be will come through others, the person being too timid to push himself forward, besides being of a melancholy turn of mind which makes him exceedingly sensitive to real or fancied slights. If the Moon is afflicted it gives a liability to slander whether that is merited or not. This position also has a detrimental effect upon the digestion. People with the Moon in this position often have an insane fear of coming to want and therefore they become avaricious and miserly, denying themselves all comforts at the present time that they may have something for a rainy day. They have very little feeling for themselves and none at all for others.

☽ ♒ *The Moon in Aquarius* if well-aspected gives the person a very vivid imagination and the power of calling images up before the mind's eye in such a manner that they seem almost tangible; besides these people are not dependent upon the faculty of reason, for their intuition is also exceedingly well-developed. In disposition they are sociable, kindly and courteous with the result that they attract many friends and are very popular in their environment, and they are helped by their friends according to the aspects of the Moon. On the other hand if the Moon is afflicted this position shows one of an exceedingly erratic mind.

☽ ♓ *The Moon in Pisces* gives a receptive mind and a fertile imagination with a disposition to indolence and self-pity, vacillation and faint-heartedness, makes one fond of dreaming rather than acting, therefore sorrow, trouble and self-undoing beset the path in life. This position not infrequently leads to mediumship, especially if Neptune is in adverse aspect, for these people are peculiarly sensitive to the flattery of spirit-controls and love anything that will stir their emotions. They are also very wordy in their expressions. If a good aspect from Venus and Mercury enables them to take up music they play with extraordinary inspiration and feeling. If the Moon is afflicted in Pisces love-affairs are apt to bring the person into trouble. If Pisces is in the Twelfth House and the Moon there at birth this will give a liability on the part of the parents to drink and thus to neglect their children who may then become the wards of charitable institutions until they reach maturity.

Aspects of the Moon to the Other Planets

☉P ☌ ☽ *The Sun parallel to or conjunction with the Moon.* No matter in what sign or house the conjunction of the Lights occurs the person will be so strongly marked with the characteristics of that sign that, lacking knowledge of his true ascendant, even the most competent astrologer is likely to be misled and judge him to be born with the sign rising in which the conjunction took place, and whatever matters are ruled by the house in which the conjunction occurs will play a very important part in the life. In the First he is an out and out egotist with very little love for others save in so far as they serve his ends, in the Seventh his world pivots on the mate, in the Tenth House or sign he will sacrifice all other considerations to rise in public life; in the Twelfth House or sign the conjunction will give a strong tendency to intemperance which will bring trouble in the life; in the Third and Ninth Houses it will brighten the mind and induce travel from which he will benefit; in the Second House it will bring wealth, especially if in good aspect with Jupiter. If the conjunction of the Sun and Moon is closer than three degrees it has a tendency to deplete the vitality and if it is also a solar eclipse and the child survives, this will be particularly noticeable all through life. People who have such close conjunctions or eclipses become listless, dispirited and out of sorts every time there is a new Moon. The conjunction or eclipse does not seem to interfere with the good effects in other departments of life.

☉ ✱ △ ☽ *The Sun sextile or trine to the Moon.* The good aspects of the Sun and Moon make for general success in life, health, fair financial fortunes, good home conditions with faithful friends and esteem in the community; they favor a rise in life because of the person's innate ability, which either gains for him the recognition of people in a position to help him rise, or impels him to carve his own way.

☉ □ ☍ ☽ *The Sun square or opposition to the Moon* makes the person vacillating and unsettled in disposition, changeable and unable to pursue a settled course in life, rash to plunge into untried ventures but lacking the persistence or continuity of purpose to carry anything to a successful conclusion. For that reason such people become failures in life; their dealings with women and people higher in the social scale such as employers, the authorities, judges, etc., are especially unsuccessful; they always have difficulty in obtaining proper employment and in keeping their positions when obtained, for they are hyper-sensitive and ready to take offense, with or without provocation. These configurations also affect the health; the body is liable to colds and recuperation is slow when sickness has overtaken the person.

♀ P ☌ ✶ △ ☽ *Venus parallel, conjunction, sextile or trine to the Moon.* The Moon is significator of marriage for a man and therefore the good aspects between Venus, the planet of love, and the Moon are good indications of a happy marriage when they occur in a man's horoscope. But in a woman's horoscope these aspects operate upon the health, for the Moon is the planet of fecundity and has rule over the female functions in particular, which are so large a factor in the woman's health, and this is much strengthened by them. These aspects give oratorical ability with a fruitful imagination, a love of pleasure, music and art. They give an engaging personality, very attractive to the opposite sex because kindly, affectionate and sympathetic, and they tend to general success in life; though the finances may be fluctuating the person usually has sufficient for the day and the way.

♀ □ ☍ ☽ *Venus square or opposition to the Moon* is an indication of trouble in marriage for a man, because the wife described by an afflicted Venus will be slovenly and of dissolute habits which will destroy domestic happiness. In a woman's horoscope it indicates a disturbance of the female functions and also gives a tendency to digestive troubles and poor circulation when in the horoscope of either sex. These aspects also give a liability to slander and public scandal as the person so afflicted is fickle and inconstant in his affections, of a sensual nature which loves to flit from flower to flower regardless of the sorrows caused by playing with the hearts of others.

☿ P ☌ ✱ △ ☽ *Mercury parallel, conjunction, sextile or trine to the Moon* gives a receptive mind and a retentive memory, two very rare qualities and therefore these aspects, particularly the sextile and trine are good indications of success in life, especially in one of the mercurial occupations, literary, clerical or traveling. People with these configurations are usually very verbose, particularly if the conjunction or trine occurs in airy signs or a sign of voice, for then the power of expression reaches a superlative degree and such people become able linguists and elocutionists; but unless there is some steadying influence people with aspects of Mercury and the Moon are not reliable because of their tendency to change their minds repeatedly in the most unexpected manner. They are inclined to look upon the bright side of life and are fond of pleasure, particularly travel.

☿ □ ☍ ☽ *Mercury square or opposition to the Moon* gives a poor memory and lack of mental stability with a tendency to indecision and worry, liability to brain storms and hysterics. These characteristics make the person unpopular and as the saying is "unlucky."

♄ ✱ △ ☽ *Saturn sextile or trine to the Moon* imparts all the best saturnine qualities to the mind and makes the person self-reliant, serious, sober and systematic, careful and thrifty in business affairs and gives success in life through tactful and diplomatic dealings with others. Such people are eminently responsible and trustworthy in all matters of honor and justice and gain great esteem in the community on that account. Their patience and persistence are inexhaustible.

♄ P ☌ ☽ *Saturn parallel to or conjunction with the Moon* is not always to be classed as a bad aspect so far as the mental qualities go for in any case it deepens the mind and gives greater power of concentration. If Saturn is strong by sign, in Libra or Capricorn, and the Moon is otherwise well-aspected, this position will also impart the virtues of Saturn though under all conditions it makes the mind gloomy and the person is subject to periodical spells of melancholy; but if Saturn is weak by sign, especially if he is in Aries and if the Moon is otherwise afflicted then his conjunction is to be judged and read the same as the square and opposition.

The effect of the conjunction also depends upon the department of life we are considering: for instance, as already said, the conjunction of the Moon and Saturn is good for concentration of the mind, but bad for the digestion, particularly in a woman's horoscope; it has also the tendency to obstruct the menses with all that that implies, and in a man's horoscope it indicates the death of the marriage partner. Similar distinctions should be made when reading the conjunctions of the other so-called malefics.

♄ □ ☍ ☽ *Saturn square or opposition to the Moon* is one of the signatures of sorrow in life for it makes the mind melancholy and full of worries so that the person is constantly carrying an atmosphere of gloom with him, and as thoughts are things this attitude of mind brings about delays and disappointments in every department of life. Such a person will experience difficulties from people and things signified by Saturn, probably parents, and if he has money he may lose it and have difficulty in getting more; thus he may be in poverty all his life. He will make more enemies than friends and become subject to slander and scandal, but the disfavor he meets is undoubtedly merited for these aspects make the mind bitter and selfish; such people are unscrupulous, avaricious and entirely unfeeling with respect to others, hence they are under the whiplash of Saturn that the sorrow and troubles which they themselves are constantly feeling may make them more mellow. If the aspect is six, five or even four degrees from being exact and if Saturn is in the exaltation sign Libra these aspects are not quite so evil in the latter part of life. They may then imply that the person has learned his lesson and as a consequence he may find himself in easier circumstances. The adverse aspects of Saturn to the Moon are very bad for the health, particularly in a woman's horoscope. There they indicate obstructions of the female functions. In the man's horoscope they either deny marriage or indicate the death of the marriage partner and their general tendency is to obstruct everything connected with the houses and signs wherein they are placed in the horoscope.

♃ P ☌ ⚹ △ ☽ *Jupiter parallel, conjunction, sextile or trine to the Moon* gives an optimistic, noble and generous disposition. The open-hearted honesty, fairness and friendliness of such people make them universally popular. These aspects strengthen both the reasoning faculties and constitution; they give a strong mind in a strong body and hence a powerful personal magnetism which may be used to great advantage in healing the sick. They have lofty ideals and a fruitful imagination with the power of acquiring wealth which will grow greater if used in philanthropic enterprises of which these people are prone to dream. These are some of the best aspects in the gamut and make for general success in life both physically and spiritually.

♃□☍☽ *Jupiter square or opposition to the Moon* impairs the reasoning faculties and brings the person trouble through litigation, lack of forethought and indecision or dishonesty. People with these aspects are too fond of ostentation and display, extravagant beyond their means and resources, prone to take desperate chances in gambling or speculation to rehabilitate their fortunes and doomed to loss, slander and sometimes bankruptcy on that account.

These aspects are also bad for health, in a woman's horoscope especially, indicating digestive and liver troubles.

♂✱△☽ *Mars sextile or trine to the Moon* gives a wonderful vitality and a strong physique so that the person is able to overcome almost any tendencies to ill-health, all of which are overruled by these aspects. The power of endurance is increased to a maximum and the person can survive hardships to which people ordinarily succumb. They give a resolute, courageous, energetic and ambitious mind of a resourceful and eminently constructive turn, and they make the person quick but not precipitate in his decisions. Thus he gains the confidence and esteem of others and earns considerable money but the nature is extremely free and generous so that money does not stay by these people. They spend it almost as fast as they get it.

♂ ☌ P ☽ *Mars conjunction or parallel to the Moon* may be either good or bad according to the sex of the person and the department of life we are considering. It strengthens the health and the vitality, particularly in the horoscope of a woman. In the horoscope of a man it would indicate a robust marriage partner of a domineering nature. With respect to the mind it would make the person very impulsive, particularly if placed in one of the common signs or in the Third or Ninth Houses. It also gives a very bad temper but not so bad as the square or opposition. If Mars is in conjunction or parallel to the Moon in Scorpio there is an abnormal sexual desire which will not be denied particularly if Venus is there also. It makes the nature very restless and unsettled for it is like mixing fire and water. In watery signs it inclines to drink.

♂ □ ☍ ☽ *Mars square or opposition to the Moon* gives a very quick temper with a tendency to hasty or impulsive expression and acts that may cause the person a great deal of sorrow and trouble. These people resent rules or regulations or any other measures that tend to curb their desires or the gratification of their appetites in whatever direction, but if they are in authority they are very domineering and exacting in their demands for instant obedience upon the part of others, nor do they hesitate to use whatever physical force may be necessary to compel obedience if they think they can do so without too great danger to themselves. Sometimes they will even take desperate chances to satisfy their spite and having an improperly balanced mind they are foolhardy in their venturesomeness so that upon occasion they will attempt to do things which no one with a sane mind would try. On account of the foregoing characteristics such people make many enemies and cause a great deal of suffering to others, particularly among members of their immediate family who cannot very well get away from them. If these aspects occur in watery signs, particularly with Mars or the Moon in Pisces the person is also an inveterate drunkard. From the standpoint of health they give a tendency to fever and accidents, trouble with the generative organs and operations which are usually unnecessary. These people are exceedingly prodigal with their money and are habitual prevaricators.

♅ ∗ △ ☽ *Uranus sextile or trine to the Moon* gives great originality and independence to the mind, which is quick, intuitive and very vivid in its imagination; hence the person has inventive ability and is attracted to the occult arts and endowed with hypnotic or magnetic powers, also the intuitional ability to study and practise astrology. If the life is devoted to electricity as a vocation the person will make a success of it. These aspects also give a peculiar fascination for the opposite sex and are likely to lead to a clandestine love affair or an unconventional union.

♅ ☌ P ☽ *Uranus conjunction or parallel to the Moon* gives similar mental and psychic tendencies and also the same liability to irregular love-affairs as the good aspects but these tendencies are not so pronounced. A secret love-affair generated under the conjunction of Uranus and the Moon may have distinctly disastrous results similar to those mentioned under the bad aspects. If the conjunction occurs in Cancer it tends to nervous indigestion; in Leo it inclines to palpitation of the heart, interferes with the rhythm of the heart-beat and gives a spasmodic action which will probably prove fatal when it has run its course. In Scorpio it inclines to perverted practices; in Sagittarius the reflex action would be felt in the lungs and similarly with the other signs.

♅ □ ☍ ☽ *Uranus square or opposition to the Moon* makes the person erratic and touchy to a degree, a walking powder magazine ready to explode at any moment, overbearing, conceited, intolerant and shunned by all who can possibly get out of his way. If such people are employers nobody can work for them and if they are employees nobody will have them. They never remain very long in any place, but are either discharged or give up their position on the slightest provocation. People with these aspects are attracted to the occult arts but they never make a success at them because of their erratic mentality. Like the other aspects of Uranus and the Moon the square or opposition also indicates a clandestine attachment either on the part of the person or the marriage partner. If it occurs in the Seventh House of a man's horoscope it proves the wife untrue so that public scandal and divorce will eventually ensue. The bad aspects of the Sun and Uranus give similar indications in the horoscope of a woman.

♆ ✶ △ ☽ *Neptune sextile or trine to the Moon* increases the faculty of imagination to a superlative degree, especially if either of the planets is in the Ninth House. Then it favors prophetic dreams and visions which bring the person in contact with the invisible worlds. It indicates ability in the occult arts and success in their practice for it makes the nature exceedingly inspirational and it also gives a kind and sympathetic disposition. The spiritual qualities mentioned may not be apparent even to the person himself but then they are latent and capable of development. It is also safe to say that at some time or other during the life people with these aspects will come in contact with and be very much attracted to the occult whether the qualities of the soul are subsequently developed or not.

♆ ☌ P ☽ *Neptune conjunction or parallel Moon* indicates the same strong psychic faculties as the good aspects, particularly if Neptune is placed in the psychic signs Cancer or Pisces. Those who were born with the good configurations of Neptune during the fourteen years when it was in the airy scientific sign Gemini are now conquering the air and perfecting scientific inventions which will make us marvel, but the children who have been born under favorable configurations during the fourteen years Neptune has been going through the psychic sign Cancer are now growing up around us as a band of mystics and when they have reached mature years they will astonish us with their spiritual insight and power. Among other things they will develop the soul of music.

♆ □ ☍ ☽ *Neptune square or opposition to the Moon* is also an indication of soul qualities similar to those of the good aspects, but under the former configurations the person will be of a negative nature and is apt to become the prey of spirit-controls and subjected to mediumship, therefore he should not attend seances.

CHAPTER XII.

SATURN, THE PLANET OF SORROW

Keynote: Obstruction

A FRUITFUL method of acquiring knowledge is by comparison of similars and contrasts of opposites; thus lights and sidelights are brought out, which otherwise may escape attention.

Applying this method to the Sun and Saturn, we remember that the keyword of the Sun is "Life," and at the vernal equinox when the Sun is in Aries, the sign of its exaltation, we may readily note the powerful effect of the crestwave of vital fluid then poured over the earth. Nature is vibrant with life, which races through the forms of all kingdoms and endues them with such abundance of vitality that they are compelled to generate in order to take care of the overflow. Life manifests as motion; but the keynote of Saturn is Obstruction, therefore that is the planet of decrepitude and decay, and consequently when the Sun is in Libra, the sign of Saturn's exaltation, at the fall equinox, Nature is tired and ready for its wintry sleep. The human frame also is energized by the solar life contained in our food, which enters our system through the head and throat, governed by the exaltation signs of the Builders, the Sun and Moon, and is eliminated by the activity of the liver and kidneys ruled by Saturn and his exaltation sign, Libra.

In youth, when the Sun forces surge through the frame, assimilation and excretion balance, but as time goes on, "Chronos" or Saturn accumulates obstructions in the organs of excretion, and elimination is gradually restricted, the avenues of life are dammed up, and decrepitude and decay turn the scales of life (Libra) towards the realm of death.

Similarly in other departments of life; where the Sun makes the social favorite, by imbuing him with optimism and a bright sunny smile, Saturn makes recluses and sours existence with frowns and pessimism; where the Sun furthers our worldly affairs and makes things run smoothly, Saturn causes provoking delays of the most inexplicable nature; all the world seems to conspire to frustrate our plans.

In the Kingdom of God all things are balanced to produce the highest ultimate good to all, and so the influence of Saturn is used to offset the exuberant life of Mars. The intrinsic nature of Saturn is *obstruction;* he is slow and persistent as Mars is impulsive and quick to change; he takes no chances, but looks before he leaps, and his cold, calculating reason misses no flaws in any scheme.

In the horoscope of a young soul Mars is dominant and the man grows along physical lines much as animals do under the law of the survival of the fittest, but gradually the thumbscrews of Saturn are put on, squares and oppositions bring sorrow and suffering; Saturn is placed above Mars in the horoscope, to frustrate and check him, till it seems as if every effort were futile because of the Saturnian obstruction.

Elijah could not hear the voice of guidance in the fire, the storm nor the earthquake, but when the tumult was over he heard "the still small voice" to cheer him; and likewise with us, while we yield to the unchecked Mars impulses our lives are too turbulent to admit of communion with the Higher Self, but when the sorrows of Saturn have chastened the unruly Mars spirit, when the night seems darkest, as in Elijah's cave, then we also may hear the voice that shall speak peace after the storm.

The leash of Saturn is not pleasant; we sometimes chafe, fret and fume while being thus held in leash, but meanwhile we ripen and are more fitted, when the obstruction is removed, to have or use that which Saturn delayed, for as we develop physical muscle by overcoming physical obstacles, so we cultivate soul power by the resistance spiritually engendered by Saturn. The teaching which he gives may be summed up in the motto: "Patient persistence in well doing."

Most of us when considering Saturn in the horoscope are inclined to look upon him as evil on account of the afflictions he brings, but that is only a one-sided view, for there is nothing evil in God's Kingdom. What appears so is merely good in the making. When we remember that the destiny shown by our horoscope is of our own making in past existences then we shall understand that Saturn only marks the weak spots in our horoscope, where we are vulnerable and liable to go wrong. When the weak points have been brought out through temptation, *and we have yielded,* the punishment follows automatically as a natural and logical sequence, for every wrong act carries in itself the seed of the punishment which brings home to our consciousness the mistakes we have made. We must hold clearly before our mind's eye that though the planets incline to a certain line of action we, as evolving Egos, are supposed to discriminate between good and evil and choose only that which is good. If we fail in this respect and *yield* to the temptation the transgression merits a just recompense under the laws of nature and these are the things signified by Saturn. *We are not punished because we are tempted but we are punished because we yielded.* Supposing for instance that Saturn is in Cancer, then it is plain that in the past we have yielded to an inordinate desire for food, that in consequence our digestive organs have become impaired and that if we do not learn frugality and discrimination in the choice of our food we shall be punished by digestive disorders. We will then be tempted to indulge in dainties and perhaps we will have an aversion for the simple foods which are best for us. The temptation, however, will cause no trouble to the stomach unless we yield and satisfy our appetite. Then the food, and not an avenging Deity, automatically punishes us until we learn to curb our appetite. Similarly in other departments of life, if Saturn is on the Ascendant. or in the Third or Ninth Houses and adversely aspected to Mercury or the Moon it causes us to brood over our troubles ana fills our lives with gloom. It gives an obstruction there to warn us that we should be more sociable and not turn our faces away from the sunshine of life. God is at the helm of the universe, His ministers are continually working with us for good, there is really no reason for blues and if we cannot see it today Saturn is going to tighten his grip tomorrow and crush harder and harder until with the sheer courage of desperation we burst his bonds and jump out into the joy and sunshine of life.

If it were not for the chastening, subduing influence of Saturn we should be liable to run amuck and burn out the lamp of life quickly in the exuberance of spirits. Saturn is well symbolized as Father Time with his hour-glass and scythe. He does not permit us to leave the school of life until the time has been run and the course is finished. Furthermore he gives to humanity many of its noblest qualities. When he lays a restraining hand upon the flighty Moon or Mercury, the swift "messenger of the gods," he deepens the mind and makes it more serious and better able to concentrate upon the problems of life. He makes the mind resourceful and better able to cope with the difficulties of our existence. Tact and diplomacy, method and system, patience and perseverance, honor and chastity, industry and mechanical ability, justice and fair-mindedness all come from Saturn when he is well-aspected and it is only when we transgress the principles for which he stands that under the influences generated by his adverse aspects he punishes us until he has brought us to our knees to pray to our Father in Heaven for forgiveness and strength to overcome our lower nature.

Saturn in the Twelve Houses

♄1 *Saturn in the First House* and well-aspected is a fortunate sign for no matter how a person may be handicapped in the start of life the ultimate success is assured through the patience, persistence, self-control and restraint of the person through a well-placed Saturn. Such people have a wonderful capacity for work. They seem never to tire and never to give up no matter what the obstacles. They have infinite confidence in themselves and their ability to accomplish that which they undertake and therefore they eventually win. But when Saturn is weak and afflicted in the First House it makes the person timid and averse to undertake responsibility; subtile, secretive, and distrustful of other people; of a gloomy disposition and inclined to seek isolation. Such people are usually shunned by others and doomed to sorrow, disappointment, delay and general trouble through life. This is also a bad sign for health, particularly in the earlier years. Bruises to the head, colds, and if Scorpio is rising, constipation; in Leo poor circulation, in Cancer poor digestion, in Libra obstruction of the kidneys, renal calculi and other urinary difficulties and so on with the other signs.

♄2 *Saturn in the Second House* when well-aspected and particularly in its exaltation sign Libra, brings money by inheritance and ability to increase it by present economy, careful, conservative investments and similar methods. Some of the very wealthiest of the world's financiers have had Saturn in this position. They obtain the money wherewith to start from ancestors indicated by Saturn and from the saturnine ray in this house they derive the business acumen and far-sighted methods that enable them not only to hold their own as so many do whose wealth comes through Saturn but also to increase the inherited estate. If Saturn is weak or afflicted, however, the life is sure to be passed in poverty.

♄3 *Saturn in the Third House* when well-aspected gives a serious, sober and thoughtful mind, capable of concentration and well able to grapple with the most profound sciences and other serious subjects in life. It gives tact, diplomacy, justice, honesty and all the other saturnine virtues of the mind.

When Saturn is afflicted in the Third House

it indicates trouble with brethren, danger when traveling, delays and disappointments in obtaining an education. It also fills the mind with gloomy forebodings, worry and general despondency.

♄ 4 *Saturn in the Fourth House,* well-aspected, shows gain from inheritance, also success from investments and administration of houses and lands, agriculture or mining property under careful and economical management. The success grows better as life advances. When Saturn is afflicted in the Fourth House it signifies the early death of one of the parents, inharmony and trouble in the home, loss of property and consequent poverty. This position whether well or ill aspected makes the person a recluse in the latter years of life.

♄ 5 *Saturn in the Fifth House* when well-aspected by the Sun and Jupiter would be good for speculation in the things that are ruled by Saturn: houses, lands and mines. This position and its aspects would also give the person a chance of appointment to public office, especially in matters connected with education. If Saturn is afflicted in the Fifth House it indicates trouble, disappointment and delay in courtship, particularly during the earlier years, or else the affections are centered upon someone who is much older than the person whose horoscope is being judged. It decreases the number of children and indicates probable death of those who are born, also that they will bring a great deal of trouble to the person.

♄ 6 *Saturn in the Sixth House,* well-aspected, gives the person ability to handle employees and workmen in general in a most efficient manner, for though such a person is quiet and subdued he is at the same time firm and serious. He has a way about him which employees respect and which calls for instant obedience to his commands without causing the resentment called forth by a blustering, bellowing Mars.

When Saturn is afflicted in the Sixth House it means a great deal of sickness in the life and if in a weak sign like Virgo the person is in danger of becoming a chronic invalid, for once he is in the grip of sickness the recuperative powers are so poor it is almost impossible for him to recover. The nature of the principal illness will depend upon the sign that is on the cusp of the Sixth House or of the Twelfth, but usually with such people many complications set in after this. Also a person with an afflicted Saturn in the Sixth House finds it almost impossible to secure employment and it is evident that such a person has indeed a hard life, being unable to earn a living when able to be about.

♄ 7 *Saturn in the Seventh House* when well-aspected denotes a marriage partner endowed with the saturnine virtues, chastity and discretion, tact and discrimination, prudence and economy, which will be of great help to the person in building up his fortunes socially as well as financially; and this is a very fortunate position save for the fact that Saturn in the Seventh House, whether well-aspected or afflicted, indicates the early death of the partner. An afflicted Saturn in the Seventh House designates a glum, gloomy, cold and disagreeable companion who is always restraining and obstructing the person. "Don't" is the word most frequently on the tongue. It also gives trouble and loss through litigation and people with this aspect should never go to law or enter into partnerships for they will always be subject to treachery.

♄ 8 *Saturn in the Eighth House* when well-aspected or placed in either of its own signs, Capricorn or Libra, gains by marriage or inheritance with the ability to properly care for whatever wealth is acquired in that manner. It is also a sign of long life and death from natural causes, but if Saturn is afflicted in the Eighth House or weak by sign, especially in Aries or Cancer, the financial prospects of the person will be decidedly worse after marriage and chronic debility may be expected.

♄ 9 *Saturn in the Ninth House* when well-aspected gives a deep, serious and thoughtful mind with ability and inclination for the study of law, science and philosophy, physics or metaphysics. It is a splendid position for a president of a corporation or college, a judge or a divine. Such people always make their mark in the world, the scope being naturally dependent upon the nature of the aspects and the line of endeavor selected by the person.

When Saturn is afflicted in the Ninth House he makes a narrow-minded bigot, critical and sarcastic; he also gives liability to trouble and loss through law, danger on voyages and trouble in foreign lands.

♄ 10 *Saturn in the Tenth House* shows a strong self-reliant and ambitious spirit with the patience and perseverance which mark a person destined to rise in life. It is the signature of the self-made man, self-made by all the sterling saturnine virtues, tact, foresight, honesty and systematic application to business. Such people are destined to become captains of industry, presidents of banks or hold other high positions involving great responsibility.

When Saturn is afflicted or weak by sign he nevertheless gives the person who has him in the Tenth House, ability to rise, but when he does rise it is by underhanded trickery and questionable business methods which in the end bring exposure, downfall and dishonor. It is said that Napoleon had Saturn in the Tenth House.

♄ 11 *Saturn in the Eleventh House* when well-aspected gives friends among the aged and wealthy who will be of benefit to the person in helping him to realize his hopes, wishes and ambitions; but when Saturn is afflicted here he should beware of seeking friends older than himself, for they will always endeavor to make use of him for personal ends and desert him when he is no longer of use to them.

♄ 12 *Saturn in the Twelfth House* gives a secluded life in a position or occupation where the person does not come into contact with the general public. When well-aspected it is good for success in an official capacity in public institutions, asylums, hospitals or prisons. When afflicted there is danger of being bed-ridden for many years, imprisoned, or employed in obscure positions.

Saturn in the Twelve Signs.

♄ ♈ *Saturn in Aries* is weak and therefore unable to express his best qualities to their full and legitimate extent even if well-aspected. Nevertheless he gives a minor measure of poise, self-reliance, discretion and tact, industry, patience and perseverance. But when Saturn is afflicted in Aries the person is quickly angered and apt to hold spite, and is also of a jealous, malicious, and vindictive disposition.

♄ ♉ *Saturn in Taurus* when well-aspected makes a person slow of speech but what he says will have weight and be well worth hearing. It gives a quiet disposition, slow to decide, but stubborn in maintaining a position once taken. These people are close-mouthed, and may be trusted to keep their own and other people's secrets well. When Saturn is afflicted in Taurus, particularly by Mercury he always causes trouble with the speech and gives a quick temper, especially if Mars is also an afflicting planet. This position makes financial difficulties.

♄ ♊ *Saturn in Gemini* when well-aspected gives a deep, one-pointed, orderly and scientific mind, adaptable to circumstances and able to cope with all the exigencies of life. Love of mathematics is usually pronounced and when literature is taken up as a vocation the more serious branches devoted to industrial and mechanical subjects are preferred. When Saturn is afflicted in Gemini, it gives trouble through brothers and sisters, literature and law, danger on short journeys. An afflicted Saturn in Gemini also gives trouble with the lungs. Such people should therefore be particularly careful not to catch cold.

♄ ♋ *Saturn in Cancer* is always weak and his virtues therefore find it difficult to express themselves when he is in this position. Nevertheless he gives reliable judgment concerning houses lands, mines etc., and gains by investing in these things;when well aspected, he favors thrift, economy and solid comfort in the home with quiet, peaceful and comfortable conditions in the latter part of life. He makes the person frugal and gives a good control of the appetite. But when afflicted he indicates domestic infelicity, the person being held back in life by a gloomy kill-joy partner who is always restraining every ambitious thought. Trouble, sorrow and disappointment increase as the life advances and to this is added ill-health, for Saturn in Cancer indicates that the stomach is weak and the gums subject to pyorrhœa, hence there is inability to properly digest the food, so that unless such people have sufficient will to curb their appetites they become the victims of chronic indigestion. Saturn in Cancer also indicates a religious tendency and an inclination toward study of the deeper sciences.

♄ ♌ *Saturn in Leo* when well-aspected gives favor from people higher in the social scale and success in obtaining public appointments where the Saturnine virtues, tact, diplomacy, discretion and system, honor and executive ability are required. The constitution of these people is not overly strong but they may maintain perfect health by the conservation of energy as indicated by Saturn. When Saturn is afflicted in Leo however, they are cruel and quick-tempered, jealous, and do not scruple to stoop to underhanded methods to satisfy an ambition. This position also indicates heart trouble.

♄ ♍ *Saturn in Virgo* gives a studious, deep, scientific mind fond of studying the deeper problems of life. It indicates an innate ability to manage others. It gives a thrifty, economical and frugal nature, but when Saturn is afflicted in Virgo the mind usually centers upon disease and the person becomes a confirmed hypochondriac. These people are the best customers of the patent medicine vendors for most of their ills are usually imaginary. This position does however, carry with it a liability to intestinal diseases.

♄ ♎ *Saturn in Libra* is exalted and very strong and therefore his good aspects bring out all the fine saturnine qualities and on that account secure for the person public esteem and recognition. The marriage partner is chaste and pure as gold. This position also brings good health and long life, but when Saturn is afflicted in Libra the marriage partner is either treacherous or removed by an early death. If the person goes to law he is likely to lose, and become the object of public disfavor. He will also be subject to urinary troubles..

♄ ♏ *Saturn in Scorpio* when well-aspected gives a rare mechanical turn to the mind, a resourcefulness under the most difficult conditions, an indomitable courage and a patient persistence before which even the most difficult construction problems must give way. Hence such people make exceedingly able engineers and are invaluable in all pioneer undertakings; they blend the fire of Mars with the forethought of Saturn and are therefore invincible. They gain by legacy, economy and thrift and their financial fortunes are much improved after marriage. Good health and a long life are also indicated, but when Saturn is afflicted in Scorpio the marriage partner is poor, dull, egotistical and exacting and the person is liable to worry and ill-health; constipation and piles are the basic causes which then affect the nerves and the whole system.

♄ ♐ *Saturn in Sagittarius* when well-aspected gives a charitable and philanthropic disposition with a desire to elevate humanity by self-help under just laws and true religious impulse. It couples all the saturnine virtues with the benevolent Jupiterian spirit of aspiration so that such people always aim to work for the public good according to their ability and station in life. Therefore they are trusted, honored, respected and in much demand for positions where these qualities are of value, in social, industrial or religious circles. When Saturn is afflicted in Sagittarius he makes the person insincere, cynical and sarcastic, ambitious to fill positions of trust and honor but for selfish purposes, liable to become involved in law and lose thereby. This position also affects the lungs and the person should be very careful not to catch cold.

♄ ♑ *Saturn in Capricorn* when well-aspected is strong and therefore his virtues are also pronounced, with honesty and integrity as staunch as the Rock of Gibraltar and the determination to work toward the desired goal no matter how long it may take. Hence in spite of all handicaps and obstacles people with a well-aspected Saturn in Capricorn ultimately achieve a large measure of success and are generally esteemed by their contemporaries. But when Saturn is afflicted in Capricorn the mind is gloomy and the person sees life from a biased point of view. There is a general sense of dissatisfaction which sometimes develops into a diseased mind. These people are cunning, underhanded and not to be trusted.

♄ ♒ *Saturn in Aquarius* when well-aspected gives a humane outlook upon life, a sympathetic and friendly disposition, very distinct and deliberate speech and a seriousness in all affairs of life. These people therefore make friends among the aged, the wealthy and the intellectual who are able to help them rise in life. But when Saturn is afflicted in Aquarius it makes the disposition shrewd, cunning and alert to prey upon others by gaining their confidence and friendship and such people therefore sink to the lower levels of society. This position also carries with it a tendency to heart trouble and varicose veins.

♄ ♓ *Saturn in Pisces* when well-aspected gives a tendency to success in some quiet peaceful line of life where these people do not come into contact with the public, such as laboratory or research work or in connection with institutions for the care of wards of the community; they are regular "home-bodies" but when Saturn is afflicted in Pisces it gives danger of confinement by a chronic disease or liability to imprisonment. The person makes many enemies who will be persistent in their persecution of him.

THE ASPECTS OF SATURN.

☉ ✱ △ ♄ *The Sun sextile or trine Saturn* endows the person who is fortunate enough to have it with some of the finest faculties in the gamut, for it brings out the best qualities in the two planets. It gives foresight, method and organizing ability with the moral stamina to carry any project determined on to a successful conclusion despite delays and obstacles. Yet the person makes no enemies in so doing, for this configuration also makes him the soul of honor, kind and considerate; he would never stoop to do anything mean for he is sincere and just in his dealings with all men, but on the other hand, when he believes a certain course of action to be right he will never swerve therefrom though heaven and earth be moved against him. These aspects bring success in political or judicial positions, also in connection with mining or agriculture. The person often benefits by legacy, but recognition and success are generally delayed till middle life.

☉ ☌ P ♄ *The Sun conjunction or parallel Saturn.* Either aspect has a very detrimental effect upon health, especially in the common signs where the resistance is fundamentally low; in Gemini, Sagittarius and Pisces it gives a tendency to tuberculosis. It does least damage in the fixed signs where the resistance is greatest, but when sickness does get a grip on the person it hangs on like grim death, for this configuration lessens the power of the body to throw off disease quickly, hence recuperation is very slow. This is especially true in a man's horoscope; in a woman's figure it affects her husband's health.

☉ □ ☍ ♄ *The Sun square or opposition to Saturn.* These aspects are adverse to that which is generally termed success, but they give an abundance of experience, so they are excellent from the standpoint of the soul. It may truly be said of the person who has either that "the best-laid plans of mice and men gang aft agley," for no matter how carefully he may plan his affairs he will be subjected to delays and meet obstacles which will thwart his desires; his marriage often is unhappy and is likely to end in divorce or early death of the partner; there is difficulty in finding and keeping employment, trouble with employers and authorities, a feeling as if he were held in leash all his life and denied expression in any direction. These are the outward experiences but they are generated by the inner nature, and until that changes he must suffer the whiplash of necessity. In the first place such a person has a tendency to crawl into a shell and shut himself in and others out. He is pessimistic and a kill-joy, has little or no regard for the feelings of others and is very obstinate. In the horoscope of a woman it signifies marriage to one much older, a person who will hold her with a very tight rein; it augurs death of the husband and often several marriages which are terminated by death or divorce.

These configurations often bring legacies, but either there is trouble and litigation over the bequests, or the person squanders the estate after he receives it. If Saturn is in Libra, his exaltation-sign, the latter part of the life may be better because the person has taken the lessons of life to heart and mended his ways.

♀ ✱ △ ♄ *Venus sextile or trine to Saturn.* The good qualities of Venus are love and affection and the good qualities of Saturn are tact, diplomacy, method and system, justice, thrift and economy, and we may therefore judge that when these two planets are configurated in good aspect they make the person faithful and true, just and honorable, diplomatic and tactful, systematic and methodical, qualities which make for success in all departments of life. Therefore a person with these aspects will be much sought as a friend and adviser, or as a person to be trusted with any commission requiring sterling honesty and ability. They make him simple in his tastes and of unimpeachable morality. Hence either is what one may call one of the luckiest aspects in the gamut.

♀ P ☌ □ ☍ ♄ *Venus parallel, conjunction, square or opposition to Saturn* brings out the evil qualities of the two planets and troubles which are thus generated usually come through the person's relations with the opposite sex. It makes him underhanded and scheming to gratify his passions, often in an unusual manner, and his perverted desires are usually directed against someone who is much younger than himself. If regular marriage relations are entered into, such a person is often a demon of jealousy which makes life a burden for the marriage partner on account of his suspicious nature. People with these afflictions are also stingy in all money matters and exceedingly avaricious. They have very poor business judgment and are therefore liable to losses, failure and bankruptcy. During the earlier years people with these configurations should beware of dealings with older people who will be prone to take advantage of them, but later on it will be their turn to prey upon the young.

☿ ✱ △ ♄ *Mercury sextile or trine to Saturn* acts as a brake upon the flighty mind and gives it a seriousness, depth and concentration which is of inestimable value in life. The forethought and profound reasoning ability indicated by these aspects insure success in whatever vocation the person may pursue. The patient persistence which permits no temporary failure to stand in the way of ultimate success, also caution and diplomacy make such people invincible in the long run. Therefore they generally become prominent in connection with some serious enterprise such as secret societies, the church or even in politics. They are in demand for high positions where a steady hand is required on the helm. But they do not usually shine for they are very quiet, subdued and serious in their manner and demeanor. They are absolutely honest, hence they make the very finest judges obtainable.

☿ ☌ P ♄ *Mercury conjunction or parallel to Saturn.* These aspects also give depth to the mind and forethought, together with all the other good qualities enumerated as resulting from the sextile and the trine, if Mercury is otherwise well-aspected; but not in so full a measure, or at any rate the person does not seem to be able to externalize them as readily, hence does not meet the same assured success as given by the definitely good aspects; he also suffers from the tendency to melancholy denoted by the square or opposition, especially if the aspect occurs in one of the common signs or in Capricorn, and if in Gemini it interferes sadly with the dexterity; such people tend to drop everything they take into their hands. These aspects also give an embarrassing timidity and if Mercury is afflicted the undesirable qualities enumerated as resulting from the square or opposition may be looked for.

☿ □ ☍ ♄ *Mercury square or opposition to Saturn* makes the person subject to trouble and delays all through life. He is thwarted on every hand by slander and secret enemies and this condition in time makes him bitter and sarcastic with the additional consequence that he is shunned by all who can possibly get away from him, and that in time leads him to become a recluse who shuts himself away to brood over his troubles. Such a person sometimes becomes a subject of melancholia of a most piteous character. These aspects also make the person cunning and untruthful. They give the same desire to study the occult conferred by the good aspects, but there is the great difference that while the good aspects of Saturn and Mercury incline to the study of occultism from unselfish motives the bad aspects impel him to ferret out nature's secrets for personal power or gain.

☽ ✱ △ ♄ *The Moon sextile or trine to Saturn* imparts all the best saturnine qualities to the mind; it makes the person self-reliant, serious, sober and systematic, careful and thrifty in business affairs and gives success in life through tactful and diplomatic dealings with others. Such people are eminently reasonable and trustworthy in all matters of honor and justice and gain great esteem in the community on that account. Their patience and persistence are inexhaustible.

☽ ☌ P ♄ *The Moon conjunction or parallel to Saturn* is not always to be classed as a bad aspect so far as the mental qualities go, for in any case it deepens the mind and gives greater power of concentration, but if Saturn is strong by sign, in Libra or Capricorn, and the Moon is otherwise well-aspected this position also will impart the virtues of Saturn, though under all conditions it makes the mind gloomy and the person is subject to periodical spells of melancholy; but if Saturn is weak by sign, especially if he is in Aries and if the Moon is otherwise afflicted, then his conjunction is to be judged and read the same as the square and opposition. The effect of the conjunction also depends upon the department of life we are considering; for instance. the conjunction of the Moon and Saturn is good for concentration of the mind, but bad for the digestion, particularly in a woman's horoscope, where it has also the tendency to obstruct the menses with all that that implies, and in a man's horoscope it indicates the death of the marriage partner. Similar distinctions should be made when reading the conjunctions of the other so-called malefics.

☽ □ ☍ ♄ *The Moon square or opposition to Saturn* is one of the signatures of sorrow in life, for it makes the mind melancholy and full of worries so that the person is constantly carrying an atmosphere of gloom with him and as thoughts are things this attitude of mind brings about delays and disappointments in every department of life. Such a person will experience difficulties from persons and things signified by Saturn, probably parents, and if he has money he may lose it and have difficulty in getting more. Thus he may be in poverty all his life. He will make more enemies than friends and become subject to slander and scandal, but the disfavor he meets is undoubtedly merited for these aspects make the mind bitter and selfish and such people are unscrupulous, avaricious and entirely unfeeling with respect to others, hence they are under the whiplash of Saturn that the sorrow and troubles which they themselves are constantly feeling may make them more mellow. If the aspect is six, five or even four degrees from being exact and if Saturn is in his exaltation sign Libra these aspects are not quite so evil in the latter part of life. They may then imply that the person has learned his lesson and as a consequence he may find himself in easier circumstances. The adverse aspects of Saturn to the Moon are very bad for the health, particularly in the woman's horoscope. There they indicate obstructions of the female functions. In the man's horoscope they either deny marriage or indicate the death of the marriage partner and their general tendency is to obstruct everything connected with the houses and signs wherein they are placed in the horoscope.

♃ ✱ △ ♄ *Jupiter sextile or trine to Saturn* gives a strong character with a deep and profoundly philosophical mind, a benevolent disposition with a strong sense of justice and fair play. All the virtues of Saturn and Jupiter are combined by these aspects and people in whose horoscope they are found will consequently gain honor and esteem in the community where they are. They will be looked upon as the pillars of society and gain prosperity commensurate with the environment in which they are placed, for these aspects give sound financial judgment, the ability to grasp opportunity when it is met, benevolence, devotion to duty, religion and all good objects in life.

♃P☌♄ *Jupiter parallel or conjunction Saturn* has the same beneficent influence as the sextile or trine, though not in as great a measure and if Jupiter is weak by sign or otherwise afflicted the aspects will probably count for very little, but in that case its effect upon the arterial circulation will be obstructive, giving a tendency to sclerosis of the arteries the same as the opposition and square.

♃□☍♄ *Jupiter square or opposition to Saturn* gives a diffident, vacillating mind unable to form decisions, always distrustful of others, indolent and inclined to drift with the tide, often a ward of society either in the poor-house or the prison, for the character is basically dishonest. These aspects also give a tendency to arterio-sclerosis.

♂ ✶ △ ♄ *Mars sextile or trine to Saturn* gives a capable, determined and energetic nature capable of intense and sustained action and of obtaining unusual results thereby. The executive ability, dominant forcefulness and endurance of these people are remarkable and consequently they are constantly accomplishing what others cannot achieve. On account of these qualities they always rise to prominent positions and are much esteemed on account of their ability but seldom liked for these aspects also make the character cruel and hard. They give a strong physique and general good health.

♂ ☌ P □ ☍ ♄ *Mars conjunction, parallel, square or opposition to Saturn.* These are thoroughly bad aspects indicating a selfish, violent, harsh and cruel nature, quick-tempered and vindictive, absolutely dishonest and untruthful; unscrupulous and liable to public disgrace and imprisonment, also to accident and a violent death, but if one of the planets is essentially dignified or exalted the evil influence is much enhanced. It should also be remembered that such serious defects do not result from one aspect alone and if the other configurations in the horoscope are good the foregoing delineation will only apply in a very mild measure.

♅ ✶ △ ♄ *Uranus sextile or trine to Saturn* is fortunate for a public career in an official capacity for it gives ambition and determination with ability to concentrate upon large problems and exercise authority, plan and systematize. It strengthens the intuition so that such people are guided by an interior insight when new and important steps have to be taken, therefore they are in demand and find positions with large corporations where they win their way through sheer ability. The mind is both mechanical and ingenious, hence this position often denotes the successful inventor, particularly along the lines of electricity.

♅ ☌ P ♄ *Uranus conjunction or parallel to Saturn* has an influence like the good aspects if the planets are elevated, in angles, essentially dignified or exalted, as Saturn in Libra or Capricorn or Uranus in Aquarius or Scorpio; but if the conjunction occurs in signs where either of the planets is weak, like Aries, Taurus, Cancer, or Leo then the influence will be detrimental and should be judged the same as the square or opposition.

♅ □ ☍ ♄ *Uranus square or opposition to Saturn* gives an unscrupulous, dishonest nature with an extremely violent temper. The outbursts are as sudden as a bolt from the blue and exhaust the person completely. These people are very eccentric and look at everything from a peculiar angle; they are treacherous, idle, indolent and altogether dangerous to the community. These aspects also indicate chronic or incurable diseases according to the signs wherein they are placed, but as said, if the other indications in the horoscope are good the influence of a single aspect will not bring out such evil characteristics and therefore the whole horoscope is to be carefully considered before judging the influences enumerated for they may be materially minimized by favorable indications in the horoscope.

♆ ⚹ △ ♄ *Neptune sextile or trine to Saturn* is good for success in worldly affairs for it brings out the saturnine virtues—honor, self-reliance, determination, etc., by which the person gains the confidence and esteem of others, but the principal effect is spiritual and therefore only felt by those who are able to respond because of other aspects in the horoscope. To them it gives the ability to delve deeply into occult and mystical subjects, also to become proficient in the art and practice of them.

♆ ☌ P ♄ *Neptune conjunction or parallel to Saturn* has the same effect as the good aspects when it occurs in a sign where either of the planets are strong as Neptune is in Cancer and Pisces and Saturn in Libra and Capricorn.

♆ □ ☍ ♄ *Neptune square or opposition to Saturn* lays the person liable to loss by deception, treachery or fraud.

CHAPTER XIII.

Jupiter the Planet of Benevolence

FROM each of the divine Hierarchies which have ministered at the birth and evolution of humanity we have received certain qualities and faculties upon which we are being nursed from nescience to omniscience and from impotence to omnipotence in life's great school. From the Lords of Venus we received the priceless gift of love which links humanity in the tenderest affection of varying degrees and makes life beautiful. From the Lords of Mercury we received the no less valuable gift of mind which enables us to conquer the material world and provide ourselves with the comforts of life, but something more is needed. The divine spark within us is ever seeking an outlet and the greater the two qualities of love and intellect grow, the stronger the upward urge, but this cannot be fully satisfied either if the Spirit seeks to raise itself to its divine source only through the love nature expressed by Venus and culminating in its higher octave Uranus. The religious fervor then expresses itself as devotion of the most sublime nature but there is still a lack. Feeling without knowledge is incomplete. Nor can the inner urge be satisfied if through the mercurial channel of intellect it attempts to raise itself to the spiritual perception of Neptune, the higher octave of Mercury, for though the intellect be sharp as a razor it is of no account when it is devoid of love. It therefore follows that *only by the wedding of love and intellect can wisdom be born.* The mercurial knowledge in itself, though neither good nor evil, may be used for one purpose or the other. Even genius shows only the bent of this knowledge. We speak of a military genius, one who has a wonderful knowledge of the tactics of war, but a man of war, whether he be a Napoleon or a common soldier, is not to be classed as wise because he deliberately crushes the finer feelings of which we take the heart as symbol. Only when the mercurial faculty of mind is tempered, blended and balanced by the heart-born faculty of love generated by the Venus ray, is wisdom born of the union. And this is the quality which the planetary spirit of Jupiter is seeking to infuse into mankind to aid them in their spiritual evolution that they may rise above the material plane and soar to higher spheres. Therefore the Jupiterian ray makes people humane, honorable, courteous, refined and generous, law-abiding and religious, cheerful and optimistic. The true Jupiterian is aptly described as a jovial fellow, and he is usually large but his heart is almost too big to find room even within his capacious chest. The corners of his mouth are always turned upward with a broad smile that can only be described as radiant and in his hearty good-feeling he is so demonstrative that when he shakes your hand the ligaments of your arm are almost sprained. He is "hail fellow well met" with everybody, always ready to give anything or anybody a boost. He seems actually grateful to you when you ask him to do you a favor and is never so happy as when working hard to help others. He would not harm a child and never gets angry on his own account but when moved to righteous indignation on account of the wrongs of others then he may be terrible in his wrath, yet he will never be cruel to the aggressor or the oppressor, but show mercy and kindness even to them as soon as they have been vanquished. Such is the pure Jupiterian, but of course he is very seldom found at the present time. Nevertheless, an increasing number of people are beginning to walk the way of wisdom and show the Jupiterian traits.

It is said that "Opportunity knocks at every man's door," yet we often hear people bewail their fate because they "never had a chance." Saturn is blamed for our misfortunes when we have learned to study Astrology; we are so intently on the lookout for evil that we usually forget to look for the good, and thus miss our opportunity. It takes Saturn thirty years to go around the horoscope, by transit, and form aspects to all planets, but Jupiter, the most beneficent influence in the solar system, goes around once in eleven years and thus the good fortunes which he may bring are at least three times as numerous as the misfortunes brought by Saturn's evil aspects.

As a matter of fact, we get from others just

what we give, each is surrounded by a subtle auric atmosphere which colors our views of others, and the thoughts, ideas and actions of others towards us. If we harbor meanness in our hearts, that colors this atmosphere so that we see meanness in others and in their actions towards us, we awaken this trait in them, as vibrations from a tuning-fork start another of the same pitch to sing. On the other hand, if we cultivate the Jupiterian qualities of benevolence, his expansive smile, his cordial attitude of mind, etc., we shall soon feel the response in our circle of acquaintances and the beneficent aspect of Jupiter will then have greater effect in making our life and work pleasant.

Jupiter is essentially dignified when found in Pisces, or in Sagittarius, the sign of aspiration. He is exalted in Cancer, the house of the Moon, for the seed-atom which furnishes the body of the incoming Ego is projected by the Moon into the sphere of Cancer but Jupiter represents the spiritual part and therefore he presides at the ingress of the Ego itself into the body. He also rules the blood in which the indwelling spirit finds expression, though his activities are confined principally to the arterial circulation. He furthers assimilation and growth, and therefore he also rules the liver. (Saturn rules the gall bladder.) Jupiterians are very fond of show and display. In their religious observances they love ceremonial and they are rather partial to the established church but often dislike any "ism" not sanctioned by society or correct form.

When Jupiter is afflicted his influence makes the person lawless, sensuous, self-indulgent, gluttonous, extravagant and careless in the payment of his obligations, hence liable to loss of health, trouble with the law and consequent social disgrace. An afflicted Jupiter makes people sporty, fond of horse-racing and gambling.

Jupiter in the Twelve Houses

♃1 *Jupiter in the First House* when well-aspected is a good sign of health and general fortune in life. It gives a good-natured, kindly disposition, a nature which breathes cordiality, honor and uprightness. These people love pleasure, particularly out-of-doors, and are fond of traveling. They have considerable executive ability and are therefore sought for positions of importance and responsibility. There is an inclination to stoutness in later years.

Jupiter afflicted on the Ascendant gives a tendency to self-indulgence, according to the sign wherein he is placed. If in Cancer the person becomes an inveterate glutton and literally makes a god of his stomach with the inevitable result that in the course of years he becomes excessively stout, the liver being particularly enlarged and as a consequence he is subjected to sickness of a serious nature. In Sagittarius it makes him an inveterate gambler who would stake his soul on the toss of a coin. In Pisces he becomes an incurable drunkard, in Scorpio a sensualist of the worst nature and so on with the other signs. It may also be said that whenever Jupiter is afflicted on the Ascendant the health suffers through some corruption of the blood.

♃2 *Jupiter in the Second House* when well-aspected, particularly by the Sun or Moon, gives great financial prosperity in life and this is a fortunate position in that respect even when Jupiter is afflicted, but then the person is liable to loss under bad directions. When Jupiter is unaspected he gives no help; the person may then be poor and starve.

♃3 *Jupiter in the Third House* when well-aspected gives a mind of a highly optimistic nature so that no matter what other obstacles there may be in life the person who has this position will always look at the silver lining of the cloud and in so doing forget the cloud itself. He will have exceptional educational advantages and what is more the education which he receives will be of great benefit to him. He will be popular among his brothers, sisters and neighbors and they will help to benefit him. Success is indicated by traveling, writing and publications. When Jupiter is afflicted in the Third House the person is liable to be in wrecks and accidents while traveling, but he will not be injured though he escape only by a hair-breadth. If Saturn afflicts he will become careless and indolent, thus forfeiting the respect and esteem of his immediate family, but if Mars is adverse they will mistrust him because of rash and imprudent acts.

♃ 4 *Jupiter in the Fourth House* when well-aspected is most fortunate for the home conditions, especially in the latter part of life. People with Jupiter in this position will do better in their place of birth than anywhere else. They will receive considerable help from the parents and probably an inheritance from them. Their business affairs will be on a solid basis and run smoothly so that at the close of life there will be a considerable accumulation according to their station and the opportunities of their environment. They pass their days in peace and end them amid friends, wealth and prosperity. But when Jupiter is afflicted in the Fourth House the person should leave his native town early in life for the conditions there will be detrimental to his success. Lavish and extravagant expenditure, love of display and kindred costly tendencies will sap his resources and bring him into bankruptcy; besides a false pride will keep him from undertaking a radical reform even when he has awakened to the fact that he ought to do so if he would save himself and the only way out of it to make a new start will be removal to another city.

♃5 *Jupiter in the Fifth House* and well-aspected increases the number of children and they will bring much profit and pleasure to the parents; it gives popularity and good friends who will be a help to the person, also a sociable and pleasure loving disposition. Gain by speculation is foreshown, high intelligence and success in educational work or the publishing or newspaper business. These people make fine teachers and have a very convincing way of putting things. If Jupiter is afflicted in the Fifth House, especially in Sagittarius, it gives a tendency towards gambling and loss thereby, a love of sports, disinclination for work, and trouble with children.

♃6 *Jupiter in the Sixth House* gives good health and success in the care and cure of the sick, faithful servants, and the respect and esteem of all with whom the person comes in contact in the course of his occupation. But when Jupiter is afflicted in the Sixth House it gives a tendency toward liver troubles, enlargement of the liver, obesity and general disorders produced by overindulgence of the appetite.

♃7 *Jupiter in the Seventh House* gives a noble, great-hearted and sympathetic marriage partner who will bring the person favor, fortune and social prestige. It is an ideal indication for marriage, also for a person seeking to take a partner or enter into partnership. He may also be assured that the partner will be noble, sincere, honest and trustworthy, and that success will come by co-operation. It is an ideal position for a lawyer for it indicates success in law and the ability to reconcile opponents. But if Jupiter is weak or afflicted the person will lose his lawsuits or suffer by misplaced confidence in his partner; marriage will be delayed or denied and when consummated trouble will arise through the indolence and self-indulgent habits of the marriage partner. Therefore wisdom would dictate that the person avoid such relationships.

248 *Jupiter in the Eighth House* when well-aspected indicates financial gain by marriage, partnerships or legacy, but when weak or afflicted it indicates lawsuits and losses in connection with these matters. A well-aspected Jupiter in the Eighth House is also a sign of an easy and peaceful termination of the life when the full course has been run.

249 *Jupiter in the Ninth House* gives a peaceful, noble, optimistic and kind-hearted disposition, with religious tendencies, broad-minded and tolerant of the opinions of others, but favoring the more orthodox and established lines of thought. The person is much esteemed in society and apt

to occupy prominent positions in church, state or in institutions of learning or philanthropic associations. This position also gives a love of travel with pleasure and gain thereby. But when weak or afflicted by sign or aspect it gives arrogance and a love of display which is out of proportion with the person's pocketbook, consequently there are lawsuits and liability to social discredit. It also shows danger when traveling.

♃10 *Jupiter in the Tenth House* when well-aspected is one of the best indications of an eminently successful and virtuous life, especially if he is supported by Saturn, Sun and Moon, for then the person will rise to a high position in the church, state or law and gain great wealth, honor and social esteem. Furthermore he will deserve all he gets for the character will be of superlative nobility. But if Jupiter be weak or afflicted in the Tenth House, particularly by Saturn or the luminaries, it shows that the character is not reliable. The person may rise but his evil deeds will find him out and therefore he will experience reversals of fortune and loss of prestige.

♃11 *Jupiter in the Eleventh House* and well-aspected gives wealthy and influential friends who may be relied upon to help the person to realize his hopes, wishes and ambitions. It also gives a sociable disposition and fondness for pleasure. In a man's horoscope it signifies that the marriage will be fruitful and that his children will be a credit and a help to him, but before judgment is rendered in this respect the wife's horoscope should also be examined to see whether it concurs, for if not then the judgment must be modified. When Jupiter is afflicted in the Eleventh House either the person meets friends who are good and sincere in their desire to help him but lack the ability or else the friends whom he attracts come to him to be benefited. In either case he will not be helped much by friends but must depend upon his own resources to attain his desires.

♃12 *Jupiter in the Twelfth House* when well-aspected brings gain and success through occupations carried on in comparative seclusion such as laboratory work, work in hospitals or asylums in an executive capacity; or in a position in one of the fraternal orders which have to do with sick benefits or in the study and practice of the mystical or occult arts. If people with Jupiter in this position are personally indigent they receive much bounty from people or institutions of a fraternal or charitable nature, but if they are well-to-do they give lavishly to these purposes. If they have enemies they also have a way of turning them to friends. If Jupiter is afflicted it makes the person indolent and improvident so that in time he usually becomes the ward of one of the charitable institutions where he lives till the end of life without either trouble or worry.

JUPITER IN THE TWELVE SIGNS.

♃ ♈ *Jupiter in Aries* gives a high-spirited, energetic and ambitious mind, always on the lookout and alert for new and progressive methods usable for advancement in the world's work; it makes a true pioneer, neither too conservative nor too impulsive, a thoughtful, but sympathetic disposition, sincere, honest and trustworthy, somewhat religiously inclined. It gives some legal or literary ability and a love of out-door games with popularity in social and business circles. But if Jupiter is afflicted the mind is not so conservative and well-balanced. There is a tendency to rash and impulsive acts; impatience and temper are shown under adverse circumstances with a consequent loss of esteem and popularity.

♃ ♉ *Jupiter in Taurus* when well-aspected gives an eminently kind and sympathetic nature to all people but a deep-seated, tender and warm love for those towards whom the relationship warrants such expression. This position also attracts wealth and gives a generous disposition to aid in philanthropic enterprises; yet Jupiter in the Second House or second sign is never lavish or extravagantly generous but rather conservative and inclined to investigate the merits of any proposition before he extends a helping hand. On the other hand he is absolutely open-handed to those who are near and dear to him. His home and his family are all in all. When Jupiter is afflicted in Taurus it inclines to extravagant expenditures for show, display and the gratification of the lower nature. Such people are great gourmandizers, fond of rich and savory foods that tickle the palate. They often experience financial difficulties and trouble with creditors, also such sickness as may result from the over-indulgence of their appetites according to other indications of the stars.

♃♊ *Jupiter in Gemini* when well-aspected gives literary ability of a high class and if that is backed by the necessary education success in this line is certain. This position also gives an inventive turn to the mind, a love of mathematics and an attraction towards the occult. Jupiter in Gemini shows that travel will bring both pleasure and profit and it gives an honorable, courteous and friendly disposition. But if Jupiter is afflicted the person is liable to meet with losses and trouble when traveling. He will have a number of hair-breadth escapes from accidents, legal and religious trouble, also difficulties with brothers, sisters and close relatives.

♃♋ *Jupiter in Cancer.* The full effect of Jupiter for good or ill is never felt until the middle life and this is especially the case when he is placed in the Fourth House or fourth sign, Cancer. When well-placed there he gives an exceedingly kindly and courteous disposition, that is at peace with all the world; he is endowed with a most vivid and fruitful imagination, a dreamer of Utopian dreams and a lover of the occult and mystical. There is also however, a practical side to the nature which makes him ambitious to attain worldly success and fortunate in his investments in houses, lands or mines, so that he will accumulate property and be well-to-do especially after middle life. This position also indicates that the person may receive much help from his parents during life and an inheritance after their death. Jupiter in Cancer makes the person very fond of the pleasures of the table but if well-aspected he will probably keep himself within such bounds that his health does not suffer. If however, Jupiter is afflicted it inclines to inordinate gluttony which will eventually corrupt the blood and cause such disease and noxious growths as result from that condition.

♃ ♌ *Jupiter in Leo* gives a truly noble nature, blending kindness and courage, self-reliance and loyalty, self-restraint and compassion, mercy and justice. It indicates, in short, a paragon of virtues nowhere excelled. It gives an abundance of vitality and a strong constitution so that it marks a leader physically, morally and spiritually, nor will such a person ever be content to follow. He craves positions of trust and responsibility, the greater the better. He will always be equal to the occasion and never abuse the confidence of those who have placed him there. Such people have an innate culture and refinement. They are fond of everything that tends to the uplift of humanity, religious, sincere; sure to win recognition and success dealing in speculative investments. When Jupiter is afflicted in Leo the person becomes cruel and sensuous, abnormally fond of pleasure and subject to loss by investments, speculation and gambling.

♃♍ *Jupiter in Virgo* gives a cautious, analytical and practical nature with an almost unerring faculty for discriminating between the seeming and the real, for sifting truth from error and arriving at facts. They cannot ferret out secrets by underhanded methods as Saturn in Capricorn which makes an ideal detective, but if Jupiter in Virgo is the judge no one is clever enough to hide the truth from him. A well-aspected Jupiter in Virgo indicates success with servants who will be found faithful and loyal, ready to do their master's bidding. It also indicates prosperity through business or professional vocations; but if Jupiter is afflicted in Virgo it gives a cynical carping and critical disposition, mistrustful of others and therefore liable to loss through servants or employees. Such people cannot succeed in business and they will find it extremely difficult to obtain or keep a position. At any rate they will serve in a very inferior capacity.

♃♎ *Jupiter in Libra* when well-aspected gives a kind, sympathetic and loving disposition, a conscientious, sociable and benevolent nature and an interest in all that makes for the uplift of humanity—music, art, literature, social intercourse, et cetera. On that account the person is popular, particularly with the opposite sex from whence gain and benefit may be expected. Success in the business and public life are shown. But if Jupiter is afflicted in Libra undue indulgence of the lower nature will bring trouble and public scandal with a consequent loss of popularity and prestige.

♃♏ *Jupiter in Scorpio* gives an ardent, aggressive and self-reliant nature, an enthusiastic, constructive and resourceful mind with the ability to meet all the exigencies of life in an efficient manner and it ensures success in practical everyday occupations, gives a large family and plenty of means to provide for them. This position also shows a tendency towards occult investigations. But if Jupiter is afflicted in Scorpio it will bring loss and trouble through the indulgence of the lower nature in an inordinate measure, love of rich and expensive food and sickness on that account.

♃ ♐ *Jupiter in Sagittarius* when well-aspected gives good fortune and general success in life, a humane, broad and philosophical mind, a reverent and religious disposition. Hence people with this position rise to the top and become leaders in their various spheres of life, finding places of prominence in church or state, scientific or philosophic enterprises or institutions. If Jupiter is afflicted in Sagittarius it makes the person sporty, fond of cheap and gaudy display, extravagant and ready to take a chance on any gamble, causes loss of social standing if born in a better environment, trouble through law, financial difficulties, narrow-minded sectarian views if inclined to be religious.

♃ ♑ *Jupiter in Capricorn* gives an ambitious nature, self-reliant and self-controlled with a desire to rise to a position of authority over others also the ability to dictate wisely and well. It gives a careful, economical disposition, and an abhorrence of waste; ingenuity, resourcefulness and some mechanical ability. These people are trust-worthy to a degree, sincere and honest in all their undertakings and hold every promise inviolate, therefore they usually rise to honor, esteem and general popularity. As already said their aim is to attain independence at the head of some business, but if they do not succeed in that and have to work for others they are best suited to be in the employ of the government, either municipal or national. On account of the implicit trust generated by their sterling characteristics of honesty, sincerity and faithfulness these people are often made the recipients of confidence from friends who feel the need of sharing their troubles with someone who can be depended upon either to give honest, disinterested advice or else to keep the secrets told them inviolate. If Jupiter is afflicted in Capricorn it makes a miser who will hoard all he can scrape together and deny himself all except the barest necessities and is consequently despised by all who know him.

♃♒ *Jupiter in Aquarius* when well-aspected gives a humane, optimistic, original and philosophic mind, fond of friends and the society of others particularly those who are interested in science or mysticism, literature and music, consequently he attracts people of that nature and they will be a benefit to him in helping him to realize his hopes, wishes and ambitions. He may possibly obtain a position of importance in some official capacity with secret or occult societies. This is a good indication of general success in life, but if Jupiter is afflicted it makes the nature restless, nervous and erratic with revolutionary or anarchistic ideas with disinclination for serious work and such people are generally disliked and distrusted.

♃ ♓ *Jupiter in Pisces* gives a charitable, sympathetic and hospitable nature which loves to minister to the outcasts of society. These people are veritable angels of mercy to all who suffer in body, soul or spirit. They are well known to those who are "sick or in prison." Being of a sensitive nature and subject to the influences from the invisible world they not infrequently have psychic experiences and become students of the occult. They love music, art and literature and if well-aspected by Venus, Jupiter in Pisces will give considerable ability as a performer; but if Jupiter is afflicted in Pisces it gives a vacillating mind, a nerveless, cowardly nature indulging in all the vices in the calendar and a generally despicable disposition—a social parasite.

The Aspects of Jupiter

☉ ☌ P ✱ △ ♃ *The Sun conjunction, sextile or trine to Jupiter.* The conjunction gives a tendency to apoplexy, especially if it occurs in Aries, but with that exception we may say that these configurations are sure indications of health, wealth and happiness; they give the person an abundance of vitality which is proof even against very severe onslaughts of disease, and should a particularly unfavorable planetary influence succeed in breaking down the constitutional resistance recovery will be so rapid as to seem miraculous. This nearly impregnable condition of health is all the more unassailable because it is backed by a disposition at once "sunny" and "jovial" and that latter characteristic also makes the fortunate possessors of these aspects beloved by all with whom they come in contact; everybody is glad to see the person with the perpetual smile, but they do more than "smile" —they *earn* the friendship universally bestowed upon them by deeds of kindness, by words of sympathy, cheer or hope as the occasion may demand. They are trusted by everybody for they never betray a trust; they have good clear heads, good judgment and executive ability so that they are well fitted to help others. These characteristics also favor their own financial fortunes so that they accumulate wealth, but theirs is never "tainted money," they never benefit by the loss of others. They are conservatively religious and may be aptly described as "pillars of society." They shine particularly in governmental offices.

☉□☍♃ *The Sun square or opposition to Jupiter* gives a tendency to indulge in habits which are bad for the health; the person is far too fond of the "good things of life" and very selfish in supplying his own comforts; he exercises little and never denies himself, with the result that the circulation becomes sluggish and as these people have a superabundance of blood their lassitude and indulgence is productive of various noxious growths and kindred disorders; sometimes a fit of anger raises the blood pressure to such a point that a vessel bursts and ends the life or leaves the person thenceforth a useless wreck. These aspects give a bombastic, haughty disposition with an inordinate love of display and thus induce to extravagance both in social and business affairs with the result that the person sometimes finds himself involved in debt which he cannot pay and then there is but a step to the bankruptcy court. A false pride often prevents these people from working honestly for others so they would rather prey upon the public as gamblers and followers of races and other so-called sports where there is an opportunity to swindle other people and get what they call an "easy" living until they land in the meshes of the law. Children with these aspects should be given special training in self-restraint, thrift and honesty, above all, religion, for they will have a tendency to scorn and scoff at religion, but perhaps a memory of a devout mother may help to keep them straight.

♀ ☌ P ✱ △ ♃ *Venus conjunction, parallel, sextile or trine to Jupiter* is one of the best signs of success and general good fortune in life. It favors the accumulation of wealth and the enjoyment of all the luxuries of life. It is a good indication of a successful and happy marriage, social prestige and the respect of all with whom the person comes in contact. It endows him with a jovial, optimistic, generous and large-hearted disposition, makes him honorable to a degree, interested and active in philanthropic measures, liberal in mind, tolerant of the views of others even where he differs radically, fond of pleasure, traveling, parties, and capable of enjoying life to the fullest extent; he loves expensive and ultra-comfortable things, a fine house, valuable books, pictures and other rich appointments.

♀□ ☍ ♃ *Venus square or opposition to Jupiter* gives the same luxurious likings as the good aspects but limits the ability to satisfy them; although such people make the most frantic efforts to present a fine front to the world they are generally found out to be shams. Their lack of business ability is often responsible for failure and bankruptcy and they are very liable to suffer losses through the treachery of others. Love and marriage also are sources of sorrow for those whom Venus and Jupiter are afflicting. They are apt to be jilted before marriage or the marriage partner will prove faithless and may desert them. These aspects also produce an amorous nature likely to take liberties regardless of the laws of decency and make the person faithless to marriage vows.

☿ ☌ P ✱ △ ♃ *Mercury conjunction, parallel, sextile or trine to Jupiter* is one of the finest assets in life for it gives a cheerful, optimistic disposition with the ability to always look upon the bright side of things and keep up the spirits in the hours of adversity; the mind is broad, versatile and able to reason correctly and to form a reliable judgment by careful deliberation; these people never decide hastily; they require time to think over what is presented to them, but once they have reached a conclusion, it will be found incontrovertible. They are successful in law or literature and much respected for their honesty and sincerity. These aspects are particularly fortunate for people who travel for business or pleasure, for they will reap both benefit and enjoyment from a migratory mode of life. It will make them "healthy, wealthy and wise" beyond the average, loved by everybody for the vital vibration they radiate upon whomever they meet.

☿ □ ☍ ♃ *Mercury square or opposition to Jupiter* gives a vacillating and wavering disposition so that the person cannot make up his mind when more than one course of action is open, hence people with these aspects often lose their opportunities through procrastination and lack of judgment; they must therefore often be classed as failures. They are liable to scandal and slander because of treacherous associates, and should not travel for it will bring them loss and trouble; they should also be extremely careful in making contracts or agreements to do or deliver certain things at a specified time for they will probably be unable to fulfill the requirements and thus trouble and loss will result.

☽ P ☌ ✱ △ ♃ *The Moon parallel, conjunction, sextile or trine to Jupiter* gives an optimistic, noble and generous disposition. The open-hearted honesty, fairness and friendliness of people with these aspects make them universally popular. These aspects strengthen both the reasoning faculties and constitution, so that such people usually have a strong mind in a strong body and hence a powerful personal magnetism which may be used to great advantage in healing the sick. They have lofty ideals and a fruitful imagination with the power of acquiring wealth which will grow greater if used in philanthropic enterprises of which these people are prone to dream. This is one of the best aspects in the gamut and makes for general success in life both physically and spiritually.

☽ □ ☍ ♃ *The Moon square or opposition to Jupiter* impairs the reasoning faculties and brings the person trouble through litigation, lack of forethought and indecision or dishonesty. People with these aspects are too fond of ostentation and display, extravagant beyond their means, lavish in their expenditures, prone to take desperate chances in gambling or speculation to rehabilitate their fortunes and doomed to loss, slander and sometimes bankruptcy on that account. These aspects are also bad for health in a woman's horoscope especially; they indicate digestive and liver troubles.

♄ * △ ♃ *Saturn sextile or trine to Jupiter* gives a strong character with a deep and profoundly philosophical mind, a benevolent disposition with a strong sense of justice and fair play. All the virtues of Saturn and Jupiter are combined by these aspects and people in whose horoscope they are found will consequently gain the honor and esteem of the community where they are. Thus they will be looked upon as the pillars of society and gain prosperity commensurate with the environment in which they are placed, for these aspects give sound financial judgment and the ability to grasp opportunity when it is met.

♄ ☌ P ♃ *Saturn conjunction or parallel to Jupiter* has the same beneficent influence as the sextile or trine though not in as great a measure and if Jupiter is weak by sign or otherwise afflicted the aspects will probably count for very little, but in that case its effect upon the arterial circulation will be obstructive, giving a tendency to sclerosis of the arteries the same as the opposition and square.

♄ □ ☍ ♃ *Saturn square or opposition to Jupiter* gives a diffident, vacillating mind unable to form decisions, always distrustful of others, indolent and inclined to drift with the tide; often a ward of society either in the poor-house or the prison, for the character is basically dishonest. These aspects also give a tendency to arterio-sclerosis.

♂ ⚹ △ ♃ *Mars sextile or trine to Jupiter.* It is the nature of Jupiter to be somewhat conservative and dignified, but when blended with the fire of Mars it gives enthusiasm and an ability to influence others and imbue them with the same feelings. It makes the nature noble, sincere, honest and straightforward. This aspect is also good for the financial prosperity of the person, for both Mars and Jupiter when well-aspected give good earning ability and favor accumulation. Jupiter is somewhat conservative in respect to expenditures, Mars is too free, but where the Martian and Jupiterian tendencies are blended by a good aspect the result is an ideal, generous nature, neither too lavish nor too conservative, able to strike a happy medium. These people have much ingenuity and constructive ability and whatever they do they put their whole heart in it. Hence they are successful in business, popular in society, fond of out-of-door sports and games. They love to travel and gain much pleasure by so doing. Mars rules the hæmoglobin in the blood which is so important a factor in health and vitality, therefore the good aspects of Jupiter and Mars increase the red blood corpuscles with the result that people with these aspects have an abundance of health, vitality, power and endurance.

♂ P ☌ ♃ *Mars parallel or conjunction Jupiter* strengthens the constitution and increases the vitality the same as the good aspects. It also indicates that the person is able to earn much money and uses it freely and generously, but the mental qualities are similar to those conferred by the bad aspects: sporty, swaggering, tricky, deceitful and untruthful, impulsive in judgment, not to be depended upon, and if the conjunction occurs in one of the watery signs, especially in Pisces, the person will probably be a drunkard, though this is not as certain as with the square and opposition.

♂ □ ☍ ♃ *Mars square or opposition to Jupiter* is the signature of the gambler and if one of the planets is in a watery sign, especially in Pisces, he will be a drunkard also, a tricky, dishonest and disreputable character who always acts through impulse. With respect to health we find that these people suffer principally from blood and liver complaints, the circulation is poor and the blood is so rich that there is danger of apoplexy.

♅ ✶ △ ♃ *Uranus sextile or trine to Jupiter* gives a broad, humane disposition and a tendency to delve into the occult arts and sciences. It favors an association with secret orders and gives promise of prosperity in life. Such a person is honest and sincere, sociable, hospitable and likely to benefit a great deal from influential friends in official positions. This position also gives executive ability and success in connection with institutions of learning.

♅ P ☌ ♃ *Uranus parallel or conjunction Jupiter* gives similar indications to the good aspects but the influence is not quite so decided, particularly if either of the planets is weak by sign or otherwise afflicted. In that case it will be found that the tendencies conferred are more like those of the bad aspects.

♅ □ ☍ ♃ *Uranus square or opposition to Jupiter* gives an impulsive nature liable to act in a sudden or unexpected manner to one's own undoing; loss by speculation, lawsuits and impulsive extravagance are also indicated, many changes both of occupation and residence, loss of friends and reputation.

♆ ✱ △ ♃ *Neptune sextile or trine Jupiter* gives an inspirational, mystical nature and success in an occupation connected with occult orders, that is to say where the character is sufficiently developed so that Neptune can make his influence felt, for then this position brings out all the noblest and most spiritual strength of both planets, and occult experiences are not infrequently the result. During the sleeping hours these people are quite conscious in the invisible worlds.

♆ P ☌ ♃ *Neptune parallel or conjunction Jupiter* gives an influence similar to that of the good aspects when Neptune and Jupiter are not afflicted, but if they are in a weak sign and aspecting the other planets by square or opposition then the influence is similar to that of the bad aspects of Jupiter and Neptune.

♆ □ ☍ ♃ *Neptune square or opposition to Jupiter* indicates lack of control of the emotions. The person is sensitive to the low psychic influences of the borderland between the seen and the unseen worlds but they are of an awe-inspiring and disgusting type, hence apt to cause hysterical conditions, such as involuntary trance and kindred disorders attendant upon negative psychism. From a material standpoint it gives danger of fraud through speculation or large companies and dealing with predatory interests should therefore be avoided.

CHAPTER XIV.

Mars the Planet of Action

FROM the Bible we learn that Jehovah was the Creator of mankind for we find His angels announcing the birth of various notable personages. Thus the conclusion is inevitable that He and they preside over the generative function and impart the quality of fertility which at that time was looked upon as a token of the favor of God while barrenness was indicated as a sign of His displeasure. This is in accordance with the Western Wisdom Teaching which tells us that in the earliest days when mankind was still in the making Jehovah and His angels guided them to great temples at the times of year when planetary conditions were propitious to generation, and men born under those harmonious conditions lived for hundreds of years without sickness or disease. It is noticeable that wild animals which are still entirely under the guidance of their group-spirits and mate only at certain seasons are also immune from sickness. Jehovah still retains control over the fertilization of the animals which are attuned to His lunar vibrations through their twenty-eight pairs of spinal nerves that correspond to the twenty-eight days of the lunar revolution and His vehicle the

Moon still measures the period of gestation for men and beasts.

But the Bible also tells us of *Lucifer* and his *fallen angels* who taught humanity to take the prerogative of creation into their own hands and instilled into them the passion that has caused sorrow, sin and death, because the holy function of generation which was intended only for temporary purposes of propagation and which works so well under propitious planetary conditions has been desecrated and made subservient to the lusts of humanity at all times regardless of the stellar rays. Yet it is a mistake to think of the Lucifer spirits as evil, for under the sway of the angels humanity was a mass of mindless automatons knowing neither good nor evil and having no choice or prerogative, but since through the martial Lucifer spirits we have learned to know good and evil we are also able by the exercise of will power to shun the evil and choose the good, to flee from vice and cultivate virtue, thereby placing ourselves in harmonious co-worker-ship with God and nature and unfolding our divine possibilities so that we may become like our Father in Heaven.

While Jehovah and His angels are thus working upon humanity from the Moon the Lucifer spirits who rebelled against His regime are located on the planet Mars and from them also we have received and are receiving many valuable gifts, chief among them *fire* and *iron.* It is well known that every *living* body is warm, for the Ego cannot manifest in the physical world save through heat, or perhaps it should be said that heat is generated in the manifestation of the Ego. But without iron, which exists in the blood in the form of hæmoglobin, there could be no oxidation and consequently no heat. That was the condition previous to the fall, so-called, when man-in-the-making was mindless. But then the Lucifer spirits came and infused iron into the blood, which made it possible for the Ego to draw into its vehicles and from that time the Ego became an *indwelling* spirit capable of evolving individuality. Thus had it not been for the Lucifer spirits man could not have become man. It is their fire and their iron that has made the world what it is today, good and bad according to the use man has made of it. The solar force focused through the Moon imparts vitality and the faculty of growth but the rays of the Sun focused upon us by the martial Lucifer spirits give us dynamic power and are the source of all activity in the world.

Power may be latent for milleniums, as exemplified in coalbeds, which are reservoirs of solar force; a furnace and engine are required to transmute and make it available as dynamic energy, but, once the sleeping giant has been roused from latency to potency it knows no rest or peace till it has expended the last ounce of its prodigious strength. Under strict control, and carefully guided into channels of useful activity, this Martian force is the most valuable servant of mankind; the most powerful agent in the world's work, an incomparable boon to humanity. But if it escapes control the servant quickly takes mastery, its inimical power of destruction and devastation is then as terrible a scourge as its beneficent use under guidance is an inestimable blessing. It is as precious as it is dangerous; eternal vigilance is the price of safety from its ravages, but without it the world would be a wilderness.

Mars, as a focus for the latent solar life, transmutes it into desire, passion and what we may call animal spirits. It is a consuming fire, more dangerous than all the nitroglycerine ever manufactured, but also more precious than any other blessing we can have or enjoy.

The Hindoo preacher, nurtured in a land governed by Saturn, the planet of obstruction, says: "Kill out desire." He dreams away his days in destitution, but as "temper" conserves the edge of the steel that carves its way through all obstructions, so the well-directed energetic desires of the martial Anglo-Saxon have wrought a marvelous transformation in the earth; they have reared a civilization beyond all which preceded it, and though perhaps brutal in many respects, there is promise in that also, according to the proverb: "The greater the sinner, the greater the saint." Parents should take a lesson from the book of nations and refrain from applying the Saturnine wet blanket to the fiery Mars spirit of children. Saturn always says "don't, don't;" his aim is to repress and obstruct. A clear fire under proper control is useful, but death lurks in the smoke and noxious gases of a smothered fire; too many "don'ts" smother legitimate ambition and frustrate accomplishment; they may drive hapless victims into ways of evil, for the dynamic energy of Mars must and will have an outlet, so beware. The worst faults of Mars are impulsiveness and lack of persistence, but he breeds no hypocrites as does an afflicted Saturn.

From Mars we receive a number of our highly-prized virtues as well as some of our worst faults. When well-aspected he gives a strong constitution and physical endurance, a positive, independent and self-reliant nature, determined and proud, generous and energetic, resourceful and quick to learn, especially when in Aries, Leo, Scorpio or Capricorn, but when he is weak by sign as in Taurus, Cancer, Libra or aspected by squares or oppositions he makes the person quick-tempered, obstinate and spiteful, inclined to drunkenness and criminal acts, cruel and hard, a bully and braggart.

People who have Mars prominent in their horoscopes are eminently practical and play an important part in the world's work. They are especially proficient in occupations where iron and fire are used for constructive purposes or where sharp instruments are handled. Soldiers, surgeons and butchers, machine workers and iron founders, engineers and men in kindred occupations are of the martial nature. They also excel in other positions where courage and intrepidity are necessary qualities.

Mars in the Twelve Houses

♂1 *Mars in the Ascendant, or First House,* when well-aspected has a most beneficial influence upon the constitution, particularly if he is in one of the fiery signs, Aries, Leo or Sagittarius, or in the sign of his exaltation Capricorn, but sometimes when a weak sign like Cancer is rising and the other planets are much afflicted Mars in the Ascendant may infuse sufficient energy into the body to tide it over the critical period of infancy. This position also gives energy, ambition, courage, self-reliance and determination which are exceedingly helpful characteristics in winning the battle of life. It indicates an enterprising and practical person who will shun no effort in order to succeed. When Mars is afflicted in the First House he nevertheless strengthens the constitution and gives muscular power and endurance. but he makes such persons rash, impulsive, headstrong and foolhardy. Thus they neglect the ordinary precautions to guard their health and become subject to fevers and other inflammatory diseases, also liable to accidents and loss of blood by lesions of varying magnitude, danger from fire such as burns or scalds, according to the nature of the afflicting planet. In this respect the Sun is usually productive of fevers and inflammations. Jupiter gives liability to broken bones or accident by railroad or rolling stock, Uranus and Saturn falls and bruises and Venus diseases caused by indulgence of the passional nature.

♂ 2 *Mars in the Second House* when well-aspected makes the nature free and generous in financial dealings with others. The person has a splendid earning capacity and will make a financial success in any business of a martial nature involving the use of fire, iron tools or machinery. It is also an indication of money by marriage or legacy, but although the money comes fast and easily, the person will not accumulate wealth as he is very generous and fond of comfort and pleasure. When Mars is afflicted in the Second House money will come just as fast as under the good aspects at times, but at other times the bad aspects make the person outrageously extravagant and inclined to be reckless in financial ventures, with the inevitable result that heavy losses are incurred and the person may find himself without a cent in the world. A competence may be made and spent several times during life. These people never give up, however, and when they have met financial disaster they immediately start to build up anew on the ruins of the old. They are then usually successful for a time again, but they can never learn to be more careful and less extravagant, hence they are always liable to repeated financial shipwreck.

♂3 *Mars in the Third House* when well-aspected makes the mind keen, bright and alert, fond of argument, quick at repartee, ingenious, inventive and resourceful, with plenty of initiative and constructive ability. But when Mars is afflicted in the Third House it gives liability to accidents on short journeys, a quarrelsome nature specially liable to get into trouble with brothers, sisters and neighbors. These people are very critical towards everybody with whom they come in contact and therefore generally feared and avoided when possible.

♂4 *Mars in the Fourth House* when well-aspected gives a strong constitution which is maintained unimpaired even in old age; the digestive faculty is particularly good and consequently the health and strength are rugged. It makes the native exceedingly aggressive in his efforts to "feather his nest" and accumulate property for old age and a rainy day. There is also likelihood of a legacy from the parents. This is a very fortunate position, especially if Mars is in Aries, Leo or Capricorn, but if Mars is weak as in Cancer or Pisces and afflicted by square or opposition. digestive troubles or dissipation will undermine the vitality and the person will become more quarrelsome and disagreeable every day he lives He will be liable to accident by fire in the home. also to fevers and inflammatory diseases. People with Mars in this position should leave their native place as quickly as possible. This may in some measure relieve the trouble.

♂5 *Mars in the Fifth House* when well-aspected gives an ardent, demonstrative love-nature. It makes the person fond of athletic exercises, sports and muscular effort, a clean, masterful man much admired by the opposite sex or a woman who is a real "pal" to her male companion. These people make excellent disciplinarians and are much beloved by their pupils if placed in positions as teachers, or better still as principals for they make much better leaders than followers. But when Mars is afflicted in the Fifth House it makes the person very fickle in his affections. It is on with the new love even before he is through with the old, an all-around flirt and therefore likely to get into a great deal of trouble. Over-indulgence of the amorous nature is liable to sap the vitality and create dangerous physical conditions. In a woman's horoscope there is grave danger of difficulty in parturition. It also threatens danger of death to a child in the horoscope of either sex. People with Mars afflicted in the Fifth House are also liable to loss through gambling and speculation in stocks, bonds and securities.

♂6 *Mars in the Sixth House* when well-aspected makes a quick, energetic worker who is likely to rise to a prominent position in the employ of someone else, therefore the larger the firm in which he seeks employment the better. But he should not attempt to start in business for himself, for people with Mars in the Sixth House always succeed better when in the employment of someone else. This position also increases the vitality and should the person on account of other planetary configurations in the horoscope become subject to disease the dynamic energy and recuperative power of Mars will soon burn out and eliminate the poisons from the body and leave it in better health than before. But if Mars is afflicted in the Sixth House there is a liability to trouble and quarrels with other employees or employer. Should the person be in the position of employer himself he will always be at variance with his employees and subject to loss by theft and dishonesty through them. They will waste his goods and have no regard for his interests. An afflicted Mars in the Sixth House also gives a liability to fevers and inflammatory diseases, danger of burns, scalds and gun-shots and accidents sustained in the course of employment.

♂7 *Mars in the Seventh House* when well-aspected gives a capable, industrious and aggressive marriage partner, untiring in the promotion of the welfare of the family, a strong personality who is bound to rule but will do so in a kindly manner. This applies to both sexes, for when in a man's horoscope the marriage partner is indicated by Mars in the Seventh House she also will be masculine and will want to take the reins of government in her own hands. However, as Mars in the Seventh House gives a tendency to an early union when the parties are both plastic they accommodate themselves to these conditions more easily than if the marriage were consummated at a more mature age. But if Mars is afflicted in the Seventh House it indicates an accident or sudden death to the marriage partner who will be of a domineering, quarrelsome nature and if one of the watery signs, Cancer, Scorpio or Pisces is on the cusp he will also be a drunkard and sex addict. This latter applies particularly if Mars is afflicted in Scorpio. Then he also brings on inflammatory diseases of the genitals or rectum.

♂8 *Mars in the Eighth House* and well-aspected brings financial benefit through the marriage partner or by legacy. In business it is also good for gain by partnerships, lawsuits or similar Eighth House matters. But when Mars is afflicted in the Eighth House the financial conditions grow worse after marriage through the extravagance of the marriage partner. Business partnerships and litigation should also be avoided for they are sure to bring loss. People with Mars in this position should not delay making their will for the end usually comes very suddenly and unexpectedly.

♂ 9 *Mars in the Ninth House* well-aspected gives a liberal, broad and progressive view upon all problems of life. People with Mars in this position are likely to take up some cause having for its object the social or spiritual upliftment of mankind in general and become very enthusiastic workers in the particular cult which has aroused their sympathies. They are fond of a roving life and benefit by changing from one place to another, especially by travel in foreign lands. They have a clean, clear and alert mentality and a taking way of presenting their views to others. Therefore they make good missionaries in whatever line of propaganda they take up. But if Mars is afflicted in the Ninth House he makes people bigoted and fanatical in their views, regular ranters who disgust all whom they try to afflict with their ideas, whether they are religious or atheistic. People with an afflicted Mars here should never travel, but remain in their native place for they will always be in danger of accidents on journeys and however much they may be disliked in their native place they will find a still worse reception in foreign parts.

♂ 10 *Mars in the Tenth House* and well-aspected is one of the best signs of success in life for it gives an ambitious, enthusiastic nature with an inexhaustible fund of energy, so that no matter what obstacles are placed in his way the person is bound to rise to the top. It gives a masterful nature and good executive ability so that the person is well-qualified to conduct business and command others. These people succeed best in Martian occupations where fire, iron or sharp tools are used in a skilled manner, as by engineers or machinists, tailors or surgeons, et cetera. When Mars is afflicted in the Tenth House it gives the same energy and ambition as the good aspects but the person will then lack discrimination and overreach himself with the result that he will incur the enmity of other people who will accomplish his downfall and bring him into disrepute in the community. Thus the life will be filled with strife, struggle and unhappiness until the person has learned to hold himself in leash, regard the rights of others and abandon his autocratic attitude and self-assertion. This position also gives liability to accident and slander.

♂ 11 *Mars in the Eleventh House* makes people leaders in their particular social set, enthusiastic in the pursuit of pleasure, brings friends among martial and athletic persons; gives energy and enthusiasm for realizing hopes, wishes and aspirations. But if Mars in the Eleventh House is afflicted it makes the person touchy and sensitive towards friends with consequent unpopularity and he is liable to overreach himself in his keen desire to realize his ambitions in life.

♂ 12 *Mars in the Twelfth House* when well-aspected may bring the person benefit from the things denoted by this house, prisons, hospitals and charitable institutions if employed in an official capacity as warden or surgeon;or as administrator of an estate or in detective work. But if Mars is afflicted in the Twelfth House the person is liable to trouble, sorrow and self-undoing all through life. He will incur the enmity of other people and may be confined in prison or an insane asylum. If Cancer or Pisces is on the cusp of the Twelfth House Mars will lead him to drunkenness and dissipation. If Scorpio is on the cusp the vitality will be sapped through sex or self-abuse. In any case Mars afflicted in the Twelfth House makes a social outcast unless there are other redeeming features in the figure.

Mars in the Twelve Signs.

♂ ♈ *Mars in Aries* gives an energetic, enthusiastic nature, impulsive, aggressive and impatient of restraint. No matter what the obstacles in the path these people will attempt the seemingly impossible and often succeed through sheer audacity. They are original, resourceful, have considerable mechanical ability and the more venturesome an undertaking appears the more it appeals to them. This position gives an abundance of vitality and a love of sport and muscular exercise. The person is just as enthusiastic in his enjoyment of recreation and pleasure as he is in his work and on that account he gets a great deal out of life. But if Mars is afflicted in Aries it gives a violent temper and a liability to accidents, burns, scaldings, fevers and inflammatory complaints. The mind is also threatened.

♂ ♉ *Mars in Taurus* and well-aspected is a good indication of an early marriage. It shows good earning power and a free, generous disposition with regard to finances; it gives an interior strength of an unconquerable nature so that the person will always gain his ends by unflagging determination and a quiet persistence that recognizes no defeat, but presses on towards the goal that he has set for himself despite all obstacles. It is also indication of money by legacy. But if Mars is afflicted in Taurus it gives an exceedingly stubborn, violent and vindictive nature. Such people will pursue their own way despite reason, argument or entreaty and if anyone attempts to thwart them in their purposes they never forgive. They also have good earning power but squander the money foolishly so that they are very often in financial difficulties and if a legacy comes to them they are more likely to lose it through legal trouble than not and they are sure also to have domestic trouble.

♂ ♊ *Mars in Gemini* when well-aspected gives a keen, active and alert mentality. People with Mars in this position never beat about the bush. They are honest and outspoken and say just what they mean perhaps at times a little too bluntly, but at any rate they are not hypocrites. They love to measure their wits against others in debate and therefore this position makes for success in law or literature. They also succeed in the engineering professions for they are resourceful, ingenious and mechanical, apt at learning and quick to grasp a problem or proposition. But if Mars is afflicted in Gemini it gives a cynical, sneering, caustic and critical disposition and makes these people feared and shunned on account of their disagreeable nature. These people are also vacillating and unable to make a decision. Thus they cannot be depended on to stand by their word or their promises and if they keep an appointment once in awhile it happens by accident. They are always in trouble with brothers, sisters and neighbors and liable to accidents when traveling. It also gives a predisposition to bronchitis, inflammation of the lungs, pleurisy and pneumonia.

♂ ♋ *Mars in Cancer* and well-aspected gives a bold, independent and fearless nature with a tendency to rebel against restraint, a home-loving disposition, very industrious and ambitious to gather and protect all things which make for comfort and luxury, so that he is a good provider for the home in every respect. But at the same time people with this aspect aim to exercise unrestricted authority over everything and everybody within the home. They tolerate no other authority there. This position makes the temper rather uncertain and gives a tendency and a desire for change of occupation, so that the person never really settles down to one line of endeavor but takes up a number of vocations and drops them suddenly. If Mars is afflicted in Cancer it brings domestic troubles, frequent and violent scenes and quarrels in the home with a tendency to move frequently from one place to another; inflammatory diseases of the stomach, and digestive ailments, also accidents by fire in the home through recklessness or carelessness.

♂ ♌ *Mars in Leo* and well-aspected gives an active, industrious and honest nature, fearless and independent in all dealings with others, a keen sense of honor and responsibility, hence makes one eminently fitted to occupy a position of trust either in a public or private concern. These people are enthusiastic and energetic either in work or play, lovers of sport and a good time generally. They are very ardent in their admiration of the opposite sex and woo the object of their affections with an intensity that carries all before it, overrides all obstacles and brings the matter to a speedy consummation. These people never beat about the bush but say what they mean in a manner that is often extremely embarrassing in its directness. They are strong and forceful in their arguments either for or against that which they believe or disbelieve and therefore they not infrequently arouse opposition on the part of those who differ from them. They are very venturesome and often take a pride in risk either in the pursuit of pleasure or business. When Mars is afflicted in Leo it gives a fiery, violent temper and a liability to fever and inflammatory diseases, palpitation of the heart, hallucinations, biliousness. There is also danger of inordinate affection, trouble in courtship, loss of children and loss through speculations. An afflicted Mars in Leo gives the same daring as when well-aspected but the danger of accident is greater because the person with the afflicted planets becomes foolhardy and reckless.

♂ ♍ *Mars in Virgo* when well-aspected gives an ambitious nature and a quick intellect, able to grasp an idea and elaborate upon it. It strengthens the mental qualities and gives a scientific turn to the mind with an ability to apply this faculty either in research work or in business. The people with this position are therefore energetic and enterprising in many of the world's industrial affairs. There their shrewdness and quick-wittedness bring them success and preferment. This is a good position for people who are engaged in any of the industries connected with the sick, such as nurses, doctors, chemists, the science of sanitation and hygiene, preparation of health-foods and kindred occupations. If people with Mars in Virgo are themselves overtaken by disease this position gives them the ability to recuperate quickly and makes them less liable to become chronic invalids as so many other Virgo people do.

When Mars is afflicted in Virgo it subjects the mind to worry and irritability, with a tendency to brood over troubles in life which are mostly illusory. No matter how or where such people are employed they are always critical toward their fellow-employees and the employer and dissatisfied with everything connected with their work. They are also of a dishonest nature and cannot be trusted in a position of responsibility. This position also makes people over-indulgent of their appetites and subject to intestinal disorders.

♂ ♎ *Mars in Libra* and well-aspected gives an ardent, demonstrative and loving nature which is very greatly attracted to the opposite sex and therefore it inclines to an early marriage. It also gives an enthusiastic love of art and beauty in all their phases and it makes the person very popular with the public or in societies of a social or religious nature. This is an excellent position for a lawyer, as it will bring much activity in this line and it is a good indication of general health. But when Mars is afflicted in Libra it makes the person very unpopular and subject to the opposition and criticism of the community; danger of public scandal on account of unfaithfulness in sex relations, for Mars in Libra always produces a strong attraction toward the opposite sex and if he is afflicted there the nature is amorous and fickle with the natural result that trouble arises by playing with the affections of others.

♂ ♏ *Mars in Scorpio* when well-aspected gives a keen, sharp and forceful mentality, a rather blunt manner and an indifference to the finer sensibilities of others, consequently these people often make themselves disliked at first until others get used to them and realize that they are not such ogres as they seem. They are very ingenious and mechanical, with indomitable courage and inexhaustible energy which carry them over all obstacles to whatever goal they set themselves. In this respect they are very selfish and ready to sacrifice whatever stands in their way. They make good police officers, soldiers and surgeons and are able to fill any other position where a dominant authority is required, or skill with sharp tools. In a woman's horoscope it shows that the husband has good earning capacity, but is rather too free and generous with his means. It also indicates the possibility of a legacy.

When Mars is afflicted in Scorpio it brings out the worst side of the passional nature and leads the person into sex excesses or causes addiction to solitary vice that saps the vitality, and unless corrected it is liable to bring the person to an early grave. In a woman's horoscope it indicates that the husband will squander his money on gratification of self, also that parturition will be a dangerous event. In either sex Mars in Scorpio indicates a quarrelsome nature and a biting tongue.

♂ ♐ *Mars in Sagittarius* and well-aspected gives an argumentative disposition and fondness of debating on subjects of a serious nature such as law, philosophy and religion. It makes the person candid and open in all his dealings with others, full of enthusiasm and ambition, anxious to appear well in the eyes of the community, although he would scorn to cater to the ideas of others where they do not coincide with his ideas of probity and justice. These people make interesting and ideal entertainers, especially in later life for they are fond of traveling and are keen observers, hence they always have a fund of interesting and instructive information which they are both willing and anxious to impart to their hearers. These people are also fond of sports and out-door exercise, in which they usually excel and a well-aspected Mars in Sagittarius is an ideal position for a lawyer. It makes for much success in that direction by sharpening and quickening the mental and oratorical faculties.

When Mars is afflicted in Sagittarius he gives a sharp tongue and a quarrelsome disposition and there is a dishonest streak in the nature, therefore such people are often found generally disliked in the community and particularly in social circles, for they seem to be always at variance with the ideas and opinions of others and adopt a most supercilious attitude toward those with whom they disagree. These people are also liable to meet with accidents when they travel and to sustain a number of broken bones.

♂ ♑ *Mars in Capricorn* when well-aspected adds much strength to the character for it gives an ambitious and enthusiastic disposition backed by an indomitable courage and a well-nigh inexhaustible energy together with a patient persistence and perseverance that are bound to overcome all obstacles and in the end reach the desired goal. Therefore people with Mars in this position are bound to rise in life, particularly if Capricorn be placed in the Tenth House. It invites the respect and esteem of the community so that people with this position are often offered public appointments in addition to their private enterprises and they serve well in posts of honor for they are naturally fitted to take great responsibilities and carry on great enterprises. The wider their scope of action the better they like it, for they are superlatively efficient.

When Mars is afflicted in Capricorn there will be a similar ambition to do great things but the person will be rash, impulsive and headstrong so that he overreaches himself and takes upon himself more than he can carry through. He will also lack the persistence and perseverance necessary to overcome obstacles and as the disposition will be basically dishonest, though he may rise on account of his enthusiasm and pretentious nature to some prominence he is certain to be shorn of his authority before very long and become an object of scorn and derision in the community. There is nothing worse than an afflicted Mars in Capricorn. It also gives a liability to accidents affecting the limbs and its reflex action on the part of the body ruled by the opposite sign, viz., the stomach, gives a tendency to gastric troubles. People with this affliction also have a hasty temper and a vindictive disposition.

♂ ♒ *Mars in Aquarius* when well-aspected makes the person quick-witted and intuitive, ingenious and original, enterprising and ambitious, a hard worker for success in whatever line he chooses in life. Hence he will gain friendship from others who are able to help him realize his hopes and wishes. These people are also very mechanical and ingenious, particularly in things connected with the electrical science. They also succeed well as managers, officials or workers in and for a philanthropic society or public utility corporation.

When Mars is afflicted in Aquarius it makes the person too independent, bombastic and resentful of authority, blunt of speech and manner toward others, and resentful in the highest degree if he is not treated with what he considers proper respect and consideration. Hence such people are very difficult to get along with and often quarrel with everybody around them. There is a tendency to loss through gambling and speculation. An afflicted Mars in Aquarius also gives a tendency to trouble with the eyes because Aquarius governs the ethers; and by reflex action the opposite sign Leo may cause palpitation of the heart.

♂ ♓ *Mars in Pisces* when well-aspected gives ability as a detective, warden of a prison or surgeon in a hospital and in kindred positions where the person does not come in direct contact with the public, but exercises authority in an obscure manner. It also gives a tendency toward secret love affairs which the person is able to hide from the public eye. But when Mars is afflicted in Pisces the indulgence of clandestine intercourse will bring trouble into the life. There is also liability to suffer from the attacks of secret enemies and to become enmeshed in the net of the law and suffer imprisonment, or it may manifest as an inordinate love of strong drink which will then cause imprisonment and make the person a ward of the community. Much trouble and many misfortunes are indicated because the nature is untruthful.

Mars in Aspect with the Other Planets

☉ P ☌ ⚹ △ ♂ *The Sun parallel, conjunction, sextile or trine to Mars.* The conjunction gives a tendency to fever, especially if it occurs in Aries, the sign which governs the head, but it is curious that people with that configuration seem also to be able to endure a much higher temperature than others, and come unscathed through such a siege of sickness as would ordinarily prove fatal. With that exception these aspects all produce a superabundance of vital energy which assures their possessor of the most radiant health all through life. They strengthen the constitution and make the person able to endure the hardest tasks; they give him a dauntless determination and courage to face the greatest odds. Given a plan to follow he may be trusted to overcome all physical obstacles for he has both executive and constructive ability together with an indomitable will which refuses to recognize defeat. The disposition is frank and open but blunt and often brusque; such people are too intensely bent on what they want to do to waste time in politeness and suavity, therefore they brush the conventionalities aside without compunction and are consequently not liked by people of too fine sensibilities, but they are men and women of action and the foremost factors in the world's work; but for their energy and enterprise the world would move much more slowly.

⊙□☍♂ *The Sun square or opposition to Mars* endows the person with an abundance of energy, and the faculty of leadership, but they are turned to purposes of deviltry and destruction; the courage implanted by the good aspects becomes foolhardiness and the person has a loud, overbearing, swaggering manner and is ready to fight at the drop of a hat; he is always in opposition to the constituted authority and ready to rebel wherever he sees a chance; he has an extremely fiery temper but holds no resentment. On account of these qualities he is universally disliked by both employers and his fellow workers, always in hot water and never stays long in any place for he is an agitator and trouble maker. These aspects also dispose to accidents in which the person may be maimed, to gunshot and knife-wounds, also to scalding, fevers, and inflammatory complaints, boils and eruptions.

Aspects to the Sun and Mars are absolutely necessary to give zest to life; even adverse aspects are better than none, for where these planets are unaspected the person is usually listless, vapid and will never amount to anything no matter how good the figure may be in other respects.

♀ * △ ♂ *Venus sextile or trine to Mars* will give an ambitious, aspiring and adventurous nature, amorous and extremely demonstrative in its affection, and very fond of sports and pleasures. It gives the person an abundance of energy and business acumen, consequently he has a splendid earning capacity, but no matter how much money he makes it just filters through his fingers, for he loves above all things to make a great outward show and display. Being a free spender he is also very popular among his associates, and being as already said of an amorous nature he marries either very early or his marriage is a very sudden and hasty one. These aspects are also indications of money by marriage or legacy.

♀ ☌ P ♂ *Venus conjunction or parallel Mars* does not always operate in the same manner, but these aspects are to be classed as good or bad according to circumstances and the matter to be judged. For instance, Mars conjunction Venus makes the person less blunt and domineering, more kind and polite, and is therefore good in that respect, but the conjunction also strengthens the passional nature, especially if it occurs in Scorpio, and in the Twelfth House it often leads to self-abuse so that in those cases it is decidedly bad. Therefore students must exercise judgment before classifying these aspects.

♀ □ ☍ ♂ *Venus square or opposition to Mars* gives a very voluptuous and sensuous disposition, liable to gross excesses in the gratification of the passions which will sap the vitality. It is likely to break down the health and constitution, leaving the person a wreck on the sea of life if it is allowed free scope. These people are altogether too generous, especially where the opposite sex is concerned. They are very extravagant and on that account spend more than they can afford on themselves, besides what they squander on their many *amours,* so that no matter how much money they make, they are generally in financial difficulty, and not infrequently they figure as defendants in the debtor's court. If Mars or Venus is in Cancer, Scorpio or Pisces there is a tendency to such a dissolute and dissipated living, such a craving for low pleasures that, if indulged, it will drag the human being down below the level of animals.

☿ ✱ △ ♂ *Mercury sextile or trine to Mars* gives a keen, sharp, ingenious and resourceful mentality. It makes the person enthusiastic over any proposition which appeals to him and he has also the ability to enthuse others and impress them with his views. He is an indefatigable worker in any cause which arouses his sympathies, but he is no visionary, he is interested only in concrete matters. These people love argument or debate, and they have an inexhaustible fund of wit and good humor, sometimes blended with a vein of sarcasm which always strikes its mark, yet never viciously nor maliciously. They also have remarkable dexterity and are able to turn their hands to whatever task is required and do it with a speed, facility and expedition that are astonishing to say the least. They cannot do anything slowly or by halves; whatever they undertake must be done with a rush, and they put their whole energy into it so that they may accomplish the task and do it well; hence these aspects give success in life, in almost any line of endeavor these people may select, but probably most in literature or the mechanical arts.

☿ ☌ P ♂ *Mercury conjunction or parallel to Mars* gives the same mental energy, enthusiasm and dexterity as the definitely good aspects but whether they are used for constructive and good purposes or for destructive and evil depends upon the other aspects, house position and sign which they occupy. If the configuration occurs in a sign where either or both are strong and well placed, as Mars in Aries or Capricorn, or Mercury in Gemini or Virgo, or if they are fortified by good aspects from the Sun, Venus and Jupiter, Mars conjunction or parallel to Mercury will operate similarly to the sextile or trine as stated in the foregoing paragraph, which see; but if Mars and Mercury are in one of the watery signs, Cancer, Scorpio or Pisces, or if either or both are afflicted by Saturn, Uranus or Neptune, the conjunction or parallel of Mars and Mercury will give the same evil tendencies as the square or opposition which are defined in the next paragraph.

☿ □ ☍ ♂ *Mercury square or opposition to Mars* makes people quick-witted, sharp and alert, quick-tempered, impulsive and excitable, liable to jump at conclusions and act before they think with the inevitable result that they are always getting themselves or other people into trouble, hence they are dangerous associates. They are born prevaricators and utterly incapable of making an exact statement. It is just as natural for them to color or exaggerate their statements as it is to breathe. They are vitriolic in their wrath and their tongues are more poisonous than the bite of a rattlesnake, hence they are either feared or hated by those who are unfortunate enough to be bound to them by environment; all who can, shun them. They are bullies who are bound either to rule or ruin wherever they are and they allow no obstacle to stand in their way which can be removed either by force or slander. They are the acme of selfishness, swagger and consummate egotism. The foregoing tendencies may of course be modified by other aspects, but if they are not, such people are a menace to society. If either Mars or Mercury is placed in the Sixth or Twelfth House or in any other position so that the bad aspect acts upon the health, there is a liability to nervous prostration, brain fever or insanity.

☽ ✱ △ ♂ *The Moon sextile or trine to Mars* gives a wonderful vitality and a strong physique so that the person is able to withstand almost any tendencies to ill-health, which will be overcome by it. The power of endurance is increased and the person can survive hardships to which people ordinarily succumb. It gives a resolute, courageous, energetic and ambitious mind of a resourceful and eminently constructive turn. It makes the person quick but not precipitate in his decisions. Thus he gains the confidence and esteem of others and earns considerable money, but the nature is extremely free and generous so that money does not stay by such people—they spend it almost as fast as they get it.

☽ ☌ P ♂ *The Moon conjunction or parallel to Mars* may be either good or bad according to the sex of the person and the department of life we are considering. It strengthens the health and the vitality, particularly in the horoscope of a woman. In the horoscope of a man it would indicate a robust marriage partner of a domineering nature and with respect to the mind it would make the person very impulsive, particularly if placed in one of the common signs or in the Third or Ninth House. It also gives a very bad temper but not so bad as the square or opposition. If Mars is in conjunction or parallel to the Moon in Scorpio it gives an abnormal sexual desire which will not be denied, particularly if Venus is there also. In watery signs it inclines to drink, and in any place it makes the person restless and unsettled, for it is like mixing fire and water.

☽ □ ☍ ♂ *The Moon square or opposition to Mars* gives a very quick temper and a tendency to hasty or impulsive expressions and acts that may cause such people a great deal of sorrow and trouble. They resent rules or regulations or any other measures that tend to curb their desires or the gratification of their appetites in whatever direction. But if they are in authority they are very domineering and exacting in their demands for instant obedience upon the part of others, nor do they hesitate to use whatever physical force may be necessary to compel obedience if they think they can do so without too great danger to themselves. Sometimes they will take desperate chances to satisfy their spite. Having an improperly balanced mind they are foolhardy in their venturesomeness and upon occasion they will attempt to do things which no one in his sane mind would try. On account of the foregoing characteristics such people make many enemies and cause a great deal of suffering to others, particularly among members of their immediate family who cannot very well get away from them. If these aspects occur in watery signs, particularly with Mars or the Moon in Pisces the person is also an inveterate drunkard. From the standpoint of health they give a tendency to accidents by fire and water, to fevers and acute inflammatory diseases, wounds and gunshot, diseases of the genitals, too copious menses, danger in parturition, and indigestion.

♄ ✱ △ ♂ *Saturn sextile or trine to Mars* gives a determined and energetic nature capable of intense and sustained action and of obtaining unusual results thereby. The executive ability, dominant forcefulness and endurance of these people are remarkable and consequently they are constantly accomplishing what others cannot achieve. Hence they always rise to prominent positions and are much esteemed on account of their ability, but they are seldom liked, for these aspects make the character cruel and hard. They give a strong physique and general good health.

♄ ☌ P □ ☍ ♂ *Saturn conjunction, parallel, square or opposition to Mars* are thoroughly bad aspects indicating a selfish, violent, harsh and cruel nature, quick tempered and vindictive, absolutely dishonest, untruthful and unscrupulous, giving liability to public disgrace and imprisonment, also to accident and violent death, and if one of the planets is essentially dignified or exalted the evil influence is much enhanced. It should also be remembered that such serious defects do not result from one aspect alone and if the other configurations in the horoscope are good the foregoing delineation will only apply in a mild measure.

♃ ✱ △ ♂ *Jupiter sextile or trine to Mars.* It is the nature of Jupiter to be somewhat conservative and dignified, but when blended with the fire of Mars it gives an enthusiasm and an ability to influence others and imbue them with the same feelings. It makes the nature noble, sincere, honest and straightforward. This aspect is also good for the financial prosperity of the person for both Mars and Jupiter when well-aspected attract money, but they differ in regard to disbursement. Jupiter is somewhat conservative in that respect, but where the Martian and Jupiterian qualities are blended by a good aspect the result is an ideal, generous nature, neither too lavish nor too conservative, but able to strike the happy medium. These people have much ingenuity and constructive ability and whatever they do they put their whole heart into it. Hence they are successful in business and popular in society. They are fond of out-door sports and games. They love to travel and gain much pleasure by so doing. Mars rules the hæmoglobin in the blood which is so important a factor in health and vitality therefore the good aspects of Jupiter and Mars increase the red blood corpuscles with the result that these people have an abundance of health, vitality, power and endurance.

♃ P ☌ ♂ *Jupiter parallel or conjunction Mars* strengthens the constitution and increases the vitality the same as the good aspects. It also indicates that the person is able to earn much money and uses it freely and generously, but the mental qualities are similar to those conferred by the bad aspects. The person is tricky, deceitful, untruthful, impulsive in judgment and not to be depended upon. If the conjunction occurs in one of the watery signs, especially in Pisces he will probably be a drunkard though this is not as certain as with the square and opposition. These people are generally plethoric and liable to apoplexy.

♃ □ ☍ ♂ *Jupiter square or opposition to Mars* is the signature of the gambler and if one of the planets is in a watery sign, especially in Pisces he will be a drunkard also, a tricky, dishonest and disreputable character who always acts through impulse. With respect to health we find that these people suffer principally from blood and liver complaints; the circulation is poor and the blood is so rich that there is danger of apoplexy.

♅ ✱ △ ♂ *Uranus sextile or trine to Mars* gives an energetic and ambitious disposition, an original, ingenious, alert, intuitive mind which is resourceful in the highest degree and able to cope with great difficulties under trying circumstances. Therefore people with these configurations are naturally of an inventive turn of mind and successful in bringing their ideas to realization. Their inventive genius expresses itself usually along electrical lines, aviation or other unusual directions for these aspects are one of the marks of the pioneer of the Aquarian age, where science and invention will reach out in directions that are now undreamed of even as possibilties. But while these people are dreamers of dreams they are also practical, energetic and enterprising in a sufficient degree to make their dreams come true in the world. They have a wide vision and a noble nature which rises over all petty distinctions of race, creed or color and recognizes in all human beings the divine spark which is the basis of universal brotherhood. They may not be exactly religious in the orthodox sense of the word, but their ideas are truly cosmic, hence they are often mistaken for visionaries by those who do not understand them.

♅ ☌ P □ ☍ ♂ *Uranus conjunction, parallel, square or opposition to Mars* gives an erratic and eccentric disposition, a violent temper of the worst nature, an unusual resentment of even the slightest restraint and gives the person a stubborn, headstrong and dogged determination to go ahead in any line of action upon which he has decided no matter what the outcome. He will listen to neither reason nor entreaty but follows his own course in defiance of all. People with these configurations often become anarchists of the reddest type for they do not stop even at the shedding of blood if other testimonies in the figure concur. They are cruel, hard and cold without a spark of true love though they may be inflamed with passion of the most burning intensity. This is particularly the case when Mars is square Uranus and either planet is placed in Taurus or Scorpio. In a woman's horoscope Mars square Uranus usually leads to seduction no matter where placed, but if in Taurus or Scorpio escape is almost impossible. The other characteristics of these planets in these configurations work themselves out according to the signs wherein they are placed so that their placement in Taurus or Scorpio work upon the sex which is governed by these signs. When one of these planets is in Scorpio if the person takes up the profession of surgery he will become very cruel and unfeeling, ready to operate for the mere pleasure of causing pain and in consequence or in pursuit of this passion he will probably take up vivisection and develop an unusual ingenuity in torturing his victims. With Mars or Uranus in Scorpio or Pisces he will be underhanded or tricky though he may show a very different front to the public. In Aries it will make a rattlebrain, in Gemini and Virgo an unusually quick mentality but quick in seeing only how to trick others; in Sagittarius it will make the person very materialistic, atheistic or fanatical against the established religion or society; thus the planets blend their nature with each individual sign.

♆ P ☌ □ ☍ ♂ *Neptune parallel, conjunction, square or opposition to Mars,* see page 402.

♆ ✱ △ ♂ *Neptune sextile or trine Mars,* see page 402.

CHAPTER XV.

Planetary Octaves

BEFORE considering the effect of Uranus and Neptune in the various signs and houses it may be expedient and illuminating to study their relations to Venus and Mercury which are their lower octaves. That such a relationship exists has been sensed by various astrological authors who by speculation and observation have learned a great deal about these two planets. What they have brought out does great credit to their sagacity, but not having had the benefit of esoteric training it is not to be wondered at that they have become confused on certain points which we shall now explain so that students of the esoteric philosophy may see how these explanations dovetail into the general philosophy of the Western Wisdom School, and thus bear out the statement that Uranus is the higher octave of Venus and Neptune the higher octave of Mercury.

The Western Wisdom teaching of the Rosicrucians states that man-in-the-making was plant-like and bi-sexual during the Hyperborean Epoch and thus able to create from himself without the necessity of co-operation with anyone else. But at that time he was without a brain and unable to think, therefore in the Lemurian Epoch the angels directed one-half of the sex force upward to the part which is now the head and used it for the formation of the brain and larynx. The process is plainly traceable in the antenatal development of the foetus which accounts for the intimate relation between the sex organs, the larynx and the brain, observable in the change of voice which takes place when the boy reaches puberty and the mental disability which follows the unrestrained abuse of the generative function. Thus it may be said that the sex function whereby new bodies are created in the physical world, and become our physical children, is closely connected with the brain and larynx which man uses to conceive the children of his brain and mind and give them vocal expression by the larynx. It is a matter of common knowledge to astrologers that man is incited to perform the generative function of the begetting of physical children by the love-ray of Venus; likewise that the ray of reason emanating from Mercury is responsible for the begetting of the children of mind and their vocal expression by the larynx, so that both Mercury and Venus are creative in their functions, one upon the physical plane, the other upon the mental plane.

Mercury is usually associated with reason and intelligence; to him is ascribed rule over the cerebrospinal nervous system, which is the medium of transmission between the embodied spirit and the world without. Thus as Neptune signifies the sub- and superhuman intelligences who live and move in the spiritual realms of the universe, but who work with and upon us, so Mercury indicates the human intelligence focused upon the terrestrial, physical world wherein we live from birth to death. Therefore it may be said that Neptune is the octave of Mercury, but there is a deeper sense.

Reference to a textbook of anatomy or physiology will show that lengthwise fissures in the spinal cord divide it into three parts which enclose a hollow tube. Each of these columns is ruled by one of the Hierarchies in closest touch with us: the lunar, martial and mercurial; one or the other predominating, according to the stage in evolution of the individual. In the spinal canal the rays of Neptune kindle the spinal spirit fire whereby the human spirit is enabled to pierce the veil of flesh and contact the worlds beyond; this vision is colored according to the column of the cord most actively excited. In the childhood days of mankind the creative force which is now turned outwards to build ships, houses, railways, telephones, etc., was used inwardly to build the organs of our body, and as the surrounding physical world is photographed upon the table of a camera obscura, so the spiritual world was reflected in the spinal canal. There man beheld the first lunar God Jehovah, whose Angels were his first tutors. Later a part of the Angels who, under the leadership of *Lucifer* had rebelled against Jehovah and who are now exiled on the planet Mars forced entrance to the spinal cord of man and incited him to abuse of the generative function. The spiritual inner vision of mankind faded when "their eyes were opened and they saw they were naked;" then they lost touch with the higher self, they saw only the person, and the docile creature of Jehovah was soon transformed to a savage and a brute under the impulses of the Lucifer Spirits, the hierarchy of Mars, but by their promptings man has also learned to conquer material obstacles, to build outwardly and become architect of the world.

To counteract the unmitigated selfishness bred by the Martian Angels, and to make mankind humane, our Elder Brothers from Mercury, human like ourselves, whose high state of evolution required the high vibration generated and prevailing in close proximity to the Sun, were required to invest the spinal cord of man also, and through their labors civilization has taken on a different form, mankind is again beginning to look inwards.

At the present time the right cerebral hemisphere is governed by Mercury, and the pineal gland, its higher octave, is ruled by Neptune who also has dominion over the spinal canal which is the avenue whereby one pole of the creative energy was originally turned upward for the building of the brain.

The ray of Neptune carries what occultists know as the Father fire, the light and life of the Divine Spirit, which expresses itself as will. This it focuses in the voluntary nervous system of the physical body governed by its lower octave Mercury which acting through the right brain galvanizes the body into speech and action, expressing the will of the indwelling spirit.

By this diversion of the creative energy the human being ceased, as already said, to be a physical hermaphrodite, a complete creative unit, and was then compelled to seek a mate in order to propagate the species. Therefore the Son, the Cosmic Christ, focused the love-ray of the Life Spirit upon Uranus, (ruling the pituitary body),who transmits it to the vital body where Venus, the lower octave of Uranus gives it expression in propagation and growth.

Between the Divine Spirit and Life Spirit on the one hand and their counterparts, the physical and vital bodies, on the other hand, is the Human Spirit ruled by the Sun, and its counterpart, the desire body, ruled by the lesser light, the Moon. But this is debatable ground contested by Jupiter and Mercury on the one side, Saturn and Mars being on the other.

The ray of Uranus is gradually forging a *second spinal cord* by drawing the lower love-ray of Venus upward and transmuting it to altruism, conquering for it the dominion over the sympathetic segment of the present spinal cord and *the left cerebral hemisphere* now ruled by the passionate hierarchy of Mars, the Lucifer Spirits. This work has been completely accomplished by the Adepts, therefore they have no need to marry for each is now a complete creative unit on both the spiritual and physical planes, having turned the bi-polar creative force, masculine and feminine, upward through the double spinal cord, illuminated and raised in potential energy by the spinal spirit fires of Neptune (Will) and Uranus (Love and Imagination). This creative energy conceives in the twin hemispheres of the cerebrum, ruled by Mars and Mercury, a vehicle fit for the expression of the spirit, which is then sent out and objectified in the world *by the spoken creative word.*

This is the secret of how the Adepts form a new body without going through the womb, and some day all humanity will attain to this standard of perfection as *spiritual hermaphrodites;* then we shall no longer be "a little lower than the angels" who create by similar methods but we shall be higher than they are now for we shall then have the reason and intellect which they lack, in addition to the complete creative power.

CHAPTER XVI.

URANUS, THE PLANET OF ALTRUISM

THE love ray of Venus goes out to the mate and blood relations but by a good aspect of Uranus it is raised beyond the realm of sex love to cosmic proportions, to love such as that which Christ must have felt when he wept over Jerusalem and said that, as a hen gathers its brood under its wing, so would he have loved to gather them to his bosom. The people who have this Uranian love therefore become builders of society; associated with every good and uplifting movement. An adverse aspect of Uranus to Venus on the other hand, has the most degrading effect on the Venus function, for it leads to disregard of the laws and conventions of society and to perversion of the sacred creative function.

Love is a much abused word, and the emotion thus miscalled is usually so tainted with desire that it is Martian passion rather than Venusian love. Coalition, the keyword of Venus, suggests a most intimate union, a blending of the very souls of two or more people who compose a family. But *Altruism*, the keyword of Uranus, hints at such an all-embracing love as our Saviour felt. Thus Uranus is the octave of Venus and anyone ready to enter the path of preparation which leads to initiation must gradually learn to outgrow the Venus love which makes the immediate family all in all and begin to cultivate the all-embracing Uranian altruism.

This goal is high and those who aim so high often fall very low. When we essay to transcend the Venus love and cultivate the Uranian altruism we are thus in great danger, and the most promising lives are sometimes wrecked by the pernicious theory of soul-mates, which leads to clandestine love affairs and perversion of the creative function. But remember this—altruism does not require return of the love bestowed upon others, it has absolutely no concern with sex; it will not lessen the love for our family, but they being nearest to us will feel the increase of our love to a greater degree than those further away, and unless our love brings forth such fruit it is not Uranian and will not further us upon the path of attainment.

Seeing this is so, we may readily understand that the great majority of humanity cannot yet respond to the higher side of Uranus, and its effect upon the morals is therefore principally perversion of sex, clandestine love affairs, free love, and disregard of conventionality; that is, of course, when aspected by squares and oppositions. Under such conditions it makes people unconventional and erratic, rebellious at the least restraint, very independent and brusque in manner, fond of pioneer work, and investigation of unusual things. They take to the higher mechanics, electricity, aviation, and the like, as a duck to water, and are rather proud of their attainments. They find prominence in literature, science, philosophy, and especially in the occult arts. Uranus also gives a high grade of musical genius when configurated with Venus, and if Uranus is well fortified by position and aspects it qualifies the person for leadership in an unusual way. It may also be said that the effects of the Uranian ray are very sudden and unexpected, whether for good or ill; it comes like a bolt out of the blue, and as we respond most easily to its evil side, these effects are generally disastrous in nature. When Uranus is on the Ascendant it adds length to the body, so that the true Uranians are usually very tall.

Uranus in the Twelve Houses

♅1 *Uranus in the First House,* even when well-aspected, makes the person very odd and eccentric in his habits, so that he seems to delight in doing exactly the things that are against the conventions and customs, just so that he may appear odd. He always finds an original way of doing things, different from that of all other people, and is very self-satisfied in his opinion that his methods and ideas are better than any one else's. If opposed he will defend his ideas to the last ditch, if Uranus is in any way afflicted. But when Uranus is well-aspected in the First

House there is usually a tolerance for the opinions of others, a spirit of give-and-take which avoids the hard feelings generated by an afflicted Uranus. Uranus on the Ascendant also makes the person very restless; there are many sudden changes in the life and it will, of course, depend upon the aspects prevailing at the time whether the changes are for good or ill; but at any rate the call of the far fields that look so green, are constantly before the mind's eye, so that the Uranians are always ready to be the pioneers in new undertakings or a new cause, just so that it is something that has not been tried before, and so offers a chance of risk and adventure.

♅ 2 *Uranus in the Second House,* which governs finance, naturally indicates a restless and unsettled state of the finances of the person. There will be many ups and downs, and even though such a person may have other good aspects that qualify him to reason accurately concerning other matters, it will be found that in the financial department he is unable to protect himself against these sudden and unforeseen losses, or gains. For him there is no such thing as a staid and solid investment, for the most unlooked-for conditions are likely to turn up and either net him an altogether unlooked-for increase or else bring about an equally unaccountable loss, all with such suddenness that there is no way of changing the matter. Therefore it is absolutely impossible to give financial advice to such people, for even if they invested in a proposition as solid as the proverbial rock of Gibraltar, it is doubtful if an earthquake would not unsettle it.

♅3 *Uranus in the Third House.* The Third House governs brothers and sisters, neighbors, education, and the mental or intellectual faculties. Therefore this position strengthens the intuitional abilities of the person, and gives a certain predisposition towards what is commonly called psychic faculties. Uranus rules the ether, hence the Third House position should make it easy for the person to cultivate spiritual sight, especially if Uranus is well-aspected with the Sun, Moon, Venus or Mercury. If Uranus is afflicted in the Third House it indicates quarrels with neighbors, brothers and sisters, probably a breaking up of the family ties, also that the education will be interfered with through the erratic, self-willed conduct of the person, and the mind will be more or less unsettled, and changeable as a weather-vane. An afflicted Uranus in the Third House also predisposes to accidents according to the nature of the afflicting planet, and particularly when on short journeys. These people, it may also be said, are subject to adventures and strange happenings on their journeys such as do not usually befall other people.

♅4 *Uranus in the Fourth House.* People who have Uranus in the Fourth House ought to leave their place of birth as soon as possible for they cannot succeed there. Both the parents and their whole neighborhood and environment will be antagonistic to them. If it so happens that the parents are wealthy they will try to disinherit a child with Uranus in the Fourth House. Even if his Seventh and Eighth Houses be well fortified, it is very doubtful if he would win in a contest for his share of the patrimony, as the public sentiment in his birthplace, where such a suit would probably be tried, would be so much against him that he would lose in the end. It would also be disastrous for such a person to marry and establish a home of his own, for peace, harmony and contentment cannot exist where the spasmodic and erratic Uranus is; that is to say, if it is afflicted. If it is well-aspected it is also doubtful if such a person would ever attempt to establish a home, for his sympathies would be too large and he would probably be identified with wider activities—a home or homes on a larger and more universal scale. This position also gives a very strong attraction towards occult science.

♅5 *Uranus in the Fifth House.* The Fifth House rules educational activities, publications, pleasures, courtship, and childbirth. The erratic

Uranus in this House will in the first place give some very unconventional ideas concerning the intercourse and relation of the sexes and usually leads to a clandestine relationship contrary to the laws of the land. A woman with this condition in her horoscope is particularly prone to be taken advantage of even though she may not consciously be guilty of inviting undue advances. It also makes parturition very difficult and if a child is brought to birth there is danger of loss by some sudden accident or unusual disease. If other influences in the horoscope give a leaning toward literature, a person who has Uranus in the Fifth House will be found to espouse some unconventional cause, like socialism, anarchism, or kindred movements, and if Uranus be afflicted by Saturn, Mars, or Neptune, the articles written by him, or the paper published by him or with which he is connected. will probably incite to bloodshed, conspiracy, and treachery, which will bring the person into trouble with the authorities. If on the other hand, Uranus be well-aspected from the Fifth House in a horoscope indicating literary tendencies, the ideas advocated on account of this Uranian influence will probably be so Utopian, idealistic, and altruistic that they will be beyond the contemporaries of the person. The love nature will also be of such a high idealistic strain that few if any will be able to respond, and this may also mitigate in a large measure the physical trouble indicated in parturition. A person with a well-aspected Uranus in the Fifth House would not gamble, and if one who has an afflicted Uranus there attempted it, he would naturally meet with loss, no matter how careful he might seem to be. With respect to the pursuit of pleasure indulged in by these people, we shall find them attracted to all new and strange things. At the present time the most of them are probably longing for the day when it will be possible for them to race in the clouds and drive aeroplanes more recklessly than they are now driving automobiles.

♅ 6 *Uranus in the Sixth House.* The Sixth House governs the employment and service, also health and disease, therefore the erratic, spasmodic Uranus in the Sixth House predisposes to occupational diseases of a strange nature, asphyxiation, mental and nervous disorders, such as epilepsy, and St. Vitus dance. Even if Uranus is well-aspected, these tendencies are not entirely abrogated, at least, a person with Uranus in this position will be very nervous and high-strung under all conditions. With respect to employers and fellow-employees this position makes the person very irritable; he is brusque and abrupt to all connected with his work and therefore liable to trouble in employment or with employees. This position gives a tendency towards mediumship and undesirable phases of psychic experiences. If Uranus is much afflicted there is also danger of obsession and insanity.

♅ 7 *Uranus in the Seventh House,* indicates a romantic, sudden, or ill-considered marriage. Sometimes a common-law or other irregular form of union is consummated under this position. Often the marriage partner is a person never thought of as a mate until the Uranian ray impels to marriage on the spur of the moment.

People with Uranus in the Seventh House are usually unfortunate in their marriage relations, because the marriage partner has the spasmodic, inconstant, independent Uranian nature, chafes under the limitation and cannot remain true to any one person, but becomes inveigled into clandestine relations with the result that the marriage is often dissolved in the divorce court and separation and estrangement follow; there is quite often a public scandal in connection with these affairs, or it may indicate the death of the marriage partner, all according to aspects.

People with Uranus in the Seventh House should never go to law, for no matter how just their cause may be they are most likely to be thwarted or checkmated by some strange, unforeseen or sudden circumstances whereby they are apt to lose their case. They should also avoid public office or position, for no matter how honest they may be themselves they are likely to become involved in scandal and trouble on that account. In short, this Seventh House position of Uranus is bad for dealings of any kind with the public or with law or partners.

♅ 8 *Uranus in the Eighth House* is a good omen, for it indicates that when life has been lived to its fullness the end will come suddenly and thus the person will be spared the long and pitiful suffering so often incident to the transition from the physical to the spiritual worlds. But knowing this it also behooves such people to have their house in readiness and order, so that when the end comes at 30 or 90 they have their affairs in shape.

This position often brings an unexpected legacy through the marriage partner when well-aspected; but if Uranus is afflicted the person may become involved in litigation on account of or in connection with the estate of someone deceased.

People with Uranus in the Eighth House often show great interest in occult subjects and become well versed in mystic lore. It also gives a predisposition to dreams and psychic experience.

♅ 9 *Uranus in the Ninth House* gives a progressive and independent mind, of an original and inventive turn, sometimes amounting to genius; the intuition is highly developed and these people indulge in constructive dreams of such a nature as transform the world in the course of time—that is, provided Uranus is well-aspected. Nevertheless they are generally looked upon as cranks because their ideas are so Utopian and far in advance of our present stage that the ordinary human beings cannot grasp them. On the other hand, if Uranus is afflicted in the Ninth House, particularly if by Mars, these people become red anarchists and are not even averse to shedding blood in order to attain what they believe is the ideal; they become fanatical in whatever cause they espouse.

This position of Uranus also indicates trouble in travel, particularly on voyages, and danger of accidents. It is one of the signs which make the explorer and pioneer in the discovery and development of new countries.

♅ 10 *Uranus in the Tenth House* indicates an original, eccentric character, with a contempt for conventions, who follows his own ideas regardless of what other people say or think, hence such people are often looked upon as black sheep and estranged from their kindred, but this they do not seem to regard as a misfortune; they are ready to offer up all, even life itself, for absolute freedom. These characteristics also bring them into public discredit and disfavor. The life is full of sudden changes for better or worse according to the other planetary aspects prevailing. If Uranus is much afflicted these people never make a success in life, but meet with continual sorrow, trouble, disappointment and reverses. When Uranus is well-aspected genius will come to the fore and is likely to find recognition in some measure at least, probably by pioneer work of some kind.

♅11 *Uranus in the Eleventh House.* Uranus being lord of the Eleventh Sign, Aquarius, is more at home in the Eleventh House than in any of the others, therefore he exerts a strong influence in bringing about strange and eccentric friendships with people of an original, creative, or inventive turn of mind who will be a benefit to the person if Uranus is well-aspected. This also indicates that through such friendships the wishes, hopes and aspirations will be promoted and reach a successful culmination. If on the other hand, Uranus is afflicted in this house, friends are apt to turn traitors or at least use the person for their own selfish ends as far as possible.

♅12 *Uranus in the Twelfth House* indicates loss of reputation, exile, and estrangement from one's kin and country, much sickness at various times of life and confinement in hospitals, if Uranus is without configuration with any other planet or even if well aspected. But if seriously afflicted it indicates confinement in prison at some period of the life, or restraint in a sanitarium on account of mental trouble, also much annoyance by the underhanded action of others. When well-aspected it brings success in connection with the occult arts or occult institutions, also by the invention of chemical processes which remain secret with their discoverer instead of being protected by patent. These people are haunted all through life by a vague fear of impending disaster.

Uranus in the Twelve Signs

♅ ♈ *Uranus in Aries* gives an original, independent nature, full of energy and ambition, ingenious, resourceful and capable of coping with difficulties, especially those of a mechanical or electrical nature. These people have a very impulsive, abrupt and brusque manner which often arouses resentment and opposition in others even though no offense may have been intended. They are seldom satisfied to remain in one place, but are fond of changes and rove about a great deal. Changes of place and position are often forced upon them because of the before-mentioned blunt way of speaking.

♅ ♉ *Uranus in Taurus* gives a very intuitive nature but stubborn and self-willed, so that when these people have made up their minds nothing in the world will turn them, but they cling to their purpose or idea with the quiet determination and persistence which neither persuasion nor threats can alter. If Uranus is afflicted they are suspicious and jealous, also subject to very sudden and unexpected reverses in financial affairs. But if Uranus is well-aspected the opposite may be judged, and comfortable financial circumstances may be looked for.

♅ ♊ *Uranus in Gemini* gives a highly original, intuitive and versatile nature, fond of scientific pursuits in general, but particularly those studies which have to do with electricity, aviation, or other similar out-of-the-way subjects. These people are broad-minded and thoroughly progressive, pioneers in all things new and modern. Among other things they generally have an inclination for the study of occultism and astrology. They are well liked among brothers, sisters, and neighbors. All this providing Uranus is well-aspected; but if Uranus is afflicted the mind becomes eccentric and full of vagaries which make the person a nuisance and a crank, disliked by everybody, particularly brothers, sisters and neighbors. This also brings trouble and liability to accident in the course of short journeys.

♅ ♋ *Uranus in Cancer.* Cancer is a psychic sign and when Uranus is there it indicates that the person is a sensitive, attuned to the psychic vibrations and capable of cultivating these powers, but whether for good or ill depends upon the aspects. If Uranus is afflicted there is a tendency to nervous indigestion for Cancer rules the stomach, and if this is not attended to serious stomach trouble may be expected. These people are liable to separation from their families, though usually much against their will, but as they are generally of a very uncertain temper, irritable and impatient, they are usually to blame for this condition and are only getting their just deserts.

♅ ♌ *Uranus in Leo* gives a very determined nature, rebellious and impatient of restraint or contradiction, with strong likes and dislikes, and an utter disregard of the conventions where the passional nature is involved. The personality is strong, forceful and self-assertive, therefore these people often incur the displeasure of others and create much opposition. They are very inconstant in affairs of the heart—"on with the new love" before it is "off with the old." In a woman's horoscope an afflicted Uranus shows difficulty in childbirth, perhaps the death of a child by accident or in a sudden, unexpected manner, also a strong tendency towards palpitation of the heart. When Uranus is well-aspected in Leo both courtship and domestic affairs run much more smoothly and it indicates original and inventive genius, particularly along educational or journalistic lines, also for entertainment and amusement of the public and gain thereby.

♅♍ *Uranus in Virgo,* when well-aspected gives a keen, original, scientific and mechanical mind, a strong and well developed intuitional faculty and a keen business bent which will make for success in life, and financial gain by the employment of others.

But if Uranus is afflicted in Virgo, the person is apt to become subject to strange ailments, a hypochondriac of a fractious and irritable turn of mind, a burden to himself and those who have to be around him. This position is also full of disappointment in the aims and ambitions of life, especially because of limitations in the employment or in dealing with employees, which the person seems unable to overcome.

♅♎ *Uranus in Libra,* when well-aspected gives literary and artistic ability of an unusual and original nature where the person follows independent lines of endeavor and expression, often in connection with occultism. This position also gives a keen intuition and an attractive personality, a vivid imagination. It signifies partnership, union, or marriage to someone who will be of a Uranian character and of much benefit to the person.

But when ill-placed or afflicted, Uranus in Libra brings sorrow, trouble, domestic difficulty and death of the marriage partner by a sudden or strange ailment or accident. Or perhaps the union may be dissolved in the divorce court, for people with the temperament described by an afflicted Uranus in Libra simply cannot remain true to one person. This position also indicates trouble with the public or the authorities on account of eccentric, anarchistic, or socialistic activity.

♅♏ *Uranus in Scorpio,* when well-aspected gives the person a forceful and determined will, bound to overcome all obstacles and achieve that which he sets out to accomplish by persistence, perseverance and dogged determination; the mind is sharp, shrewd and secretive, capable of grasping details and concentrating deeply upon whatever problem may be in hand. There is an originality and mechanical ability amounting to genius and a love for science, both occult and physical.

But when ill-aspected, Uranus in Scorpio lays the person liable to accidents and even assassination or sudden death by explosions, electricity, aeroplanes or kindred unusual agencies.

It also gives a tendency to trouble with the genitals on account of unbridled abuse of the sacred creative function, self-abuse or perversion.

♅ ♐ *Uranus in Sagittarius* gives a very strong intuitive faculty with a tendency to dreams, visions, and a very vivid imagination. This position also gives a strong inclination towards an out-of-the-ordinary belief, including the theory and practice of the occult arts. When well-aspected this position gives a strong grasp of the religious and educational problems of the day, with a philanthropic desire to work for the upliftment of humanity, a desire to travel for the educational advantages thereby to be obtained, and success in gaining these points under favorable aspects in the progressed horoscope.

When afflicted, Uranus in Sagittarius gives a very eccentric and erratic mentality, particularly with respect to law and religion. There is a rebellion against the social condition which often brings trouble with the authorities, also a desire to force one-sided views upon the world despite all protests and at all risk, characteristics which eventually bring discredit and disfavor.

♅ ♑ *Uranus in Capricorn,* when well-aspected gives an ambitious and enterprising disposition, a serious, persevering nature, and an acute sense of responsibility, with original ideas of business that bring success, especially if some line is selected that is connected with the electrical or aerial arts.

If Uranus is afflicted it gives an erratic and eccentric mind, self-willed and stubborn, bound to either rule or ruin, quarrelsome and at odds with society in general and relatives in particular. Hence this position gives a great deal of sorrow and trouble in life, frequently involving sudden changes of employment and environment.

♅ ♒ *Uranus in Aquarius,* when well-aspected is at its very best, for he is ruler of this sign and therefore in harmony with its vibrations. Hence this position strengthens the intuition and originality, and directs the energies into humanitarian lines of endeavor, unselfish devotion to the cause of friendship, and a sincere desire to help all who are in trouble. These people make many friends and generally realize their hopes, wishes, and ambitions because they are of such an unselfish nature that they desire what is good for humanity at large rather than that which is for personal gain. This position also gives considerable mechanical ability, originality and inventive genius.

But if Uranus is afflicted in the sign Aquarius, though the ambitions may be as strong and sometimes as good, and as pure as with a well-aspected Uranus, they will be of such an erratic nature that it is impossible to realize them, and they will bring trouble with friends, or pretended friends, who will seek to use the person for their own selfish ends, causing much sorrow and disappointment.

♅ ♓ *Uranus in Pisces,* when well aspected indicates a love of the occult arts and ability for development along these lines. It brings friends and associations which favor these studies. But when ill aspected it leads to mediumship, obsession, and even insanity, if this tendency to intercourse with spirits is followed to its conclusion. This position makes the mind flighty, erratic, and the person will be subject to unexpected misfortune, scandal, or suicide. All through life, even when fortune smiles and the skies are clear to all outward appearance, these people are haunted by a vague fear of impending disaster.

ASPECTS OF URANUS TO THE OTHER PLANETS

☉ ✱ △ ♅ *The Sun sextile or trine to Uranus* makes the person original, inventive and independent in his manner of conduct and personal appearance. With respect to food and certain mannerisms, he is what people call eccentric and conspicuous, yet not offensively so, given to pursuits and studies which people consider "queer" such as occultism and astrology. But he also loves delving into the unknown realms after nature's secrets concerning electricity and often becomes a successful inventor if other aspects give the mechanical ability to work his schemes out. Uranus rules the ether and now that we are nearing the Aquarian Age his vibrations will be felt in increasing measure, bringing to our ken methods of using nature's finer forces and the people with Sun sextile or trine Uranus will be the media who attract and interpret them for us as the aerials and receivers in a wireless station collect and transcribe the messages carried by the ether waves to which they are attuned. These people often rise in life through the friendship of someone above them in the social scale. They are of a very high-strung temperament but have themselves well under control, and rarely show temper or anger. They are also out-and-out idealists.

☉ P ☌ □ ☍ ♅ *The Sun parallel, conjunction, square or opposition to Uranus* makes the person very high-strung, nervous, of uncontrolled emotions and ready to fly into hysteria on any or no provocation. It predisposes to nervous disorders such as St. Vitus dance, epilepsy and lack of coordination. It makes people impulsive, unreliable, and lacking in regard for the conventionalities, highly impatient of any restraint upon their liberty and committed to the theory of affinities, soul-mates and free love, hence these people are undesirable marriage partners and likely to figure in divorce proceedings or scandals of an even worse nature. There is also danger of trouble on account of connection with anarchistic plots where the inventive faculty may find scope in the construction of explosives and infernal machines. Unless these aspects are modified by other configurations such people are among the most dangerous to society. They are liable to accidents from lightning, electricity and all through life they meet disappointment from the most unexpected quarters.

♀ ✱ △ ♅ *Venus sextile or trine to Uranus* makes the person mentally alert, of quick intuitive perception and exceedingly magnetic, especially to the opposite sex; and it also attracts hosts of friends who will be of benefit and assistance to him. These aspects give love of art, music and poetry and are a favorable indication of a happy marriage, often at a very early age or suddenly consummated. The good aspects between Venus and Uranus also sometimes bring to the subject love of a platonic nature which then acts as an inspiration in the life.

♀ ☌ P ♅ *Venus conjunction or parallel to Uranus* As in the case of Mars conjunction to Venus, so also in the case of Uranus conjunction to Venus, there is a doubt as to whether this aspect should be classed as good or evil. This must be settled in the individual horoscope where it occurs, for it may work either way, depending upon the other planetary configurations and the student will therefore have to use his judgment as to how he classes it. If Venus is otherwise afflicted in the horoscope, for instance, the conjunction or parallel will further accentuate her evil qualities and act like the square or opposition, but if she is well placed or aspected, Uranus will bring out the nobler side, the same as the sextile or trine.

♀ □ ☍ ♅ *Venus square or opposition to Uranus.* The square or opposition always brings trouble through the sex relation—quarrels, divorces, public scandals through clandestine intercourse and kindred irregularities, with loss of friends, prestige and popularity, exile from home and family and sudden financial losses through unexpected or unforeseen happenings. There is a general lack of balance, an erratic personality.

☿ ⚹ △ ♅ *Mercury sextile or trine to Uranus* gives an original, independent and eccentric mind impatient of the fetters of fashion, tradition ana convention. Such a person is strenuous in his efforts to hew a path for himself in complete liberty. Therefore this is the hall-mark of pioneers in thought and invention, the sign of genius. Their ideas and ideals are exceedingly lofty, progressive and inspiring, in fact too much so in the opinion of the average man or woman who looks upon their actions and vagaries as the outcome of a diseased mind. Nevertheless they have plenty of friends on account of their kindly and sympathetic nature. These aspects are good for a literary or scientific pursuit, also for invention, particularly those which have to do with air or electricity.

☿ P ☌ ♅ *Mercury parallel or conjunction with Uranus.* If Mercury is otherwise afflicted the conjunction and parallel are to be judged as bad aspects and read accordingly, but if Mercury is otherwise well placed and aspected the delineation given for the sextile and trine will apply.

☿ □ ☍ ♅ *Mercury square or opposition to Uranus.* Mercury in square or opposition to Uranus is the hall-mark of the true crank or anarchist with extreme ideas to tear down the social structure and undertake a radical reform without the ability to build up something better. People with these configurations are given to ranting and raving in public and their language is usually as cruel as the measures they advocate. Whatever ability they possess is usually turned to an erratic purpose and therefore they are ostracised and disliked wherever they go. They are often forced to make sudden changes to escape the consequences of their erratic conduct.

☽ ✱ △ ♅ *The Moon sextile or trine to Uranus* gives great originality and independence to the mind which is quick, intuitive and very vivid in its imagination, hence the person has inventive ability; he is attracted to the occult arts and is endowed with hypnotic or magnetic powers, also the intuitional ability to study and practice astrology. If electricity is adopted as a vocation the person will make a success of it. These aspects also give the person a peculiar fascination for the opposite sex and are likely to lead to a clandestine love affair or an unconventional union.

☽ ☌ P ♅ *The Moon conjunction or parallel to Uranus* gives mental and psychic tendencies similar to those of the good aspects and also the same liability to irregular love-affairs, but these tendencies are not so pronounced and a clandestine love-affair generated under the conjunction of Uranus and the Moon may have distinctly disastrous results similar to those mentioned under the bad aspects. If the conjunction occurs in Cancer it indicates nervous indigestion; in Leo it inclines to palpitation of the heart, interferes with the rhythm of the heartbeat and gives a spasmodic action which will probably prove fatal when it has run its course; in Scorpio it inclines to perverted practices; in Sagittarius the reflex action would be felt in the lungs and similarly with the other signs.

☽ □ ☍ ♅ *The Moon square or opposition to Uranus* makes the person erratic and touchy to a degree, a walking powder magazine ready to explode at any moment, overbearing, conceited and intolerant, shunned by all who can possibly get out of his way. If such people are employers nobody can work for them and if they are employees nobody will have them. They never remain very long in any place, but are either discharged or give up their position on the slightest provocation. People with these aspects are also attracted by the occult arts but they never make a success at them because of their erratic mentality. Like the other aspects of Uranus and the Moon, the square and opposition also indicate a clandestine attachment either on the part of the person or the marriage partner. If Uranus occurs in the Seventh House of a man's horoscope it proves the wife untrue and a public scandal and divorce will eventually ensue. The bad aspects of the Sun and Uranus give similar indications in the horoscope of a woman.

♄ ✱ △ ♅ *Saturn sextile or trine Uranus* is fortunate for a public career in an official capacity for it gives ambition and determination with ability to concentrate upon the work in hand and to exercise authority, plan and systematize. It strengthens the intuition so that such people are guided by keen interior insight when new and important steps have to be taken, therefore such people are in demand and find positions with large corporations where they win their way through sheer ability. The mind is both mechanical and ingenious, hence this position often denotes the successful inventor, particularly along the lines of electricity, aerial navigation and kindred pioneer lines.

♄ ☌ P ♅. *Saturn conjunction or parallel to Uranus* has an influence like the good aspects if the planets are unafflicted, elevated, in angles, essentially dignified or exalted, as Saturn in Libra and Capricorn or Uranus in Aquarius or Scorpio, but if the conjunction occurs in signs where either of the planets is weak or afflicted, like Saturn in Aries, Cancer or Leo, then the influence will be detrimental and should be judged the same as the square or opposition.

♄ □ ☍ ♅ *Saturn square or opposition to Uranus* gives an unscrupulous nature with an extremely violent temper. The outbursts are as sudden as a bolt from the blue and exhaust the person completely. These people are very eccentric and look at everything from a peculiar angle—treacherous, idle and indolent, malicious and altogether dangerous to the community. These aspects also indicate chronic or incurable diseases according to the signs wherein they are placed, but as often said, if the other indications in the horoscope are good the influence of a single aspect will not bring out such evil characteristics and therefore the whole horoscope is to be carefully considered before judging the influences enumerated, for they may be materially minimized by other favorable indications in the horoscope.

♃ ✱ △ ♅ *Jupiter sextile or trine to Uranus* gives a strong, independent and positive personality with an ingenious, inventive and original turn of mind. Whatever he undertakes he will carry to a conclusion or die in the attempt. This position also gives a broad, humane and benevolent disposition and a tendency to delve into the occult arts and sciences. It favors association with secret orders and gives promise of prosperity in life. Such a person is honest and sincere, sociable, hospitable and friendly to all, hence likely to benefit a great deal from influential friends in an official position. This position also gives executive ability and success in connection with institutions of learning.

♃ ☌ P ♅ *Jupiter conjunction or parallel to Uranus* gives similar indications to the good aspects but the influence is not quite so decided, particularly if either of the planets is weak by sign or otherwise afflicted. In that case it will be found that the tendencies conferred are more like those of the bad aspects.

♃ □ ☍ ♅ *Jupiter square or opposition to Uranus* gives an impulsive nature liable to act in a sudden impulsive, erratic or unexpected manner to his own undoing. Loss by speculation, lawsuits and impulsive extravagance are also indicated, many changes both of occupation and residence, loss of friends and reputation. It signifies one of an ostentatious nature given to sham and camouflage and subterfuge, generally disliked for his insincerity and double dealings; a confidence man, bunko man or cheap gambler.

♂ ✱ △ ♅ *Mars sextile or trine to Uranus* gives an energetic and ambitious disposition, an original, ingenious, alert, intuitive mind which is resourceful in the highest degree and able to cope with great difficulties under trying circumstances. Thus people with these configurations are naturally of an inventive turn of mind and successful in bringing their ideas to realization. Their inventive genius usually expresses itself along electrical lines, aviation, or in other unusual directions, for these aspects are one of the marks of the pioneer of the Aquarian Age, where science and inventions will reach out in directions that are now entirely undreamed of even as possibilities. But while these people are dreamers of dreams they are also practical, energetic and enterprising in a sufficient degree to make their dreams come true in the world. They have a wide vision and a noble nature which rises over all petty distinctions of race, creed or color and recognizes in all human beings the divine spark which is the basis of universal brotherhood. They may not be exactly religious in the orthodox sense of the word but their ideas are truly cosmic, hence they are often mistaken for visionaries by those who do not understand them.

♂ ☌ P □ ☍ ♅ *Mars conjunction, parallel, square or opposition to Uranus* gives an erratic and eccentric disposition, a violent temper of the worst nature, an unusual resentment of even the slightest restraint and gives the person a stubborn, headstrong and dogged determination to go ahead in any line of action upon which he has decided no matter what the outcome. He will listen to neither reason nor entreaty but follows his own course in defiance of all. People with these configurations very often become anarchists of the reddest type for they do not even stop at the shedding of blood, if other testimonies in the figure concur. They are cruel, hard and cold, without a spark of true love though they may be inflamed with passion of the most burning intensity. This is particularly the case when Mars is square Uranus and either planet is placed in Taurus or Scorpio. In a woman's horoscope Uranus square Mars usually leads to seduction no matter where they are placed, but if in Taurus or Scorpio escape is almost impossible. The other characteristics of these planets in these configurations work themselves out according to the signs wherein they are placed so that their placement in Taurus or Scorpio works upon the sex which is governed by these signs. When one of these planets is in Scorpio, if the person takes up the profession of surgery he will become very cruel and unfeeling, ready to operate for the mere pleasure of causing pain and in consequence or in pursuit of this passion he will probably take up vivisection and develop an unusual ingenuity in torturing his victims. With Uranus or Mars in Scorpio or Pisces he will be underhanded or tricky though he may show a very different front to the public. In Aries it will make a rattlebrain, in Gemini and Virgo an unusually quick mentality but quick in seeing only how to trick others. In Sagittarius it will make the person very materialistic, atheistic, or fanatical against the established religion or society. Thus the planets blend their individual natures with the sign.

♆ ✶ △ ♅ *Neptune sextile or trine to Uranus* gives inclination towards the occult or mystical side of life, and if either is placed in the Tenth House the person usually becomes a leader or authority in these lines, he wins at least local recognition and if other testimonies concur his fame will be national or international. Such aspects will bring direct touch with the spiritual world and success in dealing with the inhabitants of that plane. It is also productive of dreams and visions of a prophetic and inspirational nature. It strengthens the healing powers and will consequently enable the person to do a great deal of good for his suffering fellow-men. These aspects give a highly developed intuition which amounts almost to mind-reading. There is a love of travel and exploration of the physical world as well as of nature's finer realms. Nor are such people altogether dreamers, they have a strong will with excellent executive and organizing powers which will aid them in realizing their hopes, wishes and ambitions to rise in life and be at the forefront of whatever profession they select.

♆ ☌ P ♅ *Neptune conjunction or parallel to Uranus* are convertible aspects; if the planets are well placed by sign and otherwise well aspected, their effect will be similar to the sextile or trine. though not so pronounced, but if they are cadent, weak by sign, and afflicted they are only a little less evil than when aspected by square or opposition.

♆ □ ☍ ♅ *Neptune square or opposition to Uranus* brings underhanded, deceptive influences into the life which aim to undermine the reputation and make the person suffer scandal and public disfavor, sudden and unaccountable reverses in business are met with, or trouble in social affairs. There is the same love of travel and exploration as given by the good aspects but the person cannot accomplish his aims with the same facility, or if he does it is to his disadvantage and brings added trouble. He is also drawn towards the occult or mystic side of life, but his path is beset by dangers of mediumship and obsession and all through life he is filled with premonitions of danger and a vague dread of impending disaster which he can neither account for nor dispel by will or reason, hence uncertainty overshadows the life as a cloud and robs him of peace and contentment.

CHAPTER XVII.

Neptune, the Planet of Divinity

As URANUS is the octave of Venus and acts principally upon the love nature, aiming to elevate mankind in matters personal and social, so Neptune is the octave of Mercury, and altogether spiritual in its aims. As Mercury is Lightbearer of the physical Sun, so Neptune is Lightbearer for the spiritual Sun, (called Vulcan by the Western Mystics). Intellectuality, ruled by Mercury lifted us above the animal and made man, man; the Spirituality ruled by Neptune will in time raise us beyond the state of the human and make us divine.

Neptune really signifies what we may call "the gods" commencing with the supernormal beings we know as Elder Brothers, and compassing the innumerable hosts of spiritual entities, good, bad, and indifferent, which influence our evolution. Its position and aspects denote our relation to them; malefic aspects attract agencies of a nature inimical to our welfare, benefic configurations draw upon the good forces. Thus, if Neptune is placed in the Tenth House, trine to the ascendant, the person involved will have the opportunity to become a leader or prominent in a movement along mystical lines as denoted by the exalted position of Neptune. His body will be capable of receiving the finer vibrations, and of coming in touch with the spiritual world, as denoted by the trine of the ascendant. On the other hand, when Neptune is placed in the Twelfth House, whose nature is passive and productive of suffering, that position indicates that at some time, perhaps under a square from the midheaven, the evil forces, among whom are spirit-controls, will be drawn to that person and endeavor to obtain possession of the body. The conjunction of Neptune with the ascendant will make the body sensitive and usable for spiritual purposes, as well as the trine. Given the opportunity afforded by the first aspect mentioned, the man may become a pupil of a mystery school and a factor for great good in the uplift of mankind; placed under the affliction of the second aspect, he may become a helpless tool of spirit-controls: an irresponsible medium.

But there is one factor which is never shown in the horoscope, and that is the will of man. He is bound at some time in life to meet with the experiences denoted by his horoscope, and the opportunities there indicated will be placed before him one by one in orderly succession, as the clock of destiny marks the appropriate time; but how he, the free and independent spirit, meets that fated experience, no one can determine beforehand, and the man in whose horoscope the first mentioned benefic configuration occurs may not be sufficiently awake to the great opportunity before him to catch it on the wing, it may have flown before he realizes it was there. Yes, he may never become aware of the fact. On the other hand, the person in whose life the square indicates the assault by spiritual forces mentioned, may develop his spiritual muscle by resisting the onslaught and become a victor instead of being vanquished. Forewarned is forearmed.

Neptune was not discovered until 1846, but we should err greatly if we supposed the influence ascribed to it fictitious on that account, for as the person born blind lacks the organs to see the sunlight and colors, so most of humanity is still lacking the sensibility which makes them amenable to the vibrations of Neptune. (See Chapter on that subject, also on Planetary Octaves). But we are gradually developing finer feelings and becoming more able to respond to his influence. At first this influence is mostly felt by sensitives who become occultists when of a positive nature and mediums when negative, others gain from it the cunning common alike to the criminal and the detective, or it impels the weakling to take drugs which in another manner produce dreams and visions similar to those obtained by the mediumistic process.

Neptune strong in the figure gives a very vivid imagination and an artistic nature, poetic, musical or literary, a fondness of ease, comfort and beautiful surroundings. The person is easily swayed by the emotions, and when Neptune is afflicted may become subject to trances, fainting, hysteria, or psychic storms. There is a love of travel, preferably by water.

When Neptune is weak by sign or afflicted it also inclines to drink or drugs, it robs the person of ambition and makes him an indolent loafer or cheat, thoroughly dishonest, or if the horoscope is otherwise good he may become the prey of other people who will rob or defraud him. People with an afflicted Neptune should particularly avoid dealings with large corporations or they may be subjected to swindles of the most fantastic nature.

Neptune in the Twelve Houses

♆1 *Neptune in the Ascendant, or First House.* Neptune is by nature occult, prophetic and spiritual. The Ascendant signifies the body wherein we function and thus by combination of these ideas we find that Neptune on the Ascendant will give a particularly sensitive body capable of feeling the finer vibrations in nature, and according to the aspects which the planet receives, these will be either good, bad or indifferent. If Neptune is strong and well aspected to the Sun, Jupiter or Uranus, we may judge that there is an intensely mystical nature latent in the person. Whether or not it will be developed is, of course, another question depending upon opportunity and environment. On the other hand, if Neptune is afflicted, it indicates a very low mentality, perhaps even insanity. In any case the nature is visionary, romantic and generally unpractical, at least from the worldly standard. The prophetic, inspirational and visionary faculties are usually highly developed when Neptune is unafflicted in the First House. There is a love of art and music, a desire for luxury and whatever gives power and tone to life. But when Neptune is afflicted in the First House the nature is indolent, procrastinating and changeable; perverted tastes and desires come to the front and impel to acts of indiscretion which may bring grave consequences. There is indication of prostitution of the spiritual faculties; a deceptive, dishonest disposition, also a tendency to mediumship and spirit obsession.

♆2 *Neptune in the Second House* and well aspected brings gain through all things in which water plays a prominent part; also through mystic and occult matters and societies. But if Neptune is afflicted the financial affairs of the person will always be in an uncertain, chaotic state.

♆3 *Neptune in the Third House,* when well aspected enhances the mental faculties to a considerable degree. It gives ability in the direction of inspirational writing and speaking, high ideals, a devotional mind. But when Neptune is afflicted in the Third House the mind is of a low order, cunning, sometimes imbecile and idiotic, with weird and uncanny feelings and perverted appetites. Neptune in the Third House also gives a tendency to many journeys, frequently by water, but whether or not they are successful depends upon the aspects.

♆4 *Neptune in the Fourth House,* when well aspected, gives a spiritual atmosphere to the home with unusual conditions for soul-growth through the relationships there formed, but when afflicted it brings fraud and deception, unhappiness and distrust, peculiar problems and many changes of residence. There is also a liability to extreme poverty at the close of life, even confinement in a public institution of charity.

♆5 *Neptune in the Fifth House,* strong and well aspected, indicates a successful courtship of one of a highly advanced spiritual nature, success as a teacher of mystic matters, and gain by investment in things ruled by Neptune, aquatic sports and any other business in which the watery element is strong.

♆6 *Neptune in the Sixth House,* well aspected, is a favorable indication of latent psychic faculties which may be developed with profit from the spiritual point of view . But when afflicted it predisposes to the prostitution of spiritual faculties by mediumship, etc. Thus the person may become subject to spirit control and run grave danger of obsession. It also indicates trouble and loss through employees and a liability to chronic wasting diseases and deformity. Usually these tendencies are then accentuated by a sensuous nature and a self-indulgent manner of living.

♆7 *Neptune in the Seventh House* and well aspected indicates a marriage to one of an occult, inspirational nature, generally a platonic union of the most soul-satisfying nature, a true companionship of two who are really mates. It also shows success as a public speaker on occult or mystical subjects. But when afflicted, Neptune in the Seventh House shows an emotional, mediumistic, unreliable marriage partner, or there may be fraud or deception in connection with the marriage, perhaps one of the partners committing bigamy. This position also indicates one of the parasites that prey upon the public in general, or of those who become victims of public disfavor, all according to the nature of the aspects. They show whether or not this is merited.

♆8 *Neptune in the Eighth House,* when well aspected, gives gain through the marriage partner, but not through the ordinary channels of business; it comes in a peculiar manner. This position is also favorable for occult investigation and often enables the person who has it to obtain information at first hand. But when Neptune is afflicted in the Eighth House it brings loss by fraud or deception of the marriage partner, financial troubles with estates or corporations and a strange, unusual ending to the life.

♆9 *Neptune in the Ninth House* is very favorable for the cultivation of spiritual faculties; when well aspected, it brings strange visions and unusual intuitional forebodings and presentiments, also profit and pleasure in connection with long journeys or voyages.

When Neptune is afflicted in the Ninth House it makes the mind fearful and anxious, always on the *qui vive* with vague forebodings; it inclines to travel but brings trouble in that connection, also danger of legal complication and loss on that account.

♆10 *Neptune in the Tenth House,* when well aspected indicates one of high aspirations and inspirations, spiritually inclined, who has the ability to rise to leadership, fame and honor, in connection with some mystical society or in scientific research. This position of Neptune also indicates an accident to one of the parents, probably by water, while the person is still a child, but when the planet is well aspected a legacy often accrues.

Neptune in the Tenth House and trine to the Sun or Moon are sure signs of the ability to cultivate the spiritual sight in this life. A number of well-known seers have this aspect.

When Neptune is afflicted in the Tenth House it indicates fraud, deception and dishonesty which in time will bring their reward of sorrow, trouble and scandal.

♆11 *Neptune in the Eleventh House* and well aspected shows a person of high spiritual aspirations and the ability to attract others of a similar nature who will be of help to him in realizing his desires, hopes and wishes. When Neptune is afflicted in the Eleventh House it indicates deception and treachery on the part of people who pose as friends; this will bring loss and trouble. Therefore people with this position should be particularly careful whom they cultivate and admit to their friendship.

♆12 *Neptune in the Twelfth House,* well aspected, brings success in research work of a scientific or occult nature which is carried on in secret or far from the haunts of men. It also indicates a secret soul-satisfying or clandestine but honorable relationship with someone which will bring benefit to both and it not infrequently happens that this friend is in the spirit world, but the relation is much more close in such cases than it can ever be between friends who are both in the physical body. When Neptune is afflicted in the Twelfth House it gives a liability to confinement and restraint in a public institution such as a hospital, asylum, or prison, on account of secret but powerful enemies, a chronic and noisome disease or insanity due to perverted practices.

Neptune in the Twelve Signs

♆ ♈ *Neptune in Aries,* when well aspected fills a person with religious enthusiasm, though not always of the orthodox kind, and gives him the energy and ambition to push forward to the front rank in whatever line of thought and belief he espouses. There is a desire to elevate humanity to a higher and more noble plane of life and on that account this configuration or position usually brings the person forward as a public character of more or less importance, according to the general aspects and tenor of the horoscope.

But when afflicted, Neptune in Aries brings out the destructive tendencies. There is a similar desire to raise humanity to realms of happiness, but the methods are anarchistic and it incites to murder of those whom the person conceives to be the enemies of society, by bomb plot or assassination, and lays the person liable to imprisonment on account of conspiracy against the government or others in authority.

♆ ♉ *Neptune in Taurus* gives a kindly, companionable disposition and an inclination towards the beautiful and artistic in nature. He is fond of music and the pleasures of life. This is also a good omen for the acquisition of land or property. But when Neptune is afflicted in Taurus it gives a sensuous and passionate nature and a strong tendency to gourmandize which in time is bound to bring trouble and sorrow in its wake.

♆♊ *Neptune in Gemini,* well aspected, is one of the best indications of unusual mental faculties, for Neptune is the octave of Mercury the planet of mind, logic and reason. Hence this position develops the occult, prophetic and inspirational faculties. It makes the person sensitive to the finer intuitional and inspirational vibrations in nature. It is the signature of genius in one direction or another according to the conditions in the horoscope. It gives the gift of oratory and unusual literary ability, and makes the person a fine mechanician or mathematician; in short, there is no field of endeavor where mental ingenuity is required, that the person with Neptune in Gemini, well aspected, does not excel.

But when Neptune is afflicted in Gemini it indicates inability to concentrate to any good purpose. The mind is restless, chaotic and wavering, inclined to cunning, fraud and deception, or at best it makes the person a visionary and a dreamer who is apt to become the dupe of others. There is generally trouble with brothers, sisters and neighbors who cordially dislike the person in whose horoscope this aspect is found.

♆ ♋ *Neptune in Cancer,* when well aspected, gives an intuitive, sympathetic and lovable nature quick to understand the sorrows and joys of others and ready to feel for them or with them. Hence these people are generally very much liked, both in the home and in their immediate circle of acquaintances. This position also brings them in touch with the finer forces of nature and enables them to cultivate such spiritual faculties as psychometry and a species of intuition whereby they can get in touch with whomsoever or whatsoever they wish for the help and benefit of others. They are very versatile in the spiritual direction and may reach great heights by devotion, which is strongly expressed in them. But when Neptune is afflicted in Cancer it gives a very self-indulgent disposition which generally exerts a baneful influence in the home, perhaps more by inuendo than by direct malicious expression. This position also gives peculiar tastes and appetites which are apt to cause great trouble to the alimentative system and there is a strong inclination for drugs or drink.

♆ ♌ *Neptune in Leo,* when well aspected, gives a generous, sympathetic and warm-hearted disposition, a sociable nature, fond of pleasures and artistic pursuits. These people have considerable ability and success in educational pursuits because of an intimate understanding of the nature of others and the faculty of imparting to them whatever knowledge they possess themselves. They are very conscientious in their dealings with others and successful in affairs of the heart.

But when Neptune is afflicted in Leo it makes the nature super-sensual and therefore liable to disappointments in love. These people are governed by impulse rather than by reason; they lack the stamina to face an issue, are cowardly, fickle and not to be depended upon; they incur a general dislike among their acquaintances.

♆ ♍ *Neptune in Virgo.* Mercury, the planet of mind, reason and logic is exalted in Virgo, and the occult, prophetic, inspirational, spiritual, devotional and musical Neptune is the octave of Mercury, hence the blending of the Mercurial and Neptunian qualities produced by Neptune in Virgo gives exceptionally fine mental faculties with the addition of inspiration, prophetic ability, devotion to high ideals when Neptune is well aspected, for Neptune adds gentleness and sympathy to the cold Mercury; though such people are rather odd in their ideas and inclinations, especially with respect to marriage, which they usually regard from the platonic standpoint.

If Neptune is afflicted in Virgo it gives hypochondriac tendencies and an imagination of having all the ills and ailments in the universe which makes the person's life miserable. There is also a tendency to become the plaything of spirit controls, not only with respect to mediumship but such people are liable to direct obsession and when this calamity has once occurred it is very difficult to free the body from the obsessing entity.

♆♎ *Neptune in Libra,* when well aspected, gives a musical, poetic and artistic temperament and indicates a union of a highly spiritual nature which will be of great comfort and satisfaction to the person. When Neptune is afflicted in Libra, there is a tendency to clandestine, unconventional and illegitimate relations, either of the person himself or of the marriage partner, according to the nature of the aspects to Neptune. It indicates a weak and over-emotional nature which incurs and merits the dislike of those in its immediate environment.

♆♏ *Neptune in Scorpio,* well aspected, gives a desire to delve into the secrets of nature and thus it is a good position for those who work in scientific or occult research. It gives energy, enthusiasm and inspirational perception beyond the realm of reason and augurs successful accomplishment of whatever is undertaken. But when afflicted it gives a terrible temper, a sensuous and passionate nature, an inordinate desire for drink or drugs and a tendency to drowning either by accident or design.

♆ ♐ *Neptune in Sagittarius,* when well aspected increases the inspirational, devotional and religious tendencies in the horoscope. It brings dreams, visions, and occult experiences. There is love of travel and a great enjoyment of the pleasures thus obtained. When Neptune is afflicted in Sagittarius the subjects become liable to fears and forebodings; dreams of danger and visions of distress prey upon the mind, making life miserable. Sometimes they have great desires to travel but are unable to gratify them, or if they do they have trouble or accidents to contend with.

♆ ♑ *Neptune in Capricorn,* when well aspected gives a serious and contemplative nature, able to concentrate upon whatever matters come before it, hence such people are successful, keen and far-sighted business men, usually working on a large scale, or if the nature of the other aspects in the horoscope draws them toward secret work they make excellent detectives capable of solving the most intricate problems, or researchers along psychic lines; in fact they excel in any occupation where deep thought and concentration are the keys to success.

But when Neptune is afflicted in Capricorn it makes the nature melancholy, secretive and very often deceitful. These people are generally recluses and shun the society of their fellow-men.

♆♒ *Neptune in Aquarius,* when well aspected, gives an altruistic or utopian disposition with a desire to emancipate the whole world from whatsoever social, mental, moral or physical ills the person may be able to perceive. Hence these people are usually too far in advance of their time and age to be understood. They are regarded as dreamers and visionaries, idealists and, as in a sense, dangerous to society because of their originality and independence of conventions. At the same time they are very popular with the most progressive people in society. They easily apprehend Nature's finer forces and are therefore the pioneers in exploration of hitherto undreamed-of fields.

When Neptune is afflicted in Aquarius it gives similar ideas and ideals in regard to conventions. But it is only too liable to bring such people and their ideas into discredit and disgrace.

♆♓ *Neptune in Pisces,* when well aspected gives a love of mysticism and a tendency to investigate the occult. Sometimes these people develop their spiritual faculties and obtain first-hand knowledge. They are compassionate towards others, unobtrusive, retiring in their manner, well liked also often the recipients of aid from others, cheerfully and willingly given.

When Neptune is afflicted in Pisces the person is liable to suffer through mediumship, obsession and deception of secret enemies. There is danger of imprisonment and a tendency to indulge in drink or drugs which will end in sorrow and self-undoing.

Neptune in Aspect with other Planets

☉ ✱ △ ♆ *The Sun sextile or trine to Neptune* favors the possibility of developing spiritual faculties, for Neptune intensifies the higher vibrations in the aura and as some express themselves best through music these aspects make them unusually sensitive to echoes from the heavenworld, which is the realm of tone. Many people with these configurations hear the harmony of the spheres and if Mercury, the lower octave of Neptune, gives the requisite dexterity they become musicians of a high inspirational nature. In others it breeds a love of the occult which leads them into the higher life, but they usually approach it from the intellectual standpoint as psychic investigators. A few live the life and obtain first-hand knowledge.

☉ P ☌ □ ☍ ♆ *The Sun parallel, conjunction, square or opposition to Neptune* also brings the person in touch with the denizens of the invisible world by raising the vibrations in his aura, but these configurations attract the undesirable element such as are seen at the ordinary spiritualistic seance. In a watery sign Neptune induces the person to drink to excess and then the resulting acceleration of the vibratory rate frequently causes such a person to perceive the ugly and gruesome forms abounding in the lower realms of the invisible world, which are real elemental entities and not figments of his fancy as believed by people who hear him tell what he sees during delirium tremens.

♀ ✶ △ ♆ *Venus sextile or trine to Neptune* makes an inspirational musician. It gives a fertile imagination and deep emotions, a nature that is pure and chaste, hence occasionally it leads to platonic unions and companionship of the most ecstatic nature.

♀ ☌ P ♆ *Venus conjunction or parallel to Neptune* is to be judged on the same line as indicated in the cases of Mars and Uranus.

♀ □ ☍ ♆ *Venus square or opposition to Neptune* makes the person liable to sorrow, loss and trouble, especially through the marriage partner or anyone else in whom he trusts. People with these aspects should be particularly careful to avoid anything which has in it an element of chance or speculation for they are sure to lose, especially in dealing with large companies or corporations.

☿ ☌ P ✶ △ ♆ *Mercury in conjunction, parallel, sextile or trine to Neptune* makes a man peculiarly adapted to the occult art, particularly if the conjunction occurs in the Third or Ninth House or the trines are from watery signs—Cancer, Scorpio or Pisces. Such people usually succeed in occult science and often develop a supernormal faculty. They are particularly good as magnetic healers.

☿ □ ☍ ♆ *Mercury square or opposition to Neptune* gives a chaotic mind, liability to lack of memory, indolence and a disposition to dream the time away. There is a restless desire for fame frustrated by inability to fit in anywhere. Such people are liable to fraud, deception and slander, also to temptation to suicide.

☽ ✶ △ ♆ *The Moon sextile or trine to Neptune* increases the faculty of imagination to a superlative degree, especially if either of the planets is in the Ninth House. Then it favors prophetic dreams and visions which bring the person into contact with the invisible worlds. It indicates ability in the occult arts and success in their practice. It makes the nature exceedingly inspirational and it also gives a kind and sympathetic disposition. The spiritual qualities mentioned may not be apparent even to the person himself, but then they are latent and capable of development. It is also safe to say that at some time or other during the life persons with these aspects will come in contact with the occult and be very much attracted, whether the qualities of the soul are developed or not.

☽ ☌ P ♆ *The Moon conjunction or parallel to Neptune* indicates the same strong psychic faculties as the good aspects, particularly if Neptune is placed in the psychic sign Cancer. Those who have been born with the good configurations of Neptune during the fourteen years when it was in the airy scientific sign Gemini are now conquering the air and perfecting scientific inventions which will make us marvel, but the children who have been born under favorable configurations during the fourteen years Neptune has been going through the psychic sign Cancer are growing up around us as a band of mystics and when they have reached mature years they will astonish us with their spiritual insight and power. Among other things they will develop the soul of music in a hitherto unprecedented manner.

☽ □ ☍ ♆ *The Moon square or opposition to Neptune* is also an indication of the soul qualities similar to those given by the good aspects, but under the former aspects the person will be of a negative nature and is apt to become the prey of spirit-controls and subjected to mediumship, therefore people with those aspects should be very careful not to attend spiritualistic seances, "sit in the silence" or use other methods of occult development.

♄ ✱ △ ♆ *Saturn sextile or trine to Neptune* is good for success in worldly affairs for it brings out the saturnine virtues, forethought, honor, self-reliance, determination, system et cetera, by which the person gains the confidence and esteem of others, but the principal effect is spiritual and therefore only felt by those who are able to respond because of other aspects in the horoscope. To them it gives the ability to delve deeply into occult and mystical subjects, also to become proficient in the art and practice thereof.

♄ ☌ P ♆ *Saturn conjunction or parallel to Neptune* has the same effect as the good aspects when it occurs in a sign where either of the planets are strong as Neptune is in Cancer and Pisces and Saturn in Libra and Capricorn.

♄ □ ☍ ♆ *Saturn square or opposition to Neptune* lays the person liable to loss by deception, treachery or fraud in worldly matters and if he should undertake to investigate or practise the occult art he is liable to become the prey of spirit-controls and be led into mediumship with consequent danger to the health, and liability to attempt suicide.

♃ ✱ △ ♆ *Jupiter sextile or trine to Neptune* gives an inspirational mystical nature and ability to fill a position connected with occult orders, that is to say, where the character is sufficiently developed so that Neptune can make his influence felt for then this position brings out all the noblest and most spiritual strength of both planets, and occult experiences are not infrequently the result. At any rate, during the sleeping hours these people are quite active and conscious in the invisible worlds and often bring experiences back with them as dreams or visions.

♃ ☌ P ♆ *Jupiter conjunction or parallel to Neptune* gives an influence similar to that of the good aspects when Neptune and Jupiter are not afflicted, but if they are in a weak sign and aspecting the other planets by square or opposition then the influence is similar to that of the bad aspects of Jupiter and Neptune.

♃ □ ☍ ♆ *Jupiter square or opposition to Neptune* indicates lack of control of the emotions. The person is sensitive to the influences of the borderland between the seen and the unseen worlds but they are often of an awe-inspiring and disgusting type, hence apt to cause hysterical conditions, involuntary trance and kindred disorders attendant upon negative psychism, but from a material standpoint it gives danger of fraud through speculation or large companies and dealing with predatory interests should therefore be avoided.

♂ ✱ △ ♆ *Mars sextile or trine to Neptune* intensifies the emotional nature and gives a leaning toward the study and practice of occultism and mysticism. When other testimonies in the horoscope concur, the martial energy directed toward the psychic subjects denoted by Neptune often helps the person very materially in his aim to penetrate into the invisible worlds in a conscious manner.

♂ ☌ □ P ☍ ♆ *Mars conjunction, square, parallel or opposition to Neptune* makes the nature coarse and sensual, impulsive and irascible, militant and extravagant in speech and action, self-indulgent to a degree in whatever direction his passions may lead him and unable to exercise restraint over himself in any direction. It gives a fanatical spirit which may express itself in either religion or atheism and under favorable conditions such people are liable to become victims of discarnate spirits who may either use them as a medium or by obsessing them. It gives a tendency to lawlessness and participation in anarchistic schemes or plots.

♅ ✱ △ ♆ *Uranus sextile or trine to Neptune* gives inclination towards the occult or mystical side of life, and if either is placed in the Tenth House the person usually becomes a leader or authority in these lines, he wins at least local recognition and if other testimonies concur his fame will be national or international. Such an aspect will bring direct touch with the spiritual world and success in dealing with inhabitants of that plane. It produces dreams and visions of a prophetic and inspirational nature, strengthens the healing powers and will consequently enable the person to do a great deal of good for his suffering fellow-men. These aspects give a highly developed intuition which amounts almost to mind-reading. There is a love of travel and exploration of the physical world as well as of nature's finer realms. Nor are such people altogether dreamers, they have a strong will with excellent executive and organizing powers which will aid them in realizing their hopes, wishes and ambitions to rise in life and be at the forefront of whatever profession they select.

♅ ☌ P ♆ *Uranus conjunction or parallel to Neptune* are convertible aspects; if the planets are well placed by sign and otherwise well aspected, their effect will be similar to the sextile or trine, though not so pronounced, but if they are cadent, weak by sign, and afflicted they are only a little less evil than when aspected by square or opposition.

♅ □ ☍ ♆ *Uranus square or opposition to Neptune* brings underhanded, deceptive influences into the life which aim to undermine the reputation and make the person suffer scandal and public disfavor, sudden and unaccountable reverses in business are met with, or trouble in social affairs. There is the same love of travel and exploration as given by the good aspects but the person cannot accomplish his aims with the same facility, or if he does it is to his disadvantage and brings added trouble He is also drawn towards the occult or mystic side of life, but his path is beset by dangers of mediumship and obsession and all through life he is filled with a vague dread of impending disaster which he can neither account for nor dispel by will or reason, hence uncertainty overshadows the life as a cloud and robs him of peace and contentment.

For influence of Pluto see pages 728-734.

CHAPTER XVIII.

THE DOCTRINE OF DELINEATION IN A NUTSHELL

STUDENTS of the Stellar Science will find the following Table very useful in delineating horoscopes for though the planets confer many more characteristics than there given, as shown in the general reading which opens the chapter wherein the places and aspects of each planet are given, the following key-words give in a succinct manner the quintessence of the characteristics conferred by each planet according to whether it is well or ill aspected.

When the student has mastered the meaning of the positions and aspects of the various planets as given in the preceding chapters he may with the greatest of ease give a good delineation of the effect of each aspect by combining the key-words in this Table and elaborating upon them. For instance, if reading a horoscope where the Sun is trine Saturn, put down the description given in the Table as follows:

"The vital, venturesome and authoritative Sun trine the deliberative, persevering, tactful, cautious, methodical and thoughtful Saturn (then elaborate) will give John a tenacious hold on life and endow him with both courage and caution, so that while he may seem venturesome at times he will always carefully calculate the obstacles to be overcome and not attempt anything foolhardy, but accomplish his object once he has decided to go ahead. He will be systematic, orderly and methodical, also persevering in whatever he undertakes after due deliberation and forethought, hence his efforts will generally be brought to a successful issue. In dealing with others he will be thoughtful and tactful, hence usually able to obtain his desires by diplomacy. On account of these qualities he will be generally successful in life and he will lay up a fair fortune, for Saturn is also the planet of acquisitiveness."

In a similar manner students may combine the key-words of all the other planets and aspects from this Table and elaborate on them as they can. This will enable them to give a good reading of any horoscope with a little practice. For further practical demonstration of this method students are advised to study the children's horoscopes in *Rays From the Rose Cross,* where the writer makes use of it every month. These horoscopes are a mine of instruction which no student desiring to perfect himself in the stellar science can afford to be without. The key-words will bring to his mind what has been said about the general nature of the planets under consideration; this he may combine with the nature of the signs and houses where the planets are placed if a very full reading is desired.

Table of Planetary Key-Words

☉ ✱ △ The vital, venturesome, dignified and authoritative Sun.

☉ □ ☍ The lazy, ambitionless, despotic and cowardly Sun.

♀ ✱ △ The harmonious, artistic, beautiful, lovely, cheerful and suave Venus.

♀ □ ☍ The dissolute, sensual, vulgar, slothful, loud and lazy Venus.

☿ ✱ △ The quick-witted, versatile, eloquent, literary, adroit and dexterous Mercury.

☿ □ ☍ The restless, shiftless, profane, gossipy, demagogic, dishonest, untruthful, forgetful, and clumsy Mercury.

☽ ✱ △ The magnetic, imaginative, plastic and changeable Moon.

☽ □ ☍ The negative, procrastinating, dreamy, vacillating, visionary, frivolous, childish and worrisome Moon

♄ ✱ △ The cautious, deliberate, methodical, persevering, tactful, thoughtful and thrifty Saturn.

♄ □ ☍ The malicious, materialistic, melancholy, pessimistic, avaricious, obstructive, secretive and worrisome Saturn.

♃ ✱ △ The law-abiding, charitable, conservative, reverent, optimistic, opulent and benevolent Jupiter.

♃ □ ☍ The indolent, procrastinating, bombastic, ostentatious, prodigal, dissipated and lawless Jupiter.

♂ ✱ △ The gallant, enterprising, energetic, enthusiastic and constructive Mars.

♂ □ ☍ The coarse, combative, egotistic, discordant, destructive, passionate, audacious, impulsive and hot-tempered Mars.

♅ ✱ △ The advanced, romantic, original, independent, liberty-loving and inventive Uranus.

♅ □ ☍ The licentious, unconventional, fanatical and irresponsible Uranus.

♆ ✱ △ The occult, prophetic, inspirational, spiritual, devotional and musical Neptune.

♆ □ ☍ The fraudulent, vague, deceptive, dishonest and mediumistic Neptune.

THE STRENGTH AND WEAKNESS OF THE PLANETS

Shown by Elevation, Exaltation, Critical Degrees, Etc.

The foregoing delineation of the effects and influences of the planets in the various houses and signs, also by aspect and position such as parallel and conjunction, sextile, square, trine and opposition, are subject to wide modification according to the other configurations of the horoscope, and according to whether the planets are essentially dignified or in their detriment, exalted or in fall, or placed in critical degrees. The following table of planetary powers will show at a glance the signs in which the various planets are strong or weak; and when the student knows in what sign a planet rules or is exalted it is only necessary to remember that it has its fall or detriment in the opposite sign. Thus the Sun rules Leo and is exalted in Aries. Hence it is very powerful in those signs, and as the opposite signs are Aquarius and Libra it is at once apparent that when placed in these signs the Sun is comparatively weak. Another important factor which it is necessary to take into consideration is elevation. The closer a planet is to the Midheaven, the more highly it is elevated and the more powerful it is. Consulting the table of planetary powers we find that Mars rules Aries and is exalted in Capricorn. Let us suppose that in a horoscope, Mars is found placed close to the Midheaven in Aries or Capricorn and square to the Sun which is near the Ascendant. Then the evil will be very much greater than if Mars were in Libra or Cancer, the signs of his fall and detriment, and the Sun placed in the Midheaven elevated above Mars. Similarly, if the Sun were placed in Aries, its exaltation sign, close to the Midheaven in high elevation and trine to Jupiter in its own sign, Sagittarius, then both planets are very strong and their effect would be much more marked than if they were placed in the signs of their fall and debility. By memorizing this table and bearing in mind the matter of elevation, the student will be able to form a much more accurate judgment of the effect of planets in any particular horoscope than if this is not taken into consideration.

TABLE OF PLANETARY POWERS

Planet	*Rules*	*Detriment*	*Exaltation*	*Fall*
☉	♌	♒	♈ 19°	♎
♀	♉ ♎	♏ ♈	♓ 27°	♍
☿	♊ ♍	♐ ♓	♍ 15°	♓
☽	♋	♑	♉ 3°	♏
♄	♑ ♒	♋ ♌	♎ 21°	♈
♃	♓ ♐	♍ ♊	♋ 15°	♑
♂	♈ ♏	♎ ♉	♑ 28°	♋
♅	♒	♌	♏	♉
♆	♓	♍	♋	♑

Critical Degrees

Another division of the Zodiac which it is easy to remember and important to take into consideration is based upon the passage of the Moon from the first degree of Aries through the twelve signs. It takes the Moon about 28 days to go around the Zodiac and she moves with an average velocity of 13 degrees. Thus if we start with the first point of Aries and measure one day's travel, the second day will commence at the 13th degree and the third at the 26th; the fourth commences at 9 degrees of Taurus and the fifth day she starts at 21 degrees of the same sign; on the sixth day she reaches 4 degrees of Gemini; on the seventh day she starts at 17 degrees of Gemini and completes the first quarter by reaching the cusp of Cancer on the morning of the eighth day. It is evident that she will strike the same degrees of the signs composing the other three quarters during the three weeks it takes her to complete the circuit, and thus we may easily memorize the critical degrees in the folowing manner:

In the Cardinal Signs—Aries, Cancer, Libra and Capricorn, the first, thirteenth, and twenty-sixth degrees are critical.

In the Fixed Signs—Taurus, Leo, Scorpio and Aquarius, the ninth and twenty-first degrees are critical.

In the Common Signs—Gemini, Virgo, Sagittarius and Pisces, the fourth and seventeenth degrees are critical.

It has been found that when a planet is within orb of three degrees of one of these critical points it exercises a much stronger influence in the life than it would otherwise. Therefore students will also do well to remember this and should a planet be in a sign of fall or detriment, but in a critical degree, it is thereby strengthened and will do more good or bad according to its nature and the aspect it has. On the other hand, if a planet is in its exaltation sign, highly elevated and in a critical degree, its aspects will be exceedingly powerful and make themselves felt much more in the life than would otherwise be the case.

Mercury Before and After the Sun

Another important point which is only too often overlooked is the position of Mercury with regard to the Sun. When Mercury is in a lower degree of the same sign as occupied by the Sun, or in any degree of a preceding sign, he rises before the Sun and, so to speak, carries the rays of the Day Star forward. But when he is placed in a higher degree of the same sign as the Sun or in the sign following that occupied by the Sun, then he rises after the Orb of Day and is, so to speak, overshadowed. Therefore it has been found that when Mercury, the planet of mind, logic and reason, rises *before* the Sun, it gives a keener, better intellect than when he follows the luminary.

Are You Helping Your Stars?

One not infrequently hears students of Astrology express their annoyance at the way the stars work. They complain that the evil directions are always on time and marked in their effect, while very often the good directions seem to have little or no influence and they wonder why. Have you ever realized that you cannot possibly get something for nothing, any more than you can create something out of nothing. This holds good whether you want a loaf of bread, a position, favors, or anything else. If at any time you seem to get something without paying for it, you will have to settle later, and settle with interest, for it is nature's law of Justice that nothing is given for nothing. There must be an equivalent in one way or another; the scales may be tipped in one direction for a long time, but as surely as the pendulum swings equally to each side of the neutral point, so surely will the scales of justice swing, and swing until the balance is reached.

This holds good in Astrology; it is said that "God helps the man who helps himself;" you may also say that *the stars help the man who helps himself,* for they are God's ministers and it should always be remembered that *the stars show tendencies, they mark times when opportunities are ripe, but they never under any circumstances compel anyone to act in this, that or the other manner.* But neither are the directions haphazard events, they are lessons and experiences for us, of which we may avail ourselves, or not, as we choose within certain limits. For instance, the Moon comes to a square of Mars, and it will bring to us an opportunity to lose our temper,and get into trouble thereby, then when the trouble is over and we sit down to reflect on the occurrence we will most likely say to ourselves: Well, what fools we were to allow a little thing like that to play havoc with our happiness. On the other hand if the Astrological student uses his knowledge in the proper manner, then he should know what the effect of the Moon square Mars will be, he should resolve beforehand to be calm and say: Here is an opportunity for me to rule my stars. I am going to keep my temper well under control so that no matter what happens, I shall maintain my equilibrium. Then, when the opportunity comes along to lose his temper he may stand firm. Although he may feel the passions surging *within,* he may stand outwardly quiet, keep a cool head and when the danger is past he will have gained a victory and learned the lesson which it was intended he *should* learn. Or suppose it is a square of the Moon to Saturn; this will cause people to worry and look upon the dark side of life,but the astrological student may say to himself when such a configuration is approaching: No, I am not going to worry; worry will not help matters, it hinders, because it takes from me all my strength, wherewith otherwise I could overcome conditions. I am going to look at the bright side of the matter and see what I can do to remedy this trouble.

As a matter of fact most of the things we worry about never come to pass, and if the student can learn under this planetary direction to keep his equilibrium, to stop worrying, then he has ruled his stars and learned an important lesson. Thus, if he helps his stars by learning the lessons which they are endeavoring to teach him, the evil directions will not have the same power over him as if he simply sits down and folds his hands saying: "Well, I cannot help it, I am under the evil directions and naturally things are bound to go wrong in every particular." There is in the horoscope a dominant factor, namely, the Individual Will; bear in mind that the *horoscope shows only tendencies and it has no power whatever to compel you; compulsion is from within yourself.* You, in the final analysis, are the dominant factor in that horoscope, and can by an exercise of sufficient will power rule your stars. It is admitted that we are all weak, and therefore not able to exercise the necessary will power at all times; but that is exactly why these evil directions are sent to us, to enable us to cultivate a stronger will to do the right thing at the right time and it depends upon ourselves whether we shall be compelled by circumstances from without or by our own will from within. Surely that is the proper way, and astrological students above all other people ought to be able to guide their lives safely amid the rocks and shoals of existence, because they have proper warning, they know what is coming, and they should prepare for it.

On the other hand it is asked: Why do the good directions not bring a corresponding measure of benefit? And the answer to that question is, for the same lack of co-operation. It is as absolutely necessary to help our stars in one direction as to hinder them in the other. Are you out of a position with perhaps the family exchequer running low and no means in sight wherewith to replenish it, but your hopes centered upon a strong favorable direction such as perhaps a trine of the progressed Moon to the ruler of the Sixth House or the Sun? Under these conditions you feel sure, from an astrological standpoint, that you are going to obtain a good position which will put you on easy street. Very well, you may be sure that the opportunity will come, but do not expect it to be laid in your lap without a single effort on your part; if a thing is worth having it is worth going after, it is worth making the very best efforts to get it; do not neglect any detail, dress yourself carefully, but not showily when you go to see the person who has it in his power to bestow the favor, remember, first impressions are important; have all your ammunition ready in the shape of recommendations and everything else that you would have were you not depending upon an astrological aspect to help you get the position. Use every proper means of impressing the prospective employer with your ability and you may depend that your effort will be successful.

for *you have helped your stars,* you have grasped your opportunity. Or, are you about to embark in a business venture with some one else and you feel very confident because the Moon is trine to the Sun and Venus in the Seventh House? Be careful that you do not lay aside your caution on that account, thinking that under such a direction no one can come into your partnership who is not all right. If you do, you neglect your part and you will have no reason whatever to blame the stars if later on it is shown that the person is not all you expected him to be. Nothing is needed in the world today in the same degree that we need common sense, and this applies to the department of astrology, as well as to every other department of life. Opportunity may be likened to a toboggan slide between ourselves and our desires; it is necessary for us to make an adequate initial effort in order to launch our sled upon this incline, but once we have done our part, then everything will go along swimmingly under favorable directions, for then the stars are with us to impress others in our behalf, or to strengthen our penetrative power so that we may know what is best for us.

If you want to know positively the power of directions, even transits, as we call the actual position of the stars in the sky, take an ephemeris and note the moon's aspects for the current month. When the Moon is in opposition to Mars you will find in people a general lack of energy and ambition, they would rather tear down than build. When we have a conjunction of Mars and the Moon, people will be active and energetic, but impulse rather than common sense will govern, hence they will accomplish little good, and may do harm without intention. But when the Moon and Mars are trine, there will be a general desire among people to do something of a constructive nature, and they will meet with success in such efforts. And last, but not least, when the Moon is square to Mars it will make people irritable, quarrelsome, destructive, ready to fly at each other, unreasonable and unmanageable.

CHAPTER XIX.

Mind and the Ruling Planet

WHEN we wish to study the character, disposition and temperament of anyone we must first realize that the mind is the keystone of the arch of the human personality. But character, disposition and temperament do not depend so much upon the quality of mind, whether it be keen, sharp, and alert or slow and plodding, as upon what channels it takes for its expression. Intellects of the first magnitude are sometimes put to perverted use to the detriment of the community and the individual who thus misuses his divine heritage, while a slow and very inferior mind may minister to many in lowly but loving meekness and reap sheaves of soul-growth thereby. Thus it is not sufficient to determine the quality of the mentality; we must also ascertain what is the channel of its expression. To judge that or any other matter thoroughly really involves consideration of the horoscope as a whole, separately and apart from its bearing upon all other matters. But in a general way the character and disposition may be learned from the Sun, Moon, Mercury, Ascendant and the ruling planets.

It has become the custom of many astrologers

to take the lord of the rising sign as the ruler of the horoscope. That is correct in Medical Astrology because the Ascendant represents the body, but when we want to judge the character which is the combination of all the forces focused through the horoscopical wheel of life the matter is different. Then we must find what planet has the most dominant influence in the life and that is then the life ruler regardless of whether or not it is the ruler of the Ascendant. To find that planet, look first to the lord of the Ascendant. If he is elevated, essentially dignified or angular and strongly aspected, remember, it matters not whether the aspects are good or bad as long as they are close and plentiful (for if it were only the good aspects that made the ruler then there would be only good people in the world. But we know that there are people of all shades of character and therefore it is necessary to select the ruler according to the aspects, regardless of whether they are good or bad), and above all, if the aspects are close, then the lord of the Ascendant is also the ruling planet, for he will exercise the most potent influence in the life.

On the other hand if another planet is more highly elevated than the ruler of the Ascendant, if it is exalted, essentially dignified or placed in an angle and its aspects are more plentiful or closer than the aspects of the lord of the Ascendant, then judge that that planet will be the ruler of the horoscope and exercise a dominant influence in the life regardless of the fact that it is not the ruler of the rising sign.

But if there are two planets running neck-and-neck in the race for rulership, so to speak, with no strongly marked difference in favor of one or the other so that it is difficult to make a choice, do not utterly discard one and choose the other, for then they will both be very active in the life and must be classed as co-rulers.

The Influence of Ruling Planets
Well Aspected

☉ *The Sun as Ruling Planet.*

When the vital, courageous and ambitious well aspected Sun is ruler, it gives dignity to the whole nature, a lofty pride that would not stoop to do anything small, mean or degrading, a fine and noble courage that may show itself on occasion as much by disdainfully ignoring the attacks of an adversary whom he considers too far beneath his notice as by a fight to the death for a principle. There is an intense craving for recognition and leadership which will make it very difficult for him to occupy a subordinate position; also an intense warm-hearted, affectionate and demonstrative nature.

♀ *Venus as Ruling Planet.*

When the refined, luxurious and musical well aspected Venus is ruler of the horoscope it gives a tender, loving, even amorous nature which craves love as we all desire air, for love is the very life breath of such people. They are extremely fond of children and usually have many pets which serve as avenues for their expression of love. They are also pleasure-loving and fond of social intercourse, neat and artistic in their ideas and in the decoration of their homes. They love jewelry and anything else that adds beauty to the life; they are luxurious in all their tastes, very amiable and much beloved by all; their greatest fault is an inordinate love of ease and an aversion to soiling their hands.

☿ *Mercury as Ruling Planet.*

When Mercury the planet of reason, expression and dexterity is the well aspected life ruler it gives a keen, quick-witted mind which craves knowledge as a thirsty man craves water and absorbs it as readily, a mind that solves, apparently without effort, the most intricate problems. Thus there is ability in the various branches of mental endeavor, science and literature, but these people are also very apt and forceful orators and have an extraordinary dexterity so that they can usually turn their hands to anything. They are fond of traveling and very successful as salesmen and agents.

☽ *The Moon as Ruling Planet.*

When the romantic, imaginative and restless well aspected Moon is the life ruler, the people born under its influence are indeed rolling stones and far fields always look greenest to them. Therefore they have an overwhelming desire for travel and change which generally does not permit them to stay in one place longer than necessary to earn the money which will enable them to go to the next. They have a most vivid and fanciful imagination and a romantic nature entirely foreign to any practical endeavor; listless, restless and unstable as the tide that comes and goes, flotsam and jetsam upon the sea of life. They are generally mediumistic, though usually unconsciously so, but are otherwise quite harmless though utterly irresponsible and untrustworthy where anything requiring an effort is concerned.

♄ *Saturn as Ruling Planet.*

When the serious, sagacious and profound well aspected Saturn is life ruler, the people born under its influence are of a profoundly thoughtful, serious nature. They have a keen sense of responsibility and are full of forethought, hence trustworthy and reliable advisers; they are systematic, orderly and have good executive ability, frugal in their tastes, thrifty and saving; just to a degree, but their justice is cruel, hard and untempered by the slightest degree of mercy. They are chaste, sober and exemplary in their lives but they have neither mercy nor pity for those who are unable to overcome faults or habits or who otherwise become delinquent to the laws of society. They care little or nothing for pleasure or the society of others and generally keep their own counsel and company; they are highly respected, esteemed and trusted in the community but neither care for nor merit the *love* of their fellow men.

♃ *Jupiter as Ruling Planet.*

When the jovial, genial and generous well aspected Jupiter is life ruler, the people born under his influence are ensouled by a great desire for honor, respect and esteem in their community. Therefore they aspire to be pillars in the church, legal lights, or to fill an honored position in the pulpit; failing this they enter by preference one of the professions as lawyer or doctor. They are cordial, genial people with a jovial smile and a hearty handshake that make one glad to meet them wherever they go, so they are always welcome. They are law-abiding and just but inclined to temper their justice with mercy; and while they themselves live lives beyond reproach they are kind, forgiving and lenient to those of a weaker morality whose lives are smirched by sin and crime, hence they are philanthropic and always ready to give to charity and benevolent work. They are not only respected and esteemed but beloved in the community where they reside.

♂ *Mars as Ruling Planet.*

When the enthusiastic, energetic, constructive and militant Mars is the well aspected life ruler, the people born under the influence of his dynamic rays are eager for the fray and battle of life. They are ensouled with an ardent desire to conquer the world. To them it does not so much matter what they do so long as it affords an adequate outlet for the constructive energy which, figuratively speaking, threatens to burst them unless released. The bigger and more difficult the undertaking, the more they exult; hence they become the pioneers and pathfinders of civilization, the engineers and contractors who build our cities and the highways and byways that connect them, who develop the resources of the world and turn them over to others to use. They are extremely impatient of restraint and will brook no interference with their plans or methods. These people govern others and bend them to their will by the whiplash of sheer force for they have neither tact nor diplomacy but win by the merit of might. They earn money easily and spend it as lavishly and foolishly. They are extremely extravagant and when reverses come they are down and out for the time being but they never stay down; the indomitable inner force soon accomplishes rehabilitation and with it the old reckless ways of living reassert themselves. They are generally foolhardy to a degree, hence liable to accidents and a violent end.

♅ *Uranus as Ruling Planet.*

When the original, romantic and eccentric well aspected Uranus is life ruler the character is idealistic, unconventional and utopian. These people are generally out of patience with the conventional ways of living and determined in their efforts and endeavors to break the shackles of society and live a bohemian life. They are full of fads and given to unusual beliefs, too advanced for the majority. At the same time they are pioneers of a new age in which many of the ideas we now consider utopian will be modified so that they will be held by all. These people are also the inventors of the world, in touch with the higher worlds where ideas merge from the Divine Mind to impinge upon the minds of those who are sufficiently sensitive to grasp them and bring them to birth for the use of humanity. The Uranians are very headstrong and always ready with an argument to defend their ideas and secure a convert to their cults; odd in dress, in food, in ideas, they are a class apart.

♆ *Neptune as Ruling Planet.*

When the occult and mystical well aspected Neptune is life ruler we have a person of a most peculiar power whose chief mark is a strange expression of the eye which must be seen to be appreciated. It is as if he looked right through and through whatever is before him, but it is not necessary to discuss this type for there are so few that they are very seldom encountered by the average astrologer and only an occultist can know and judge another occultist.

The Influence of Afflicted Ruling Planets

When the life rulers are afflicted by the conjunction, parallel, square or opposition from the other planets, especially from the malefics—Saturn, Mars, Uranus and Neptune—they affect the life in an inimical manner which may be outlined as follows:

☉ *The Sun as Ruling Planet.*

When the cowardly and arrogant afflicted Sun is life ruler, people born under his debilitating influence are egotistical in the extreme, full of swagger, self-importance and arrogance. If they obtain authority over anyone whom they think they can overawe they will rule such dependent with a rod of iron, trample upon his tenderest feelings without a twinge of conscience or compunction, but if they themselves come under the authority of another these spineless weaklings will then cringe, creep and cater to the slightest whim of their master though they hate him with an intense hatred that is only kept in check by their fear. They whine and wheedle at the faintest frown though ready to spring and devour him if only they dared. It is the signature of one of the most despicable characters in the gamut.

♀ *Venus as Ruling Planet.*

When the slovenly, slothful and lazy afflicted Venus is ruler of the horoscope the persons are sensual and profligate, untidy and slatternly, of depraved, perverted tastes and utterly disreputable in their conduct; they are social parasites. They use loud and obscene language and are fond of music of a clanging, jarring nature. They love revelry and debauch, their affection expresses itself in coarse lusts, unbridled passion, free love and moral perversion. They revel in spangles and tinsel, loud, clashing colors and cheap imitations of beauty and worth.

☿ *Mercury as Ruling Planet.*

When the untruthful, dishonest and clumsy afflicted Mercury is life ruler the people under his influence are either entirely mentally unsound so that they must be confined for their own good in proper institutions, or they are so cunning that they are able to hide their mental bias and prey upon society as thieves, pick-pockets, defaulters and criminals of similar nature. They are notoriously untruthful and prefer misleading others to telling the truth, even where it is of no benefit to them. They are either dull of comprehension or of such consummate cunning that they seem to be driven by a resistless force to get the best of some unsuspecting person. They excel as confidence men, badgers and in similar unsavory occupations. They are thoroughly unreliable and dishonest in all their dealings; neurotic and perverted, scabs on society. These people are also inveterate talkers and always ready to criticise, slander or ruin the reputation of others. They are a menace to society in all their activities.

☽ *The Moon as Ruling Planet.*

When the changeable and visionary afflicted Moon is life ruler it makes the persons extremely restless and averse to labor of any kind, fidgety and always on the move; if they cannot travel from one city to another, they move from one house to another and from one situation to another as often as possible and they infuse the same restlessness into whomsoever they come in contact with. If the afflictions are very severe the mind suffers and their mental phases coincide with the changes of the orb of night.

♄ *Saturn as Ruling Planet.*

When the morbid, melancholy and malicious afflicted Saturn is life ruler he robs life of all joy and brightness so that these people become recluses and melancholy misanthropes; so miserly and avaricious that they will starve themselves and forego the comforts of life even when they have ample means to satisfy them. They are cruel, hard and suspicious of the acts and motives of others and if they take up work as a detective they become human ferrets, bloodhounds who will hound their prey to death and gloat over his misery. If anyone frustrates such people they will hold spite forever and aim to get even, if it takes a lifetime. But the end of these people is always bad; sometime or other they overreach and fall into the trap they have set for others. They usually die an ignoble death and the world gives a sigh of relief when they pass out.

♃ *Jupiter as Ruling Planet.*

When the indolent, bombastic and egotistical afflicted Jupiter is the life ruler the person is often a parasite on the social tree, a gambler, confidence man and speculator, sporty, fond of display and ostentation; he wears loud clothing, paste diamonds and cheap jewelry. He is usually met with in pool rooms, on race tracks and in similar places; playing poker or playing the ponies are among his favorite means of earning a living; he is very loud and egotistical, anxious to attract attention no matter how; he often figures in court proceedings on account of shady transactions or immoral conduct or unpaid bills, for he is an adept at obtaining credit for everything he wants and never pays the price of his expensive tastes if there is any way of avoiding a settlement of his debts. Among the laboring class he usually figures as a demagogue and agitator, inciting to strikes and riots, but he is always ready to sell out a striking union to the employers. We find them among the typical Italian padrones, as keepers of sweat-shops, and in similar occupations.

♂ *Mars as Ruling Planet.*

When the arrogant, egotistical and foolhardy afflicted Mars is life ruler the person is an egotist of the first water, bound to attain to his wishes by force or destruction if other means fail; in fact he prefers to bulldoze others to do his will rather than to have them submit without a struggle. He is a first-rate slave driver, section boss on the railway, in a construction camp and similar places, a liar, braggart, bouncer, or pugilist, a daredevil willing to risk his life and the lives of others at any moment and in any undertaking.

♅ *Uranus as Ruling Planet.*

When the stubborn, erratic and independent afflicted Uranus is life ruler the mentality is usually so obsessed in one direction or another that such people become fanatics and generally also there is an excessive sensuality and perverted taste. They are always ready and anxious for an argument as a means of airing their ideas but they are so hypnotized by their own particular fad that they are never convinced and can never see when the argument goes against them. They always espouse the most radical and unconventional ideas.

♆ *Neptune as Ruling Planet.*

When the mediumistic, neurotic and self-indulgent afflicted Neptune is life ruler, the persons are of a dreamy, neurotic and negative nature, apt to become the medium of disembodied spirits or even obsessed by them. They are likely to evolve psychic powers of a low grade such as involuntary clairvoyance, crystal gazing, etc., and if they are unable to develop these faculties they often simulate mediumship and other psychic gifts for the purpose of duping or defrauding others. They have a strong faculty of imitation and easily become adepts at deception.

The Signs as Mental Significators

When the *Cardinal* Signs, Aries, Cancer, Libra and Capricorn, are on the angles, that is to say, the Ascendant, Midheaven, Fourth and Seventh Houses, it is a general indication that the person is mentally alert, quick to grasp an idea, active and enthusiastic in whatever work he undertakes; one who has organizing and executive ability and is capable of carrying whatever enterprise he may start to success; a bold, brave, indomitable spirit. This is especially true when many planets are in Cardinal Signs and these people may be classed as the business men of the world.

When the *Fixed* Signs, Taurus, Leo, Scorpio and Aquarius are on the angles it indicates a thoughtful but slow and plodding type of mind which requires time to come to a decision. They always look before they leap but when they have made up their minds they adhere to the course mapped out with a remarkable patience and perseverance which in the end insure success. They are very reliable and can be depended upon to keep their word and meet their obligations. Their principal fault is that they are too apt to get into a rut and become narrow-minded. They are very original and may be classed as the inventors of the world. These delineations are especially true when many planets are in Fixed Signs.

When the *Common* Signs, Gemini, Virgo, Sagittarius and Pisces, are on the angles the mind is flighty and superficial, wavering and versatile. These people are often very quick to grasp a point and form a decision, but just as ready to forget and change their minds. They are adepts at imitation and often pretend to virtues or abilities entirely foreign to their nature. They are easily swayed by the winds of emotion; one moment they may be highly elated over some small matter and the next a trifling trouble bows them down to earth. They are inconstant and unreliable in all their dealings with others because they do not know their minds two minutes in succession. They constitute the agents and middlemen of the world, where they occupy a subordinate or serving position. These delineations are particularly apt when many planets are in Common Signs.

Mental Effect of the Rising Sign

When there are no planets on the Ascendant the rising sign has considerable influence on the type of mind.

♈ *Aries* rising gives an energetic, enthusiastic and ambitious type of mind, but inclined to rash and impulsive acts and a quick temper.

♉ *Taurus* rising gives a stubborn, headstrong and selfish nature, envious, covetous and malicious when angered.

♊ *Gemini* rising gives a quick, alert and versatile mind, easily adaptable to conditions but so fluidic that it lacks the ability absolutely essential to sustained effort and lasting success.

♋ *Cancer* rising gives a negative, imaginative and receptive type of mind, sometimes of a rather morbid nature, reserved and mistrustful; but when such a person has made up his mind to do something he is usually very tenacious in his adherence to his ideas; sympathetic, hospitable and kind.

♌ *Leo* rising gives a frank, open, ambitious mind; a powerful will and a proud, honorable and kind disposition but inclined to be hasty, quick-tempered, sensual and apt to go to extremes.

♍ *Virgo* gives a critical, scheming and ingenious mind, able to evolve ideas galore but usually lacking the initiative to carry them out unless prodded by others. These people are very selfish, self-centered and reserved. They do not take other people into their confidence and they seldom become really familiar with anyone.

♎ *Libra* rising gives an easy-going but kindly and sympathetic type of mind which is unable to grasp or cope with the exigencies of existence. Therefore these people drift along the stream of life, taking as much of the sweet as they can get and using every effort to avoid the bitter. They crave approbation and in return adore their friends and are usually bound up in them.

♏ *Scorpio* rising gives a dual type of mind. This is one of the most mystical of the twelve signs. Some times it is symbolized as an eagle representing the lofty, aspiring type soaring as does the eagle into the ether. At other times it is typified as a serpent which crawls in the dust, and again as a scorpion. There is also considerable occult significance in the fact that the serpent has the sting in its head and the scorpion has it in its tail. But for the present purpose we will judge the two latter as one.

The Scorpio type of mind denoted by the eagle is thoughtful, reserved and inclined to lofty ideals; dignified in demeanor, proud and with perfect control of the temper. These people are very reserved and generally keep their own counsel.

The other type when Scorpio is represented by the serpent is entirely different; deceitful, shrewd and secretive; past finding out; sensual and unforgiving; jealous and passionate, with a very sharp tongue and fiery temper.

♐ *Sagittarius* rising gives an energetic, aspiring, benevolent mind but rather lacking in ambition. These people are usually of an ardent, affectionate disposition and sometimes very demonstrative.

♑ *Capricorn* rising gives a tactful, diplomatic, deep and thoughtful type of mind but selfish, envious and covetous. These people are apt to get into a rut and become very narrow, and when they are crossed they hold spite and plan revenge. They are self-reliant and persistent in whatever they undertake.

♒ *Aquarius* rising gives a good intellect, a friendly, sympathetic and humane disposition, but these people are very original and independent; they will brook no interference with their vagaries and pursue their own course regardless of what others say or think, sometimes even against their own reason and just to assert their independence.

♓ *Pisces* rising gives a sentimental and romantic type of mind, inclined to worry and restlessness, apt to turn to the occult, and to mystical ideas. The mind is very sensitive and often takes on the conditions of others with the effect of unsettling and troubling the person.

CHAPTER XX.

YOUR LUCK IN LIFE

HEALTH, wealth and happiness are to most people the prime objects of life, and whoever has them is rightly considered lucky, though, as we have endeavored to show, luck is very closely linked to merit, and we have earned what we have either in this or former lives and what we lack in fortune or ability we may acquire in this or later lives by good use of our opportunities.

Thus health and disease, vocational ability, social and financial fortunes, marriage, etc., are shown in the horoscope as outlined in the following pages.

HEALTH AND DISEASE

The subject of health and disease is thoroughly elucidated in that part of the book which deals with medical astrology, but those who do not care to go into the depths of the subject will find the following general hints helpful in determining the matter for ordinary purposes:

The main indicators of health and disease are the Sun, Moon and Ascendant, together with the planets in the First House or just above the Ascendant. The twelve signs of the Zodiac confer a vitality of differing degrees and when there are no planets near the rising sign it is of much greater importance than otherwise. The signs may be classed as follows:

Aries, Taurus, Leo, Scorpio and Sagittarius are strongly vital signs.

Gemini, Virgo, Libra and Aquarius are moderately vital.

Cancer, Capricorn and Pisces are signs of weak vitality.

Both the Sun and the Moon affect health in all horoscopes, but the Sun is the particular significator of health for men and the Moon has the same function in a woman's horoscope. Thus, if a boy is born at a New Moon which is a total eclipse, he will have very poor chances of surviving. The same may be said of a girl born at the Full Moon when that is eclipsed.

If the Sun is strong by sign, well aspected by Mars or by the benefics, if he is in essential dignity, exaltation or elevation in a male horoscope, it indicates the possession of a strong vitality and presages a life blessed by good health. If the Moon is similarly placed in a woman's horoscope the same effect follows.

On the other hand if the luminaries are in weak signs in the Sixth or Twelfth Houses or afflicted by Saturn, Mars, Uranus or Neptune, the vitality is weak and much sickness will result unless, from childhood, care is taken to follow the laws of health and hygiene. It must be borne in mind that *the horo-*

scope shows only tendencies which work out infallibly if we drift with the tide of life. But on the other hand, it does not show the factor of the human will, which being divine may enter in and by proper efforts in the right direction correct, at least in a large measure, the limitations.

It is a good indication of health when a strong sign rises with Jupiter or Venus close to the Ascendant and well aspected. But if a weak sign is on the Eastern horizon, and the life forces are further sapped by Saturn, Uranus or Neptune in the rising sign, a life of suffering is foreshown.

With respect to Mars it has been found that his presence on the Ascendant strengthens the constitution when he is well aspected but predisposes to feverish or inflammatory complaints when he is afflicted.

It should be understood that the Sun, Venus, Mercury, the Moon and Jupiter do not afflict save by square or opposition, whereas the conjunction and parallel of Saturn, Mars, Uranus and Neptune are considered inimical as well as the square and opposition.

The afflictions from *Cardinal* Signs, Aries, Cancer, Libra and Capricorn, indicate acute ailments which usually run their course and leave no particular trace.

The afflictions from *Fixed* Signs, Taurus, Leo, Scorpio and Aquarius, indicate organic or hereditary tendencies which are difficult to conquer and usually become chronic.

The diseases indicated by *Common* Signs, Gemini, Virgo, Sagittarius and Pisces, are convertible. They may be entirely overcome or run their course until they become chronic, according to the mental temperament of the person in whose figure these are found.

The places of the malefics, Saturn, Mars, Uranus and Neptune always indicate weak points in the anatomy and the place of Saturn is particularly sensitive; no matter whether he is afflicted or not it is always a danger point. By knowing the parts of the body which are ruled by the different signs it is easy to see where the weak links in the chain of human health are located:

Aries rules the head and face.
Taurus rules the neck and throat.
Gemini rules the lungs, arms and shoulders.
Cancer rules the breast and stomach.
Leo rules the heart and dorsal region of the back.
Virgo rules the abdominal parts.
Libra rules the kidneys and loins.
Scorpio rules the genitals and rectum.
Sagittarius rules the hips and thighs.
Capricorn rules the knees.
Aquarius rules the ankles.
Pisces rules the feet.

Thus if Saturn is placed in Leo it will indicate that the person is subject to heart trouble. If it is in Pisces it will indicate cold feet. The hot and inflammatory Mars afflicted in Aries, the sign which rules the head, would indicate a tendency to fevers, and so on with the other planets.

There are three nebular spots located in the zodiac, namely: the Pleiades in 29 degrees of Taurus; the Ascelli in 6 degrees of Leo, and Antares in 8 degrees of Sagittarius. If the Sun or Moon are found in these places and afflicted by a malefic, be careful of the eyes, or if one of the malefics are in one of these places afflicting the Sun and Moon the same judgment holds good.

With these general indications the ordinary student should be able to judge a horoscope with respect to health and disease and should a more thorough examination be desired, a study of the matter in the part dealing with Medical Astrology will give the necessary information.

The Social and Financial Fortunes

The vocation, financial fortune and social standing, like all other matters, should be judged from the whole horoscope, but the Second, the Sixth, the Eighth and the Tenth Houses with their lords are the chief significators.

The Second House indicates what the person earns by his own efforts. When Jupiter, Venus, the

Sun, the Moon or Mars are well aspected and placed in the Second House or lord thereof they attract wealth commensurate with the number and closeness of their aspects and their position as to dignity, exaltation or elevation. But if Saturn, Mars, Uranus or Neptune are elevated and afflict the Sun and Moon it is a sure sign of financial misfortune.

Jupiter in the Second House is moderately generous but Mars makes a free spender and consequently the money he brings goes about as fast as it comes. Saturn in the Second House, or its ruler, makes the person thrifty and saving but he will find it difficult to make ends meet unless Saturn is in his exaltation sign Libra and well-aspected by Jupiter; then fortune comes by legacy or in the latter part of life. Uranus in the Second House and in good aspect to Jupiter or the Sun and Moon is also a good indication of financial fortune.

The Eighth House: The planetary influences which bring financial fortune through the person's own efforts when operating through the Second House bring money through the marriage partnership or legacy when operating through the Eighth House. Thus Jupiter in the Eighth House indicates money by marriage or partnership if well-aspected by the Sun, Moon, Venus or the lord of the Seventh House. But if aspected by Saturn or Uranus it shows a legacy. Mars in the Eighth House well aspected shows a husband, wife or partner with good earning capacity but too free a spender. The other indications enumerated as acting through the Second House may be similarly applied to the Eighth.

Vocation

When the majority of the planets are well aspected and above the Earth or when the Sun is in good aspect to the Moon and Mars it is generally easy for the person to obtain a situation and when the Sun is in good aspect to Jupiter it gives promise of a lucrative occupation. But when the majority of the planets are below the Earth, weak and afflicted, or when the Sun is in bad aspect to the Moon, Mars or Jupiter, it is usually difficult for the person to find employment.

To find the employment in which the person will be most likely to succeed consider the nature and significance of the Houses and Signs which hold the majority of the planets.

When the majority of the planets are in the *Fiery* Signs, Aries, Leo and Sagittarius, it indicates as profitable the occupations in which the metals and fire play a prominent part, as those of machinists, engineers, chauffeurs, smiths, cutlers, barbers, surgeons, soldiers, also hazardous and dangerous vocations.

If the majority of the planets are found in the *Earthy* Signs, Taurus, Virgo and Capricorn, it indicates success in agriculture, horticulture, gardening, land, mines, timber, building materials and as contractor for buildings, houses; dealers in foodstuffs, both in the raw and cooked states, such as the grocery business, in restaurants or as grain dealers, chemistry, etc., also dress goods and clothing; in short everything that comes out of the Earth to nourish, clothe and shelter the physical body.

If the majority of the planets are in the *Airy* Signs, Gemini, Libra and Aquarius, it indicates success in clerical, literary, or artistic pursuits; occupations principally involving brains or travel, as those of accountants, bookkeepers, agents, messengers, expressmen, architects, civil engineers, mechanical draughtsmen and designers, lecturers, scientists, electricians, aviators, inventors, and all similar occupations in which mind is a principal factor.

If the majority of the planets are in the *Watery* Signs, Cancer, Scorpio and Pisces, the person should seek occupations in which fluids are prominent, as those of sailors and fishermen, ship builders and ship owners, marine engineers, and other occupations on shipboard; manufacturers and dealers in liquid refreshments, etc.

The ruling planet also has an important bearing on the life-work, and the occupations signified by the different planets may be stated as follows:

⊙ *The Sun* as life ruler indicates a leader—it may be of a state as king or president, or of a province or city as governor or mayor, or as head of a corporation, whether large or small. Thus when the Sun is life ruler, especially if it is in the Tenth House, it indicates a government position or employment in an executive capacity.

♀ *Venus* as life ruler indicates employment in an artistic capacity as a musician, singer, actor, theatrical agent, manufacturer or dealer in millinery or fancy goods, laces, embroidery and women's clothing; candy and confections, flowers or ornaments, etc.

☿ *Mercury* as life ruler indicates success in literature or on a lecture platform; as printers, publishers, or bookkeepers; as school teachers, express agents, mail carriers, commercial travelers, stenographers, secretaries, office workers and all other clerical and traveling occupations.

☽ *The Moon* as life ruler signifies success as traveling salesmen, railroad employees, ticket agents and other positions concerned with the transportation of the public; car builders, hotel keepers, dealers in fluidic commodities, nurses, obstetricians, fishermen, sailors and others employed on shipboard and in the shipping trades.

♄ *Saturn* as life ruler signifies all employments connected with the earth such as agriculture, gardening, mines, building and building materials; diplomats, judges, politicians, police, jailers, detectives, secret service agents and all whose work is accomplished by stealth and strategy; night workers and those engaged in slow, plodding, laborious work.

♃ *Jupiter* as life ruler signifies success in the professions, as lawyers, judges, clergymen, ambassadors, cabinet officers, senators, congressmen or other positions of public trust; bankers, financial agents, physicians, benevolent or social workers.

♂ *Mars* as life ruler signifies employments in which iron and sharp instruments are prominent, as used by soldiers, surgeons, smiths, founders, engineers, and in all dangerous occupations.

♅ *Uranus* as life ruler signifies employments in which air, electricity, thought power and genius are chief factors, as those of inventors, electricians, aviators and those interested in supernormal or superphysical subjects such as psychology, phrenology, magnetic, divine or mental healing; also in connection with co-operative colonies, socialism, and advanced ideas of life and living.

♆ *Neptune* as life ruler indicates occupations involving the occult, watery and psychic elements; also those in which fraud and deception are rampant because the genuine psychic article is so rare. These occupations include those of astrologers, mediums and clairvoyants. Neptune also produces some highly inspirational musicians.

CHAPTER XXI.

Marriage and Offspring

THERE was a time when man-in-the-making was male-female and able to beget children without the assistance of another, but when one pole of the creative force was directed upward to build the brain and the larynx mankind ceased to be bisexual and thenceforth each male or female had to seek its complement to accomplish the begetting of children. Therefore marriage was instituted by the angels as a sacrament and the sacred rite of generation was performed under their supervision in great temples at certain times of the year when the interplanetary lines of force were propitious for propagation. The rest of the time all lived together in the paradisiacal bliss of chaste companionship. Therefore parturition was painless and sickness and sorrow were unknown.

But when, under the guidance of the fallen angels, the Lucifer spirits, mankind commenced to exercise the creative function for pleasure regardless of the stellar ray, death entered and the woman began to bring forth her children in sorrow and suffering. For though a minister may *legally* marry people, he, being ignorant of the stellar script, cannot see if the basic harmony necessary to truly mate two souls is present. Therefore, alas, most marriages fail to bring the happiness and satisfaction of soul which mark the companionship of true mates. Besides there is the pain of parturition incidental to mismating and the increased suffering of the ego which is building its body under inharmonious prenatal conditions. Surely, a heavy toll to pay for ignorance of the stellar science! Worse still, in the great majority of cases where people do know astrology or where they are informed of its pronouncement in their case, they refuse to heed its warning voice when it is contrary to their desires. They often even hate the astrologer who has the temerity to tell them that sorrow is in store if they wed. Therefore it is at best a thankless task.

But this matter is so important at our present stage of evolution, it has such far-reaching consequences both for the individual and for society, that it is really criminal to leave to chance the choice of a mate. Fortunately we are nearing the Aquarian Age and there is no doubt that people will then study the stellar script; perhaps they will institute matrimonial bureaus maintained by the church or state, with a view to guiding the growing generation in the right direction. If children whose nativities are harmonious could visit at each others' homes and become playmates the attachment would undoubtedly ripen into love with the years. Then marriage would not end the romance as it unfortunately does in the majority of unions consummated at the present time, but it would intensify love and happiness year by year. The bond of affection would grow stronger and aid the soul growth of those under its magic spell as no other relation can.

Children would not be accidents then. They would be loved into life and they would scarcely miss the heaven they had left for they would find in their homes a heaven on earth. Therefore we pray that the time may soon come when each community will have its matrimonial bureau conducted upon the astrological basis where parents may send their child's birth data and receive in return the name and address of another child who will be harmonious as a mate. If the parents of both feel satisfied with respect to family connections, etc., the children could be made acquainted; if not, other names could be submitted by the bureau until one suitable according to both the social and astrological standards was found. The children could then become playmates, and there is no doubt that in time their affection would grow into a love that would satisfy the youthful sentiments of romance. Later an ideal marriage would crown their happiness.

Nor should we wait for the church or state to take the initiative. If parents who believe in astrology would form associations, maintaining a central bureau where the horoscopes of their children could be kept on file, grouped and classified with a view to finding true mates for them, it would give such a practical demonstration of the worth of astrology that in twenty five years enough cases could be pointed out to arrest the attention of conservative people.

Harmony and Discord

Man is, as Paul says, spirit, soul and body. Therefore the blending of two beings in perfect harmony requires that they be in accord on the spiritual, moral and physical planes, symbolized in the horoscope by the Sun and Moon (Spirit or Ego), Mars and Venus (soul or sex) and the Ascendant governing the physical body. These significators taken together with the sign on the Seventh House and the planet therein show the innate agreement or discord between people so far as the matrimonial relationship is concerned.

The physical harmony is judged by comparison of the rising sign of the two persons involved. Fiery signs agree, so do earthy, airy or watery signs. But a person with a fiery sign rising cannot successfully mate with one who has a watery or earthy sign on the Ascendant. It is like mixing fire and water, or heaping earth upon fire. Fire will only combine with fire and air. People having a watery sign on the Ascendant may harmonize with a person having an earthy sign rising, or vice versa. But neither the earthy nor watery signs will mix with the fiery triplicity.

On the moral plane the relationship is governed by Mars and Venus. If Venus in the horoscope of one person is in the same sign and degree as Mars in the horoscope of another person, there will be love at first sight when they meet, but the attraction will be sexual and unless there are other powerful signs of harmony, Mars will dominate Venus, especially if Mars is situated in the Seventh House or highly elevated above Venus in the other person's horoscope.

When the Sun in one person's horoscope is on the place of the Moon in the other person's chart harmony is shown on the spiritual plane.

The ideal marriage requires the blending of the two charts in all these particulars and the happiness will depend upon the measure of agreement as indicated. There are unions where people are sexually mated but have entirely different characteristics in other respects and vice versa. Therefore the two charts must be examined in their entirety to give a reliable judgment.

The following will explain the indications for marriage in the individual horoscope of both sexes.

Men's Marriages

An early marriage is indicated in a man's horoscope:

(1) When he is born in the light of the Moon, at the time she is progressing from the new to the full, provided she is placed in the Fourth, Fifth, Sixth, Tenth, Eleventh or Twelfth House.

(2) When the Moon and Venus are strong and well aspected with a number of the other planets in the fruitful signs, Cancer, Scorpio, or Pisces.

(3) When the Moon and Venus are in the Fifth or Seventh Houses which rule courtship and marriage.

(4) When a fruitful sign is rising with Cancer, Scorpio, or Pisces in the Fifth or Seventh Houses.

(5) When Venus and Mars are dignified, elevated, strong and well aspected.

(6) When Jupiter or Venus, or both, are in the Seventh House well aspected.

A late marriage is shown in a man's horoscope:

(1) When he is born in the dark of the Moon; that is to say, when the Moon is going from the full to the new and she is placed in the First, Second, Third, Seventh, Eighth, or Ninth Houses.

(2) When the Moon or Venus are afflicted by Saturn, Mars, Uranus or Neptune, especially if either of these planets is placed in the Fifth or Seventh Houses.

(3) When Saturn, Mars, Uranus or Neptune are in the Fifth or Seventh Houses.

(4) When the Moon is square or opposition to Venus or Jupiter they bring trouble in courtship and consequent delays of the marriage.

Marriage is denied or is accomplished with great difficulty:

(1) When Saturn is in Scorpio which rules the genitals, or if the Moon is there parallel, conjunction, square, or opposition to Saturn the planet of obstruction, for then there is little or no desire for sexual intercourse, hence such people generally remain bachelors.

(2) When the Moon, or Venus, the planet of love, is afflicted in the Saturnine sign Capricorn, especially if the affliction comes from Saturn, the planet of obstruction, many obstacles to marriage present themselves and it is doubtful if they can be overcome, hence it is unlikely that the person will marry.

(3) When the Moon is square or opposition to the Sun it is difficult for the person to make up his mind on any subject, and if the Moon is placed in the First, Second, Third, Seventh, Eighth or Ninth Houses, this will make it particularly difficult to come to a decision regarding marriage. If at the same time there is an affliction from Saturn he will never make up his mind, hence marriage will not be consummated.

(4) When the Moon is in the last degrees of a sign she is said to be void of course, and if at the same time she makes no aspect to other planets, it shows a lack of attraction to the opposite sex, which will probably prevent the person entering the marriage relation.

Women's Marriages

An early marriage is indicated in a woman's horoscope:

(1) When she is born in the light of the Moon, that is to say, when the orb of night is going from the new to the full, and the Sun is placed in the Fourth, Fifth, Sixth, Tenth, Eleventh, or Twelfth Houses.

(2) When the Sun and Venus are in one of the fruitful signs, Cancer, Scorpio, or Pisces, and well aspected.

(3) When the Sun, Venus, and Mars are well aspected, especially if in the Fifth or Seventh Houses, which govern courtship and marriage.

(4) When a fruitful sign is rising, with Cancer, Scorpio, or Pisces in the Fifth or Seventh Houses.

(5) When the Sun, Mars, and Venus are dignified, elevated, well and strongly aspected.

(6) When Jupiter or Venus is in the Seventh House well aspected.

A late marriage is shown in a woman's horoscope:

(1) When she is born in the dark of the Moon, that is to say, when the Moon is going from the full to the new, and the Sun is in the First, Second, Third, Seventh, Eighth, or Ninth Houses.

(2) When the Sun and Venus are afflicted by Saturn, Mars, Uranus or Neptune, especially if placed in the Fifth or Seventh Houses, which govern marriage and courtship.

(3) When Saturn, Mars, Uranus or Neptune are in the Fifth or Seventh Houses.

(4) When the Moon is square or opposition to Venus or Jupiter, delays and trouble in courtship and marriage may be looked for.

(5) When the Moon is parallel, square or opposition to Uranus, the octave of Venus, that also will bring delays.

Marriage is denied or accomplished only with great difficulty:

(1) When Saturn is in Scorpio, the sign which rules the genitals, or when the Sun is there parallel, conjunction, square, or opposition to Saturn, the planet of obstruction, the desire nature is held in check, hence when either of these conditions is found in a woman's horoscope it is safe to judge that she will remain a spinster.

(2) When the Sun, or Venus the planet of love, is afflicted in the Saturnine sign Capricorn, particularly if the affliction comes from Saturn, the planet of obstruction, there will be many obstacles to marriage and it is very doubtful if under the circumstances a marriage will result.

(3) When the Sun and Moon are afflicting each other by square or opposition it makes the person vacillating on any subject, and if the Sun, which is significator of marriage for a woman, is placed in the First, Second, Third, Seventh, Eighth, or Ninth Houses, this will make it particularly difficult to come to a decision regarding marriage. Should there be at the same time an affliction between the Sun and Saturn it will effectually prevent the person from making up her mind, hence marriage will not be consummated.

(4) When the Sun by progression makes no aspect to the other planets it indicates a lack of attraction to the opposite sex, which will probably prevent her from entering the marriage relation.

Happiness, Sorrow and Bereavement

The masculine Sun is the particular significator of the marriage partner in a woman's horoscope, and the feminine Moon signifies the spouse in a man's chart. Hence when the Sun and Moon are in good aspect to each other, or to Venus, the planet of love, or Jupiter, the planet of benevolence, happiness and joy are assured in the married relationship, particularly if these planets are placed in the Seventh House.

On the other hand, Saturn, Mars, Uranus or Neptune, afflicting the Sun in a female figure, or the Moon in a man's chart, indicate sorrow and trouble through the marriage relation. If they are placed in the Seventh House the testimony is all the more potent, and it is also foreshown that the marriage will be dissolved.

In this respect, Saturn and Mars indicate death of the marriage partner; Uranus may also bring about this ending if afflicted by Saturn or Mars, but otherwise it points rather to a clandestine relationship which will probably bring about the dissolution of marriage by desertion or divorce.

Second Marriages

If one or more of the malefics, Saturn, Mars, Uranus, and Neptune, are found in the Seventh House, and the Sun or Moon are in a fruitful sign, Cancer, Scorpio, or Pisces, or in the double-bodied signs, Gemini or Sagittarius, it is likely that the person will marry several times, and probably to his sorrow.

If the Sun or Moon are aspected to a number of planets placed in double-bodied signs, Gemini, Sagittarius, or Pisces, especially if these signs are on the Seventh House, two or more marriages are likely to occur. When the ruler of the Ascendant is placed in the Seventh House well aspected to other planets and in a double-bodied sign, Gemini, Sagittarius, or Pisces, it indicates a plurality of marriages.

Description of the Husband or Wife

In a man's horoscope the planets to which the Moon makes an aspect by progression after birth, indicate the women to whom he will be attracted, together with their character and disposition, which are determined by the signs that the planets are in and the aspects which they make. For illustration, let us suppose that the Moon in a certain person's horoscope comes first to a sextile of the Sun in Leo, and that the Sun is aspected by a trine to Jupiter, then we shall find the description of the wife by looking up the disposition and character in the chapter of the Sun under the Sun in Leo and the Sun trine Jupiter. This would indicate a lady of ambitious disposition, a noble character, a blonde and of florid complexion. If on the other hand, we find that the Moon after birth makes a square to Mars in Scorpio, and Mars in turn square to Venus, then it would show a woman of a very lewd, slothful and slovenly nature who would be domineering, quarrelsome, and extremely difficult to get along with. Similarly for the other planets.

In a woman's horoscope the husband is described by the planets to which the Sun makes an aspect by progression, these planets to be taken in connection with the sign where they are found and the planets with which they in turn form configurations, and the method is the same as indicated in the case of the Moon in a man's horoscope. It should be remarked, however, that when the significator of the marriage partner, aspected by the Sun or Moon, is retrograde or weak by sign, as Saturn in Aries or Jupiter in Gemini, the attraction is not strong enough to culminate in a marriage but will probably indicate only a passing attraction. Therefore the student must use his judgment in these respects.

Children

Whether a person will have children or not cannot be judged from his or her individual horoscope with any degree of accuracy for this matter is not dependent on one only, therefore the horoscope of the prospective parents should be compared and the individual indications blended, then if both horoscopes show a fruitful nature many children will be born, but if both are only moderately fertile, or if one is very fruitful and the other barren, the forecast must be made accordingly.

The indications shown in the individual horoscope may be interpreted as follows:

The Moon is the planet of fecundation and therefore the most important significator; next comes Venus, the planet of love and attraction; and last, Jupiter, the planet of benevolence. If either of these planets is in the Fifth House, which indicates children, and in one of the fruitful or double-bodied signs, Cancer, Scorpio, Pisces, Gemini, or Sagittarius, it is an indication that the person has a fruitful nature and will have a number of children who will be of a good and pleasant disposition. A similar judgment may be formed if the Eleventh House is thus invested. For if we turn the horoscope upside down so that the Seventh House becomes the First, then it will show the marriage partner's figure, and the Eleventh House is then his Fifth House indicating children, therefore both the Fifth and Eleventh Houses should be considered in this matter. But as already said, the true state of conditions cannot be forecasted save by blending the actual figures of both parents.

When the violent, turbulent Mars, or Saturn, famed in ancient mythology as a destroyer of children, or the Sun or Uranus, are in the Fifth or Eleventh Houses, they either prevent the birth of children or destroy them during childhood. This is particularly true if Aries, Leo or Capricorn are on the cusps of either of these Houses.

When the Moon is in Cancer, Scorpio, Pisces, Gemini, or Sagittarius, in good aspect to Jupiter or Venus, a large family is indicated.

But when the Moon is in Aries, Leo, or Capricorn, and afflicted by one of the malefics or by the Sun, the marriage is usually barren. Saturn and Venus in the Seventh House is also a sign of a marriage without issue.

If there is a difference in the testimonies of the Fifth and Eleventh Houses the judgment must be modified accordingly.

CHAPTER XXII.

Progression of the Horoscope

Fate or Free Will

WHEN a chain is subjected to strain, imperfections in any of its links become manifest, and the weakest link will break first. Similarly, in the case of the body, there are certain inherent weak points and these are indicated in the horoscope. From the moment of birth we subject the body to a constant strain, and in time the weakness of the various points becomes manifest as disease. The movement of the planets after birth measures the time when any particular link is liable to break. This motion of the planets in the horoscope is called "Progression." Study and practice of medical Astrology require knowledge of how to progress the planets in the horoscope, and we shall therefore take up that subject in connection with the message of the stars relative to disease.

When the Sun rises in the East the day is young and the labors allotted to each are still before us. Gradually the Sun progresses across the arched vault of the heavens, and marks the time set for the performance of our various duties, for keeping our appointments, for taking nourishment, rest and recreation; and when it has run its course through the day and has ceased to illuminate our sphere of action, its absence invites sleep until the dawn of a new day shall present opportunities for continuation of the activities left in abeyance from the previous day. If the Sun remained stationary at any certain point of the sky it would not serve as a time marker but as it is, all events of our lives are fixed by its progression.

The horoscope is a chart of the heavens for the time when the mystic Sun of Life rises and awakes us from the long sleep between two lives; then we are born in the physical world, to continue the labors of a previous life, to keep the appointment there made with friend or foe; to reap the joy or bear the sorrow which is the fruitage of our former existence on earth; and as the progression of the Sun marks the changing time of day and year, as it ushers in season after season in orderly sequence and changes the appearance of the Great World, the Macrocosm, so progression of the horoscope, a veritable 'Clock of Destiny,' registers accurately when the tendencies, shown by the natal horoscope will culminate in events; it measures the periods of prosperity and adversity; it warns of impending temptation and tells from what quarter it will come, thus aiding us to escape if we will but listen to its warning. The natal horoscope shows unerringly weak points in our character or constitution, but the progressed horoscope indicates when previous indulgence of harmful habits is scheduled to bring sorrow or sickness; it tells truthfully when crises culminate; thus it warns us to be on the alert at critical moments, and fortifies us in the darkest hour of calamity, with hope of surcease of sorrow and sickness at a definite time, hence the importance of knowing how to progress the horoscope.

But, some may say, if all is thus foreshown, it argues an inexorable destiny decreed by divine caprice; what use is there then of striving, or knowing; let us eat, drink and be merry, for tomorrow we die. If we were born into this life on earth for the first and only time, to live here for a while and then pass away from this sphere never to return, fate and favoritism independent of justice would seem to rule. Such cannot be the case; in a world where everything else is governed by law, human existence must also be reducible to a system, and we hold that a reasonable solution of the mystery of life is given by the Twin Laws of Being, the Law of Rebirth and the Law of Causation.

That which has a beginning must have an end, and conversely, that which is without ending can never have had a beginning. If the human spirit is immortal and cannot die, neither can it be born; if it will live to all eternity, it must have lived from eternity, there is no escape from this truth; pre-existence must be accepted if immortality is a fact in nature.

In this world there is no law more plainly observable than the law of alternating cycles, which decrees succession of ebb and flow, day and night, summer and winter, waking and sleeping. Under the same law man's life is lived alternately in the physical world where he sows seeds of action and gains experiences according to his horoscope. These, the fruits of existence here, are later assimilated as soul powers in the spiritual world; birth and death are thus nothing more than gateways from one phase of man's life to another, and the life we now live is but one of a series. The differences of character, nobility or brutality, moral strength or weakness, possession of high ideals or low instincts, etc., are certain signatures of soul power or soul poverty. Finer faculties are the glorious garments of gentle souls wrought through many lives in the crucible of concrete existence by trial and temptation. They shine with a luster which illuminates the way and makes it easier for others to follow. Coarseness of calibre proclaims the young in Life's School, but repeated existences here will in due time smoothe the rough corners, mellow and make them soulful also.

The horoscope shows this difference in the texture of the soul and the aspects indicate how the soul is ripened by the kaleidoscopic configurations of planets in progression, which fan the fires in the furnace of affliction to cleanse and purify the soul of blemish, or brighten the crown of virtue when victory is won, but though the planets show the tendencies most accurately there is one indeterminable factor which is not shown, a veritable astrological "x,"—*the will-power of the man,* and upon that rock astrological predictions are ever liable to founder; that, at times, is the Waterloo of even the most careful and competent astrologer, yet the very failure of well-founded predictions is the blessed assurance that we are not fated to do thus and so because our horoscope shows that at a certain time the stellar rays impel us in a given direction. In the final analysis we are the arbiters of our destiny, and it is significant, that while it is possible to predict for the great majority of mankind with absolute certainty that the prediction will be vindicated, because they drift along the sea of life directed by the current of circumstance, predictions for the striving idealist fail in proportion to his spiritual attainment of will power which rouses him to self assertion and resistance of wrong.

A beautiful little poem by Ella Wheeler Wilcox gives the idea in a most pleasing form:

"One ship sails East and another sails West,
With the selfsame winds that blow;
'Tis the set of the sail
And not the gale
That determines the way they go.

"Like the winds of the sea are the ways of fate,
As we voyage along through Life;
'Tis the act of the soul
That determines the goal,
And not the calm or the strife."

CHAPTER XXIII.

Different Methods of Progression and the Reason for Them

BESIDES the physical world in which we live, move and have our being at the present time, where sunshine and rain, storm and snow, heat and cold affect our physical being in various ways, a world of finer substance permeates the denser matter, and the forces indigenous to that realm impinge upon our souls, as feelings, desires and emotions, because the soul is clothed in substance from that world. Mystics therefore call this realm in nature the Desire World. A still more subtle substance, an ocean of Thought, pervades both the Desire World and the Physical World, and as the mind is composed of substance from that region, it senses the waves of thought generated by other spirits endowed with mind.

Here in the physical world, Time and Space are prime factors of existence, but in the Desire World distance is practically eliminated because spirits having dropped the mortal coil travel with the speed of lightning, and as spiritual sight pierces the densest substance, light there is never obscured, so there is no night, neither does heat and cold affect the soul, hence there is no seasonal division either, to mark time as definitely as in the physical world. But nevertheless, there is a certain sequence of events. In soulflights from place to place on the globe, we sense the nature of intervening country in spite of speed, but in the World of Thought, to think of a place, is to be there instanter, neither is there past or future; events are not separated by time, or places by space, but all is one eternal *here* and *now.*

As the science of Astrology is founded in cosmic fact, there are also three stages in progression from incipient events in the World of Thought, to accomplished facts in the Physical World, and there are two methods of horoscopic progression pertaining to the finer realms besides the actual movement of planets observable in the Heavens.

Suppose a pole billions of miles long stuck into the earth at the Equator, and at right angles to the poles, then, as the earth turns upon its axis, the end of the pole would describe a circle in the heavens; this the Astronomers call the "Celestial Equator," and the position of a heavenly body on this line is measured in degrees and minutes of "Right Ascension," from the point where the sun crosses the equator at the vernal equinox. This axial rotation of the earth brings a new degree to the zenith, or Meridian about every four minutes, and by the rules of one system of progression we may calculate how many degrees of Right Ascension come to the Meridian position from birth to the formation of a certain aspect.

The intervening degrees are then converted to time at the rate of 1 degree equals 1 year.

The other system of progression is founded upon the orbital revolution of the earth, but in this system the positions of the planets are expressed in degrees of Longitude and measured on the ecliptic or Sun's path, from Aries 0 degrees to Pisces 29. The measure of time is the same as in the system first mentioned: 1 degree equals 1 year, but there is this important difference, that while the earth takes only 4 minutes to turn 1 degree upon its axis, it requires 24 hours to move 1 degree in its orbit.

Thus, by one system of progression all the aspects that govern events in a life of 60 years would be formed in 60 times 4 minutes, which equals 4 hours or one-sixth part of a day.

By the other system, formation of aspects for the same period of life would require 60 days, or 2 months, or one-sixth part of a year.

Thus coming events cast their shadows before, but the shadow varies in length according to the exaltation of the sphere of life whence it is cast.

From the sublime height of the World of Thought, where all things have their inception in the eternal, the progression of events in a life are silhouetted upon the screen of Time while the infant is still upon the threshold of birth, but the shadow is so short, 1-360 part of a day being equivalent to a year, that an error of 4 minutes in the given time of birth would throw predictions out a whole year. Few people know their birth hour to the minute, therefore this system of progression is of little use and little used.

Shadows of events projected from the denser Desire World are longer and more definite; it does not require great delicacy or precision to calculate progression at the rate of 1-360 part of a year equal to 1 year. By this method an error of 2 hours in the given time of birth would only cause an error of 1 month in predictions; this system therefore gives universal satisfaction, and is most commonly used. In the following pages we shall explain a simplified method of this system of prediction, whereby mathematical calculation of events for a whole life may be performed in a few minutes by any intelligent child who can add and subtract.

The Adjusted Calculation Date

When a child is born at 7 A. M., in New York, and another at 6 A. M., in Chicago, a third at 1 P. M., in Berlin, a fourth at 2 P. M., in St. Petersburg, and a fifth at 12 noon in London, the Observatory clock at Greenwich would point to noon, at the exact moment when all these children were born, hence though the clocks in their several birthplaces pointed to different hours, the Greenwich Mean Time of their births would be identical:—noon. And as the planets' places in the ephemeris are calculated for Greenwich, noon, it would be unnecessary to make corrections;

we should simply place each planet in the natal horoscopes as tabulated in the ephemeris. This would be most convenient, but the saving of calculation in a natal horoscope where the G. M. T. is noon, fades into insignificance before the facility this gives in progressing the planets for years subsequent to birth, as required to predict events, for in natal horoscopes where the G. M. T. is before or after noon, the places of the planets must be calculated for each year just the same as at birth. We have evolved the following simple method of saving this calculation and of copying the progressed planets direct from the ephemeris into any horoscope.

Theorem I.

If the Greenwich Mean Time of birth was *before* noon, it is evident that the planets' places in the ephemeris are calculated for a *later* time and also that, as they progress at the rate of a day (of 24 hours) for a year, they will reach the Longitude given in the ephemeris some day within a year after birth.

Theorem II.

If the G. M. T. of birth was *after* noon, it is plainly to be seen that the planets' places in the ephemeris for the year of birth are calculated for an *earlier* time than birth, and that the position there given corresponds to a certain day in the twelvemonth *before* birth.

Furthermore, if we can find the date in the twelve-month before birth, or after as the case may be, when the planets were in the degree and minute of longitude registered in the ephemeris, we may use that date as a starting point of calculation instead of the birthday, and as aspects formed during the travel of the planets from the position given on any noon to the noon next following, indicate events in the corresponding year of life, the same starting date may be used for any year. Therefore, once that adjusted calculation date has been found, no further calculation is required to progress the planets in that horoscope; they may be simply copied from the ephemeris. It is only necessary to bear in mind that the horoscope thus erected does *not* apply to the year *from birthday to birthday,* but from the adjusted calculation date of one year to the same date of the next. There are two methods of finding this date; the first is the more difficult and not so accurate, but it shows the philosophy of the correction better than the second method, and we therefore give examples of both.

We will use the figure No. 26 (Medical Astrology Section), which is the horoscope of a man who died of hemorrhages in June, 1918, to illustrate how the adjusted calculation date is found, but defer description of the case and its crises. The man was born April 24, 1884, Longitude 95 W., Latitude 42 N., at 2 P. M., True Local Time. We first find the G. M. T. by adding to the local time of birth 4 minutes for each degree the birthplace is west of Greenwich.

True local time of birth, April 24........ 2:00 P. M.
Correction for 95 degrees W. Long...... 6:20

Greenwich Mean Time of birth Apr. 24 .. 8:20 P. M.

In compliance with Theorem II, we subtract from the birthdate, April 24, a correction of 8 hours and 20 minutes which the G. M. T. is past noon. The measure of time used in this system is as follows:

24 hours correspond to 12 months.
2 hours correspond to 1 month.
1 hour corresponds to 15 days.
4 minutes correspond to 1 day.

According to this scale we subtract
from .... April 24, 1884
Correction for 8 hours—4 months
Correction for 20 minutes—5 days
—4 months, 5 days

Adjusted Calculation Date ..... December 19, 1883

We may, however, find the Adjusted Calculation Date much more accurately and with less labor by the following fourfold rule:

Rule

(1) Find the interval from G. M. T. to the *following* noon.

(2) To this interval add the Sidereal Time for Greenwich noon on the birthday, as given in the ephemeris. The sum of these is the Sidereal Time of the Adjusted Calculation Date.

(3) When the G. M. T. at birth is A. M. of the birthday, or P. M. of the preceding day, *count forwards* in the ephemeris till you find a day having the required S. T.; that is the Adjusted Calculation Date.

(4) When the G. M. T. at birth is *P. M.* of the birthday or A. M. of the succeeding day *read back wards* in the ephemeris till you find the day having the required S. T. which designates it as the Adjusted Calculation Date.

We shall use the same example as before to demonstrate this method.

Section 1 directs us to find the interval between G. M. T. and the following noon. Please observe this, the *following* noon, for all depends upon this being accurately understood.

From .... April 25, 12:00 Noon
Subtract G. M. T............. April 24. 8:20 P. M.

Interval from G. M. T. to next Noon, 15 hrs. 40 min.

By Section 2 of Rule:
Add S. T. of birthday
as given in ephemeris .... 2 hrs. 11 min.

S. T. of Adjusted Calculation Date .. 17 hrs. 51 min.

By Section 4 of Rule:

As G. M. T. is P. M. we read backwards in the column of the ephemeris giving S. T., until we come to Dec. 19, 1883. On that day the S. T. is 17 hrs.,51 min., and the A. C. D. is therefore Dec. 19, 1883.

Thus, by both methods we have arrived at identical results, but slight discrepancies may appear in using the proportional method because that makes no allowances for long and short months, hence the method last demonstrated is more accurate as well as easier. If this man had been born two hours later, the Adjusted Calculation Date would have been November 19, 1883. Where children are born *late* in the year and *early* in the morning, the Adjusted Calculation Date may run into January or February of the next year. *It is therefore very important to state the Adjusted Calculation Date by year* also, in this case December 19, 1883.

Now, that we have arrived at the point where we are to make use of our A.C. D. to progress the man's horoscope and show how accurately it marks the crises, the first application of the date to the horoscope is a crucial point, and the student is earnestly warned to overlook no word in our description so that he may acquire understanding of the principle. Once having grasped the point, an immense amount of labor will be saved, so it will pay to follow our instructions to the letter.

Write in the margin of your ephemeris for 1884 opposite the birthday (April 24), December 19, 1883.

Opposite April 25 write December 19, 1884. Opposite April 26 write December 19, 1885, and so on, as shown below. Every day after birth corresponds to a certain year of life which starts on the day written in the margin, and the planets in line with any A. C. D. indicate the events for twelve months from that date.

Dec. 19, 1883....Apr. 24	Dec. 19, 1897....May 8
Dec. 19, 1884....Apr. 25	Dec. 19, 1907....May 18
Dec. 19, 1885....Apr. 26	Dec. 19, 1916....May 27
Dec. 19, 1886....Apr. 27	Dec. 19, 1917....May 28
Dec. 19, 1887....Apr. 28	Dec. 19, 1918....May 29

The motion of the Sun and planets from day to day is slow, and as we count a day for a year, we may liken their progression to the short hand on the clock of destiny: they indicate the year when a certain condition shown in the natal horoscope has ripened, and is ready to manifest as an event. The swift moving Moon is the long hand; it marks the months when aspects culminate in events. Therefore we divide its motion during the year commencing with any adjusted calculation date, by 12, but for rough figuring we may consider the Moon's travel in the progressed horoscope one degree a month.

Planetary aspects alone do not operate, however; an aspect of the progressed Moon or a New Moon is required to focus the hidden forces. Therefore crises shown by the planets are sometimes retarded beyond the time when the aspect culminated and we may think we have safely escaped, but the first aspect of the Moon which excites it will prove that "though the mills of the gods grind slowly, they grind exceeding fine." The finer forces lose none of their in tensity by lying latent in Nature's lock-box of events.

Now let us see how the planets worked in the horoscope we have just given. In the year 1915 we find the progressed Sun, the life-giver, had reached the conjunction of the Midheaven, Gemini 5-0. The New Moon on May 2, 1916 fell in Taurus 11-44, square to the radical Mars; on the 31st of May the second New Moon was in Gemini 9-40 in conjunction with the radical Saturn in the M. C., which latter had been obstructing the capillaries of the lungs; thus hemorrhages resulted. At this time the young man, who had become a very efficient astrologer, began to realize that he was entering a critical period and did all possible to overcome its influence. But a succession of lunations during the year 1916 afflicted his Midheaven and Saturn by square and opposition in the sign ruling the lungs, Gemini, made a constant struggle necessary. With the negative sign of Virgo on the Ascendant, with Uranus in the First House square to Venus in Gemini, and with Jupiter afflicted by a square of the Moon, both the venous and arterial circulations were restricted, preventing deep breathing and complete oxygenation of the blood in the lungs.

In the Spring of 1918 this young man, after consulting his own horoscope, unfortunately made up his mind that he would pass out on a certain day, and made all necessary arrangements for his funeral. This state of mind was very dangerous to one in his weakened condition and to one with his negative Ascendant. He precipitated the crisis even before its normal time, as we will show.

We will now proceed to find what brought about the crises that terminated the life on June 1, 1918. We first find where the progressed planets were at that time. We take the date May 28, 1884 for the places of the progressed planets on the Adjusted Calculation Date, Dec. 19, 1917. We now progress the Sun and Moon 5 1-2 months beyond this date to June 1, 1918. If we subtract the Moon's longitude on a given day from its place on the following day, the difference is its motion during the 24 hours intervening, which corresponds to a year of life in progression. Division of this by 12 gives us the rate of its monthly travel.

Moon's place on A. C. D. Dec. 19, 1917,
(May 28 in ephemeris for 1884)...Cancer 27.11
Moon's place on A. C. D. Dec. 19, 1918,
(May 29 in ephemeris for 1884)..Leo 11.14

Moon's travel by progression from Dec. 19, 1917 to Dec. 19, 1918 .... 14.03

Dividing 14 degrees 3 minutes by 12 gives the Moon's monthly travel as 1 degree 10 minutes. This we add to its place for each month as shown in the following table:

Dec. 19, 1917 ♋..27.11	Mar. 19, 1918 ♌.. 0.41
Jan. 19, 1918 ♋..28.21	Apr. 19, 1918 ♌.. 1.51
Feb. 19, 1918 ♋..29.31	May 19, 1918 ♌.. 3.01

As we see above, the progressed Moon was in Leo 3.01 on May 19, 1918, and as it moves 1 degree 10 min. per month, in the 13 days to June 1st it would travel 0 degrees 29 min., reaching Leo 3.30, and making a square to the radical Sun.

On Dec. 19, 1917, the progressed Sun was in Gemini 7.29. We count forward from Dec. 19th to June 1, 1918, 5 1-2 months, and as the Sun moves 58 minutes per year, making 5 minutes per month, in 5 1-2 months the progressed Sun would arrive at Gemini 7.56, conjunction to Saturn.

The New Moon on May 10, 1918 fell in Taurus 19.00, conjunction to the radical Neptune. This was the day the young man had chosen as the day of his death, but the crisis was not reached until the transiting Sun reached the conjunction of Saturn in Gemini 8:33, the night of May 30th. At the same time Saturn was transiting conjunction to radical Mars and square to radical Sun, depleting the vitality,and the transiting Moon and Neptune were square to the radical Sun. All this was too much for him to endure in his weakened condition and he began to sink. June 1st when the transiting Moon reached the square to Saturn and the Midheaven, and the opposition to the Ascendant, he passed into the great beyond.

Thus we see that we cannot base judgment upon merely one affliction. We must look to the progressed planets, the strong transiting planets, and particularly to the New Moon to excite a natal affliction.

Progression of the Angles

Besides the progression of planets which we trust has been sufficiently elucidated, we must also note a similar forward movement of the houses, but these must be calculated by the same method as when casting a natal figure, save that we use the Sidereal Time for the day which corresponds to the year for which we wish to progress the horoscope. In relation to the man's horoscope we have studied, the critical year was 1918, and May 28 in the ephemeris for 1884 corresponds. We bear in mind that birth occurred at 2:00 P. M., True Local Time, in Lat. 42 N., Long. 95 W., for these factors are used in placing the degrees on the houses just as in the natal chart; the only change is using the S. T. of the progressed birth day.

	H.	M.	S.
S. T. at noon previous to progressed birth-day, 1918 (see ephemeris for 1884, May 28)	4	25	0
Correction of 10 seconds for each 15 deg. birthplace is West of Greenwich.....	0	1	3
Interval from previous noon to birth....	2	0	0
Correction of 10 secs. per hr. of interval..	0	0	20
Sidereal Time of progressed birth.......	6	26	23

With this S. T. we turn to the Tables of Houses for the Latitude of birth place, and erect a horoscope with twelve Houses in the usual manner; we may further insert the planets' places on the A. C. D. for 1918, then we shall have a complete separate horoscope for the year, which we may compare with the natal chart. Some Astrologers use that method, but we advise another, which we think facilitates comparison and judgment of aspects between the natal and progressed position of the planets in a degree unattainable by any other system; it is illustrated in the various figures used in this book.

We write the natal chart in ink, as that is unchanged during life; we also draw a large circle outside it, to contain the progressed position of the planets. These and the houses we write in their proper places, but lightly, and with pencil, so that they may be easily erased and the horoscope erected for another year without the necessity of rewriting the natal chart.

But no matter how placed, two full horoscopes with 24 houses, 18 planets, a couple of dragons' heads, each with its respective "tail," and two Parts of Fortune, make quite a maze, and if the full galaxy of aspects, including biquintiles, sesquiquadrates and other highsounding nonsensicals are to be figured out the astrologer will surely so lose himself in the mathematical labyrinth that he will be unable to read a syllable of the message of the stars. During the first year of his astrological study, one of the writers being originally of a mathematical turn, had the habit of constructing figures, and tables of aspects, so fearfully and wonderfully made that they beat the proverbial "Chinese puzzle;" they were veritable "Gordian Knots," and the destiny of a human being was so tangled in each, that neither the writer who had concocted the abomination, nor anyone else could ever hope to disentangle the poor soul involved. May he be forgiven; he has mended his ways, and is now just as zealous to eliminate all non-essentials from the horoscope, but having been enmeshed in the maze of mathematics, his experience should serve as a warning. Our minds, at best, are but feeble instruments to fathom fate and surely we shall have the greatest chance of success by applying our science to the most important factors, and these are usually the simplest.

If this be granted, the question presents itself: What are the essentials and what may be eliminated with advantage to clear the progressed horoscope of useless, befogging elements?

First, with regard to the progressed houses, only two vital points produce results when aspected: the Midheaven, which is spiritual in nature, and the Ascendant, which is a significator in material matters. We shall treat that subject later; for the present we confine ourselves to the argument that it will facilitate judgment of the progressed horoscope if we leave the ten unessential cusps out, and draw two dotted lines with pencil to mark the progressed Midheaven and Ascendant.

In the second place, the student may readily convince himself by looking through the columns of any ephemeris, that the motion of Neptune, Uranus, Saturn and Jupiter, during the two months which represent progression for a life of 60 years, is so slow that they seldom form an aspect not registered in the natal chart. In rare cases where an important aspect is formed, the fact is easily seen, and the planet should then be entered in the outer ring of the progressed horoscope, but in the great majority of cases it is better to leave these planets out, and enter only the progressed positions of the Sun, Moon, Mars, Venus and Mercury.

In conclusion of our treatment of the method of Progression, two important points must be mentioned: The Midheaven at a given Sidereal Time is the same for all Latitudes, so that two children born at the same S. T. would have the same sign and degree on the M. C., but if one were born in Alaska and the other in Mexico, the Asc. would vary much and change the grouping of planets in the houses very considerably, with the further result that planets which influence the First House affairs in one horoscope affect Twelfth House matters in the other, etc. Thus the lives of these people would be very different.

The same argument applies to the progressed horoscope of a person traveling North or South from his birthplace. His progressed M. C. remains unchanged, but he receives the forces from a different ascending figure, according to the Latitude where he resides, and the grouping of planets relative to the progressed Ascendant varies accordingly. As examples we may state that both writers have left their birthplace; one traveled 2,000 miles West, but is close to the same Latitude as her birthplace, hence both her M. C. and Asc. are the same as if she had remained in her native city.

The other writer was born in Latitude 56 N., and now lives in Latitude 32. Had he remained in the far North, his progressed Ascendant would in (1912) be Virgo 6°, exactly conjunction to Mars' place at birth, but the Ascendant of his new home is Virgo 0 degrees, and in this latitude he will not feel the effect of the Mars ray for a number of years.

The other important point we had in mind is the necessity of being definite in regard to the year for which we progress. Perhaps a person tells us that a certain event occurred when he was 26, and another in his 50th year. Such statements are ambiguous, and give no safe working basis. The Astrologer may go home and do an immense amount of work to no use, because he thought the person meant that one event occurred when he, the person, was between 26 and 27 years of age, and a later consultation reveals that he meant the year between his 25th and 26th birthdays. Pin them down to the year, 1850, 1900, or whatever it may be, but never accept a person's age as a starting point.

On the same principle, never predict that an event will happen when a person is so and so old;

that also is ambiguous and gives them no satisfaction; give the year and month; never hedge; never predict anything of which you are in doubt; when you are satisfied a prediction is justified, speak fearlessly, *but tactfully;* believe in the stars, and the stars will fully justify your faith.

Some Important Points

When judging the effects of directions it is of the greatest importance to bear in mind the tenor of the nativity, for even weak aspects which are in harmony with the tendencies foreshown in the natal figure will be much more active than a strong aspect which is contrary to the radical indications. Supposing, for instance, that there are strong testimonies of sickness and accident, as Mars in Sagittarius in the Midheaven square the Sun in Pisces in the Twelfth House and square Saturn in Virgo in the Sixth House; then the progression of Mars to square of the radical Ascendant would undoubtedly precipitate an accident or a fever of a serious nature, but if the Sun were trine Mars and Jupiter the effect of Mars square Ascendant would produce little if any discomfort. Similarly with all the other directions, and if the student neglects to take into consideration this all-important point, he is likely sometime to make a great mistake and wonder why a seemingly powerful direction produced no result in one case, while in another a very weak aspect had such a far-reaching effect. Aspects between two progressed planets are unimportant.

Another important point to remember is that aspects of the progressed to the radical planets operate in proportion to the power of the radical planet in the nativity. Let us suppose, for illustration, that in a certain figure the Sun is elevated in Leo and aspected to a number of the other planets—it matters not whether the aspects are good or bad so long as they are close—then even a weak aspect from a progressed planet to the Sun will have a marked result. On the other hand, if the Sun in that horoscope received no aspect, or only one or two weak ones, then even a strong aspect of a progressed planet would have little effect.

It should also be noted that a good aspect from a progressed planet to a planet that is much afflicted in the nativity would produce small if any benefit. In short, and to sum up, progressed aspects operate only in the measure that they are in harmony with the trend of the nativity and the planet wherewith they are blending.

The third important point to remember when judging the effects of directions is that an aspect from a progressed to a radical planet is never in itself sufficient to produce results; a harmonious aspect from the progressed Moon or a lunation is absolutely essential to bring the tendency to fruition. That is to say, if the progressed Sun comes to square of radical Saturn, a sextile or trine aspect of the progressed Moon or of a lunation will pass unnoticed; no effect will be felt until either the progressed Moon or a lunation comes into conjunction, square, or opposition to Sun or Saturn, and vice-versa, if the progressed Sun comes to a trine of the radical Jupiter a square or opposition of the Moon will not affect it, it must wait for a sextile or trine. For this reason directions are sometimes delayed in their action beyond the time of their culmination, and at other times they are somewhat hastened because a lunar aspect of the requisite nature occurs slightly in advance of the time when the aspects of the planets are complete.

It also happens that in cases where the event indicated by an aspect involves two people the aspects of the planets by progression may be complete in one person's horoscope and fertilized by a harmonious aspect without producing a result, because the aspect in the other person's horoscope has not yet matured. In this connection we remember the horoscope of a lady whose Venus was placed in the Eighth House showing a late marriage. In her 45th year the progressed Sun reached conjunction Venus but neither engagement nor marriage resulted; then the Sun and Venus came into conjunction in the horoscope of a gentleman of her acquaintance bringing an engagement quickly followed by marriage. Thus one had waited for the other, and unless such a contingency is taken into consideration the astrologer is most liable to meet his Waterloo when forecasting events.

CHAPTER XXIV.

Progressed Solar Directions

WHEN the Sun forms a conjunction, sextile, square, trine or opposition to one of the planets by progression the influence begins to manifest when the Sun is 1½ degrees from the exact aspect, and it is felt until the Sun is 1½ degrees past the point of culmination. And as the Sun moves about one degree a day, and the time measure of directions is that one day equals a year, we may say that the influence of the solar aspects is felt for a period of three years. Their effects are particularly strong at times during this period when aspects of the progressed Moon or lunations vivify them.

The parallel is different from the other aspects. In the case of the slow-moving planets it lasts for a considerable number of years so that a parallel of the Sun and Saturn may operate for ten or more years, and a parallel of the Sun and Jupiter nearly as long.

It may also be noted that the conjunction and parallel act principally upon the health, while the other aspects also affect the business, social standing, etc. Thus under the parallel of the Sun and Saturn there would be a very protracted state of ill-health, while the parallel of the Sun and Jupiter would strengthen the constitution materially.

☉ P ☌ ✱ △ ♀ *The Sun progressed parallel, conjunction, sextile or trine to radical Venus.*

If the radical Venus was well aspected these directions will bring a three-year period of unusual pleasure and enjoyment into the life. If the person is not already married an attachment will be formed and ripen into marriage of an ideal nature. If the horoscope shows artistic ability, this will receive a great impetus during the activity of this direction, and it will bring honor and social preferment.

☉ □ ☍ ♀ *The Sun progressed square or opposition to radical Venus.*

If the radical Venus was afflicted, these directions will bring a period of petty annoyances, social disgrace, trouble and sorrow, with a tendency to be slovenly and to look upon the dark side of life, but it can be overcome if the person will strive to be careful of his morals and personal appearance. "Where there's a will there's a way."

☉ P ☌ ✱ ☿ *The Sun progressed parallel, conjunction or sextile radical Mercury.*

If Mercury was well aspected at birth this will mark a period of unusual mental activity, so that the person will be able to further his ambitions and succeed in business by new ventures, If the natal figure shows literary ability this is the time to make all efforts to produce something worth while. It is a good and profitable time to travel either for pleasure, in search of inspiration, or for the good of whatever business he may follow. Advertising will be found a most effective way of promoting business success under this direction.

☉□☿ *The Sun progressed square to radical Mercury.*

The Sun cannot reach the square of Mercury until late in life, and in comparatively few lives at that, therefore its effects can only be conjectured and it has no importance.

☉ P ☌ ✱ △ ☽ *The Sun progressed parallel, conjunction, sextile, or trine to radical Moon.*

If the Moon was well aspected at birth these directions bring a period of success and popularity. It increases the honor and esteem which the person enjoys in his environment, it brings favors from influential persons, employers, or the authorities, and if marriage has not already been contracted, this direction will most likely bring about a successful union. It is also an excellent time to form partnerships.

☉□☍☽ *The Sun progressed square or opposition to radical Moon.*

If the Moon was afflicted at birth this marks a very evil period, replete with domestic unhappiness if the person is married; discredit among the people with whom he is associated in business or socially, perhaps imprisonment; loss by dishonesty of the partner, financial stricture or even bankruptcy. He is also likely to suffer severely from ill health, and if either the Sun or Moon are in Cancer, Scorpio or Pisces he may become a chronic drunkard.

☉✶△♄ *The Sun progressed sextile or trine to radical Saturn.*

If Saturn is well aspected in the nativity these directions will bring a steadying and consolidating influence into the life so that the person will be able to discharge his duties in a most effective, systematic and tactful manner. He will have greater opportunities for advancement than before, and will be able to assume the added responsibilities with credit. Much benefit may be expected from older people who will be drawn to him with full confidence. Investments in land, mines, houses, and similar things will prove profitable when made under this direction, and in general it gives a very deep insight into all problems of life.

☉ P ☌ □ ☍ ♄ *The Sun progressed parallel, conjunction, square or opposition to radical Saturn.*

If Saturn was afflicted in the natal chart these directions mark a period of very evil influence. This is especially true of the parallel, which lasts about ten years; the other aspects are only active during the usual three years. Under these directions the person suffers disappointments and delays in everything he undertakes. No matter how carefully he may plan, something is sure to crop up to thwart him, and this is apt to breed a spirit of worry and pessimism which makes life seem a hopeless battle, with everyone conspiring to checkmate him. Financial difficulties make matters harder, and he is liable to incur the opposition of employers or the authorities. To crown it all, the health suffers, especially under the parallel; his vitality will be very low, and the recuperative power almost *nil*. All will depend on whether he can look for the silver lining to the cloud, and strive to learn the intended lessons, or whether he simply sinks down under the load and gives up. Forewarned is forearmed and students of Astrology have at least the knowledge that these trials are only passing. They know when brighter days will come.

☉ P ☌ ✱ △ ♃ *The Sun progressed parallel, conjunction, sextile or trine Jupiter.*

If Jupiter is well aspected at birth these aspects are among the most fortunate in the whole gamut of directions, for they indicate a period of financial prosperity, where every undertaking succeeds, hence speculation, investments, and new ventures in business will bring success and gain, the person will rise in popularity and esteem in the community or his immediate sphere of associations; he may gain much credit in connection with philanthropic or charitable undertakings, and he will enjoy much social success and domestic happiness. There is a tendency to travel or changes which will bring both pleasure and profit, and ambitions that for years seemed impossible of realization are likely to be gratified. Under these directions lasting friendships of benefit to the person are often formed. They also strengthen the constitution and bring radiant health, but the exuberance of animal spirits may later, under evil directions, bring disease. If this is guarded against the increased flow of vital fluid given by these directions will have a lasting beneficial effect on the health.

☉ □ ☍ ♃ *The Sun progressed square or opposition to radical Jupiter.*

If Jupiter is afflicted at birth these directions denote a period of trouble and trials. Someone near and dear will pass out of the person's life, either by estrangement or death; lawsuits, financial losses and social disaster are threatened, with much opposition from other people. If he invests money or speculates each venture will prove a failure because of deception and misrepresentation of those with whom he deals. If he makes a change of business or travels to another city he will meet with worse conditions, the health will suffer and domestic infelicity will result.

☉ P ☌ □ ☍ ♂ *The Sun progressed parallel, conjunction, square or opposition to radical Mars.*

If Mars is afflicted at birth these aspects mark an extended period of a very evil nature. There is a state of rash and reckless excitement which is apt to lead the person to do the most foolhardy things, hence a liability to squander his money, wreck his prospects in life, become crippled by an accident, or indulge in excesses which bring on fevers, boils, or inflammatory complaints. He should be particularly careful not to handle fire, hot water, explosives or firearms, and be guarded by insurance against loss by fire, sickness or accident. The reputation is also likely to suffer by scandal, therefore he should exert all his energy and will power to act with all the discretion possible to him and so endeavor to rule his stars.

☉ ✱ △ ♂ *The Sun progressed sextile or trine to radical Mars.*

If Mars is well aspected at birth these directions indicate a period of adventure when the person will be imbued with a powerful spirit of activity, enterprise and industry; he will become acquainted with people of a pioneering instinct or in some way receive an impulse that will start him upon a new venture in life which will bring him success, friends, and prosperity. He is likely to travel in search of new fields and to be very restless in seeking an outlet for the energy which threatens to burst him, but he is also too prone to squander the money which seems to come so easily. If he were wise he would be a little less generous, for when this aspect passes off, it is likely that the golden days are over.

☉ P ☌ □ ☍ ♅ *The Sun progressed parallel, conjunction, square or opposition to radical Uranus.*

If Uranus is afflicted at birth these aspects mark a very critical period in the life. The person becomes very irritable and short-tempered. He is liable to tax the patience of friends and relatives to the breaking point so that a separation or estrangement occurs. He will be repellent to others, rash, erratic, liable to do the most strange and unexpected things. He may rush into litigation when he has not the shadow of a case or cause, just for the mere insane love of quarreling. Thus he is likely to disgrace himself permanently in the eyes of all who know him, or, depending upon what other aspects are in force at the time, it may be someone close to him who causes the disgrace which then reflects upon him on account of the friendship or relationship.

☉ ✱ △ ♅ *The Sun progressed sextile or trine to radical Uranus.*

If Uranus is well aspected at birth and the person is of a sufficiently advanced type to respond to this influence, these aspects mark a period of great spiritual and mental acceleration; the originating, organizing, and inventive faculties become greatly enhanced, so that he is able to formulate ideas, perfect inventions, and organize enterprises in a most surprisingly efficient manner, with little or no effort. There may be sudden and unexpected gains through inventions, investment or speculation, and if he is not already interested in advanced thought or occultism he will most likely be attracted during this period and obtain a good start before the aspect wears off.

☉ P ☌ □ ☍ ♆ *The Sun progressed parallel, conjunction, square or opposition to radical Neptune.*

If Neptune is afflicted at birth these aspects mark a critical time for those who can respond to the spiritual influence. They are then hypersensitive and likely to develop an undesirable phase of involuntary spiritual sight or apt to become entranced or obsessed by spirits from the invisible world who seek a medium to gratify their desires, which are usually bad. The person may also most easily become the victim of a hypnotist and get into trouble through fraud, deception and disadvantageous changes, or loss by speculation in large companies where the stock is watered.

☉ * △ ♆ *The Sun progressed sextile or trine to radical Neptune.*

If Neptune is well aspected at birth these aspects mark a period of spiritual awakening, when the person may receive an initiation which will develop his spiritual powers and open the invisible worlds to him, if he is sufficiently developed. For others it may develop the faculty of inspirational music, and yet other people may experience a period of unexampled love and bliss, but the majority cannot respond to this influence.

☉ P ☌ * △ M.C. *The Sun progressed parallel, conjunction, sextile or trine to radical Midheaven.*

These aspects bring a period of profit, preferment, honor and recognition, favors from the authorities or employers, added social prestige, and a general advancement of the worldly affairs.

This is a good time to make special effort for obtaining an increase of income for all endeavors in that direction will have a favorable stellar influence behind them and are therefore more likely to succeed than at other times.

☉□☍ M.C. *The Sun progressed square or opposition to radical Midheaven.*

These aspects mark a period of discredit when slander and enmity threaten the honor and social standing. It is therefore best for the person to be very circumspect in all he does or says, for trouble with the authorities may result in imprisonment, or if with employers it may bring loss of position. Financial fortunes are also threatened.

☉ P ☌ ✱ △ Asc. *The Sun progressed, parallel, conjunction, sextile or trine radical Ascendant.*

These aspects mark a period of general good fortune, radiant health and happiness. Whatever the person undertakes seems to prosper.

☉□☍ Asc. *The Sun progressed square or opposition to radical Ascendant.*

These aspects mark a period of ill-health, especially in a woman's horoscope. There is also a great deal of trouble and general so-called "bad luck."

CHAPTER XXV.

Progressed Lunar Directions

THE Moon travels through the Zodiac at an average rate of between twelve and thirteen degrees a day, and as the day in the art of progression is taken as a time measure equivalent to a year, we may say that the Moon by progression from birth to death travels at the rate of between twelve and thirteen degrees a year, or about one degree per month. Thus in the course of about twenty-eight years she circles the whole horoscope and forms all the aspects that can be formed to all the planets in the radical figure, and she may thus travel two or three times around the horoscope in the life of the average man or woman. It is her passage around the horoscope that makes the life fruitful of events for the aspects of the planets themselves which indicate the year when a certain influence is ready to be reaped as ripe destiny and produce events in the life, do not of themselves cause either good or ill effects unless an aspect of the progressed Moon or a lunation brings the matter to a focus and marks the month when the occurrence will take place. Therefore sometimes even strong aspects between the Sun and planets, or between the planets themselves, are barren in effect when not fortified by a progressed lunar aspect or a lunation of the same nature.

Neither do the lunar aspects have an influence of their own, or at least if they have, it is not very marked unless the lunar aspect agrees in nature with the primary direction then in force.

These are important points which the student should always bear in mind. It should also be noted that the aspects of the progressed Moon to progressed planets produce little or no effect and the influences set down below are with respect to the radical planets.

☽ P ☌ ✱ △ ☉ *The Moon progressed parallel, conjunction, sextile or trine to radical Sun.*

These aspects mark a rather prosperous period in life, bringing important changes for the better. Not infrequently marriage results which is both successful and happy. An increase of business if the person is an employer, or a raise in salary if he is an employee, may be looked for at this time, for superiors and those in a position to bestow favors are in a generous mood and ready to give the person credit for all that is good in him.

☽ □ ☍ ☉ *The Moon progressed square or opposition to radical Sun.*

These aspects indicate a time of trouble and loss. There is a tendency to difficulty with employers or customers which will bring loss of employment or business; the mind is vacillating so that the person cannot make up his mind what to do, and thus he is apt to lose opportunities which might bring gain and instead they bring loss. He will experience trouble with the opposite sex, particularly the marriage partner if he is in the state of matrimony. The health will suffer and there is a change for the worse in all the affairs of life.

☽ P ☌ ✱ △ ♀ *The Moon progressed parallel, conjunction, sextile, or trine to radical Venus.*

If Venus is strong and well aspected in the natal chart this period will be one of pleasure and profit both, for the person will make new friends and have opportunities to advance himself both socially and financially. These aspects also frequently indicate the commencement of courtship or the culmination of courtship in marriage, in a man's horoscope. They bring good health and a happy, cheerful frame of mind, so that the whole world seems bathed in sunshine. This is, in short, a period of general success and happiness.

☽ □ ☍ ♀ *The Moon progressed square or opposition to radical Venus.*

If Venus was afflicted at birth this marks a period of considerable trouble and disappointment. A courtship may be broken off or a marriage dissolved by separation. The financial fortunes are likely to suffer and the health is apt to be poor. Snubs and ostracism may be expected in the social relation and the person should be particularly careful with the opposite sex, for while this direction is operative there is considerable liability to trouble from that source. Knowing what is doing and the nature and duration of the influence, he should try to rule his stars by keeping as cheerful a frame of mind as possible, schooling himself to act wisely in the matters which are particularly shown as danger points.

☽ P ☌ ✳ △ ☿ *The Moon progressed parallel, conjunction, sextile or trine to radical Mercury.*

If Mercury was well aspected at birth, these directions will bring out the mental powers and it is therefore a favorable time to take up any study which the person may feel attracted to. If any important changes have been in contemplation this is the time to make the move, for under these directions success is sure to attend in a much larger measure than under less favorable influences, and if he has any important matters to settle with brothers, sisters or neighbors, he will reach a favorable conclusion with them much more quickly than at any other time.

☽ □ ☍ ☿ *The Moon progressed square or opposition to radical Mercury.*

If Mercury was afflicted at birth the person will need to exercise a great deal of care during the operation of these planetary influences, for there will be a tendency to rash and indiscreet speech; thereby the person may lay himself liable for libel or slander. It is also likely that if any deeds or legal papers are signed during this time it will be to the person's detriment and he will later regret it. He should also be very careful of his expressions in correspondence and if he is a literary man he should be doubly careful or his writings will be more than likely to cause trouble for himself or others. The mind will be much disturbed and he should neither travel nor make changes but endeavor to keep himself as quiet as possible during this time.

☽ P ☌ ♄ *The Moon progressed parallel or conjunction radical Saturn.*

If Saturn was afflicted in the natal chart this is a very critical period. In a woman's horoscope it indicates ill-health, worry and trouble. In the horoscope of a man, if he is married, it indicates domestic difficulties or ill-health of the wife. There is trouble, delay and disappointment in all the affairs of life and a tendency to worry over things and become morbid and melancholy.

☽ □ ☍ ♄ *The Moon progressed square or opposition to radical Saturn.*

If Saturn is afflicted at birth, these aspects mark a very evil time, particularly with respect to health and the conditions in the home. They produce a disturbed frame of mind with irritability and a tendency to worry, a pessimistic outlook on life; gloom and despondency seem to be the rule, the financial affairs also suffer and care should be taken to make no changes or investments at this time. The only remedy is to try to keep as philosophical an attitude as possible, looking for the silver lining of the cloud and endeavoring to learn the lessons that are to be taught during this period.

☽ ✱ △ ♄ *The Moon progressed sextile or trine to radical Saturn.*

If Saturn was well aspected in the natal chart these aspects mark a successful and prosperous period when one will gain recognition of a lasting nature in his sphere of life. He will be able to take on added responsibilities and acquit himself of the trust with credit. If any investments in houses, lands or mines are contemplated this will be a very favorable period to undertake such matters. This time will be epoch-making in the life when a new, solid and stable foundation for success will be laid, upon which the edifice of a successful life may be reared.

☽ P ☌ ⚹ △ ♃ *Moon progressed parallel, conjunction, sextile or trine to radical Jupiter.*

If Jupiter was well aspected at birth, these aspects mark a period of success and general good fortune. The health is excellent, or if the person has been sick improvement may be looked for at this time. The frame of mind will be happy and he will enjoy all the pleasures of life. It is a particularly good time to travel for he will meet a friendly and cordial reception everywhere. The financial fortunes will be benefited if investments are made under these directions, or if the business is pushed to the best of his ability. This is an epoch when things take a decided turn for the better, and if the person takes proper advantage of the opportunities then presented to him this time will be long felt in the life.

☽ □ ☍ ♃ *The Moon progressed square or opposition to radical Jupiter.*

If Jupiter was afflicted at birth the person should be very careful of his diet during the time when these aspects last, for there is a tendency to excesses which will cause disease by making the blood impure. He should also be very careful not to lose his temper because if there is any danger of apoplexy shown in the natal figure it is more likely to manifest under these stellar influences than at any other time. Keep as cool as possible and avoid all stimulating food and liquors. Do not under any circumstances undertake to speculate while these directions last for loss is certain and there is a liability to be deceived or defrauded by others. There is also a danger of domestic troubles and loss by lawsuits or similar matters. The social prestige is likely to suffer on account of haughty, bombastic and overbearing manners, therefore the person should be careful and moderate in everything and also hold himself well in check.

☽ P ☌ □ ☍ ♂ *The Moon progressed parallel, conjunction, square or opposition radical Mars.*

If the radical Mars was afflicted these aspects mark a very evil period. In a woman's horoscope they indicate, for one thing, bad health, and in a man's, violent quarrels in the home. There is a tendency to be quarrelsome, foolhardy and reckless, with the result that the person may sustain bodily injuries or accidents, also a tendency to the over-indulgence of the lower passional nature which may bring trouble in its train, therefore he should be very careful in his dealings with those of the opposite sex. Unless great care is taken slander and social discredit are sure to result. These directions also make the person very reckless and extravagant in financial matters, liable to form hasty and erroneous judgments, therefore if papers are signed at this time disaster is very likely to follow. These directions are among the most reliable in operation and the person rarely escapes without suffering loss or injury in some manner, therefore the greatest care should be taken during this period.

☽ ✶ △ ♂ *The Moon progressed sextile or trine radical Mars.*

If Mars was well aspected at birth these aspects mark a period of considerable activity in the life which will be to the benefit of the person involved. A great deal of vital energy is accumulated and this dynamic force naturally must have an outlet in some way, hence this is a good time for the expansion of business or undertaking new enterprises; they are sure to succeed if the person is not too precipitate in his efforts but uses a grain of caution in the expenditure of this great energy. These aspects are particularly active among those who work with or deal in the martial elements of iron and fire, such as soldiers, surgeons and engineers; to them they bring honor and promotion.

☽ P ☌ □ ☍ ♅ *The Moon progressed parallel, conjunction, square or opposition radical Uranus.*

If Uranus was afflicted at birth these aspects mark a very critical period, when the person is apt to make a sudden and unexpected change which will have a disadvantageous effect upon the life, therefore he should guard carefully against such a contingency. There is also a liability to the formation of a clandestine relationship which will bring sorrow and trouble to the person, hence he should avoid association with the opposite sex and when this is unavoidable he should be very circumspect in his manner and behavior, for under these directions people are very likely to judge him severely for the slightest semblance of wrong-doing. There is a tendency to irritability and cruelty of speech which is likely to cause domestic unhappiness and the loss of friends that will later be regretted very much, therefore the person should endeavor to curb himself; in fact it would be better to avoid his friends as much as possible during this time.

☽ ⚹ △ ♅ *The Moon progressed sextile or trine to radical Uranus.*

These are excellent aspects for those who are sufficiently advanced to respond. If Uranus was well aspected at birth, the original, intuitive and inventive faculties will find an outlet at this time which may be very advantageous to the person. If he is interested in the study of advanced thought or occultism this is a particularly good time to pursue such subjects, for an expansion of consciousness may most easily result under these directions, friendships are formed with advanced people who will be of benefit to the person, and advantageous changes or removals may be made, hence it marks an epoch in the life which is likely to leave a permanent mark for good.

☽ P ☌ □ ☍ ♆ *The Moon progressed parallel, conjunction, square or opposition to radical Neptune.*

If Neptune was afflicted in the natal chart these directions mark a period of weird and uncanny experiences, when the person is likely to come under the spell of hypnotism or mediumship or have visions or begin to hear voices, but all these experiences are of an undesirable character and should therefore be guarded against as much as possible. It would be very unwise under these directions to enter the seance room of a spiritualistic meeting where the conditions favor such manifestations, and if the aspects occur from watery signs—Cancer, Scorpio, or Pisces—there is a strong tendency to form a drink or drug habit which may operate to the sorrow and trouble of the person for all the rest of his life. As these aspects produce a mental and physical lassitude, when the vital forces are low and the person negative, such undesirable influences are particularly apt to gain a foothold. There is also a danger from plots by secret enemies which tend to bring the person into discredit and trouble. He may even suffer imprisonment or be confined in a hospital through ill-health, for Neptune rules prisons, hospitals, insane asylums, and similar places. Great care should be taken in all dealings with others.

☽ ✱ △ ♆ *The Moon progressed sextile or trine to radical Neptune.*

If Neptune was well aspected at birth these directions may bring a slight extension of consciousness and if the solar aspects to Neptune are also in force at the same time an initiation may be looked for by those who are sufficiently advanced to respond to this influence. But to the majority of people it will probably mean only a pleasant time, a feast of music or some similar experience.

☽ P ☌ Asc. M. C. *The Moon progressed parallel or conjunction radical Ascendant or Midheaven.*

These aspects bring changes in the life, but whether these are good or bad depends upon the other influences operating in the horoscope at the time.

☽ ✱ △ M. C. *The Moon progressed sextile or trine to radical Midheaven.*

If other influences agree this is a time of beneficial changes, preferment and honor, and general success in the various departments of life.

☽ □ ☍ M. C. *The Moon progressed square or opposition to radical Midheaven.*

These aspects indicate loss of prestige, trouble and anxiety, financial loss, especially if dealing with women. It is a bad time to travel or make changes.

☽ ⚹ △ Asc. *The Moon progressed sextile or trine to radical Ascendant.*

These aspects bring beneficial changes, financial prosperity, and general good fortune.

☽ □ ☍ Asc. *The Moon progressed square or opposition to radical Ascendant.*

These aspects mark a period of trouble. Ill-health may be looked for, and if any changes or removals are made they will be to the person's disadvantage.

CHAPTER XXVI.

Mutual Planetary Directions

ASPECTS between two progressed planets have little or no potency, but when a planet by progression comes into aspect with a *radical* planet it operates for good or ill, according to its nature and the power of the radical planet in the horoscope.

In the following paragraphs we have set down these tendencies, and it matters not whether Venus progresses to a good aspect with radical Saturn, or Saturn progresses to a good aspect with radical Venus, the effects are as noted in the first paragraph, and similarly with the other aspects following.

♀ ♄ ✱ △ *Venus and Saturn in good aspect by progression* indicate a period of financial success, gain in social prestige and emotional exaltation. The religious and devotional nature is likely to receive an awakening.

♀ ♄ P ☌ □ ☍ *Venus and Saturn in evil aspect by progression* indicate a period of sorrow and trouble. Both the health and reputation suffer; delays, disappointment and losses are frequent and annoying. Others will seek to impose upon the person; death or separation from loved ones, and other disagreeable experiences are met. The mind is gloomy and inclined to worry.

☿ ♄ ✱ △ *Mercury and Saturn in good aspect by progression* mark a good time to undertake new responsibilities, make investments in houses, mines, lands, or similar property, undertake study or research work of a deeper nature, and make important contracts which will prove of lasting benefit to the person. It is a good time to deal with agents and elderly persons, or to undertake journeys for a serious purpose.

☿ ♄ P ☌ □ ☍ *Mercury and Saturn afflicted by progression* indicate a time of delays and disappointments with a tendency to look upon the dark side of things. It is a bad time to undertake new responsibilities, deal with elderly people or sign legal papers. The person is liable to slander and loss of reputation.

♂ ♄ ✱ △ *Mars and Saturn in good aspect by progression* mark a period when the person will be very enterprising yet tactful and diplomatic, courageous but not foolhardy, strong and dignified, better able to shoulder the responsibilities of life than at any other time. If he makes proper use of these qualities he will gain financially, also in honor and respect among his associates.

♂ ♄ P ☌ □ ☍ *Mars and Saturn in bad aspect by progression* make the person very foolhardy and impulsive, hence there is a liability to accident under these directions. Occasionally when the horoscope shows violence there is a tendency to crime and bloodshed which may result in imprisonment. All the vices of the character seem to come to the fore at this time, and loss of temper is the least among them. The greatest care should be taken to keep the animal nature down and hold a firm check upon all the undesirable traits in the character.

♀ ♃ P ☌ ✱ △ *Venus and Jupiter in good aspect by progression* bring financial benefits, and a rise in social position and esteem. They make the person more kindly, sympathetic and considerate, hence increase his popularity. It is a good time to travel and enjoy life. Investments made under this influence are generally successful, and the health is excellent, or if the person has been ill this marks the period of convalescence and recuperation, when life takes on a rosier hue.

♀ ♃ □ ☍ *Venus and Jupiter afflicting each other by progression* indicate a period of mild domestic trouble, small financial losses and a tendency to extravagance and wastefulness, pecuniary difficulties on that account, and possibly lawsuits. There is also some loss of prestige in the social circle or the person's environment.

☿ ♃ P ☌ ⚹ △ *Mercury and Jupiter in good aspect by progression* indicate a very successful period in the life. The person will probably travel with both pleasure and profit to himself. He will have good health and be in the best of spirits, so that life in general will take on a very rosy hue. There are indications of gain by investments and in the general course of his business, and it is a good time to enter into contracts and agreements, especially for literary work.

☿ ♃ □ ☍ *Mercury and Jupiter afflicted by progression* mark a troublesome time, when the person is liable to become involved in lawsuits and lose thereby. He should be very careful not to sign papers or enter into agreements, for there will be trouble and misunderstanding, involving financial loss; also if he lends money to other people they will endeavor to impose upon him and defraud him, and dealings with agents and commission men should be particularly avoided.

♂ ♃ ⚹ △ *Mars and Jupiter in good aspect by progression* mark a period in life when the usual conservatism of Jupiter is blended with the martian enthusiasm, hence the person will become more enthusiastic and enterprising so that he is likely to extend his business and be successful in gaining an added income thereby. He should be careful, however, not to overreach himself at this time. These aspects also work upon the devotional nature and may sometimes express themselves as religious enthusiasm when the person turns over a new leaf and becomes a better man or woman than before.

♂ ♃ P ☌ □ ☍ *Mars and Jupiter in evil aspect by progression* mark a danger point in the life when the person is liable to wreck his whole career by acts which are definitely criminal, or by losses due to ostentatious display and extravagance, or he may become interested in some wildcat mining scheme or speculate upon the stock exchange in such a reckless manner that he loses all he has and becomes a pauper. The health is also likely to suffer under this direction; impurities of the blood may cause growths, tumors, boils, and kindred afflictions. Altogether it is a very evil time and the person should guard himself very carefully against yielding to any of these influences.

♀ ♂ ✱ △ *Venus and Mars in good aspect by progression* mark a period of pleasure and enjoyment when an attachment of a lasting nature may be formed with someone through an enthusiastic courtship. There are also indications of financial gain and an increase of popularity.

♀ ♂ P ☌ □ ☍ *Venus and Mars in evil aspect by progression* mark a period of impulse and recklessness when the person is likely to act in a most indiscreet manner that may cause great trouble in life. If married there will be some domestic unhappiness. Financial losses and discredit are also shown, therefore the person should endeavor to hold himself in check and avoid any temptations that may come in his path.

☿ ♂ ⚹ △ *Mercury and Mars in good aspect by progression* mark a time when the person is generally successful in all affairs of life, especially where the mental qualities are called into action, for this will make him keen, shrewd and sharp, quick to see a point and grasp an advantage, hence financial gain is also indicated. This is a good time for advertising and extending the person's business, entering contracts and agreements, and dealing with agents and middlemen. It is good for literary work of a lighter nature, and an excellent time to travel. The health is good and there is a feeling of cheerfulness, joy and optimism.

☿ ♂ P ☌ □ ☍ *Mercury and Mars in evil aspect by progression.* This is a critical time when the person is liable to act on impulse, to speak and act impulsively without due deliberation and forethought, hence he is likely to get into trouble or suffer loss through the sharp practices of other people. He should therefore be very careful not to sign papers or enter into agreements, and there is danger of accident and trouble if the person travels. It is a bad time for changes or extensions of business.

♂ ♅ ✱ △ *Mars and Uranus in good aspect by progression* indicate a good period for perfecting inventions or starting new and original enterprises. Friendships of a beneficial nature are often made under these directions, and not infrequently a psychic awakening takes place through associations with people, or groups of people, of a Uranian nature.

♂ ♅ P ☌ □ ☍ *Mars and Uranus in evil aspect by progression* mark a very dangerous time in the person's life. There is a liability to accidents of an unusual nature, a breaking up of conditions, estrangement from friends, and the person is liable to find himself suddenly alone in the world. Sometimes there is a psychic awakening but always of an undesirable nature.

♂ ♆ ✱ △ *Mars and Neptune in good aspect by progression* mark a time of good health and high spirits for advanced people, but the majority do not feel its influence.

♂ ♆ P ☌ □ ☍ *Mars and Neptune in evil aspect by progression* produce a neurotic condition in those who can respond to its influence. There is also a liability to be defrauded or victimized in some unaccountable manner.

♀ ♅ ✶ △ *Venus and Uranus in good aspect by progression* give a probability of some financial gain and it is likely that the person will have what he considers a good time, involving probably a romantic love affair, but it is likely to leave a sting behind. This direction insures the aid of friends and increases the popularity of the person for the time being.

♀ ♅ P ☌ □ ☍ *Venus and Uranus in evil aspect by progression* are a fruitful cause of domestic unhappiness and divorce. This direction is likely to bring about a scandal on account of immoral conduct. Lawsuits and financial loss are also threatened, and the person is likely to act in a most erratic manner.

♀ ♆ ✶ △ *Venus and Neptune in good aspect by progression* indicate a period of success in social matters, happiness and enjoyment of life for those who can respond to this direction. The person is particularly apt to indulge in the building of air castles and the concoction of roseate daydreams which are of no particular avail but serve to make the period thoroughly enjoyable.

♀ ♆ P ☌ □ ☍ *Venus and Neptune in evil aspect by progression* are likely to bring some psychic experience of a disagreeable nature connected with mediumship or hypnotism. There is a tendency to sensuality and immorality, occasionally the indulgence in drinks or drugs which will cause sorrow and trouble to come to the person.

☿ ♅ ∗ △ *Mercury and Uranus in good aspect by progression* make the native active mentally, bring unexpected pleasures, give impulse to mental work, make the mind keen and give a desire for occult investigation. Many are attracted to and become interested in altruistic and humanitarian work under this aspect.

☿ ♅ P ☌ □ ☍ *Mercury and Uranus afflicting each other by progression* make the native unconventional, erratic and restless, create a nervous, wayward state of mind, and may bring unexpected lawsuits.

☿ ♆ ∗ △ *Mercury and Neptune in good aspect by progression.* The mind is active and inclined to the study of Astrology and Mysticism. The native is apt to travel by water and make changes. Only those who are advanced along spiritual lines feel the effect of Neptune.

☿ ♆ P ☌ □ ☍ *Mercury and Neptune in bad aspect by progression.* Persons under this influence should guard against investments in corporations. The mind is disturbed by evil thoughts and the morals may be lax if such a tendency is shown in the natal horoscope.

♄ ♃ ♅ ♆ *Saturn, Jupiter, Uranus, and Neptune* seldom form aspects by progression on account of their slow motion.

CHAPTER XXVII.

TRANSITS

THE progressed positions of planets are the principal significators of events, but the transitory positions of the planets in space at the actual time of events strengthen or weaken effects of aspects in the progressed horoscope, according to whether they are akin in nature or not. The New Moons are particularly potent. These so-called *Transits* are seen in the ephemeris for the actual year of events.

The Increasing or Decreasing Moon

Among the points in Astrology which bother the beginner, is when the Moon is increasing in light or decreasing. Astrological works frequently use these expressions when tabulating the effects of various configurations. But so far as we know, no explanation has been given elsewhere, and we trust the following may make the subject clear to students.

Each month the Moon comes into conjunction with the Sun, and this conjunction of the luminaries is called a *lunation or New Moon.* After the conjunction or New Moon, she may be seen in the western sky close to the horizon as a tiny crescent; day by day the lighted surface grows larger; at the time of the opposition to the Sun she has increased her light to the fullest capacity, and at that time we speak of her as a full Moon; she then rises in the eastern sky at the same time as the Sun sets in the west. From that time for another fortnight it will be observed that she rises later and later in the night; at the same time the illuminated part of her disc decreases until just before the next conjunction or new Moon, early risers may observe her in the eastern sky just before sunrise as a tiny crescent upon the vault of heaven. Thus the Moon is increasing in light from the time of its conjunction or new Moon to the opposition, or full Moon, and from the full Moon to the next New Moon it is decreasing in light. The times of the New Moon, Full Moon and eclipses are given each month in our *Simplified Scientific Ephemeris,* which see.

Transits of Neptune, Uranus, Saturn and Jupiter are important,and when the student has become familiar with the mysteries of the progressed horoscope but not before, he may profitably write the ephemeral position of these planets outside the progressed horoscope and watch their effect, also the aspects of the New Moons. But be sure, at first, to keep the progressed horoscope down to first principles, for fancy aspects are "the stuff dreams are made of," the warp and woof of astrological romances which fade away into moonshine and leave the astrologer discomfited. It is comparatively easy to wield the shuttle of imagination with natal, progressed and transiting planets, each set with its corresponding houses, and a multitude of aspects to choose from, but simple judgment based upon the prime essentials of a horoscope is almost invariably justified by events.

♄ ☌ ☉ ☽ ♀ ♃ *Saturn transiting the radical Sun, Moon, Venus or Jupiter.*

These transits lower the vitality and act as a damper on the spirits of the person; there is a tendency to colds, gloom and melancholy, delays and disappointments, and if Saturn should turn retrograde passing and repassing these points, quite a long time of trouble and anxiety results.

♄ □ ☍ ☉ ☽ ♀ ♃ *Saturn transiting square or opposition radical Sun, Moon, Venus or Jupiter.*

These aspects will produce similar effect to the conjunction but more intense, and falls, bruises, or broken bones are often additional results.

♄ ⚹ △ ☉ ☽ ♀ ♃ *Saturn transiting sextile or trine the radical Sun, Moon, Venus or Jupiter.*

These aspects do not produce any benefit so far as has been observed.

♄ ⚹ △ ☿ *Saturn transiting sextile or trine the radical Mercury.*

These aspects steady the mind and make it more capable of concentration when Saturn is direct, or when he is retrograde, but aspecting Mercury by *square or opposition,* fear, worry, melancholy, gloom and trouble result; then it is also dangerous to travel.

♄ ☌ ♂ ♅ ♆ *Saturn transiting radical Mars, Uranus or Neptune.*

These transits always mark a time of trouble, *no matter what the aspect,* but the nature of the trouble is best determined by the house and sign where the afflicted planet is located.

♄ ☌ M. C. *Saturn transiting the radical Midheaven.*

This aspect always produces slander, discredit and loss of prestige.

♄ 6-12 *Saturn transiting the Sixth or Twelfth House or the Ascendant.*

These positions have an inimical effect on the health, according to the signs which are on the cusps of these houses.

♃ ✱ △ ☉ ♀ ☿ ☽ *Jupiter transiting sextile or trine the radical Sun, Venus, Mercury or Moon.*

These aspects bring health, happiness and financial benefit in accordance with the radical indications. If Jupiter retrogrades he is not so active but the period of good is protracted by his repeated direct passage over the good aspects.

♃ □ ☍ ☉ ♀ ☿ ☽ *Jupiter transiting square or opposition radical Sun, Venus, Mercury or Moon.*

These aspects are not very evil because evil is out of harmony with the basic nature of Jupiter.

♃ ☌ ♄ ♂ ♅ ♆ *Jupiter transiting or aspecting radical Saturn, Mars, Uranus or Neptune.*

These aspects produce no appreciable results because the basic natures of these planets are entirely different. This is on the same principle that tuning forks of different pitch do not respond to one another.

♅ ☌ ☉ ♀ *Uranus transiting radical Sun or Venus.*

These transits produce romantic attachments, Bohemian pleasures, unconventional experiences; when Uranus is retrograde this may last for a long time, but when he is in evil aspect immorality, scandal and divorce may result.

♅ ☌ ♂ ☽ ☿ *Uranus transiting radical Mars, Moon or Mercury.*

These aspects of Uranus to the radical Mars, Moon or Mercury have a tendency to make the person rash, reckless, foolhardy and erratic, sometimes to the point of insanity if other testimonies in the horoscope concur, the phase of the mental disturbance varying from violence when induced by Mars, to mild idiocy when produced by the Moon.

♅ ☌ ♄ ♂ ♆ *Uranus transiting or in evil aspect to radical Saturn, Mars or Neptune.*

These transits cause trouble according to the house and sign where Uranus is located. Good aspects produce no benefit as far as we have observed.

♆ ☌ ☿ ☽ *Neptune transiting radical Mercury or Moon.*

These aspects bring a spiritual awakening accompanied by dreams and visions of an elevating nature. These aspects are also good for travel, but the bad aspects make the mind unclean, polluted and criminal if the radical horoscope allows, so that the person may commit a crime and suffer imprisonment. Mediumship is also often the result of these transits.

PART II

Medical Astrology

AFTER AN EXTENSIVE PRACTICE OF MANY YEARS, THE FOLLOWING TREATISE IS SUBMITTED AS EMBODYING THE AUTHORS' EXPERIENCE, GAINED BY SUCCESSFUL DIAGNOSIS OF MANY THOUSANDS OF HOROSCOPES

[But we want to make it clearly understood that we do not cast horoscopes for money, or tell fortunes. Our work is a strictly humanitarian undertaking. To us, Astrology is a phase of religion.]

CHAPTER XXVIII.

Astro-Diagnosis of Disease

PARENTS have an exceptional opportunity and may lay up much treasure in heaven by judicious care of growing children based upon knowledge of tendencies to disease revealed by the horoscope. The writers rely implicitly upon the horoscope's testimony and though in a few cases doubts have been expressed as to the correctness of our diagnosis, because it varied from that of practitioners in personal touch with the patient, subsequent developments have invariably vindicated our judgment and proved the far-reaching penetration of Astrology which is as much in advance of the X-Ray as that is superior to a candle, for even though the X-Ray were capable of illuminating the entire body to such an extent that we could see each individual cell in activity, it could only show the conditions of the body at a given moment. But the horoscope shows incipient disease from the cradle to the grave, thus it gives us ample time to apply the ounce of prevention, and maybe escape an illness, or, at least, ameliorate its severity when disease has overtaken us. It indicates to the day when crises are due, thus forewarned we may take extra precautionary measures to tide over the critical point. It indicates when the inimical influences will wane and fortifies us to bear present suffering with strength born of the knowledge that recovery at a specific time is certain. Thus Astrology offers help and hope in a manner obtainable by no other method; for its scope is wider than all other systems, and it penetrates to the very soul of Being.

An Important Warning

If letters of fire that would burn themselves into the consciousness of the reader were obtainable, we would spare no effort to procure them for the purpose of warning students on some particular points in connection with the practice of medical Astrology; these are:

Never tell a patient a discouraging fact.
Never tell him when impending crises are due.
Never predict sickness at a certain time.
Never, *never* predict death.

It is a grave mistake, almost a crime, to tell sick persons anything discouraging, for it robs them of strength that should be husbanded with the utmost care to facilitate recovery. It is also wrong to suggest sickness to a well person, for it focuses the mind on a specific disease at a certain time, and such a suggestion is liable to cause sickness. It is a well known fact that many students in medical colleges feel the symptoms of every disease they study, and suffer greatly in consequence of auto-suggestion, but the idea of impending disease implanted by one in whom the victim has faith is much more dangerous; therefore it behooves the medical astrologer to be very cautious. If you cannot say anything encouraging, be silent.

This warning applies with particular force when treating patients having Taurus or Virgo rising or the Sun or Moon in those signs. These positions predispose the mind to center on disease, often in a most unwarranted manner. The Taurean fears sickness to an almost insane degree, and prediction of disease is fatal to this nature. The Virgos court disease, in order to gain sympathy, and though professing to long for recovery, they actually delight in nursing disease. They beg to know their symptoms, the crises, and delight in probing the matter to the depths; they will plead ability to stand full knowledge and profess that it will help them; but if the practitioner allows himself to be enticed by their protestations, and does tell them, they wilt like a flower. They are the most difficult people to help in any case, and extra care should be taken not to aggravate their chances by admissions of the nature indicated.

Besides, though the writers have used medical Astrology for many years and with astonishing success, and though Astrology, as a science, is absolutely exact and infallible, it must not be forgotten that there remains nevertheless the chance of mistaken judgment on the part of the practitioner and the chance that the person whose horoscope he is judging may assert his will to such an extent that it overrules the indication in the horoscope. He may change his mode of life without knowing what would have happened if he had gone on as before, and thus he may be in no danger at the time when the tendency to sickness shown by the horoscope arrives; it is cruel to unsettle his mind in any case. Naturally, the young student would be most liable to make a mistake in judgment, but no one is immune. We remember a case that came to our notice recently. One of the most prominent European astrologers predicted for a client in South Africa that on a certain date he would have a severe hæmorrhage of the lungs. The poor man wrote to us for help, but though liability to colds in the lungs was shown, we saw no serious trouble at the time predicted, nor has hæmorrhage been experienced in the year elapsed between that time and the present writing.

Some students have a morbid desire to know the time of their own death, and probe into this matter in a most unwarranted manner; but no matter how they may seek to deceive themselves there are very few who have the mental and moral stamina to live life in the same manner, if they knew with absolute certainty that on a certain date their earthly existence would be terminated. That is one of the points most wisely hidden until we are to see on both sides of the veil, and we do wrong, no matter what our ground, to seek to wrest that knowledge from the horoscope.

Moreover, it has been well said that "the doctor who prescribes for himself has a fool for a patient," and this applies to diagnosis of one's own horoscope with tenfold force, for there we are all biased; either we make too light of conditions, or we take them too seriously, particularly if we investigate the time and mode of death. We remember a case where an intellectual woman, principal of a private school in New York, wrote asking for admission to our correspondence class, "if we thought it worth while, as she was going to die the first week in March." She gave us all the aspects upon which she based her judgment, and as one of the writers had just emerged hale and hearty from similar configurations, she gave the lady in question a good talking to that straightened her out; she told the lady she (the writer) expected to live to a ripe age. Now that lady is thinking of a useful life, she has learned to forget death. Astrology is too sacred to be thus misused. Let the student forget about his own horoscope and devote his knowledge to helping others; then it will aid him in accumulating treasure in heaven as no other line of spiritual endeavor will.

Planetary Polarities

When we study magnetism we are dealing with an invisible force; and ordinarily we can at best state the way it manifests in the physical world, as is the case whenever we deal with any *force*. The physical world is the world of effects; the causes are hidden from our sight, though they are nearer than hands or feet. Force is all about us, invisible and only seen by the effects it produces.

If we take a dish of water, for illustration, and allow it to freeze, we shall see a myriad of ice crystals, beautiful geometrical figures. These show the lines along which the water congealed and these lines are lines of force which were present before the water congealed; but they were invisible until the proper conditions were furnished them and they became manifest.

In the same way there are lines of force going between the two poles of a magnet; they are neither seen nor felt until we bring iron or iron filings into the place where they are, when they will manifest by arranging the filings in an orderly pattern. By making the proper conditions we may cause any of the nature forces to show their effects—moving our street cars, carrying messages with lightning speed over thousands of miles, etc., etc.; but the *force* itself is ever invisible. We know that magnetism travels always at right angles to the electric current with which it manifests; we know the difference between the manifestations of the electric and the magnetic current, so dependent upon one another, but we have never seen either; though they are about the most valuable servants we have today.

Magnetism may be divided into "mineral" and "animal" magnetism, though in reality they are one, but the former has very little influence upon animal tissue, while the latter is generally impotent in working with minerals.

The mineral magnetism is derived directly from lodestones which are used to magnetize iron, and this process gives to the metal thus treated the property of attracting iron. This kind of magnet is very little used, however, as its magnetism becomes depleted, is too weak in proportion to its bulk, and principally because the magnetic force cannot be controlled in such a so-called "permanent" magnet.

The "electro-magnet" is also a "mineral" magnet. It is simply a piece of iron wound around with many turns of electric wire; the strength of the magnet varies as the number of turns of wire, and the strength of the electric current that is passed through it.

Electricity is all about us in a diffused state, of no use for industrial purposes until it is *compressed* and forced through the electric wires by the powerful *electro-magnets.* We must have *magnetism* in the *first* place before we can get any electricity. Before a new electric generator is started the "fields," which are nothing but electro-magnets, must be magnetized. If that is not done they may turn it till the crack of doom, at any rate of speed they please, and it will never light a single lamp nor move a grain of weight; all depends upon the magnetism being there *first.* After this magnetism is once started it will leave a little behind when the generator is shut down, and this so-called "residual magnetism" will be the nucleus of force to be built up each time the generator is started afresh.

All bodies of plants, animals and men are but transformed mineral. They have all come from the mineral kingdom in the first place, and chemical analysis of the plant, animal and human bodies brings out the fact beyond cavil. Moreover, we know that the plants get their sustenance from the mineral soil, and both animal and man are eating mineral when they consume the plants as food; even when man eats the animals he is nevertheless eating mineral compounds, and therefore he gets with his food both the mineral substances and the magnetic force which they contain.

This force we see manifesting in "Hæmoglobin," or the red coloring matter in the blood, which attracts the life-giving oxygen when it comes into contact with it in the millions of minute capillaries of the lungs, parting with it as readily when it passes through the capillaries which all over the body connect the arteries with the veins. Why is this?

To understand this, we must acquaint ourselves a little closer with the way magnetism manifests as seen in industrial uses.

There are always two fields or a multiple of two fields in a generator or motor, every alternate "field" or magnet being "north-pole" and every other one, "south-pole." If we wish to run two or more generators "in multiple" and force their electricity into the same wire, the first requisite is that the magnetic current in the field-magnets should run *in the same direction.*

If that were not the case, they would not run together; they would generate currents going in *opposite* directions, blowing their fuses. That would be because the poles in one generator, which should have attracted, repelled, and vice-versa. The remedy is to change the ends of the wire which magnetizes the fields; then the magnetic current in one generator will become like the current of the other, and both will run smoothly together.

Similar conditions prevail in magnetic healing; a certain vibratory pitch and magnetic polarity were infused into each of us when the stellar forces surged through our bodies and gave us our planetary baptism at the moment when we drew our first complete breath. These are modified during our pilgrimage of life, but in the main their initial impulse remains undisturbed and therefore the horoscope at birth retains the most vital power in life to determine our sympathies and antipathies as well as all other matters. Nay more, its pronouncements are more reliable than our conscious likes and dislikes.

Sometimes we may meet and learn to like a person, although we have a feeling that he has an inimical influence on us for which we cannot account, and therefore strive to put aside; but a comparison of his horoscope with our own will reveal the reason and if we are wise we heed its warning, or as surely as the circling stars move in their orbits around the

Sun we will live to regret our disregard of this handwriting on the wall.

But there are also many cases when we do not sense the antipathy between ourselves and a certain person, though the horoscope reveals it, and if we see the signs when comparing the two horoscopes we may feel inclined to trust our feelings rather than the stellar script of the horoscopes. That also will in time lead to trouble, for the planetary polarity is certain to manifest in time unless both parties are sufficiently evolved to rule their stars in a large measure. Such people are few and far between at our present stage of evolution. Therefore we shall do well if we use our knowledge of the stellar script to compare our horoscopes with those at least who come intimately into our lives. This may save both them and us much misery and heartache. We would advise this course particularly with regard to a healer and his patients, and with reference to a prospective marriage partner.

When anyone is ill, resistance is at the lowest ebb, and on that account he is then least able to withstand outside influences. So the vibrations of the healer have practically unrestrained effect, and even though he may be ensouled by the noblest of altruistic motives, desiring to pour out his very life for the benefit of the patient, if their stars were adverse at birth, his vibratory pitch and magnetism are bound to have an inimical effect upon the patient. Therefore it is of prime necessity that any healer should have a knowledge of Astrology and the law of compatibility, whether he belongs to those who admittedly heal by magnetism and the laying on of hands or to the regular schools of physicians, for the latter also infuse their vibrations into the patient's aura and help or hinder according to the agreement of their planetary polarity with that of the patient.

What has been said with regard to the healer applies with tenfold force to the nurse, for he or she is with the patient practically all the time and the contact is so much more intimate.

For healer, nurse and patient, compatibility is determined by the rising sign, Saturn, and the Sixth House. If their rising signs agree in nature so that all have fiery signs rising, or all have earthy, airy, or watery signs rising, they are harmonious, but if the patient has a watery sign rising, a nurse or a docter with fiery signs will have a very detrimental effect.

It is also necessary to see that Saturn in the horoscope of the nurse or healer is not placed in any of the degrees of the zodiac within the patient's Sixth House.

With respect to marriage the planetary polarity is shown principally by a consideration of the feminine Moon and Venus in a man's horoscope, for they describe his attractions towards the opposite sex, and in a woman's horoscope the masculine Sun and Mars have a similar significance. If these planets are harmoniously configurated and the signs on the cusps of the Seventh Houses of the prospective partners agree, harmony will prevail, especially if the Sun, Venus or Jupiter of one person is placed in the Seventh House of the other. But if the planets mentioned afflict one another, or the Seventh Houses of the parties are out of harmony, or if Saturn, Mars, Uranus or Neptune of one is in a degree included in the Seventh House of the other, it is the handwriting on the wall which indicates that the planetary polarities are inharmonious and that sorrow is in store for them if they allow their evanescent emotions to draw them together in a bond of unhappiness; for it is easy to change the field wires on two electric generators so that their polarities will agree, but it is extremely difficult to reverse the planetary polarity of one person to make it agree with that received by another at his planetary baptism.

CHAPTER XXIX.

The Law of Correspondences

IT IS said in the Bible that God made man in His likeness, and from hoary antiquity seers and sages have noted a correspondence between the *macrocosm,* the great world, and the *microcosm,* the little world, or man. This is again expressed in the hermetic axiom which is the master-key to all mysteries: *"As above, so below."* Therefore we may note that the various parts of the human body are correlated to different divisions of the vaulted arch of heaven and the marching orbs that move through it. As the creative forces within the womb act upon the ovum and gradually build the fœtus, so also the stellar rays from the macrocosmic body of mother nature are active upon man. It is their activity which we note in the process of evolution whereby that which is now man has come up through the lower kingdoms to his present stage of completion, and it is by the same rays that he will gradually evolve to the divine stature where he will indeed be like the Father in Heaven, consequently we may note the correspondences between the signs and planets and the different divisions of the human body as follows:

Pathogenic Effects of the Twelve Signs

♈ *Aries* rules the head, the cerebral hemispheres, the various organs within the head, and the eyes, but the nose is under the rulership of Scorpio.

Thus any affliction in Aries will react upon the head, producing headaches, neuralgia, coma and trance conditions, diseases of the brain and cerebral hemorrhages.

♉ *Taurus* rules the neck, throat, palate, larynx and tonsils, lower jaw, ears, and occipital region. The cerebellum is also under the rule of Taurus, so are the atlas and cervical vertebræ, the carotid arteries, jugular veins, and certain minor blood vessels.

The diseases to which these regions are subject are goitre, diphtheria, croup and apoplexy. As each sign always reacts upon the opposite, afflictions in Taurus may also produce venereal diseases, constipation, or irregular menses.

♊ *Gemini* rules the arms and hands, shoulders, lungs, and the thymus gland, also the upper ribs, therefore afflictions in Gemini cause pulmonary diseases, pneumonia, pleurisy, bronchitis, asthma and inflammation of the pericardium.

♋ *Cancer* rules the œsophagus, stomach, diaphragm, pancreas, the mammae, lacteals, upper lobes of liver, and thoracic duct, hence afflictions in Cancer produce indigestion, gas in the stomach, cough, hiccough, dropsy, gloom, hypochondria, hysteria, gall stones, and jaundice.

♌ *Leo* rules the heart, the dorsal region of the spine, the spinal cord, and the aorta, therefore the afflictions in Leo cause regurgitation, palpitation, faintings, aneurism, spinal meningitis, and curvature of the spine, also arterio-sclerosis and angina pectoris, hyperæmia, anæmia and hydræmia.

♍ *Virgo* rules the abdominal region, the large and small intestines, the lower lobes of the liver, and the spleen, therefore afflictions in Virgo produce peritonitis, tapeworm, malnutrition, interference with the absorption of the chyle, typhoid fever, cholera, and appendicitis.

♎ *Libra* rules the kidneys, the suprarenals, the lumbar region of the spine, the vasomotor system and the skin, hence afflictions in Libra produce polyuria, or suppression of the urine, inflammation of the ureters which connect the kidneys with the bladder, Bright's disease, lumbago, eczema and other skin diseases.

♏ *Scorpio* rules the bladder, urethra, and genital organs in general, also the rectum and the descending colon, the sigmoid flexure, the prostate gland, and the nasal bones; hence afflictions in Scorpio produce nasal catarrh, adenoids, and polypi, diseases of the womb and ovaries, various venereal diseases, stricture, and enlargement of the prostate gland, irregularities of the menses, leucorrhœa, rupture, renal stones and gravel.

♐ *Sagittarius* rules the hips and thighs, the femur, ilium, the coccygeal and sacral regions of the spine, the iliac arteries and veins, sciatic nerves, hence afflictions to Sagittarius produce locomotor ataxia, sciatica, rheumatism, and hip diseases. Furthermore, as each sign has an influence upon its opposite, afflictions in Sagittarius may also cause pulmonary troubles. It is also noteworthy that broken bones are caused by this sign.

♑ *Capricorn* governs the skin and the knees, but it has also a reflex action on the stomach, which is governed by the opposite sign Cancer. Hence afflictions in Capricorn produce eczema and other skin diseases, erysipelas, leprosy, and digestive disturbances.

♒ *Aquarius* rules the ankles, the limbs from the knees to the ankles, and has also a reflex action on its opposite sign Leo, hence afflictions in Aquarius produce varicose veins, sprained ankles, irregularities of the heart action and dropsy.

♓ *Pisces* rules the feet and toes. It also has a reflex effect on the abdominal region governed by the opposite sign, Virgo, hence afflictions in this sign indicate trouble and deformities of the feet, intestinal diseases and dropsy. It also produces a desire for drink and drugs which may bring about delirium tremens. Consumption is sometimes found to be a secondary result of cold in the feet contracted by an afflicted Pisces.

Pathogenic Effects of the Sun

The Sun rules in the very first place the vital fluid which is specialized through the spleen, transferred to the solar plexus, and thence distributed over the whole body. This vital fluid is invisible to ordinary humanity, but to those gifted with the spiritual sight it appears as a rose-colored fluid which is like the electricity in the wires of a telephone or telegraph system. When the wires designed to carry electricity are minus the electric fluid they are dead and the telephone or telegraph instruments do not respond. Similarly, when for some reason the invisible vital fluid ceases to flow through any part of the human organism in sufficient quantity, that part of the body will not perform its proper function, and therefore disease results, continuing until some obstruction has been removed and the path cleared for the vital fluid. On that account an afflicted Sun always causes disease, particularly in a man's horoscope, and in a woman's nativity the Moon, which is the collector of solar forces, takes the same office or function. The heart and the *pons varolii,* or vital knot, situated in the brain, are the principal parts of the body ruled by the Sun. When the Sun is well aspected in Leo or Aries radiant health may be looked for. But on the other hand, when he is afflicted he produces the various ailments according to the sign wherein he is placed at the time. These disabilities may be set down as follows:

☉ ♈ *The Sun afflicted in Aries,* the sign which rules the head, gives a tendency to aphasia, loss of identity, brain fever, cerebral hæmorrhage, and meningitis, cerebral anæmia or congestion of the blood, faintings and headaches.

☉ ♉ *The Sun afflicted in Taurus* gives a tendency to quinsy, diphtheria, and polypus of the nose. In the Pleiades (Taurus 29°), eye trouble.

☉ ♊ *The Sun afflicted in Gemini* gives a tendency to pleurisy, bronchitis, and hyperaemia of the lungs.

☉ ♋ *The Sun afflicted in Cancer* gives a tendency to anemia, dropsy, dyspepsia, and gastric fever.

☉ ♌ *The Sun afflicted in Leo* gives a tendency to palpitation of the heart, backache, and spinal affections. In the Ascelli(Leo 6°), eye trouble.

♍︎ ⊙ *The Sun afflicted in Virgo* gives a tendency to interference with the assimilation, peritonitis, typhoid fever, and dysentery.

⊙ ♎︎ *The Sun afflicted in Libra* gives a tendency to Bright's disease and eruptions of the skin through overheated blood, for Saturn rules the skin and Libra is his exaltation sign.

⊙ ♏︎ *The Sun afflicted in Scorpio* gives a tendency to renal calculus, genito-urinary and menstrual disturbances, uterine and ovarian affections.

⊙ ♐︎ *The Sun afflicted in Sagittarius* gives a tendency to sciatica, paralysis of the limbs and pulmonary diseases. If the Sun is in Antares (Sagittarius 8°) and afflicted by one or more of the malefics there is danger of disease of the eyes.

⊙ ♑︎ *The Sun afflicted in Capricorn* gives a tendency to rheumatism, skin diseases, and digestive troubles.

⊙ ♒︎ *The Sun afflicted in Aquarius* gives a tendency to varicose veins, dropsy, palpitation of the heart, and poor circulation.

⊙ ♓︎ *The Sun afflicted in Pisces* gives a tendency to perspiration of the feet, also intestinal troubles, typhoid fever, et cetera.

Pathogenic Effects of Venus

On account of her rulership of Taurus and Libra, Venus is responsible for a number of affections of the throat and kidneys, also maladies due to gastronomical indiscretions, lack of exercise, sedentary habits, poor circulation of the venous blood, excess of amorous indulgence and dissolute living, hence she brings obesity, tumors, cysts, poor circulation, venereal diseases, tonsilitis, and various other disorders. Her general effect when placed in the twelve signs may be classed as follows:

♀ ♈ *Venus afflicted in Aries* gives a tendency to catarrh in the head, mucus, and, by reflex action in Libra congestion of the kidneys.

♀ ♉ *Venus afflicted in Taurus* gives a tendency to mumps, headaches affecting the occipital region, goitre, tonsilitis, and glandular swellings of the throat. By reflex action in Scorpio this also brings venereal diseases or other troubles peculiar to the genitals.

♀ ♊ *Venus afflicted in Gemini* gives a tendency to corrupt blood, pulmonary inefficiency, whitlows. warts, and dropsy.

♀ ♋ *Venus afflicted in Cancer* gives a tendency to distended stomach, gastric tumor, and nausea.

♀ ♌ *Venus afflicted in Leo* gives a tendency to spinal affections, backache and enlarged heart.

♀ ♍ *Venus afflicted in Virgo* gives a tendency to weakened peristaltic action of the intestines, tumors, tapeworm, and worms in children.

♀ ♎ *Venus afflicted in Libra* gives a tendency to uremia and polyuria; by reflex action in Aries, headaches.

♀ ♏ *Venus afflicted in Scorpio* gives a tendency to varicocele, venereal diseases, uterine prolapsis or tumors, painful menstruation and other female complaints, and by reflex action in Taurus, throat affections.

♀ ♐ *Venus afflicted in Sagittarius* gives a tendency to tumors and kindred diseases in the hips, and, by reflex action in Gemini, bronchial and pulmonary affections.

♀ ♑ *Venus afflicted in Capricorn* gives a tendency to gout in the limbs, and, by reflex action in Cancer, digestive troubles, nausea and vomiting.

♀ ♒ *Venus afflicted in Aquarius* gives a tendency to varicose veins, and, by reflex action in Leo, heart trouble.

♀ ♓ *Venus afflicted in Pisces* gives a tendency to tender feet, bunions, chilblains, gout, and, by reflex action in Virgo, abdominal tumors and intestinal disorders.

Pathogenic Effects of Mercury

Mercury rules Gemini and Virgo, therefore his afflictions manifest in diseases related to these signs. as bronchitis, pulmonary and respiratory troubles. He also rules the right cerebral hemisphere, the motor segment of the spinal cord, and the vocal cords, hence locomotor ataxia and nervous and vocal disorders are among his manifestations; so is deafness. The following effects may be noted when he is afflicted in the twelve signs:

☿ ♈ *Mercury afflicted in Aries* gives a tendency to brain fever, nervous headache, vertigo, neuralgia, and, by reflex action in Libra, nervous disorders of the kidneys, and lumbago.

☿ ♉ *Mercury afflicted in Taurus* gives a tendency to stuttering, hoarseness and deafness, and by reflex action in Scorpio, nervous affections of the genito-urinary system.

☿ ♊ *Mercury afflicted in Gemini* gives a tendency to gout in head, arms, and shoulders, bronchitis. asthma, asphyxiation, pleurisy, and, by reflex action in Sagittarius, nervous pains in the hips.

☿ ♋ *Mercury afflicted in Cancer* gives a tendency to nervous indigestion, phlegm, flatulence, and drunkenness.

☿ ♌ *Mercury afflicted in Leo* gives a tendency to pain in the back, fainting, and palpitation of the heart.

☿ ♍ *Mercury afflicted in Virgo* gives a tendency to flatulence, wind colic, short breath, and nervous debility.

☿ ♎ *Mercury afflicted in Libra* gives a tendency to suppression of urine, renal paroxysms, lumbago, and, by reflex action in Aries, vertigo, nervous headaches and eye trouble.

☿ ♏ *Mercury afflicted in Scorpio* gives a tendency to pains in bladder and genitals, menstrual trouble, and, by reflex action in Taurus, stuttering or hoarseness and deafness.

☿ ♐ *Mercury afflicted in Sagittarius* gives a tendency to pain in the hips and thighs. By reflex action in Gemini, cough, asthma and pleurisy.

☿ ♑ *Mercury afflicted in Capricorn* gives a tendency to rheumatism, especially in the knees; pains in the back, skin diseases, melancholy; by reflex action in Cancer, nervous indigestion, flatulence.

☿ ♒ *Mercury afflicted in Aquarius* gives a tendency to shooting or gnawing pains in the whole body, varicose veins, corrupt blood and, by reflex action in Leo, palpitation, and neuralgia of the heart.

☿ ♓ *Mercury afflicted in Pisces* gives a tendency to gout in the feet, or they are tender and subject to cramp, or, by reflex action in Virgo, a general weakness, lassitude, worry, and sometimes tuberculosis, deafness.

Pathogenic Effects of the Moon

The Moon rules the œsophagus and stomach, the uterus and ovaries, the lymphatics and the sympathetic nervous system, the synovial fluid. When afflicted she produces dropsical and menstrual troubles, uterine and ovarian afflictions, dyspepsia, eye trouble, and lunacy, according to the sign, house and nature of the afflicting planet. She has particular rule over the mother during pregnancy.

☽ ♈ *The Moon afflicted in Aries* gives a tendency to insomnia, headache, lethargy, and weak eyes.

☽ ♉ *The Moon afflicted in Taurus* gives a tendency to sore throat, and if in Taurus 29° with the Pleiades and afflicted by Saturn, Mars, Uranus, or Neptune, eye trouble results; by reflex action in Scorpio, menstrual or other trouble with the genitals.

☽ ♊ *The Moon afflicted in Gemini* gives a tendency to catarrh of the lungs, asthma, bronchitis and pneumonia, rheumatism in the arms and shoulders.

☽ ♋ *The Moon afflicted in Cancer* gives a tendency to cancer of the stomach, dropsy, obesity, bloating, digestive troubles, and epilepsy.

☽ ♌ *The Moon afflicted in Leo* gives a tendency to backache, disturbed circulation, convulsions, and heart trouble; if in Leo 6°, eye trouble.

☽ ♍ *The Moon afflicted in Virgo* gives a tendency to disorders in the bowels, abdominal tumors, dysentery, and peritonitis.

☽ ♎ *The Moon afflicted in Libra* gives a tendency to Bright's disease, abscess of the kidneys, uræmia; by reflex action in Aries, headache or insomnia.

☽ ♏ *The Moon afflicted in Scorpio* gives a tendency to disturbed menses, bladder troubles, hydrocele, and other genito-urinary disturbances; by reflex action in Taurus, throat troubles.

☽ ♐ *The Moon afflicted in Sagittarius* gives a tendency to blood affections, hip disease, and, sometimes, a broken femur; by reflex action in Gemini, asthma.

☽ ♑ *The Moon afflicted in Capricorn* gives a tendency to articular rheumatism, lack of synovial fluid, eruptions of the skin, and, by reflex action in Cancer, digestive troubles.

☽ ♒ *The Moon afflicted in Aquarius* gives a tendency to varicose veins, ulcers of the leg, dropsy, and, by reflex action in Leo, hysteria, fainting, and heart trouble.

☽ ♓ *The Moon afflicted in Pisces* gives a tendency to drink, drug habits, tender feet, and, by reflex action in Virgo, abdominal disorders of various kinds.

Pathogenic Effects of Saturn

Saturn is the planet of obstruction, crystallization and atrophy. By his action the circulation or passage of bodily fluids, such as the blood, lymph, or urine, is impeded, and by this stagnation waste materials are retained instead of being eliminated. Thus they form various deposits in the body, building the skeleton, which is *constructive,* hardening the arteries and articulations, which is *destructive.* Saturn rules the gall bladder, where he forms the painful gallstones, and by virtue of his exaltation power in Libra he crystallizes the renal stones and gravel which cause such suffering to those who have these concretions. By retention of the urea he causes the painful rheumatism and gout which often manifest in deformity of the joints that so often disfigures and disables the sufferers therefrom. He rules the pneumogastric nerve, and by his restrictive action through that medium he may at any moment slow down the heart action, stop digestion, suppress the urine and stool under the emotions of fear and worry generated by him. Thus he has the power to bring every bodily function to a standstill.

Saturn also rules the teeth and the skin. By his action the teeth decay, leading to malnutrition, the synovial membranes are hardened, making the spine and limbs rigid; he makes the skin tough as the years go by. Saturn is at home in Capricorn, and by his reflex action in Cancer he interferes with the peristaltic action which is necessary in the digestion of food; he then causes antiperistalsis, or vomiting. His general activities in the body are destructive and tend to end the life of the organism.

Saturn generally hurts by falls, bruises, and colds. He predisposes to chronic and deep-seated ailments, and his victims are difficult to reach because he imbues them with fear, worry, and pessimism, so that they refuse to believe in the possibility of a cure and cannot be induced to take a cheerful look on life.

The presence of Saturn in any part of the horoscope constitutes an affliction in itself, therefore we may note the following effects in the twelve signs, whether he is aspected by squares, oppositions, trines or sextiles, but naturally his effects are somewhat more inimical when in evil aspect.

♄ ♈ *Saturn in Aries* gives a tendency to headache, colds, catarrh, deafness, and chills, cerebral anæmia, dental decay, tartar, faintings, and, by reflex action in Libra, renal disorders.

♄ ♉ *Saturn in Taurus* gives a tendency to phlegm, diphtheria, quinsy, mumps, croup, decay of the lower teeth, choking, and by reflex action in Scorpio, stricture, constipation and similar disorders.

♄ ♊ *Saturn in Gemini* gives a tendency to rheumatic pains in shoulders and arms, bronchitis, pulmonary consumption, asthma, and, by reflex action in Sagittarius, sciatica and hip diseases.

♄ ♋ *Saturn in Cancer* gives a tendency to pyorrhœa, dyspepsia, gastric ulcer and cancer, nausea and belching, scurvy, jaundice, gallstones, anæmia, and stricture of the œsophagus.

♄ ♌ *Saturn in Leo* gives a tendency to curvature of the spine, muscular inefficiency of the heart, weak back, arterio-sclerosis, and sclerosis of the spinal cord.

♄ ♍ *Saturn in Virgo* gives a tendency to weakened peristalsis of the intestines, abated absorption of chyle, obstruction of the *ileum caecum* and transverse colon, appendicitis.

♄ ♎ *Saturn in Libra* gives a tendency to locomotor ataxia, renal stones, gravel and sand, Bright's disease, suppression of urine, malnutrition, and, by reflex action in Aries, headache, toothache, and other disorders of the head.

♄ ♏ *Saturn in Scorpio* gives a tendency to sterility, suppression of the menses, stricture, constipation, hæmorrhoids and, by reflex action in Taurus, nasal catarrh, hoarseness, phlegm, and other throat affections.

♄ ♐ *Saturn in Sagittarius* gives a tendency to contusions of the hips and thighs, sciatica, gout, and hip disease; by reflex action in Gemini, bronchitis, tuberculosis, and other Gemini affections.

♄ ♑ *Saturn in Capricorn* gives a tendency to articular rheumatism, eczema, erysipelas, and other diseases of the skin; by reflex action in Cancer, jaundice, gallstones, and dyspepsia.

♄ ♒ *Saturn in Aquarius* gives a tendency to weak ankles, easily sprained, and, by reflex action in Leo, curvature of the spine, sclerosis and other affections of the heart, back and arteries.

♄ ♓ *Saturn in Pisces* gives a tendency to cold feet, rheumatism and bunions, also tuberculosis due to cold and wet feet, and, by reflex action in Virgo, dropsy.

Pathogenic Effects of Jupiter

The liver is the great center of the Jupiterian activity; there he forms glycogen from the waste products of the portal blood-stream. The great central vortex of the desire body is also in the liver, and when an extra effort is to be made, Mars draws upon the glycogen storehouse of Jupiter for fuel. Saturn too is active in the liver, forming the gall, urea, and uric acid.

It is somewhat difficult for the average student to segregate and combine the varied functions of this organ, but if we bear in mind that Cancer is the exaltation sign of Jupiter and the opposite sign Capricorn is the home of Saturn and the exaltation sign of Mars, we shall more readily understand that the great benefic, Jupiter, endeavors to store in the liver the glycogen so necessary to the bodily activity. This, Mars, the opposing exaltation ruler, recklessly scatters by expenditure of muscular energy, and he is aided and abetted in his destructive activities by Saturn, who produces gall and urea which he deposits during the muscular work as uric acid in the various parts of the body where it manifests as gout and rheumatism. Saturn also makes the liver torpid and causes constipation.

Jupiter rules the adrenals and arterial circulation, hence his afflictions cause formation of adipose tissue, fatty degeneration of muscles, tumors, and morbid growths, enlargement of organs, waste of sugar and albumen as in diabetes and kindred diseases. Blood-poisoning, hyperæmia and apoplexy are due to afflictions of Jupiter.

The following effects may be noted when Jupiter is afflicted in the twelve signs:

♃ ♈ *Jupiter afflicted in Aries* gives a tendency to dizziness, cerebral congestion, sleepiness, thrombosis, fainting, ulcerated gums of upper jaw, and, by reflex action in Libra, diabetes and depression due to lack of adrenal secretion.

♃ ♉ *Jupiter afflicted in Taurus* gives a tendency to gourmandize, hence plethora and apoplexy, ringworm and carbuncles follow; also ulcerated gums of mandible; by reflex action in Scorpio, catarrh of the nose and nosebleed.

♃♊ *Jupiter afflicted in Gemini* gives a tendency to pleurisy, blood affections, congestion of the lungs, pulmonary apoplexy; by reflex action in Sagittarius, broken bones, gout and rheumatism in hips and thighs.

♃♋ *Jupiter afflicted in Cancer* gives a tendency to gourmandize, causing dilation of the stomach, dyspepsia, liver complaints, jaundice, and dropsy; by reflex action in Capricorn, which rules the skin, pimples and similar eruptions.

♃♌ *Jupiter afflicted in Leo* gives a tendency to apoplexy and fatty degeneration of the heart, the valve action is weakened, the circulation sluggish at times and at other times there are palpitation and feverish conditions; by reflex action in Aquarius, swollen ankles.

♃♍ *Jupiter afflicted in Virgo* gives a tendency to enlarged liver, often ulcerated, jaundice.

♃♎ *Jupiter afflicted in Libra* gives a tendency to melancholy due to diminished adrenal secretion, renal abscess, diabetes, skin eruptions due to sluggish action of kidneys; by reflex action in Aries, congestion of brain, coma and vertigo.

♃♏ *Jupiter afflicted in Scorpio* gives a tendency to enlarged prostate gland, uterine tumors, urethral abscess, dropsy, hydræmia, excess of urates and strangury; by reflex action in Taurus, apoplexy and nosebleed.

♃ ♐ *Jupiter afflicted in Sagittarius* gives a tendency to rheumatism and gout; by reflex action in Gemini, pulmonary apoplexy and corrupt blood.

♃ ♑ *Jupiter afflicted in Capricorn* gives a tendency to various skin diseases, and, by reflex action in Cancer, digestive ailments, dropsy, jaundice, and fatty degeneration of the liver.

♃ ♒ *Jupiter afflicted in Aquarius* gives a tendency to milk-leg, swollen ankles, and, by reflex action in Leo, apoplexy and palpitation.

♃ ♓ *Jupiter afflicted in Pisces* gives a tendency to swollen, perspiring feet, and, by reflex action in Virgo, enlarged liver, abdominal tumors, jaundice, and diseased intestines.

Pathogenic Effects of Mars

The ancient Egyptian sages called Cancer the sphere of the soul, and when the mystic Sun of life goes through this moist, fruitful lunar sign the seed-atom of the ego's physical body is planted. While the embryonic body grows unconsciously as a plant grows, the mystic Sun of life passes through Leo, Virgo, and Libra. In the fourth month of gestation it passes through the second of the watery signs, Scorpio. Then the spirit dies to its heavenly home and is immured in its earthly prison house by Mars, who chains it with the silver cord and thus brings about the quickening. Then the Sun of life proceeds through Sagittarius, Capricorn, Aquarius, and when after the nine months have been completed it has passed through the last of the watery signs, Pisces, the flood-gates of the womb are opened and the ego is launched upon the sea of life under the auspices of the martial sign Aries, where the giver of life, the Sun, is exalted.

During the gestatory period Mars has given to the body iron, especially in the form of hæmoglobin, and with the first breath oxidation of this substance commences to produce the heat so necessary to life and consciousness. This operation is continued all through life, and thus to the Martian ray falls the important task of supplementing the Sun in the maintenance of the vital spark until the mystic Sun of life has completed its circle and reached the sign where the quickening took place. Then Scorpio gives the body its death-sting, Mars and his friend Saturn cut the silver cord, and the freed soul soars as an eagle into the empyrean seeking the celestial spheres which are its true home. Therefore Scorpio is symbolized both by a scorpion and an eagle.

On account of his mission as *aide* to the Sun in the maintenance of life, Mars ever aims to cleanse the body of filth and waste accumulation so that the fires of life may burn brightly, hence, when the gourmandizing habits of Jupiter and Venus have clogged the system, or the obstructive tendencies of Saturn have poisoned the body by stoppage of elimination,

Mars lights the fire of fever and inflammation to burn out the refuse and give the system a new lease on life and energy. Thus many of the pathogenic effects of Mars aim at a constructive end.

But Mars not only aids the vital process of the life-giving Sun, who is exaltation ruler of Aries; he is himself exaltation ruler of Capricorn, where Saturn, the planet of death, holds sway, and between those two thieves the Sun, the Lord of Life, is crucified, suffers and dies, while they part his physical garment. The role of Saturn in this process has been described in the appropriate chapter, and of Mars it may be said that by his recklessness he predisposes to accidents by burning, scalding, wounds, or gunshot. He rules the genitals through Scorpio, and depletes the vitality and causes genital disorders by passional excesses, hæmorrhage, rupture of blood vessels. Excessive menses and hæmorrhoids show his activities in the blood; hernia and contagious diseases are also manifestations of the martian ray. As Mars is a malefic, his presence in any sign or house constitutes an affliction in itself, regardless of his aspects, but naturally his pathogenic effects are worse when he is aspected by square or opposition than when he is fortified by sextile or trine.

His effects in the twelve signs may be more specifically stated as follows:

♂ ♈ *Mars in Aries* gives a tendency to sunstroke, cerebral hæmorrhages or congestion, inflammation of the brain, brain fever and delirium, shooting pains in the head, insomnia, and wounds in the head; by reflex action in Libra, inflammation of the kidneys, renal hæmorrhage and renal calculi.

♂ ♉ *Mars in Taurus* gives a tendency to mumps, enlarged or inflamed tonsils, suffocation, adenoids, diphtheria, polypus and nosebleed, goitre, inflammation of the larynx; by reflex action in Scorpio, excessive menstrual flow, scalding urine, venereal ulcers, enlargement of the prostate gland and strangury.

♂ ♊ *Mars in Gemini* gives a tendency to hæmorrhage of the lungs, pneumonia, bronchitis, cough, wounds or fractures of hands, arms, and collarbone; by reflex action in Sagittarius, fractured femur, and sciatica.

♂ ♋ *Mars in Cancer* gives a tendency to milk-fever, inflammation, ulceration and hæmorrhage of the stomach, dyspepsia.

♂ ♌ *Mars in Leo* gives a tendency to muscular rheumatism in the back, overheating of the blood, enlargement of the heart and palpitation, pain in the heart, suffocation and fainting (*angina pectoris*), inflammation of the pericardium.

♂ ♍ *Mars in Virgo* gives a tendency to typhoid, inflammation of the bowels, peritonitis, worms, diarrhœa, cholera, and ventral hernia, appendicitis.

♂ ♎ *Mars in Libra* gives a tendency to inflammation of the kidneys, excess of urine, hæmorrhage of the kidneys, and renal stones; by reflex action in Aries, brain-fever, sunstroke, pains in the head.

♂ ♏ *Mars in Scorpio* gives a tendency to excessive menses, scalding urine, gravel, sand, and renal stones, inflammation and ulceration of the ovaries and uterus, also of the vagina and urethra, varicocele, enlargement of the prostate gland, stricture and strangury, venereal ulcers and hæmorrhoids; by reflex action in Taurus, inflamed tonsils or larynx and nosebleed.

♂ ♐ *Mars in Sagittarius* gives a tendency to fracture or dislocation of the femur, sciatica, and ulcers of the thighs; by reflex action in Gemini, pneumonia, bronchitis and coughs.

♂ ♑ *Mars in Capricorn* gives a tendency to carbuncles, erysipelas, smallpox, chicken pox, measles, pimples, itch and other eruptive or inflammatory skin diseases; by reflex action in Cancer, dyspepsia and ulcerated stomach.

♂ ♒ *Mars in Aquarius* gives a tendency to varicose veins, fracture of the leg and blood-poisoning; by reflex action in Leo, heart failure, overheated blood, fainting and palpitation.

♂ ♓ *Mars in Pisces* gives a tendency to deformities of the feet, or accidents to them, corns, bunions and perspiring feet; by reflex action in Virgo, ventral hernia, inflammation of the bowels and diarrhœa.

Pathogenic Effects of Uranus

Uranus rules the ether which is the medium by which the light rays are transmitted, hence he has considerable influence over the eyes and is responsible, when afflicting the Sun or Moon, for various diseases of the eyes, or even blindness. This is especially the case when the Sun or Moon is placed in the Pleiades (Taurus 29°), or the Ascelli (Leo 6°) or Antares (Sagittarius 8°).

Modern astrologers have not yet had time to tabulate the full effects of Uranus in all the signs, and as for the pathogenic effects still less is known, but he is said to be exalted in Scorpio and our own experience seems to indicate that Uranus has a very marked evil influence on the sex which is ruled by this sign, producing most deep-seated venereal diseases. By reflex action or affliction to planets in Taurus (ruled by Venus) where the organ of coordinated action is located, he produces erratic movements, as seen in St. Vitus dance, contortions, spasms, tetanus, cramps, hiccough and hysteria.

As ruler of the ether and gases he is responsible for injury and shock by electricity which travels through the ether. Nitrogen, a gas, is the base of a number of compounds whose characteristic Uranian instability makes them highly explosive, and Uranus is thus responsible for such deaths and injuries as occur on that account, especially if placed in the Eighth House.

♅ ♉ *Uranus in Taurus* gives a tendency to diminished pituitary secretion and consequent abnormal growth.

♅ ♊ *Uranus in Gemini* gives a tendency to spasmodic asthma, colds, and a dry, hard cough.

♅ ♋ *Uranus in Cancer* gives a tendency to hiccough, produced by the erratic action of the diaphragm, also to a hard, dry stomach cough and cramp of the stomach, gas and flatulence.

♅ ♌ *Uranus in Leo* gives a tendency to palpitation, spasmodic heart action, spinal meningitis and infantile paralysis; by reflex action from Aquarius similar effects are now observable

♅ ♍ *Uranus in Virgo* gives a tendency to flatulence, and abdominal cramps.

♅ ♎ *Uranus in Libra* gives a tendency to intermittent action of the kidneys and venereal eruptions of the skin; by reflex action in Aries, sudden and violent headaches, shooting pains in the head, and hallucinations.

♅ ♏ *Uranus in Scorpio* gives a tendency to miscarriages, abortions, and venereal diseases, and in the Fifth House he causes painful and difficult parturition, generally involving the use of instruments and often the infant is severely or fatally injured or stillborn.

♅ ♑ *Uranus in Capricorn* usually works by reflex action in Cancer, but as the children with this position are still young (this is written in 1918) the full effects are as yet unknown.

Pathogenic Effects of Neptune

Neptune, the octave of Mercury, works principally upon the nervous system (ruled by Mercury) and at times produces frenzy where the person is beside himself on account of religious or other excitement. At other times he produces lethargy, coma, catalepsy, trance or mediumship, where the bodily energies are in abeyance while the psychic powers are in a state of hyperactivity. He rules the spinal canal, which is filled with ether during life. (It is true that surgeons tap it and draw out a fluid, but they may also draw water from a steam boiler because the steam condenses to water). This luminous gas is called *the spinal spirit fire* by occultists, and by vibrating the pineal gland, also ruled by Neptune, spiritual sight is produced, but it depends upon the rate and pitch of these vibrations what the person sees. By prayer, concentration and meditation, a state of religious ecstasy may be produced where he sees the celestial hosts, or if a lower rate of supernormal vibration is produced by drink or drugs he sees demoniac shapes as related by sufferers of delirium, which is due to Neptune, especially in the watery sign Pisces. The pathogenic influence of Neptune is most evil in the Sixth House (or the sixth sign, Virgo) indicating disease, or in the Twelfth House (or the twelfth sign, Pisces) which governs sorrow, trouble and self-undoing. If these two houses are occupied by Taurus and Scorpio, the signs ruling the throat and genitals, there is an abnormal and perverted passional desire which gives a tendency to self-abuse and perversion of a still worse nature. The mind, ruled by Mercury, the lower octave of Neptune, is morbid in its brooding upon unsavory subjects, and parents with children having Neptune in the Sixth or Twelfth Houses will do well to watch them carefully, especially if Neptune is in opposition to Uranus; that covers a number of those who are now, in 1918, reaching puberty, for Neptune has been going through the psychic sign Cancer while Uranus was in the opposite sign Capricorn.

We have found that Neptune square Saturn and Jupiter brought mental disturbances; Neptune conjunction Mars in Aries, square Uranus and the Moon in Cancer caused temporary instability of a periodic nature; Neptune conjunction Moon square Uranus caused spirit control. We have also seen many other indications, but the full effects of Neptune have not yet been systematically observed. We are working to that end, however, and hope in future years to be able to present a fairly full tabulation.

THF DUCTLESS GLANDS

Their Role and Rulers

It is well known to the esoteric astrologer that the human body has an immense period of evolution behind it and that this splendid organism is the result of a slow process of gradual upbuilding which is still continuing and will make each generation better than the previous until in some far distant future it shall have reached a stage of completion of which we cannot even dream. It is also understood by the deeper students that in addition to the physical body man has finer vehicles which are not yet seen by the great majority of human beings, though all have within them latent a sixth sense whereby they will in time cognize these finer sheaths of the soul. The occultist speaks of these finer vehicles as the *vital body,* made of ether, and the *desire body,* made of desire stuff, the material whence we draw our feelings and emotions, and with the addition of the *sheath of mind* and the physical body these complete what may be termed the personality which is the evanescent part distinct from the immortal spirit that uses these vehicles for its expression. These finer vehicles interpenetrate the dense physical body as air permeates water and have particular dominion over certain parts thereof, because the physical body itself is a crystallization of these finer vehicles in the same manner and upon the same principle that the soft fluids of a snail's body gradually crystallize into the hard and flinty shell which it carries upon its back. For the purpose of this dissertation we may say broadly that the softer parts of our bodies which we commonly call flesh may be divided into two kinds, glands and muscles. The vital body was started in the Sun Period. Crystallization from that time on in that vehicle has developed what we now call glands and to this day they and the blood are the special manifestations of the vital body within the physical vehicle, and therefore the glands as a whole may be said to be under the rule ot the life-giving Sun and the great benefic, Jupiter. For it is the function of the vital body to build and restore the tone of the muscles when tense and tired by the work imposed upon them by the restless desire body which was started in the Moon Period. The muscles are therefore ruled by the wandering Moon, which is the present vantage point of the angels, the humanity of the Moon Period, and by the impulsive and turbulent Mars, where the so-called "Fallen Angels," the Lucifer spirits, dwell; that is to say as a whole, for the student must carefully note that individual glands and particular groups of muscles are under the rulership of other planets as well. It is as when we say that all who live within the United States of America are citizens of that country, but some are subject to the laws of California, others to those of Maine.

We know the Hermetic axiom, "*As above, so below,*" which is the master key to all mysteries, and as there are upon the earth, the macrocosm, a great many undiscovered places, so also in the microcosm of the body do we find unknown countries that are a closed book to the scientific explorers. Chief among them has been a small group of the so-called "ductless glands," seven in number, namely:

The *Pituitary Body,* ruled by Uranus.
The *Pineal Gland,* ruled by Neptune.
The *Thyroid Gland,* ruled by Mercury.
The *Thymus Gland,* ruled by Venus.
The *Spleen,* ruled by the Sun.
The two *Adrenals,* ruled by Jupiter.

They have a great and particular interest for occultists, and they may be termed in a certain sense "the seven roses" upon the Cross of the body, for they are intimately connected with the occult development of humanity. Four of them, the Thymus Gland, the Spleen and the two Adrenals, are connected with the personality. The Pituitary Body and the Pineal Gland are particularly correlated with the spiritual side of our nature and the Thyroid Gland forms the link between. The astrological rule over these seven glands is as follows:

The Spleen is the entrance gate of the solar forces specialized by each human being and circulated through the body as the vital fluid, without which no being can live. This organ is therefore governed by the Sun. The two Adrenals are under the rulership of Jupiter, the great benefic, and exert a calming, quieting and soothing effect when the emotional activities of the Moon and Mars or Saturn have destroyed the poise. When the obstructive hand of Saturn has awakened the melancholy emotions and laid its restraint upon the heart, the Adrenals' secretions are carried by the blood to the heart and act as a powerful stimulant in its effort to keep up the circulation, while the Jovial optimism struggles against the Saturnine worries or against the impulse of Mars, which stirs the desire body into turbulent emotions of anger, rendering the muscles tense and trembling, dissipating the energy of the system; then the secretion of the Adrenals comes to the rescue, releasing the glycogen of the liver in a more abundant measure than usual to cope with the emergency until the equipoise has been again attained, and similarly during whatever other stress or strain. It was the knowledge of this occult fact that prompted the ancient astrologers to place the kidneys under the rulership of Libra, the Balance, and in order to avoid confusion of ideas we may say the kidneys themselves play an important part in the nutrition of the body, being under the rulership of Venus, the Lady of Libra, but Jupiter governs the Adrenals, with which we are now particularly engaged.

Both Venus and her higher octave, Uranus, govern the functions of nutrition and growth, but in different ways and for different purposes. Therefore Venus rules the Thymus Gland, which is the link between the parents and the child until the latter has reached puberty. This gland is located immediately behind the sternum or breast bone; it is largest in ante-natal life and through childhood while growth is excessive and rapid. During that time the vital body of the child does its most effective work, for the child is not then subject to the passions and emotions generated by the desire body after that comes to birth at or about the fourteenth year. But during the years of growth the child cannot manufacture the red blood corpuscles as does the adult, for the unborn, unorganized desire body does not then act as an avenue for the martian forces which assimilate the iron from the food and transmute it into hæmoglobin. To compensate for this lack there is stored in the Thymus Gland a spiritual essence drawn from the parents, who are symbolized by Venus, the ruler, and with this essence provided by the love of the parents the child is able to accomplish the alchemistry of blood temporarily until its desire body becomes dynamically active. Then the Thymus Gland atrophies and the child draws from its own desire body the necessary martian force. From that time, under normal conditions, Uranus, the octave of Venus, and ruler of the Pituitary Body, takes charge of the function of growth and assimilation in the following manner:

It is well known that all things, our food included, radiate from themselves continuously small particles which give an index of the thing whence they emanate, its quality included. Thus when we lift the food to our mouth a number of these invisible particles enter the nose and by excitation of the olfactory tract convey to us a knowledge of whether the food we are about to take is suitable for this purpose or not, the sense of smell warning us to discard such foods as have a noxious odor, etc. But besides those particles which attract or repel us from food by their action upon the olfactory tract through the sense of smell, there are others which penetrate the sphenoid bone, impinge upon the Pituitary Body and start the Uranian alchemistry by which a secretion is formed and injected into the blood. This furthers assimilation through the chemical ether, thus affecting the normal growth and well-being of the body through life. Sometimes this Uranian influence of the Pituitary Body is eccentric and therefore responsible for strange and abnormal growths which produce the unfortunate freaks of nature we occasionally meet.

But besides being responsible for the spiritual impulses which generate the before-mentioned physical manifestations of growth, Uranus, working through the Pituitary Body, is also responsible for the spiritual phases of growth which aid awakened man in his efforts to penetrate the veil into the Invisible Worlds. In this work it is, however, associated with Neptune, the ruler of the Pineal Gland,

and it will therefore be necessary, in order to properly elucidate, that we study the functions of the Thyroid Gland, ruled by Mercury, and of the Pineal Gland which is under the domination of his higher octave, Neptune, simultaneously.

That the Thyroid Gland is under the rule of Mercury, the planet of reason, is readily realized when we understand the effect which the degeneration of this gland has upon the mind, as shown in the diseases of Cretinism and Myxedema. The secretions of this gland are as necessary to the proper functioning of the mind as ether is to the transmission of electricity, that is to say, upon the physical plane of existence where the brain transmutes thought into action. Contact with and expression in the invisible worlds depends upon the functional ability of the Pineal Gland, which is altogether spiritual in function, and is therefore ruled by the octave of Mercury, Neptune, the planet of spirituality. But Neptune operates in conjunction with the Pituitary Body ruled by Uranus, the planet of wisdom, as has already been stated.

Scientists have wasted much time in speculation upon the nature and function of these two little bodies, the Pituitary Body and the Pineal Gland, but without avail, and principally because, as Mephistopheles says so sarcastically to the young man who wants to study science under Faust:

"Who e'er would know and treat of aught alive
Seeks first the living spirit thence to drive;
Then are the lifeless fragments in his hand;
He lacks, alas! *the vital spirit band.*"

No one can really and truly observe the physiological functions of any organ under such conditions as exist in the laboratory, on the operating table, or in the dissection or vivisection chamber. To arrive at an adequate understanding one must necessarily see these organs exercising their physiological functions *in the living body,* and that can only be done by means of the spiritual sight. There are a number of organs which are either atrophying or developing; the former show the path we have already traveled during our past evolution, the latter are finger-posts, indicating our future development. But there is still another class of organs which are neither degenerating nor evolving; they are simply dormant at the present time. Physiologists believe that the Pituitary Body and the Pineal Gland are atrophying because they find these organs more developed in some of the lowest classes of life, such as worms, but as a matter of fact they are wrong in their ideas; these organs are only dormant. Some have also suspected that the Pineal Gland is in some way connected with the mind, because it contains certain crystals after death, and the quantity was much less in those who were mentally defective than in people of normal mentality. This conclusion is right, but the Seer knows that the spinal canal of the living is not filled with *fluid;* that the blood is not *liquid,* and that these organs have no *crystals* in them when the body is alive; these assertions are made with full knowledge of the fact that the blood and the spinal essence are liquid when drawn out of the physical body, living or dead, and the contents of the Pituitary Body and the Pineal Gland *appear* crystalline when the brain is dissected; but the reason is similar to that which causes steam drawn from a steam boiler to condense immediately upon contact with the atmosphere, and molten metal drawn from a smelter's furnace to crystallize immediately upon withdrawal therefrom.

All these substances are purely spiritual essences when inside the body; they are then ethereal and the substance in the Pineal Gland, when seen by the spiritual sight, appears as *light.* Furthermore, when one Seer looks upon the Pineal Gland of another who is then also exercising his spiritual faculties, this light is of a most intense brilliancy and of an irridescence similar to but transcending in beauty the most wonderful play of the Northern Lights, the *Aurora Borealis,* ever witnessed by the writer, and he has seen them many times. It may also be said that the function of this organ seems to have changed in the course of human evolution. During the earlier epochs of our present stay upon the earth, when man's body was a large, baggy thing into which the spirit had not yet entered, but was there only as an overshadowing presence, there was an opening in the top and the Pineal Gland was within it; it was then an organ of orientation, giving a sense of direction. As the human body condensed, it became less and less able to endure the intense heat which prevailed during that time and the Pineal Gland gave warning when the body was brought too near one of the many craters and active volcanoes which were then erupting the thin earth crust, thus enabling the spirit to guide it away from these dangerous places. It was an organ of direction which operated by feeling, but feeling has since been distributed over the skin of the whole body, and this is an indication to the occultist that some day the senses of hearing and sight will also be similarly distributed so that we shall both see and hear with our whole body and thus become still more sensitive in those respects than we are now.

Since then the Pineal Gland and the Pituitary Body have become temporarily dormant to make man oblivious to the invisible world while he learns the lessons afforded by the material world; but the Pituitary Body has manifested the Uranian influence sporadically in abnormal physical growth, producing freaks and monstrosities of various kinds, while Neptune, working also abnormally through the Pineal Gland, has been responsible for the abnormal spiritual growth of medicine men, witches and mediums of spirit controls. When they are awakened to normal activities these two ductless glands will open the door to the inner worlds in a sane and safe manner, but in the meantime the Thyroid Gland, ruled by

Mercury, the planet of reason, holds the secretion necessary to give the brain balance.

In the future the ductless glands are destined to play a prominent role; their development will accelerate evolution greatly, for their effects are mainly mental and spiritual. We are now nearing the Aquarian Age; the Sun is therefore beginning to transmit the highly intellectual vibrations of this sign which accounts for the intuitions, premonitions and telepathic transmission now so prevalent. In the final analysis these phenomena are due to the awakening of the Pituitary Body, ruled by Uranus, the lord of Aquarius, and every passing year will make them more manifest.

CHAPTER XXX.

Thirty-Six Example Horoscopes

IN ORDER to further aid the student of the stellar science we present a number of horoscopes of people who have come to us for help in their trouble. We therefore know these cases to be authentic and trust that our delineation of their various ailments by means of astro-diagnosis may prove a true guide.

We have made an attempt at classification of these horoscopes, but as there are generally symptoms of several diseases in each horoscope it has been impossible to draw hard and fast lines in the grouping, and the student will therefore have to rely mainly on the headlines for indications of what the figure shows.

The first 22 horoscopes are found on pp. 624-634.

The last 14 figures are attached to their respective readings.

Sex as a Factor in Disease

It is our earnest conviction, that the less we dwell upon sex, the less we read about it and think about it, the purer we shall be mentally, and also less liable to danger of morbid habits, for these are often formed by overstudy of the sex question, and persons having a tendency in that direction should be discouraged in attempts to discuss the matter at all. In planning this chapter we had at one time thought it possible to escape mention of the subject, but more mature thought based upon much study of health and disease from the mystical standpoint has convinced us that we must go back to the allegorical Garden of Eden for the starting-point of pain and sorrow, as fully explained in our literature. The effects of continued transgression are with us today as a matter of actual fact, abuse of sex is in the most literal sense the primal source of sorrow, disease and degeneracy under which the world is groaning, and in a work of this nature it is obligatory to show the causes so that the remedy may be found and applied. Therefore we shall attempt to show the prenatal influences revealed by the horoscope as a warning to parents that marriage is a sacrament, and not a license to sex abuse, and that "the sins of the fathers are indeed visited upon the children." At the same time, of course, an innocent child is not born with the tendency to a certain disease, its former living has made it liable to a specific weakness, and for that reason it is drawn by the Law of Association to parents from whom it may obtain a body subject to that particular ailment. Thus parents are only instruments in fulfilling the self-made destiny of the child. If we thoroughly realize that fact, and can be persuaded to live pure and wholesome lives, so that we may draw to ourselves souls of a kindred virtuous nature, how much better for all the world. To drive this point home, the writers undertake to paint the loathsome picture of degeneracy, that the picture of purity may be the more attractive by contrast.

In this connection we present first figure No. 1, which is that of a boy, in 1912 about 16 years of age. The Fourth and Tenth Houses, the planets in them and their rulers show the parents. The parent who most influences the life is shown by the Tenth House configurations, and the Fourth House indicates the one least concerned in the child's destiny.

In this figure Gemini is on the Midheaven, and Mercury, its ruler, is square the Moon from cardinal signs. Neptune is conjunction Mars in the Tenth House and square the Sun in the mercurial sign Virgo. This establishes well the morbid, neurotic nature of the father, and his instrumentality in depriving the boy of the faculty of speech and of coordination of muscular movements; the boy cannot walk, but staggers.

The mother's part is described by Sagittarius on the Fourth House. Jupiter, the ruler is in Leo in conjunction with the Dragon's Tail, (the Moon's Western Node), which has an influence similar to Saturn. It is also square to Saturn and Uranus, these being in conjunction in Scorpio. This describes her as being a lewd woman; degenerate, committed to the dreadful theory of soul-mates, affinities, free love and all kindred abuses. These lewd tendencies she imparted to the boy. The affliction to Leo affects the heart, and as Saturn is the embodiment of obstruction, restraint and suppression, we may know that the heart action is very weak, (had the affliction come from Mars his dynamic energy would have caused palpitation). Scorpio has rule over the sex organ, Uranus and Saturn there give tendency to self-abuse, and on the well known principle that mutilation of that organ affects the voice, we have in this configuration an added reason for the poor boy's inability to speak. The affliction coming from fixed signs shows the deep rooted constitutional nature of the evil, and what may come of conception during a drunken debauch.

The Guardian of the Threshold

Horoscope No. 2 shows one of the most remarkable psychic conditions we have ever come across. Its portents in some respects are plain to any astrologer, but investigation by one of the writers into this person's past life adds sidelights and gives depth to the meaning of configurations not otherwise obtainable; also to the writer, who made the spiritual investigation two years before the horoscope was cast, it was a revelation to note how the mystic facts he remembered so well, were inscribed in this little wheel of life. To enable the student to properly appreciate the remarkable case we relate the story of how we came into connection with the person, what we attempted to do, and what actually happened.

In the fall of 1910, a friend told us the sad case of a young boy confined to his bed, lying upon his stomach and elbows, persistently gazing at a certain spot in a corner of the room, as if fascinated, his whole frame continually shaking with sobs and moans. At request of the friend we visited the unfortunate boy, and found that the object which drew his gaze, with a power similar to that whereby the snake charms a bird into its fangs, was an elemental of the most horrible type we have ever seen. Standing by the bedside we directed a stream of force towards the base of the poor victim's brain, and thus drew him towards us in an endeavor to break the spell, but the fiend held the consciousness charmed to such a degree that there was evident danger of rupture of body and soul. We therefore desisted, and, with the fearlessness born of inexperience, decided to fight the elemental upon his own plane of being. But the Elder Brother who is our Mentor sought us that evening; he advised caution, and investigation of the genesis of the monster before we took action.

Research of the memory of nature developed the fact that in its last life the spirit embodied in the youth had been an initiate of the Order of Jesus, a Jesuit, and a zealot of the most ardent type, cruel and unfeeling in the highest degree, yet perfectly impersonal, with no other aim in life save to further the interests of his Holy Order. The health, wealth, reputation or life of others he sacrificed without qualm of conscience, so that the order was benefited;

he would have offered himself up as freely, for he was sincere to the core. Love was as foreign to his nature as hate, but sex was rampant; it tore his strong soul to shreds, yet it never mastered him; he was too proud to show his passion even to one who could have gratified it, and so he developed the secret habit. It must not be supposed that he became an abject slave in that respect; he, the immortal spirit, fought his lower nature by prayer, castigations, fastings and every other conceivable means; sometimes he thought he had conquered, but when he least expected it the beast in him rallied, and the war waged as fiercely as ever. Many times he was tempted to mutilate himself, but he scorned such a course as unworthy a man, especially when that man had taken the vows of priesthood. At last he succumbed to the strain; vigorous manhood was succeeded by a middle age of delicate health, constant pain increased his mental anguish and sympathy was born of suffering; he was no longer indifferent to the tortures of victims of the Holy Office. Being by nature a zealot and enthusiast in whatever direction his energies were exerted, the pendulum soon swung to the other extreme, Paul-like, he fought to protect whom he had previously persecuted, he incurred the enmity of the Holy Office, and finally, broken in body, but dauntless of spirit he fell a victim to the torture to which he had subjected so many.

By the sincerity of his nature, and his later life he earned the right of admission to a Mystery School and prepared for the privilege of working as an Invisible Helper in future lives. The Law of Association drew him to birth in an American family who were former friends, and from them he received a nervous organization tuned to the high pitch required for his experience.

Saturn opposes the life-giving Sun, suppresses the nervous energy of Mercury, and obstructs the Venus (venous) circulation, by hindering secretion of urine and elimination of poisonous matter through the kidneys which are ruled by Libra, the sign of Saturn's exaltation where he is placed in this natal figure. As the planets which he opposes are placed in Aries, ruler of the head, his disordering influence manifests through the brain and mind, as well as the genito-urinary system. The morbid condition of these parts caused by Saturn's repressive influence on the kidneys is further accentuated by Uranus conjunction the Moon in the Sixth House which indicates the health, under the sign ruling the generative organs, Scorpio. As the horoscope shows tendencies resulting from our actions in past lives, it is evident that the self-abuse of this person must bring him to birth under a stellar ray affecting the health in that particular manner, for when the soul has been over come by any particular besetting sin in any life, death does not pay all any more than removal to another city pays our debts in our present abode. When we return, temptation will again confront us until we conquer our weakness. It is the task of this poor soul to extract the essence of virtue and chastity from the burning embers of passion and secret vice. May God help him and strengthen his arm in the terrible combat. Only Astrology, the Master Key of Compassion, can adequately reveal to us the struggle and anguish of the soul, and save us from the crime of despising one in conditions of depravity.

The before-mentioned aspects were from Cardinal and Fixed signs, which indicate that which is almost unalterable destiny. But Neptune on the Ascendant, in a Common sign, Gemini, points to a condition in the making. He is trine to Saturn, the afflicter of the mind, and supported by the dynamic energy of Mars.

Neptune indicates the invisible spiritual hierarchies which work with and upon us, and when placed in the Twelfth House it is evident that sorrow and distress may be expected from them. This position renders the person liable to be preyed upon by spirit controls, but the trine to Saturn and the sextile to the Sun, Venus and Mercury protect him against influence from outside sources. Thus he became a prey to the demoniac embodiment of his former actions, the terrible creature known to mystics as "Guardian of the Threshold," which the neophyte must pass ere he can enter consciously into the Invisible World. This dreadful shape had drawn its being from acts of cruelty committed by the man in his bygone life; it had fed upon the curses of his tortured victims, and gorged itself upon the odor of their blood and perspiration, as is the wont of elementals; it was a monster in every sense of the word. Death of its progenitor rendered it latent, but in the new birth figure time was marked for retribution upon the clock of destiny. When the Moon by progression reached Mars' natal place in the Twelfth House, his dynamic energy galvanized the monster into new life, and the troubles of the poor lad had commenced. The hate, anger and malice stored in the monster radiated back upon him pang for pang and his negative Gemini nature crumpled under the onslaughts of the demon. When we saw the thing it appeared as a shapeless jellylike mass with many large greenish eyes imbedded at different parts of its body. Every few seconds a sharp pointed, swordlike projection shot out from the most unexpected places in its body and pierced the poor lad who lay cringing upon his bed. Then, although the monster had no mouth, wherewith to laugh, it seemed convulsed with fiendish glee at the fear and pain it had given. At other times, one or another of the eyes seemed to dart from the monster,projected upon what resembled an elephant's trunk and it would halt within an inch of the victim's eyes, gazing into them with a compelling power of awesome intensity.

There being so many good aspects to help him, it is not likely that he will succumb, and when the Sun reaches conjunction of Jupiter's place in the natal figure and the Moon has passed the square to the Sun's natal place, a distinct turn for the better may be looked for. In the meanwhile the poor soul must struggle alone with its self-made demon. Had not the secret habit sapped vitality in the former life, birth under a stronger sign would have given greater power of physical endurance and rendered victory more certain.

Disease of the Eyes

This malady is due to rays from certain nebulous parts of the Zodiac; the Pleiades in Taurus 29, the Ascelli in Leo 6, and Antares in Sagittarius 8. When the Sun or Moon is in orb of one of these places, and afflicted by Saturn, Mars or Uranus, or vice versa, when Saturn, Uranus or Mars is in these nebulous parts afflicting the Sun or Moon, trouble is indicated, but if care is taken in the case of children having this tendency to disease it may be greatly modified or entirely avoided. The light in schoolrooms calls for attention on general principles, but where a child has incipient eye trouble the parent ought to request proper placement of the child in a modified light; reading by lamplight or in the dusk should not be permitted, and window shades in the home ought to be of a soothing color. With civilization and life in cities the eyes have become habituated to short focus and cannot quickly adjust themselves to variation of range as can those of sailors and plainsmen. When a child's horoscope indicates weak eyes, residence in a rural district, if possible, may be of immense value in preserving the vision, for exercise of the eye muscles by frequent adjustment of focus from short to long range, and vice versa, will materially aid to strengthen the eyes. It is a fact, that much eye strain is due to congestion of the ciliary muscle, which adjusts the lens to range of objects, and of the muscle which contracts the iris. Each time the latter fails to act quickly too much light enters and the retina is hurt. Life in the open while the child's muscles are still limber will do wonders towards correcting such defects, and even grown persons may derive vast benefit from outdoor life provided the eyes are properly shaded at first. Careful osteopathic treatment of the eyes has also a most beneficial effect of stimulating circulation and limbering the muscles.

Subtile Indications of Spiritual Sight

It is a well known scientific fact, that sensation depends on ability to feel and interpret vibration in air and ether, according to the sense involved. Ancient seers devised the Staff of Mercury as a symbol of its effects, and among other spiritual secrets embodied in the undulating forms of the twin serpents, is also this, that Mercury is the originator of all vibratory movement. Hence he is a prime factor in production of sensation and mental processes arising in the consciousness as a result. An elevated, well aspected Mercury therefore makes our senses acute and the mind keen; an afflicted Mercury either dulls the senses, or makes the person hypersensitive; in either case an abnormal state of the brain mind is produced which causes suffering according to house, sign and affliction; even a good aspect of a so-called evil planet, though it brings out the virtue of that planet, also carries with it a touch of the darker side because even the best of us have something in our inner natures which vibrates to that phase of the planet's nature.

But, besides this roundabout way of acquiring knowledge through vibrations in the air and ether inaugurated by Mercury and interpreted by slow processes in the brain mind where spirit and matter meet, *there is a direct path to knowledge* symbolized by the staff around which the serpents twine. This is the ray of Neptune, the octave of Mercury, which puts us in touch with the spiritual worlds. But, observe this, the staff and the serpents are not separate, the staff goes *through* the winding forms of the serpents, and thus we learn that in our present condition spiritual knowledge is dependent on the brain mind for concrete expression, and through the brain mind the latter is colored according to the aspects of Neptune.

Experience has proved that the afflicted stellar ray from certain parts of the Zodiac already mentioned, interferes with the etheric vibration sensed by the retina of the eye, and thus impairs the physical sight. If, in the same figure, Neptune is focused through one of these places, the so-called "blind spot," which is *blind* because unresponsive to the etheric mercurial vibrations is sensitized by the spiritual ray of Neptune, and thus it may be that a person physically near sighted, or even blind, may view the spiritual worlds hidden from people whose sight is focused by mercurial vibrations. The aspect of Neptune determines the grade and nature of the spiritual sight evolved, as illustrated in various horoscopes herewith. These were picked to demonstrate other points, but it occurred to us that the phase just mentioned is worthy of notice. It may be well, however, to warn students against absurd conclusions; we do not say that everyone afflicted with eye trouble by Antares, Ascelli or the Pleiades is gifted in return with spiritual sight. The woman in horoscope No. 5 is much afflicted physically, but Neptune is out of orb, and she derives no vision from his ray. Spiritual vision may also be undeveloped in many who have the aspect well defined, but in those cases it is in process of unfoldment, and will yield *easily* to proper exercises. Where this aspect is a square or opposition it is wise, however, to refrain from any attempt to seek illumination, for in those aspects lurk great danger from spirit controls, elementals, etc., which is amply illustrated in horoscope No. 2, where the opposition of Neptune to Antares is responsible for the awful vision of the Guardian of the Threshold. There the physical sight is not impaired, but in horoscope No. 3, defective eyesight is shown by affliction from the Ascelli and like trouble comes from Antares in No. 4. In one the trine from Neptune produces voluntary vision of the super-physical realms, but in the other his focus is square, hence the spiritual sight obtained is intermittent and not under control.

We have spoken of Mercury as originator of all sense vibrations, auditory, olfactory, visual, etc., and of Neptune as its octave; to forestall questions we may say that in the spiritual world separateness ceases, sensations merge, so that sound and sight, voice and vision are one. The Neptune ray carries both, but undeveloped seers suffering from the involuntary faculty, "see" or "hear" as it suits the entities which obtain admission to them through this ray.

Horoscope No. 3 shows the inimical influence of the nebulous spot in Leo 6, the Ascelli, on the sight. This dangerous degree was rising at birth with the Moon in close conjunction, and the Sun also in orb. Saturn in 24 degrees of Libra is just within orb of a square to the Sun in Leo 0 degrees, and as a result of these various afflictions the person is compelled to use bifocal glasses. There is a compensating advantage, however; Neptune in elevation and trine to the Ascelli (with Sun, Moon and Ascendant in orb), has endowed him with spiritual sight over which he has perfect control, as the student may readily see by examination of Mercury, the best fortified planet in the horoscope. Saturn, by sextile, from the sign of his exaltation,gives steadiness, persistence and concentration; Jupiter by trine from the house he rules, expands the mind, makes it religiously inclined and benevolent; Venus, by sextile, adds kindliness and love of beauty. Thus it is evident that in this horoscope the relation of Mercury and its octave, Neptune, to physical and spiritual expression of mind, is well illustrated. Neptune is most highly elevated and Mercury is most strongly aspected. Neither is afflicted, therefore he is not liable to hallucinations. but weighs his experiences in the scale of logic. Compare this horoscope with that of the poor young man afflicted by the Guardian of the Threshold (No. 2), where Neptune is in the Twelfth House in conjunction with Mars, and where Mercury is afflicted by the opposition of Saturn, all from Cardinal signs; contrast of the two figures will bring out some fine points,

In horoscope No. 5 we see the Moon in the Sixth House, about three degrees from Antares, and Saturn is in the Twelfth House within 4 degrees of an opposition to Antares, about 7 degrees from exact opposition to the Moon; thus his natal influence was minimized. Had the opposition been close or exact, blindness from birth would have been inevitable, but fortunately it was a weak aspect and the vision was not seriously affected until the Sun by progression entered the Twelfth House, passed the opposition to the Moon, then opposition to Antares and arrived at conjunction with Saturn. These points of contact in the horoscope marked crises in the disease of the eyes. Saturn being the afflicter, the nerves and muscles crystallized until sight of one eye was lost and the other eye is almost blind. In November, 1912, the Moon had progressed to the square of the Sun's place at birth. That was the final crisis which vivified the before-mentioned aspects. Neptune makes no aspect to the points of the Zodiac mentioned, hence the spiritual sight is deeply dormant.

Horoscope No. 4 is the most afflicted of all; the Dragon's Tail, the Sun and Antares are in conjunction. That alone is sufficiently severe; the condition is further aggravated, however, by a close square of Neptune and Mars to the Sun, and the affliction to the eyes is increased by a conjunction of Saturn with the Pleiades which occurs in the Twelfth House. Thus this horoscope shows the person then born to have very weak eyes, and as a matter of fact she can scarcely read even when holding book or paper a few inches from the eyes and using a magnifying glass; but the square of Neptune to Antares has opened her spiritual senses to a certain extent so that she hears spirit voices and at times has visions. These manifestations, being uncontrolled by her, are very unsatisfactory of course, but prove the effect of Neptune aspecting these points in the Zodiac.

The Dragon's "Head" and "Tail" (☊—☋)

As it has often been a sore puzzle to students what are the "Dragon's Head" and "Tail" (called the Moon's nodes in the ephemeris), and why one is supposed to be good and to further all that comes under its benefic ray, while the other is considered extremely evil, it may be well to show the reasonableness of the philosophy.

First, let us say for the information of students not versed in astronomical terms, that "nodes" are points where a planet, traveling in its orbit, crosses the Sun's path; as for instance, the earth does at the equinoxes. This is explained from both the astronomical and mystic sides in our *Simplified Scientific Astrology,* and also the revolution of the Moon's Nodes.

Speaking from the convenient geocentric viewpoint,the Sun crosses its eastern node each year at the vernal equinox, 50 seconds of space in advance of the point where it crossed the previous year; as the Sun travels 15 degrees per hour, 50 seconds of space are traversed in about 3 seconds of time.

The Moon rises about 50 minutes later each night; applying the same measure, 50 minutes of time correspond to about 3 minutes of space, and the Moon's nodes recede just that much every day.

Thus the Sun travels around the circle of the Zodiac in one year, but requires 27 times as many thousands (27,000 years), to complete the precessional circle of its nodes, the equinoctial points. The swift moving Moon circles the Zodiac in 27 days and its nodes make a full revolution in 1000 weeks or 19 years. (These figures are only approximate.)

In the case of the Sun the place where it crosses the earth's equator in the east is always regarded as the first point of Aries, no matter where in the constellations it falls because of precession. This procedure is perfectly justified because the life-giving qualities ascribed to the Sun in Aries are observable as soon as it has crossed the equator; then the seeds sprout, the mating season commences and the whole creation seems stirred by the solar ray to bring forth. Therefore astrologers say that the Sun is exalted in Aries, and Aries is understood to be the first 30 degrees from the equinoctial point, the eastern node of the Sun, where he crosses the equator at the vernal equinox.

On the same principle the western node of the Sun, the point where he leaves the northern hemisphere for the winter months, is called the first point of Libra, and Saturn, the planet of obstruction and suppression is here exalted; he is the reaper with his scythe, he mows down the fruits of the solar ray, he suppresses life and joy, the gladsome voices of our feathered friends are hushed in his presence, and the earth goes down to its wintry grave under his withering influence.

As the Moon gathers and reflects the solar light upon earth, this borrowed light is similar to the direct ray in certain respects; no matter where its eastern node (called the Dragon's Head), falls in the signs, the effect upon affairs wherewith it is connected by conjunction is like that of the Sun in Aries, which makes nature sing with joy; it furthers and accelerates personal matters in a most benevolent manner, it so to speak, oils the wheels of life in the particular department where it is conjoined with a planet. On the other hand, the Moon's western node, (called the Dragon's Tail), corresponds to Libra where Saturn is exalted and if in conjunction with a planet it exerts an influence of suppression and obstruction similar in effect to the chill blasts of winter ushered in by the saturnine exaltation.

Horoscope No. 6 shows its part in breaking the femur (thigh bone) of a woman. Its position in the Twelfth House indicates confinement; the square of the Sun from the Midheaven is a further natal affliction. In December, 1908, the full Moon was in exact conjunction, and Jupiter, ruler of the Sixth House (which shows sickness), was in exact square to the Dragon's Tail, also in exact opposition to her Sun. Thus indications of trouble were many. Sagittarius, which has dominion over the hips and thighs, occupies the Sixth House, so the femur was broken when the lady slipped on an icy pavement just outside her house. No. 4 shows the Dragon's Tail in conjunction with the Sun near the fixed star Antares which has an inimical influence on the sight, and the poor woman who is thus afflicted is in great danger of blindness.

The Moon's nodes are tabulated in our *Simplified Scientific Ephemeris,* the position being given for every day; their places at birth are found by simple proportion, and the diagram herewith will explain that these points are called the "Dragon's Head" and the "Dragon's Tail" because the paths of Sun and

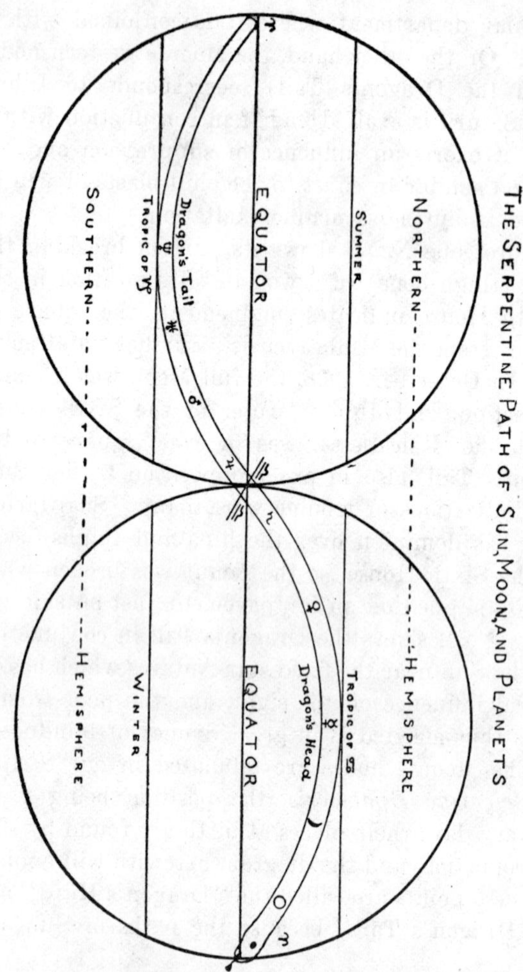
The Serpentine Path of Sun, Moon, and Planets
Northern- - - - - - - - - - - - - - - -Hemisphere
Summer
Tropic of ♋
Equator
Equator
Dragon's Tail
Dragon's Head
Tropic of ♑
Winter
Southern- - - - - - - - - - - - - - - -Hemisphere

planets appear serpentine when drawn upon a plane surface.

Disease of the Ears

The Twelfth House indicates the confining influences in life. Mercury there in conjunction with the Sun limits the spirit, and deafness hampers its search after knowledge. The same happens if Saturn, Mars, Uranus or Neptune afflict, also when the mercurial signs, Gemini or Virgo, are on the twelfth cusp and Mercury is afflicted, (no matter where in the figure it is placed). We append horoscopes of people who are suffering from this malady ;No. 7 is the horoscope of a woman who is gradually losing her hearing. Mercury, Venus and the Sun are in close conjunction in Pisces, the twelfth sign, which is in the Twelfth House. Blood, lymph, and the invisible vital fluid, called "nerve force" by science, are the builders of our bodies; each planet, except Uranus and Neptune, has dominion over one of their constituent parts.

☿ *Mercury* rules the nerves, particularly the cerebro-spinal system, and the invisible rose colored vital fluid which flows in the visible nerve sheath.

☽ *The Moon* also rules the nerves in a general way, but has special dominion over the nerve sheaths of the body, the sympathetic system and the lymph.

♃ *Jupiter* governs the arterial circulation.

♀ *Venus* rules the venous blood.

♂ *Mars* rules the iron in the blood.

☉ *The Sun* rules the oxygen.

♄ *Saturn* has dominion over the mineral deposits carried by the blood, which causes the arteries and other parts of the body to harden.

When a planet is in very close conjunction to the Sun, three degrees or less, it is said to be *combust;* its ray is, so to speak, burned up in the terrific heat of the Sun, and thus the afflicted planet is unable to properly exercise its function in the life of persons born under that configuration. It is also evident that as the weakest link of a chain is the first to give, so the disability would show itself in a part of the body otherwise afflicted.

Horoscope No. 7 has both Venus and Mercury combust in the Twelfth House; we may therefore conclude that there is a lack of nerve force or vital fluid, and that the venous circulation of the ear is obstructed. Thus congestion is inevitable, and the hearing becomes less and less acute. Osteopathy is excellently equipped to deal successfully with a case like this; were the configuration in a fixed sign we might not feel optimistic, but *flexibility* is the salient characteristic of the common signs, so we see no reason why with patience and perseverance a cure may not be consummated.

As said, Saturn rules the earthy mineral matter carried by our blood; from this the bony structure is formed, also concretions in the softer tissues. Therefore the skeleton is also under the dominion of Saturn.

In horoscope No. 8, the auditory disability comes through the fixed signs Leo and Scorpio; this makes it more difficult to remedy, particularly as Saturn is the afflicter and throws his malefic ray upon Mercury from an angle. Science thought at one time that the tympanum was the only, or at least the main factor in hearing, but realizes now that as much or more depends upon the bony structure. It is the nature of Saturn to obstruct and as Scorpio rules the organs of excretion, we may easily see that this important function is impaired, and that waste products have difficulty in passing kidneys and colon. The whole system becomes clogged in consequence, and as Mercury in the Twelfth House marks the ears as weak, it is only natural that the auditory nerve becomes clogged and the bony parts of the ear grow denser in the course of time.

Sour milk or buttermilk has a particularly wholesome influence in clearing up a clogged system. Many people rebel against the use of milk in quantity because of an idea that it aggravates constipation; that is true in the beginning, but after a short time the system will accommodate itself to the diet, which will be then found superlatively cleansing, wholesome and nutritious. Greens and fruits will also aid a person afflicted as in horoscope No. 8 to eliminate the waste and effect a cure in time.

Disease of the Vocal Organs

Among the subjects germane to thorough knowledge of Astrology are the similar effects of intrinsically opposite factors; Saturn is called evil, and Jupiter good, but when Saturn is well fortified in a horoscope it has an exceedingly desirable effect, and an afflicted Jupiter is the very reverse of beneficial. Thus there is a good side to each so-called "evil" planet, and every "good" planet has also an undesirable phase. The signs of the Zodiac are said to rule certain parts of the body, but each sign has also subsidiary dominion over the part ruled by its opposite sign; affliction of Gemini may cause bronchitis, or weaken the arms and shoulders, but sciatica, a Sagittarius disease, may also result. Taurus rules the throat; it has great sympathy with Scorpio, the sign that rules the generative organs, hence we note the change of voice in boys at the time of puberty; also woman, when she forsakes the path of chastity and lives a life of debauch acquires a coarser voice. Taurus rules the larynx, but Mercury governs the air which stirs the vocal cords to vibration; thus organic affliction is indicated by affliction of Taurus and Scorpio, but functional disability by the position and aspect of Mercury. There is a similar relation between Taurus (ruling the vocal organs) and Mercury (ruling the air which passes through the larynx) as between instrument and player. If Taurus (and Scorpio) are unafflicted the vocal organ is in good condition, but an afflicted Mercury may nevertheless cause a functional disorder of the speech. The reverse may also happen, namely, that a well fortified Mercury partially overrides the effect of a Taurus affliction. This is well exemplified in horoscope No. 9; Saturn, Neptune and the Sun conjoined in Taurus cause a throat affection, but Mercury is in a sign of voice, Gemini, (Libra and Aquarius are the other signs of voice) and in conjunction with Jupiter. The woman suffers constantly from throat trouble, but as a good musician draws melody from a dilapidated instrument, so, by the aid of her well placed Mercury, this woman is able to express herself better than many whose vocal organs are sound; in fact, she teaches elocution.

Horoscope No. 3 has a singularly well fortified Mercury; there is no affliction to Taurus or Scorpio, and the gentleman has a powerful voice capable of filling the largest halls without effort, yet not too loud for the smallest; but Mercury in Leo, a bestial sign, and Saturn in Libra, a sign of voice, are obstructive of perfect vocalization, therefore the gentleman has at times a certain halt or hesitancy of speech.

It follows as a matter of course that disabilities of speech are more easily remedied than those that are organic; patience, practice of vocal and breathing exercises such as teachers of voice culture give, (these are entirely different from the dangerous

Hindu breathing exercises) are almost sure to restore normal conditions.

Horoscopes Nos. 9, 10 and 11 have Saturn and Neptune conjoined in Taurus; as a consequence all have throat trouble, and also disorder of the genital organs. Nos. 10 and 11 have both undergone operations for removal of certain parts, and Mercury in Scorpio centers the thoughts of No. 10 upon sex, causing intense torture, as it is impossible to gratify the craving. Saturn in a fixed sign is certainly a sore afflicter, the reaper of fruits from a past life, and if there is to be any solace it must come through knowledge of the cause, prayer, and the patience engendered thereby.

Disorders of the Mind

Before closing discussion of maladies peculiar to the head, mention must be made of insanity, though the underlying causes can only be hinted at in a work of this kind; but the student is referred to *The Rosicrucian Cosmo-Conception* for a thorough explanation of the cosmic agencies concerned in building the brain, and a key to the astrological correspondences. Here we only give the essential facts.

The brain and larynx were first built by the angelic host from the Moon (Luna), who used part of the sex force for that purpose, hence the intimate connection between these organs. "Lunacy" is often induced by misuse of the sex force, and "lunatics" frequently have a flaw in the speech. When boys reach puberty the voice changes; the speech of a fast woman becomes coarse, and degenerate men acquire effeminate voices. In Italy singers anxious to cultivate a high tenor voice have become eunuchs to achieve their purpose.

Into the system thus built by the lunar host under Jehovah, rebel Angels led by Lucifer, the Spirit of Mars, insinuated themselves, and inculcated passion, sex abuse and rebellion against the rulership of the Angels of Jehovah. To offset their influence our Elder Brothers from Mercury were commissioned to foster reason that man may in time learn to guide himself. All the great Hierarchies work in our bodies constantly, but the three mentioned have particular dominion over sex and sense; each invests one of the three segments of the spinal cord. The sublimely spiritual hierarchy of Neptune works in the spinal canal and cerebral ventricles to awaken spiritual senses which, when evolved, enable the imprisoned spirit to pierce the veil of flesh and contact superphysical realms. The Lucifer Spirits dominate the left cerebral hemisphere which now is our principal organ of thought. The Mercurians have dominion over the right hemisphere, which will come into activity in the future and elevate mankind to a higher, nobler plane of life, give us the power over the lower nature and make us Christlike. The lunar Angels hold sway in the cerebellum which is the instrument of coordination. In this veritable "Tree of Knowledge" the fight is fought between forces which make for the emancipation of man and agencies which aim to keep him dependent, as explained in Rosicrucian Christianity Series, Lecture No. 14, "Lucifer, Tempter or Benefactor?"

Such are the teachings which explain the deep reason back of astrological dicta, and any qualified seer may easily perceive the various agencies at work in the human body; such are few, however, and the student of Astrology has reason to thank God day by day for the blessed science which is of greater benefit than any measure of spiritual sight. Though the writers are firm believers in the law of compensation which gives to each exactly what he has earned, neither more nor less, we cannot free ourselves from the feeling that our measure of spiritual faculties has been heaped and shaken down. We feel very, very grateful for the privilege and added usefulness in service which this gives us. Nevertheless, were the alternative placed before us involving choice between loss of spiritual faculties and loss of our knowledge of Astrology, we should not hesitate one moment, but decide at once in favor of our beloved science, neither ought this surprise anyone who will give the matter a moment's thought. It is true that spiritual sight, even in its rudimentary form enables us to see the condition of the human body to the minutest detail, and thus affords a much easier means of diagnosis than Astrology, but though it penetrates to the innermost core of the bone, mere clairvoyance is superficial compared to Astrology for it shows only present conditions of the body. To find the causes which led up to that state and judge of future tendencies, it is necessary to consult the memory of nature. We should have to do that personally, and this, time would not permit, as we are handling hundreds of cases, but a simple astrological figure,which we may commission one of our students to cast, reveals as much at a glance. There are delineated the causes of mental, moral and physical disorders; it shows accurately the stages that have been passed and the crises yet to come. It also indicates the direction from which a remedy may be looked for and the most favorable time for administering the same. It helps people Here and Now, and the astrologer who lives up to his privilege has a mission so high and so holy that the office of priest (in the esoteric sense) pales into insignificance by comparison. Let the aspirant to this great knowledge remember that he stands upon holier ground than Moses before the burning bush, when he looks at a horoscope. Through that circle-symbol of infinity an immortal soul is laid bare, and woe to him who dares to look with profane gaze, for no matter how that soul may have been smirched in its pilgrimage through matter, it is essentially divine and dear to the Father, yea, perhaps even more precious, than the righteous who do not need mercy and compassion. This has been somewhat of a digression, but we have no apologies to offer, for we preach Astrology as a religion and feel the necessity of emphasizing this phase in season and out, if by any means we may inculcate in others the reverence which we ourselves feel for this divine science.

Returning to the astrological consideration of insanity, and in view of what has been said we may note that the horoscope shows how, in the spinal canal, rays of the various hierarchies blend, and Astrology tabulates the resultant mental conditions as follows:

People not congenitally affected, who have cardinal signs rising, particularly if cardinal or fixed signs also invest the Midheaven and Nadir, rarely become insane. The active nature forbids morbid tendencies and blues, disappointment is quickly thrown off and hope springs eternal in the cardinal breast urging to renewed struggle with conditions. It is said that the exception proves the rule, and when Capricorn rises the saturnine rulership gives a tendency to melancholy which under certain aggravating circumstances may provoke suicide, particularly when the ruler is cooped up in the Eighth House, as we see in horoscope No. 12. Virgo, a common sign, devoid of stamina, holds the Sun, Saturn, Venus and the Moon in this, the house of death; this robs the person of joy in life and impels him to end it under stress of sorrow. Knowledge on the part of an astrologer friend has so far forestalled the calamity, and it is hoped, may save the poor man from committing so grave a crime.

When a Fixed sign rises at birth of a normal child, chances of insanity in later life are so exceedingly remote as to be almost negligible, especially if a Fixed or Cardinal sign is also on the Midheaven.

In our extended practice, we know of no exception; the rigid, set and inflexible nature of the Fixed signs seems to protect the mind under all exigencies of stress.

It therefore follows that the mentally unbalanced come principally from those born with Common signs on the angles. The intrinsic nature of these signs is *Flexibility;* as a reed in the wind people under these signs are swayed hither and thither by circumstances; they have no stamina or stability, and take reverses much to heart, while they last. Sorrow seems to overwhelm them and balance is easily lost

It is a distinctive feature of the Rosicrucian teachings that pupils in the Western world must be given a reason for every dictum, so as to forestall criticism as much as possible, for it retards development every time it is indulged. The Rosicrucian teachings therefore aim to forestall questions at every point by giving reasons for every dictum, so that the critical mind may be weaned away from this attitude. We are ardently looking for the day and reign of Christ, the Friend of man; we do not know when He will come, no man knows, but Paul said that when He comes we shall be like Him. Adverse criticism and skepticism were not traits of His character and anything that will aid to eradicate these undesirable characteristics hastens the glad day of *Universal Friendship.*

The reason has been given in *Simplified Scientific Astrology* why the Ascendant rules the body as a whole; it (or its opposite) is the place of the Moon at conception. In the Bible angels are mentioned as heralds of birth and their lunar home is the focus whence the spirits enter our terrestrial sphere on their return to physical life. They fashion the etheric mould for our present instrument, and direct the growth of the fœtus. Therefore the Ascendant and the Moon show the organic disabilities which lead to mental disorder. The congenital idiocy resulting from lack of proper adjustment between the vital body and the physical vehicle has been thoroughly described in the *Rosicrucian Cosmo-Conception,* together with causes producing the same during prenatal life. Astrologically this condition is produced by an affliction of the Ascendant, that is to say, the Moon's place at conception, which throws the angle of the stellar ray out of parallax to the mother's body and the physical vehicle is built in such a manner that the head of the vital body is several inches above the skull. Thus the nerve centers are askew, preventing the ego from properly controlling its instrument This is one of the configurations which produce idiocy and St. Vitus' dance. Uranus and Neptune are especially concerned in producing this latter phenomenon.

Saturn is the cause of melancholy and depression. Mars and Uranus produce the muscular and violent forms of insanity. Horoscopes 13 and 14 illustrate these peculiarities. No. 13 also shows the connection between puberty and the mental state. Gemini is rising, with Taurus and Mars intercepted in the

Sixth and Twelfth Houses, from whence come disease and confinement. The Moon is in Taurus, which rules the larynx; she is in conjunction with Neptune, square to Mercury, and Mars is in Scorpio, which rules the generative organs. There we have at once the tendencies to a disease, which is further accentuated by the fact that Neptune in Taurus squares the Sun in Leo, and Leo has rule over the heart, and is the prime factor in circulation upon which the life of the body depends; thus the threatened illness may be set down to trouble with the blood, produced by a nervous affection. Puberty occurs at the time when the Moon is in the opposite quarter from its place at birth. She entered Scorpio, the opposite of Taurus which held her at birth, at the time when the child was nearly twelve years of age. Up to that time the little girl had been bright, but the conjunction with Mars in Scorpio precipitated the period and robbed the growing child of vitality sorely needed at that time. The initial periods were few, but left her depleted of strength to withstand the square to Mercury and the opposition of the Moon to its radical place. (The radical place of a planet is its position at birth.) This affliction of Mercury, the ruler, by the Moon at birth, was thus excited and insanity showed itself in consequence. As the affliction comes from fixed signs, we may judge it will be impossible to overcome, and the best that can be done for the poor soul is to pray for the day of its release, that it may have a better chance in a future embodiment.

No. 14 is the horoscope of a young man. The common sign, Gemini, is rising, the ruler, Mercury, is in the Eighth House, the house of death, and Uranus and the Moon are in opposition to Mercury. This configuration, is similar to that of No. 12, and has the same significance, namely, suicidal tendencies under nervous strain, and this augur is all the more dangerous as it comes from fixed signs. Mars and Neptune in Taurus give a desire for drink and the Sun in a watery sign accentuates this tendency. Under such circumstances the man has several times tried to end his life in a most extraordinary manner. Jupiter in Sagittarius, square to Saturn in Pisces, increases the looseness of his morals and makes him dishonest. He will forge and steal in order to satisfy his passion and craving for drink and questionable society. Leo on the Second House with Uranus and the Moon in close conjunction, shows that he spends what he gets in dissolute living.

There is one redeeming feature in the horoscope: Venus in the Midheaven sextile to his ruler, and trine to the Moon. He has energy and artistic ability which, it is hoped, may in time rouse the better qualities and make him a man. But again we reiterate that with the affliction from fixed signs the obstacle is almost insurmountable.

In conclusion the student's attention is directed to the Third and the Ninth Houses, which will also have an influence on the mind. Planets therein act according to the intrinsic nature expressed in the key word of each.

Pulmonary Diseases

Horoscope No. 15 is the chart of a woman who, among other things, was afflicted with pulmonary trouble.

Virgo is rising and Mercury, the ruler, is trine at birth, but unfortunately he is combust, a term which has been previously explained as meaning that the heat of the Sun burns up the ray of any planet placed too close thereto. The disease was not congenital however, although the Moon was square to the Ascendant. But Virgo people, we have seen, are extremely fond of being sick. When once they have had a little pain, they magnify and nurse it and are loath to let it go. The square of Neptune in Aries to Uranus caused St. Vitus' dance at about the age of four years when the Moon reached the conjunction of Saturn (which is 21:15 Capricorn) and the opposition to Uranus. This was the beginning of her illness. She afterwards regarded herself as an invalid and nursed sickness. Saturn in opposition to Jupiter added to the trouble by restricting the arterial circulation. At the time of puberty the Moon was in Gemini in opposition to its place at birth. This excited the above mentioned square between the radical Moon and the Ascendant; it also caused the periods to be irregular and troublesome. The blood must have an outlet and the square of Neptune to Jupiter in Cancer, which rules the stomach, caused hæmorrhages when the Moon came into conjunction with the Dragon's Tail in Sagittarius (the opposite sign to Gemini), and the radical square of the Ascendant and the Moon were again excited. Then also the lungs became affected. In April, 1909, the progressed Moon squared the natal positions of Saturn, Jupiter, and Uranus. This inimical force from the house of death, the Eighth, ended the life.

As we feel that this cannot be reiterated too often, we repeat our injunction to students never to let a patient know that there is any danger or that there is a crisis ahead. Particularly, please remember, *particularly,* if it is a Virgo, for he has no chance at all if he knows what is coming.

Horoscope No. 16 shows the natal configuration of an actress. Sagittarius is rising; Jupiter and the Moon are in close conjunction in Gemini, a mercurial sign, and are supported by a trine of the Sun; thus she had a most healthy constitution at birth, so far as the lung power is concerned. Mars and Mercury are also in an airy sign, giving energy to respiration and it thus seems as though this person were singularly well fortified against pulmonary trouble. But Saturn, Neptune and the Dragon's Tail in Taurus in the Sixth House, give a tendency to colds and contraction of the throat. Uranus in Virgo produces convulsive movements of the diaphragm and abdominal region; he is square to Jupiter and the Moon, and thus we see how graphically the stellar script pictures the tendency to convulsive coughing and hæmorrhages which nearly brought the young woman to an early grave when Mars, by progression, came into conjunction with the radical Sun and vivified the square to Saturn. We rejoice to say that the good aspects first mentioned enabled the young woman to weather the storm; but close attention to diet, regular living and above all absolute continence are required to regain full physical strength, for there is much evidence to show that license played an important part in reducing the life forces and robbing her of the needed strength at the critical period.

Diseases of the Stomach

Horoscope No. 17 presents a number of diseases, but all have their root in an insatiable appetite fostered by the fact that the person is a professional chef. Venus in Taurus gives discrimination in food, and the sextile to Mercury in Cancer causes the mind to run in the direction of preparations wherewith to tickle the palate. But the Moon being ruler of Cancer, the rising sign, which has dominion over the stomach, shows that over-indulgence of the appetite will result disastrously. The distended stomach presses upon the heart, of which the Sun, our life-giver, is ruler. This planet is in Gemini, the sign which has dominion over the lungs, and square to Mars in Pisces. Mars rules the iron in the blood and the Sun gives us oxygen, thus this square shows that the blood will lack in that life-giving element. The conjunction of the Sun with Uranus in Gemini produces spasmodic motion of the lungs and labored inspiration to obtain sufficient oxygen wherewith to supply the system; thus we have the condition called asthma. Saturn and Jupiter are in Virgo which rules the abdomen, square to the Sun and Uranus in Gemini, showing lack of circulation and a tendency to ulcerous growths, and there is a general lack of nutrition in the whole system because of the great energy required to eliminate waste from the enormous quantities of food which this person consumes. Sad to say, however, persons in that occupation protest that they cannot help tasting, and that in spite of all ills they must eat to excess. It were wiser of course, to seek another profession and train the system to moderation.

In horoscope No. 18 we have the natal configurations of another chef; they are similar to those delineated in No. 17. Cancer, the sign of the stomach, is rising, with Mars and the Sun close to the Ascendant; thus the forces of this individual will be directed principally toward the stomach, and the opposition of the Moon shows disastrous results which eventually resulted from gratifying his ravenous appetite. The Sun is life and motion, Mars is dynamic energy, and the excessive activity centered in the stomach to take care of digestion causes this organ to be inflamed. Nature is not a jerry-builder; she builds substantially and well, or our bodies could never stand the abuse we give them as well as they do, but even the healthiest organism must give way in time under such dreadful strain. As indicated by the Sun and Mars, an ulcer developed from the internal heat, ate through the stomach and relieved the poor soul of its misused body. Neptune in Taurus, the sign of the palate, was of course also a contributing factor. It is not to be supposed however, that anyone who has Cancer rising or many planets in Cancer, is necessarily going to die of the disease to which that name has been given, but it would be the part of wisdom to train children with such conditions to abstain from overeating, for it is a truism that more people die from overeating than from starvation.

Diseases of the Heart

As the heart is the seat of physical life, its natural ruler is the Sun. The solar sign is Leo. But it is a mistake to think that palpitation of the heart is necessarily shown by an affliction to the sign Leo. Indeed, there are many cases where overindulgence of the appetite indicated by the sign Cancer distends the stomach, which presses upon the heart producing what the person then believes to be heart trouble. This was the case in horoscopes Nos. 17 and 18; both believed their heart trouble to be the primal cause of the illness under which they were suffering, while in reality it was only one of the effects.

But No. 3 shows a case of organic weakness of the heart. The Sun is at home in the fixed sign Leo and receives a square from Saturn the reaper; thus it is evident that the heart was a weak link in the constitution and would cause trouble in time, unless care was taken. Unfortunately of course, parents knew less about Astrology a generation ago than today, when the science is coming to the fore. The energy of which this horoscope is full, was allowed to spend itself unrestrained with no thought given to coming disaster.

Venus and Jupiter, the planets ruling the venous and arterial circulation, are in opposition. Venus is in Gemini the sign of the lungs, and when the Sun progressed to the square of Venus' radical place, and Uranus transited the Sixth House, illness began; breathing became labored as indicated by the square of the life-giver to the lungs. Uranus in opposition to his natal place in Cancer produced the convulsive movement known as the stomach cough, and thus for years this illness robbed the man of vital energy; but these afflictions passed and because of attention to right living the system has been left none the worse for the experience. Moreover, the suffering of the soul has resulted in growth that he might not otherwise have obtained.

Horoscope No. 19 shows another case of heart disease. The Sun and Neptune are conjunct in the Eighth House, in opposition to Mars. As this conjunction is in the sign Gemini and in the house of death, it is easy to see the portent. The dynamic energy of Mars tears everything to pieces, accelerates motion, causes palpitation etc. The Sun and Neptune in Gemini show a likelihood of a hæmorrhage of the lungs, resulting from over activity of the heart. The Moon and Saturn in Leo show the obstructed passage of the blood, for the keynote of Saturn is obstruction and retardation; thus the valves of the heart become leaky and the backward flow of the blood called regurgitation takes place.

Leo also rules the spinal cord and malefic configurations there may produce hunchback and kindred disabilities.

Horoscope No. 20 is the figure of a beautiful boy, well formed and healthy, who became afflicted with curvature of the spine. Here we find the Moon in conjunction with the Dragon's Tail in the Twelfth House, square to Saturn and Uranus in Scorpio. At five and one half years of age the Moon had progressed to the square of its own place; this and the conjunction with Saturn and Uranus in Scorpio, brought on his affliction. After enduring eight years of torture he died, having been taken from one free dispensary to another and used by the doctors to practice on. Each doctor tried a new cure. He was in plaster casts for years but to no purpose. The mother is represented by Neptune in conjunction with Mars, careless and of dissolute habits; she was glad of the opportunity to place the boy anywhere in order to shirk the responsibility of caring for him. The boy died when the Moon had progressed to an opposition of its own place; it was also then in square to Uranus and Saturn.

Diseases of the Kidneys

The kidneys are ruled by Libra and Scorpio both. That is to say, the functional activity of secretion of urine comes from Libra, but the bladder and urethra through which elimination takes place are ruled by Scorpio. Renal stones and gravel would result from an affliction to Libra, for they are formed in the peduncle of the kidneys. These would also result from an affliction to Scorpio, causing faulty elimination and consequent retention of calcareous matter in the system. Diseases of the ureters are under Libra.

Horoscopes Nos. 3 and 21 are examples of how the stars indicate diseases of the kidneys. In both cases Saturn is in or near an angle and square to the Sun, and in his sign of exaltation. Libra, which rules the kidneys, is also elevated. This latter point may not be apparent to beginners who look at No. 3 and find Saturn, as they would say, *down* in the Fourth House, but the nadir of the birth place is Midheaven or Zenith of an opposite point on the earth, and planets at either of these points are found to have an added power.

In the two examples mentioned, Saturn, the planet of obstruction, prevents secretion of urine but does not interfere with elimination ot that which has been secreted. But in horoscope No. 8 where he is posited in the sign Scorpio square to Mercury, we have a case where the formation of gravel and renal stones is shown to result from incomplete elimination. A person with such a configuration ought to be extremely careful not to drink hard water, for this may cause a painful ailment. Only filtered water should be used for purposes of cooking and drinking. Sour milk, buttermilk and grape juice are great solvents. We may further say that to boil water will not soften it, and the fur which gathers in a tea kettle where hard water has been boiled is no evidence to the contrary, for that scaly formation was obtained from the water which evaporated; what remains in the kettle for use is as hard as ever.

In horoscope No. 7 we find Saturn in Scorpio square to Mars. Saturn produces the obstruction of the blood known as hæmorrhoids, and the dynamic energy of Mars causes rupture of the congested places; thus we have the painful bleeding well known to so many sufferers. As a secondary result constipation adds to the malady, because persons afflicted with the first named disease shrink from the added pain of the stool, and do not respond to nature's call. A prolonged rest seems to be the only physical means which is really effective. Nature however, will be very much aided by proper osteopathic manipulations, and a diet consisting principally of milk.

Accidents to Hips and Arms

Sagittarius rising, or in the Sixth or Twelfth House is responsible for broken bones and accidents. Under the chapter on the Dragon's Tail we saw how the person described in horoscope No. 6 fell upon the ice and broke her hip. No. 21 has even stronger indications of accidents and probably the life will end in an untoward manner. Sagittarius is rising, Saturn is exalted in the Midheaven exactly square to the Sun, and Neptune is elevated at the nadir also squaring the Moon; thus both luminaries are afflicted. As the Sun is lord of the house of death these auguries presage an untimely end. The only hope lies in the sextile of Jupiter to the Sun which gives hair-breadth escapes. This man's life has been jeopardized many times in railroad wrecks, automobile accidents, etc., but although he has thus been near the gate of death many times, the benefic ray of Jupiter has so far preserved his life and no bones have yet been broken. The woman described in horoscope No. 22 has not been so fortunate; her arms and legs have been accidentally broken several times, for Mars and the Moon are in Sagittarius in the Twelfth House, also in opposition to Jupiter. The Sun and Mercury are in the Eighth House in opposition to Neptune and these planets are square the first mentioned positions. Saturn, her ruler, is square to Venus so that she attracts accidents and never escapes being hurt.

Diseases of the Limbs

In horoscope No. 7 we find Mars in Aquarius square to Saturn, and from this affliction it is evident that there is an obstruction of the blood in the lower limbs, which produces varicose veins. Horoscope No. 17 shows Mars in the sign Pisces in opposition to

Saturn and Jupiter. It is the nature of Saturn to obstruct, and his conjunction with Jupiter shows that the circulation is poor. Mars in Pisces produces heat, inflammation and swelling of the feet, because of the stagnated blood. We have already seen that the person there described is gluttonously inclined, and therefore it is no wonder that stagnation of the blood produces such painful afflictions as indicated by these configurations. The remedy of course is self-evident; it is moderation.

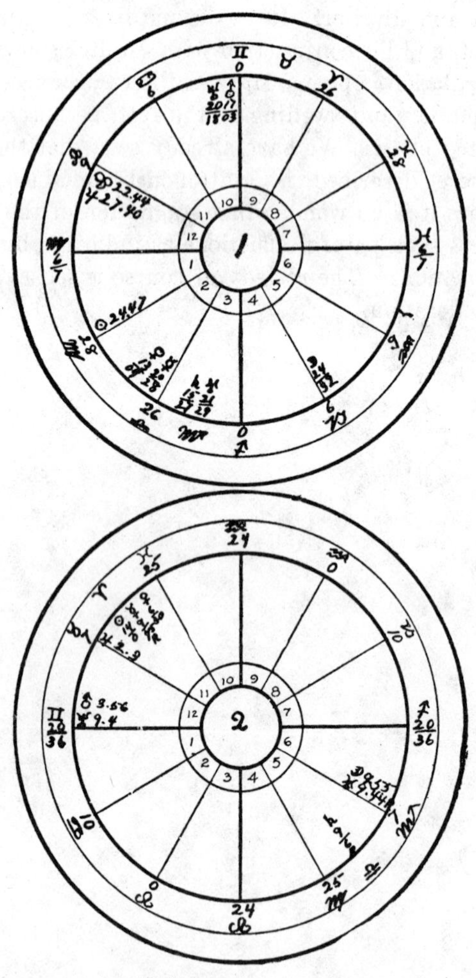

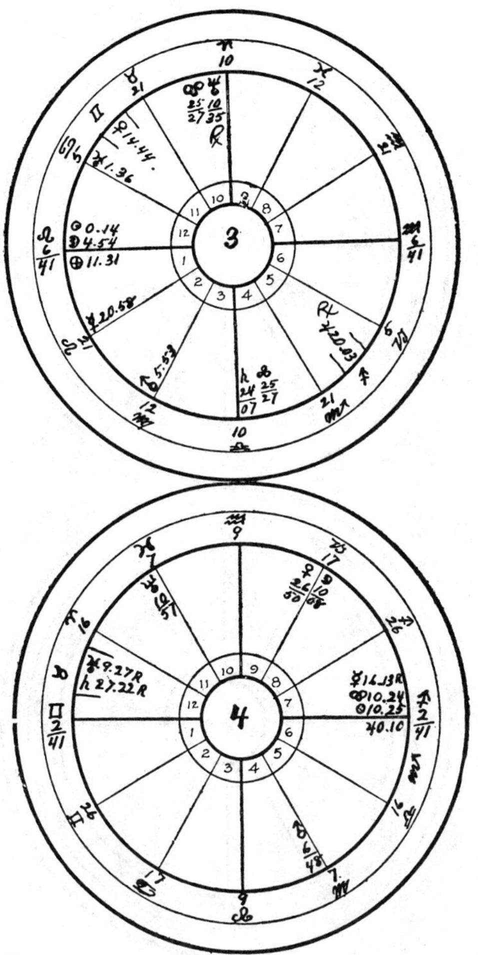

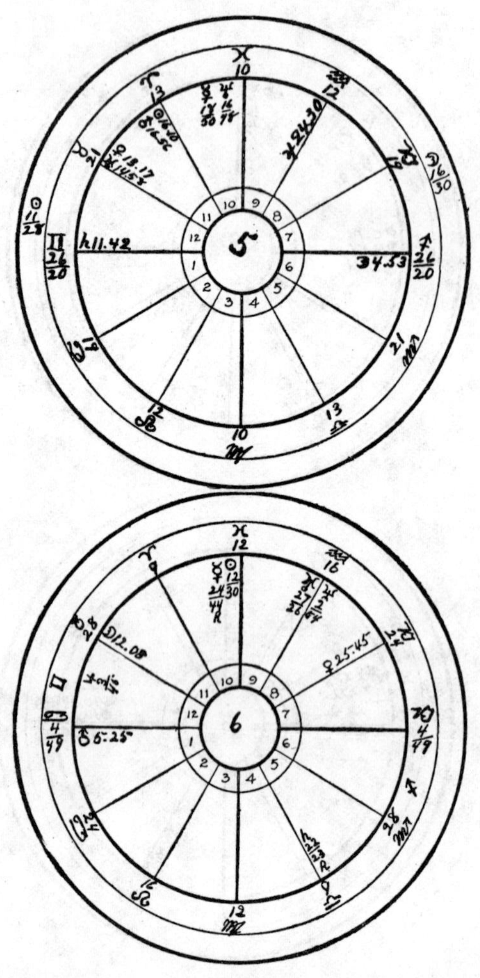

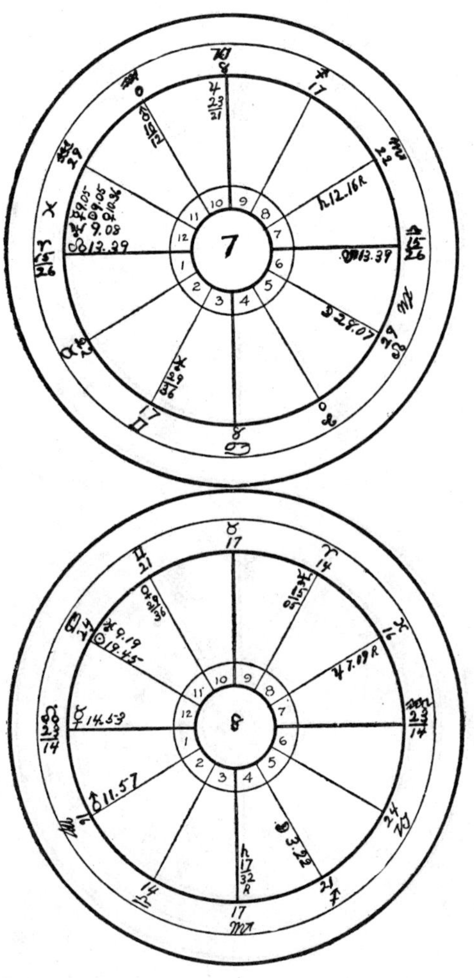

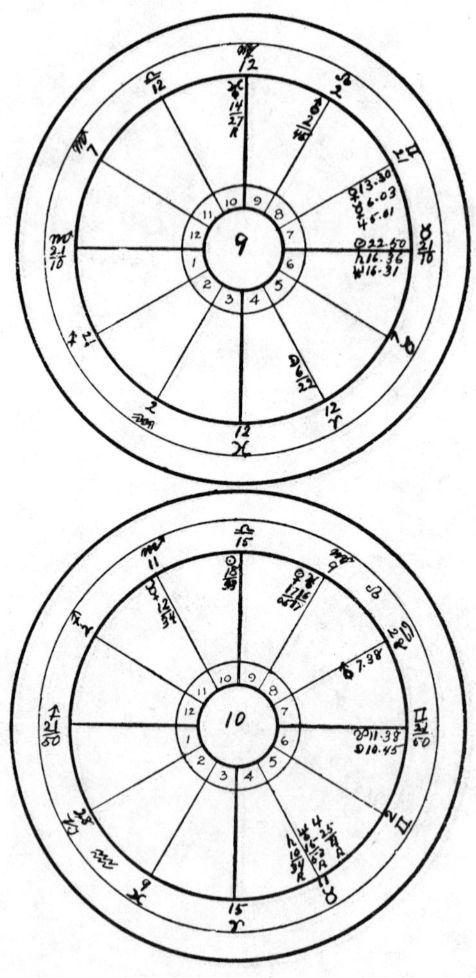

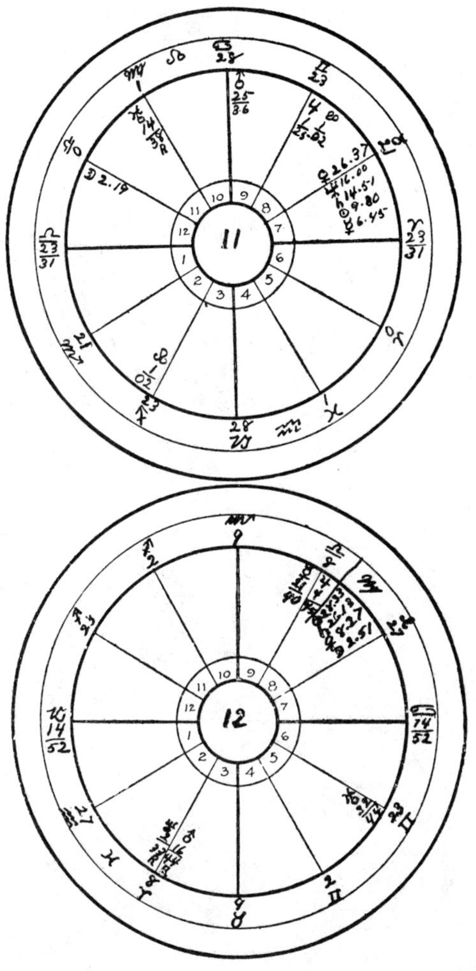
11
12

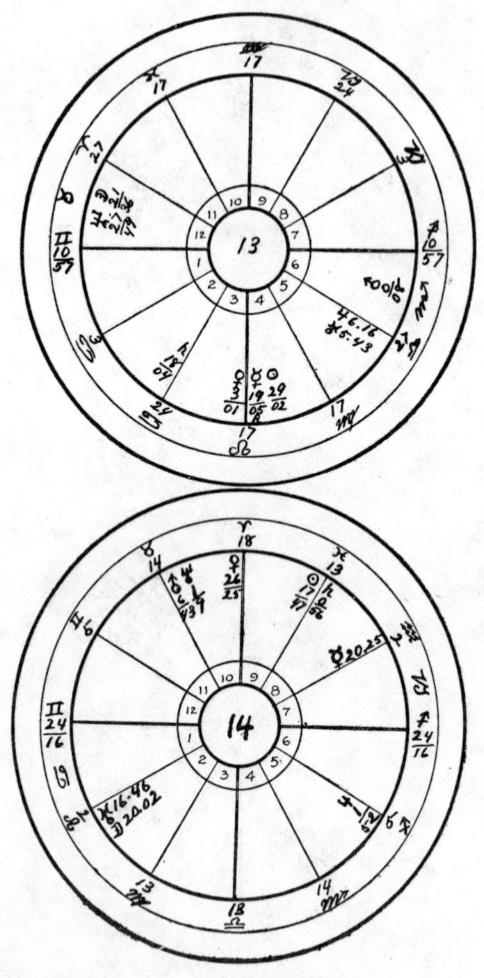
13
14

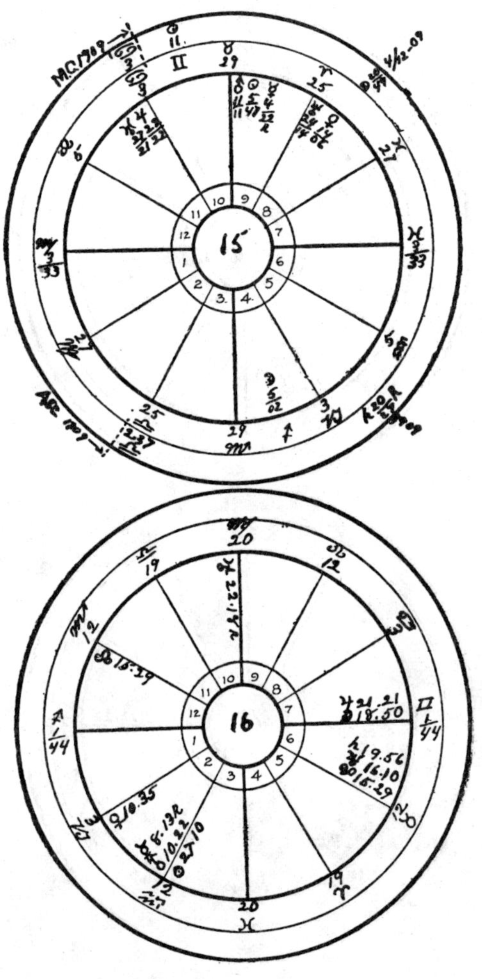
M.C. 1909
15
16

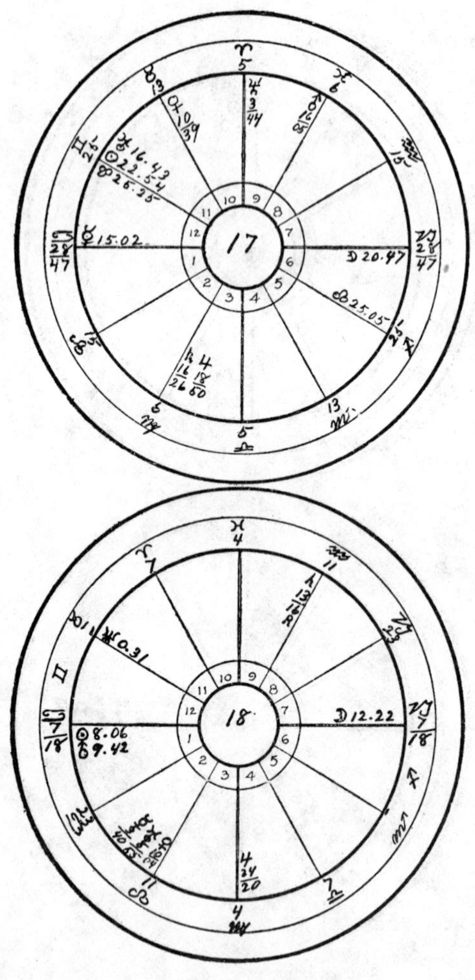
17
18

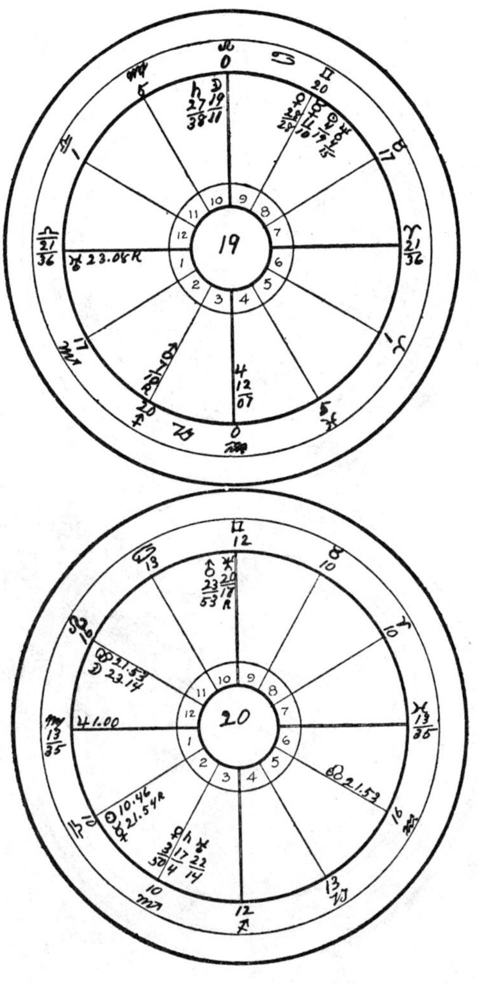

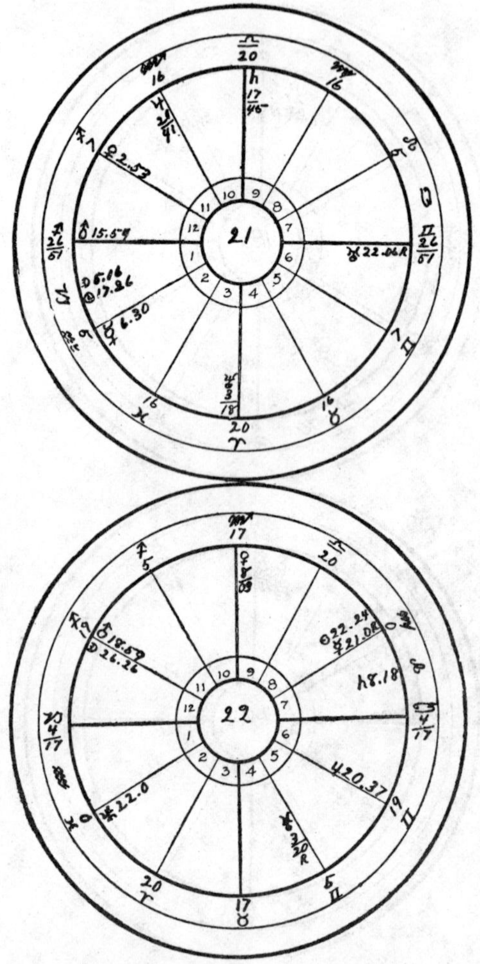

No. 23.—Insanity and Spirit Control

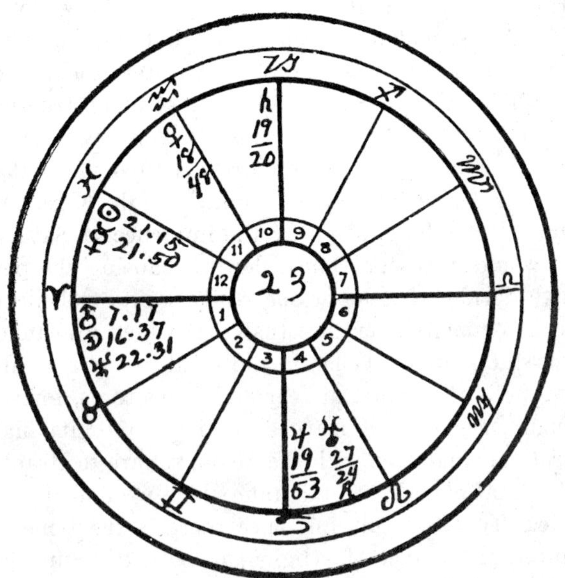

In judging this horoscope we look first to the mentality, as this is always the most important factor in the treatment of a patient. Mercury and the Moon are the two principal factors in determining this point, though, of course, all the planets have their bearing on that as well as on any other subject. Here we find that Mercury is combust and that it is with the Sun in the Common sign, Pisces. That in itself is not a very good augur; we further find that the Moon is in conjunction with Neptune in Aries, that it is square to both Saturn and Jupiter, and that therefore the mind must be of a weak and unstable nature. Mars, the Moon and Neptune in Aries would in themselves make a person erratic, but when we find, as here, that Luna is square to Jupiter, the planet of religion, also to Saturn, the planet of obstruction and negation, it naturally causes a very evil condition. The opposition of Jupiter to Saturn shows that whatever desire for religion Jupiter might engender, would always be opposed by the influence of Saturn, who would counsel "Don't, don't," causing the person to deride what he or she really wants to believe. It is a common experience that that which we cannot understand, appears chaotic and erratic to our minds. Neptune is the planet of fear and chaos to us, for the human race has not learned to live up to its high vibrations, and this, with the Moon, square to Uranus makes that chaotic mental state which we find in this circle. To offset this influence there is the trine of Jupiter, the planet of religion, to both the Sun and Mercury; but even this influence will not be able to break the condition entirely, though there is no doubt this great redeeming power has had an effect in staving off the evil day when the mind will break down entirely. As usual, the marching orbs in their circling dance come to a point where the string of each aspect is touched which then produces the tone of either harmony or discord that impels us to actions which we call good or evil; so also in this case. The time marked on the clock of destiny by the hand of

God was April, 1913; then the lunation fell in conjunction with the radical Moon in Aries. This naturally excited the radical square to Saturn and Jupiter, also their opposition, and thus the climax was precipitated; the person became violently insane.

We may look for the immediate cause that precipitated that calamity to the radical position of Neptune and Uranus. These, the octaves of Mercury and Venus, in a square position will always bring the person in contact with spirits who have left the body, or who have never inhabited a body such as we have at the present time.

During aspects like the above, they would have an excellent chance to use this poor person as a tool for their nefarious practices, for naturally those spirits which come under a square are not what we would call good in any respect; they have no benevolent designs for helping their victim, no matter what they may profess in that direction.

The question then comes: What can we do for a person in that condition? We have a good aspect to the Moon and Neptune, which is the sextile of Venus. Neptune rules music—classical string music in particular—and Venus in Aquarius gives the person a love of just that kind of music, which will soothe the mind. This configuration also gives a love of bright colors and sunshine which will help to tone the system. She should not be allowed books, but should have a complete rest from all mental effort, the brightest conversation possible, and a vegetarian diet. With these there is a probability that the evil configuration may be overcome and the person restored to mental health, though that will never be robust.

No. 24.—Heart Trouble, Insufficient Oxygenation, Eye Trouble, Death

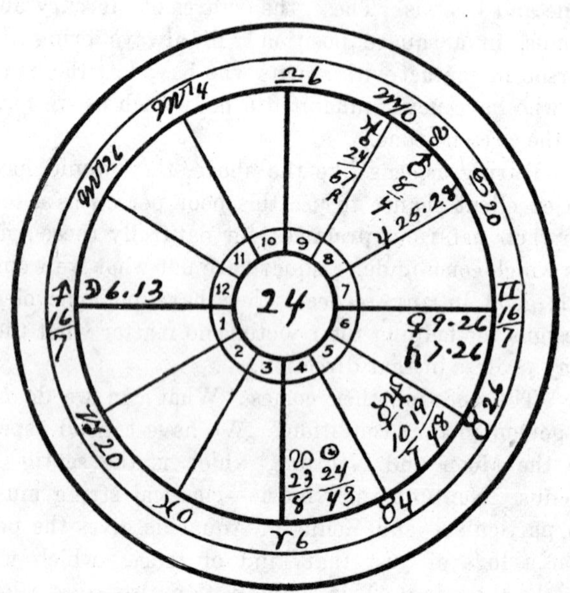

Good Aspects: Mars trine the Moon, sextile Saturn; Uranus trine Neptune; Jupiter sextile Neptune and Uranus.

Bad Aspects: The Moon conjunction Antares, opposition Saturn and Venus; the Sun conjunction

Dragon's Tail, square Jupiter; Mercury square Mars.

The Moon on the Ascendant in Sagittarius makes the patient restless and unstable, but not shiftless, because the Moon is also trine to Mars. This gives her much more energy than usually possessed by Sagittarians. Even the opposition of the Moon to Saturn and Venus, which robs life of its joys and makes her melancholy, is, in a certain sense, a help; it gives her a persistence and resistance that will not allow her to give in to disease. Mercury square Mars shows that she has a very quick temper, and as Mercury is in Taurus, the sign of voice, the unfortunate characteristic will find expression in an unbridled tongue. This will hurt her very seriously from a physical standpoint (not to speak of the even more deplorable spiritual injuries), for Mars is in Leo, the sign of the heart, and that always predisposes to palpitation. He is sextile to Saturn, but even good aspects to Saturn are physically inimical. The Sun, which is ruler of the heart, is in conjunction with the saturnine Dragon's Tail. The nerves also are affected by the square of Mars to Mercury, hence the heart is far from normally balanced, and the outbursts of temper which this person is apt to indulge in on the slightest provocation may cause heart failure at some time, by putting an undue strain on this organ and interfering with the already sluggish circulation, which is shown by the square of Jupiter to the Sun and the Dragon's Tail, also by the conjunction of Venus with Saturn, and their opposition to the

Moon; Jupiter and Venus being governors respectively of the arterial and venous circulations.

The head is particularly congested because the Sun conjunction the saturnine Dragon's Tail occurs in Aries, the sign of the head, and Saturn, the planet of obstruction, is in Gemini, the sign of the lungs, in conjunction with Venus. This shows interference with the circulation of the venous blood in the lungs. The Moon, which governs the tidal air, is in opposition, showing that an insufficient amount of air is inspired into the lungs to cleanse the blood of its poisonous carbon dioxide, and the presence of Saturn shows a hardening of the tissues, which is apt to develop into tuberculosis. You will also notice that Jupiter, the ruler of the Ascendant, is in the Eighth House square to the Sun and the saturnine Dragon's Tail in the Fourth House, and all are in Cardinal signs. This is a strong testimony of an accidental death, and Mars in the Eighth House, in the sign Leo, which rules the heart, shows that hæmorrhages may be the cause which will end the physical life.

If this person had been taken hold of in time and taught self-control, this serious condition could probably have been avoided; even now a frank statement concerning the great danger that undue excitement may cause, should help her to govern her temper, and thus lengthen life.

The Moon conjunction Antares, and opposition to Saturn shows that the eyes are in danger also, and Saturn in Gemini, which is a mercurial sign, shows nervous affection. The conjunction with Venus would suggest a congestion of the muscles of the eyes, which may be greatly relieved by osteopathic treatment.

A healer with Leo rising, and Saturn not in Gemini, would be best able to handle the case.

No. 25.—Heart Trouble, Tuberculosis, Kidneys

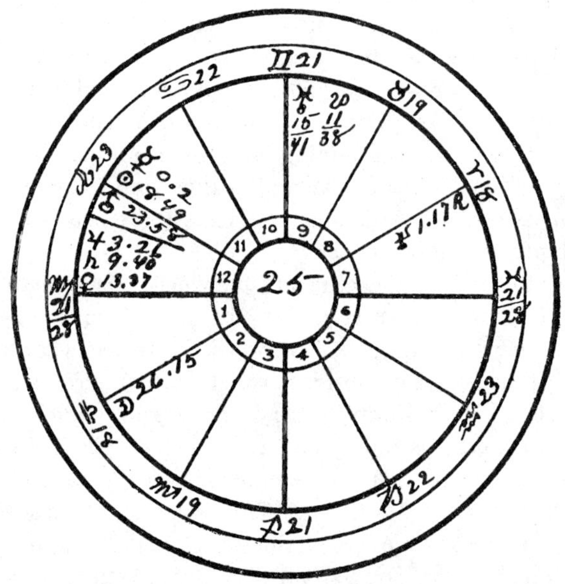

We judge first the mental calibre of our patient. Four Common signs are on the angles, and this at once describes the nature as weak and vacillating. Mercury square the Moon further accentuates this wavering and flightiness of her mind, and Saturn conjunction Venus and Jupiter in the Twelfth House robs life of its joy, making this woman subject to melancholy and morbid fear. This characteristic is somewhat ameliorated by the sextile of the Sun to Uranus, which fosters altruism, and the trine of Mercury to Neptune, which gives spiritual perception, thus aiding to dispel gloom by directing the mind from sorrows which are but fleeting, to the eternal verities. To sum up, she is prone to be either "down in the dumps," or "up in the air," and it is necessary to strive to cure her of both depression and elation, which are alike harmful. Equipoise must be cultivated to aid in attaining and maintaining health. Were Fixed signs on the angles this would be next to impossible, but with Common signs there she is more adaptable and reachable.

Regarding the ailments to which this woman is subject, we note first Uranus in high elevation, conjunction the Dragon's Tail, whose influence is saturnine, that is to say, obstructive, crystallizing, and hardening. Both are in the airy sign Gemini, which governs the lungs, and square to Saturn in the Twelfth House, which denotes confinement—in prison, hospitals or upon a sickbed. This gives us at once the key to the trouble. Sometimes the tidal air is almost stopped by the Dragon's Tail and the square of Saturn; Uranus prevents asphyxiation by the convulsive movement of the lungs known as coughing, which clears away the obstruction and enables the heart to again circulate the blood.

The blood is unable to throw off its poisonous carbonic acid because of the obstructive power of the Dragon's Tail in Gemini, and the square of Saturn to Uranus in the sign of the lungs. The arterial and venous circulations are also impeded by the conjunction of Jupiter and Venus with Saturn, hence, malnutrition and carbonic acid poisoning are in evidence. The hardening of the lungs and consequent cough, label the case as tuberculosis.

Elimination of urine is retarded by the square of Mercury to the Moon, which is in the latter part of Libra, the sign of the kidneys. Mercury governs the sensory nerves, while Mars rules the motor nerves and muscles. Mars is in good aspect, showing that the mechanical apparatus is in good condition, but that the trouble is nervous. This may be alleviated by manipulations, and so may the sluggishness of the bowels indicated by Saturn in Virgo. The Mars hour would be the best time, the Sun hour next. Besides this treatment dry rubs with coarse gloves will stimulate the skin and aid in eliminating carbonic acid from the system. Whole wheat bread toasted, plenty of fresh milk given while still warm (for then it contains the maximum quantity of the ether which is so necessary to restore the vital body), and as much green uncooked food as the patient can take should be given, for that also contains a maximum of ether. Onions are particularly valuable nerve-builders.

A person with Taurus rising, whose Saturn is not in the degrees included within the patient's First or Sixth House, will make the best healer for this patient.

No. 26.—Tuberculosis

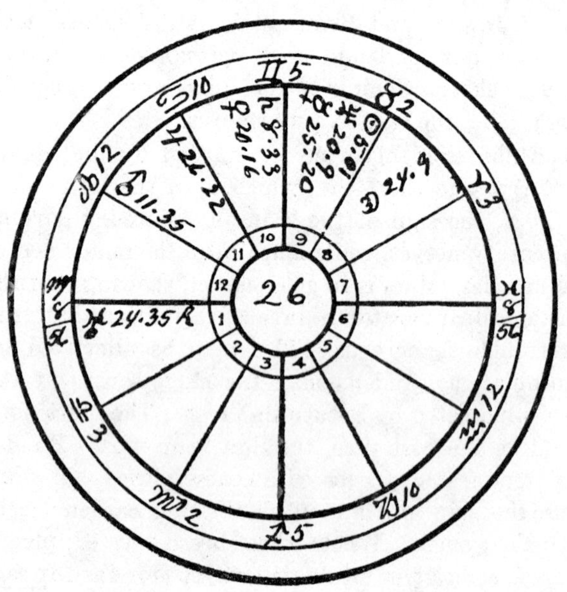

Good Aspects: Uranus trine Mercury and Neptune; Moon sextile Venus; Saturn sextile Mars.

Bad Aspects: Moon conjunction Dragon's Tail; (☋ 22-33 ♈) ; Moon square Jupiter; Sun square Mars; Uranus square Venus.

This is the horoscope of our friend, James Casey, who wrote such helpful articles in the "*Rays.*" He passed into the invisible worlds in June, 1918, and as he has no relatives connected with our society who might read this diagnosis and feel badly on that account, he gave us permission to use it for the benefit of his fellows. He was born on April 24, 1884, 2:00 P. M., in Harlem, Iowa, and became afflicted with tuberculosis while living in Denver, Colo., the Mecca for all who are afflicted with this disease.

You will notice that Saturn, the planet of crystallization and obstruction, is placed in Gemini, the sign which rules the lungs, and although Saturn is the highest elevated planet in the horoscope, besides being unafflicted, there is always a weak spot in the anatomy where he is found. The hot, inflammatory and disruptive Mars is in Leo, the sign which governs the heart, square to the Sun, which is ruler of Leo, in the sign Taurus, which governs the throat and all the passages there. This is a configuration which usually produces fevers, inflammation, wounds and hæmorrhages. Thus there was a tendency in the system toward tuberculosis, and you will furthermore notice that there are four Common, flexible signs on the angles, the Sixth House sign, Virgo, being on the Ascendant with the spasmodic Uranus afflicting Venus, the ruler of the venous circulation, which is placed in Gemini, the sign ruling the lungs. Uranus gives a tendency to coughs and spasms, so you see that the condition is very well outlined in the horoscope. The four common signs show that when he became subject to illness the Virgo nature was too weak to throw it off and he simply made up his mind that he was going to die from it, hence there was no help. If he had been able to throw off the feeling of impending death and to struggle against the sickness there is no doubt that with this horoscope he could have overcome.

For a more detailed analysis of the conditions which resulted in death, see pages 477-480.

No. 27.—Adenoids and Constipation

In this figure the planets occur in four groups: Neptune is in conjunction with Mars, Saturn in conjunction with Uranus, Mercury in conjunction with the Sun, and Jupiter in conjunction with the Moon. The last two groups are also squaring each other. Venus is alone and forms a trine to Jupiter. Note also that the Sun is parallel to Neptune and Mercury, and Venus is parallel to Mars.

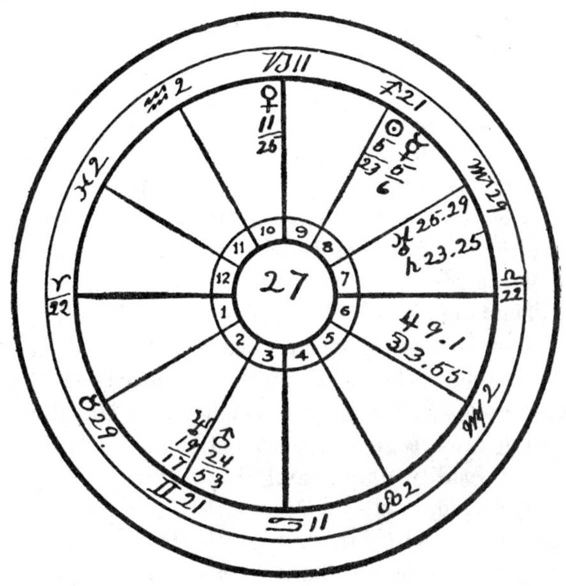

This is the horoscope of a young woman born Nov. 27th, 1896, 2:15 P. M., Tacoma, Wash. We note first that there are Cardinal signs on the angles. showing her to be active in nature. But she acts more from impulse than from reason. This characteristic is shown by the fact that the Moon is square to Mercury and the Sun. Naturally as both the Moon and Mercury are significators of mind, any inharmonious aspects between them are detrimental. Add to this the further fact that Mercury is combust or burned up by its close proximity to the Sun, and it is very evident that we may expect to do very little with this person by reason. This does not mean that she is of an evil mental disposition; she is quite the reverse, as shown by the conjunction of the Moon with the planet of benevolence, Jupiter, and the trine between this last named planet and Venus, the planet of love and pleasure.

The trouble for which this young woman has consulted us is adenoids, which cause extreme difficulty in breathing. The condition is very clearly shown in the horoscope. When we remember that afflictions in one sign always give a reflex action in the opposite, we shall readily understand that Saturn, the planet of obstruction, in conjunction with Uranus, the planet of spasmodic action in the sign Scorpio, is certain to interfere with the rhythmic breath through the Taurus region comprising the throat and lower part of the head. Furthermore, Scorpio also governs the nose, as you will realize when you remember that the most prominent feature of the true Scorpio person is an aquiline nose of generous dimensions. Thus an afflicted Saturn located in Scorpio, which causes an obstructed rectal region and constipation, also at the same time gives a tendency to throat trouble and obstruction of the nasal passages.

In the case of this patient we find the condition aggravated by the square of the Sun and Mercury to the Moon and Jupiter. The Sun and Mercury being placed in Sagittarius are therefore active in the opposite sign Gemini, which governs the lungs, and as the Moon governs the tidal air in the lungs the square of these planets will naturally affect the breathing.

Now for the remedy; it seems far-fetched to attempt to rectify an obstruction in the throat by working on the anus. Nevertheless, Saturn, the planet of obstruction, conjoined with Uranus, the planet of spasmodic action in Scorpio, shows that at certain times the sphincter muscles of the anus are so tightly closed that it is impossible for the diaphragm to move. Under ordinary conditions there is an inbreathing through the anus which regulates the air pressure in the bowels, a fact that is not generally known, but when the sphincter muscles are congested by a configuration of so severe a nature as this one, this automatic regulation stops and the diaphragm is then unable to work with the necessary freedom; therefore the lungs are deprived of the necessary tidal flow of air. So, to relieve this condition an adjustable mechanical dilator should be used. It should be noted that *there are two sphincter muscles* to operate upon, the inside one being located just a little way inside the anus.

After a few treatments of this kind the bowels should be kept open by the use of the proper laxative foods such as prunes, figs *and not forgetting coarse whole wheat bread.*

There is no doubt that this person has resorted to mouth breathing, which has aggravated the throat trouble, but by consistent continuance of the treatment here outlined she will soon experience less difficulty in breathing and it will then be an easy matter to learn to breathe through the proper channels, the nostrils.

A healer having Leo on the Ascendant and whose Saturn is not in Virgo would probably be the best one to help this patient.

No. 28. Accidents to Head, Poor Oxygenation

Good Aspects: Saturn sextile Jupiter, trine Mars and Uranus.

Bad Aspects: Jupiter opposition Mars and Uranus; Moon opposition Venus; Sun and Mercury square Uranus, Mars and Jupiter.

This is the horoscope of a man born on March 16, 1865, at 3 P. M., in England, and it affords a good example of how accidents and also crises are shown in the horoscope. The main affliction comes from the fact that the Sun and Mercury are in close conjunction in the Eighth House, occupied by Pisces. This itself is unfortunate for the reasoning faculty. They are both square to Jupiter in Sagittarius, which also has a strong influence upon the mind. But worst of all, they are square to Mars, the planet of dynamic energy, impulse, etc., and Uranus, the planet of lightning-like action, which precludes forethought. When action is dictated by intuition generated under good aspects, all is well and the person is better off than when he is forced to use the comparatively slow

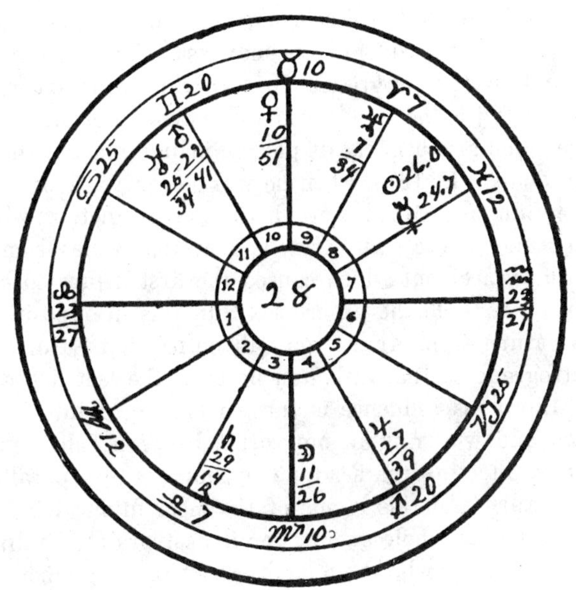

reason. But when it is generated under the adverse aspects of the square and opposition, it results in such rattle-brained foolhardiness and absolute lack of thought and intelligence that the person is generally mentally incompetent. So we see at the very first glance that we have here before us a person who on account of weak mentality is apt to get into trouble and accidents. But the injuries which he has received in consequence of his lack of forethought were all to the head and as the horoscope does not show any serious affliction to Aries, which rules the head, except that Mars and Mercury, which rule the two hemispheres of the cerebrum, are square, what then caused these accidents, we may ask. The answer is found in the progression of the Sun, which corresponds with the time when this person was injured, the Moon also bearing its part in bringing about these accidents. In 1876, when he was eleven years of age, the Sun and Moon were both in conjunction with Neptune in the sign Aries and at that time he met with an accident which caused the first injury to his head. In 1896 the progressed Sun was in opposition to Saturn from Aries; you will notice that Saturn is retrograde so that although he is in the last degrees of Libra his influence is thrown backward into that sign and works as an opposition between Libra and Aries, affecting the head. The Sun was also parallel to Saturn and this is one of the most inimical influences in the whole gamut, for it destroys all vitality of the person who is under its sway for a number of years. (One of the writers can testify to this from personal experience, having felt it for ten or twelve years.) At the same time the progressed Moon was in opposition to Mars and Uranus and square to the Sun and Mercury at birth; thus there were very severe afflictions at that time and the poor man suffered a considerable injury.

The third accident came in 1908, at the age of forty-three. At that time the Sun was in opposition to the Moon's radical place and the progressed Moon was in conjunction with Uranus and Mars, square to the Sun and Mercury, radix. The opposition of the Sun to the Moon occurred from Taurus, which governs the lower part of the head, where he was hurt.

In consequence of these various accidents the man is now suffering from chronic headaches and he is on the verge of insanity. Various doctors have been called on for advice but no one is able to put his finger on the seat of the trouble. Consulting our ephemeris we find that during the man's lifetime Saturn will continue to retrograde further back into Libra, and that his influence in Aries is becoming stronger with every year. Saturn always causes bruises and depression; we are therefore satisfied that there must be a depression of the skull and an examination should be made to find this and have it removed. But the square of the Sun and Mercury to Mars and Uranus in Gemini, which rules the lungs, shows also that there is something the matter with the oxygenation of the system, and Saturn in Libra indicates that there is a scarcity of urine. These defects can be remedied by breathing exercises and through regulating the diet. When that is done there will be at least a large measure of relief.

A healer with Aries rising, whose Saturn is not in Aquarius, will be best able to look after this patient.

No. 29.—Goitre

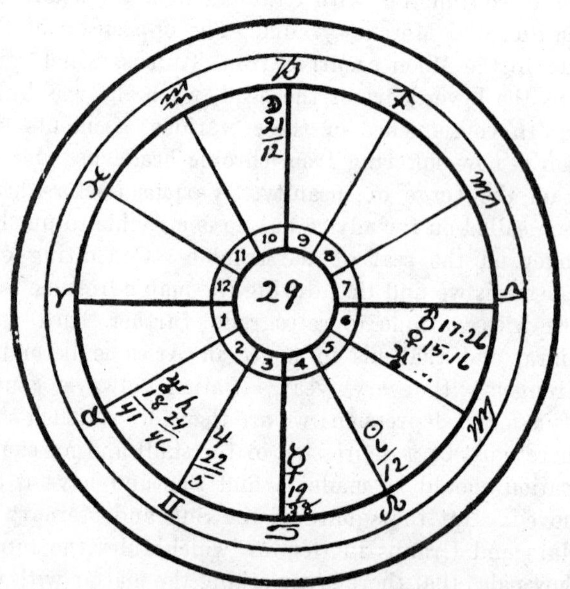

As the hour of birth of the person in this horoscope is not known, we place Aries in the First House, Taurus in the second, etc.

Mercury and the Moon are significators of the mind, and we find them in opposition. This in itself is not a sign of good mentality. We further find that Jupiter in the mercurial sign Gemini is square to

Uranus in Virgo 16-20 and Mars is also in the sign Virgo; thus all the significators point to a weak, and even an erratic mentality. In the last few years Mercury has, moreover, progressed past the natal places of Uranus and Mars, thus accentuating the trouble.

A person may, however, have a weak mind and yet it may not become entirely unbalanced, provided there are no other malefic aspects between the natal planets or the progressed positions. The person may be constitutionally below the stature of the normal mind, and still retain unto the last sufficient hold upon himself or herself so that it does not become an actual disease.

When we look for the signs of disability in a horoscope like the present, we turn to the aspects for our information. Saturn, it appears, is in conjunction with the Dragon's Tail (☋ 26-10 ♉), and this adds to his malefic influence; he is further in conjunction with Neptune in 18 degrees of Taurus, and also with the fixed star Alcyone in 29 degrees of Taurus. As Saturn is the planet of obstruction and Taurus rules the throat we naturally look for some obstruction in that region, and we find that a concretion has taken place, a growth, a crystallization known as Goitre, a disease which also further bears out the indications in the former aspects which we have discussed.

Were it not for good aspects which we have not hitherto mentioned, namely, the sextile of Saturn to Mercury and its trine to the Moon, this person would certainly have become an inmate of an insane asylum, but this is one of the few cases where Saturn really helps in a material sense, for even his good aspects will obstruct when coming to the other planets; but when this obstruction is applied to the Moon, the flightiest planet of all, and to Mercury, the one next to her in swiftness and instability, both of them significators of mind, Saturn does really help to hold the flighty mind in check, and such a weak mental condition as the one found here will be vastly benefited by these aspects, whereas if there are no evil aspects the sextile of Mercury and Saturn will strengthen the mind in a wonderful degree.

As Saturn in Taurus always affects the functions of the opposite sign, Scorpio, namely elimination, it is of great importance to see that both kidneys and bowels act freely with a person like this. Nothing but distilled water should be taken into the system on any account. As the muscles of the neck are always strained in hill and stair climbing, a person with this disease should be housed on a level and on the lower floor of the house. A vegetarian diet consisting of uncooked food is preferable to any other, and it is particularly necessary to get the vegetable salts which may tone the body and bring the standard of general health as high as possible; lettuce is the best single vegetable for this purpose.

No. 30.—Weak Back and Limbs, Eye Trouble, Deafness

Good Aspects: The Moon sextile to Uranus and Jupiter; the Sun sextile to Mars; Venus trine Jupiter.

Bad Aspects: Saturn opposition to Neptune; the Sun and Mercury square to Jupiter and Uranus.

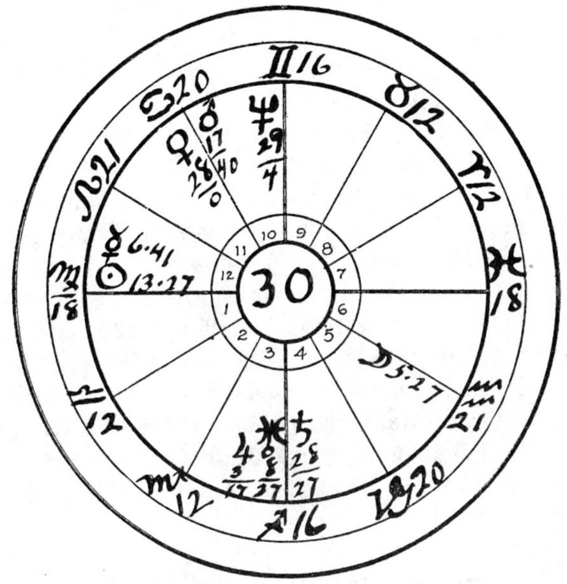

This is the horoscope of a young man born on September 6, 1900, at 6:00 A M., and the disability complained of is a weakness in the back and limbs, which prevents him from moving about normally

Astrologically we find that this is due to several causes. In the first place, there are four Common signs on the angles, the Sixth House sign, Virgo, being on the Ascendant which governs the condition of the body. It is a vital point in that respect. This in itself shows his somewhat indolent nature and a tendency to give up very easily. We also find Mercury, the ruler of the Ascendant, in the Twelfth House, denoting hospitals and chronic illness; he is square to Jupiter and Uranus, which are placed in Sagittarius, the sign which governs the hips and the great sciatic nerve. The Sun, the giver of life, is also square to Uranus, the planet of irregularity, which is conjoined with Jupiter in Sagittarius. And finally, Saturn, the ruler of the bony structure and its articulations, is placed in Sagittarius in opposition to Neptune, in Gemini. All these configurations naturally tend to bring about the conditions complained of if nothing is done to prevent; but in this case, with four Common, flexible signs on the angles, with the life-giving Sun sextile to Mars, the planet of dynamic energy, and with the Moon sextile to Jupiter, the planet governing the arterial blood, it is quite possible to obtain relief by means of exercises which will remove the sluggish conditions.

But we also find other weaknesses of a serious nature latent in this horoscope. Uranus is in conjunction with the nebulous star Antares in Sagittarius 8°, square to the Sun and Mercury. This implies a grave danger to the sight and also to the hearing because of Mercury being in the Twelfth House. These conditions can certainly be overcome if the ounce of prevention is applied. We take it that because the man is not able to otherwise occupy himself he is an inveterate reader and this will bring trouble if persisted in. Massage of the head in the region of the eyes and ears, and exercise of the limbs and body will aid in restoring this young man to health. A healer with Taurus on the Ascendant whose Saturn is not in the patient's Sixth House will probably have the most persistence in the performance of this work.

No. 31.—Eye and Ear Trouble, Poor Circulation

Mercury, the significator of mind, rises *before* the Sun and is in the Twelfth House, conjunction Neptune, its higher octave. This shows that the mind is naturally inclined toward the higher and more spiritual things of life, though Jupiter square Mercury from the house of mind indicates that under severe afflictions this woman may at times follow the example of Job and reason with God concerning the hard fate she has to bear. The Moon, which is the other significator of mind, square Venus, shows us that considerable sorrow may be expected in this life; but the conjunction of Mercury with the mystical Neptune in the Twelfth House gives her a certain degree of spiritual development, which brings much comfort through her communion with the higher worlds, compensating her for her isolation. Jupiter in the Midheaven trine to the Ascendant causes her to look upon life from a more hopeful angle than even people who are not at all afflicted (in comparison with her), and the strength of her hope is bound to help her in a degree beyond human measure; for even as the person who gives way to worry and melancholy

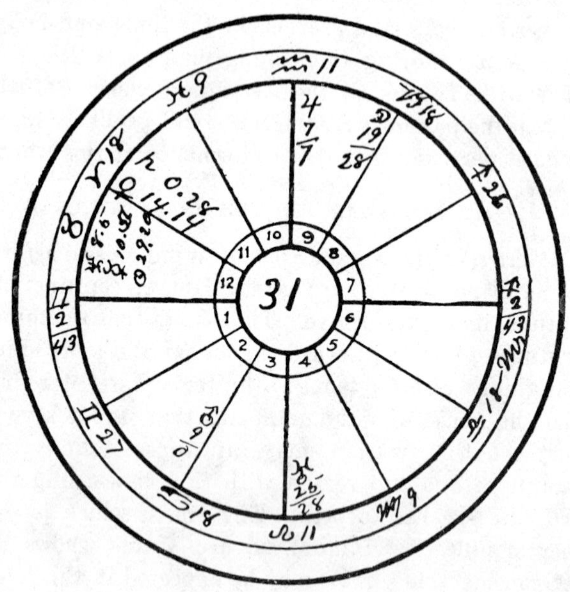

is thereby made more unhappy or unhealthy, so also the person who constantly keeps an optimistic spirit is bound to gain thereby correspondingly in health and happiness. The Sun on the Ascendant, even though it is afflicted by a square of Uranus, is nevertheless a valuable asset in recuperation. The Sun sextile Saturn will give her a persistence, a tenacity of life, that will not let go despite all discouragements.

This woman has been deaf since she was five years of age and this disability is indicated by the position of Mercury in the Twelfth House, by his conjunction with Neptune, and his square to Jupiter. This latter aspect indicates that it is sluggish circulation of the blood which is responsible for the disability. These aspects of Mercury also make her dumb, particularly because Mercury is in Taurus, which governs the vocal organs. She has nevertheless learned to talk, showing that there is no organic disability but only a functional weakness.

But these are not all of the poor woman's afflictions. You will notice that the Sun is in Taurus 29. In other words, it is in conjunction with the Pleiades, a nebular spot in the Zodiac. It is also square to Uranus and parallel to Mars. Therefore the eyes are sorely afflicted; one is almost blind, the other not much better, so that there is danger that she may lose her sight entirely.

On account of her afflictions and the position in which she has been placed, this woman has been unable to get an education. Nevertheless, by persistence, indicated by Saturn sextile the Sun, she has accomplished much. She writes a really beautiful letter which tells how she was in comfortable circumstances up to 1906, when the earthquake in San Francisco deprived her of her all, and still she has not given up hope. Her mental attitude, inspired by her Sun conjunction Ascendant and sextile Saturn, is justified in quite a large measure. The trouble comes from Saturn, the planet of obstruction, in Aries, the sign which governs the head, and the square of Jupiter, the planet which governs arterial circulation, to Mercury in Taurus, the sign which governs the throat. There are also signs of malnutrition, indicated by the presence of Mars in Cancer, the sign which governs the stomach, square Venus, which governs the venous circulation. If the system could be given the proper amount and kind of food and the head and neck massaged with special attention to manipulations of the ears and eyes, conditions might be considerably relieved and further progress of deterioration stopped. An Aquarian whose Saturn is not in Libra or Scorpio would have a most beneficial effect in this case.

No. 32.—Hæmorrhoids, Blindness, Latent Spiritual Sight

In the case before us we have not the hour of birth, and will therefore insert the signs in their respective Houses, commencing with Aries in the First, Taurus in the Second, etc. This person was born November 27, 1867.

Good Aspects: Sun and Mars trine Neptune.

Bad Aspects: The Sun and Mars conjunction Antares; Saturn and Mercury square Jupiter; Mars conjunction the Moon and Venus; Saturn conjunction Mercury, Jupiter square Sun, Uranus square Neptune.

Regarding the mentality of this person, we find that the conjunction of Saturn and Mercury, particularly in the Eighth House sign, Scorpio, clouds the mind with gloom. The Moon, which is the other significator of mind, conjunction Mars in the Ninth

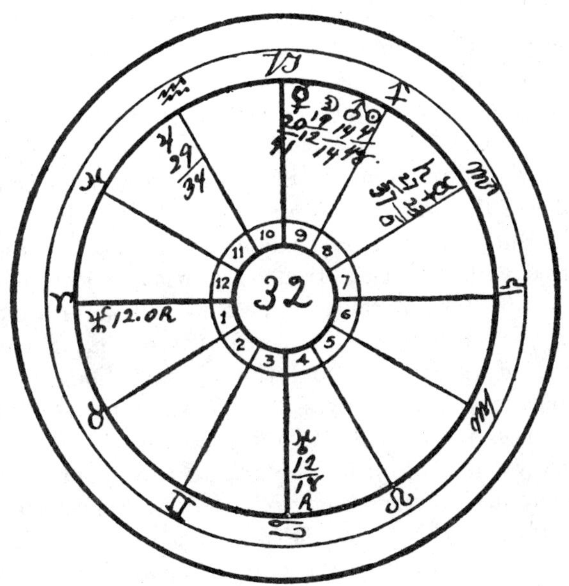

House sign, Sagittarius, would have the tendency to make the patient rebellious against misfortune. This tendency is somewhat softened and toned down by the presence of Venus in conjunction with these planets, and we may therefore conclude that this person is apt to be very much depressed in mind whenever misfortune overtakes him; that he rebels, at least inwardly, very strongly against the blows of fate, though Venus may prevent him from expressing his disappointments.

With regard to the ailments to which this person is subject, we find in the first place that Jupiter square to Mercury and Saturn, the latter being in Scorpio, which rules the rectum, gives a tendency to constipation and hæmorrhoids. This configuration also interferes with the circulation of the arterial blood. His disability is further enhanced by the square of Jupiter to the Sun, the latter planet being ruler of the organ which circulates the vital fluid.

But there is a great misfortune in this life, compared with which the troubles previously mentioned pale into insignificance. The Sun and Mars are in conjunction with the fixed star Antares in eight degrees of Sagittarius, and this configuration always brings trouble to the eyes, though it may not result in blindness from birth. In the present case the crisis came when the Sun had progressed to the opposition of Uranus, at the same time striking the square to Neptune. In that year the Moon also was in conjunction with Neptune in the sign Aries, which rules the head. This kindled the double fire of Mars and the Sun at birth, with the result that inflammation of the eyes made the man blind beyond hope of recovery.

It may seem strange that the writers selected this horoscope for analysis, as the patient is beyond help, but it offers certain points which it will be well for the student to impress upon his mind. You will notice that Mars is trine to Neptune, and that the Sun is only about seven degrees from a trine to Neptune. The culmination of the latter aspect will occur before even the vital body is brought to birth. This is a very good indication that *the spiritual sight may be awakened* in this person and that it will compensate, or more than compensate, for the loss of the physical faculty. There is, however, as you will also note, the square of Neptune and Uranus which makes for mediumship; on that account it would be advisable for this person to be very closely on his guard during the time when the spiritual faculty is being developed, and until he is perfectly safe and balanced in the other world; and it would be a great privilege for a healer receiving such a case to aid a person stricken by the misfortune of blindness to cultivate the latent faculty shown by the horoscope.

No. 33.—Heart Trouble, Dropsy

Good Aspects: Jupiter trine Mercury; Saturn trine Mars.

Bad Aspects: Saturn square the Sun, Moon and Venus; the Moon opposition to the Sun and Venus; Mercury square Neptune; Mars conjunction Uranus.

We consider first the mind of this woman, to obtain the key to her condition, for the mind is the most important factor in bringing about disease and curing it. You may call that Christian Science or whatever you please, the fact remains and has been made use of by all successful healers, either consciously or unconsciously, no matter to what school they belong. And there is more healing in a cheery word from the physician in whom the patient has faith, than in all

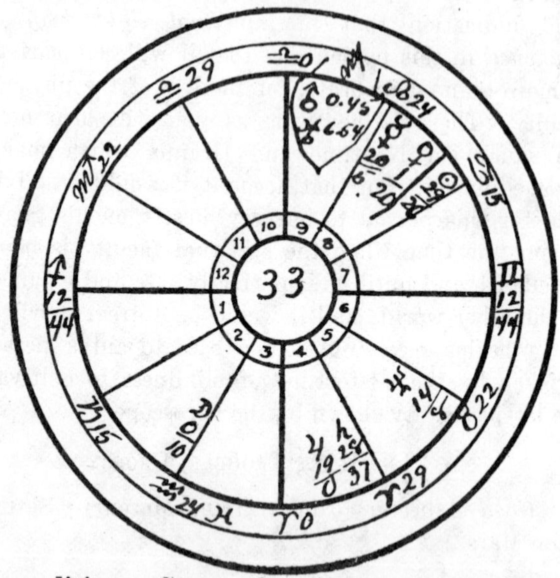

his medicines. Conversely, when the doctor gives up hope and makes a long face, the patient dies unless he "*gets mad,*" or "*spunky,*" as once happened to the writer when he was broken down from overwork. He went to a hospital to get nursing and quiet, and had to engage a regular doctor to comply with the rules. He knew that his condition would not change till the Moon did, and lay patiently waiting, though the case was approaching a crisis, for his mind was too lethargic to set to work; *he expected the Moon to do it all* at the proper time. But on the day of the New Moon his doctor came in with another, and both had faces a yard long. They did not think he had another hour to live; and he laughed, but it made him "mad," and he commenced to work on himself with the result that the dropsical swelling which had almost reached the heart, was gone in a few hours and he was out in the sunshine getting a dose of new life. Before a month had elapsed he had not only left the hospital behind, but had written *The Rosicrucian Philosophy*. There is no doubt that the fluid could not have been eliminated before the change of the Moon, but the co-operation of his mental attitude was necessary to help the lunar forces, and combined with proper action it brought results. Similarly in every case, the right attitude of the mind must be cultivated or cure is impossible.

This figure shows an unfortunate person, for the mind is in a bad state. Saturn is square to the Sun, Moon and Venus. The Moon, which signifies the instinctual mind, is in opposition to the Sun and Venus, robbing life of all joy, making her pessimistic and prone to look only on the dark side. Mercury, the planet of reason, is square to Neptune, the planet of spiritual perception, all these testimonies tell us that nothing we may say is likely to make her cheer up.

Such a poor person is a burden to herself and her associates all through life, so they shun her while she is able to take care of herself, that is to say, while the body is in comparative health; but the af flictions which make her mentally miserable also have their effect on the body, for as we mould the lines of our face to an exact expression of our habitual mode of thought, so are also our other organs shaped and built by this force, and the evil effects show themselves as disease. The Sun, Venus and Mercury in the Eighth House indicate that when sickness comes she is going to let it take its course, and will make no effort to fight for life.

The nature of her sickness is seen to be heart trouble, from the fact that the Sun is on the cusp of Leo, which governs the heart, in conjunction with Venus, which governs the venous circulation, and opposed by the Moon, which rules the liquids of the body. The Sun, Venus and the Moon are squared by Saturn, the planet of obstruction, and thus we see that there was a natal tendency to poor heart action and faulty elimination of liquids.

In 1913 the Sun progressed to the conjunction of Uranus and Mars. The aspects of the Sun are always effective for three years, one and one-half years before the aspect is exact, and a like period after. Therefore it was still active in 1914, when the Moon progressed to the conjunction of Saturn and thus enlivened this square to the Sun, Moon and Venus. Neptune, the watery planet, also reached the natal Sun by transit, and the poor soul was released by the total obstruction of the liquids; in other words, the dropsical condition stopped the heart.

The main effort in such cases should be to get the person to fight. If she could have been made to see that it was her gloomy outlook on life that was responsible for her sickness and that if she did not fight here and now, she would have a harder fate to face next time, it might have helped. No person who is naturally pessimistic can change over night, but he can do a whole lot to cultivate optimism if given years, and we should strive to inculcate this attitude of mind in all, *besides trying to be cheerful ourselves,* for that is a healer's greatest asset.

No. 34.—Sex, Eye and Throat Trouble

The type of mind is denoted particularly here by the square of Saturn to the Sun. This occurs from Cardinal signs, Saturn being essentially dignified and therefore very powerful, while the Sun is in Libra, the sign of its debility and greatest weakness. Life and joy come from the Sun, while Saturn gives gloom and death. Therefore we readily see that this person must be subject to gloom and melancholy. The sextile of Uranus to Mercury, the significator of mind, tells that the person is endowed with an almost uncanny lightning-like intuition, and the square of Uranus to the Moon and Venus shows that she is indiscreet and too weak for her own good. You will notice that this square occurs from the Fixed signs, Leo and Scorpio, and it is therefore a condition which would be very difficult to overcome. Leo governs the heart, and Scorpio the generative organs, and thus her secret is told in the horoscope in unmis-

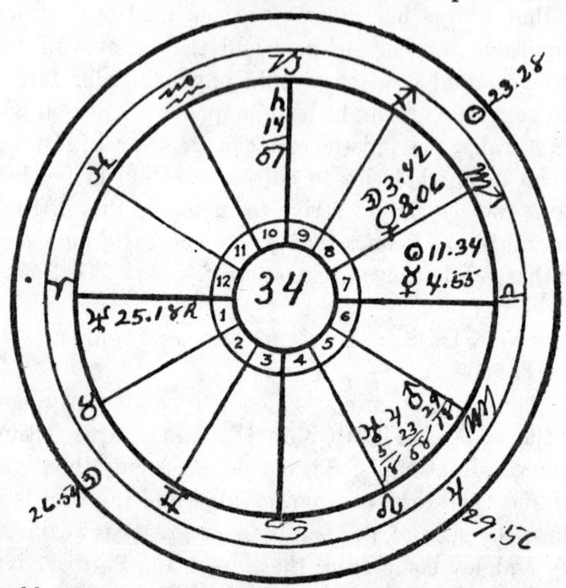

takable terms. When such secrets of the soul are revealed by this sacred science, it shows us also the hidden springs which are causes of the acts we are only too prone to condemn, and it teaches us that we should pity rather than censure a soul impelled by such an almost irresistible force as here revealed.

The act itself should, of course, never be condoned, but the tenderest kindness and the greatest effort to succor should be given to the one who is thus afflicted.

The horoscope is, as you know, the clock of destiny, and the position taken by the planets at birth give certain tendencies for life. From that natal position the planets move on to different positions with every year that passes, as the hands of a clock move around its face; thus they bring to pass events foreshown at birth. Now you will notice that the Sun is in eleven degrees of Libra in this horoscope, so at nineteen years of age the Sun entered the sign Scorpio. At twenty-two it reached the conjunction with the Moon and Venus and a couple of years later the square with Uranus was reached. During this period the unfortunate tendency spoken of developed and the seeds of disease were sown which resulted in a number of operations, both in the lower regions and in the throat, for you must remember that the opposite is always afflicted. The generative organ can never be hurt without in some measure its counterpart, the larynx and throat, also being affected. During the years which intervened between that time and 1914 the Sun had pursued its path through Scorpio, and reached the affliction of Jupiter, which occurs from the sign Leo in 23 degrees. This square was also augmented by the fact that the Moon in its circle around the horoscope had been going through Taurus, so that was an opposition of the progressed Sun and Moon, both of them squaring the planet

Jupiter at the same time. The Sun's square to Jupiter will for a few years be an affliction to this poor person. Uranus at birth was also on the Ascelli in Leo, the nebulous spot that is so dangerous to the eyes, and from there it squares the Moon. This, also, is another danger which faces this person, for, as you know, eye trouble is very often the accompaniment of indiscretion.

Now comes the question as to what can be done for this poor person. As we have often stated, the first effort should be toward instilling hope into the mind. Persons suffering with melancholy are always centering their thoughts upon self, always seeing their own desperate position which appears to them more hopeless than that of any other. If their interest can be diverted from self then the battle is more than half won; that should be the first consideration of the healer.

A simple diet should be prescribed and no highly seasoned dishes permitted a person of this nature. The sextile of Uranus to the Sun and Mercury and the trine of Neptune to Jupiter shows that an appeal along the higher lines, an appeal to the better and nobler nature will not meet with a rebuff and it is possible on account of these positions to elevate this person's ideas and ideals so that she may become a servant of humanity instead of driftwood upon the ocean of life. You will note that all the good aspects are from Cardinal and Fixed signs, that the Common signs are void of planets, hence there is a great deal of hope. There is energy in this person, and when this energy has been turned in the right direction, when she has become thoroughly aroused, then the great sinner may become the great saint, and a blessing to humanity.

No. 35.—Solitary Vice, Tuberculosis

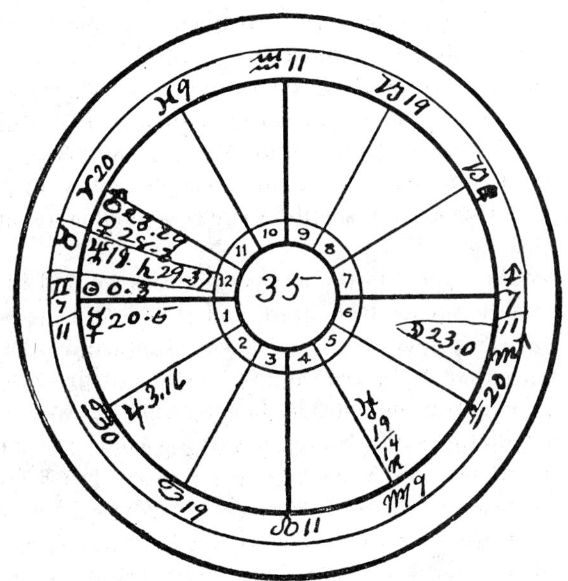

Good Aspects: Neptune trine Uranus; Uranus sextile the Moon; Jupiter sextile Venus.

Bad Aspects: Mars conjunction Venus; Sun conjunction Saturn; Uranus square Mercury; Neptune opposition the Moon.

This is the horoscope of a woman born May 21, 1883, at 5 A. M., Longitude 88 West, Latitude 44 North. The student will at once note that five of the nine planets are placed in the Twelfth House, which governs sorrow, trouble, and self-undoing. This has been a characteristic feature in the life. She is a competent worker in her vocation, stenography and bookkeeping, but has, nevertheless, found herself unable to obtain employment at various times and has been at those times on the verge of starvation. This is due to the opposition of Saturn and Neptune from the Twelfth House to the Moon in the Sixth, the house of employment. Jupiter, though exalted in the Second House and sextile Venus, is unable to offset this.

With respect to the mental qualities we find that Mercury is square to Uranus, and the Moon in opposition to Neptune. This makes her skeptical, critical, very peculiar and spasmodic in her mental processes, with an extremely morbid imagination. Uranus is placed in the Fifth House, governing courtship and the relations among the sexes prior to marriage, and therefore, squared to Mercury, it indicates an unconventional turn of the mind, with a tendency to promiscuous relations, involving public criticism and slander. That in itself is an extremely unfortunate configuration and condition in a life, but it is only one of a number of afflictions which point in the same direction, for in the Twelfth House, the house of sorrow, trouble, and self-undoing, we find Mars, the planet of dynamic energy, conjoined with Venus, the planet of love, in the fiery sign Aries, another inflammatory sex condition; and last, but not least, we note Neptune in Taurus, opposition to the Moon in Scorpio, which governs the generative organs. This latter is the worst of all for it makes the mind almost insane upon this subject, conjuring up before the imagination morbid pictures, and where the configuration occurs from the Sixth and Twelfth Houses it is a certain indication of inveterate self-abuse. Naturally such practices in time undermine the health and disease shows itself in the weakest parts of the body according to the indications of the horoscope. In the present case we find Saturn on the cusp of Gemini in conjunction with the Sun. Gemini is the sign which rules the lungs, and the conjunction as we see is almost exact, wanting only 26 minutes. Thus the cold, crystallizing saturnine forces are hardening the lungs and producing the disease we know as tuberculosis, which is slowly sapping her vitality and carrying her toward an early grave. It may be noted in passing that her mother succumbed to tuberculosis at the very moment when she gave birth to this child. Mars by progression has now arrived close to the place of Neptune at birth. This will unfortunately in all probability accentuate the morbid craving indicated by Neptune opposition to the Moon, so that if left to herself the end will not be very far off.

Tuberculosis though serious is not, however, necessarily fatal if she can be put under restraint so that it becomes impossible for her to gratify the passion for solitary vice that saps her vitality. Thus the spells of gloom which are also resultant from the conjunction of Saturn and the Sun in the Twelfth House can be overcome if she can be given a brighter outlook upon life. Then the usual measures employed against tuberculosis may probably save her. The occult has an intense attraction for her, indicated by the exact trine of Neptune and Uranus, also by Uranus sextile to the Moon. By playing upon those strings and giving her a new interest in life it may be possible to win her away from her present morbid channels of thought. At any rate salvation from the evil configurations should always be sought through the good aspects and substituting the higher for the lower may help this poor soul out of her condition. Very little can be done physically until the mental condition is changed. A healer with either Libra or Aquarius rising and whose Saturn is not in Libra or Scorpio would be beneficial, but much firmness is needed here and therefore probably the Fixed sign would be preferable.

No. 36.—Horny, Venereal Growths and Kidney Trouble

Good Aspects: Mercury sextile Jupiter; the Moon trine Venus.

Bad Aspects: The Sun conjunction Uranus; Mars conjunction Venus; Neptune square to Saturn.

This is the horoscope of a young man born in Boynton, Missouri, October 11, 1889, at 6:00 P. M. It is a strange case which has puzzled all the doctors who have been consulted. About five years ago all

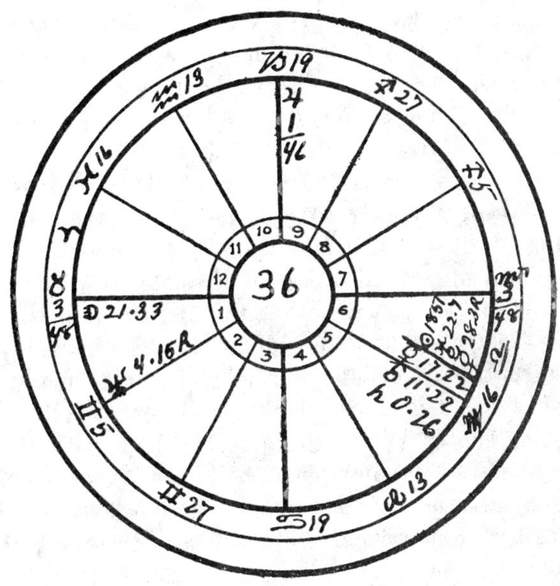

the joints in arms, legs and neck commenced to grow stiff, so that by degrees he became unable to move. At the same time there appeared, instead of the nails, a strange horny growth on fingers and toes; this grows to a certain length or stage of development and then it begins to suppurate. This facilitates the removal of the growth and when that has been completed the suppuration ceases, but immediately a new growth begins to form. Lately the jaws have also commenced to grow stiff, so that now the young man can no longer eat with comfort.

The very first glance at the horoscope shows us Uranus, the planet of spasmodic action, in conjunction with the Sun, and in the sign Libra, which rules the kidneys. We also note that Uranus is parallel with Mars, the planet of dynamic energy; this shows at once that the action of the kidneys is spasmodic and irregular so that instead of the poisons being eliminated from the body by these organs they are retained and naturally contaminate the whole system. But we also find that this patient is poisoned to a greater extent than ordinarily by a venereal disease contracted about seven or eight years ago; this is shown as a tendency in the natal horoscope by the conjunction of Venus, the planet of love, with Mars, the planet of dynamic energy, in the Fifth House, which governs courtship and the relations of the sexes before marriage. Saturn is also there with his obstructive hand and square to Neptune, the planet which governs strange and unusual conditions. Neptune is in the sign Gemini, which rules the hands and fingers. About seven years ago, when the Moon was in Pisces by progression, the sign which governs the toes, it was in opposition to Venus, Mars and Saturn and square to Neptune. We base our judgment that the disease was contracted at that time on the fact that the afflicting planets are in Common or flexible signs; hence it could have been avoided without much effort. As it is, the most drastic measures for purification of the blood must be adopted; the patient should be brought to California, treated with daily sun-baths to facilitate copious perspiration, and given nothing but water and fruit juices until the system has been cleansed.

Planetary Hours

Measures for the alleviation of pain and disease cannot always be deferred to a propitious time, but where that is possible the student will find that remedial treatments given under the propitious planetary rays are much more efficient and successful than when applied haphazard. Therefore the following hints may be found valuable.

Surgeons who have watched and tabulated these matters inform us that the operations performed while the Moon is increasing in light (see p. 521) are generally more successful, less liable to cause complications and more quickly healed than operations performed when the Moon is decreasing in light.

When a surgical operation seems unavoidable consult the ephemeris and if the Moon is going through the sign which rules that part of the body where the operation is to be performed defer it for a day or two till the Moon gets well into the next sign. This will minimize the danger of complications, and not infrequently the symptoms change so that operation is avoided.

Always look to the benefics and the good aspects in a horoscope for directions concerning how and when to treat. Suppose the Sun, the giver of life, is square to Saturn, the planet of stagnation and death. The tendency is to rob the person of vitality and if he is taken ill recuperation will be very slow. Then, to give the most effective and energizing treatment apply the principle of the day and hour rulers as given in our *Simplified Scientific Astrology;* choose the Sun's day (Sunday) and the hours ruled by the Sun on any day. Treatments on Mars' day (Tuesday) and the hours ruled by Mars on any day, will also build up wonderfully. Similarly with the other planets, their virtue and power is greatest during the days ruled by them.

But the so-called malefics also have their virtues. Poultices intended to draw suppuration from a wound, or bring a boil to a head are most efficacious on the hot and inflammatory Mars' day (Tuesday), or in the hours of Mars on any day, but applications made to disperse a swelling are most successful when applied on the day of Saturn, the planet of suppression, or in his hours on any day.

Treatments received on the day and in the hours of the planets which are well aspected in the patient's horoscope are always more powerful and beneficial than they would be if given in the hours and on the days ruled by planets afflicted when he was born.

Six tables of Planetary Hours covering the twelve months, usable for both North and South Latitude, will be found in *Simplified Scientific Astrology*.

CONCLUSION

We have now given an exposition of the methods we use in diagnosis of disease. This we trust will enable the student to work out the subject for himself in greater detail. And as he uses it unselfishly to aid suffering human beings, the spiritual qualities will be developed in him so that *the message of the stars* revealed in each horoscope will be as an open book. Thus used, this wonderful science will aid him to lay up treasures in heaven as nothing else in the world can do. And we pray God that this book may be the means of fostering soul growth in all who aspire to follow the dual commandment of Christ:

"*Preach* the Gospel and *heal* the sick."

IMPORTANT NOTICE

Despite all we can say, many people write enclosing money for horoscopes, forcing us to spend valuable time writing letters of refusal and giving us the inconvenience of returning their money. Please do not thus trouble us, as it will avail nothing. We use Astrology only for healing purposes. If you are sick we will gladly help you, but we do not advise people in worldly affairs either gratis or for pay.

Table of Contents

PART II.

Medical Astrology

Index to Natal Astrology

—A—

Abel, tragedy connected with, 15
Abiff, Hiram, builder of Solomon's Temple, 23
highest initiate of old system, 24
Adam, man, humanity, number of, is nine, 52
Adept, a complete creative unit, 345
can form new bodies without going through the womb, 346
Adjusted Calculation Date, how to find, article, 470-480
Ailments, acute, afflictions from cardinal signs, 440
convertible, or chronic, from common signs, 441
organic or hereditary, from fixed signs, 441
Altruism, must supersede egoism; relation of Saturn and Jupiter to, 39
Amulets, effective and ineffective use of, article, 60-67
Angels, fallen, are Lucifer Spirits, 569
were human in Moon Period, 62
Angles, of the horoscope, are first, fourth, seventh, tenth houses, 73-74
Animals, archangels, their group-spirits, 62
Antares, in Sagittarius 8°, a danger to eyes, 546
Aquarian Age, at end of, new race born, 11
length of, approximately 2000 years, 12
probably final preparatory day before Sixth *Epoch*, 13
seven hundred years before definitely ushered in, 27
Aquarius, effect when Sun in, 136, 137, 155
influence of, when rising, 108, 109, 437
rules the ankles, 441
ruled by Saturn, 64, and by Uranus, 358, 365
Aquarius-Leo, age of, indicates new phase of religion, 27
Archangels, human in Sun Period, 62
Aries, children of, effect when Sun in, 119-120, 150
influence when rising, 92, 93, 434
rules head and face, 441
when Sun entered sign of, by precession, 17, 24

Aries-Libra, age of, indicates a day of judgment, 25
Aryan Epoch, divided into three ages: 12, 25-29
Aryan Age, Moses to Christ, Aries-Libra, 12, 25
Piscean Age, Roman Catholicism, Pisces-Virgo, 12, 25
Aquarian Age, to come, Aquarius-Leo, 12, 27
Aryan Epoch, development in, 16
rainbow seen first time at opening of, 19
Aryo-Semitic Race, when called out, 11
Ascelli, Leo 6°, one of three danger spots to eyes, 564, 545
Ascendant, at birth, or its opposite, is Moon's place at conception, 88
important factor in horoscope,88
ruler determines mineralogical affinity, 63
See also Rising Sign.
Aspects, lunar, little, if any, influence of their own, 500
adverse, or good, never to be judged singly, 168, 415
Astrologers, advice to younger ones, 70, 71
see aura if endowed with spiritual sight, 41
unable to determine strength of will of native, 71
Astrology, belief in requires belief in previous and future lives, 57
founded on cosmic fact, 468
horary, author's experience in, and philosophy of, 67
of enormous benefit in attainment of spiritual growth, 54
three factors in, bring mystic message of stars, 71
Atlantean Epoch, early third, 14; duration of, 12; latter third, 11
Atlantis, development of egoism during latter third, 16; home of the Bull, 19; last of, destroyed by water, 16; when submerged, 18
Aura, colored by planetary rays, 42

—B—

Barrenness and fertility, under control of Jehovah, 303
Bible, astrological key needed to open otherwise "closed book," 19
discussion of events and principles of, Chapter I, 3-30
light given on obscure passages of, 3
translation of word "serpent" in, 21
Birth, best time for, article, 67-70
occurs with first breath inhaled, 89
rising sign at, or its opposite, is Moon's place at conception, 89
Birth stones, amulets, etc., value of, 60-67

Black magician, dependent upon Neptunian ray, 50
Bode's Law, proves Neptune does not belong to our solar system, 53
Body, parts of ruled by planets, 441
Brain, angels helped to form, 342
Bull, properly worshiped by Atlanteans, 17

—C—

Cadent houses, 3rd, 6th, 9th, 12th, indicate work, voluntary and forced, 74
Cain, tragedy connected with, 15
Cancer, effect when Sun in, 125-126, 152
 influence when rising, 96, 97, 435
 rules breast and stomach, 441
 sphere of the soul, ruled by Moon, 6
 watery in nature, 14
Cancer-Capricorn, age of, early third of Atlantean Epoch, 14
Capricorn, effect when Sun in, 135-136, 155
 fish part of, symbolizes state of life under water, 14
 influence when rising, 106-108, 436
 part fish and part goat, 7
 ruled by Saturn, 6
 rules the knees, 441
 solstitial point, will see inauguration of new cycle, 16
Cardinal signs, nature and keyword, 80
Cattle, possession of, desired by ancient nations, 17
Celestial Centaur (Sagittarius), shows savage ideal, 15
Chaos, Saturn is door to, 6
Children, indications for, in horoscope, 460-461
 desired and loved into life, 450
 of Israel, left flesh pots of Egypt, 27
Christ, abrogated sacrifice of others, 28
 announces himself as the Great Shepherd, 19
 called disciples fishers of men, 26
 came and inaugurated new teaching, 25
 heavenly mother of, 9
 must be born within, 10
 newborn, within, actual experience, 10
 raised widow's son, 24
Christian Rosenkreuz, reincarnation of Hiram Abiff, 24
Circulation, venous and arterial, restricted, prevents deep breathing and oxygenation, 477
Clairvoyance, undesirable, is result of adverse aspects of Uranus, 48

—F—

—G—

—J—

—K—

—L—

—N—

—O—

—P—

—Q—

—R—

—S—

—V—

—W—

—Z—

Index to Medical Astrology

—A—

Abdominal cramps, Uranus in Virgo, 565
Abdominal Disorders, Moon in Pisces, 552
Abdominal Tumors, Jupiter in Pisces, 559; Moon in Virgo, 552; Venus in Pisces, 548.
Abortions, Uranus in Scorpio, 566
Abscess of kidneys, Moon in Libra, 552
Accidents, Mars predisposes to, 561
Adenoids, 646; afflictions in Scorpio, 542; Mars in Taurus, 562
Adrenals, Jupiter rules, 557, 570, 571. *See also* Jupiter afflicted in Libra.
secretions of, deficient, Jupiter in Libra, 558
Afflictions. *See* each Sign and Planet by name.
Alcoholism. *See* Drunkenness.
Anemia, afflictions in Leo, 542
Saturn in Cancer, 555. *See also* Hydraemia.
Aneurism, afflictions in Leo, 542
Angels, fallen, Lucifer spirits, 569
present vantage point of, is the Moon, 569
Anger, writer "gets mad" and lives, 666, 667
Angina pectoris, afflictions in Leo, 542; Mars in Leo, 562
Ankles, swollen, Jupiter in Aquarius, 559; Jupiter in Leo, 558
weak, Saturn in Aquarius, 556
Antares, Sagittarius, 8°, 546
Antiparistalsis, afflicted Saturn, 554
Antipathy, revealed in horoscopes, 537
Aphasia, loss of power of speech, Sun afflicted in Aries, 545
Apoplexy, afflicted Jupiter, 556; afflictions in Taurus, 541; Jupiter in Leo, 558; Jupiter in Scorpio, 558; Jupiter in Taurus, 557
Appendicitis, Mars in Virgo, 563; Saturn in Virgo, 555

Aquarius, afflictions, diseases, parts of body ruled by, 543
passage of mystic sun through, 560
Aries, afflictions, diseases, parts of body ruled by, 541
Sun in, gives strong vitality, 545
Arms, accidents to, Mars in Gemini, 562, 621
Arteries, diseases of, Saturn in Aquarius, 556
Arterio-sclerosis, afflictions in Leo, 542; Saturn in Leo, 555
Ascelli, Leo 6°, 545
Asphyxiation, Mercury in Gemini, 549
Assimilation, poor, Sun afflicted in Virgo, 546
Asthma, afflictions in Gemini, 541; Mercury in Gemini, 549; Mercury in Sagittarius 550; Moon in Gemini, 551; Moon in Sagittarius, 552; Saturn in Gemini, 554
Astrology, infallible but for patient's will, 530
judgment of astrologer fallible, 530-531
preferable to spiritual sight for diagnosis, 606

—B—

Back, affections of, Mars in Leo, 562; Saturn in Aquarius, 556
Backache, afflictions in Leo, 545; Mercury in Capricorn, 550; Mercury in Leo, 549; Moon in Leo, 551; Sun in Leo, 545; Venus in Leo, 547
Baptism, planetary, given with first complete breath, 536
Belching, Saturn in Cancer, 555
Bladder, inflammations, Mercury in Scorpio, 550; Moon in Scorpio, 552
Blindness, aspects indicating, 662-664
Blind spot, sensitized by Neptune, 590
Bloating, Moon in Cancer, 551. *See also* Dropsy.
Blood, affections of, Jupiter in Gemini, 558; Jupiter in Sagittarius, 559; Mercury in Aquarius, 550; Moon in Sagittarius, 552; Venus in Gemini, 547
circulation of venous, 547
not liquid, as supposed, 576
overheating of, Mars in Aquarius, 563; Mars in Leo, 562
stagnation and obstruction of in lower limbs, 622, 623
venous, ruled by Venus, 600
Blood poisoning, afflicted Jupiter, 557; Mars in Aquarius, 563
Blood vessels, rupture of, Mars causes, 561
Bodies, all are transformed mineral, 535. *See also* Body.

—C—

—E—

—L—

—M—

—O—

—P—

—R—

—S—

—T—

—U—

The Rosicrucian Fellowship

There was a time, even as late as that of Greece, when *Religion, Art* and *Science* were taught unitedly in the Mystery-temples. But it was necessary to the better development of each that they should separate for a time.

Religion held sole sway in the so-called "dark ages." During that time it bound Science and Art hand and foot. Then came the period of the Renaissance and *Art* came to the fore in all its branches. Religion was strong as yet, however, and Art was only too often prostituted in the service of Religion. Last came the wave of modern *Science,* and with iron hand it has subjugated Religion.

It was a detriment to the world when Religion shackled Science. *Ignorance* and *Superstition* caused untold woe, nevertheless man cherished a lofty spiritual ideal then; he hoped for a higher and better life. It is infinitely more disastrous that Science is killing Religion, for now even *Hope,* the only gift of the gods left in Pandora's box, may vanish before *Materialism* and *Agnosticism.*

Such a state cannot continue. Reaction must set in. If it does not, anarchy will rend the cosmos. To avert a calamity *Religion, Science* and *Art* must reunite in a higher expression of the *Good,* the *True* and the *Beautiful* than obtained before the separation.

A spiritual religion, however, cannot blend with a materialistic science any more than oil can mix with water. Therefore steps were taken to spiritualize Science and make Religion scientific.

In the thirteenth century a high spiritual teacher,

having the symbolical name, Christian Rosenkreuz—Christian: Rose: Cross—appeared in Europe to commence that work. He founded the mysterious Order of Rosicrucians with the object of throwing occult light upon the misunderstood Christian religion and to explain the mystery of life and being from the scientific standpoint in harmony with religion.

In the past centuries the Rosicrucians have worked in secret, but now the time has come for giving out a definite, logical and sequential teaching concerning the origin, evolution and future development of the world and man, showing both the spiritual and scientific aspects; a teaching which makes no statements that are not supported by reason and logic. Such is the teaching promulgated by the Rosicrucian Fellowship. It satisfies the mind by giving clear explanations and neither begs nor evades questions. It holds out a reasonable solution to all mysteries but, and this is a very important "but," *it does not regard the intellectual understanding of God and the Universe as an end in itself;* far from it. The greater the intellect, the greater the danger of its misuse. Therefore the *scientific teaching is only given in order that man may believe and start to live the religious life* which alone can bring true fellowship.

The International Headquarters

of the Rosicrucian Fellowship

Having formed the Rosicrucian Fellowship for the purpose of promulgating the Rosicrucian teachings and aiding aspirants on the path of progression, it became necessary to find a permanent home and facilities requisite for doing this work. To this end a tract of land was purchased in the little town of Oceanside, California, ninety miles south of Los Angeles and forty miles north of San Diego, the southwesternmost city of the United States.

Southern California offers exceptional opportunities for spiritual growth on account of the etheric atmosphere being denser than in any other part of the world, and *Mt. Ecclesia*, as the Rosicrucian Fellowship headquarters is called, has been particularly favored in this respect.

The work of building was started in the latter part of 1911. As of 1973, the grounds have been greatly beautified and numerous buildings erected, some of which now take the place of the old original ones.

The *Pro-Eccelsia* or *Chapel,* in which two 15-minute services have been held daily since its dedication in December, 1913, was thoroughly renovated in 1962. A devotional service with lecture continues to be conducted on Sundays. The public is welcomed at all services in the Chapel.

The *Ecclesia,* or *Healing Temple,* the center of our spiritual healing activities, was dedicated on Holy Night of 1920. A healing service is conducted here each evening; only Probationers attend.

The *Administration Building* was completed in 1917 and renovated in 1962. On the second floor are offices for the various departments: Esoteric, Correspondence Courses, Editorial, Foreign Languages, Accounting, etc. On the first floor are the Shipping Department and the Printshop, where our monthly Letters and Lessons, *Rays from the Rose Cross,* pamphlets, etc., are printed. A letterpress was used until 1972, when an offset press was installed. The increase in sales of our books has necessitated the printing of most of them elsewhere.

The *Dining Hall* or *Cafeteria* was built in 1914, enlarged in 1939, and renovated in 1962. Only vegetarian meals are served to workers and guests.

The *Rose Cross Lodge* was built in 1924, for the use of guests and workers. After numerous repairs, it is now used largely for storing the books we sell.

The *Sanitarium Building* was opened in 1939 and used for a number of years to house and treat patients suffering from non-contagious diseases. It is now our Guest House, used by visiting members and workers. Numerous cottages built since 1962, with renovated older ones, provide living quarters for workers.

The *Healing Department Building* was completed in 1940. Here the secretaries carry on the correspondence pertaining to the Healing Work.

Palm, eucalyptus, and other trees, along with a profusion of shrubs and flowers, make this a place of beauty and inspiration.

THE PLANET PLUTO

Although discovered only about forty years ago, and of very slow motion, the planet Pluto has now considerable seemingly reliable astrological data gathered about it. By inserting Pluto in old charts, and taking the keys handed down in mythology, it has been possible to fashion many keywords and keyphrases which enable astrologers to interpret correctly the influence of this planet in any sign, house, and aspect.

These keywords are numerous and include such well-known ones as transformation, transmutation, redemption, regeneration, degeneration, death and rebirth, unity, cooperation, dictatorship, disappearance, underworld, gangster, and coercion. It will be seen that these are very largely connected with the eighth house, the house of inheritance and death.

In mythology Pluto was God of the nether world, called Hades, or the Hell of orthodoxy, where burns the Eternal Fire. This fire corresponds to sex, the procreating force. When analyzed, Pluto indicates all phases of sex, and, as sex activities are the strongest in matters of life and death, so this planet may well be termed the powerhouse of the planetary family. It should not be strictly termed a malefic, we believe, but rather as uncompromising, giving no favors, and demanding that benefits be earned.

Pluto can well be allocated to the underworld, for the word means *wealth*, being applied to him because *corn*, the wealth of early times, was sent from beneath the earth as his gift. Plutus, the God of Wealth, was represented as blind, indicating that when man focuses his attention on material things he fails to see the more worthy things around him. Truly, "the love of money is the root of all evil."

Our word *plutocrat* is derived from Pluto, and means power of domination through wealth derived from sources other than one's own labor. Such wealth is within the jurisdiction of the eighth house, the natural zodiacal position of Scorpio. It stems from inheritances, legacies, bonuses, windfalls, insurance, and similar sources. It has been earned in a previous incarnation and comes from hidden sources as an inheritance in the present life.

Pluto and Proserpina, his wife, ruled over the Spirits of the dead in the Lower World; here we have a direct analogy with the eighth house rulership of death. Pluto and Proserpina are correlated with the male and female principles in Nature, the principles of procreation.

Another correlation with eighth house matters becomes evident when we consider the function of Ceres, Goddess of Corn and mother of Proserpina, from whom the word *cereal* is derived. In the growth-cycle of corn, as of most plants, an old plant dies, but the seed from which it sprang is buried and regenerates --- out of death comes rebirth.

Pluto, generally accepted as ruler, or co-ruler with Mars, of the sign Scorpio, governs the excretory organs which control the sewage system of the body, as well as municipal sewage systems. Here we see Pluto's role as regenerator and transformer, for all excretory matter, when buried in the earth, is transformed, regenerated, or redeemed, and will reappear, phoenixlike, in other forms.

On its positive side, Pluto works for unity through organization. The regeneration of body and mind takes place when sense gratification is discontinued, the life forces ascending through the serpentine spinal cord as a fluid or gas, vitalizing the pineal gland, which comes under the rulership of the spiritual Neptune. Then men may soar to great heights by the force of a renewed mind. As a result, the Plutonian rulership is converted or transferred to the head sign Aries (ruled by Mars), the seat of thought and of the pineal gland.

On its negative side, Pluto engenders tyranny, dictatorship, and organization for the purpose of domination. Thus Pluto influences the lords of the underworld, gangsters, and murderers. When in the eighth house of a natal horoscope, it may indicate a mysterious death, possibly through surgery, or after disappearance.

In its adverse aspects, Pluto has been likened to the Dweller on the Threshold (the composite elemental entity created on the invisible planes by our untransmuted evil thoughts and acts in past lives). In its positive aspects, it has been compared with the Holy of Holies. No planet can indicate more depraved or drastic conditions, or, conversely, more exalted heights of spirituality.

The essential qualities of a planet's "spiritual nature" must coincide with the essential qualities of the sign it rules. Therefore, in a study of Pluto, it is necessary also to consider the sign Scorpio, concerning which considerable authentic information has come to us through past centuries, and of which Pluto and Mars are generally accepted by leading astrologers as co-rulers.

As a fixed, watery sign, Scorpio may be likened to ice, compressed and immobile. As an emotional significator it is feeling in its most intense form. It is the source of desire-power from which all humanity derives its emotional pabulum, to be transmuted through love for the regenerating of Life. From this source, all living things derive their creative expression and perpetuation. Because we have used this power in many ways during many incarnations, all human beings have a great area of "submerged" desire-potential, unseen in the present lifetime, which stems directly from our affiliation to this resource. This mutual affiliation has been referred to by many thinkers as the "collective unconscious."

In terms of a conventional, orthodox viewpoint

we may say that Scorpio represents or symbolizes the "source of evil." This expresses the attitude of people who see life as black or white---essentially good or essentially evil. Such a concept has been, and still is, necessary, because it serves as a guidepost for the conduct of evolving humanity.

As man evolves, however, his love-consciousness becomes more spiritualized and his intelligence more developed. Self-love becomes love of mate and progeny, and, eventually, "brotherly love;" the forces of sexuality are raised in vibratory quality to extend into levels of creativity and mental power. Through it all the consciousness of the individual ripens and matures into desire for improvement, expansion into wider acquaintance with the universe and other people, and, ultimately, for wisdom and realization of ideals. Thus life is not "entirely black" or "entirely white," but a process of developing. Scorpio, through the eighth house patterns, makes possible the extension of experience into the transcendent expressions of the ninth, tenth, eleventh, and twelfth houses---those ruling the mind, social standing, friends, and sorrow.

Scorpio appears evil only to the mind that sees evil as a "static entity." When viewed in a more dynamic context, Scorpio is the source of all love, all aspiration, and, through fulfillment of relationship-experience, the source of all wisdom.

There is an unpleasant psychological factor involved in the Scorpio vibration which must be considered, and that is the frustration of the unreleased generative urge. This creates a congestion in the desire nature which results in myriad emotional, nervous, and mental ills that may afflict humanity in almost any phase of development. It is true that there are a few persons in incarnation at any time who do not require this form of release, but they are few and far between.

It is natural and healthy that people, generally speaking, experience the fulfillment of the mating urge in the companionship of love-relationship. Not many Egos are yet physiologically or emotionally ready for a life of celibacy, and it would be dangerous, individually and to society, for most people to undertake such a life at their present stage of development.

This, however, is not intended as an argument for indiscriminate use of the sex force for purposes of propagation or pleasure. This same force, when conserved, can be transmuted into spiritual force and released in the form of mental creativity and epigenesis. For people who are aware of the true nature and ultimate goal of the creative agent now termed "sex force," and of the means of channeling it upward, there is no need to experience the frustration and ailments which occur when it is entirely unreleased.

An unfulfilled Scorpio (or Pluto) in the natal chart, however --- that is, a configuration in which it does not appear that this force will be released legitimately either for propagation or creative purposes --- indicates the possibility that the person may yield to expressions of cruelty, dishonesty, murder, and other destructive impulses as a substitute satisfaction for this thing which, in his desire nature, screams for gratification. As the physical body may erupt with boils due to unreleased toxic conditions, so the consciousness may erupt with all kinds of black urges to release a potent desire urge. The history of humanity's development as a sexual organism is riddled with chapters of fear, perversion, disease, and madness, because so many people have lived, emotionally, by standards ranging from false puritanism to promiscuity, completely removed from the process of natural experience and healthy, loving fulfillments.

We are finally beginning to get at the roots of these emotional diseases and are being forced to the conclusion that life cannot be well lived unless it is based on a philosophy of healthy, constructive, loving, and happy releases. The remedy for emotional diseases is found in enlightened, spiritualized education, plus the vitalized determination to live healthy, expressive, beautiful, and loving lives, in relation to self and to others. In this way the desire resource is transmuted and expressed in terms that make for evolution, as well as the redemption of karmic debts into spiritualized consciousness.

The most significant lessons Pluto would teach will be learned, and the highest potential of Scorpio will be realized, with the development of pure minds, pure thoughts, and pure living. Then the adverse aspects of planet and sign will be powerless to affect us, and we will be able to make tremendous spiritual growth under their benign influences.

ANCIENT AND MODERN INITIATION

By MAX HEINDEL

• •

I am not come to destroy, said the Master of masters, but to fulfill.

• •

This illumined book bridges the abyss between the ancient Teachings of Initiation known in Pre-Christian Eras and that of Christ for the modern world.

PART I.—THE TABERNACLE IN THE WILDERNESS

The Atlantean Mystery Temple—Brazen Altar and Laver—East Room of Temple—Ark of Covenant—Sacred Shekinah Glory—New Moon and Initiation.

PART II—THE CHRISTIAN MYSTIC INITIATION

Annunciation and Immaculate Conception—Mystic Rite of Baptism—The Temptation—The Transfiguration—Last Supper and Footwashing—Gethsemane, the Garden of Grief—The Stigmata and the Crucifixion.

A Splendid Index and Seven Illustrations

TEACHINGS OF AN INITIATE

By MAX HEINDEL

This book is compiled from the writings of an Initiate of the Rosicrucian Order.

It comprises a series of lessons issued by the author to his students, together with various public addresses. A few chapter headings will give an idea of the contents of the book:

The Scientific Method of Spiritual Unfoldment.
The Death of the Soul.
Our Work in the World (three chapters).
Mystic Light on the World War (three chapters).
The Secret of Success.
The Sign of the Master.
Religion and Healing.

Max Heindel is well qualified to impart esoteric knowledge on these subjects, by virtue of his various Initiations into the Mysteries. TEACHINGS OF AN INITIATE contains the later fruit of the author's extensive occult investigations. It is of value to both the beginner and the advanced student of occultism. Indexed for ready reference.

MYSTERY OF THE DUCTLESS GLANDS

By A STUDENT

In developing this fascinating subject the writer has delved deeply into the esoteric information in Max Heindel's writings and has also presented authentic physiological data as taught by Medical Science.

TABLE OF CONTENTS

•

•

THE ROSICRUCIAN FELLOWSHIP

Oceanside California, U.S.A.

THE ROSICRUCIAN MYSTERIES

By Max Heindel

The author has written the sublime truths of the Western Wisdom Teachings in almost narrative style in this book intended specially to give busy people a solution to life's basic problems as contained in the mind- and heart-satisfying Rosicrucian Philosophy.

LIST OF CONTENTS

Chapter 1.—The Order of the Rosicrucians and the Rosicrucian Fellowship: Spiritual Wave; Christian Rosenkreuz; Choice of Author as Messenger of Brothers of the Rose Cross.

Chapter 2.—The Problem of Life and Its Solution; Necessity for Independent Thought; Three Theories of Life—Materialistic, Theological, Rebirth; Soul and Breath; We Are Eternal (poem).

Chapter 3.—The Visible and Invisible Worlds: The Chemical Region; The Etheric Region; The Desire World; The World of Thought; Logos and "the Beginning"; Christ or Creed (poem).

Chapter 4.—The Constitution of Man: The Vital Body; The Desire Body; the Mind; Soul differentiated from Spirit.

Chapter 5.—Life and Death: Invisible Helpers and Mediums, Interpenetration of Vehicles; Death, Purpose, Reason for Seeking Long Life; Panorama of Past Life, Rupture of Silver Cord, Method of Reviewing entire Past Life; Purgatory, How Evil is Purged, A Place of Cleansing not of Punishment; The First Heaven, Reaping of Good, Fulfillment of Constructive Desire, Children, Light and Color; The Second Heaven, "The Great Silence," Preparation of Future Environment; The Third Heaven, Preview of Coming Earth Life, Preparations for Rebirth; Birth and Child Life; The Mystery of Light, Color, and Consciousness; Education of Children; Mt. Ecclesia, a Description of the Headquarters of The Rosicrucian Fellowship.

Twenty pages of Index enable the interested reader or student to turn instantly to any desired topic.

THE ROSICRUCIAN FELLOWSHIP
Oceanside, California, U.S.A.

OCCULT PRINCIPLES OF HEALTH AND HEALING

By MAX HEINDEL

Second Edition

Culled with great care from the many books, lessons, letters—even from hitherto unpublished notes—of this Western Seer and Initiate and brought together in one volume.

The Heart of the Western Wisdom Teaching pertaining to Health and Healing

PARTIAL LIST OF CONTENTS

Man and His Vehicles
General and Specific Causes of Disease
The Rosicrucian Fellowship Method of Healing
The Science of Nutrition
Astrology as an Aid to Healing
Therapeutic Basis of Light, Color, and Sound
The Scope of Healing
The Real Nature of Death

Bound in Green Cloth and Stamped in Gold

25 Chapters 244 Pages Index

THE ROSICRUCIAN FELLOWSHIP
Oceanside California, U.S.A.

THE WEB OF DESTINY

By Max Heindel

Sixteen of the ninety-seven monthly lessons sent out to his students by this illumined teacher. They are the fruitage of true esoteric research.

•

TABLE OF CONTENTS

Four Parts—Sixteen Chapters—Index

•

•

THE ROSICRUCIAN FELLOWSHIP

Oceanside California, U.S.A.

GLEANINGS OF A MYSTIC

By MAX HEINDEL

The author of this book is recognized as a true Seer and Mystic. His broad spiritual insight is shown in the opening words of this book:

It is no rare occurrence to receive questions relating to Initiation, and we are also frequently asked to state whether this order or that society is genuine, whether the initiations they offer to all comers who have the price are bona fide. For that reason it seems necessary to write a treatise on the subject so that students of the Rosicrucian Fellowship may have an official statement for reference and guidance in the future.

In the first place let it be clearly understood that we consider it reprehensible to express condemnation of any society or order, no matter what its practices. It may be perfectly sincere and honest *according to its light.* We do not believe that we rise in the opinion of discriminating men and women by speaking in disparaging terms of others; neither are we laboring under the delusion that *we* have all the truth and other societies are plunged in Egyptian darkness.

CHAPTER HEADINGS

Initiation: What It Is and Is Not—Sacrament of Communion—Baptism—Marriage—The Unpardonable Sin and Lost Souls—Magic, White and Black—Our Invisible Government—Sound, Silence, and Soul Growth—Mysterium Magnum of the Rose Cross—Why I Am a Rosicrucian—and many others. There are thirty-four chapters and an Index.

• •